The making of Mauritian Creole

Analyses diachroniques à partir des textes anciens

edited by

Philip Baker
&
Guillaume Fon Sing

BATTLEBRIDGE
PUBLICATIONS
2007

BATTLEBRIDGE
PUBLICATIONS

United Kingdom and Sri Lanka
www.battlebridge.com
pb@battlebridge.com

Westminster Creolistics Series
ISSN 1470-3750

1. *From contact to Creole and beyond* (Philip Baker, ed.)
2. *Changing meanings, changing functions* (Philip Baker & Anand Syea, eds)
3. *Pidgin and Creole Linguistics* (revised, expanded edn) (Peter Mühlhäusler)
4. *St Kitts and the Atlantic Creoles* (Philip Baker & Adrienne Bruyn, eds)
5. *From French to Creole* (Chris Corne)
6. *Spreading the word* (Magnus Huber & Mikael Parkvall, eds)
7. *Comparative Creole Syntax* (John Holm & Peter L Patrick, eds)
8. *Twice as meaningful* (Silvia Kouwenberg, ed.)
9. *The making of Mauritian Creole* (Philip Baker & Guillaume Fon Sing, eds)

Forthcoming:

Black through white (Angela Bartens & Philip Baker, eds)

Simplicity and Complexity in Pidgins and Creoles (N Faraclas & T Klein, eds)

Copyright

Battlebridge Publications holds copyright for the volume as a whole
but copyright of individual articles belongs to their named authors

Cataloguing data

Title: The making of Mauritian Creole. Analyses diachroniques à partir des textes anciens.
Editors: Philip D Baker and Guillaume Fon Sing
Includes bibliographical references and index.
ISBN 978-1-903292-14-3
1. Creole languages – Lexicon. 2. Creole languages – Grammar. 3. Creole languages – History.

Cover picture

The cover picture (untitled) comes from the *Atlas* which accompanies Louis
de Freycinet's multi-volume *Voyage autour du monde (...)*, Paris, 1824-1844.
It is reproduced by courtesy of the Trustees of the British Library
The cover was designed with the assistance of Pradeep Ihalage.

Printing

Tharanjee Prints, 506 High Level Road, Nawinna, Maharagama, Sri Lanka

Table of Contents

The Corpus of Mauritian Creole texts
    Philip Baker, Guillaume Fon Sing, & Vinesh Y Hookoomsing   1

Definiteness and Specificity in Mauritian Creole: a syntactic and semantic overview
    Diana Guillemin   63

The development of the noun phrase in Mauritian Creole and the mechanisms of language development
    Anand Syea   93

Conjunction and ditransitives: some functional domains covered by *avec, et,* and *ensemble*
    Sibylle Kriegel & Susanne Michaelis   113

Ena et *gagne* : à propos de la genèse de l'expression de l'existence et de la possession / propriété en créole mauricien
    Guillaume Fon Sing & Daniel Véronique   133

L'absence de marqueurs préverbaux et les fonctions du marqueurs zéro
    Peter Stein   157

The resumptive pronoun *li* in Mauritian Creole
    Diana Guillemin   173

Comparative Creole typology and the search for the sources of Mauritian Creole features
    Anthony Grant & Philip Baker   197

La concordance
    Guillaume Fon Sing   217

Elements for a sociolinguistic history of Mauritius and its Creole (to 1968)
    Philip Baker   307

Letter to the Colonial Office of the conditions of emancipated negroes in the Mauritius
    J A Lloyd   335

Index   341

A CD containing the complete versions of all 60 texts in our corpus and a concordance which allows the user to search for all the occurrences of any word will be made available in the early part of 2008. Details will be posted on our website:
www.battlebridge.com

Un concordancier informatique comprenant un moteur de recherche et la version complète des 60 textes de notre corpus sera disponible début 2008. Les détails seront annoncés sur notre site:
www.battlebridge.com

The Corpus of Mauritian Creole texts

Philip Baker
Guillaume Fon Sing
Vinesh Y Hookoomsing

The search for old texts

The collection of Mauritian Creole (MC) texts on which this book is based has a long history. The process began in May 1975 when, after 16 months in Africa, Baker returned to Mauritius. There he met up with Vinesh Hookoomsing and Peter Stein, both former students of the Université de Provence in Aix-en-Provence whom he already knew. Between them, they already had copies of several old texts, but they were agreed on the desirability of carrying out a thorough search of Mauritian libraries in order to expand their collection.

The search began at the Carnegie Library in Curepipe where they found copies of Chrestien (1822 and 1831) and Descroizilles (1867), among others. Chrestien (1822) was in very poor condition. It was impossible to turn over a page without part of the page flaking off. It had also suffered greatly from insect damage, leaving large holes on every page.[1] They restricted their examination to the first lyric, comparing it with the 1831 edition. Insofar as insect damage permitted, the text appeared to be identical in the two editions.

Photocopies of the texts were clearly needed in order that they might each have their own copy of each of the texts. This proved to be a problem: the Carnegie Library did not possess a photocopier at that time and its rules would not permit any of the texts to be removed from the library. After much discussion, it was agreed that the texts could be taken to the nearest photocopier, in a barber's shop two streets away, provided that they were accompanied by a member of staff. Thus the collection began.

Visits to the Mauritius Institute, the Mauritius Archives, and the municipal libraries of Port Louis and Rose-Hill/Beau-Bassin quickly added several more texts to the collection. This led them to discuss the possibility of republishing the texts in a book. At that time Laurence Nairac, another former student of the Université de Provence, had just launched a small publishing concern, *Chien de Plomb*.[2] She expressed great interest in publishing such a book but it was eventually decided to wait until Baker and Stein had searched for additional texts in Europe before making any firm plans. Several more items were found there, mainly manuscripts in archives.

The possibility of *Chien de Plomb* publishing the book came to an end in 1979 (?) when it was learned that a yacht on which Laurence Nairac was travelling had disappeared without trace off the northern tip of Mauritius. A further setback came with the publication of Chaudenson's (1981) *Textes anciens....* This included several texts they had come to regard as their own discoveries: Grant's letter dated 1749, Bernardin de St Pierre 1773, Milbert 1812, Freycinet 1827, Lambert 1828, Nicolay 1835, and a small selection of

---

[1] When Baker revisited the Carnegie Library in 2000, the copy of Chrestien (1822) could no longer be found there and the index card for it had been removed from the catalogue. However, since Benoît (1998) includes the introduction to the 1822 edition, it is seems that the copy formerly in the Carnegie Library may not have been the only surviving one as had been feared.

[2] The name comes from a very old lead figure of a dog overlooking the entrance to Port Louis dockyards.

items from Chrestien 1822 and 1831. But of course they had no proprietorial rights over these; these texts were available to anyone who took the trouble to search for them, as Chaudenson had done. His book also included five extracts from 18th century court records and the M Carabas text from ca. 1850 which they had not known about. For their part, they had by this time amassed about 20 texts not in Chaudenson (1981), including Lolliot 1855, De Chazal 1860, Anderson 1885, and Soulsobontemps 1925, and a more than dozen shorter items. Baker had additionally found the picture, now used on this book nearly 30 years later, and obtained permission from the British Library to reproduce it. Nevertheless, the publication of Chaudenson's book led them to postpone any plans for publication in the short term.

From time to time, during the 1980s and 1990s, Baker and Hookoomsing separately came across additional MC texts, mainly in 19th century newspapers, but there was no serious discussion of publication plans.

A new initiative arose in 2002 with the arrival of Guillaume Fon Sing, as an exchange student from the University of Provence, at the University of Westminster where Baker taught a course on Creole languages. Fon Sing took an immediate interest in the old MC texts and a plan for putting all of them on computer quickly emerged. He began the laborious task of typing them towards the end of 2002 and continued after his return to France the following year.[3] From this, the idea emerged of making a concordance of all these texts and this in turn created renewed interest in a book based in some way on these texts. A "book planning session" was held as part of the Westminster Creolistics Workshop in April 2004. Given that the number of texts available by that time – 58 – was too great to include in a single book, it was proposed that all the texts should be made available on a CD and/or on the internet and that, while a limited number of texts of special interest and/or importance might be printed in the book itself, the book should be devoted mainly to articles dealing with the evolution of MC.

A further setback occurred on 26 December 2004 when Baker's house in Sri Lanka was hit by the tsunami. All his papers relating to Mauritius and MC were submerged in 2,5 metres of sea water, damaging the legibility of many of them while others were simply washed away and never recovered.

In the spring of 2007 it was learned that Furlong & Ramharai (F&R) had just published *La production créolophone* and that, with the exception of extracts from some of Anderson's gospels[4] and a letter dating from 1908, all the pre-1930 texts in their book also formed part of our corpus. This, at first, appeared to be yet another serious setback. However, the number of texts contained both in F&R and the present corpus is 23 (of which four of the texts are in some way incomplete in F&R, as indicated in the following pages) which means there are 35 texts in the corpus which are not included in F&R. Nevertheless, the choice of texts printed in the present volume is inevitably influenced to some extent by the range of texts in F&R.

The choice of texts

After much discussion, the editors decided to include the following texts in this book:

- All pre-1820 texts, regardless of whether or not they are currently available in print elsewhere.
- Almost all post-1820 and pre-1930 texts which are not included in F&R or which are not otherwise easily obtainable. Thus Baissac's 1880 and 1888 books are excluded,

---

[3] The only text of significant length not typed by Fon Sing is Decotter 1920 which Stein had typed some years earlier and kindly made available to the editors.

[4] The extracts are from the gospels of St Mark and St John, and from the Acts of the Apostles. Curiously they include nothing from St Matthew, the only translation published by Anderson while he was living in Mauritius.

since they can easily be found in libraries. Exceptionally, it was decided not to reproduce Anderson (1885) in full, primarily because of its length and the fact that it is a translation. It is nevertheless a very important text because it includes certain grammatical features of modern MC which are absent from Baissac (1880, 1888), and because it employs a unique orthography. Extracts to illustrate these aspects of his work are thus included.
- A selection of the writings of Chrestien (1822, 1831, 1838, 1839) and Lolliot (1855).

The chosen texts are set out below. Where a text is reproduced in full (regardless of how short or long it is), references to it in other articles included in this book are to the date it was written (insofar as this can be determined) only. This is printed in bold characters and followed by a, b, c, etc. where there are two or more texts from the same year, e.g. **1777, 1818b, 1839f**, etc.

The overall plan is that each text is preceded by general information about it (author, circumstances in which written, etc. – insofar as these things are known). Following each text attention is drawn to any significant linguistic or orthographic features contained in it.

The chosen texts

Texts **1734, 1777, 1778, 1779, 1784, 1793, 1822b**, and **1823** are all from court records. The people who recorded court proceedings were expected to write in French regardless of how far the language actually employed in giving evidence deviated from French. However, they also had to work quickly at times in order to keep up with what was said in court. In consequence they occasionally wrote down short snatches of evidence from slaves with little or no attempt at translation (or "standardization"). A limitation of such data is that it is not always easy to determine the precise point at which the scribe switches from French to Creole (cf the **1777** and **1793** examples).

1. **1734** Affaire Pierrot; coups et blessures[5] [Mauritius Archives, JB 1]

   Il auroit aperçu un noir qui estoit blessé et qui lui auroit dit **moy fini mouri**, *... et le dit enfant fu* **sakabar** (Chaudenson 1981: 77).

This text provides the first attestation of *moi* as subject pronoun and, more significantly, of *fini* as a preverbal perfective marker. *Mouri* is not found in any later text; the verb 'die' is consistently found thereafter as *mor(t)*. A further point of interest is that the speaker is identified as being "de Guinée" whereas **sakabar** is of Malagasy origin (Chaudenson 1981: 77; see the Concordance for more details).

2. **1741** Letter written by Grant, Baron de Vaux

Grant appears to have been a French citizen with Scottish connections. At least one of his descendants, Charles (author of Grant 1801), moved to Britain following the French Revolution.

   Creole ladies (...) season their favourite dishes, which they call *Caris* and *Plots* with the hottest spices (Grant 1801: 194).

3. **1749** Letter written by Grant, Baron de Vaux

   ... they will direct their hand to the point where it [Madagascar] lies and exclaim, in their corrupted French, **ça blanc là li beaucoup malin; li couri beaucoup dans la mer là haut ; mais Madagascar li là** (Grant 1886: 166).

---

[5] In the Mauritius Archives texts for which Chaudenson is the immediate source, both the words immediately following the date (e.g. Affaire Pierrot) and any words preceding the quotations which are not in bold or italics (e.g. Réponse d'un esclave...) are also those of Chaudenson.

Grant's **1749** sentence is striking in that it closely resembles modern MC except that *beaucoup* no longer functions as an adjectival intensifier (as in *beaucoup malin*) and that the verb *courrir* is now obsolete. However, from the text immediately preceding the words quoted above it would appear that the slave was probably referring to the crew of the ship collectively in which case *ça blanc là* and the first two examples of *li* would all be plural. The sentence also includes two examples of zero copula, both preceded by **li**. (See Guillemin, *this volume* for an alternative interpretation of **li** in this position.)

4. **1769** Sentences reported by Bernardin de St Pierre

    Le patron me dit dans son mauvais patois : "**ça n'a pas bon, Monsié**". *Je lui demandai s'il y avoit quelque danger, il me répondit:* "**Si nous n'a pas gagné malheur, ça bon**" (Bernardin de St Pierre 1773: I, 257).

This brief text provides the first attestations of *n'a pas* as the predicate-initial negator, preceding both zero copula and the verb *gagné*.

5. **1777** Affaire du Chevalier de la Poëze [Mauritius Archives, JB 29]

    Ayant demandé à ce noir pourquoi il inquiétait cette négresse, le noir lui répondit: quesque cela te fout, **moi voulé baiser ly**.

    Ce noir se sentant frappé lui dit en le menaçant du poing **pourquoy toi battre moi qui toi faire moi**.

    Toi va paye moi ça, *avance si tu l'oses*.

    Viens si tu es **capable qui toi faire toi battre moi**.

    Qui toi vouler faire moi, Battre si toi oser.

    Moi voulé baiser ça négresse là. (Chaudenson 1981: 78)

The third 1777 example above includes the first attestation of *va* as preverbal future marker.

6. **1778** Interrogatoire de Louis, esclave [Mauritius Archives, JB 29]

    A répondu que **jamais, mentir n'a pas bon** (Chaudenson 1981: 78).

7. **1779** Affaire La Douceur [Mauritius Archives, JB 33]

    A répondu **Pardonne moy, Monsieur, moy n'apa été batté ça Blanc là** (Chaudenson 1981: 78).

8. **1784** Affaire Rouillon [Mauritius Archives, JB 42]

    Réponse d'une esclave à son maître qui lui reprochait sa paresse:

    Moi vieux, Monsieur, Moi malade, vendez moi.

    Moi faire bien et vous battez mon corps.

    Le maître après la mort de la femme s'adresse en créole à son mari:

    Papa, votre femme fini mort, moi tué ly (Chaudenson 1981: 78).

9. **1793** [Mauritius Archives, JB 78]

    … *qu'il ne vouloir pas avoir* **la guerre avec lui** (…)

    ah mondieu tirez cet homme

    moi n'a pas vouler la guerre avec camarade

A version of this text is included in Scarr (1998).[6] In 2000, Baker was able to examine the original in the Mauritius Archives and to make some minor corrections which are incorporated above.

Note that the second occurrence of **la guerre** appears to be a verb 'to fight' and is unambiguously attested as such in some later texts. Only two other cases are known of an MC noun derived from a French article and noun which subsequently also became a verb: **lasas** 'to hunt' (<la chasse) and **lapes** 'to fish' (< la pêche).

10.   1802 Milbert's MC data

Milbert visited Mauritius in 1802 and his two-volume book provides an informative description of life in the island at that time. However, as indicated in Baker (1976: 28-30), there is reason to doubt the authenticity of at least some of his MC examples. His first example, which refers to monkeys, is remarkably similar to Haitian one which was published anonymously in *Cri des colons contre un ouvrage de Gregoire* : « *La littérature des Nègres* » (Anon. 1810) just two years before Milbert's book appeared:

ça petit di monde là n'a pas voulé palé pour na pas travail

singe, ça p'tit monde, qui malin trop ïo pas vlé palé, pou que ïo pa fair travail

The upper line is from Milbert (1812: I, 240-41), the lower from Anon. (1810: 39). Examples which similarly state that monkeys don't want to speak in order to avoid having to work (as the slaves do) can be found in both English and French Caribbean territories in the 19th century. It is thus possible, but rather unlikely, that this saying might have been introduced into Mauritius by visitors or settlers with prior experience of the Caribbean. However, what is particularly suspicious here is « palé » rather than *parlé*. French vowel + r in closed syllables remains distinct from vowel alone in MC, in contrast to the French Creoles of the Caribbean, all of which have *palé* rather than *parlé*. Of the many occurrences of this verb in our concordance, Milbert is the only author to write the word without an *r*. There is also no other evidence in our corpus that monkeys were ever known as *petit di monde* in Mauritius.

Monsié, pas di tout, *répondit-il,* **moi venir voir femme à moi** (Milbert 1812: I, 271).

The striking feature in the above example is *femme à moi* for 'my wife'. This structure is attested in northern Haiti and Guadeloupe (Goodman 1964: 53) but is not found in any other MC text at any time.

... *les nègres appeler nos matelots* "ça li nègre blanc" (Milbert 1812: I, 274).

The above example is entirely consistent with other MC texts.

- « *Je lui demandai des indications en l'appelant* « **papa** » (*c'est le nom qu'on donne généralement aux noirs esclaves, de même qu'on appelle* **maman** *les négresses privées de liberté*) : « **Moussié,** *répondit-il,* **moi n'est pas papa ; moi libre comme vous-même, comme moussié** *tel et tel* » (Milbert 1812: II, 71).

N'est pas is not found in any other MC text but might be due to a simple mishearing of *n'a pas*. Milbert goes on to indicate that the slave mentioned the names of particular white men and that he replaced these with *tel et tel*. The use of *Papa* as a term of address for male slaves is mentioned by Bernardin de St Pierre (1773) and is also illustrated in the 1784 example above.

---

[6] Baker is grateful to Derek Bickerton for having brought this text (and also **1823**) to his attention.

> Ah ! moi voir comme li venir dans mon li qui ; quand maître avez zoté chimise, vous laissé si chaise, moi assisé, disi, remué comme ça disi chaise, bouton li veni dans mon li qui (Milbert 1812: II, 180-81).

As noted in Baker (1976: 29), this text is somewhat aberrant in its failure to observe the usual correspondence between French *ch* and MC /s/, its use of some words not attested elsewhere, e.g. *disi* 'dessus', and above all *zoté* for 'ôter'. There is no other example in the entire MC corpus of a liaison consonant being agglutinated to a vowel-initial verb. Examples of this can, however, be found in Ducoeurjoly's (1802) *Manuel* of Haitian Creole. That said, it is entirely possible that a domestic slave would have employed some French features not heard in the speech of field slaves in his MC.

Taken together, Milbert's data cannot be dismissed as fraudulent since he did visit the island and was therefore exposed to MC. But it seems probable that he did consult some of the available literature on Caribbean créolophone territories on his return to France – it would be entirely natural for him to take an interest in them – and that examples of Creole speech contained in them may have influenced his memory of what he had heard in Mauritius a few years earlier. Whatever the case, it would be unwise to assume that any feature found only in the above examples formerly existed in MC.

11. 1805 Thomy Pitot's observations on Bernardin de St Pierre (1773)

More than 30 years after the publication of B de St Pierre's *Voyage à l'Isle de France*, Thomy Pitot, a white Creole of the island, presented a refutation of Bernardin de St Pierre's negative portrayal of its slave-owner inhabitants at a meeting of the *Société d'Emulation Intellectuelle*. In its published form, the refutation, a 70 page-long document contains an annex in MC in the form of a dialogue between the author and a slave. The latter is presented as a happy *noir Mozambique (…) chantant, dans sa langue, quelques couplets*. He is therefore not a Creole slave born on the island, but he shows native mastery of MC, the *lingua franca*. It is not known whether the dialogue was actually rendered as such or just read out, or merely referred to during the meeting. Whatever the uncertainties of its presentation (and reception), the fictitious dialogue between a leading figure of the Isle de France white elite and a *noir Mozambique, entre la fleur et la vigueur de l'âge, paré d'un simple langoutis*, constitutes the first elaborate text in MC.

Question. Vous bien content, donc, Papa?
Réponse. Hé ! Hé ! pourquoi mô n'a pas content?
Q. Qui bon nouvelle donc faire vous content comme ca?
R. Ah ! ben oui ; mo connais nouvelle moi ; mo content comme ça même.
Q. Où vous couri, papa?
R. Mô couri bitation, donc.
Q. Vous maître li bon, hein papa?
R. Ah ! hé !… oui, va, li bon même.
Q. Vous n'a pas gagné coups de fouette?
R. Coups de fouette? di mounde faire son zouvraze li gagne coups de fouette? mô n'a pas volor, moi, mô n'a pas maron, pourquoi mô gagné coup de fouette?
Q. Vous gagné bien manzé, papa ?
R. Mo gagné manioc, mo gagné maye.
Q. Ça même?
R. Qui encore va gagné ?
Q. Vous manzé maye sec, donc ?
R. Non, va.
Q. Qui manzé encore ?
R. Ah! bé! mo ramasse brède à soir, mô n'a pas couri la pesse? mô gagne posson, gagne sévrettes ; - mô n'a pas zardin donc? mô gagne ziromon, bananes.
Q. Mais, papa, vous n'a pas simise, donc, vous n'a pas kilotte; n'a rien?

R.	Si fait, dans mô case,[7] y en a.
Q.	Qui donne vous ça?
R.	Quequefois, m'sié li donné. Quequefois mô asséte.
Q.	Où vous gagné l'argent pour asséter ?
R.	Hé ! Hé ! vendé cosson, vendé tabac, dimanse travaille pour di mounde.
Q.	Mais, papa, quand vous malade, qui soigné vous?
R.	Ah ! hé ! n'a pas l'optal, n'a pas sourzin?
Q.	Vous, noir bitation, ou bien vous commandèr?
R.	Mô noir bitation.
Q.	Vous n'a pas envi vini commandèr?
R.	Ma foi, non : mô n'a pas bisoin ça, moi.
Q.	Papa, vous y en a femme, ou bien vous tout cèle?
R.	Mo y en a femme.
Q.	Li zoli, vous femme?
R.	Hé! hé!... ... ça blanc - là?[8]
Q.	Dire donc ; li zoli, hein?
R.	Mô trouve li zoli, va.
Q.	Vous conné bon Dié, papa?
R.	Hé! hé! mô n'a pas conné bon Dié pour blanc, moi : mô conné bon Dié qui dans mon paye.
Q.	Li bon ça bon Dié-là qui dans vous paye, hein?
R.	... Y en ça qui bon, y en a ça qui mauvais.
Q.	Vous per ça bon Dié là qui mauvais?
R.	Non, va : quand ça qui bon, li content moi, ça qui mauvais n'a pas capave faire moi di mal.
Q.	Qui li va donné vous, ça bon Dié là qui bon?
R.	Ah! bé! li n'a pas donné moi n'a rien; li empesse moi gagné grand malher; quand mo mort li faire moi arrive dans mo paye!
Q.	Vous bien content, vous paye, donc papa?
R.	Ah! – ... soûrement mo bien content.
Q.	Qui meyer, vous paye ou bien Maurice?
R.	Hé! ... Maurice bon, mon paye li bon aussi ...
Q.	Mais, papa, quand vous capave quitte Maurice pour alle dans vous paye, vous va allé?
R.	Hé! hé! mô n'a pas pense ça, moi, qui mô va faire dans mô paye? mô n'a pas saclave?
Q.	Ah! bin ; quand vous arrive dans vous paye, vous n'a pas libe donc?
R.	Non va ; mô saclave la guerre ; quand mô arrive là ; zotte prend moi encore pour vendé moi. Quand mô fini mort, mô va allé dans mon paye, à v'là tout.
Q.	Comment zotte faire la guerre dans vous paye?
R.	Hé! missié, li tard, oui ; laisse mo allé.
Q.	Allons, bonsoir, papa.
R.	Ah! ça, bonsoir, m'sier.
Q.	Bonsoir.

This is the earliest text yet known in which the first person subject pronoun is written *mo* (also *mô* in this text). It is used in subject position to the exclusion of *moi* throughout the entire text. This contrasts with Chrestien's texts (see below) in which the first person subject pronoun is always *moi*. Variation between *mo* and *moi* in subject position is found in many later texts including Descroizilles (1867). Examination of the texts favouring one or other form of the 1st person pronoun strongly suggests that it was slaves who first began to use the *mo* form and that whites were reluctant to adopt this form for several decades (cf Baker 1976: 46-48). Pitot's text also includes three examples of the first person singular possessive adjective two of which are written *mô* while the other is written *mon*. This might be seen as a very early example of denasalization but it is perhaps more likely

---

[7] In all other texts, the word for house has an agglutinated article indicating the pronunciation /lakaz/.
[8] The question mark here is perhaps a misprint for the exclamation mark.

that the phonetic and semantic similarity of *mo* and *mon* and the far greater frequency of the pronoun than the possessive adjective favoured the extension of the former to the latter role.

This is also the first text in which short forms of verbs are found in positions where short forms are required today: *alle, arrive, donne, empesse, laisse,* and *ramasse.* Note that these all have infinitives in –er in French. Exceptionally, there are several occurrences of the French verb *gagner* in this text but there are examples of both *gagne* and *gagné* in positions where the short form is required today. Most of the short forms are in the replies of the slave rather than the questions of the white man. Apart from *gagné* the only two verbs in the slave's replies which have long forms where short forms are required in modern MC are *conné/connais* and *vendé*. Note that these both have infinitives ending –re which suggests that the development of short and long forms of verbs began with the majority of regular –er verbs,[9] and only later extended to other verbs. As with *mo* in subject position, there is evidence to suggest that the use of short and long forms in different grammatical contexts was initiated in slave usage (see Corne 1982: 67-72).

Other features of Pitot's text worthy of note are:

- Absence of distinction in the case of nominative and possessive *vous*.
- The first attestation of *y en a* 'have'.
- Fr. *pays* is written as *paye*, with a final mute 'e' instead of 's'. The concordance shows this to have been a very common spelling of this MC word in the 19th century, implying that it was pronounced [pej] rather than [peji].
- *libe* without the prefinal 'r'
- Speech-based variants of the same word: *missié, m'syer* (< Fr. *monsieur*).
- Absence of any indication that the *la* of *la guerre* is not an article but is agglutinated to *guerre*.
- *Meyer* (< Fr. meilleur) is a surprisingly standard form; one would have expected *plis bon* instead.

12.   1816 Le Brun's Journal

The following text differs from all the others in this collection. Jean Le Brun was a protestant minister born in the Channel Islands. During his first few month in Mauritius he kept a diary. His entry for 9 juillet 1816 contains the description in French of a visit he received from *une Mauricienne de couleur* which made a deep impression on him. In the margin, at 90 degrees to the entry in French, is the text reproduced below. Baker's interpretation of this is that Le Brun attempted to write down as far as he could remember exactly what she had said but he would have been constrained by his lack of mastery of MC at this time. In other words, I think that what he has written is the MC parts that he remembered linked together with French words expressing the sense of what he believed she said. (For instance, it seems highly improbable that anyone who said *nous n'a pas connai n'a rien* would mix this with French first person plural verb forms such as *sommes, aimions,* etc.)

> *Qu'est-ce donc qu'un veritable chrestien?*
>
> *La mère dit:* Nous n'a pas capables de dire vous ce que c'etait, mais nous connai que depuis que sautres allons entendre vous nous trouvons nos coeurs changès *autrefois nous aimions valles courir aux comédies mais appresent nous trouvons* quet chose qui dire n'a pas bon pour chretiens. Chretiens na pas preche contre Dieu. Avant vous te vini, nous n'a pas connai n'a rien sautres pretes na pas été instruire sautres, nous vivres comme bête. Mais au jour d'huit nous connai un petit peu. Nous connait *nous sommes grands pecheurs,* nous connaie *avons besoin lagrace de Dieu pour senger coeur,* nous connai n'a pas Baptême qui faire nous autres chretiens, oui avant nous te croire ça. Car mère dire nous ça nous été

---

[9] Bollée (2007: 57) points out that the short and long forms of such verbs are the two forms which occur with by far the greatest frequency.

pauvre ingnorans na pas connai na rien di tout nous té croire quand pauvre fini mort tout fini avec nous (Council for World Mission Archives, School of Oriental and African Studies, University of London).

One point of linguistic interest is that there are three examples of *sautres*, all of which seem more likely to refer to 1st rather than 2nd person plural, one of *nous autres*, and none where /zot/in any spelling has unambiguous 2nd or 3rd person reference. Were the text more reliable, this might suggest that MC once had /zot/as an all-person plural pronoun. But no other text yet known offers any support for this.

13-15 **1818a/b/c** Data collected by Freycinet in 1818

Freycinet's voluminous *Voyage autour du monde (...)* contains some six pages on early 19th century MC, which he describes as follows:

> Indépendamment du français, qui forme la base du langage à l'Ile de France, une sorte de patois a été inventé par les noirs, qui, ne pouvant se plier à notre syntaxe, prononcer nos mots difficiles, et saisir la valeur propre de quelques-unes de nos expressions, les ont travestis à leur manière. Peu à peu l'usage a fait loi ; et peut-être ne seroit-il pas sans intérêt aujourd'hui d'examiner les règles de cette langue créole, qui n'est pas dénudée de charmes.

Freycinet's plan of a grammatical description unfortunately did not materialize, but he managed to include in his brief account a story reproduced in a slave's style (**1818a**) and a translation of a La Fontaine fable by Chrestien (**1818b**), to illustrate the existence of two distinct varieties of MC, the slave's and the master's:

> On conçoit en effet que chacune des races noires qui existent dans la colonie a dû altérer le français d'une façon particulière, et que ce nouveau langage a dû se régulariser ou conserver sa rudesse originelle, selon les idées et le degré de culture d'esprit de ceux qui le parlent. On distingue donc le créole mozambique de celui des noirs indiens, malais et malgaches, et plus encore du créole usité, par goût et par habitude, par les mulâtres et les personnes riches de l'île. Je donnerai un exemple de ceux de ces dialectes qui diffèrent le plus entre eux : tels sont le créole malgache et le créole des Européens, si je puis m'exprimer ainsi.

The story narrated by the slave, but obviously not transcribed by either the slave or Freycinet, shows according to the latter *la nature des idées, la rudesse de langage, et la manière de raconter des noirs de pioche mozambiques*.[10]

13. **1818a** Le Chasseur (CONTE EN LANGAGE CRÉOLE DE L'ILE-DE-FRANCE)

Acoute zaut'[11] mo parlé! Enne zour ça nous té[12] la sasse cerf Grand-Rivière. L'her solé lévé, mo pour alle prend mon poste au pavé; mo passe drète cote ça grand pié di-bois piant Aughiste conné là; à v'la mo sivre la rivière pour saute l'aut' côté : mo ramasse enne tondre, mo guette li; li encor fimé. Ah Ah ! qui dou-monde qui té pass' là ! N'a pas nous zence - ça, zaut' fait que lévé.	Écoutez, vous autres, moi va parler! Un jour, comme cela, nous sommes allés à la chasse du cerf à la Grande-Rivière. A l'heure du soleil levant, moi allé pour prendre mon poste au pavé (au chemin); moi passé juste à côté de ce grand pied de bois puant (sorte d'arbre) qu'Auguste connaît là; et voilà moi suivre la rivière pour passer de l'autre côté; moi ramasse un *tondre*;[13] moi regarde lui; lui encore fumer. Ah ah! quelle personne a passé là ! Ce ne sont pas de nos gens

---

[10] L'auteur semble faire ici une confusion entre créole malgache et créole mozambique [Fon Sing].
[11] *Zaut'* pour *vous autres*, ou *les autres*. *Zaut'* signifie aussi parfois eux.
[12] *Té*, pour *été*, ou plutôt *avons été*.
[13] *Tondre*, morceau de bois creusé, rempli de coton charbonné, qui sert d'amdou aux noirs.

Aster[14] mo baisse en bas pié[15] frambouése; comm' ça mo trouve la tarace. Comment dou-monde entré dans di-bois[16] en montant piti la-ravine là! Mo dir non! marron[17] même ça, fanigasse! Parié noir madam Lissir, ça qui té couri[18] n'a pas lontems là. Mo sivré la tarace, mo sivré, mo sivré, sivré, mon fizi en bas mon le-bras; mo marce comment ici comment ça; gros pié di-bois di fer tombé là; mo senti la fimé, mo dire: non, zaut' n'a pas loin! Mo faire dé pas, mo baisse en bas comme ça, mo trouve son la-caze, couvri ensembre[19] bacoua marron. Mo dire: non! n'a pas comm' ça, asper[20] va! Mo va alle dréte son la-porte même.

Mo marce, mo commence arrive[21] proce li même, a v'la mon li-pié marcé la haut[22] enne brance sec, li faire[23] cararaca; hi-i-i-i-i, papa! comment[24] cerf, mo dir' vous; our-r-r-r-r-r dans di-bois pa-pa-pa-pa-pa. Mo crié: « Arrête là, zanf …! » Li diré « Non va! na pas toi la zourdi. » Mo parti moi. « Comment! to n'a pas sivré zaut'! — Bon! to pense qui mo béte! Bon morceau[25] dou-monde comm' ça, mo tou sel, mo all' taque zaut' : hé hé ! laisse zaut' couri pito! »

cela, eux autres ne font que de se lever.

Alors moi baisse sous un framboisier; de cette manière moi trouve la trace (empreinte des pieds). Comment quelqu'un seroit entré dans le bois en montant par cette petite ravine là! Moi dire non! ce doit être un noir marron cela, enfant de g…! Je parie que c'est le noir de madame Lessur, celui qui s'est sauvé il n'y a pas longtemps. Moi suivre cette trace, je la suis, je la suis, je la suis, mon fusil sous mon bras; moi marcher par-ci et par-là: un gros pied de bois de fer est là par terre; moi sentir la fumée, moi dire: non, les autres ne sont pas loin! Moi faire deux pas, moi baisse en dessous comme ça, j'aperçois leur case, recouverte avec du vacouas[26] sauvage. Je dis: Non! il n'en sera pas ainsi, attends, va ! Je vais aller droit à leur porte même.

Je marche, je suis près de les atteindre ; mais voilà que mon pied marche sur une branche sèche qui fait cararaca ; hi-i-i-i-i-I (signe d'un prompt départ), papa ![27] comme un cerf, vous dis-je ; our-r-r-r-r-r (signe d'une course rapide) dans le bois pa-pa-pa-pa-pa (bruit des pas précipités); je crie: « Arrête-là, j… f…! » Eux dirent: « Non, va! ce ne sera pas toi aujourd'hui. » Je m'en vais moi. « Comment (dit l'un des auditeurs), tu ne les as pas poursuivis! — Bon! penses-tu que je sois une bête? Tant de personnes comme cela, moi tout seul, moi aller les attaquer. Hé hé! laisse-les se sauver plutôt! »

---

[14] *Aster*, à cette heure, alors, maintenant.

[15] *En bas pié*, en bas du pied, dessous, sous.

[16] *Di-bois* pour *du bois*. Ordinairement les noirs joignent notre article au substantif, et n'en font ainsi qu'un seul mot ; on en voit de fréquens exemples dans ce morceau : comme *la-ravine*, pour *ravine* ; *le-bras*, pour *bras* ; *la-case*, pour *case*, maison ; *li-pied*, pour *pied*, &c.

[17] *Marron* signifie proprement *sauvage*. On donne ici ce nom aux nègres esclaves qui se sauvent de chez leur maître pour aller vivre dans les bois.

[18] *Couri*, courir, partir, se sauver.

[19] *Ensembre*, ensemble, avec.

[20] *Asper*, espère, attends.

[21] *Commence arrive*, signifie j'arriverai bientôt, à l'instant.

[22] *La haut*, sur, dessus.

[23] *Li faire*, elle fait.

[24] *Comment*, comme.

[25] *Bon morceau*, un grand nombre, une grande quantité.

[26] Feuille d'une sorte de palmier.

[27] *Papa*. Nous n'avons pas en français l'équivalent de ce mot créole, qui signifie *monsieur d'une classe inférieure*; en pareil cas nous dirions *mon garçon*. Ce nom donné par un noir à un autre est toujours un signe de respect; il en est de même du mot *maman* pour les femmes.

Mo alle dans son boucan, mo trouve bon morceau la plime tanke,[28] ensemble la peau batate, mo dir' vous! La plime paye-en-qui, la paye maye en milon. Lon-tems zaut' té là! Mo quitte là, mo sivre la rivière, touzour mo alle dans mon poste, mo tende comment dou-monde marce, tsiaka, tsiaka, tsiaka, tsiaka. Aster mo arrêté: mo trouve Marezanne, missié[29] Desfontaines là. Li vini, manami,[30] farau,[31] ensemble zipe guingan Karikal, pariaka mi dans lé-rein; li arrive proce moi, mo dir' li : « Ou to allé, pit...! » Li n'a pas conné[32] qui li va fair encor; li fini sézi![33] Aster li dir' moi: « Ah! mon Dié, papa, mo dimande vous grâce; mo va donne vous ça qui vous voulé; laisse moi couri. — Vouti[34] f…. moi l'camp! Qui mo fair toi moi! »

Aster mo laisse li allé, mo dir' li : « Couri. » Mo sivré touzour sentié pour gagne dans mon poste. A v'la mo arrive bord la rivière là; mo trouve ça vié noir Moudiawa,[35] missié Carrière là;[36] li azise bien là haut roce,[37] la pesse[38] madam-céré,[39] fiou, fiou, fiou, fiou, fiou, fiou; mo dir' li : « To fini pri,[40] papa. — Eh bien! qui li va dire encor! » Mo dir' li : « Amene[41] to pagné ici. » Mo guette[42] là dans; mo trouve bon zangui,[43] camaron bon morceau, mo dir'

J'entre dans leur *boucan*[44] ; je trouve quantité de poils de *tenrec*, avec des pelures de patates, je vous l'assure ! des plumes de pailles-en-cul, de la paille de maïs en meule. Il faut que les autres (ces gens), aient été là long-temp ! Je m'éloigne de là, je suis la rivière, toujours pour me rendre à mon poste ; j'entends comme quelqu'un qui marche, tsiaka, tsiaka, tsisaka, tsiaka (imitation du bruit que fait une personne qui marche sur des feuilles sèches). A cette heure je m'arrête : je trouve Marie-Jeanne, de ce M. Desfontaines. Elle vient, mon ami, requinquée, avec une jupe en guingan de Karikal, un paliacat autour des reins; elle arrive près de moi, et je lui dis: « Où vas-tu, p… ? » Elle ne sait pas encore ce qu'elle doit faire; elle reste stupéfaite! Maintenant elle me dit: « Ah ! mon Dieu, *papa*, je vous demande grâce; je vais vous donner ce que vous voudrez; laissez-moi partir. — Veux-tu me f… le camp! Que ferois-je de toi, moi ! »

Alors je la laisse aller, et je lui dis : « Va-t-en. » Moi suivre toujours le sentier pour gagner mon poste. Voilà que j'arrive au bord de cette trivière là; je trouve ce vieux noir, Moudiawa, de M. Carrière que vous connaissez; il est assis à son aise sur une pierre, à la pêche des *madame-céré*; fiou, fiou, fiou, fiou, fiou, fiou (imitation du bruit que fait la ligne quand on la jette dans l'eau). Je lui dis: « Te voilà pris, papa! — Eh bien! que va-t-il dire encore? » Je lui dis: « Approche ton panier ici. » Je regarde dedans; je trouve de bonnes anguilles,

---

[28] *La plime tanke*, mot à mot, la plume tanrec. Les noirs appellent indistinctement *plumes*, les poils, les cheveux et les plumes proprement dites.
[29] *Missié*, monsieur.
[30] *Manami*, mon ami.
[31] *Farau*, élégant ; mais plutôt, requinqué.
[32] *Li n'a pas conné*, elle ne connoît pas, elle ne sait pas.
[33] *Li fini sézi* ; littéralement : *elle est finie saisie*, elle est saisie, stupéfaite, interdite
[34] *Vouti*, veux-tu.
[35] *Moudiawa*, nom d'une caste particulière de noirs Mozambiques.
[36] *Là*, celui que vous connoissez. Plus haut on a : *bord la rivière là*, ce qui signifie, *la rivière que vous connoissez, la rivière dont on a parlé déjà*.
[37] *Bien*, à son aise. *La haut roce*, sur une roche, une pierre.
[38] *La pesse*, à la pêche.
[39] *Madame-céré*, madame-céré, sorte de poisson ainsi nommé.
[40] *To fini pri*, tu es pris, te voilà pris ; ou littéralement *toi fini pris*.
[41] *Amène*, apporte.
[42] *Guette*, regarder, jeter les yeux.
[43] *Zangui*, anguille.
[44] Lieu où l'on fait la cuisine.

vous! Sifé va,[45] zoudi là, mo va faire cari moi; mo prend tout, mo mette dans mon boursac: mo laisse li ninque dé[46] piti madam-céré même; apré li couri. Mo arrive dans mon poste; mo resté zousqu'à midi, mo n'a pas tendé[47] na rien; apré mo tendé lé voix li-cien donné,[48] Enne piti mament mo tendé cote[49] Bazile là bas, di-i-i-i-i! Hé! mo dir', là dans sa,[50] va! Aster, enne piti mament encore, Grand-Louis appelle moi; mo prend mon cimin,[51] mo vini.	une grande quantité de camarons,[52] je vous l'assure ! Oui, par ma foi, aujourd'hui même, je vais faire un cari,[53] moi; je prends tout, je le mets dans mon bissac: je ne lui laisse rien que deux petits madame-céré; après quoi li s'enfuit. J'arrive à mon poste; j'y reste jusqu'à midi sans rien entendre; après j'entends la voix des chiens donner. Un petit moment après j'entends du côté de Bazile là-bas, di-i-i-i-i (imitation de l'explosion d'une arme à feu)! Hé ! dis-je, celui-là est dans le sac, va! Alors, un petit moment encore après, Grand-Louis m'appelle; je me remets en route, et je reviens.

Freycinet (1827: 407-11)

A notable feature of Freycinet's text is the sporadic use of the hyphen to mark articles which are agglutinated to nouns, e.g. la-ravine, di-bois, etc. This is similarly a sporadic feature of **1818b**, which raises the unanswerable question of whether Freycinet or Chrestien was the innovator of this convention.

14. 1818b Earliest translation of a La Fontaine fable into Creole

During his two-week stay in Mauritius, Freycinet obtained a draft of an MC translation of *Le Lièvre et la Tortue* by François Chrestien (see **1822** for details). Creole translations of some of La Fontaine's fables were subsequently to appear in Reunion and in several of the créolophone islands of the Caribbean, but Chrestien was the first to do this. However, such translations were to form only a small proportion of his overall output in MC.

Freycinet was very favourably impressed by Chrestien's work and this caused him to evoke *la possibilité de reproduire en créole un grand nombre de morceaux de notre littérature*, a view firmly rejected 60 years later by Baissac (1880). The version of this fable which Chrestien published four years later differs in a number of details. For that reason the 1818b and 1822 versions are set out side-by-side below. Differences between the two versions are printed in bold. Comment on these differences follows.

LE LIÈVRE ET LA TORTUE

1818b	1822
Ein' **torti** avec **lièvre** été voulé parié **Ein** zour qui va mié galoppé Pour arrivé drette **ein** li-pié banane: « Tout d'bon, maman **torti**, vous y en a trop l'arzent	Ein' **Torti** avec **Lièvre** été voulé parié **Ein'** zour qui va mié galoppé Pour arrivé drette **ein'** li-pié banane: « Tout d'bon, maman **Torti'** vous y en a trop l'arzent,

---

[45] *Sifé va*, pour *si fait va* ; oui, par ma foi.
[46] *Ninque dé*, rien que deux.
[47] *Tendé*, entendu. *Na rien*, il n'y a rien, rien.
[48] *Lé voix li-cien donné*, la voix des chiens donner (terme de chasse).
[49] *Cote*, du côté.
[50] *Là dans sa*, celui-là est dans le sac.
[51] *Cimin*, chemin, route.
[52] *Camaron*, sorte de crustacé.
[53] *Cari*, sorte de ragoût de l'Inde fortement épicé.

« **Vou l'esprit** li maron dans milié la savanne, Avec moi là vous lité a présent ? Dir' **lièvre** avec **torti** qui coute li tranquille N'a pas pèr mon zami ; **torti** répond' li, Vous, ça qui blancs appell' di-monde **azile**,« Moi **porte** mon **la-case**, et li **réd'** mon li-pié ; Mais c'est égal, moi va parié, Moi **connois** comment moi va faire : **Mésuré vous cimin ; chaqu'ein'** son l'esprit. Quand fini mesuré ; à v'la **ti** té parti, P'tit papa **lièvr'** crié li : « **Mon** commère **Emmen'** la gazett', **prend** gard' vous ennuyé ! Quand vous trouvé galant, n'a pas besoin causé ; Quand mêm' couroupas, **vou p'tit** frère **Passé vous** à côté, Ou bien moi va gagné. Et p'tit papa **lièvre** amisé, Cassé bouquet pross' la rivière, Dans l'herbe frais roulé, sauté, Et **torti là touzour** marcé. Lièvre à la fin guetté Li voir **torti** dans bitte Li voulé galoppé bien vite Mais son nation **là** trop tourdi, Et li té **perdé** son pari.	» **Vou - l'esprit** li maron dans milié la savanne. « Avec moi là vous lité a présent ? Dir' **Lièvre** avec **Torti** qui **couté**-li tranquille. « N'a pas pèr mon zami **Torti** répond' li, Vous ça qui blancs appell' di-monde *agile* « Moi, **porté** mon **la caze** et li **rèd'** mon li-pié « Mais c'est égal, moi va parié, « Moi **connais** comment moi va faire ; « **Mesuré vou - çimin; chaquein'** son l'esprit; » Quand fini mesuré ; à v'la **li** té parti. P'tit papa **Lièvr'** crié li : « **mon** commère, «**Emmèn'** la gazett', **prends** gard' vous ennuyé ! « Quand vous trouvé galant n'a pas besoin causé « Quand mêm' couroupas, **vou - p'tit** frère, « **Passé - vou'** à côté « Ou bien moi va gagné. » Et p'tit papa **Lièvre** amisé, Cassé bouquet pross' la rivière, Dans l'herbe frais roulé, sauté, **Ramass' l'astron pour son soupé** Et **Torti - là touzours** marcé. Lièvre à la fin guetté Li voir **Torti** dans bitte. Li voulé galoppé bien vite, Mais son nation **li** trop tourdi, Et li té **perdi** son pari.
Freycinet (1827: 411-12)	Chrestien ([1822] 1831: 25-26)

Some of the changes in the 1822 version look like improvements made by Chrestien in the intervening period, for example the initial capitals for Lièvre and Torti, the use of italics and the change from z to g in *agile* to indicate that this word is French rather than MC, the modernization of *connois* to *connais*, and perhaps the addition of –s in *prends gard'*. Other changes cast some doubt on the accuracy of the **1818b** version. Two verbs, *coute* and *porte* in the **1818b** version, were published as *couté* and *porté* in 1822. The *ti* in *à v'la ti té parti* (1818b) can only be a misprint for *li* (as in 1822).

Noteworthy features common to both the 1818b and 1822 versions are:

- The inconsistent use of a hyphen to indicate agglutination, e.g. di-bois, la-bousse, là-sasse, li-zié (as was mentioned earlier).
- The past tense marker occurs in its disyllabic form *été* only when following a consonant; following a vowel, the abbeviated form *té* is used.
- The first person subject pronoun is systematically *moi* (instead of *mo* or *mô* as in **1805**, many other texts, and in all texts from the 1840s onwards).
- The completive aspect marker is invariably *fini* and is not always distinguishable from the verb *fini* ('to finish').

Two other features of Chrestien's spelling found here and in his later work include:

- Frequent and seemingly unnecessary omission of a final vowel (unpronounced in French) and its replacement by an apostrophe, e.g. gard', red', ramass'.
- Use a hyphen to link possessive *vou(s)* to the following noun, e.g. *vou – l'esprit*. His intention was no doubt to alert his readers to the fact that *vou(s)* followed by a

hyphen corresponded to French *votre* and *vos*. This practice was not followed by other writers.

15.   1818c Tchéga

On pages 403-05, Freycinet writes about the *Chéga, ou plutôt* **Tchéga**. (This word of Bantu origin is today invariably pronounced *sega*). He gives the titles, but not the lyrics, of five segas poplar at that time: **Chéga** *de Magasin-Bon-Goût,*[54] *Air mozambique;* **Chéga** *de Maman Jeanne, Air mozambique; Autre* **Chéga** *Mozambique; Quatrième* **Chéga** *Mozambique; et* **Cari Lalo***, Air malgache.* He adds that *Le nom de* **chéga** *se donne aussi à une danse mozambique qui pourroit être comparée au* **fandango** *des Espagnols.* He also provides the first attestation of the word "**tamtam**" (Freycinet 1827 *Historique* volume 1, deuxième partie, livre 2).

16.   1818d Further papers and communications relative to the slave trade at the Mauritius and Bourbon, and the Seychelles

moi n'a pas connais parler François, ni les autres non plus (Port-Louis 7/8/1818)
        (British Parliamentary Papers - Slave Trade vol. 69, p 37).

17.   1822a Ratsitatane's trial

At the request of the then ruler of Madagascar, the British agreed to have the troublesome Prince Ratsitatane sent to Mauritius and be imprisoned there. Ratsitatane managed to escape from prison and is alleged to then have met up with a group of maroons with whom he planned to carry out a series of attacks on whites and their property, but accounts of this vary considerably. He was eventually caught and brought to trial. Such records of the trial as survive contain only the few examples in MC which follow.

> 26 fev 1822
>
> **Anglais monte français restez. Dimain nous voulé la Guerre avec zotres pour Touyé vous.** f 94
>
> *Sur quoi Brutus lui avait dit* **Si pas qui ça betise là** *et s'est en allé.*
>
> *Le nommé Brutus a passé devant leur boutique et leur a dit en passant,* **vous ne savez pas vous autres que ça prince malgache qui au bagne fini sorti là haut montagne pour faire la Guerre,** *sans dire si c'était aux blancs ou aux noirs.* f 170
>
> *Lui a demandé «* **hé bien qui ci ça** *et lui a dit* **c'est ça lé Roi malgache qui fini aller làhaut montagne qui z'autres guetter ; que Jupiter a repété qui bétise ça est ce qui moi capable quitter mon maître pour ça le Roi malgache là »**. f 175
>
> 27 fev1822
>
> **Lui Lapaix était marron bon à vini** f 210.
>
> *A répondu* **Si vous peur laisse moi faire tout seul, moi capable avec Tonnerre** f 218.

The proceedings also included early attestations of two MC words: **simbou** F 223 ('roll of cloth put on the head to support a heavy object') and **langouty** F 352 (Colonial Office, CO167/64, Extracts from Trial of Ratsitatane)

18.   1822b Chrestien's first publication: *Les essais d'un bobre africain*

Chrestien has been described as an administrator and *interprète auprès du Tribunal pour le patois mauricien* (Sauzier [n d] cited by Hookoomsing 1979).

---

[54] Baissac (1888) cite un couplet de cette chanson:
> Quand mo passé magasin Bon-Goût,
> Mo léquier sauté, mo lipieds côlé.

Benoît (1998) was able to find a copy of this extremely rare first edition,[55] thanks to which one learns that, immediately below the title of this publication are the words:

> *Petit recueil de poésies, composé de Chansons choisies et corrigées, et de quelques Fables traduites de Lafontaine, en créole; suivies de méditations mélancoliques.*
> Par un AMATEUR[56]

This first edition contains 17 items in MC: eleven songs and six translations of La Fontaine fables. Note that Chrestien's name does not appear on the title page

The *bobre africain* refers to a single-string musical instrument re-created by the African slave and, metonymically, to the player, in this case the amateur poet and his MC rendering of French songs and fables. Chrestien's *Essais* is the first attempt at literary composition in MC, so the instrument has to be tuned, the audience prepared and the work dedicated to and blessed by friends, well-wishers and esteemed personalities. He starts with an "avant-propos nécessaire", which opens as follows:

> Il est fort difficile *le Créole* ; surtout de façon à en conserver la prononciation, qui en fait une partie du mérite, et à le plier aux règles de la poésie. (…)

Referring to his country – *mon pays* - which boasts of so many brilliant, accomplished and respectable people, he argues:

> Mon pays, dis-je, n'a point encore produit de grammairien pour son patois ; pour cet idiome simple et naïf dans lequel nous avons dit et nos premiers sentimens et nos premiers besoins et dont les expressions ramènent ces souvenirs attachans par lesquels on semble rétrograder dans la vie et conjurer un instant ce sable inflexible qui règle nos fugitives années.

He then goes on to explain how he would proceed to create some sort of an orthography in order to get closer to the MC pronunciation rather than to French (see below).

He would also appeal to the reader for his compositions, written *avec ce faible qu'on a pour sa patrie et dans le désir de donner quelque relief à son patois qui n'est pas sans agrément*.

Chrestien's translation of a La Fontaine fable in this 1822b publication is given above in order to compare it with an earlier version; see **1818b**. The lyrics of two of his songs are reproduced below, while those of a third, *Mr et Mme Denis*, are given in full and discussed in Stein (*this volume*).

LE JALOUX

AIR : *Je veux être un chien, à coups de pieds, &a.*

Ensemble mon frêr' Sans-Façon
A soir nous té conduir' Lizon
Ça n'a pas difficil' pour croire?
A v'là quein' sacré l'africain
En passant attrap' son la-main.

(On parle.) Eh! Papa soldat, quand même la plime poule dans vou-sapeau, avec grand couteau amare dans vou-lé-rein, moi n'a pas pér vous, si vous connois? ça femme-là pour moi tout sel' moi n'a pas la mode malgaçe.. Vous tendez?

(Continuation de l'air.)

Moi dir' li fant-d' cien
A coup d'pieds à coup*d'poings
Moi cass' ton la-guél' dans ton maçoire!

Comm' nous la gorze été gratté
Dans ein' la-cantin' nous rentré
Ça n'a*pas difficil' pour croire

---

[55] See note 1 above.
[56] These words are not included in the second (1831) edition.

> Garçon qui té vidé flacon
> Fair' li-zié doux avec Lison?

(On parle.) *Mon zami, fair' vou-louvraze tranquille hem?. vous-maître n'a pas mette vous là pour guetté les*filles?..*

> Moi dir' li fant-d' cien
> A coup d'pieds, &a.

> V'la qui nous commencé lassé
> Avec Lison nous assisé!
> Ça n'a pas difficil' pour croire?
> Ein' noir à-bord qui té passé
> Tout-iniment tir' son condé?..

(On parle.) *Papa matelot doucement vous in-pé, ça n'a pas goudron pour vous manié!*

> Moi dir' li fant-d' cien
> A coup d'pieds, &a.

> Comment nous té passé bazard
> Nous dé marcé en bas l'hangard
> Ça n'a pas difficil' pour croire?
> Moi voir' dans noir ein' vié-maman
> Avec Lison parl' tout douç'ment.

(On parle.) *N'a pas ça, maman gàteau, vende vou-marçandise mais n'a pas besoin montre l'esprit mon femme, moi n'a pas content ça?*

> Moi dir' li fant-d'çien
> A coup d'pieds à coup de poings
> Moi cass' ton la-guél dans ton maçoire!

(Chrestien [1822] 1831: 10-11)

Another lyric from this publication is *Le Pauvre Diable*, probably Chrestien's best known lyric. However, the somewhat distorted version of this which appears, without acknowledgement, in Dumas' *Georges* (1843) is probably even better known. The two versions are printed side-by-side below. The main reason for doing this is that Dumas is a well-known author whose books are reprinted from time to time. As a consequence, this lyric is frequently « discovered » and taken to be a genuine example of MC. The reasons why this is a distorted version of Chrestien's original are interesting.

It has long been recognised that Dumas could only be, at most, part author of this book. The main reasons for this are (a) the descriptions of the mountains and the flora of Mauritius are so detailed and accurate that only someone who had spent a considerable amount of time in Mauritius could have written them; and (b) that the names of many characters in the book are the names of real people, French and British, who lived in that island in the first decade of British rule (from 1812). The chief Mauritian "suspect"[57] as co-author or sole author is Félicien Mallefille who left Mauritius as a boy in 1822 and is known to have been friendly with Dumas in Paris in about 1840 (as indicated in the introduction to the 1974 edition of this book) but his (co-) authorship has never been confirmed. Nevertheless, history provides two very important pieces of supporting evidence which are not widely known. Chrestien (1822) was the first popular publication in MC aimed at the literate general public and must have made quite an impact, being republished twice. It is thus not unlikely that Mallefille would have known some of its songs when he left in 1822. The differences (in bold typeface) between the Chrestien original and the Dumas version set out below are all consistent with someone attempting to recall the lyrics of a song they had heard as a child in a language they had had little

---

[57] This word is appropriate because Georges of the title gives a very unflattering picture of the whites. He hates them because they will not accept him as an equal while he is at the same time sexually attracted to white women whom he pursues with some success. The book outraged Mauritian whites when copies reached the island and it is said that some copies were burned in public.

opportunity or reason to use for about 20 years (with the exception of one obvious typographical error: *maigache* for 'malgache'). The other evidence comes from the plot of the second half of the book which is in most respects the story of the Malagasy prince Ratsitatane. He was imprisoned in Mauritius in about 1821 at the request of the then Malagasy ruler who suspected that the prince was planning to overthrow him. In Mauritius, Ratsitatane bribed the prison guards to let him escape and he fled to the hills. There he is said to have met up with a group of maroons and become their leader. He is then alleged to have planned a serious of attacks on white-owned property, stealing guns and food (but information about this varies considerably). He was eventually caught and brought to trial. Some court records survive and include a few slave responses in MC. The whole Ratsitatane affair was undoubtedly the biggest news story in the Mauritius of 1822 and turned the prince into a folk hero as is still the case today. This seems to have been the inspiration for the second half of the plot of the "Dumas" book, except that it is Georges who escapes from prison and goes on to lead the maroon attacks against the whites. A boy who left Mauritius in 1822 would not forget the details of the most exciting event of that year. It thus seems certain that Mallefille made, at the very least, a major contribution to "Dumas'" *Georges*.

Chrestien ([1822] 1831: 16-17) **Le Pauvre Diable.** Air: *Du petit matelot.*	Dumas (1843: 129-30)
Moi resté dans ein' p'tit la-caze Qui faut baissé quand pour rentré ; Quand mon la-têt' dans son faitaze Mon li-pié là haut son plancé.. (*bis*.) Moi n'a pas besoin la limière A soir quand moi voulé dormi Car pour moi trouvé la lin' claire N'a pas manqué trous Dié merci.. (*bis*.)	Moi resté dans *un* p'tit la caze Qu'*il* faut baissé *moi* pour entré ; [] Mon la tête *touché* son faitaze *Quand* mon li pié *touché* plancé. Moi *té* n'a pas besoin *lumière*, *Le* soir, quand moi voulé dormi ; Car, pour moi trouvé *lune* claire, N'a pas manqué trous, Dié merci !
Mon li-lit ein' p'tit natt' malgace Mon l'oreiller, morceau bois-blanc ; Mon gargoulett', ein' vié cal'basse Ou moi mett' l'arack zour de l'an. (*bis*.) Quand mon-femm' pour fair' badinaze Sam'di comm' ça vini soupé Moi fair' couit dans mon p'tit la-caze Bréd' diboute et moutouc grillé.. (*bis*.)	Mon *lit est un* p'tit natt' *maigace* [sic], Mon l'oreill*é* morceau bois blanc, Mon gargoul*ette un'* vié calbasse *Où* moi met l'arack, zour de lan. *Quand mon* femm' pour fair *p'tit ménaze*, Sam'di comme ça vini soupé, Moi fair' *cuir*, dans mon p'tit la caze, *Banane sous la cend'* grillé.
Dans mon coffre n'a pas ferrire Zamais moi n'a pas fermé li ; Dans bambou comm' ça sans serrire Qui va fouill' mon quat' langoutis. (*bis*.) Dimanç' quand moi gagné zournée Si moi y en a morceau tabac Pour fair' faro mon la-fimée Moi mett' li dans pip' couroupas. (*bis*.)	*A* mon coffre n'a pas *serrure*, *Et* jamais moi n'a [] fermé li. Dans bambou comm'ça sans *ferrure* Qui va *cherché* mon [] langouti ? *Mais dimanch' si* gagné zournée [] Moi *l'achète un* morceau d'tabac. *Et tout la s'maine, moi fais* fumée *Dans grand pipe, à moi carouba.*

Points of particular interest are (1) the grammatical inaccuracy of *té n'a pas* (5th line of the first verse). The tense marker *te* can only follow the negator. (2) The use of the French copula *est* in the first line of the second verse. MC has only zero copula in such a structure. (3) The author has clearly forgotten the word *couroupas* which represents Makhuwa /kurupa/, the giant African land snail whose spiral shell can grow to 15 cm or more and which could easily be adapted for use as a pipe. The modern MC pronunciation is /kurpa/. *Carouba* is not a word found in any other text.

19.   **1823** Mauritius Archives JB 151

Tiens voilà ton fusil   moi fini casse la et si mon été en a couteau, moi va bien arrange toi, coquin détachement. (As reported by Scarr 1998 in a footnote)

Scarr gives what appears to be a very free translation of this: 'Hang on to your gun - I'll end up smashing it - and if I had a knife with me I'd see to you, you coward of a detachment'. The reason for gaps before and after *moi fini* is not obvious, nor is it apparent that *casse* is necessarily a verb here. No other example of the first person subject pronoun written *mon* is known in MC. One would expect this to be written *moi*, as in the two other cases in this text, or *mo*. There is also no indication of why *coquin* is translated as 'coward' (rather than as 'scoundrel' or 'rascal').[58]

20.   **1826** An expletive

Ac fait fout (Mauritius Slave Trade, Minutes of Evidence 13-23 May 1826, in British Parliamentary Papers – Slave Trade I, p 19)

21.   **1830** A hymn in MC

... the talent for communicating [religious] instruction is not possessed by all; and the [language] spoken and understood by the slave population of the Mauritius is a peculiar <u>French patois</u> in which an English person even after a long residence, rarely attains such a proficiency as to be able to apply it fluently to the sacred subjects of religion* (*see Note C) (Vicars 1830: 13).

It is very desirable that they should be well acquainted with the French language, for without this foundation time would be lost before a facility of communication could be acquired;... (Vicars 1830: 17-18).

HYMN
Après quéques bonnes années
Qui va passé vit' vit'ment ;
Comment nous zaut va sanzé.
Quand nous allé l'enterrement !

Moi na pas capab resté
Bien long-tems là-haut la terre ;
Mon âme li allé Bon-Dié,
Mon li corps dans cimitière.

Quand Bon-Dié va fair' l'appel,
La trompette va sonné fort !
Si-pas moi tremblé tout sél,
Quand va lévé tous les morts !

Si-pas, comment li <u>a</u> fair',
Comment li va zizé moi?
A'sterè - la, ça fair' moi pèr,
Maziné ça grand lè roi !

Tout-d'bon moi va fair' la prière,
A'sterè - là qui moi vivant,
Faut pas moi gagné misère,
Pour li pini moi long-tems.

Seigneur Bon-Dié pardonné moi,
Et fair' moi ein bon lè quèr,
Pour moi capab' servi toi,
Pour moi gagné vrai bonher !

---

[58] In December 2000, Baker visited the Mauritius Archives but was unable to find Scarr's text in JB151.

> Moi fair' mon possib' vous plair',
> Caque zour moi na pas fair' mal;
> Malade vini, na pas pèr,
> Quand-même la mort, c'est égal   (Vicars 1830: 61, note C)

The language of this hymn is consistent with other texts of the period. Note that all verbs have their long forms, consistent with white usage at this time. The *a* in the first line of the third verse is probably a misprint for *va* because this occurs as the future marker on seven other occasions and because no subsequent example of *a* in this role is found until 1860. One point of interest is *nous zaut* in the first verse since this does not appear to signify exclusive first person plural here (cf the **1816** text).

Vicars does not name the author of this hymn (but it is clearly not himself).

22.   1831 Les Essais d'un Bobre Africain. (second, expanded edition)

Chrestien's dedication of this second edition was to a lady in France, separated by the wide ocean, most probably for ever, and includes the words:

> C'est sous vos auspices que j'ai osé faire parôitre cette seconde édition de mes poésies créoles. Puissé-je ainsi, par le patois naïf de nos heureux climats, rappeler dans votre mémoire les premières et douces années de la vie et exciter un instant ce pur sourire que le cœur accorde, si volontiers, aux souvenirs de la patrie (...).

Finally, to his friends, he wrote:

> Puisez un grain de folie
> Dans le gaulois du pays

F&R state that this second edition contains only five MC items not in the first edition. This is not the case (as the words *Augmentée de près du double* on the title page clearly suggest). The 1831 edition in fact includes ten MC items not in the 1822 edition (of which six were translations of La Fontaine). F&R wrongly indicate that four of these were published for the first time in the 1869 edition. They also accidentally omit the final MC item in the 1831 edition, *Les animaux malades de la peste*, which we reproduce below.

Les Animaux Malades De La Peste.
TRADUCTION LIBRE DE LAFONTAINE

> Ein' zour comm'ça,
> Dans tout pays grand'terre,
> Ein' bien mauvais malad' qui zaut' dir' *Choléra*,
> Avec tous zanimaux eté fair' grand' la-guerre,
> Et maniér' li té travaill' là,
> N'a pas long-tems tous va dans cimetière.
> Lé-roy lion à s'tér dir' zautres : " Mon z'enfans
> " Moi té tendé quand blancs y en-a mauvais zaffaire
> " N'a pas besoin fouillé long-tems ;
> " Pour fair' bon dié fini son la-colère
> " Y-en-a quéqu'zein qui touyé son lé-corps,
> " Allons voir, à s'tér là, qui mérité pour mort
> " Et quand mêm' zautres là n'a pas couri la messe,
> " Parlez zautres péçés comment dire à confesse :
> " Moi, pour bien dir', moi n'a pas va caçié
> " Quéqu'fois cabrit moi té manzé
> " Quand pour sauvé zautres gagné paresse
> " Et souvent, quand moi faim,
> " Moi manzé son gardien. "
> Zacot, qui couté li, dire à s'tér là : - " Mon maître
> " En vérité - dié vous trop bon !
> " Qui celle - là va pensé vous n'a pas té raison

" Manzé cabrit ou bien mouton ?
" Et ça n'a pas ein' grand l'honnér, peut-être,
" Pour son gardien qui mort dans vous lé-dents ! "
Comm' ça zacot té dire et zautres tous contents.
Tigre, Loulou, été parlé chaquéne
Quand son tour arrivé
Mais, ma foi, n'a pas té la peine
Ça zens là n'a pas fair' péçé
Et zautres tous li doux, li sazes
Sirop di-miel dans zaut visazes
Comment mam'zell avant marié.
Pauvre bourriqu' qui branlé son la-tête
Pour conté son paquêt arrivé à s'tér là :
- " Moi là n'a pas voulé faire ici l'embaras,
Li dir, " ein' zour, qui peut-être moi bête,
" Moi passé dans l'habitation
" Ou prêtres fair' planté son bréde et son loignon,
" Quand prend di-bien l'égliz' sis pas ça malhonnête ?
" Mais l'herbe senti bon, diable dans mon l'esprit
" Morceau fataqu' moi té manzé tout crid,
" Ça n'a pas té pour moi, moi parlé sans malice.
- Couh ! à v'la tout zaut la-bouce à ster - là li bouilli,
Zautres crié : - " Condir' li la police
" L'herbe qui pour *jésuit* ça coquin - là manzé,
" Ça même fair' bon Dié façé,
" Et son la tête à s'ter là faut coupé ! "
- Ma foi son compte été fini bien vite,
Et li, ça zour là mêm' n'a plis besoin marmitte.

Quand pour zizé ça qui rice ou qui fort,
Pauvre diable, tout sél, qui toujours tort! (Chrestien 1831: 53-54)

23. 1832a *La Grand'maman*

Although not published until 1838 (or 1839, see below), three of the four MC pieces contained in Chrestien's *Album Tropical* are individually dated 1832, of which we have chosen *La Grand'maman* to reproduce here.

LA GRAND'MAMAN

chanson philosophique.

DANS LE SENS DE LA PROCLAMATION AUX NOIRS, DU GÉNÉRAL COLVILLE (JUIN 1832)

Air : *Mon épouse fait ma gloire &a.* (du Sénateur)

1
Colas tous les jours vous boire
Plitôt couté - moi causé ;
Vous - la trop content z'histoire
Qui fair' vous l'esprit viré ?
N'a pas vaut-mié vous croir' moi
Fair' vous comment l'autrefois ;
Travaillez
Toujours gais
Après - ça vous va dansé
Et zamais vous gagné batté ! (*)

2
Et puis quand fini la danse
Vous capable boire ein' coup
Mais gardez - ça pour Dimance
Pour zaut' n'a pas grondé vou ;
Dans la s'maine mon zenfans
Fair' vous - maîtres li contens.
Travaillez
Toujours gais
Après - ça vous va dansé
Et zamais vous gagné batté.

---

* Observez l'époque. [This is Chrestien's own footnote – eds]

3

Quand moi sorti dans la messe,
Ça moi n'a pas cacié vous,
Vous papas dans mon zênesse
Été fair' moi li-ziés doux ;
Et Sam'dis, après soupé,
Moi dir' vous tchéga roulé !
    Travaillez
    Toujours gais
Après-ça vous va dansé
Et zamais vous gagné batté.

4.

Quéqu'fois comme'ça dans l'office
Quand fini l'ouvraz' pour blancs
Li rend' moi pitit service
Et tous lés dés nous contents ;
Mais zamais, bon-Dié connaît
Nous z'enfans mauvais sizet
    Travaillez
    Toujours gais
Après ça vous va dansé
Et zamais vous gagné batté.

5.

Mais moi té souffri misère …
Vous papa fini manqué !
Moi sivré - li dans cim'tière
Et puis pour moi consolé
Tous les mois moi prend mari ; –
    (avec une larme)
Ça n'a pas fair' blié li !
    Travaillez
    Toujours gais
Après ça vous va dansé
Et zamais vous gagné batté.

6.

Gouvernèr mêm' dans son lettre
Va parlé vous comment moi ;
Ça mêm' comment dir' vous maître
Ça mêm' Grand Papa ma foi ;
Si vou - yen-a l'*ambition*
Si vous tendé la raison,
    Couté li
    Son l'esprit
Va dir' vous : Dansez, causé,
Mais zamais quitté travaillé.

Chrestien (1838: 270-72)

24. **1832b** *Faire serment*

((Jean-Pierre)) Le défenseur :	Il a vue M.Durand et Lamour après crocher dans bagasse. Est-ce long-temps avant la rixe que M.Durand a frappé Lamour ? R : Oui, long-temps ; M. Durand a frappé Lamour avec un morceau de bagasse et de suite Lamour a jeté à terre.
((Augustin))	R : Tout ça zaffaire là, aussi, moi n'a pas connais. Q : Vous connais faire serment ? R : Non. Q : Vous connais bon Dié ? R : Non.
((Charles))	Q : Vous connais faire serment ? R : Sarron ? Q : Vous connais faire serment ? R : Ah ! Sarment ? oui. Q: Comment vous faire? R : Faire sarment bon Dié.
((Jean-Baptiste))	Q : Vous connais faire serment ? R : Non. Q : Vous connais bon Dié ? R : Moi connais. Q : Comment vous faire serment? R : Moi pas encore allé l'église. Q : Vous n'a pas connais faire serment ? R : Moi n'a pas connais.
((Figaro))	Q : Vous connais faire serment ? R : Non. Q : Vous connais bon Dié ? R : Oui. Q : Comment vous jurez bon Dié ? R : Moi connais jurer bon Dié, quand moi parle la vérité li va soulage moi.

> Q : Combien bann'années vous y enna ?
> R : Quatorze.   ((Il a trois fois cet âge)) (*Le Cernéen* 18 mai 1832)

25. **1832c** Letter from Pèdre.

A letter to the editor signed "Pèdre, esclave de MM Pitot" (but obviously written by a Franco-Mauritian) ends with the following words:

> … je passé mes journées à chanter sur un air Mozambique, en m'accompagnant de mon Bobre: **Tété tombé, tété dibouté** (*Le Cernéen* 5 juin 1832).

26. **1835** Nicolay's *Proclamation* (Pour noirs esclaves dans Maurice)

This is the only official publication known in English, French, and MC.[59] The tone of the MC version is extremely patronizing e.g. **[eine noir bon sizet] mérité pour appelé lé Roi son papa!** or **ça mois qui vini là, qui appelé** *Février.* The text is reproduced in full in both Chaudenson (1981: 115-20) and F&R (pp 101-10).

27. **1837** Souvenirs

The MC samples in Maure (1840) are dated 1837 by Baker & Hookoomsing (eds, 1987) because that is when he returned to France after many years in Mauritius. The first sample refers to the revolutionary period and the second apparently to the later 1820s. But there is no guarantee that, when he came to write his memoirs, he would remember the precise wording used up to forty years earlier.

> ça citoyen la République été un bon blanc ; avec li toujours bon poids (Maure 1840: 70)

Maure complains that, although there have been protectors of slaves etc., nothing is done for those with full civil rights but in difficulties. Example:

> *Mama Rita dans un bureau particulier d'indemnité*
>
> - N'a pas ici qui appelle bureau l'indignité ?
> - Oui: qui vous voulé ?
> - Moi vini Trois-Islots, moi y en a, en [sic] noir, en [sic] négresse et en [sic] petit créole; o vela [sic][60] papier qui parlé. Moi pauvre, moussié ; gouvernement donné moi morceau du riz, moi misère. Blanc diré moi, ici donné l'argent, moi vié, n'a pas capable travail.
> - Sizé, bonne femme. (*On avance un fauteuil*)
>
> *Ici commence une scène dégoûtante. La cupidité, qui veut arracher à la misère sa dernière ressource, prend tous les masques, toutes les formes, use de tous les moyens pour y parvenir.*
>
> - Comment vou appelé ?
> - Moi appelé Rita, Mama Rita ; moi créole Madame Magon, Ville Bague li qui été affranchi moi.
> - Vous voulé l'argent, bonne femme ?
> - Qui na pas voulé, tout dimande [sic][61] content l'argent, moi ici, moi voulé.
> - Eh ben, nous va donné vous. Vous na pas zenfans ? na pas papa, na pas mama ?
> - Personne, moussié. Moi vié comme ça, comment moi va gagné papa, mama ? na pas personne, moi tout seul.
> - Si nous donné vous cent piastres, vous va content ?
> - Grand merci, bon Dieu, moi va bien content…(Maure 1840: 352-53).

---

[59] But note that Chrestien's *La Grand'maman* makes reference to a Proclamation aux Noirs, du Général Colville (Juin 1832). It is not impossible that there may also have been an MC version of this but no copy if known.

[60] An apparent error for avela 'voilà'. The preceding three *en* also seem to be typesetting errors.

[61] An apparent error for dimonde 'person'. The book was printed in France and, given the mention of money, it is likely that the typesetter, unfamiliar with MC, might have interpreted handwritten *dimonde* as *dimande* (demande).

28. **1838 *Album Tropical***

Chrestien's *Album Tropical* is clearly marked with 1838 as its year of publication (even if it did not actually appear until the following year; see 1839e) but, as noted above (1832a), three of its four MC items are individually dated 1832. The fourth, which is missing from F&R but reproduced here, must have been written several years later since Victoria did not become Queen until June 1837.

DOMINGUE,
ARRIÈRE PETIT FILS DU DOMESTIQUE DE
PAUL & VIRGINIE,
A SA MAJESTÉ LA REINE VICTORIA

Madame la Reine !

Vous grand Madame blanc, moi pauvre noir …. Comment moi va capable causé avec vous ? — Mais, si vous connais, en bas nous la peau comment di-bois ébenne, y-en-a morceau léquèr pour content vous, pour béni vous comment dire nous maman même, pour dire vous grand merci la liberté qui vous tonton été faire nous gagné et pour prier bon Dié pour li soulaze vous dans l'ouvraze, bon morceau qui vou y en a, pour condire tous ça grands l'habitations là qui dans vous zordres !

Moi té dans mon la-caze tranquile après commande mon vouve pour la-pèce pour mon pitits …. A v'la moi tendé tout d'ein coup : « Nous lé-Roi fini mort … Nous bon lé-Roi fini manqué ! » —Ah ! mon Dié ! Moi dire, grand malhèr fini arrivé ! — petit moment moi tende encore … : « Y-en-a eine zène Madame, bon madame, zolie madame, son famille même, qui fini vini la Reine. — Moi soupiré à s'tèr, mon léquèr li fané comment à soir quand di vent frais vini dans la montagne ! — et puis moi voir encore tout dimonde après dire vous : Salam, salam, — zautres tous voulé crire vous, soldats sortis ensemble zautres pavillons, zofficiers tous contens, tous farauds, la mizique soufflé, canon tiré !! — eh ! eh ! moi dire, moi aussi voulé s'en mêlé, quand même moi vié, quand même mon l'esprit n'a pas connois parlé, di-monde qui bon n'a pas va pousse - moi, pèt-être ? — et puis, Madame la Reine, moi prié vous pour vous n'a pas façé avec moi : moi prié bon Dié aussi pour vous toujours ça va bien, pour vous toujours content, pour qui zamais la guerre vini faire vous çagrin ! — et puis si vous mariez …. ah ! par exemple Madame la Reine moi engaze vous pour vous marié, moi : — Faut vous prend eine bon garçon, eine *bon-vivant* (comment zautres parlé) qui tout di-monde va dire « li bien », qui va content vous bien comme il faut, qui son l'esprit va travaille la zournée pour vous - la-bouce touzours rié. — Quéque zour, pèt-être, vous va gagné zenfans qui va dire vous : — *maman maman !* — Si vous connois, ça parole - là li douce comment sirop di-miel ; li faire sauté léquer comment soleil quand li sorti dans la*mer après qui l'oragan fini ! Et puis ça mari là, ça zenfans là, tout ça là va comment vous même et nous tous va content zautres comment vous même.

Moi tombe dans vous li-piés.

29. **1839a Letter from *Zean ensemble Prosper***

Moussié La Gazette,

Vous ti dire Moussié Sirandale fin' donne nous boire zour Noël di vin, la bierre ensemble la liquère. Laut' zour vous ti dire Gouvernère bête à cause li causé quiqu' çose qui li n'a pas coné : à c't hère vous même qui bête, vous parle ça qu'vous n'a pas coné. M. Sirandale ça même qui zize pour nous, li ti donne ene grand bal dans son la case. Coument nous ti hérés! Assise dans fauteuils; boire dans verre zize; domestiques na pas manqué, zendarmes !.!. y en a di vin, y en a la bierre, y en a la liquère; tout madame di l'eau cologne dans moussoir. Mo même la misique avec Prosper. Moussié Sirandale dire nous comme ça moutié français, moutié anglais: amisez mo z'enfants, badinez ; ça même nous banne année azourdi. A v'la tout la nouit nous dansé, zisqu'à viélon na pas capabe marcé;

colophane na pas. Sitôt la LIBERTÉ finie, nous tire galop zisqu'à nous fine soûlé ! Moussié Sirandale même toné.

Y en ena dispite même : Myrtil qui fin trouvé son femme avec Philogène là haut grénier.

L'hère nous maziné pour quitte bal, a v'la camrades saut' dans parc cabris, ça povre moussié Sirandale pour dire li merci, prend trois cabris, coupe son la tête, f..... la haut l'épaule ; la tête même quitte divant la porte. La zoie aussi gagne malhor ; quatre fine saboulé. Pauvre Moussié Sirandale ! Son zendarme où li ? Après donne la liquère tout zènes filles la Rivière Grampant. l'hère pour TIOMBO PIOSSE, COURAZE NA PAS li zié bourlé coument piment, li plié raide, reinté qui n'a pas pelle reinté même, pa la moutié all' l'hôpital. A soir vini cabris la zoie, tout ça dans marmite.

A v'la Moussié la Gazette, ça qu'vous na pas ti coné ; Si vous na pas voulé croire moi donne di l'eau béni : mo boire .

ZEAN ENSEMBLE PROSPER
MISICIENS LA RIVIERE GRAMPART
(Le Cernéen, 1.1.1839)

30. 1839b Letter from Caroline *qui vend' bouquet derrière l'Eglise Zanglé*

Vou ti dir moussié Sirandale ti donn' enne bal pour noirs la rivière Grampart ; qui fer vous n'a pas coz sa qui grand zize au Port té donne zènes filles, banané – av'la enne famé bal cenne là. Na pas pour dir, mais si fé va ça grand blanc là li bien content neingresses va ! Y ty en a partout, plein son la salle, plein son la varangue, plein son cabinet. Violon ronflé là dans, na pas badiné. Femme grand zize, son mamzelles, zot' tout vine appiyé dansé avec nous comment dir zot servant' comment nous. Grand zize aussi li dansé, mais dommage, son li pié fine cassé enne coté pov' diabe. Av'la blanc qui na pas fier là. Quand même vous la peau li noire, zot' na pas embrasse. Na pas blié coz' ça dans vous la gazette pour nous gagne encore enne bal. Nou liquerre na pas va content tant qui nous na pas va danse enne galop avec gouverner li même.

Salam don, moussié la gazettte.

<u>Caroline</u>, qui vend' bouquet derrière l'Eglise Zanglé.
(*Le Cernéen* 3.1.1839)

31. 1839c Anecdotes

… Mais qui va faire, mo blizé, mo fine libre, na pas capable servi mon maître encore…
… Eh bien ! figure, ou li ton sabre donc – Mo na pas yana. (*Le Cernéen*, 4.1.1839)

32. 1839d *Un coin du feu à la campagne*

François Chrestien died or soon after 1840. This could be the last of his compositions to have been published although, to judge from **1839e**, there may well have been several more.

Quelques fois aux grelots de la folle saillie ;
Sous des voiles légers la morale s'allie. F. Ch.

Un coin du feu à la campagne
ou
Fonclair et Pierrot
(La scène se passe dans la caze de Pierrot)

Fonclair (habitant entrant) : Bonsoir, Pierrot mais qui toi gagné donc ? ... Ton li-ziés li rouzes comment zozeau foudé, toi n'a pas causé et toi l'air triste comment di-monde qui fini cassé son pipe ?

Pierrot, ancien commandeur (half and half) : Ma foi, moussié, moi n'a pas cacié vous ; moi té après comment vous voir moi là ; et, pour dire vous la vérité, moi lé boire eine petit coup ; parce qui eine côté moi bien aise, et pis eine côté moi moi çagrin.

Fonclair Comment toi çagrin ... Qui capable faire toi la peine à s'tèr la ? A vlà tout ton camarades fini gagné zautres bonhèr, tout ton famille, tout ton zamis fini libres ! ... Est-ce qui ton zaffaires n'a pas allé bien ... Est-ce qui ton poules fini gagné la rouzeole aussi ?

Pierrot N'a pas ça, moussié ; grand merçi Bon Dié, mon poules, mon coçon, mon cabrits, tout mon famille ça va bien. Mais ça n'a pas empèçé qui moi çagrin !

Fonclair Diable ! ... Mais ciplique moi ça ein pé ?

Pierrot Ah ! mon Dié, moussié, vous même va voir sis pas moi raison. Vous connois moi libre longtemps moi ; défint vous papa, qui Bon-Dié va béni li toujours, été donne moi la liberté, morceau l'arzent, morceau la terre, et pis li dire moi comme ça : « Pierrot, mon garçon, quand toi voulez resté moi, restez ; moi va soigné toi, quand toi malade comment l'autrefois ; moi va donné toi cinq roupies tous les mois et toi va sivre la bande comment toujours : si toi voulez allé, allez, mon garçon. A s'ter - la toi capable faire ton volontés. » Moi dire ou di-l'eau été vini dans mon liziés, quand moi té tendé vous papa causé comme ça ? Et moi réponde li tout de suite « ah ! Mon Dié, moussié, comment vous capable pensé qui moi va quitté vous ? ... Moi qui fini habitié dans vous lacaze, dans vous l'habitation ? ... Moi, qui fini voir lévé tous ça zenfans là qui mon femme été son nénaine ? Zamais ! Moussié, zamais ! Ou bien ça jour là mon l'esprit va fini çaviré. » Comme ça moi té parlé, et manière vous bon papa été guetté moi, li encore là divan mon li ziés. Mais n'a pas ça à s'ter, moussié ; vous connais bien aussi qui mon papa, qui sivré la mode malgace, été y-en-a dés, trois femmes dans l'habitation ? Son dernier pitit, mon frère été resté dans séclaves zisqué à s'ter - la, li té dans sicriers ; pour bien dire, dans la main eine blanc qui bein soigné son zens ; bon la caze, bon vivres, bon lahardes, bons médecines ... Car n'a pas manqué blancs qui soigné son zapprentis à s'tèr ! Mais zènes-zens, vous connais, tout ein-pé *fouca-fouca* ? Zautres n'a pas couté, paroles grand monde, zautres sivré mauvais l'esprit et ça li maziné qui tant qui li n'a pas faire son farces, zamais li va croire li libre tous d'bon ; et farces là, vous connois qui sis-ça ? Eh ! Bien, moussié, li été rentré dans vagabondaze !!

Fonclair Mais qui sis-ça métier là, Pierrot, vagabondaze, zamais encore moi té tendé eine parole comme ça ?

Pierrot Ma foi, moussié, moi nommé li à pé-près comment moi té tendé blancs parlé ; mais ça n'a pas métier ; ça eine manière emmène vous lé-corps pour vous promené la zournée, dans la mizique et dans bazar ; comment li cien qui fini perdi son maître ; pours vous n'a pas travaille, pour rammasé malade dans la cantine et dormi dans la rie. Et voir vous même sis-pas moi raison pour moi çagrin, à s'tèr - là qui moi fini tendé qui la police commencé s'en mêlé et qui mon petit frère va faire mette li en prison ?

Fonclair Faire vous consolé, mon pauvre Pierrot ; moi voir bien sa doit faire vous la peine, mais allez vous causer ensemble vous frères. Quand di-monde fini goûté la prison, et fini la misère fini taqué li morceau, li capable connois qui tout di monde doit travaille, doit sivre la zistice ; et qui n'a pas y-en a liberté qui capable empèçe vous faire faire vous l'ouvrage et vous devoir.

11e avril 1839, Le Bobre Africain (*Le Cernéen,* 18 avril 1839)

33. **1839e** *Scènes populaires de l'époque*

This is not an MC text but an advertisement which mentions seven Chrestien titles of which only two are currently known, *Un coin du feu à la campagne* (**1839d**) and *Adresse de Domingue à la reine Victoria* (1838). The collection of all Chrestien's works in MC is thus not yet complete.

A puzzling feature of this newspaper advertisement is that it implies that *Album Tropical* had not yet gone on sale even though it bears the date "1838" and includes the letter to Queen Victoria mentioned below. In addition, *Un coin du feu à la campagne* had been published in the same newspaper just three months earlier. (Perhaps the latter was a provisional version?)

En attendant l'Album Tropical, (...), M. F. Chrestien offre au Public les SCENES POPULAIRES DE L'EPOQUE, en patois créole, et intitulées :

> Un coin du feu à la campagne ;
> La veillée de village ;
> Pierrot dans les embarras de la paternité ;

Se débitant au bureau du Cernéen ; prix deux shillings comptant.

Incessamment, et suivant le succès de cet essai :

> Adresse de Domingue à la reine Victoria ;
> Pierrot dans la diplomatie ;
> Les appâts d'un bal du faubourg.

Enfin, plus tard :

> Les brigands de la Plaine des Roches, (...)   (*Le Cernéen* 11.7.1839)

34.   **1839f** La liberté fine gagné

1. Grand nouvelle fini vinie,
La liberté fine gagné ;
La Reine qui bien content nous,
Li voulé qui nous posé.
A c't'hère qui nous mamzelles,
Plis souvent si nous va piossé :
   En avant, marçons,
   La case Anderson,
   Parasol sous l'bras,
     la peau bef dans li pié
   Bardeau la haut la tête (bis).
	2. Comment vous v'lez nous travail,
	M'sié Sirandale li même causé ;
	Li dir com' ça : à c't'hère vous libres,
	Vous pitit piossé n'a pas.
	Au port li va gagne ène métier,
	Ene métier bien <u>attitré</u>.
	   En avant, etc.

3. A c't'hère la qui nous servantes,
Travail na pas bésoin,
Dourmi na pas va manqué,
Ça même qui nous métier
Mo tende côte l'hôpital
Viélon commence ronflé.
   En avant, etc.
	4. Dommaze nous li pié faire mal,
	Soulié ein pé zéné.
	Blizé tir pour marcé,
	Apporte li dans la main.
	Sitot trouvé calesse
	Bien vite attace costime (1)
	   En avant, etc.
	
	(1) Ceci veut dire cothurne

5. A c't'hère là faut nous faraud.
Zènes gens na pas manqué,
Zaconats, zindiennes, mousselines,
Di l'eau Cologne en bas lé bras ;
Fané, fané partout,
Vous coné dans bal faire çaud.
   En avant, etc.
	6. Bon dié ! bon dié ! comment nous héré !
	Ça bal là tout d'bon famé :
	Gateau, paté, di vin,
	Na rien qui fine blié
	Bal même moussié Sirandale
	Na pas ti zoli comme ça.
	   En avant, etc.

7. Nous papa même ça grand blanc là,
Li donne la peine pour son pitit
Li faire semblant allé Seycelles :
All' voir, li alle l'Angleterre.
Li grand cam'rade la Reine,
Ça même nous gagne cadeau.
   En avant, etc.
	8. La police empèce promener,
	M'sié Finniss fini mâté ;
	Gouverner li v'lé causé,
	Grand blanc dir li, assez ;
	Quand même bitation fine sec,
	Mo v'le mo zenfans héré.
	   En avant, etc.

Le Cernéen 7 mai 1839

35. **1840a** Lloyd's report on what happened to the former slaves

Lloyd was an engineer who came to Mauritius from India, bringing with him his own elephant which he used to travel to and from work. He was responsible for the construction of many of the bridges which survive to this day. (For more on Lloyd, see the chapter devoted to him in Hollingsworth 1965.)

In 1840, he sent a detailed report on what had happened to the former slaves to the Colonial Office in London. His text, never published before, is reproduced as an annex at the end of this book. It includes only a few words in MC.

36. **1840b** Newspaper extracts

   Çà manioc, coup de poing
   Çà n'a pas bon jamais manze l'aloi
   Tayèr mousié, li na pas conne ça
   N'a pas voulé, di zoeuf n'a pas y en a   (*Le Cernéen* 3 oct 1840)

37. **1846** Cirandane Çampec

While it has been the intention of the editors of this volume that comment on the selected texts should be predominantly linguistic in nature, they feel that this particular booklet merits special treatment because it had eluded all efforts to locate a surviving copy over the past 32 years – until Hookoomsing at last succeeded.

On discovering *Cirandane-Çanpéc: ou Enigmes créoles*

Vinesh Y Hookoomsing

Tradition demands that I begin with the opening ritual of a session of riddle-playing:

   Q   Sirandann?   [an invitation to play riddles]
   A   Sanpek!   [acceptance of the invitation]
   Q   Ki ti ekrir premye liv sirandann dan Moris?
                   (Who/what wrote the first sirandann book in Mauritius?)
   A   *Lame ek plim!*   ([A] hand and [a] pen!)

The answer is appropriate not just because it corresponds to the logic of the *sirandann*, but also because the first collection of Mauritian *sirandann* is an anonymous publication. The date and place of publication of *Cirandane-Çanpec ou Enigmes Créoles dédieés à Lady Gomm*, as well as the name of the publisher, are well known, but the identity of its author has remained a mystery. Maybe rightly so, because the *sirandann*, and riddles in general, belong to collective oral tradition which, in former times, was popular throughout Europe, Africa, and many other parts of the world.

The publication itself has for many decades eluded researchers and antiquarians interested in Creolia. Until recently, the only proof of its existence was its inclusion in Toussaint & Adolphe's authoritative *Bibliography of Mauritius*. Further evidence came from one of my persistent searches at the Mauritius Archives which confirmed that *Cirandane- Çanpéc* (C-Ç) had actually been published and was sold at the Malartic fancy-fair organized by Lady Gomm in 1846. In its issue of 20 August that year *Le Cernéen* reported the event in both English and French. The English version reads as follows (Hookoomsing 1989: 22):

> Scarcely have you entered, than you are assailed by dealers of both sexes who offer you their wares; now you are presented with biographical notices, verses and acrostics on General Malartic in all languages; then a fair dame entreats you, in the Creole patois, to buy her SIRANDANES;...and all this for the moderate sum of one shilling; why it is absolutely nothing.

It is reasonable to believe that copies of C-Ç found their way to private collections and were also deposited at the Archives and public libraries and institutions such as the Mauritius Institute. Yet, unlike the *blue penny* stamp for which Lady Gomm is best known,[62] the collection of *sirandann* dedicated to her is nowhere to be found in Mauritius.

Both Baissac's *Etude sur le patois créole de Maurice* and *Folk-lore de l'Ile Maurice*, have near identical sections on "Sirandanes" but without any mention of C-Ç. But then Baissac gloriously ignores all the publications in MC of his contemporaries and predecessors.

The present project created the need for a fresh search for *Sirandanes-Çanpec*, now greatly facilitated by technology. Random browsing on the internet is very much a lottery. I kept on losing until one day a lucky click opened the website of University of California Library, Santa Barbara, and gave me access to the web page of its Special Collections. Among them was *Mauritius*, described as follows:

> **Mauritius Islands** [sic] **Collection.** About 250 books and pamphlets, in French and English, most printed in Port Luis [sic]. Includes numerous Creole writings and descriptions of Mauritian life from the early 19th century onward.

Among the items listed in the Collection, just after Antoine Chelin's *Le Theatre à L'ile Maurice*, the enigmatic title seems to have been put on hold for that special occasion, in its original form, with just a few minor distortions in the entry: "Cirandane – Canapec: *Ou Enicmes Creoles*. Port-Louis, Maurice, De L'Imprimerie de E. Baker, 1846."

I am grateful to Edward C Fields, Information Services Supervisor at the Department of Special Collections, for sending me the Mauritiana list and especially for the scanned copy of the precious document, a perfect replica of the original.

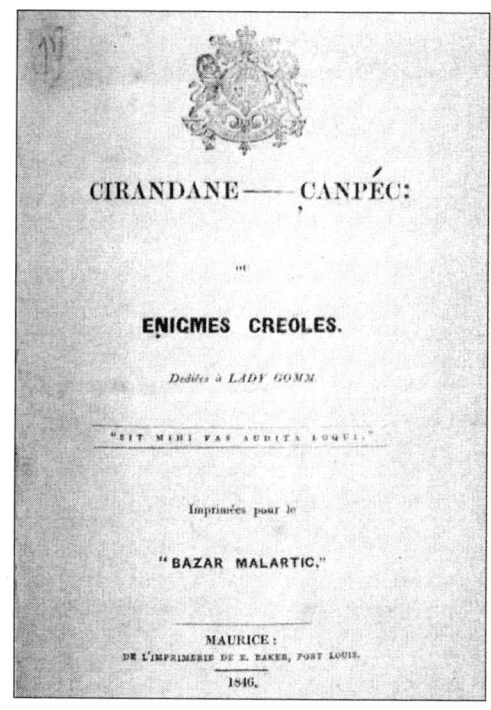

---

[62] This was the first postage stamp to be issued in Mauritius but the words "POST OFFICE" were printed on it instead of "POST PAID". Lady Gomm wanted to be the first person to use the new stamps for invitations to a ball she was holding and did so, instead of waiting for the stamps to be reprinted. She thus became responsible for one of the world's rarest and most valuable stamps.

The cover bears the seal of official sponsorship, reflected in the British coat of arms at the top. This is further confirmed by the stated purpose of printing C-Ç: "Imprimées pour le Bazar Malartic". Malartic was governor of Isle de France during the troubled period of the French Revolution. After his death in 1800, the French inhabitants of the island decided to erect a monument in gratitude for his good governorship. The project was however not completed when the Colonial Assembly was dissolved and Decaen took over in 1803. In his voluminous biography of Malartic, Raymond d'Unienville (2006: 443) describes how the project was later revived by Lady Gomm:

> Lady Gomm trouva regrettable qu'on laissât inachevé le tombeau de Malartic, éminent prédécesseur de son mari. Elle prit les choses en main en 1846, fit appel à la générosité des colons, établit une liste de Dames Patronnesses dont elle prit la tête et toutes ensembles elles organisèrent une kermesse intitulée Bazar Malartic. (...) Le Bazar Malartic rapporta en deux journées près de 6 000 piastres et avant la fin de l'année le tombeau reçut son obélisque.

A further interesting detail is the Latin inscription on the cover:

SIT MIHI FAS AUDITA LOQUI

This is a quotation from Virgil's *Aeneid*, Book VI, which appears to have been popular among learned societies of the 18th and 19th centuries. John Wesley, founder of the Methodist Church, uses it in the concluding part of his sermon *On Faith*, where he stresses the importance of Revelation, without which "how little certainty of invisible things did the wisest of men obtain!" before quoting Virgil: "how warily he begins, with that apologetic preface, – *Sit mihi fas audita loqui?* – 'May I be allowed to tell what I have heard?'".

Edward Baker, whose name appears on the cover and on the last page of C-Ç, was a missionary priest and printer attached to the London Missionary Society in Madagascar in 1827, and was involved in the publication of the Bible in Malagasy. Following the expulsion of all foreigners from Madagascar in the 1830s, he moved to Mauritius and established his printing house in Port Louis. The works published by him included some of his own literary titles as well as textbooks and religious materials for the Anglican schools run by Reverend Jean Le Brun. According to Furlong & Ramharai (2007: 114), this background would make him a candidate for the authorship of C-Ç,

C-Ç is just a collection of 52 riddles, without any commentary or note. A simple, straightforward and plausible explanation of its 'authorship' would be that it was the work of one or, more probably, several of the "Dames Patronnesses"[63] who were responsible for the organization of the 'Bazar Malartic'. The idea of producing it as part of the fund raising activities probably came from Lady Gomm, which would explain the dedication inserted in the title. Baker's part – and contribution – as printer was to have it printed for the Bazar. The Latin inscription on the cover may be attributed to the missionary priest he was.

The *sirandann* are numbered 1 to 48, followed by an additional four which are not numbered and are typographically distinguished from the numbered collection. Out of the 48 *sirandann* in C-Ç, 45 appear in Baissac, many of them in identical or near-identical wording and content (see Table). While assuming that oral tradition, which Baissac claims to be his only source, could have transmitted the totality of his corpus through Mmâ Telesille and Ppâ Lindor, the high level of correlation between the two sets leads me to conclude that Baissac had full knowledge of C-Ç and its content and that he must have used it at least as a complementary source.

---

[63] The 'Dames Patronnesses' were "Lady Gomm, Mmes Wilson, d'Epinay, Dioré, Rémono, Colin, Lemière, Harrison, E Salesse", according to *Le Mauricien* of 24 July 1846 (D'Unienville 2006: 443, note 2).

The *Cirandane Çampéc* (C) riddles and their equivalents in Baissac (1880, 1888)

MD = Minor differences of orthography and/or content only; CS = Conceptually similar; European = Of European origin. African = of African origin; Shared = Attested in at least one Indian Ocean Creole and at least one Atlantic Creole, even though of unknown origin.

	Cirandane Çampéc	Baissac	Answers C = Cirandane Çampéc, B = Baissac	Comments (Origin)[1]
1	Piti batte maman.	Pitit batte manman	C *La cloce*, B *Lacloce*, F Cloche, E Bell.	MD (Shared)
2	Dileau diboutte	Dileau diboute	C & B *Canne*, F Canne à sucre, E Sugar cane.	MD (African)
3	Bois d'ibœnne dans dileau	Boisdebène dans dileau	C: *Anguy*, B: *Zanguïe*, F Anguille, E Eel.	MD
4	Yana einne grand-maman, li faire piti, li faire piti, li coumande boucoup piti natte, tout son piti dourmi par terre.	Mo grandmanman li beau fère nattes tout so pitits dourmi partére	C *Ziromon*, B *Ziraumon*,[2] F Citrouille, E Pumpkin.	CS[3] (African)
5	Vous zoindre einne grand bande doumounde; quand vous encore loin, li dire vous bonzour; quand vous finne arrive proce, zotte n'a pas dire n'a rien.	Mo zoinde ene grande bande doumounde; quand mo loin, zautes dire moi bonzour; quand mo proce, zautes napas dire narien	C *Gournoye*, B *Gournouïes dans bôrd dileau*, F Grenouïlles, E Frog.	MD
6	Tant-que li vivant, n'a pas parlé; qua li finne mort, li parlé.	Vivants napas causé, morts causé	C *Barvatte*, B *Barvades*,[4] F Plante légumineuse, E Pigeon peas.	CS
7	Tout noirs mon papa li pied torte	Tout so noirs mo papa zautes lipieds torte	C *Li cien fizi*. B *Liciens fisi*, F Chiens de chasse à tir, E Gun dogs.	CS
8	Dileau pendi	Dileau en pendant	C & B *Coco*, F Coco, E Coconut.	MD (Shared)
9	A soir li prom'né partout, li zour son la tète en bas, son li pied la haut	Asoir li promné partout, grandzour so latête en bas, so lipieds en lére	C *Soursouri*, B *Soursouris*, F Chauve-souris, E Bat.	CS
10	Yana einne grand bande marmaille, qua solé coucé, vous trouve zotte tout clair, qua solé lévé, zotte tout cacié	Mo éna éne grand bande marmaille ; soléye lévé zautes caciéte, soléye coucé zautes sourti	C *Zétoille*, B *Zétoiles*, F Etoiles, E Stars.	CS, with reversed sequencing of events

[1] As indicated in Baker (2004). Where no origin is indicated, the riddle could be a local (Mauritian) creation.
[2] French *çiraumon* but ultimately from Tupi *jirumum*.
[3] Baissac (1880: 404) also provides another, looser CS variant: *Mo grandmanman zamés oulé dourmi lâhaut so natte, li quitte so natte li dourmi par tére*.
[4] From Malagasy *ambáravátry*, known in Mauritian French as *embrevade*.

11	Mo maré [sic; error for maré] dans einne piti çimin, zamé mo va pozé, zamé mo va tourné.	Mo marce dans éne ptit cimin, zamés mo va posé, zamés mo va tourné	C *La Rivière*, B *Larivière*, F Rivière, E River.	MD (African)
12	Dans dileau yana la corde.	Cinque brances dans dileau	C *Zouritte*, B *Zouritte*,[5] F Poulpe, E Octopus.	CS
13	Li mince corps, li yana boucoup lé dent, li n'a pas la bouce, i capabe manzé li-zour, la nouy sans pozé, tant qui vous voulé.	Li éna lédents li napas labouce, li capave manzé lanouite lézour sans posé	C *La scie*, B *Lascie*, F Scie, E Saw [n].	MD
14	Tout mon piti noir mette boné rouze.	[Not in Baissac][6]	C *Coq*, F Coq, E Cock.	MD
15	Brède dourmi.	Brédes dourmi	C *Ziromon*, B *Ziraumon*,[7] F Citrouille, E Pumpkin.	MD
16	Li n'a pas lé dent, li manzé tout lé zour dipi bomatin zousqu'à soir, zamé li avalé	Touzours li manzé zamés li avalé	C *Moulin canne*, B *Moulin cannes*, F Moulin à cannes, E sugar mill.	CS
17	Brède galoupé.	Brédes galpé	C *Yévre*, B *Yéve*, F Lièvre, E Hare.	MD
18	Mo yana einne bande piti noir, zour zotte féte, zotte habillé tout en rouze.	Mo éna éne banne ptit bonhomes : zour zaute féte zautes tout habillé en rouze	C *Cévrette*, B *Piments*, F Chevrette (crevette) / Piments, E Shrimps or prawns / Chillies.	MD, but different answers. (Shared)
19	Eine laquée, sept lapattes, quatre zoreilles, la guelle dans la boue.	Guéle dans guéle, sette lapattes, quate zoréye	C *Li cien manze dans marmitte*. B Licien manze dans marmitte. F Un chien mange dans une marmitte. E Dog eating from a cooking pot.	CS (European)
20	4 pattes la haut 4 pattes, 4 pattes aspère 4 pattes, 4 pattes n'a pas vini, 4 pattes allé, 4 pattes resté.	Quate pattes làhaut quate pattes aspère quate pattes ; quate pattes napas vini, quate pattes allé, quate pattes resté	C *Çatte la haut çèze aspère lé rat, lé rat n'a pas vini, çatte allé, çèze resté.* B *Çatte làhaut cése aspère lèrat ; lèrat napas vini, çatte allé, cése resté.* F Un chat sur une chaise attend un rat, le rat ne vient pas, le chat s'en va, la chaise reste. E Cat on a chair waits for a rat, the rat doesn't come, the cat goes away, the chair remains.	MD (European)
21	Mo beau léve li enlére, li touzours même léve li la haut li toujour bas.	Mo yana einne quiqu' çoze, qua même léve li la haut li toujour bas.	C *Lé bas*, B *Lébas*, F Un bas, E Stocking.	CS (European)

[5] From Malagasy *horita*.
[6] Baissac has a very different riddle to which the answer is *coq*: *Courone dans mo latéte, zéprons dans mo lipieds, mo léroi dans basse-cour, mé mo papas léroi.*
[7] Ultimately from Tupi *jirumum*.

22	4 pilé 1 vané.	C *Çouval pouce mouce*, B *Çouval pousse mouces : so lipieds pilé, so laquée vané.* F Un cheval qui chasse les mouches. E A horse repelling flies.	MD
23	Yana 14 pieds dipi son lécou zousqu'à son lé reins, qua vous mizoure tout son corps né qu'einne pied dimi	C *Homar*. B *Homard*, F Homard (langouste), E Lobster.	MD (European)[8]
24	Mo yana einne piti noir son l'espri dans son néné	C *Li cien*, B *Licien*, F Chien, E Dog.	CS
25	Mo yana trois noirs qui travaillent toujour dans même place, zamé zotte n'a pas avancé, zotte n'a pas arquilé.	C *Cilindres Moulin.* B *Cylindes moulin.* F Cylindres d'un moulin (à sucre). E Cylindres in a sugar mill.	MD
26	Qui marcé la tête en bas.	C *Coulou soulièt* [sic], B *Coulou soulier*, F Clou d'un soulier, E Nail of a shoe.	MD (European)
27	Mo yana einne piti noir son l'esprit dans son la patte.	C *Couval,* F Cheval, E Horse.	
28	Qui yana son lezo la haut son la peau.	C *Barique,* B *Barique divin*, F Barrique (de vin), E Barrel (of wine).	CS (European)
29	Quand mo allé bégné la Rivière, mo laisse mon tripe la caze.	C *Matelat* [sic], B *Latoële matelas,* F (La toile recouvrant) un matelas, E (Cover of) a mattress.	MD
30	Qui ça qui li zour li plein et la nouy li vide	C & B *Soulié,* F Soulier, E Shoe.	CS (European)
31	Qua mo allé la Rivière mo çanté, lhére mo tourné mo ploré.	C *Barique Galère,* B *Barique galère,* F Barillet, E Small barrel.	MD (European)
32	Si vous lavé pas, prétte moi li; si vous lavé, n'a pas pretté.	C & B *Battoir,* F Battoir, E Washerwoman's beetle.	MD (European)
33	Mo louvrage zamé fini	C *Ramasse bouteilles cassées*; B *Ramasse vèrres boutêye*; F Ramasser des bris de bouteille / verre. E Collecting the glass of broken bottles.	MD
34	Quate pattes monte làhaut quate pattes ; quate pattes allé, quate pattes resté.	C *Licien apré zaco.* B *Licien làhaut cése.* F Un chien poursuivant un singe / un chien sur une chaise. E Dog chasing a monkey / dog on a chair.	MD - but different answers

[8] See Baissac's footnote (p. 417) : « Cette ineptie et les deux suivantes ne sont rien moins que créoles : c'est par rancune que nous les citons. » His note refers to this *sirandann* and to nos. 21 above and 32 below.

35	Mo té va boire divin, si té yana dileau, mo boire dileau pass'qui n'a pas dileau	Mo boire dileau à cause napa dileau !	**C & B** *Navire tombé au sec.* **F** Naviree échoué à marée basse. **E** A ship grounded in low water.	CS
36	Si zotte vini, zotte n'a pas va vini, mé si zotte n'a pas va vini, zotte va vini.	Si zautes vini zautes napas va vini, mé si zautes na pas vini, zotte va vini.	**C** *Z'habitant plante p'tit pois, li père pizon vinne manzé.* **B** *Doumounde plante pitits pois: li père pizons vine manzé.* **F** Un homme plante des petits pois: il a peur que les pigeons ne viennent les manger. **E** A farmer/someone plants peas but is afraid that pigeons will come and eat them.	MD
37	Tourou sans fond	Tourou sans fond	**C & B** *Bague,* **F** Bague, **E** Ring.	Identical (European)
38	Yana einne band bêbette qui travaille dans même l'endroit, zotte tendé l'einne à l'autre, mé zotte n'a pas capable trouvé zotte figuire ou zotte vizage	Iéna éne banne bébêtes qui travaille dans même l'endroit, zautes tendé éne a l'aute, més zamés zautes capave trouve zaute figuire.	**C** *Moutouc,* **B** *Moutoucs,*[9] **F** Asticots, **E** Maggots.	MD
39	Einne band Mam'zelle au bord cimin zotte tout baisse la tête.	Iéna éne banne mamzélles dans bord cimin, zautes tout latéte enbas	**C** *Banane,* **B** *Pieds banane,* **F** Bananiers, **E** Banana trees.	CS
40	Mo expédié einne Commissionnaire, sitôt li gagne la réponse mo finne coné.	Mo envôye éne ptit noir comission, sitôt li fine gagne laréponse mo coné.	**C** *L'hameçon,* **B** *Lhamçon,* **F** Hameçon, **E** Fish hook.	MD[10]
41	Li manze son tripe et li boire son disang en même temps.	Mo coné éne mamzelle li manze so tripe, li boire so disang.	**C** *La lampe,* **B** *Lalampe,* **F** Lampe (à huile), **E** Oil lamp.	CS (European)
42	Bancal au bord di leau.	Casse bancal dans bord canal.	**C** *Grounouille,*[11] **B** *Gournoüies,* **F** Grenouilles, **E** Frogs.	MD (African)
43	Mo yana boucoup zouli l'assiette bien fine, quand li tombé zamé cassé.	Mo éna boucoup lassiétes bien fin, zautes beau tomber, zamés cassé.	**C & B** *Feilles.* **F** Feuilles, **E** Leaves.	MD
44	Mo yana piti barique qui tini dé sorte divin.	Mo éna barique av dé qualités dileau.	**C** *Dizef,* **B** *Ene dizéf,* **F** Oeuf. **E** Egg.	MD
45	Yana belle la caze, rempli p'tit Mazambique ladans qui travaille tré bien	[Not in Baissac]	**C** *Mouce dimiel,* **F** Abeille, **E** Bee.	MD

---

[9] Word of unknown origin.
[10] Variant in Baissac (p. 398) : Mo envôye éne lette, mo coné lhére décacétte li .
[11] This word is written *gournoye* in no. 5.

46	Yana la caze qui peinte en verd par dohors, en blanc en didans et tout ça qui demére là dans, zotte tout noir.	Mo lacase tout en bardeaux, endans éne bane p'tit mazambiques habille en blanc.	**C** *Z'attes,* **B** *Zatte,* **F** Atte, *Annona squamosa*, **E** Sweet-sop.	CS
47	Mo yana dé bassin bien zouli, gazon tout tout en tour, çaqu'ienne einne l'Ilote dan milié, quand zotte débordé, vous trouve son dileau coulé çaqu'einne dans son coté ; mé, canal qui fourni dileau ans tout lé dé bassin, vous n'a pas capable trouvé.	**C** *Lizié,* **B** *Liziés,* **F** Les yeux, **E** Eyes.	MD
48	La terre li blanc la semence li noire liquér récolté	Latére blanc, lagrains noir	**C** *Papier L'écritire Z'amitié;* **B** *Papier sembe lécritire;* **F** Papier, écriture, (et amitié); **E** Paper, writing, (and friendship).	CS[12] (European)
	Qui la Plaine qui plis haut ?	[Not in Baissac]	**C** *Cé la plaine line,* **F** La pleine lune, **E** Full moon.	
	Qui différence entre einne Zize et einne escalier ?	[Not in Baissac]	**C** *Einne Zize faire vous lève la main, l'escalier faire vous lève li pied.* **F** Un juge vous fait lever la main, l'escalier vous fait lever le pied. **E** A judge makes you raise your hand; a staircase make you raise your foot.	
	Dans qui mois lé femme parlé moins ?	[Not in Baissac]	**C** *Mois Février,* **F** Février, **E** February.	
	Quand vous coupe dipain, qui li dire ?	[Not in Baissac]	**C** *Li di-mini.* **F** Il di(t)-minue.	

---

[12] See also: Baissac (1888: 415): lamain sémé, liziés récolté? *Crire av lire.*

38. 1850 Moucié Caraba

This text was first published by Chaudenson who established that its author was Aristide le Père de la Butte and that it *a dû être rédigé au plus tard vers 1850* (1981: 121). On the same page he remarked that *il présente en outre l'intérêt de pouvoir être comparé à la version de ce même conte donnée en 1880 par Charles Baissac*. With a view to facilitating just such a comparison, we print the two versions side-by-side below.

Our concordance of texts (*this volume*) suggests that there are two apparent errors of transcription in the 1850 version, in the words written *arla* or *avla* (< Fr. *voilà*) and *are* or *ave* (an abbreviation of Fr. *avec*) respectively. In Chaudenson's transcription, there are 5 tokens of *avla* as against 44 of *arla*, and 2 tokens of *ave* compared with 4 of *are*. In the concordance as a whole, there are more than 300 tokens of *avla* (including variant spellings) but none of *arla* other than in this text (in modern MC, this is *ala*); and there are more than 500 tokens of *ave* or *av* but the earliest example of *are* other than those in this text is not found until 1929. (Baker [1996] suggests that the change from *av* to *ar* is due to Bhojpuri influence; see also Kriegel & Michaelis, *this volume*). There are probably more ways of writing *r* cursively than most other letters of the alphabet. Given that neither *avla* nor *av*(e) is attested beyond the mid-20th century, it is entirely understandable that anyone familiar with modern MC would be inclined to interpret an uncertain *v* in these two words as *r*. We have thus changed the *r* of these words in the Chaudenson transcription to *v* below (which also corresponds to the spelling in Baissac's version).

Chrestien's (1822) *Avant propos*, includes a mention of the "traducteur si plaisant du *Chat-botté*" (Benoit 1998: 112), which indicates that an MC version of this story was already in circulation at that time. This does not, however cast any doubt on Chaudenson's datation *vers 1850*: the grammatical and orthographic features of the 1850 version are very much consistent with those of other texts immediately preceding and following that date. Nevertheless, if Baissac "modernized" the 1850 version, it seems likely that the author of the latter had himself done the same to a version written 30 or more years earlier.

Zistoire Moucié Caraba	**Z'histoire ene çatte qui té éna botes**
Acoute bien zotte, a force sa zistoire la li gou y en a capable gagne dourmi, mo dire vou.	
Eti y en a a enne vié blan qui ti gagne troi piti ; li ti y en a enne moulin, enne bourique ensemble enne satte. Enne zour, sa vié bonome la, li gagne gran malade, pour mor même, li appelle son troi piti, li dire, mon piti, mon piti, avla mo va mor, napa la peine zotte appelle blan au por pour faire la partaze parcequi toi qui pli gran la, mo donne toi mon moulin, toi mo donne toi mon bourique, et toi qui pli piti la mo donne toi mo satte. – Avla, comman li encore parlé la, son labouce sèque tou din cou, li mor même.	Té iéna éne vié blanc qui té éna trois pitits : li té éna éne moulin, éne bourique ensembe éne çatte. Éne zour ça vié bonhomme là li gagne grand malade pour môrt méme. Li apéle so trois pitits, li dire zautes : « Mo pitits, avlà mo pour mort ; napas lapéne zautes apéle zense au pôrt[1] pour fére la partaze ; toi, àcause to plis vié, mo done toi mo moulin ; toi, mo done toi mo bourique, et toi qui plis pitit, mo done toi mo çatte. » Avlà coment li encore après causé, éne coup là so labouce séc. Li môrt méme.
– Astore sa qui piti la qui té gagne satte, li sagrinne, li dire mo gran frère la qui té qui gagne moulin, li va faire moudre diblé dans son moulin, lotre li va sarrié lafarine avec son bourrique, zotte dé va gagne l'arzen, mé mouan	L'hére zautes tourne dans cimiquière, pitit là qui té gagne çatte, li çagrin, li dire : Mo grand frère qui té gagne moulin li va moule diblé, li va gagne larzent ; laute là va çarié lafarine av so bourique, li va gagne larzent ;

---

[1] Le port, Port-Louis, c'est par excellence la ville, *urbs; zense au pôrt*, les gens de la ville en suspicion auprès des *« zhabitants »*.

qui té gagne enne faye satte la, qui mo va faire, mo va mor fin.

Avla son dé gran frère li dire, arranze toi mor fin quan to voulé qui nous embrasse. – Astore sa qui pli gran li dire moi mouan alle moudre diblé dans mon moulin, lotre dire moi mouan alle donne l'erbe mon bourique, avla zotte dé courir.

– Astore sa qui pli piti la dire, quan mo va fini touille mon satte, mo vande son la po ave dou mounde pour faire barsaque taba, mo coui son laviande, apré mo manze li, qui mo va faire, mo va mor fin. Coman li té souplaigné la, satte été dourmi en ba lili astore li sourti, li dire : mon mètre, mon mètre, napa bisoin vous sagrinne, quan voulé coute moi, vou va vini rice. Son mètre dire : qui toi faye satte couman toi, pito to alle sasse lé ra pour to manzé. Satte li entété, li dire : mon mètre, quan vou voulé don moi sa qui mo demande vou, vou va vini rice. Son mètre dire : hé bin qui to voulé. Satte mo voulé botte avec enne sac. Son mètre dire : hé bin mo va coute toi pacequi mo conné to bien malin. Avla son mètre donne li sa qui li té demandé.

Avla astore satte metté son botte dans son li pié, li amarre son sac dans son lé rin, astore li allé, li allé, li allé zousqua li arrive dans enne gran carré doublé, astore li ouvri bien la bouce son sac, li mette la dan bon morceau laceron, li té amare enne pti la corde bien longue, astore li arquillé, li cacié dans fon boursaille, rien que son li zié même té dohore, mo dire vou, un poti moman, avla enne gran B... lièvre vini cri, cri, cri, cri, avla li voir la lasseron, li antre dan son sac pour li manzé ; manami ! satte trouve sa, li halle son piti lacorde tou din cou, avla lièvre fini pri. Avla lièvre li dire : grasse papa satte, grasse papa satte, mo napa faire encore. Satte na pas coute tou sa. Li touille, apré li mette li dans son sac.

zautes dé napas va môrt faim ; més moi là qui té gagne néque éne çatte qui mo a[2] fére ? Mo va touye li, mo va couit so lavianne[3], mo va manze li ; aprés ça, qui mo a fére, mo va blizé môrt faim !

Côment li té encore plaigné là, çatte té dourmi enbas lilit. Avlà so dé grand frères dire li : Aranze toi, môrt faim quand to content, qui nous embrasse[4]! Acthére là so grand frére dire come ça : Mo alle méte diblé dans mo moulin. Laute frére dire come ça : Mo alle coupe lhérbe pour mo bourique. Avlà zautes dé allé.

Lhére zautes fine allé çatte sourti enbas lilit, li dire comme ça : « Mo ptit méte, couté : napas lapéne vous cagrin[5] ; quand vou vlé acoute moi, vous a vine rice qui apéle rice. » So méte dire li : « Qui to a fére ? Éne çatte pitit coment toi, toi qui a capave trouve manzé pour dé doumounnes ? » Çatte li entété, li dire : « Mo méte, done moi ça qui mo dimande vous, aprés lésse moi fére, wou a voir !» So méte dire li : « Eh ben ! causé. Qui to vlé ? – Mo vlé botes sembe éne sac.» So méte done li ça qui li dimandé.

Çatte méte so botes, li prend so sac, li amare li dans so léreins, aprés li allé, li allé zisqu'à li arive dans éne grand lapléne acote té iéna bon morceau iéves. Li prend so sac, li méte làdans bon morceau lastrons, li ouvert labouce ça sac là li amare éne ptit lacorde bien longue ; aprés li arquilé, li caciéte enbas feilles, so liziés tout séle dohors, mo dire vous. Avlà éne papa iéve vini, cri, cri, cri, cri. Li arive dréte av lacorde éne coup : li làdans[6], manami ! Iéve crié : grâce, papa çatte, mo napas fére encore ! Çatte napas acoute li, li touye li. Aprés, li amare so lipiéds, li ouvert so vente, li foure éne ptit dibois làdans, li méte li dans so boursac, li alle drétte lacase léRoi.

---

[2] *A* pour *va*.
[3] *Lavianne* plutôt que *laviande*.
[4] Mot à mot, en quoi nous embrassons-nous. Nous est sujet puisqu'il précède la verbe.
[5] *Cagrin*, chagrin. Il est verbe, comme nous l'avons établi.
[6] *Làdans*! Là dedans! Interjection qui répond à notre ca y est! c'est dans le sac.

Avla astore li allé, li allé, li allé. Li arrive cote la caze lé roi, li voulé entré, soldat qui té la garde la porte lé roi napa voulé lésse li entré. Avla lé Roi qui tende dou monde barbouille barbouille dan son la porte, li dire : mé qui barbouille dan mon la porte la don. Son domestique dire li : enne faye satte sa qui dire li voulé parlé parlé ave vou. Lé Roi dire : hé bin, laisse li entré.

Avla satte entré, li dire lé Roi : lé Roi, avla enne lièvre mon mètre, Moucié Caraba envoye pour vou. Lé Roi dire : dire gran merci Moucié Caraba.

Lendimain avla satte li alle encore ave son saque, li mette la dan enne pognée la farine maille la, li cacié encore. Avla enne perdri li trouve sa la farine maille la, li entre dan sac pour li manzé, avla satte li halle encore son piti la corde, li gagne sa perdri la.

Avla li alle encore la caze lé Roi, li dire lé Roi : lé Roi, avla enne perdri mon mètre envoye pour vou. Lé Roi appele son doumistique, li dire : donne-moi enne cou boire sa satte la, avla satte boire, quan la fini boire li dire : sifé va ! Mon di san li fané. Gran merci lé Roi. Apré bon dié vou même mon mètre.

Avla coman satte dessande sacalié pour li couri, li trouve sartié apré mette souval carosse lé Roi. Li dire : qui faire sa carosse la. Sarretier dire li : pour lé Roi alle proumener ensemble son mamzelle dans la gran soumin bor la rivière la.

Avla satte fine tendé sa, li galoupé ti, ti, ti, ti, ti, san posé ;
avla li arrivé, li dire : mon mètre, mon mètre quan vou voulé coute moi, zourdi même vou va vini rice.

Çatte vlé entré, avlà soldat qui té monte lagarde dans laporte léRoi, li barre li cimin. Més çatte entêté. Avlà léRoi qui tende doumoune cause fort dans so la porte li dire : « Més, qui çaça qui sipite come ça dans mo laporte, don ! » So soldat là réponde li : « Éne faye[7] çatte qui dire li vlé parle av vous. Eh ben ! lésse li entré.»

Çatte souye lipieds dans laporte, li entré, li tire iéve dans so boursac, li dire léRoi : « léRoi, avlà éne ièvre qui mo méte Moussié Carabas té laçasse pour vous. » Avlà léRoi bien content li répondé : « Dire grand merci Moussié Carabas. » Çatte allé.

Lendimain grand bomatin çatte alle dans éne grand carreau diblé, so sac zamés quitté. Li comence encore encore, li méte so sac enbas, li ouvert so labouce, li méte làdans bon morceau lafarine maïe, après li caciéte enbas vitiver dans bôrd carreau. Avlà éne perdrix qui vire viré pour manze ça lafarine là ; perdrix entré, çatte hisse éne coup so ptit lacorde : làdans méme ! perdrix maillé.

Li améne perdrix là lacase léRoi, li dire léRoi : « LéRoi, avlà éne perdrix qui mo méte Moussié Carabas té dire moi done dans vous lamain.» Avlà léRoi bien content, li apéle so domestique : « Donnez-moi éne coup à boire à ça çatte là[8]. » Avlà çatte li boire. Lhére li fine boire li dire : « Sifét va ! mo disang fané ! Grand merci, léRoi ; après Bondié vous même mo méte. »

Avlà comment li dicende léscalier, enbas peron lavarangue li trouve éne bélébéle carosse av quate çouvals làdans ; li dimande av cocé : « Hé wou ! Qui fére ça carosse-là, don ?» Cocé dire li : « Ça ? carosse pour léRoi alle promené av so mamzéle grand cimin làbas bôrd larivière. »

Lhére çatte fine tende ça, li galpé lacase so méte, ti, ti, ti, ti, taillé méme, sans posé.

Li arivé, li dire so méte : « Quand vous vlé acoute moi, àzourdi même vous pour vine rice qui apéle rice. So méte dire li : «Bien sir mo va acoute toi, àcause mo coné to malin coment sipas. Causé éne fois ! » Cate dire li : « Ah ben ! anons allé !»

---

[7] Faye du français failli; « un failli chien », disent les matelots.
[8] Ici le conteur veut que le Roi parle français: «Donnez-moi un coup à boire à cet homme-là » ; ce sont de ces phrases qui s'impriment à jamais dans une mémoire.

Astore li amene son mètre bor la rivière, li dire li : tire vou la harde, entre dan di lo, son mètre dire : qui faire entre dan di lo fré fré la. Satte dire : entré toujour moucié vou va voir. Avla quan son mètre fine entré dan di lo, li armasse tou son laharde, li cacié li en ba roce (guette voir son malice, sa satte la). Avla astore li monte li lor rempar la rivière, li guette si pa carosse lé Roi vini.

An piti moman, li voir carosse lé Roi vini gran trin. Avla li cri : à mouan, à mouan ! ah ! moundié ! bondié ! avla marron volore la harde mon mètre apré bègne dan di lo. Avla lé Roi tende sa li faire arrête son carrosse, avla satte alle parle li, li dire lé Roi : lé Roi, mon pauvre mètre Moucié Caraba qui té envoye touzou lièvre ave perdri la, li té vini pour bégné dan di lo. Avla couman li té apré bégné, marron vini volore tout son la harde (al voi li même qui té cacié la harde son mètre en ba roce oui). Avla lé Roi dire son doumistique : galoupé, ouvre mon l'armoire, apporte enne ressanze pour Moucié Caraba. Manami !

Moucié Caraba fini mettre sa la harde lé Roi, a force li zouli, doumounde na pas capave conne li, piti lé Roi napas capave guette li drette. La noui, li zour ça piti lé Roi rève, rève Moucié Caraba même.

Astore Moucié Caraba fine entré dan carrosse lé Roi, satte galouppe divan. Li arrive coté en a enne gran bande apré casse maille, li dire zotre : acoute bien mon zami, si lé Roi dimande zotre pour qui sa maille là, dire moucié Caraba ça, si zotre na pas dire, mo va faire mon gri gri ave zotre, n' pas va y en a enne qui va doubouté dimain bon matin, arranze zotre. Manami ! Avla sa noir la tendre sa, à force père, caca caca tou sel.

Avla satte couri, astore carrosse lé Roi passé. Lé Roi dire : pour qui sa maille la mon zami ? Zotre tou répondé : pour Moucié Caraba ça ! Avla satte vini coté enne lotre bande noir apré coupe canne, li faire zotre père aussi. Lé Roi passé : pour qui sa canne la mon zenfan ?

Li améme so méte bôrd larivière, li dire li : « Tire tout vous linze, ente dans dileau. » So méte dire li : « Qui fére ente dans dileau frés là ! Entré, mo dire wou, napas létemps causecausé àçthére. » So méte ente dans dileau ; çatte ramasse tout lahardes so méte, li caciétte enbas roce, li dire : « Réste là, aspéré mo vine çaca vous. » Li quitte so méte dans dileau, li monte bôrd rempart[9] pour guétte guétte carosse léRoi passé.

Avlà comment li assisé là li voir carosse léRoi vine grand galop drétte ac li. Avlà li lévé, li crié : « A moi ! A moi ! Bondié ! Bondié ! Marrons fine volor tout linze mo méte qui après baigne dans dileau !! » Awouah ! li même qui té caciéte linze enbas roces.

LéRoi tende ça crié là, li fére aréte caléce ; ça méme çatte té voulé. Li alle cotte léRoi, li dire li come ça : « LéRoi ! LéRoi ! mon pauvre méte, Moussié Carabas, vous coné ça qui touzours envôye vous ièvre av perdrix là, coment li après baingne so lécorps dans dileau, marons féque volor tout so linze ! » LéRoi dire av so domestique : « Galpé lacase, ouvért mo larmoire, améne linze pour Moussié Carabas. Vané méme, pendgare li gagne larhime dans dileau frés là. »

Avlà Msié Carabas méte so linze LéRoi. Mo dire ous, sifet va ! àforce li vine zoli lafille[10] léRoi napas capave guette li drétte, li blizé bésse bésse so liziez. Çatte guétte zautes éne coup, li maziné, li rié. Lésse zautes !

Çatte galpé divant carosse. Li trouve éne grand bande noirs qui après casse maïe, li dire zautes : « Acouté mézamis, si léRoi dimande zautes pour qui ça bitation là, dire li pour Moussié Carabas ; si zautes napas cause come ça, mo fére mo sourcié av zautes, napas iéna éne qui pour dibouté dimain bomatin. Aranze zautes. » Tout ça noirs là àforce zautes pére, zautes lazambes fébe, mo dire wous !

LéRoi passé, li guéte bitation là, li dire ça noirs qui après casse maïe : « Pour qui blanc ça maman bitation là ? » Zautes tout néque éne labouce : « Pour Moussié Carabas. » LéRoi qui ti assisé dans so carosse li dire : « Ah monami ! Sifet va, ça qui apéle rice ! »

---

[9] Nos rivières, pour la plupart profondément encaissées, coulent entre deux rives à pic, deux « remparts ».
[10] Le mot fille d'ordinaire ne prend pas l'article ; mais nous sommes à la Cour, la langue s'élève.

Zotre tou répondé : pour Moucié Caraba ça ! Astore doumestique lé Roi qui té size derrière carrosse, li tonné, li dire : cou ! Manami ! Sifé va ! Ça qui appelle risse.

Satte été toujour couri divan. Avla li arrive cote enne gran la caze gran couman légliz. Ça la case té lacase enne loulou. Satte li entré, li dire comme ça loulou : loulou mo napa té voulé passé dan vou la porte san mo vini dire vou bonzour. Loulou dire : to bin fé mo piti. Avla zotre dé cozé, cozé, astore satte li dire : mo té tendé loulou quan vou voulé vou capable fondre enne cou, vou vini lion ou bien alphan, sa qui vou liquierre content. Loulou dire : to va voir tou ta lor mon piti. Avla li fondre enne cou, li vini lion. Monami ! Satte trouve sa, à force père li saute par la fenêtre, li monte la hau la caze, troi fois li manque tombé mo dire vou, a coze botte qui té dan son lipié glisse glisse la hau bardo. Avla loulou crié, napas père mon piti, dissandé. Avla satte dissandé, li dire : couman mo té père papa loulou. Mé loulou vou té sanzé pour vini lion, esqui vou va capable sanzé pour vini zozo ou bien lira. Oui mo capable. Avla li fondre in cou, li vini lira. Manami, satte guette sa, li saute la hau li, li empigne son latête même, li touille, apré li manze li.

Couma li té fine manzé sa loulou la, li tendre carrosse lé Roi entre dan la cour. Li alle ouvri la porte carrosse, li dire : ça la caze mon mètre, vini proumouné proumouné, vou va voir.

Avla lé Roi, son mamezelle, moucié Caraba dissandé, zotre proumouné proumouné par tou. Avla lé Roi dire : sifé va, mo qui lé Roi mo hanté, mon la caze napa zouli couman pour vou Moucié Caraba.

Avla satte amène zotre dan enne gran la salle manzé coté té y en a enne gran latable, été y enna paté, bonbon toute sorte et divin qui té gou comman zamé divin été gout.

Avla zotre tou size a table, sa qui manzé, manzé, sa qui boire, boire. Avla tou din cou lé Roi dire : Moucié Caraba quan vou voulé, mo va marié mo piti ave vou. Manami ! Avla sa piti lé Roi tendre sa, li voulé dire son papa gran manzé, sa qui boire, boire.

Avla tou din cou lé Roi dire : Moucié Caraba quan vou voulé, mo va marié mo piti ave vou. Manami ! Avla sa piti lé Roi tendre sa,

Çatte galpé touzours divant ; li arive drète éne lacase qui grand coment léglise ; li entré : ça té lacase Louloup. Li dire : «Louloup, Louloup, mo napas ti vlé passe divant vous laporte sans dire vous bonzour. » Louloup dire li : « To té bienfét, mo pitit. » Avlà zautes dé cause causé. Çatte dire av Louloup, guétte bien so siprit ça çatte là : « Mo té tende dire quand vous vlé vous capabe fonde éne coup pour vine lion ou bien zalphant, ça qui vous léquére content. » Louloup dire li : « To a voir talhère, mo pitit.» Coment li dire ça, li fonde éne coup même, li vine éne gros lion. Çatte trouve ça, àforce li pére li saute lafenéte, lésse li sauté, li monte làhaut bardeaux. Louloup blizé rié, li crié : « Napas pére, pitit, dicendé. » Çatte dicendé, li dire Louloup : « Manman ! napas péle pére qui mo té pére, papa Louloup ! Més, Louloup, vous té zanzé pour vine lion, esqui vous capabe zanzé pour vine zozo oubien lérat ? » Louloup dire : « Sifét, mo pitit, mo capabe. » Avlà li fonde éne coup, li vine lérat. Çatte, manami ! pése li dans so latéte méme, li touyé li, li manze li.

Avlà coment li féque manze ça Louloup là, li tende carosse léRoi vine dans lacour ; li alle ouvert laporte carosse li prye léRoi dicendé sembe so pitit av Missié Carabas. Çatte dire léRoi : « Ça lacase là pour mo méte, Moussié Carabas ; vine promené, vou à voir. »

Avlà léRoi prômené, proméné ; li guété, li guété ; napas péle bélebéle lacase mo dire ous !

Quand çatte fine féré zautes proméné tout quiquepart, li féré zautes assise dans éne grand lasalle àcote té iéna éne grand latabe rempli pâtés, brioces, pralines, bonbons tout sorte ; té iena gouyaves, té iéna zacques, té iéna caramboles, té iéna vavangues, papayes, cocos, mambolos, zanblongues, té iéna tout ça qui té iéna ; més, monanmi ! ti éna éne divin, qui ti divin côment zamés divin ti divin !

Avlà léRoi coment li sise à table li dire : « Sifét va, moi qui léRoi, mo honté mo lacase napas zoli coment pour vous, Moussié

li voulé dire son papa gran merci, mé son la bouce sèque aforce liquierre content.	Carabas. » Lhére zautes tout zautes fine assise à tabe, ça qui manzé manzé, ça qui boire boire. Avlà léRoi goûte ça divin là, éne coup li dire Msié Carabas : « Moussié Carabas, quand vous vlé, mo marié vous sembe mo pitit. » So mamzéle léRoi li tende ça, monami, àforce li content li vlé dire, grand merci, mo papa ; narien sourti, son labouce séque.
Moucié Caraba qui té povre diable comman mo même la, li demande pa mié. Avla zotre alle léglize pour marié. Quan fini marié lé Roi donne enne gran bal. Li faire satte size à cote li a table. Avla quan lève de table, satte passe à cote son mètre, li dire : hé bin mon mètre qui mo té dire vous nne zour ? Son mètre dire : sifé va, to appelle satte couman zamé été y en a satte.	Msié Carabas qui té pauve coment moi méme li dire : «Mo béte moi ! sipas vous croire mo va dire non.» Zautes lévé, zautes méte légants, zautes alle léglise, zautes marié. LéRoi done éne grand bal, li fére çatte sise à table acote li : avlà àçthére çatte fine vine grand missié. Quand soupé fini avlà çatte léve so place ; li passe àcote so méte li dire li : « Ah ben, mo méte, qui ous croire ? menti ça qui mo té dire vous éne zour la ? » So méte dire : « Sifét va ! to éne çatte coment zamés té éna çatte. »
Quan fini soupé, satte li alle dan son la sambre pour li dourmi. Avla mo sivre li pour mo tire so botte. Quan so botte fini tiré, pour gran merci li f... moi enne cou de pié au qui, mo tombe ici.	Avlà çatte coment li alle dans so laçambe pour dormi, mo sivré li pour mo tire so botes. Lhére mo fine tire so botes, pour dire moi grand merci li envôye moi éne coudepied qui fére moi tombe ici pour raconte vous ça zhistoire là. So finition zhistoire çatte qui té éna botes[11].
(Chaudenson 1981: 121-24)	(Baissac 1880: 121-40)

39. 1855a Pierre Lolliot's *Poésies créoles*

Apart from this collection of poems, published in 1855, and articles in *Le Mauricien* and *Le Cerneen* referring to it, we have not been able to discover any information whatsoever about the author. There does not appear to be anyone living in Mauritius today who has this surname. However, there is a collection of poems in French, published in Mauritius in the 1840s, by one Isidore Lolliot who is also the author of an article which appeared in *Le Mauricien* newspaper in 1845. It is thus possible that Isidore and Pierre were one and the same person but it is probably more likely that the two were merely related to one another (possibly brothers or father and son). The fact that *Poésies créoles* was printed on *Le Mauricien*'s press and yet this newspaper provided no information about its author might suggest that he had close links with *Le Mauricien* and was possibly one of its employees.[12]

Rather than inform us about the author, the newspaper coverage the publication of *Poésies Créoles* was used as an occasion to celebrate the memory of François Chrestien, to express the nostalgia of their readers for their childhood days with which MC remained closely associated, and to lament the anticipated death of the language as a result of

---

[11] Nous devons ce conte à l'obligeance de M F de la B, que nous remercions de sa précieuse collaboration. Alors que dans presque toutes les productions soi-disant écrites en créole, la langue fait au français des concessions un peu bien nombreuses, elle conserve ici sa physionomie dans toute son originalité. Le conte finit, comme tout vrai conte créole doit finir, par le coup de pied traditionnel qui fait tomber le conteur devant son auditoire.

[12] PB is responsible for the speculation in this paragraph. The remainder was written by VYH.

emancipation. Referring to the liberated slaves, one of the *Cernéen* articles contained the words: *zot conn' caus' français aster* ('they know how to speak French now').

This publication contains a total of 24 texts, half of which are adaptations of La Fontaine's *Fables*. The preface, written entirely in MC and dedicated to MM A de Rochecouste and E de Chazal, is reproduced below. The human qualities and life style attributed to these men give an indication of the traditional aspects of Creole philosophy and way of life which Lolliot valued so highly. Of his 24 poems, we have chosen to include three of his original pieces: *Si mo té va zozo, P'tit bengali,* and *Ein' vié noir av' so pitit*.

A MM A de Rochecouste and E de Chazal

Zot dé là zot voir bien, mo dir' ça sans menti,
Tout sels fin' conn' gardé touzours zot zenr' créole;
Zot léquer là zamais té donn' nous démenti;
Zot té touzours zot mêm' sans zamais zoué rôle,
Et té marcé tout dret' sans zamais zot çanzé,
Sans baiss' à*droite à*gauce et sans fair' la*poussière,
Sans qui zamais personn' té par zot écrasé.
Mo conné pouquoi ça! zot té tourné derrière
Pour guet ein pé cimin qui créoles l'aut' fois
Té touzours conné sivre, et zot léquer té dire
Qui ça la*route là, quand mêm' cimin dans bois,
Fin' marqué par l'honner comment là haut la*cire;
Aussi, zot na*pas hont' met' zilet la*toil' blé
Et quand mêm' pour sourti met zot çapeau la*paille,
A*cauz' qui zot conné qui zilet là doublé
Semb' ein léquer qui bon et qu' en*bas son p'tit maille
L'aut la*couvri zot front qui zamais té courbé.
Si mo té çoisi zot pour parrains mo l'ouvraze,
Na*pas à*cauz' zot riç' et qui mo per tombé;
Non, personne mo croir' va tini ça langaze,
Car zamais mo té conn' ni flatté, ni menti.

Si mo té va zozo

1.
Si mo té va zozo,
Mo té va batt' lé zaile
Quand mo voir vous, coco,
A force qui vous belle.

2.
Pour çanté mon çanson,
Mo té va çoisi brance
A côt' ça p'tit gazon
Vous té crasé dimance.

3.
Si mo té va bouquet,
Mo té va çoisi place
Dans milié vous corset
Quand vous guett' dans la glace.

4.
Ou bien pouss' dans jardin
A côt' ça p'tit tonnelle
Qui çaque grand matin
Voir vous touzours plis belle.

5.
Et si mo té di l'eau
Qui coul' là haut la mousse,
Mo té va pour tombeau,
Çoisi vous p'tit la bouce !

(Lolliot 1855: 77-78)

P'tit bengali

1
Bord la rivière
Dans la fouzère,
Quand to sauté
Quand to çanté,
To camarades,
Par to roulades
Tout désolés,
Vite envolés ;
Zot gagné honte,
Ça na pas conte
Tant to zoli
P'tit bengali !

2
To ptit tapaze,
To gazouillaze
Fair' cardinal
Qui zénéral,
Dressé la tête,
Resté tout bête
Et cerç' ein coin
Qui na pas loin,
Là haut ein' zarbre,
Comment ein' marbre
Pour dibouté,
Quand to çanté.

3
Çaque p'tit plime,
Dans to costime,
Li plis brillant
Qui diamant.
To la bec rose
Na pas quiq' çose !
To p'tit li pié
Capav' défié
Pour so finesse,
So zentillesse,
Quand mêm' dicrin
Ça qui plis fin.

4
Bon dié mo croire
Pour qui to boire,
To badiné,
Té maziné
Bord la rivière
Met' la fouzère ;
Quand pour di l'eau
To boir' morceau,
To fair' av' brance
To révérence,
Qui to zoli
P'tit bengali !

5
Ah! qui dommaze
Qui dans la caze
Souvent zenfants,
Qui si méçants,
Ein'a malice
Pour zot caprice,
Enfermé toi
Toi p'tit lé roi,
Sans prend la peine
Donn' toi la graine
Ou bien di l'eau
Tout p'tit morceau.

6
Quand to misère,
Sans mêm' ein' frère
Dans to prison,
To p'tit çanson
Li semblé dire,
Dans so délire :
Ah! p'tits zenfants
Qui si méçants,
Dans la fouzère,
Bord la rivière,
Laiss' moi sauté,
Laiss' moi çanté.

(Lolliot 1855: 107-10)

Ein' vié noir av' so pitit

Pitit
Papa, tout d'bon l'autfois, te gagn' lé temps margoze,
Ein' lé temps ou li noirs té pour blancs ein' quiq'cose
Qui zot capav' loué, qui zot capav' vendé
Comment morceau la terre ? Ah cauzé mo tendé !
Est-ce qui vrai tous blancs té fair' nous la misère,
Té nèque batt' batt' nous, té touzours en colère
Bo matin zisqu'à soir et té néq maziné
Ça qui fair' plis di mal, ça qui plis raffiné
Pour qui zot mett' av' nous ? Moi qui dans zot la caze
Qui fin' lèv' ensemb' zot, qui comprend zot langaze,
Zamais moi, mo va croir' qui zot la même ça
Qui té blancs l'autre fois et qui blancs zourd'hi là.

Papa
To conné, mon p'tit, souvent faut voir pour croire,
Ça qui té vrai l'aut'fois, zourd'hi là li z'histoire ;
Mais noirs zot capav' dir' grand merci bon Dié,
Ça lé temps là zot tous na pas doit blié.

Pitit

Mais pourtant mon papa, ça qui mo té tend' dire
Té bien vrai — Zot tous là, zot té vin' dans navire
Comment tout ça tas befs qui vin' Madagascar ;
Blancs té prend ça qui forts, mett' ça qui fail à part
Pour bien tiré parti quand zour qui fair' la vente,
Et Gouvern'ment pour ça té fair' payé patente.

Papa

Eh ben to voir, mon p'tit, qui na pas z'habitants
Qui té tous sels la cause et faut pa croir' tous blancs
Té mauvais — Na pas ça — Té gagn' aussi bons maîtres
Qui té conn' sogn' nous bien, et qui na pas té traitres ;
Pour ein' qui té méçant, té gagné cent qui bons.

Pitit

Mais vous tous té z'esclav' ; dir' moi pour qui raisons ?

Papa

Pour qui raisons, si pas ; mais faut pa qui to croire
Qu' à présent faut touzours qui nous çanté victoire.
Gouvern'ment té tort donn' nous la liberté
Avant qui li té sir si nous capav' litté ;
Mais pour to comprend bien si mon cauzé li ziste,
Et pour to na pas croir' mo léquer inziste
Et na pas dir' merci ça qui fair' li di bien,
Mo va saye dir' toi : guett' nous vié li cien,
Si nous va tiré li dans l'endroit qui so place,
Ou li nou nourri li, sans montré li la çasse,
To croir' qui si nous va largué li dans grand bois
Li va rodé zibié et trouvé primier fois ?
Na pas ; li va sauté, galpé sans son la çaine,
Mais quand la faim vini, li va dans grand la peine,
Et nous qui va la cauz', car il fallait montre li
Comment faut li travail avant laiss' li courri.

Pitit

Alors dir' mo papa, ça qui fallait zot faire,
Pour av' la liberté na pas donn' nous misère ?

Papa

Mo va dir' toi pitit, moi qui néq' ein' pauv' noir,
Ça qui fallait zot faire, à cauz' qui mo té voir :
Fallait pas tant pressé tir' nous dans l'esclavaze,
Fallait bien voir avant si nous léquer té saze
Assez pour bien senti qu' ensemb' la liberté
Nous couraz', nous travail, tout té doit augmenté.
Comment nous vié li cien, fallait nous conn' la çasse
Avant qui nous galpé, sans nous billet de passe.
Ah! dans commencement, té na pas comment nous !
Tous noirs, to voir mo p'tit, té manqué vini fous ;
Mais semb' la liberté, personn' té pensé dire,
Qui faut l'honner marcé, pour son la route sire ;
Qui faut touzours travail, plis encore qu' avant,
Pour gagné dans la caz' touzours morceau l'arzent
Pour quand malad' vini : touzours dans la cantine
Là même té zot place, et souvent la cousine
Na pas té fimé, mêm' pour morceau dou riz sec.
Comment pauv' p'tits zozos, z'enfants ouvri la bec ;
Mais papas semb' mamans sans conné qui zot faire,
A force zot tourdis, croir' zot na pas misère.
Aussi, quand choléra té tap ensemb' nous tous,

> Li té trouvé tous noirs, sans ein' pauvre trois sous,
> Dourmi là haut la terr' sans mêm' ein' couvertire
> Isés par la boisson, par mauvais nourritire,
> Sans souci zot la vie et sans pens' zot zenfants,
> Ça pitits qu' avant là tous noirs té si contents.

PITIT
> Ça qui vous dire là comment dir' ein' z'histoire :
> Pour ça pauvres zenfants, mo na pas capav' croire
> Qui zot papas laiss' zot sans sogn' zot p'tit morceau
> Quand vous, quand vous guett' moi, vous li ziés pleins di l'eau.

PAPA
> Si mo ploré, z'enfant, à cause qui la terre
> Va bientot couvri moi ; mo pens' tout la misère,
> Quand mo na pas va là, qui va tomb' la haut toi,
> Si to na pas travail, si to na pas croire moi.

PITIT
> Na pas per vous, Papa, Blancs va donn' moi l'ouvraze,
> Quand zot va voir qui moi bon p'tit noir plein couraze.
> A présent là sirtout qui mo fin' comprend' bien
> Qui mêm' la liberté sans travail li na rien.

(Lolliot 1855: 117-21)

One additional Lolliot text, *Ein vié blanc avare semb' so pitit*, is reproduced within Stein's article (*this volume*).

Although the content of Lolliot's poems is very firmly rooted in local culture, some of his orthographic choices tend, paradoxically, to revert back to French-based orthography and to thus go against the evolutionary trends in the writing of MC already noted above and used, albeit inconsistently, in Chrestien's publications. And the popularity of Chrestien's work ensured that his conventions influenced many others. The most striking feature is Lolliot's complete disregard for the use of the hyphen as a means of signalling that a French article or adjective was an integral part of the corresponding MC noun, e.g.:

Pitot	Freycinet	Chrestien	Lolliot	
di mounde	*dou-mounde*	*di-mounde*	*di mound'*	'person'
–	*li-pié*	*li-pié*	*li pié*	'foot'
bon Dié		*bon-Dié/Bon-dié*	*bon Dié*	'God'

However, it must be pointed out that Chrestien himself did not always follow his own rules. In a few cases, he dropped the hyphen as in *léquer* 'heart' (instead of *lé-quer*). A few similar examples can be found in Lolliot, as well as examples of both (a) hesitation between separating the French article from the noun and writing the MC item as a single word, and (b) partial agglutination:

full agglutination:	*léquer, nàme, aulié, zépaules* (but : *l'épaule*)
hesitation:	*di mound'* / *dimound'* ; *di bois* / *dibois*; *z'affaire/zaffaire*;
partial agglutination:	*di l'eau* / *di leau*; *lé zaile, di zouitre*

The functional subject / object distinction for the first and second singular personal pronouns is found in some texts from **1805** onwards and occurs consistently in Lolliot's poems. This distinction is not found in any of Chrestien's publications and is also absent from several other pre- 1840 texts. Sporadic examples of denasalized forms of the three singular possessive pronouns are found from **1818a**. The denasalized forms occur to the exclusion of nasalized forms in all but one of the 1839 *Cernéen* texts,[13] as well as in

---

[13] The exception is **1839d**, the one written by Chrestien.

Cirandane-Çanpec (**1846**) and *Moussié Caraba* (*circa* **1850**). Lolliot hesitates between nasalized and denasalized possessives but the latter predominate.

	subject	object	possessive
Pitot[14]	mô, li	moi, li	mon, son
Freycinet	mo, to, li	moi, toi, li	mon, to(n), son
Chrestien	moi, toi, li	moi, toi, li	mon, ton, son
Lolliot	mo, to, li	moi, toi, li	mo(n), to(n), so(n)

The distinction between the verb *fini* and the completive aspect marker [fin] (generally written *fine* or *fin*, non existent in Chrestien and also in *Proclamation*, is present in all the 1839 *Cernéen* texts (except **1839d**, the one written by Chrestien) and also in subsequent texts. Lolliot uses elided *fin'* as aspect marker as in (1) and (2) but, curiously, also *fini* as in (3) and (4).

1) Zot dé là, zot voir bien, mo dir' ça sans menti,
   Tout sels fin' conn' gardé touzours zot zenr' créole; (Dedication)
2) Après zot fin' allé, l'autre dimound' encore
   La porte vini tapé (*Zeanne*, p 4)
3) Marmit' ein zour té proposé
   Panelle fair' ein' p'tit voyaze.
   Panelle fini réfisé,
   A cauz' qui li trouvé plis saze
   Resté tranquil' dans so ptit coin (*Marmite av' Panelle*, p 33)
4) Pour li gagné di lait ein' maman cèvr' ein zour
   Fini quitté so la cour. (*Loulou, cèvre av' p'tit cabri*, p 45)

The use of both *fin'* and *fini* as the aspect marker in Lolliot's poems seems to indicate that, despite the evidence of earlier texts, the phonetic distinction between the preverbal marker and the verb 'to finish' was not yet complete in all varieties of MC, and that this poet may have spoken a somewhat conservative variety. His choice of monosyllabic *fin'* or bi-syllabic *fini* in particular instances may be for versification purposes (i.e. the need for a particular number of syllables in a rhyming verse).

For discussion of the grammaticalization of *fin'*, see Fon Sing (2005).

40-48 **1855b-1855j** Newspaper correspondence in MC

The publication of Lolliot (1855) appears to have encouraged *Le Mauricien* newspaper to publish correspondence in MC on several occasions between April and September 1855, and sometimes in verse. All these examples are reprinted below.

F&R (2007: 155-57) announce the **1855b** text but curiously and presumably by accident, print only the first 25 lines of this adding to it, as if part of the same text, the whole of **1855e**.

40. **1855b**

MISSIÉ LA GAZETTE
Autréfois, vous conné, ça dans lé temps margoze,
Noirs n'a pas té capav' dir' ça qui zot pensé;
A présent, Dié merci, li na pli la même çoze
Çaquein' capav' écrir', çaquein' capav' causé.
Mo va donc dire vous, ça qui dans mo la tête
Car mo croir' qui vous bon et qui vous va content
Donne mo lécritir' place dans la gazette.

---

[14] Pitot's dialogue uses the invariable polite form 'vous' for the second person (S/O) and for the possessive form.

Mo voulé conn' ein pé, pourquoi dipis longtemps
La misèr' tappe av' nous dans ein' sorte manière
Qui nous tire la langue en verté pas trop fort.
Lé rat dasn son p'tit trou, tangue dans so tannière,
Zacot mêm' dans grand bois la montagne Grand Port,
Na pas tir' la ficel' comment nous qui zens libres.
Malbars zot vir' viré dans milié grand cimin,
Zabitants, mo tendé, n'a plis capav' donn' vivres;
Tous blancs la tête en bas, comment dans grand çagrin.
Pourquoi donc tout ça là? Mo na pas capav' croire
Qui laguer' qui la cause ! Y-ein-a quiq' çose de pli
Dans temps français, ma foi, ça n'a pas ein' zistoire.
Zamais nous té conn' ça! Quand sourti dans lilit,
Au moins té sir manzé, çaquein' Dans son la case
Té gagné maï-mouli, bon ration can manioc
Ou bien quiq'çoze enfin, Pour tirer son la raze;
Tandis qu'à présent là, li capav' fitter croc
Dou riz n'a pas vini Dans fond pauvre marmite;X
Pourtant mo tendé dir' qui Français av' Anglais
Zot' fin' Donné la main ; qui zot met mêm' lévite
Parce qui zot laguer' dans ein' pays qui frais
Et qui Français capav' prête plein zot zamis.
Enfin ça qui bien sir, zot' fin' fair' cammarades
Comment p'tits dames céré fair' av' p'tits gouramis
Zot' vasiseaux navigué tous dans même la rades.
Ici mêm' vous voir ot' donné poignées de main,
Tire çapeau, papa, faire grand politesse,
Quand zot tourné lé dos, na pli dir' "Quel gredin!"
Tout ça fini passé. Li lé temps la tendresse
Donc, vous voir bien, Missié, qui de ça côté là,
Zaffair' na pas all' mal et mo bien sir la Reine
Ti dir' lé roi Français en causant, Eh vous là?
Acetez bien mon di sicre et vous va croir' sans peine
Comment moi, qui par là, commenc' fin' augmenté.
Mo va dir' vous quiq'çoze et ça n'a pas mensonze,
Mo conné qui Français à présent boir' di thé :
Guet' Malbars ; quand vini, zot na pas manz' bred' sonze
Mais quand voir nous mangé, zot' aussi gouté ein pé
Après ça, croire moi, zot faire boui grand marmitte
Avec morceau safran, mêl' av' piment rapé.
Tout ça té pour dire vous qui di sicre vend' vite.
Mais vous va répond moi, qui donc qui vous pensé,
Qui fair tout ça di mal ? Vous conné, moi mo bête
Mais là dans mo l'esprit n'a pas va balancé
Vous voulez mo causé ça qui dans mo la tête :
Eh ben, vous mem' va voir, si pas mo gagn' raison.
Pourtant mo per ein pé, zot four' moi dans prison
Ah bah ! tant pis pour li! Gouvernement la cause
Car si li ti va vlé tiré dé trois sacs l'or,
Malabars n'a pas té va fair' tous sortes quiq'çose
Vend' di bois, vend' posson, marsandises dehors,
Zot té doit piocher et non pas fair' commerce
La ter' n'a pas manqué, y-ein-a plein la forêt,
Pour trouver n'a pas loin, faut pas all' la recerce
Lé bras mêm' qui na pas, mais terrain li tout prêt.
A présent, tout ici, dans la main malabars même,
Cinois fin' enfoncés, pourtant zot zens bien fins!
Volailles dans panier dizef pour dans carême,
Malbars meme qui vendé. – Qui band' famé grédins !

Si mo té gouverner, mo té va met zendarmes
Dipi soleil lévé, zisqu'à soleil coucé
Rod' rod' zot tout partout av' bons batons pour zarmes,
Et mo té va pez' zot' ! mais faudrait dépécé,
Car sans ça vous va voir, zot va touque Maurice,
Mette tous blancs la pioce et tous zens libr' aussi.
Nous gagné divant nous, ein famé précipice
L'odér qui dans son fond senti lognon roussi,
Faut veil au grain papa ; faut met' zot tous l'ouvraz
Tous ça scélérats-là, sans ça ma foi, missié
Pays-ici va perdi semb' zot vagabondaze ;
Car la moitié malbars, guet travail l'aut' moitié
Mo té pour continié, mais mo largue mo plime.
Eh vous là ? La vérèt' fin' arriv' Pavillon
Qui nous va divinis ? Qui sacré plat léguime ?
Choléra, la misère et la vérette bon,
Na pli besoin na rien, vaut mié fermé la boutique
Allé voir mo zenfants comment zot tous ça va,
Ah, ça la malle là, qui mauvaise pratique,
Pli tard, mon cer missié, moi fini lette là.
(*Le Mauricien* 21 avril 1855)

41. **1855c**

Nous demandons pardon à notre collaborateur Jean Pierre Louis*, d'avoir omis sa signature au bas de la lettre patoise insérée dans un de nos derniers Nos**. C'est vraiment une spécialité amusante et rare que celle qu'il nous a décelée et qu'il nous décèle encore aujourd'hui***. Nous pouvons lui affirmer que c'est un vif plaisir pour nous de l'imprimer et si il en éprouve lui-même à apprendre son succès près de nos lecteurs, qu'il le sache de notre bouche. La plaisanterie maniée avec la naïveté et l'esprit de notre collaborateur fait rire et ne fâche pas.

P.S : L' autre jour quand vous té donn place mo lecritire
      Vous prot' finn' blié mette mo signatire

* Il s'agit très probablement de celui qui a écrit la série de poèmes publiés dans le m. de 1855.
** Voir le long poème du 21 avril 1855
*** Il s'agit d'un poème de 36 vers, à propos d'une nouvelle parue dans *La Sentinelle* :

[« Mo té lir bon matin qui bientôt dans milice,
Comment soldats tout d'bon, nous va tous engazés,...]   (*Le Mauricien* 24 avril 1855)

42. **1855d**

Vous qui doit conné tout, pisqué vous La Gazette,
Fair' moi plaisir Missié, dire moi la verté,
Car ça qui mo tendé, cass' ein' pé mo la tête,
Sans li capav' entré; pourtant li répété
Par tant di mond' ici, qui faut croir' qui li ziste ;
Mais li bien étonnant et vous va dir' moi ça ;
Paul Emile, Francois, Zean Marie av' Auguste,
Tous mo voisins enfin, dir' moi qui comme ça
A présent nous gagné pour Cef la Colonie
Ein' famé Gouverner' qui bien content nous tous
Qui n'a pas vin' ici, pour faire l'économie
Et quand nous, va plaigné, va bien écouté nous.
Moi, mo trouv ça si fort, qui mo pas vlé croire
Et pourtant si li vrai, comment mo va content !
Dire moi, cer Missié, si na pas z'histoire?
Comment li va famé, si la port' Gouvern'ment

Té va touzours ouvert, pour laisse entrer di monde,
Pour caus' ein pé zaffairs, pour conné si li bon
Percé barriqu' en bas, ou prend li par la bonde
Vendé rhum par ptits coups ou laiss' li par gallon

Mo tendé z'employés qui faire zot la fière
Na pli va guetté nous comme si nous li cien,
Na pli va front' fronté, zot va guette derrière
Et faire ça qui capav' pour fair' l'ouvraze bien.
Cefs mêmes dsn bireaux, va vini plis honnêtes.
Faut espérer, Missié, qui zot va vini bons bébètes
Et na plis va trait' nous comm' ein' troupeau
Qui nous tous conné bien et qui son nom moutons.
Tout ça, li bien zoli ; mais y-ein-a l'autre çose
Qui faudrait fair' encor' et qui té va famé,
Qui té va dans çapeau fair' metté riban rose ;
Sais pas si vous comprend? Mo vlé dir' faut ramé
Pour tirer nous navir' qui dans di l'eau pourrie ;
Faudrait donc Gouvernèr donn' nous ein pé la main
Pour nous capav' gagné morceau bef la boucerie.
Faut pas comment touzours, dir', nous va voir dimain,
Lé temps fini vini. Si vous vlé vous bourrique
Hissé bien son çarette et donné vous l'arzent,
Faut vous nourri li bien, faut arrêt' laboutik
Pour prend morceau di son ; alors vous bien comprend
Qui li va gagn' liquer pour fair' bien son l'ouvrage

Vous bourrique va gras, vous poce li va lourd ;
Vous, vous va plein l'arzent, li, li va plein courage
Mais Gouvernèr mo croir', va fair semblant li sourd.
Domamaze qui mo bête et qui mo pauvre Diable,
Sans ça, mo té va dir' : Ecouter Zénéral. »

(Le Mauricien 26 avril 1855)

43. **1855e**

Avant qui causé, faut mo dir' vous qui moi.
Zot apélé moi Zean ! mo mitié garde-çasse,
Pour veillé tous çasser qui çasse sans la loi.
Dans milié la forêt, là même qui mo place.
A présent là, laiss' moi tir' ein pé mo bagout .
Mo té l'aut' zour à soir, dans mo pauvre la case
Après crasé piment pour met' dans brèd' dibout
Ein plat qui va touzours trouvé dans mo ménaze,
Quand mo guetté par ter', brill' ein' morceau papié
Qui té doit servi moi pour ramassé quiqu' çose ;
Ça qui mo baiss' en bas, mo li zié li bourrié
Comment quand peppermint fair' léffet so la dose.
Vous conné qui ci-ça ? mo lequer té sauté
A cause papié là, té morceau la gazette
Qui té dir tout dimound', qui dans so la bonté,
Ein' Gouverner Français, Ah ! Qui Français honnête,
Té vlé rendé visite av' nous bon Zénéral,
Et qui dans quiques zours, li té va vin' Maurice.
Ah zamais vous va croir, qui di bien qui di mal
Mo léquer té senti ! mo té fair' sacrifice

Plitôt perdi mo place et resté sans l'arzent
Qui na pas vin' en vil' pour voir ein' fois encore,
Avant qui mo crêvé, Français qui mo content,
Et zot Pavillon là, Pavillon tricolore

> Qui té pour nous l'aut' fois, dans temps M'sié Malartic,
> Alors mo ti zène ! ... Ah ! mais mo capav' dire
> Quand même mo léquer li sec comment mastic,
> A présent qui li vié, qui li té vin' la cire
> Quand mo té maziné, qui comment l'autrefois,
> Mais non ! ... assez causé, pourtant rend moi service
> Dir' ça gouverner là qui si blancs contents li,
> Anglais, Français, tous zens qui resté dans Maurice,
> Qu'ein vié vié noir aussi, ti vini pour voir li,
> Na pas té pèr quitté, so licien, son la case,
> Fair' si pas qui la rout' son bâton dans la main
> Pour voir avant li mort ça z'habits ça visaze
> Qui Bon Dié sel conné, si li va voir dimen.
>
> (*Le Mauricien* 25 mai 1855)

44. **1855f**

> M'sié Croolc
>
> Faut convini Missié, qui dans vous la peintire,
> Mang' Fizet là si bien, qui va dir' li vivant.
> Faut qui vous pleinl'esprit, pour dans tout so natire
> Vous capav' peintiré ça frit qui si çarmant,
> Qui li faire vini plein di l'eau dans la bouce.
> Quand même zot dé là, neque là haut papié,
> Va dir tout' d'bon qui zot dans zardin Pamplemousse
> Sans menti, mangues là, vous fin' si bien copié,
> Qui çaquein quand voir li, pour manzé gagn' l'envie ;
> Qui vius fair' mo lédents neque faire crouc-crouc.
> Croire moi, mo dir' vrai, zamais dans mo la vie
> Mo té voir ein' dessin comment pour vous M'sié Croolc
>
> (*Le Mauricien* 28 mai 1855)

45. **1855g**

M'sié la Gazette

Comment mo té tonné bon matin, quand mo té voir qui personne na pas té racont' ça zoli la Comédie qui Zofficiers Anglais té donné l'aut' zour! Pourquoi ça Misié la Gazette?

> Pourtant Z'Anglais, Francais, zot tous fin' camarades
> Et quand Français zoué tous zofficiers allé ;
> Mêm' qui zot gagn' ein loze entre dé colonnades,
> Qui zour concert M'sié Zeorz', nous tous nous doit rapp'lé,
> Té fin' bien arranzé semb' pavillons tout sorte,
> Bouquets, bell' la bouzie, enfin semb' si pas quoi,
> Zisqu'à brances coco, qui té pleins dans la porte,
> Si tant qui noirs té croir' ça la fête lè roi,...
> Pitêt' qui Français na pas comprend langaze
> Qui tous Z'Anglais parlé ; mais dir' moi, qui ça fait ?
> A'vlà moi par exemple, est-ce qui dans la case
> Zamais mo parl' Anglais ? Pour menti n'a pas fait.
> Mo conn' neq' dé trois mots, Goddam avec by love
> Very well, good morning, How ar' you my dear Sir
> Give me my hat ou bien Boy, give me my glove.
> Pour all' la Comédie et prend morceau plaisir
> Na pas bisoin comprend !... Parol' mo capav dire
> Qui ca z'officiers là té zoué pour tout d'bon;
> Aussi la sall' té plein. Capitaines navire,
> Zanglais qui dans bireaux, caporals ein' galon,

       Dé galons, trois galons, soldats ensemb' zot femmes,
         Té neque rodé place. Et lozes ! Fallait voir.
       Zofficiers, nèq' là dans, av' plein belles Madames:
         Dans la salle, partout, na pas té fair' noir noir
       A cauz' qui M'sié Racel té bien sogn' tous son globes
         Racel là vous conné, li même qui çarzé
       Allim ! Allim ! la lampe ; aussi tous ça bell' robes,
         Na pas ein té gâté; tout té bien arranzé.
       Gouverner té là mêm' ensemb' tout son famille,
       Zizes, tous gros gros zens, té cauz' cauz' ensemb' li
         Et faire li la cour comment si li p'tit fille.
         Tout dans la Comédie an verté té zoli.
        Eh' vous là ! … mo dir' vous, zamais mo là va croire
         Vié comment zot dir'. Na pas ça neq' z'histoire,
        La poudre li metté pour li gagn' civés blancs
       Fallait voir li l'aut soir, galpé galpé dans loze
       Donn' la main par ici, par là, fair ' papillon,
       Fair' galant semb' mamzel', pour senti prend zot rose.
        Zènes zens divant li blizé baiss' pavillon.

Mais tout ça là na rien. La Comédie là qui li ! Vous vlé mo racont' vous li. Ein Missié té baiss' ein l'autre, l'autre là té rend' li, après zot té boir' ensemb', zot té rié, rié zisqu'à n'a pas bon. Après ça zot té la guerr' ensemb' encor' ; zot té tomb' par ein la fenêtre ; après ça ein' Missié qui té rice té fine vine domestique ; l'autre so camrade té cacié dans la cave et pis tous sortes quiq' çoses. Primier pièce là mo té bien cout' ; mais les zaut' ma foi mo té voir tout di monde rié tant, qui mo té tant rié voir zot rié qui mo té malade mo côté. Tout de bon vous là, zamais quand vous voir Anglais dans la rie, vous capav' qui zot' mêmes qui faire la Comédie qui farce comme ça.
        Ein p'tit Noir.

                             (*Le Mauricien* 27 juillet 1855)

46.   1855h

M'sié la Gazette,

Mo na pas comment mo va faire, neque vous qui pour moi sourti dans mon zéné. –Ein malbar fine donn' moi 4 poules avec ein coq pour faire ein lettre pour qui li dire merci zens qui vlé malbars gagne plein femmes. Rend' moi service dire moi comment faut faire ou plitôt mette li dans vous papié pour li arrivé. Mo croir qui li fine donne moi 4 poules av' ein coq pour fair' voir qui malbars aussi doit gagne trois quatre femmes.

       Salam, Salam, Salam, Bara Sirdas la Reine !
      Moi qui néquein Malbar, mo vlé dir' sans menti
   Pourquoi tous z'habitants zot si tant dans la peine,
      A cauz' qui vous, Sirdars, fin' fair' zot averti
    Qui vous léquer content qui tous Malbars gagn' femmes
     Plis qui zot gagn' bizoin, pour laver, pour canzer,
      Zot qui zisqu'à présent té tant miser' Madames
     Pour peign' zot grands civés et fair' coui zot manzer.
       Z'habitants là vous voir, zot tous là zot canaille ;
    Zot néq' contents plaigné ! Zot n'a pas vaut trois sous,
   Zot cerce gagn' l'arzent, néq' pour sogn' zot marmaille
    Pour envoy' zot l'écol', et zot bisqué voir nous
     Laisse tous nous pitits galpé dans tous la rie
     A cause qui nous sirs qui nous mèm' qui bientôt
       Va prend blancs pour malbars et met' zot l'équirie
      Pour sogn' nous zanimaux, zot qui fair' zot zabot
       Et qui dir' qui Malbars ein' bien mauvais race,
      Qui nq' content volor et qui gagn' trop l'arzent.
   Grands Sirdars, vous raison mett' ein pé dans nous place

        Et pensé qui Bibis faut qui nous gagné tant
    Qui nous tous va soulé. Comm' ça mêm' son manière
      Pour nous na pas çagrins fin' quitté nous papas
        Pour vin' travail ici, dans ça pays misère,
      Où li nous fair' na rien, mais à côt femm' na pas.
    Et pis guett' à présent ; nou tous nous contents Tirques
        Ein' famé nation, qui conné ça qui faut,
    Et qui mo bien facé mo vin' voir neq' dans cirques
      Car vrai, li conné bien ça qui femmes li vaut.
    Vous croire qui tous blancs comment zot na pas faire ?
        Awoa, mo conné plein Missiés qui contents
    Quand même dans grand zour, fair' semblant gagn' zaffaire.
    Pour all' voir'… Mais laiss' zot. –Nous va fair comment blancs.
      Et grand merci, Sirdars ; nous va fair' plis encore
        Caqu'ein va gagn' sérail, comment Omer-Paça
      Et nous va lèv' bon matin semb' l'aurore
    Comment mo tend' blancs dire … Vous Sirdars qui v'lé ça –
      Pour di sicre ma foi, ça qui capav' va faire :
      Pourvi nous gagn' douriz et qui nous gagn' bibis
    Restant na pas pour nous, ça na pas nous zaffaire.
      Si nous té vin' ici, néque pour faire pitits.
    Ainsi donc na pas cout' ça qui z'habitants dire
      Et laiss' nous, Grands Sirdars, fair' ça qui nous voulé,
      Dire zot désiré tout ça qui zot écrire
    Car zotte tous là vous voir, neque bon pour guêlé.
                                 (*Le Mauricien* 1er août 1855)

47.   1855i

M'sié La Gazette

Mo té va rié bon quer, quand mo té lir' 'Commercial' si mo na pas té va senti dans son requête qui farce, quiq'çose qui pi. Li vlé moq' zens la Minicipalité mais mo trouv' tous noms qui li té donn' zot bien zis. Si son cef appel' Bagoût, té mett' li exprès pour saye litt' av' Gouvernement ; si son second là appell' Poupon à cauze nous encore z'enfants qui na pas conné tous nous droits ; msié L'Escalier là pour nous qui faut nous fair' tout ça qui nous capav' pour monter ; misyé Gros Lizié doit faire nous comprend qui nous lé temps na pas loin ; m'sié Calfat li là pour dir' nous na pas per' coups-de-vent qui Gouvernement va souffler semb' nous ; m'sié Martin té nommé pour touye tous ça carapattes qui sice nous di sang ; m'sié coco sec pour fair' voir qui nous capav' marcé sans nous bisoin cacié nous front ; m'sié Avale tout cri, pour fair' per tout ça p'tits li ciens qui neq' conn' zappé ; m'sié Coq di bois, m'sié Zozo pour çanté quand nous na plis va misère ; m'sié La Daube, pour donné manzé ça zens qui na plis va gagn' gouvernement pour nourri zot ; misié Canal pour dir' nous qui ça zour là va gagn' ein famé lessive pour faire ; m'sié Gros la tête pour ramass' bon sens pour zens qui ein'a bisoin ; m'sié Bacoa pour amarr' la main ça qui conn' prend tous les dés côtés et m'sié Bonhomme pour faire voir qui comment nous tous va contents, nous tous va bons.

Mo té va continié si mo té va sir qui 'Commercial' na pas pratiqué mais tous sa z'Abé qui dans son papier là fair' moi per.

    Salam m'sye La Gazette,
              Ein' P'tit Noir.

                                    Le Mauricien 9 août 1855

48.   1855j

Madame Fréry

Après tous compliments qui tous blancs fin' fair' vous
Laiss' moi, qui neq'ein noir, seyé dir' vous, Madame,
Ça qui dans mo léquer ! Pour dir' qui quiq'çose doux
L'aut' fois té dir' di miel. Qui té va croir' qu'ein' femme

Té va vin' ici pour fair' di mound' menti,
Et pour fair gagn' honté tous mouces là haut rose !
Violon dans vous la main li cauzé, li senti ;
Ça qui li dire là na pas appell' quiq'çose ;
Li plis doux qui di miel mêm'ça qui vin' Bourbon.
Mais faudrait bêt' pour croir' qui di bois gagn'ein' nâme !
Na pas possible ça ; vous là, vous ein démon
Et vous té vin' ici pour rend' nous fous, Madame.
Vous fair' nous blié tout quand nous tend' vous vini ;
Vous fair' tout nous di sang arrêt' dans nous la veine,
Car dans vous violon là gagn' nâm' Paganini
Quand vous çant' vous çagrin, quand vous dire vous la peine.
Vous fair' sourti la voix dans ein morceau dibois
Et pis vous va dir' nous qui vous na pas malice
Moi, quand mo va voir vous, mo va fair' sign' la croix
Ou bien mo va port' plaint' contre vous la Police.
Pourquoi perdi di mound', quand vous, dans Paradis,
Vous beauté, vous talent va fair' vous gagn'ein place ?
Saint Pierre, son gardien, comment zenfants va pris
Et va donn' vous la clé sans fair' mem'ein grimace.
                                        Ein' noir.

(*Le Mauricien* 28 septembre 1855)

49. 1860 Catéchisme Créole

The only copy of this text known to us is in the British Library. It contains no information as to authorship or place of publication. It was sent to the director of this library by a private individual who, in an accompanying letter, identified the author as "Mr E de Chazal, a sugar planter of Mauritius". This is almost certainly the same E de Chazal mentioned in the dedication to Lolliot's (1855) poems (see above).

Demande : Qui ti faire nous, et qui faire nous vivre tous les zours ?
Réponse : Nous Papa qui dans ciel, nous Seigneur qui tout sél Bondié, dans ciel et la haut la terre.
D. Est-ce qui Bondié faire tout qui chose ?
R. Oui, Bondié faire tout, quand na pas Li, na pas té va yenna narien qui ti vivant.
D. Qui sentiments nous dévré yenna pour Bondié ?
R. Nous dévré content Li, tout nous liquère, tout nous name, tout nous siprit, tous nous la force.
D. Pour qui faire Bon Dié ti faire nous ?
R. Pour nous vine son pitits, son zenfants même, pour nous content Li, pour nous content faire dibien, comment Li content neinque faire dibien, et pour nous capave rende service, et gagne bonhère par nous dibien.
D. Est ce qui nous va vivre touzours la haut la terre à cote nous à présent ?
R. Non, nous va quitte eine zour ça la terre là, et si nous bons, nous va vivre coment [sic] zanges dans ciel.
D. Qui ci ça ciel ?
R. Ciel, son condition meme à cote zanges vivre ; zote tous content camrades, et zote tous hérés à cote zote Papa qui dand Ciel.
D. Et si nous na pas bons, à cote nous va allé ?
R. Nous va alle à cote diables avec mauvais siprits, dans l'enfer.
D. Qui ci ça l'enfer ?
R. L'enfer, son condition la vie diables meme avec mauvais siprits ; zote na pas capave reste ensemble ça qui bons ; zote sauve loin zot Papa qui dans Ciel.
D. Comment nous capave vine bons ?
R. Nous capave vine bons quand nous conné cé qui Bon Dié ti dire doumounde pour montre zotre siprit ; après ça quand nous faire ça qui nous conné Bondié ti dire nous faire pour nous bonhère.
D. Qui va donne nous la force vivre coume ça ?

R. Nous Papa meme qui dans Ciel, qui ti vine la haut la terre, qui ti laisse doumounde voir Li dans eine lé corps comment doumounde meme, et coume ça ti faire cé qui ti bizouin pour tire nous péchés.
D. Coument doumounde ti appelle Bon Dié quand Li ti vini la haut la terre ?
R. Doumounde ti appelle Li « EMMANUEL » et ça nom là, dans son langage nation qui ti voir Li, voulé dire : « BonDié toujours ave nous » après ça zotre ti appelle li « NOUS SEIGNERE JESUS CHRIST ».
D. Coument Li capave ide nous tire nous péchés, astère qui doumounde n'a pli capave voir li.
R. Par son parole qui Li ti dire, et qui nous capave conné quand nous fine conne lire LA BIBLE, et par son siprit qui entre dans nous name, pour faire nous comprend son Parole qui a montre nous bon chimin.
D. Coument vous appelle ça siprit la ?
R. Nous appelle li SAINT ESPRIT ou bien ça qui soulaze nous, CONSOLATEUR.

FIN

Quand zote fine conne lire mo va montre zote l'autre quichose, qui Siprit Jésus Christ meme, ou ça qui <u>Saint Esprit</u> ti montre nous.

50.   1865 *Soirées d'abat-vent. Souvenirs de chasse.*

This small collection of lyrics and poems by Henry Pitot contains three items in MC. All three are reprinted in F&R (2007: 161-67) and so are not reproduced here. This publication appears to have been popular since a second edition was printed in 1878.

51.   1867 *Navire fine engazé. The "Mauritius" in danger.*

This is probably the longest single creative text produced in MC during the whole colonial period, with a total of almost 1,000 lines. It dates from the time the prosperity of *L'âge d'or* was rapidly coming to an end. Although written in a humerous style and sold to aid a charitable cause, the author comments of many of the problems then facing Mauritius. Since this text has recently been published in full in F&R (2007: 172-99), we will not include it here but a short extract commenting on MC can be found in Baker (*this volume*).

Spelling in this text is somewhat inconsistent, suggesting that it was written very hurriedly, but these inconsistencies are revealing. He hesitates between *té* and *ti* as the anterior marker, but the latter is dominant. While examples of l/n variation can be found earlier,[15] he is the first and only author to employ the spellings *nané* and *nanné* (for French *l'année*).[16] Some of his words with initial z deriving from French plural s have rarely if ever been seen in other texts. *Zerrata* (for *errata*) is obviously a humorous but attractive invention. There could also be some intended humour in *zanglais, zéconomie, zédication, zoder,* and *zopital* (corresponding to French *anglais, économie, éducation* and *hôpital*), all of which are generally attested elsewhere with an initial *l* in MC. A few of the words he uses are worthy of mention:

1. *papa*: *Jisqu'à canne meme, li dire Papa!* apparently meaning 'until the sugarcane itself says it can no longer cope' (this interjective expression is not attested elsewhere); *Ça qui Papa la Pli* 'that's truly torrential rainfall' (*mama* is far more commonly used as a superlative).
2. *morceau*: This seems to be a favourite word, being used to designate a small quantity or part in a wide variety of contexts: *morceau dibois; morceau l'arzent; Compagné gagné boucoup, zami vrai pitit morceau; Morceau la Haut Flacq, morceau oussi Moka* (parts of these districts); *Na pas colère, zami, ça morceau badiné* ; and *li posé ptit morceau*.

---

[15] Baker believes that /nene/ 'nose' is not a case of reduplication but in fact derives from French *le nez* with agglutination of the article and the initial *l* being changed to *n*.

[16] The initial *n* here may have been favoured by the existence of the semantically overlapping term /banane/ meaning 'years' (but the *ban* does not derive from the homophonous plural marker – see Baker 2003: 135-39) as well as 'New Year's Day'.

3. Nouns derived from verbs: ***Dourmi*** *appellé encore, mais li na pas vini; Anous faire eine zistoire, Anous ramasse **blagué**, qui nous tiré à soir.*

This is also the first text to make extensive use of *pour* as marking futurity alongside *va*. Its predominance in combination with *ti* to express conditionality is quite striking on the introductory page, *Avla tout son causé Sans-Souci*, with seven occurrences of *ti pour* and only two of *ti va*.

A final observation is that this text contains several references to ethnic varieties of MC. *Langage Blanc* is said to be changing; one example given is described as being like an incomprehensible *sirandane* (riddle), other examples are described as being *langage, comça Madame Serrée*. On one occasion he refers to the MC of Indian immigrants with the words *ça malbar causé*, and he includes a few examples of their speech containing Indian words *li **bourbac**; dans tout bon dileau, **capra** sale li lave!; **Cousparvani**, travaille ou bien n'a pas travaille* [bold lettering added]. The Indian terms reflect the increasing Asian numerical dominance of the population and a feeling of linguistic insecurity among the authentic "Crioles".

52. 1880 *Etude sur le patois créole mauricien*

Charles Baissac (1831-92) was born in Port-Louis but was sent to France at the age of 12. He returned to Mauritius in 1854 (Prosper 1978: 319). He subsequently became *professeur de français* at the Collège Royal, then even more than today, by far the most prestigious boys' school in the island. Since this book and his subsequent collection of folk-tales (1888) were both published in France, he may have returned to France in retirement but we are unable to confirm that.

Baissac's *Etude* was among the earliest grammars of a French Creole to be published and has remained ever since the most quoted source of information on MC. Apart from a lengthy Introduction (pp i-lvii) and the grammar proper, it also includes two stories and sections on *Proverbes et dictons, Locutions,* and *Sirandanes*. The first of the two stories, *Z'histoire éne çatte qui té éna botes,* is printed above side-by-side with an earlier version of the same story (pp 35-40). Both stories and the MC parts of *Proverbes et dictons* and *Locutions* are included in our concordance.[17]

53. 1885 *L'Evangil selon S. Matthié*

Samuel Anderson was born in Mauritius and was the son of a Scottish protestant minister and his Mauritian wife. He was educated at the Royal College where his English and French teachers were respectively the novelist Walter Besant and Charles Baissac. After being ordained as a minister himself, he began translating the gospels into MC. In 1884 he sent a manuscript of *L'Evangil selon S. Matthié dan langaz créol Maurice* to the British and Foreign Bible Society (BFBS) in London and, in an accompanying letter wrote:[18]

> The Mauritian Creole language is a wide-spread and permanent one (...). [It] must have originated with the Malagasy and African slave population during the French occupation [sic] before the close of the last century, and soon became what it is to this day, emphatically the language of the poor and the labouring classes in the Island, irrespective of the many other languages and dialects in use there.
> More than 350,000 out of the 360,000 souls that make up the population of that British Colony understand and speak the Mauritian Creole. It is spoken by the English and French and all the European inhabitants, also by the Indian coolies and traders from the Bombay, Madras and Calcutta presidencies, by the Chinese, Malagasies, Africans, etc. in

---

[17] The concordance includes Baissac's (1888) version of the *Sirandanes* in preference to the marginally different version included in Baissac (1880).
[18] All extracts from correspondence quoted here were collected by Baker at the BFBS archives in London during the 1980s. The archives have since moved to Cambridge University.

the island, for it is the only medium of communication between all the other languages and dialects spoken there (letter dated 17 March 1884; BFBS Archives).

The BFBS referred Anderson's letter and gospel translation to Walter Besant. His reply indicated that he held a very low opinion of people of racially mixed descent (such as Anderson).[19] Besant was highly critical of Anderson's deviations from French orthographic conventions, in particular his (inconsistent) use of k where French would require c or qu. But Besant indicated that his knowledge of MC was insufficient for him to comment on the quality of the translation. He thus passed the manuscript on to a Miss Dick, almost certainly the daughter of G F Dick, Colonial Secretary to Mauritius in the 1820s and 1830s, and who had probably spent much of her childhood on the island. Meanwhile, Besant's criticisms were relayed to Anderson (in suitably diplomatic terms). Anderson replied:

> I (...) hasten to say that I studied the question very carefully before deciding to write the Creole Gospel phonetically. Were I to write for some ten thousand French scholars who do not require the Creole Gospel I would keep to the French orthography and the task would be the more easy for me, but as my purpose is to give the Gospel to more than 350,000 souls who do not read French and yet use Creole... I determined to write phonetically (letter dated 5 August 1884, BFBS Archives)

The BFBS also received an undated letter from Miss Dick. She informed them that *the expressions are all good and dreadfully créole...* On this recommendation, the BFBS decided to print the gospel, and copies were subsequently distributed in both Mauritius and the Seychelles.

Soon after the publication of *S Matthié* Anderson moved to France. All subsequent correspondence between him and the BFBS concerning his translations of the other three gospels and the Acts of the Apostles was written in Paris. So far as is known he never returned to Mauritius. It follows that his translations of the three other gospels and the *Acts* cannot reflect subsequent changes in spoken MC. Extracts from each of the latter are included in F&R (2007: 289-305) but the include nothing from *S Matthié*. We have nevertheless decided not to reprint this text because of its length and because it is a translation. However, it is important to mention some of its features.

Orthographic conventions adopted by Anderson include:

- **oa** for [wa] where French orthography has *oi*.
- Consistent use of **ein** for [ẽ] regardless of the spelling of the corresponding French word, e.g. **einvité, biein, zanciein** for French *invité, bien, [les] anciens*.
- Consistent use of **ïn** to represent the palatal nasal, e.g. **gaïn** for French *gagne*.
- Consistent use of **k** where French has *qu* followed by *i* or *e*, e.g. **parski, kek** for French *parce que* and *quelques*.

While he was the first to employ **k** in this way for writing MC – a very radical step to take in the 1880s – he was curiously very conservative in other respects. He generally writes MC nouns which have an initial syllable wholly derived from a French article as two words, e.g. **la rivier, lé ker, la cour** (for French *rivière, coeur,* and *court*). While regularly replacing French *j* with MC **z** in most words, J is retained in Biblical proper nouns, e.g. **Jésu, Jan, Jac, Jérusalem,** etc. One oddity is his consistent writing of **prosh** (for French *proche*) with **sh**. No other author represents the final consonant of this word as having this sound.

---

[19] In the part of his biography dealing with his time at the Royal College in Mauritius, Besant mentions Anderson by name and refers to him as "that cheeky half-caste boy". The autobiography, which was published posthumously in 1902, makes no reference to Anderson's gospel translations.

Grammatically, the most significant new feature of this text is the use of /ban/ without any article as a marker of plurality:

> **kan band cef prétr avec zans scrib ti voar tou ça mirac...**
> 'when the chief priests and scribes saw all those miracles...'
>
> **band solda gouverner, condir dan palé**
> 'the governor's soldiers led [him] into the palace'
>
> **li ti anvoy band so domestic pour appel zans ki ti fine einvité pour vine mariaz**
> 'he sent his domestics to call the people who had been invited to come to the wedding'

While Baissac (1880) only hints at the emergence of the overt copula /ete/ in a footnote, Anderson makes extensive use of this in locative phrases :

> **li al divan zot, ziska ki li ti fine arriv laho l'androa acot ça pti zanfan là ti été**
> 'he went ahead of them, until he reached the place where that little child was'
>
> **parski acot to trézor li été, là mem to lé ker ossi va resté**
> 'because where your treasure is, is the same place as where your heart will remain'

Although he generally uses **avec** and **av** as reflexes of French *avec* (but with a much wider range of meanings; see Kriegel & Michaelis (*this volume*), he is the only author to make occasional use of another variant, **vec**:

> **larg zot, é améne zot vec moa**
> 'release them, and bring them to me'

54.   1888 *Le folk-lore de l'île Maurice*

Baissac's collection of folk-tales comprises 28 stories.[20] Since editions of these are readily available in libraries and bookshops today, we are not including any examples of these here but all the stories are included in the concordance. *Le folk-lore* also includes a selection of *sirandanes* which is almost identical to those contained in Baissac (1880), but it is the 1888 *sirandanes* which we have chosen to include in the concordance. Of the 48 numbered riddles contained in the 1846 *Cirandanes, Çampéc* collection, 45 closely resemble those Baissac (1888). These are printed side-by-side for ease of comparison on pp 30-34. This book also contains a section on *La chanson*. We have excluded these from the concordance because, while the lyrics probably date from the early part of the 19th century, they cannot be accurately dated. They are also mainly fragmentary and the meaning of the words is not always apparent.

55.   1892 *Le cyclone du 29 avril 1892*

A collection of Henri Antelme's work was published posthumously in 1923. This includes one poem in MC as well as the author's own French translation of this. Both are reproduced in F&R (2007: 327-31) and, for that reason, are not repeated here.

56.   **1897** The first advertisement in MC?

It is not certain that the following is the first newspaper advertisement in MC but it is the earliest we have yet found.

Rs 55,000 pour donne piblique!!!
Cadeau qui Magasin Singer donné pour Noël ecque banané !!!

Vrai valère eine billet Trésor Singer ! ! ! Qui ci ça ein biyet Trésor (Singer)? Ça eine vrai biyet et lontant pareil common tout ça biyet gouvernement Maurice la, mais qui fine

---

[20] F&R (2007) curiously misattribute these to another Baissac publication (1884).

marqué dans so lédo ça nom "Singer" qui tout dimoune conné. — Zote croire qui dans 950,000 Roupies qui dimoune fine payé Magasin Singer dipis mois Jillet 1883, jousqu'à aster là, capable gagne encore 550,000 Roupies en biyet marquer Singer qui encor déhor. Ouv'lé donne eine souvenir SO BANNE CLIAN MAURICIEN parce qui éna plis qui 14 banané qui zote appiye li plis dipis ça grand diffé qui ti éna en 1893 et aussi parce que Magasin Singer toujours gagné, so maîte sozir ça la fin l'anné là qui plin bénédiction, ecque bon sentiment li fine décidé qui dipis le 15 Décembre 1897 jusqu'à le 15 Janvier 1890 tout seil, tout ça qui amène eine biyet trésor Singer va éna droit pour asté Rs 5.50 marçandise avec eine biyet de Rs 5 et capable asté pour Rs 11.00 marçandise avec eine billet Rs 10 mais touzour ce qui marqué Singer derrière zot lédo. "Condition" ça cado la necque pour dimoune qui va asté marçandise contan dipis le 15 Décembre 1897 jousqu'a 15 Janvier 1890, mais ce qui paye par morço et ce qui loué marçandize dipis le 15 Décembre 1895 jousqu'a 15 Janvier 1898, mais ce qui par morço et ce qui loué marçandize na pas capable gagne ça — Tout marçandise qui éna dans "Magasin Singer", et tout ce qui fecque arrivé par la malle française pour Noël ecque banané capable asseté et paye dans sa manière la pendan ça manière la pendant ça bon mois la. Tout prix marçandise dans Magasin Singer dipis 1894 na pas fine augmenté pendan ça bon mois – là, laho çaque marçandise zote ziste prix marqué. — Ou doite rode dans tout biyet qui ou éna et ce qui ou va gagné, tout vrai billet "Singer" pour profiter *ça bon ocazion là*.

(L'*Albion*, 17 décembre 1897)

There appears to be a mistake in the first word of the sentence beginning *Ouv'lé donne eine souvenir...* above but we cannot identify precisely what was intended. One would expect the start of this sentence to mean 'It [Magasin Singer] wants to give a souvenir...". In the 19th century, the verb 'to want' had two forms, usually written *voulé* and *v'lé*. *Ouv'lé* might be either a previously unrecorded variant of, or typo for, *voulé* but both the absence of an overt subject and the apostrophe after *v* would seem to rule that out. But it cannot also be that *Ou* and *v'lé* have been accidentally run together as if a single word because the second person pronoun would not make sense here.

57.   **1917** *Zozef Zan*

This poem, written in pencil, was discovered after the death of Léoville L'Homme. A photograph of the manuscript and other details are provided by F&R (2007: 324-26)

1. Zozef Zan, n'a pas faire to malin,
  Mo fine comprend qui to oulé.
  To prend moi pour ène ti fille la vie.
  Missié Zozef, n'a pas faire lé fanor !
  N'a pas croire qui to pipengaille
  Qui pou file la-haut mo tonnelle.

2. Toe'ene vagabond, n'espèce milate,
  Si to marié, to famme à misère.
  To fer vantar parce qui to la peau
  Couler goyave quand li fine mir.
  Mo préfère Zamor quand même'li notr.
  Avlà ène zhomme, li, li travaille

3. Quand même so civé pas bien droite,
  So lé bras fort, so lé quér bon,
  Si nous gagne pitit, au moins so vente
  N'a pas pou reste sans manzer.
  Li a donn' moi rob', quand même zaconat,
  N'a rien, mais moi va content li !

4. Li a content moi. Pou nourri moi,
  Li a capav travaille bourloque.
  Quand li a rentré à soir,
  Mo li quer va manze, manze li,
  Tellement mo content li.
  Zozef Zan, to pipengaille
  N'a pas pou file lé haut mo tonnelle

58.   1920 Locutions et proverbes

A good many years ago, Peter Stein copied out by hand all the MC sayings and proverbs given in Decotter (1920). He later transferred these to computer, numbering them as he did so, arriving at a total of 437. We are grateful to him for making these available to us. F&R list *Les 265 locutions et proverbes de Nemours Decotter* citing the same publication, but this is 172 fewer tha Stein found! We have not attempted to account for this substantial difference.

For reasons of space, we have decided not to reproduce any of Decotter's MC sayings and proverbs here but all are included in our concordance.

59. 1925 *Zistoire trésor bonnefemme Magon*

Until recently we, and everyone we know who has read this story, felt confident that this was the first work of fiction in MC which was not written by a Franco-Mauritian. But an entry in the *Dictionnaire de Biographie Mauricienne* reveals that we were wrong and that Philogène Soulsobontemps is a pseudonym adopted by Marie-Joseph Robert René Le Juge de Segrais (1893-1977; not to be confused with, although no doubt related to, Xavier Le Juge de Segrais, author of the *Zolies Zistoires* books published between 1939 and 1976).

The entry in the *Dictionnaire* indicates that M-J R R Le Juge de Segrais led a very active life which included his involvement in the making of silent movies of *Georges* (see pp 16-17 above) and *Paul et Virginie* in France in the 1920s and an involvement in printing in France, the Ivory Coast and, for many years, in Japan. The *Dictionnaire* entry even appears to indicate that this story was actually printed in France rather than in the small village of Bois des Amourettes on the southeast coast of Mauritius (which surely never had its own *imprimerie*, contrary to what is indicated in the publication itself).

This story is reprinted in full in F&R (2007: 365-74) and thus – but with considerable regret – we refrain from reproducing it here. One curious orthographic feature of this publication is that the preposition meaning 'on', normally written **lor** in modern MC, is consistently written *or*. This spelling is not found in any other text.

60. **1929** Pou' Zénie

Auguste Esnouf, under the pseudonym Savinien Mérédac, published a number of articles in the review *L'Essor* in the period 1926-1939. A selection of these are reprinted in F&R (2007: 375-422). *L'Essor* also published the following poem in MC (not in F&R 2007), attributed to "POLYTE G". This would appear to be a pseudonym, but we have not been able to identify the author.

1. Qui to oulé ? qui éna ? qui faire ?
   En bas pied mangue to vine cizé ?
   N'a péna zour, n'a péna l'hère
   Mo zoreille tende to causé.

2. Ena l'aut' place à côte mam'zelles
   Are zènes gens rié, dansé :
   Moan, mo la case touzours tout sèle,
   Assembe moan qui to vine sassé ?

3. Na péna l'arzent dans mo poce,
   Mo lipieds pas conne mette souliers,
   Mo néné plate, mo civés brosse,
   Qui faire are moan to batte liziés ?

4. Pas bizin tracasse mo la vie,
   Assez pointères dans grand cimin !
   Sourte divant moan, Mam'zelle Zénie,
   Zozo bulbul pa' oquipe martin

POLYTE G. (*L'Essor*, No 121, 15 novembre 1929)

This is the earliest text yet known in which *are* 'with' is found.

References

1734 *see* Chaudenson 1981.
1741 *see* Grant 1801.
1749 *see* Grant 1886.
1777 *see* Chaudenson 1981.
1778 *see* Chaudenson 1981.
1784 *see* Chaudenson 1981.
1793 *see* Scarr 1998.
1802 *see* Milbert 1812.
1818a *see* Freycinet 1827.
1818b *see* Chrestien 1818.
1818c *see* Freycinet 1827.
1818d *see* Anon.
1822a *see* Colonial Office 1822.
1826 *see* Anon. 1826.
1850 *see* Chaudenson 1981.
1860 *see* [de Chazal] 1860.
1897 *see* L'Albion
1917 *see* L'Homme 1917

Anderson Samuel 1885 *L'Evangil sélon S Matthié (dan langaz créol Maurice)*. London: British and Foreign Bible Society
Anon. 1810 *CRI des colons contre un ouvrage de Gregoire: "la littérature des Nègres"*. n p: no publisher.
Anon. 1818 Further papers and communications relative to the slave trade at the Mauritius and Bourbon, and the Seychelles. *British Parliamentary Papers – Slave Trade*, vol. 69, p 37.
Anon. 1826 Mauritius slave Trade, Minutes of Evidence 13-23 May 1826. *British Parliamentary Papers – Slave Trade*, vol. 1, p 19.
Anon. 1846 *Cirandane Çampéc*. Port Louis: E Baker.
Antelme, Henri 1923 *Sous le ciel de l'Ile de France*. Paris: Jouve et Cie.
Baissac Charles 1880 Etude sur le patois créole mauricien. Nancy: Imprimerie Berger-Levrault.
—— 1884 *Récits créoles*. Paris: Oudin et Cie.
—— 1888 *Le folklore de l'île Maurice*. Paris: Maisonneuve & Larose.
Baker, Philip 1976 Towards a social history of Mauritian Creole. MA dissertation [originally written as a BPhil dissertation but later upgraded], University of York.
—— 1996 On the development of certain prepositional forms in Mauritian and other French Creoles. Véronique, Daniel (ed.) *Matériaux pour l'étude des classes grammaticales dans les langues créoles*. Aix-en-Provence: L'Université de Provence.
—— 2003 Quelques cas de réanalyse et de grammaticalisation dans l'évolution du créole mauricien. Kriegel, Sibylle (ed.) *Grammaticalisation et réanalyse. Approches de la variation créole et française*. Paris: CNRS, 111-41.
—— 2004 Sur les origines africaines et européennes des devinettes mauriciennes de Baissac (1880, 1888). Coveney, A, Hintze, M-A, et Saunders, C (eds) *Variation et francophonie*. Paris: L'Harmattan, 51-85.
Baker, Philip & Hookoomsing, Vinesh Y 1987 *Diksyoner kreol morisyen. Dictionary of Mauritian Creole. Dictionnaire du créole mauricien*. Paris: L'Harmattan.
Benoît, Norbert 1998 *Un poète et chansonnier créole du dix-neuvième siècle. François Chrestien (1767-1846) (...)*. Quatre Bornes: Editions NSB Associates.
Bernardin de St Pierre, J-H 1773 *Voyage à l'Isle de France*. Paris: Merlin, 2 vols..
Besant, Walter 1902 *Autobiography of Sir Walter Besant*. London: Hutchinson.

Bollée, Annegret 2007 *Deux textes religieux de Bourbon du 18e siècle et l'histoire du créole réunionnais.* London: Battlebridge.
British Parliamentary Papers, *see* Anon. 1818, Anon. 1826.
Chaudenson, Robert 1981 *Textes créoles anciens: La Réunion et Ile Maurice. Comparaison et essai d'analyse.* Hamburg: Buske.
Chrestien François 1818 Le lièvre et la tortue. Freycinet 1827: 411-12.
—— 1822 *Les essais d'un bobre africain.* Isle Maurice.
—— 1831 *Les essais d'un bobre africain.* Port-Louis: G Déroullède. [second, enlarged edition]
—— 1838 *Album tropical ou Recueil de pièces inédites et autres de porte-feuille de François Chrestien, et faisant suite au Bobre Africain.* Port-Louis.
—— 1839 Un coin du feu à la campagne ou Fonclair et Pierrot. *Le Cernéen* 18 avril 1839. Port-Louis.
Colonial Office 1822 [Extracts from the trial of Ratsitatane.] Public Record Office, Kew: CO 167/64, f 94, 170, 175, 210, 218, 223, 352, ms.
Corne, Chris 1982 A contrastive analysis of reunion and Isle de france Creole French. Baker, P & Corne, C *Isle de France Creole. Affinities and origins.* Ann Arbor: Karoma, 7-129.
De Chazal, E 1860 *Catéchisme créole.* [no publisher or place of publication indicated].
Decotter, Nemours 1920 *Les proverbes français expliqués avec leurs équivalents en anglais – augmentés parfois de proverbes créoles.* Port Louis : General Printing & Stationery Cy Ltd.
Descroizilles, Henri Charles 1867 *Navire fine engazé or the Mauritius in danger.* Port-Louis: E Dupuy & F Dubois.
Ducoeurjoly, S J 1802 *Manuel des habitants de Saint-Domingue.* Paris: Lenoir.
Dumas, Alexandre 1843 *Georges.* Paris.
D'Unienville, R 2006 *Malartic,* Mauritius.
Fon Sing, Guillaume 2005 Créolisation et grammaticalisation: le cas de *fin* en créole mauricien. *Actes des VIIIèmes Rencontres Jeunes chercheurs de l'Ecole Doctorale 268 'Langage et langues',* Université de Paris 3, mai 2006, pp 25-28
F&R *see* Furlong & Ramharai 2007.
Freycinet, Louis Claude Desaulces de 1827 *Voyage autour du monde exécuté sur les corvettes de S.M. l'Uranie et la Physicienne pendant les années 1817, 1818, 1819 et 1820 (....),*Paris, vol. 2.2.
Furlong, Robert & Ramharai, Vicram 2007 *La production créolophone. Vol. 1. Des origines à l'indépendence.* Mauritius: TIMAM.
Goodman, Morris 1964 *A comparative study of Creole French dialects.* Mouton: The Hague.
Grant, Baron de Vaux 1886 *Letters from Mauritius in the eighteen century.* Mauritius
Grant, Charles 1801 *History of Mauritius, (...).* London.
Hollingsworth, Derek 1965 *They came to Mauritius.* London: Oxford University Press.
Hookoomsing, Vinesh Y 1987 L'emploi de la langue creole dans le contexte multilingue et multiculturel de l'Ile Maurice. Une etude de son importance en tant que langue commune et des implications sociolinguistiques de son élaboration en mauricien, These de PhD, Universite Laval, Quebec.
—— 1989 Prefas. Anon. (ed.) *Sirandann Sanpek. Zistwar an Kreol,* Mauritius: Ledikasyon pu Travayer, p 22.
Kriegel, Sibylle & Michaelis, Susanne 2007 Conjunction and ditransitives: some functional domains covered by *avec, et,* and *ensemble. This volume.*
L'Albion 17 décembre 1897, Mauritius.
[Lambert, Richard] [1828] 1888-92 Catéchisme en créole de l'Ile Maurice en 1828. *Bulletin de la Société de Linguistique de Paris* 7: 122-32
Le Brun, Jean 1816 Journal, [ms] London Missionary Society Collection, School of Oriental and African Studies, University of London
Le Cernéen 18 mai 1832, 5 juin 1832, 1, 3 & 4 janvier 1839, 18 avril 1839, 7 mai 1839, 11 juillet 1839, et 3 octobre 1840. Port-Louis.

Le Juge de Segrais, Xavier 1939 *Vingt zolies zistoires Misié Lafontaine dans créole Maurice avec 74 zolies zimages.* Mauritius.

Le Mauricien 21, 24 & 26 avril, 25 & 28 mai, 27 juillet, 1 & 9 août, et 28 septembre 1855. Port Louis.

L'Essor 15 novembre 1929, Mauritius.

L'Homme, Léoville 1917 *Zozef Zan.* Ms.

Lloyd, J A 1840 Letter to the Colonial Office. Ms. Public Record Office, Kew, London.

Lolliot, Pierre 1855 *Poésies Créoles.* Port-Louis: Imprimerie du *Mauricien,*

[Maure André] 1840 *Souvenirs d'un vieux colon de l'Ile Maurice.* La Rochelle: Frédéric Boutet.

Mauritius Archives [Legal documents JB1, JB29, JB33, JB42 – see Chaudenson1981; JB78, JB151 – *see* Scarr 1998]

Milbert, Jacques Gérard 1812 *Voyage pittoresque à l'Ile de France, au Cap de Bonne Espérance et à l'Ile de Ténériffe.* Paris, 2 vols.

Nicolay, W 1835 Proclamation. Pour noirs esclaves dans Maurice. *Recueil des lois, ordonnances, proclamations, notes et avis du gouvernement publiés à l'Ile Maurice pendant l'année 1835.* Port-Louis.

Pitot, C Thomi 1886 *Souvenirs historiques de l'Ile de France (2ème partie)* Port Louis : Mercantile Record Company.

Pitot, Henry [1865] 1878 *Soirées d'abat-vent.* Port-Louis: Mercantile Record and Commercial Gazette.

Pitot, Thomy (1805) Quelques observations sur l'ouvrage intitulé *Voyage à l'Ile de France. Revue historique et littéraire de l'Ile Maurice* 2: 372-74, Port-Louis.

Prosper, Jean-Georges 1978 *Histoire de la littérature mauricienne de langue française.* Mauritius: Editions de l'Océan Indien.

Scarr, Deryck 1998 *Slaving and Slavery in the Indian Ocean,* Basingstoke: Macmillan.

Soulsobontemps, Philogène 1925 *Zistoire trésor bonnefemme Magon.* Bois des Amourettes: Imp. Grandporienne.

Stein, Peter 2007 L'absence de marqueurs préverbaux et les fonctions du marqueurs zéro. *this volume.*

Toussaint, A & Adolphe, H 1956 *Bibliography of Mauritius (1502 – 1954).* Port Louis; Government Printing.

[Vicars, ()] 1830 Representation of the state of government slaves and apprentices in the Mauritius; with observations by A RESIDENT who has never possessed either land or slaves in the colony. London.

Wesley, John, Sermon 122 On Faith, in *Sermons on Several Occasions,* published on line by The Christian Classics Ethereal Library, www.ccel.com.

Philip Baker worked in Mauritius for MBC TV and L'Express newspaper 1965-67 but the interest in MC which this aroused led him to study linguistics formally and many publications have resulted. He is currently Professor of Linguistics at the University of Westminster, <phildbaker@yahoo.co.uk>.

Guillaume Fon Sing est actuellement Attaché Temporaire d'Enseignement et de Recherche (ATER) à l'Université de la Sorbonne Nouvelle (Paris 3). Il achève sa thèse de doctorat sur les créoles français et enseigne la linguistique française, <gfonsing@yahoo.fr>.

Vinesh Y Hookoomsing is Professor of Linguistics at the University of . Mauritius. He wrote his PhD on the importance of Mauritian Creole as the common language of multilingual Mauritius and the sociolinguitistic implications of its development as *Morisyen.* He has led the team officially set up to develop harmonized standard orthography for MC, <hyvinesh@hotmail.com>.

Definiteness and Specificity in Mauritian Creole: A syntactic and semantic overview

Diana Guillemin

Introduction[1]

The goal of this article is twofold. I look at the expression of Definiteness and Specificity in Mauritian Creole (MC), and argue that they represent distinct categories of meaning. The definite determiner is shown to be a phonologically null element, while the post nominal and post clausal morpheme *la* is shown to be a Specificity marker on definite noun phrases. A secondary goal of this paper is to suggest that the means by which a language expresses semantic features like Definiteness and Specificity is a consequence of the denotation of nouns in that language.

The modern MC determiner system is quite different from that of its lexifier. While in French, all common nouns must occur with a determiner in argument positions, MC admits bare nouns in various syntactic configurations, yielding, in the case of mass nouns [±definite] interpretations, and in the case of count nouns, either a [±definite] plural or [+definite] singular interpretation.

My analysis is inspired by Chierchia's (1998) Nominal Mapping Parameter, which assumes that the denotation of nouns varies across languages, and that this variation may be responsible for the different distribution of bare nominal arguments. NPs[2] can be either predicates or arguments, and only the latter can occur without a determiner in argument positions. I also adopt Longobardi's (1994) seemingly incompatible theory that only DPs can be arguments, NPs cannot. Longobardi analyzes determiners as operators binding variables, converting predicative NPs into referential arguments. But, determiners also serve to assign semantic features to their complement NPs; Definiteness and Specificity are properties of DPs, not NPs.

I claim that nouns in MC come out of the lexicon as argumental, kind-denoting terms, with a default plural interpretation. The occurrence of bare nouns with a [+definite] singular interpretation is accounted for in terms of a null definite determiner which forces the realization of a Number Phrase, and converts argumental nouns into cardinality predicates. This projection is not realized for mass nouns, and they are shown to pattern differently in the grammar. While bare mass nouns can occur in any argument position, regardless of their Specificity feature, non-Specific count nouns are barred in subject position in MC.

In support of my analysis of Definiteness and Specificity as distinct categories of meaning, I resort to semantic definitions from the literature, and provide numerous

---

[1] I am grateful to fellow contributors to this volume for their helpful comments on an earlier draft of this article. Some of the more important of these are mentioned in the text or in footnotes.

[2] Abbreviations used in this paper include: **1.PL**: 1st plural pronoun; **2.SG.F**: 2nd singular pronoun, Formal form of address; **3.SG**: 3rd singular pronoun; **arg**: Argument; **ASP**: Aspect; **COMP**: Complementizer; **D**: Determiner; **DefP**: Definiteness Phrase; **DEM**: Demonstrative; **DemP**: Demonstrative Phrase; **DP**: Determiner phrase; **LF**: Logical Form; **MC**: Mauritian Creole; **MP**: Minimalist Program; **NEG**: Negation; **N**: Noun; **NP**: Noun phrase; **Num**: Number; **NumP**: Number phrase; **PF**: Phonetic Form; **PLU**: Plural; **POSS**: Possessive; **pred**: predicate; **PST**: Past tense; **SG**: Singular; **SP**: Specificity; **SpP**: Specificity Phrase; **Spec**: Specifier; **UG**: Universal Grammar; **VP**: Verb Phrase.

examples from modern MC. My syntactic analysis is within the framework of Chomsky's Minimalist Program (1995), which makes the assumption that functional items are the locus of semantic features, that drive movement in the syntax. My analysis points to a mapping of semantic type and syntactic category.

This article is organized as follows: In Section 1, I present some background on the emergence of the MC determiner system. In Section 2, I look at the semantic properties of bare count and mass nouns in various syntactic configurations and provide evidence for a null definite determiner equivalent to the English and French definite articles. Section 3 is an overview of how the other determiners in MC modify count and mass nouns. In Section 4 I provide semantic definitions of Definiteness, Specificity and Deixis, and give further examples to show that Definiteness comprises nuances of meaning, to which both the English and French definite articles are insensitive. Section 5 comprises an overview of the syntactic framework adopted for my analysis. Section 6 is the analysis and Section 7 concludes this article.

1. Early changes

1.1 The loss of the French determiners

Early in the stages of creolization, the French definite articles and partitive determiners incorporated into a large number of the nouns that they modified, leaving the emergent creole without the means of expressing the contrasts of (in)definiteness and singular vs. plural. It seems that the French determiners, which serve to mark these semantic contrasts, were not recognized as separate morphemes, but were taken to be an integral part of the nouns that they modified (Baissac 1880; Chaudenson 1981; Baker 1984; Grant 1995; Strandquist 2005). The examples that follow serve to demonstrate the processes that affected a large number of nouns.

In the case of both consonant initial and vowel initial count nouns, the singular definite article incorporated into the noun:

- Le coeur (the heart) → *leker* (heart)
- La fenêtre (the window) → *lafnet* (window)
- Le lit (the bed) → *lili* (bed)
- L'année (the year) → *lane* (year)
- L'idée (the idea) → *lide* (idea)
- L'opération (the operation) → *loperasyon* (operation)

In the case of many vowel initial count nouns, the plural form of the noun starting with /z/ as a result of liaison with the plural determiner transferred into MC:

- Des/les animaux (animals/the animals) → *zanimo* (animals)
- Des/les étoiles (some stars) → *zetwal* (star)
- Des/les oranges (oranges/the oranges) → *zoranz* (orange)

It may also be the case that some consonant initial nouns derive from the plural form:

- Les bras (the arms) → *lebra* (arm)
- Les doigts (the fingers) → *ledwa* (finger)
- Les pieds (the feet) → *lipye* (foot)

In the case of many mass nouns, the partitive determiner *de, du* incorporated into the noun:

- De l'huile (some oil) → *dilwil* (oil)
- Du thé (some tea) → *dite* (tea)
- Du vin (some wine) → *diven* (wine)

In the case of some French feminine mass nouns, which are consonant initial, the definite article *la*, from the partitive *de la* incorporated into the noun:

- De la bière (some beer) → *labyer* (beer)
- De la boue (some mud) → *labu* (mud)
- De la farine (some flour) → *lafarin* (flour)

However, not all nouns end up with an incorporated article, e.g.:

- Le chat (the cat) → *sat* (cat)
- La chaise (the chair) → *sez* (chair)
- La robe (the dress) → *rob* (dress)

The immediate consequence was that nouns occurred without a determiner (other than *ça … là*), yielding ambiguous interpretations between [±definite] for mass nouns, and [±definite] singular and plural for count nouns, as shown:

	Features	French	MC	English
Count nouns	singular [–definite]	une table		a table
	plural [–definite]	des tables	latab	tables
	singular [+definite]	la table		the table
	plural [+definite]	les tables		the tables
Mass nouns	[–definite]	de l'eau	dilo	water
	[+definite]	l'eau		the water

Table 1: The ambiguous interpretation of bare nouns in very early MC

1.2 A new determiner system

Over a period of some 150 years, new functional items emerged in the MC determiner system, namely:

- The singular indefinite determiner *enn*, derived from the French *un/une*.
- The demonstrative *sa* derived from the French demonstrative *ce/ces*. Unlike its French source, it is not specified for Number.
- The specificity marker *la*, which is derived either from the French demonstrative particle *là* or the homophonous locative adverb, or both. Like *sa*, it is not specified for Number. *La* is post-nominal, while all other determiners are pre-nominal.
- The plural marker *bann*, derived from the French *bande* ('group'). It is unspecified for the feature [±definiteness].

MC has retained the count mass distinction of its lexifier, but, unlike French, it does not grammaticalize Gender and its nouns do not inflect for Number.[3]

By the late 1880's the MC determiner system was in place. The new functional items served to mark all the semantic contrasts that could no longer be expressed following the loss of the French determiners. However, bare nouns continue to occur in various syntactic configurations, and this represents a significant divergence from French, where all nouns, with few exceptions, must occur with a determiner in argument positions.[4]

The next section comprises a brief overview of the emergence of the MC determiners.

---

[3] In French, the singular and plural forms have the same phonological form in the case of consonant initial nouns. They differ in the case of vowel initial nouns as a result of liaison with the plural determiner.
[4] These exceptions include, e.g. coordinate constructions, as in *Père et fils se ressemblent* 'Father and son (s) look alike', *Spectacle son et lumière* 'Sound and light spectacle', and in idiomatic expressions or proverbs, e.g.: *Pierre qui roule n'amasse pas mousse* 'A rolling stone gathers no moss'.

1.2.1 The singular indefinite 'enn'

From its first attestations in 1818, *enn* unambiguously marks nouns as singular and indefinite:

(1)   *Enne zour ça nous té la sasse cerf Grand-Rivière.* **(1818a)**[5]
       one day when 1.PL PST hunting stag Grande-Rivière
       One day when were hunting stag at Grande-Rivière
       Un jour que nous chassions des cerfs à la Grande-Rivière

(2)   *mo ramasse enne tondre,* **(1818a)**
       1.SG pick up a firelighter
       I picked up a firelighter, / J'ai ramassé un ligot,

1.2.2 The demonstratives 'ça ... là'

In the first instantiations of MC, the demonstratives *ça .. là* are used exactly as in French, in that *là* is a demonstrative reinforcer, not used independently of *ça*.[6] However, while French has the singular *ce* and the plural *ces*, the same phonological form /sa/ is used with both singular and plural NPs in MC. I gloss *là* in these early examples as DEM (for demonstrative), as opposed to SP (for Specificity):

(3)   *ça blanc là li beaucoup malin* **(1749)**
       DEM white DEM 3.SG much clever
       These white men are very clever[7] / Ces blancs là sont très malins

(4)   *Moi voulé baiser ça négresse là.* **(1777)**
       1.SG want make love DEM negress DEM
       I wanted to make love to this negress. / Je voulais faire l'amour avec cette négresse.

(5)   *Vous per ça bon Dié là qui mauvais?* **(1805)**
       2.SG.F fear DEM god DEM COMP evil
       Do you fear those evil gods (spirits)?[8] / Vous craignez ces dieux (esprits) malfaisants?

1.2.3 The occurrence of ça witout là

There are a few occurrences of *ça* without *là* in early MC, but such use subsides by the mid 19th century.[9] The use of *sa* without *la* is recurring in modern MC, but only when the noun is modified by a relative clause. Its use with an unmodified noun is ungrammatical in MC (see Section 3.4).

(6)   *mo trouve ça vié noir Moudiawa,* **(1818a)**
       1.SG saw DEM old black Moudiawa
       I saw that old Moudiawa slave / J'ai vu ce vieux noir Moudiawa

(7)   *ça prince malgache qui ..* **(1822)**
       DEM prince Malagasy COMP
       That Malagasy prince who ... / Ce prince malgache qui ...

---

[5] In conformity with the overall editorial policy, wherever a text is reproduced in full in the corpus of MC texts (pp 1-61), I refer to it by date only (printed in **bold** characters).

[6] The term 'demonstrative reinforcer' was coined by Bernstein (1996). They are the proximate *ci* and distal *là*, which, as the term suggests, are used with demonstratives, e.g.: *cet homme ci* ('this man'), *cet homme là* ('that man'). To my knowledge, there are no occurrences of the proximate *ci* in the creole.

[7] I had interpreted *ça blanc là* as singular, but Philip Baker (p c) suggests that the context makes it more probable that the speaker was referring to the white crew as a whole.

[8] I assume that the speaker is referring to more than one 'god' or 'spirit'. "The Supreme being of the African is the Creator, the source of life, but between him and man lie many powers and principalities good and bad, gods, spirits, magical forces, witches to account for the strange happenings in the world" (Wiredu 2007).

[9] The use of *sa* without *la* is most probably the source of this morpheme in Seychellois Creole (SC), where it functions both as a definite determiner and as a demonstrative. SC does not have the Specificity marker *la*.

1.2.4 The use of *là* without *ça*

While in French, and in early MC, only an NP can intervene between a demonstrative and its reinforcer, *là* starts to appear in a clause final position as shown:

(8) ça grand pié dibois pian Aughiste conné **là** (1818a)
DEM big tree wood smelly Auguste know SP
This big foul smelling tree that Auguste knew
Ce grand arbre puant (là) qu'Auguste connaissait

This is the first example of *ça* + NP + *relative clause* + *là*, where both *ça* and *là* have scope over the head noun (here *pié*), and this patterns with the use of these particles in modern MC. Around the same period, *là* starts being used on its own, without the pre-nominal demonstrative *ça*. In (9), its interpretation may be ambiguous between a specificity marker and a locative adverb:

(9) Comment doumonde entré dans dibois en montant piti laravine **là**! (1818a)
as people enter in wood by climbing small ravine SP / there
As people entered the woods by climbing **that** small ravine/the small ravine **there**
Comment les gens entraient dans la forêt en montant par **cette** petite ravine (là)/la petite ravine (qui est) **là**

But there is no doubt in (10) and (11) that *là* is used to mark anaphoric definiteness on *Torti* and *Bourriqu'* both of which have discourse antecedents. Note that *la* forces a singular reading of the subject NP:

(10) Et Torti **là** touzours marcé (1818b)
and tortoise SP still walk
and the tortoise was still walking / et la tortue marchait toujours

(11) Bourriqu' **là**, moi dir' vous, content comment léRoi (Chrestien 1831)
donkey SP 1.SG tell 2.PL happy as king
The donkey, I tell you, was happy as a king
La bourrique, je vous dis, était heureuse comme un roi

1.2.5 The plural marker 'bann'

The plural maker *bann* is the last of the 'determiners' to grammaticalize[10]. MC did not have a single morpheme plural marker until the mid 1880's. Prior to its occurrence, *tout/tous* ('all') was commonly used to mark [+definite] plural:

(12) Quand nous sorti dans l'églize **Tout** blancs guetté nous passé (Chrestien 1822)
when 1.PL come.out in church **all** white watch 1.PL go by
When we came out of the church **the** white men watched us go by
Quand nous sortions de l'Eglise **les** blancs nous regardaient passer

But *tout/tous* is a universal quantifier, which could only mark NPs that were both plural and [+definite]. From 1850 onwards we see the appearance *eine bande*, derived from the French *une bande* ('a group'), used to express an indefinite number/quantity, i.e. [–definite] plural, as shown in the following examples:

(13) Avla satte vini coté enne lotre **bande** noir... (**1850**: 123)
so cat come near an other group black...
So the cat came by another group of slaves...
Voilà que le chat arriva auprès d'une autre bande de noirs..

The next example, from a translation of the Bible, is the first occurrence of *band* as a functional item in the early creole, where it serves to mark only plurality:

---

[10] Arends (1995) comments on the late grammaticalization of a plural marker in several pidgins and creoles.

(14) *éne dan **band** profet* (Anderson 1885: 14)
    one in PLU prophet
    'one of the prophets' / 'quelqu'un des prophètes' (*Matthew* ch.16 v.14)

The grammaticalization of *bann*, unspecified for the feature [±definiteness], triggered the final stage in the grammaticalization of *la*, which was able to also mark both singular and plural NPs. In the following example, the occurrence of the plural maker between the demonstrative particles patterns as in modern MC:

(15) *Namcouticouti qui té faire vous tout ça **bande** malices là*[11] (Baissac 1888: 107)
    Namcouticouti who PST make 2.SG.F all DEM PLU mischief SP
    It is Namcouticouti who has played all these tricks on you
    « C'est Namcouticouti qui vous a fait tous ces tours-là » (Baissac 1888: 106)

In sections that follow, I provide examples from modern MC to show the interpretations of bare count and mass nouns in existential constructions, as preverbal subject, direct object, and prepositional object. The aim of the analysis is to provide evidence for a null definite determiner in MC, equivalent to the English *the* and French *le/la/les*.

2. Bare nouns

2.1 Count nouns

2.1.1 Existential constructions

Existential constructions have been shown to admit only indefinites (Milsark 1979). In MC, existential sentences are with *ena*, meaning 'have', which is derived from the French *Il y en a* ('there is') → *y en a* → *ena*.[12] In (16), the bare nouns *sant*, *pyes teat* and *poem* have a default plural interpretation:

(16) *Ti ena pyes teat, sant, poem.*[13] (Legallant 2002: 51)
    PST have play song poem
    There were plays, songs, poems.
    Il y avait des pièces de théâtre, des chansons, des poèmes.

---

[11] This example is, to the best of my knowledge, the only example of *bande* as a plural maker (as opposed to a lexical item meaning 'group') in Baissac (1888).

[12] See Fon Sing & Véronique, *this volume*, for a detailed analysis of *ena*.

[13] I have faithfully reproduced the orthography of each author. The form *sant* is a not the correct form, and is obviously copied from French *chant*, 'song'. The correct MC form is *sante*.

[15] As rightly pointed out by two reviewers, bare count nouns are grammatical in sentences like *Televizyon finn kase* ('The TV is broken') and *Zwazo finn manz tu lagren* ('The bird has / Birds have eaten all the seeds'). In the case of the former sentence, one would generally assume that there is only one TV thus the NP behaves somewhat like a unique noun. If there were more than one TV, one would say e.g. *Televizyon dan salon inn kase* ('The TV in the lounge is broken'). When the noun is modified by a relative clause, it patterns differently from a bare noun, and it is beyond the scope of this paper to also discuss modified nouns. In the case of *zwazo*, note that the bare noun translates either into a definite singular (in which case speaker and hearer must share knowledge of the bird in question), or into an indefinite plural. In order to have a [+definite] plural, the noun must be modified by *bann*, as in *Bann swazo finn manz tu lagren* ('The birds have eaten all the seeds'). Furthermore, the two sentences: *Televizyon finn kase* and *Zwazo finn manz tu lagren*, are tensed clauses. Note that my example (19) is a <u>non-tensed affirmative clause, with a stage level predicate, uttered out of context</u>, hence the ungrammaticality of the utterance. There are a number of factors that can license the occurrence of a bare noun in subject position, and these include (other than the interpretation of the noun itself) the presence of operators such as Tense, Modals, adverbs of quantification, etc. For example, a statement like *Zom vini* ('man come') is meaningless out of context, but *Tulezur zom vini* ('Everyday men come') is grammatical. This topic is discussed in Guillemin [*forthcoming*] 'Noun interpretation and function of determiners in MC'.

2.1.2 Subject

Bare singular count nouns can occur in subject position under certain conditions. For example, in (17), the names of the animals function like proper names, they are referential NPs, whose reference was previously established in the discourse. The characters were first introduced into the story as *Misié Lion* ('Mr. Lion') and *ène bourique* (a donkey):

(17) *Lion costé   are   li .... Bourique napas ti   peir* (Le Juge de Segrais 1939: 15)
    lion approach with 3.SG ...donkey NEG PST afraid
    (The) Lion moves close to him .. (the) Donkey is not afraid
    (Le) Lion s'approche de lui .. (la) Bourique n'a pas peur.

Bare count nouns commonly occur as subject in conversation, where the referent is known to both speaker and hearer. For example, in answer to a question such as *Kot lisyen?* ('Where's the dog?') when referring to the pet dog, one would answer *Lisyen deor*. Common count nouns also can also occur without a determiner when they are the subject of an individual level predicate, which derive a generic interpretation, as in:

(18) *Dodo kontan pistas*
    dodo like   peanut
    Dodos like peanuts / Le dodo aime les cacahuètes

In this case, reference is not being made to a specific dodo, but to the genus 'dodo'. When the predicate is a stage level predicate, which cannot derive a generic reading, and when the noun is not referential, a bare count noun is ungrammatical in subject position of a non-tensed affirmative clause, and the following utterance is meaningless:

(19) *zom   deor
    man outside
    ≠ A / the man is outside; ≠ (The) men are outside[15]

2.1.3 Direct object

When a bare count noun is the direct object of a verb, it can be [+definite] singular, as with *laport* in (20), where the narrator is referring to a particular door, [−definite] singular as with *sak* in (21) or [−definite] plural as with *guni* in (22):

(20) *pa kapav uver **laport*** (Chiffone 1980 : 82)
    NEG able open door
    not able to open the door / pas capable d'ouvrir la porte

(21) *Bann dimunn ki   sarié **sak***, (Anon. 1980: 90)
    PLU people COMP carry bag
    The people who carry a bag, / Ceux qui charrient un sac,

(22) *Ena bann kuder, ki   ramas **guni***   (Elizier 1980: 2)
    have PLU mender COMP pick up gunny bag
    There are the menders, who pick up gunny bags
    Il y a les ravaudeurs, qui ramassent des sacs en jute

In order to dispel any ambiguity in interpretation, the indefinite article *enn*, or plural marker *bann* must be used. Note that when the direct object is marked by *bann* it is always [+definite]:

(23) a. *ki   sarié enn   sak*   b. *ki   sarié bann sak*
       COMP carry a/one bag   COMP carry PLU bag
       who carry a bag   who carry the bags
       qui charrient un sac   qui charrient les sacs

A bare count noun is never [+definite] plural in an argument position.[16]

2.1.4 Object of preposition

When a bare count noun is the object of a preposition, it is always [+definite] singular (excepting generics), as with *latab* in (24):

(24) Li   vinn   direk   lor   latab (Salamut 1980: 20)
      3.SG come   straight on   table
      It comes straight onto the table / Ça vient directement sur la table

For a [−definite] singular, *enn* must be used, and for a [+definite] plural, *bann* must be used, as in the case of a direct object. A bare count noun cannot yield a [−definite] plural interpretation when it is the object of a preposition, except in generic sentences:

(25) Zako   dormi   dan pye
      monkey   sleep   in   tree
      Monkeys sleep in tree / Le singe dort dans l'arbre/un arbre/des arbres

2.2 Unique nouns

Unique nouns are inherently referential, and generally occur without a determiner as in the following examples, where they occur as subject, direct object, and prepositional object:

(26) dimunn ti   kwar   ki   **later** li sant   liniver (Ah-Vee 2002a: 72)
      people PST   believe COMP   earth   PM centre universe
      People thought that the earth was the centre of the universe
      Les gens pensaient que la terre était le centre de l'univers

(27) dimun anvi get   **soley** (Ah-Vee 2002a: 73)
      people want look sun
      people want to look at the sun / les gens veulent regarder le soleil

(28) 6 banane dan **siman**, dan **disab**, dan **soley**, dan **lapli**; (Virahsawmy 2007)
      6 year   in concrete   in   sand   in   sun   in   rain
      six years in concrete, in the sand, in the sun, in the rain
      six ans dans du ciment, dans du sable, dans le soleil, dans la pluie

2.3 Mass nouns

2.3.1 Existential constructions

Mass nouns in MC pattern like mass nouns in English in their ability to occur without a determiner. In existential constructions they are [−definite]:

(29) Mem si ena **dilo**   mo   konn kwi !¹⁷   (de Salle Essoo 2006)
      even if have water   1.SG know cook
      Even if there is water I know how to cook / Même s'il y a de l'eau je sais comment cuire

2.3.2 Subject

Bare mass nouns can occur in subject position where their interpretation can be [±definite]. They are [+definite] when there is a discourse antecedent, [−definite] otherwise, as shown in (30) and (31) respectively:

---

[16] The bare noun *Dodo* in the generic example (18) translates into a bare plural in English and into a definite singular in French. Generics are a special case. The NP is [+definite] but whether it is singular or plural is not relevant to this analysis.

[17] The speaker is a charcoal burner, who explains that he can keep the fire going, even when there is water around.

(30) *Ler* ***disik*** *tarde mulin,* (Elizier 1980: 2)
when sugar linger mill
When the sugar lingers at the mill / Quand le sucre s'attarde au moulin

(31) ***Dife*** *ranpli dan lorizon* (Virahsawmy 1977)
fire fill in horizon
Fire engulfs the horizon / Du feu engouffre l'horizon

2.3.3 Direct Object

Like bare count nouns, mass nouns that are the direct object of a verb can be [±definite], depending on the context. If their reference has been established in the discourse, they are definite, as with *disik* in (32), otherwise, they are indefinite, as with *dil'huile* in (33):

(32) *Met **disik** lor leng* (Camle 1980: 50)
put sugar on rope
(We) put the sugar on the rope / On met le sucre sur la corde

(33) *Lère li pu asté **dil'huile**, li na pas énan bouteille* (Asgarally 1977: 92)
when 3.SG MOD buy oil 3.SG NEG have bottle
When he is to buy *oil*, he doesn't have a bottle.
Quand il est pour acheter *de l'huile*, il n'a pas de bouteille.

2.3.4 Object of preposition

When object of a preposition, bare count nouns can also be [±definite]. *Disable* is definite in (34) and both *dile* and *dimiel* are indefinite in (35):

(34) *Soonil montré li bann marque lor **disable*** (Asgarally 1977: 89)
Soonil show 3.SG PLU print on sand
Soonil shows her the prints on the sand / Soonil lui montre les traces sur le sable

(35) *Sembou la ki plen ora ar **dile** ek **dimiel**[18]* (Virahsawmy 2003)
sembou SP comp full to the brim with milk and honey
That sembou which is full to the brim with milk and honey
Ce sembou qui est plein jusqu'au ras de lait et de miel

2.4 A phonologically null definite determiner?

In his typological study of 'Articles', Himmelmann comments that 'count nouns cannot be used in core argument positions without a marker for definiteness or specificity' (2001: 832), a view shared by Longobardi (1994) who derives the principle that 'DP can be an argument, NP cannot', though D can be a phonologically null element (1994: 628). If this is indeed the case, then the occurrence of bare nouns that yield a definite interpretation provides evidence for a phonologically null determiner in MC, equivalent to the English and French definite articles. I will represent it as δ for expository purposes.

However, the view that only DPs can occur in argument positions is challenged by Chierchia (1998), who argues that the denotation of nouns varies across languages, and that this variation may be responsible for the different distribution of bare nominal arguments. In some languages, for example Chinese, all nominals are by default argumental, and they can occur in argument positions without a determiner. In others, such as the Romance languages, all nominals are predicates, and since predicates by definition cannot function as arguments, such a language should disallow bare nominal arguments altogether (1998: 355). There are also languages like English, in which nouns

---

[18] A *sembou* is a container for milk that pilgrims put on their heads for the Cavadee festival. This comes from the Tamil word for the roll of cloth placed underneath the object carried on the head (Baker p c).

can freely be predicative or argumental - singular count nouns need a determiner, while mass nouns and bare plurals can occur without a determiner.[19]

Chierchia classifies NPs in terms of the parameters [±arg, ±pred]. NPs that are [+arg, pred] are kind-denoting terms, or Generalized Quantifiers, while NPs that are [–arg, +pred] are predicates; they have an extension that can restrict the range of a quantifier. An analysis of the denotation of bare nouns in MC is beyond the scope of this paper, but they have been shown to pattern like English bare plurals in the grammar.[20] Carlson (1978) proposed that the complex properties of bare plurals can be explained by assuming that they refer to kinds. On the basis of their similarity to English bare plurals, I assume MC nouns to come out of the lexicon as kind-denoting terms, with the parameters [+arg, –pred], and a default plural interpretation. However, an important difference between MC bare nouns and English 'bare' plurals is that, while the latter comprise N + plural morphology, MC nouns are strictly bare, and yet have a default plural interpretation.

While Longobardi (1994) and Stowell (1989) agree that head nouns in the N position always refer to kinds, they differ from Chierchia in their claim that all NPs are predicates. They analyze determiners as operators binding a variable, whose range is the extension of the natural kind referred to by the head noun. The function of a determiner is to convert a predicative NP into a referential expression.

However, determiners also serve to assign to their complement NPs the semantic features of (in)definiteness, specificity and deixis, amongst others. These are features of DPs, not of NPs; only DPs can be arguments of a proposition that can yield a value True or False. Thus, despite my claim that nouns in MC are argumental, I adopt Stowell's (1989) and Longobardi's (1994) principle that only DPs can be [+ referential], and assume that when bare nouns occur in argument positions, they are DPs and not NPs (excepting generics perhaps). I attempt to reconcile these seemingly incompatible theories in my analysis in Section 6.

Prior to attempting an analysis of the environment in which null δ occurs, I will look at other determiners to establish how the various semantic features are assigned to NPs in modern MC. This analysis will also serve as a comparison with the French determiner system.

3. An overview of modern MC determiners

3.1 The indefinite singular *enn*

The indefinite singular article *enn* performs a similar function to French *un/une* ('a/an') from which it is derived. It unambiguously marks a noun as singular and indefinite, and serves to introduce a new referent into the discourse:

(36) *Ena enn lot problem* (Carpooran 2005: xiii)
  have an other problem
  There is another problem / Il y a un autre problème

(37) *Kolo fek aste enn bisiklett koulerr blé* (Maingard 2002: 101)
  Kolo ASP buy a bicycle colour blue
  Kolo has just bought a blue bicycle / Kolo vient de s'acheter un vélo bleu

An NP marked by *enn* can freely occur in existential sentences, and in internal argument positions, as in the above examples. However, they are admitted in subject position only if

---

[19] Both Carlson (1978) and Chierchia (1998) argue that English bare plurals are indeed bare in the sense that there is no phonologically null determiner.
[20] This current work forms part of a larger project, where, in a chapter on 'Noun interpretation in MC' I establish that MC bare nouns pattern like English bare plurals.

they are [+specific], as in (38) where the NP *enn dodo* can only refer to a previously mentioned set of dodos:

(38) *Enn   dodo   ti   kontan pistas*
      A/one dodo   PST   like   peanuts
      A dodo/one of the dodos liked peanuts / Un (des) dodos aimait les cacahuètes

Indefinite subjects are also admitted in generic sentences:

(39) *Enn dodo   li   kontan pistas*
      a   dodo   3.SG   like   peanut
      A dodo likes peanuts / Le dodo aime les cacahuètes

Singular indefinites are otherwise barred in subject position, and, out of context, an utterance like (40) with an indefinite singular subject of a non-tensed affirmative clause is meaningless:

(40) *?Enn dodo vini*
       A   dodo arrive

3.2 The plural marker *bann*

I claimed that MC bare nouns have a default plural interpretation when they occur in existential sentences. In argument positions, plural nouns are generally marked by *bann*, which is standardly defined as a plural marker (Baker & Hookoomsing 1987; Virahsawmy 2004; Carpooran 2005). It is in complementary distribution with cardinal numerals, and is unspecified for the feature [±definiteness]. A noun marked by *bann* can also occur in existential sentences, where the meaning is roughly equivalent to English 'some N':

(41) *Dan tou lang   ena   **bann mo**   ki ....*   (Carpooran 2005: xxv)
      in   all language have PLU   word   that
      In all languages there are (some) words that ...
      Dans toutes les langues il y a des mots qui ...

When a simple noun (i.e. unmodified by an adjective or relative clause) which is marked by *bann* is in an argument position, it is always [+definite], as shown in the next three examples, where *bann rityel* is the subject of a verb, *bann formil* is a direct object, and *bann geto* is the object of a preposition. In all three cases, no previous mention of the noun is required for a definite interpretation.

(42) ***Bann rityel*** *azir kouma enn veyikil   institisionel ek kiltirel*   (Romaine 2002: 128)
      PLU   ritual act like   a   medium   institutional and cultural
      The rituals act like an institutional and cultural medium
      Les rituels agissent comme un véhicule institutionnel et culturel.

(43) *pou introdir   **bann formil***   (Carpooran 2005: xxv)
      to introduce PLU   formula
      to introduce the formulae / pour introduire les formules

(44) *ki sorti dan geto   et ki   exprim lavi dan **bann geto***   (Romaine 2002 : 128)
      who come in   ghetto and who express life in PLU   ghetto
      who come from ghettos and who express life in *the ghettos*
      qui sortent des ghettos et expriment la vie dans *les ghettos*

The fact that *bann* + N in argument positions yield a [+definite] interpretation may have prompted Anon. (2004) to define this morpheme as a [+definite] plural determiner, equivalent to plural *the*. But this fails to account for the occurrence of *bann* + NP in existential sentences, such as (41). Nor does it account for the indefinite interpretations of the NPs *bann gran linguist*, *bann santiman profon* and *bann sante relizie* in the following examples, where the noun is modified by an adjective:

(45) **Bann gran linguist** *finn demontre   ki   langaz   relizie* ... (Romaine 2002: 127)
PLU   great linguist   PST   demonstrated   COMP language   religious ...
Famous linguists have shown that the language of religion ...
De fameux linguistes ont démontré que le langage de la religion ...

(46) *li   exprim* **bann santiman profon**, (Romaine 2002: 128)
3.SG   express   PLU   feeling   profound
he expresses profound feelings / il exprime des sentiments profonds

(47) *atraver* **bann sante relizie** *   an Kreol*   (Romaine 2002: 128)
through   PLU   song   religious   in creole
by means of religious song in creole / à travers des chants religieux en créole

However, when the noun modifier is a relative clause, as opposed to an adjective, the plural marked NP is always [+definite] when it occurs in an argument position:

(48) **Bann dimunn** *ki   ti   kiontribiye ladan ti*... (Federation of Preschool Playgroups 2002: 119)
PLU   person   COMP   PST   contribute in   PST
The people who contributed to this were ...
Les personnes qui ont contribué à celà étaient ..

(49) *pu   nu   rapel*   **bann moman** *ki   ena   zot   lenportans dan listwar Kreol   Morisyen* (Hookoomsing 2002: 25)
for 1. PLU   remember   PLU   moment   COMP have   3. PLU.POSS   importance in   history creole Mauritian

for us to remember the moments that have their importance in the history of Mauritian Creole
pour nous rappeler les moments qui ont leur importance dans l'histoire du créole mauricien

(50) *ambarke dan* **bann relizion institisionel** *ki   prezan dan Moris* (Romaine 2002: 128)
embark in   PLU   religion institutional   COMP   present in   Mauritius
embarked in the institutional religions that are present in Mauritius
embarqué dans les religions institutionnelles qui existent à Maurice

An interesting question which arises from this analysis is why is it that, in argument positions:

o bann + N is [+definite]
o bann + N modified by an adjective is [–definite]
o bann + N modified by a relative clause is [+definite]?

Furthermore, given that bare nouns have a default plural interpretation, why does the language need a plural marker?

3.3 The Specificity marker *la*

While all determiners in French are pre-nominal, MC has the post-nominal *la*, which modifies both count nouns and mass nouns. This morpheme has been defined as a definite article, equivalent to English *the* and French *le/la/les* (Baker 2003; Virahsawmy 2004). However, in their *Dictionary*, Baker & Hookoomsing (1987) also identify the "specificity" feature of this morpheme, and define *la* as: "semantically very similar to 'the', which marks the specificity of a noun or noun phrase and occurs as the final element of the latter, e.g. *lalin-la* 'the moon', *lari ki al Moka-la* 'the road which leads to Moka" (1987: 170, *my italics*).

Unique nouns in MC usually occur without a determiner. The specificity maker *la* deprives them of their uniqueness, and is used only when a specific instance or aspect of the noun is the intended meaning, as in the following example, where the author is describing how the sun feels when they are working in the sugar cane fields:

(51) *Soleil la tapé, li   cuit   ou   la peau.* (Asgarally 1977: 1)
sun   SP beat   3.SG   cook   2.PLU.POSS   skin
That sun beats upon you, it cooks your skin / Ce soleil tape, il cuit votre peau

The specificity marker *la* encodes an element of deixis which is not always present in English *the* or French *le/la/les*, consequently, a unique N + *la* translates into a demonstrative, as opposed to a definite article.

The other example that Baker & Hookoomsing give to demonstrate the specificity feature of *la* is a noun modified by a relative clause: *lari ki al Moka-la*, which they translate as 'the road which leads to Moka'. The presence of *la* with this complex NP is not required for a [+definite] interpretation, as shown:

(52) Lari ki al Moka byen long
  road COMP go Moka very long
  The road that leads to Moka is very long / Le chemin qui mène à Moka est très long

As pointed out by Baker & Hookoomsing (1987), the presence of *la* marks the specificity of the NP (*lari*). This morpheme can only be used to modify an NP that has a discourse antecedent. When a noun is modified by a relative clause, and marked by *la*, it translates into a demonstrative phrase:

(53) Lari ki al Moka **la** byen long
  road COMP go Moka SP very long
  That road that leads to Moka is very long / Ce chemin qui mène à Moka est très long

Ledikasyon pu Travayer (2004) define *la* as a 'suffix denoting specificity'. The term 'suffix' suggests that it is not categorized as an independent morpheme, and this explains the frequent use of a hyphen between the NP and *la* in current literature, e.g.:

(54) Lerla, profeser-la lir lartik- la (Ah-Vee 2002b: 73)
  then teacherSP read article SP
  Then, the/that teacher reads the/that article / Ensuite, le/ce professeur lit l'/cet article

However, its definition as a 'suffix' fails to account for the occurrence of this morpheme when it is disjoint from the noun that it modifies, e.g. with the complex NP in the following example, where *la* marks the head noun *travay*, and not the noun modifier *standardizasyon*:

(55) sa travay standardizasyon -la (Hookoomsing 2002 : 29)
  DEM work standardization SP
  This work of standardization / Ce travail de de normalisation

Nor is its definition as a 'suffix' justified in the following example, where *la* modifies the head noun *lang* and not the verb *rantre* which immediately precedes it:

(56) Tu sa bann lang ki pe rantre la (Rungoo 2002 : 98)
  all DEM PLU language COMP ASP enter SP
  All these languages that are being introduced / Toutes *ces langues* qui sont introduites

3.3.1 La with singular count nouns

We have that bare count nouns are ungrammatical in subject position as in (19) unless they are referential NPs that function as proper names, as in (17), or in generic sentences as in (18). When these last two interpretations are not the intended ones, a [+definite] singular common count noun in subject position must be marked *la*. In this case, *la* translates into either a definite determiner or a demonstrative. It marks anaphoric definiteness and forces a singular interpretation of the count noun:

(57) Tifi **la** galoupé li trappe so ti toutou. (Asgarally 1977: 52)
  girl SP run 3.SG catch 3.SG.POSS small dog
  The girl runs she catches her small dog / La fille court elle attrape son petit chien

(58) *Problem* **la** *poze dan enn leta miltileng* ... (Carpooran 2002 : 67)
   problem SP pose in a state multilingual
   That problem arises in a multilingual state / Ce problème se pose dans un état plurilingue

3.3.2 La with plural count nouns

We have noted in Section 3.2 that *bann* + N yield a [+definite] interpretation when in an argument position. The presence of *la* adds deictic force; it is used only when the NP is referential, and this translates into a demonstrative in English and French:

(59) *enn fwa* **bann** *zanfan* **-la** *mor, fer zot leve aswar* ...²¹ (Carpooran 2005: 147)
   once PLU child SP dead make 3.PLU get up night
   Once those children are dead, (she) gets them up at night ...
   Une fois que ces enfants sont morts, (elle) les réveille la nuit ...

(60) *li ti pe ramass sa* **bann** *zistwar* **la** *an 1888* (Hookoomsing 2002: 26)
   3.SG PST ASP collect DEM PLU story SP in 1888
   he was collecting those/these stories in 1888 / il recueillait ces histoires (là) en 1888

3.3.3 La with mass nouns

We have seen that a bare mass noun in subject position can be [±definite] (see examples (30) and (31)). Another example follows:

(61) *Letan* **disik** *inn tap ladan,* (Anon. (ed.) 1980: 14)
   when sugar ASP bump into
   When (the) sugar has bumped into .... / Quand du/le sucre a tapé dedans ...

When a mass noun in subject position is marked by *la*, it translates either into a definite determiner, or into a demonstrative:

(62) **Dilo la** *ti tied* (Virahsawmy, n d)
   water SP PST warm
   The/that water was warm / L'/cette eau était tiède

When the NP is in an internal argument position, *la* translates into a demonstrative, and *sa* is also often present:

(63) *pu anvoy* **disik la** *abor* (Elizier 1980: 2)
   to send sugar SP on board
   to send that sugar on board / pour envoyer ce sucre à bord

(64) *E ler zot pu sarié* **sa** *sarbon* **la** (Anon. 1980: 78)
   and when 3.PLU MOD carry DEM charcoal SP
   And when they will carry this/that charcoal / Et quand ils vont charrier ce charbon (là).

3.4 The demonstrative sa ...la

The MC particle *sa* is a weakened form of the French demonstrative adjectives *ce/ces*, and like its French source, it is pre-nominal, but unlike the French demonstratives, it is not marked for Number. As in French, the demonstrative can be used with count and mass nouns, but it differs from French *ce/ces* in that it is ungrammatical when used on its own with unmodified nouns:

(65) a. **Sa bebet*   b. **Sa bann bebet*   c. **Sa dite*
       DEM insect   DEM PLU insect   DEM tea

The demonstrative *sa* is generally used in conjunction with the post-nominal Specificity marker *la*, where it serves to mark the deictic value of *la* as proximate. In this respect it performs a similar function to the French demonstrative reinforcers *ci/là*:

---

[21] This quote is taken from the definition of ***Dainn***, a witch who is reputed to kill children, then bring them back to life during the night to perform evil deeds.

(66) a. *Sa (bann) bebet la* b. *Sa dite la*
      DEM PLU   insect SP   DEM tea SP
      This/these insect(s)   This tea

The presence of an adjective does not license the occurrence of *sa* without *la*:

(67) a. **Sa bebet ble* b. **Sa dite lavani*
      DEM insect blue   DEM tea vanilla

In modern MC, *sa* can be used without *la*, only when the noun is modified by a relative clause or a prepositional phrase:

(68) *sa senk domenn ki neseser pou definisyon enn lang ofisyel* (Carpooran 2002 : 68)
     DEM five category COMP necessary for definition a language official
     Those five categories that are necessary for the definition of an official language
     Ces cinq domaines qui sont nécessaires pour la définition d'une langue officielle

(69) *sa lespas politik propis pu langaz Kreol* (Legallant, 2002: 51)
     DEM space political favourable for language creole
     that political space which is favourable to the creole language
     cet espace politique propice à la langue créole

The demonstrative *sa …la* can be used to introduce a new discourse referent, when it is present in the situational context, as in (70), which is the opening sentence of a conference presentation, and the speaker is referring to her paper:

(70) **Sa papye la** *so bi se…* (Dholah 2002: 79)
     DEM paper SP 3.SG.POSS aim is
     This paper, its aim is … / Cet article, son but c'est ..

It is not possible to use *la* on its own to introduce a new discourse referent, suggesting that when this morpheme is used in conjunction with the demonstrative *sa*, its deictic function is different from when it is used on its own. I address this point in Section 4.5.

The above overview served to show how determiners modify count and mass nouns in various syntactic environments in modern MC. The definite determiner has been shown to be a phonologically null element, equivalent to the definite article in English and French, while post-nominal *la* serves to mark only NPs that are both [+definite] and [+specific]. *La* adds an element of deixis which is not always present in the English and French definite article. The function of *la* is closer to that of the demonstrative in these languages, and this morpheme cannot be defined simply as a definite article.

In support of this claim, I resort to semantic definitions Definiteness, Specificity and Deixis from current literature.

4. Semantic definitions

4.1 Definiteness

I assume Definiteness to be a universal category of meaning that finds expression in natural language. While languages like English and French use articles to mark the (in)definiteness contrast of NPs, many other languages do not have articles and it could be assumed that there is no structural representation of this feature in their grammar. However, all languages are able to establish the referential properties of nouns, be it by articles, by word order, or by the use of a demonstrative when the reference of bare nouns has to be made absolutely clear.

4.2 The 'Familiarity' theory of definiteness

In English and French, the definite article serves to indicate that the NP has the feature [+definite]. Traditionally the meaning of *the* has been explained in terms of the contrast with the indefinite article *a/an*, which is used to introduce a new referent in the discourse, while the definite article *the* signals a familiar referent. Christophersen notes that 'For the proper use of *the*, it is necessary that it should call up in the hearer's mind the image of the exact individual that the speaker is thinking of' (1939: 28). The interesting thing is that the *the*-form supposes that the hearer knows it, too.

The contrast between indefinite NPs and definite NPs is that the former introduce new referents in the discourse, while the latter pick out particular elements that the hearer can identify, either by information supplied in the discourse, or through shared knowledge. The claim is that indefinites cannot have antecedents in the discourse, whereas definites must.

4.2.1 Incomplete definite descriptions

Heim (1983, 1988) rejects the traditional 'Familiarity theory' of definiteness associated with Christophersen and Jespersen, and points to the superiority of Karttunen 's (1971) theory, which substitutes *discourse referent* for *referent*. Thus the requirement for a definite NP is that it picks out an already familiar *discourse referent*, while an indefinite NP always introduces a new *discourse referent*. Given that a discourse referent may not necessarily have a referent, this solves the problem of definite NPs that fail to refer, as in the following examples:

(71) He was the son of a tailor. (Though the tailor in question may have more than one son)

and:

(72) Towards evening we came to the bank of a river (In spite of the fact that every river has two banks) (Christophersen 1939: 140)

Russell had noted that: '... *the*, when it is strictly used, involves uniqueness; we do, it is true, speak of "the son of So-and-so" even when So-and-so has several sons, but it would be more correct to say "a son of So-and-so"' (1905: 481).

4.2.2 Singular and plural definite descriptions

Russell (1905) identified two basic requirements for the correct use of a definite description, namely *existential commitment* and *uniqueness*. In other words, a definite description of an individual asserts the existence of a unique individual so described. Russell's theory however, failed to account for the use of *the* with plural count nouns and mass nouns, when this morpheme clearly cannot encode a 'uniqueness requirement'. In its plural use, *the* has been likened to the universal quantifier like *all* or *every*, but Kearns (2000) points out that the terms are not always interchangeable, as in for example:

(73) a. All men are mortal
   b. Every man is mortal
   c. ? The men are mortal

Unlike *all* or *every*, *the* cannot be completely independent of a particular context, but like the proportional quantifiers, *many, few, most*, and *several*, *the* expresses a proportion of a given set of things or individuals, which must be identified in a discourse for clear interpretation. The oddity of the (c) example above is that the utterance can only apply to a subset of men, not to all men as in the (a) and (b) examples. Like singular definite descriptions, plural definite descriptions are dependent on a particular context for interpretation. The quantificational analysis of *the* thus predicts the 'Familiarity' effect in the sense that it expresses a proportion of a set, which the hearer must be able to identify for clear interpretation.

The 'Familiarity' and quantificational theories of definiteness in fact overlap in the work of Christophersen, who writes of the plural form of *the* that "It stands for a particular part of what is denoted by the zero-form, marked off with precise limits" (1939: 36).

4.2.3 *Referential and attributive uses of definite descriptions*

Strawson (1950) and Donnellan (1966) differentiate between two main uses of definite descriptions: the referential (or identifying) use, and the attributive (or denoting) use. They challenge Russell's (1905) theory on the grounds that it fails to account for the referential uses of definite descriptions, but recognizes only their denoting function. When a definite description is used referentially, there is a presupposition or implication that a particular someone or something fits the description, and they want the audience to pick out or think of the right thing or person that fits the description. "No such presupposition is present in the attributive use of definite descriptions" (Donnellan 1966: 289).

Definite descriptions that do not involve uniqueness and do not denote specific reference are defined as 'incomplete definite descriptions'. They are dependent on the context of their utterance, unlike 'complete' definite descriptions', such as the phrases like "the author of Waverley" and "the eighteenth king of France" (Strawson 1950: 338) which pick out a unique individual regardless of any particular context. French and English use a definite article with all definite descriptions, regardless of whether they serve to refer or simply to denote. In the latter cases, it could be argued, as suggested by Lyons (1999), that '*the* is not lexically specified as definite - it is a "minimal Det with no semantic content, which acts as a semantically empty filler of the DP specifier in the absence of any other occupant. The is thus analogous to pleonastic *it* in subject position, ... the is a pleonastic Det" (1994: 29, emphasis in original).

4.3 Stages of Familiarity

Jespersen (1933) identified several 'Stages of Familiarity' ranging from complete unfamiliarity, which corresponds to indefiniteness, where an indefinite article is used, to complete familiarity, as with proper nouns, where the use of a definite article is made redundant. In between those two, there are various stages of familiarity which are dependent on the discourse or the situation of utterance, and for which both English and French use the definite article.

Christophersen (1939) classified these different types of definite descriptions, in terms of the contexts in which objects are referred to, namely, *explicit contextual basis*, *implicit contextual basis* and *situational basis*.

Hawkins (1978) builds on the work of Jespersen (1933) and Christophersen (1939) in his seminal work on Definiteness and Indefiniteness, where he identifies 8 usage types of the definite article. He reduces these to two anaphoric uses, four situational uses, and some unidentifiable uses. They are:

(i)   Direct anaphora
(ii) Associative anaphora
(iii) Visible situation use
(iv) Immediate situation use
(v)   Larger situation use, relying on specific knowledge about the referent
(vi) Larger situation use, relying on general knowledge
(vii) Unidentifiable uses

In the sections that follow, I will provide MC and French translations of some of Hawkins' examples, to illustrate how the different categories of definiteness are marked in the creole, while offering a comparison with French.

4.3.1 Anaphoric uses

In (74) a new referent is introduced in the discourse by an indefinite NP, and the next example is the second mention of the referent:

(74) Fred was discussing an interesting book in his class. (Hawkins 1978: 86)
 Fred ti pe diskit **enn liv** interesan dan so klas.   MC
 Fred discutait d'un livre intéressant dans sa classe.   French

(75) I went to discuss *the book* with him afterwards. (Hawkins 1978: 86)
 Mo'n al diskit **liv la** ek li apre.   MC
 J'ai été discuter *du livre* avec lui après.   French

Where 'the book' is understood as referring to the same individual as the preceding indefinite description, and is part of a singleton set or authors. We have here a case of <u>direct anaphora</u>. While English and French use definite determiners, MC has the post-nominal specificity marker *la*.

In (76) a definite description is used for a newly introduced discourse referent, marked by the definite article in both English and French:

(76) He is friendly with *the author*. (Hawkins 1978: 86)
 Li kamwad ek **so loter**.   MC
 Il est ami avec *l'auteur*.   French

If the above example is an utterance which immediately follows sentence (74), there is no previous mention of the author, but s/he is understood as being the author of the previously mentioned book. This is a case of <u>associative anaphora</u> (Hawkins 1978:100). The use of the definite article in English and French is possible not just because a book has an author, but because this is shared knowledge by speaker and hearer. Note that in this case, MC uses the possessive pronoun *so*.[23]

However, the following is also a case of associative anaphora, and while both English and French have a definite article, MC has a bare noun:

(77) Mary stopped to look at a house. *The door* was open. (Hawkins 1978: 101)
 Mari ti arete pu get enn lakaz. Laport ti uver.   MC
 Marie s'est arrêtée pour visiter une maison. La porte était ouverte.   French

In this case, even though the relationship is one of associative anaphora, the use of *so* would imply that the house had only one door. If more than one door was being referred to, the plural marker *bann* would be used:

(78) Mary stopped to look at a house. The doors were open.
 Mari ti arete pu get enn lakaz. Bann laport ti uver.   MC
 Marie s'est arrêtée pour visiter une maison. Les portes étaient ouvertes.   French

4.3.2 Immediate situational uses

Situational uses of definite descriptions, like associative anaphoric uses, do not require a discourse antecedent. In the case of a visible situation use, Hawkins points out that the definite article may often overlap with demonstratives. In the case of an object being in the field of vision of both discourse participants, the speaker may utter either of the following:

---

[23] Philip Baker suggests that the use of *so* in this case is more typical of rural rather than urban areas, and claims that *loter la* is definitely possible here (p c).

(79) Pass me *the bucket*, please (Hawkins 1978: 103)
   Pas mwa seo, do[24]   MC
   Passe-moi le seau s'il te plaît   French

(80) Pass me *this/that bucket*, please (Hawkins 1978: 103)
   Pas mwa sa seo la, do   MC
   Passe-moi ce seau-là, s'il te plaît   French

As in English and French, MC may use a demonstrative with a first mention of an object which is visible in the situational context. It is not possible to use the specificity marker *la* on its own in this case, unless there was a previous mention of the object.

When the object is not visible, a demonstrative is not appropriate. English and French use a definite article and MC has a bare noun:

(81) Don't go in there, chum. *The dog* will bite you. (Hawkins 1978: 103)
   Pa al laba, monwar. Lisyen pu mord twa.   MC
   Ne vas pas là-bas, mon vieux. Le chien va te mordre.   French

No dog need be visible, nor does the hearer need have prior knowledge of the referent.

4.3.3   Larger situational uses

Typical examples of larger situation uses of definite descriptions include for example reference to 'the mayor' or 'the church' by residents of a particular town, or reference to 'the president' or 'the queen' by residents of a country. While English and French use the definite article, MC has a bare noun:

(82) *Larenn Langleter*
   queen England
   The Queen of England / La reine d'Angleterre

There are also unique nouns, such as 'the earth' or 'the moon', when the speaker appeals to the hearer's general knowledge about entities which exist in his/her world, and where we have seen that MC uses bare nouns.

4.3.4   Unfamiliarity uses

The unfamiliarity uses of definite descriptions are those where there is a modifying NP, or relative clause or prepositional phrase, which serve to establish a definite referent for the hearer without the need for previous mention. The information provided makes set identification and location possible, e.g.:

(83) I remember *the beginning of the war* very well ...(Hawkins 1978: 139)
   Mo byen rapel kumansman lager ...   MC
   Je me souviens bien du début de la guerre ...   French

Hawkins also identifies 'unfamiliarity uses' of the definite article, when the hearer is given no means to identify the object, when there is no presumption of prior knowledge, and no associative link between the referent and other previously mentioned individual, as in:

(84) My wife and I share *the same secrets* (Hawkins 1978: 102)
   Mo fam ek mwa partaz bann mem sekre   MC
   Ma femme et moi partageons les mêmes secrets   French

If *bann* is left out, we have a [+definite] singular reading:

---

[24] I use the exclamation *do* which does not express anything except that it is a friendly, casual expression. There is no word for *please* for the singular, casual form of address in MC. For the formal form of address, *siuple* is used.

(85) *Mo   fam   ek   mwa   partazmem   sekre*
     1.SG wife and 1.SG share same secret
     My wife and I share the same secret / Ma femme et moi partageons le même secret

In summary:

- For <u>direct anaphora</u>, MC uses the specificity marker *la*. This corresponds to Donnellan's (1966) and Strawson's (1950) 'referential' uses of definite descriptions and to what Jespersen (1933) and Christophersen (1939) identify as having an <u>explicit contextual basis</u>. These descriptions satisfy Russell prerequisites of *uniqueness* and *existential commitment*. They are known to both hearer and speaker, and are the only definites that are also [+specific].

- For <u>associative anaphora</u>, When it is assumed that there is only one referent, either the possessive pronoun *so* or *la* is used. When there is more than one referent, a bare noun is used to refer to a single one, and *bann* is used to refer to the totality of referents. There is no overt definite determiner. This use of a definite description fits into Christophersen's <u>implicit contextual basis</u>. The referent exists, but may not be known to the hearer.

- In the case of <u>visible situational uses</u>, either a bare noun or a demonstrative is used. As in English and French, there is an overlap between definite determiners and demonstratives when these are used in an 'immediate situational use', when the object is visible.

- In the case of an <u>immediate situation use</u>, where the referent is not visible, English and French use a definite article, and MC has a bare noun.

- In the <u>larger situation uses</u>, MC uses only bare nouns.

The above analysis provides evidence that Definiteness and Specificity are distinct phenomena. While a definite NP selects an individual or individuals in a set of possible individuals, an NP that is both definite and specific relates to pre-established discourse referents. "Definiteness expresses the discourse pragmatic property of familiarity, while specificity mirrors a more finely grained referential structure of the items used in the discourse. A specific NP indicates that it is referentially anchored to another discourse object" (von Heusinger 2002: 247). This view is shared by Pesetsky (1987) who coins the term *d-linking* (discourse linking) to define the phenomenon of Specificity.

4.4   Specificity

4.4.1   *Specific and non-specific indefinites*

Specificity and non-specificity in fact, have more commonly been associated with indefinites, when these occur in sentences with operators such as modals, propositional attitude verbs and other quantificational NPs. This can lead to an ambiguous interpretation of some utterances, such as:

(86)   Paul wants to buy a monkey.

However, the following utterances leave no room for ambiguity:

(87)   a. <u>Specific</u>
          Paul wants to buy [a monkey]$_i$. He saw it$_i$ at the market yesterday
          [A x: MONKEY(x)] WANT(p, BUY(p, x))
          There is a specific monkey that Paul wants to buy.
       b. <u>Non-specific</u>
          Paul wants buy a monkey. He will look for one at the market.
          WANT (p,[A x: MONKEY(x)] BUY(p, x))
          Paul wants to buy a monkey, any monkey, and he hopes to find one.

In the case of indefinites, contextual information dispels the ambiguity with regard to their [±specificity] feature, which can also be disambiguated in a formal representation as shown. In (87a), where Paul has a specific monkey in mind, 'MONKEY' has scope over 'WANT', and the NP can be pronominalized, as shown by the co-indexation. This is not the case in (87b), where the verb has scope over the NP, and there may be no monkey.

The non-specific and specific readings correspond to what Quine (1960) termed 'opaque' and 'transparent' readings, and what Fodor & Sag (1982) define as an 'existential' and a 'referential' reading, respectively. In their opaque or existential reading, indefinites have narrow scope, and in their transparent, or referential reading, they have wide scope. A specific NP refers to a particular individual, while a non-specific NP simply refers to a class of objects or to any individual fitting the description denoted by the NP.

A specific NP is characterized by the "certainty of the speaker about the identity of the referent" (von Heusinger 2002: 245). In the case of definites both hearer and speaker are able to identify the referent; in the case of indefinites, only the hearer has knowledge of the referent.

Partee (1970) draws a parallel between specific indefinites and referential definites, and between non-specific indefinites and attributive definites. The first two "exist" within a particular universe of discourse; the latter two need not necessarily exist. We have seen that [+specific] definites have a strong discourse antecedent; [+specific] indefinites also require a discourse antecedent, but it is a weaker link, as in the following example: "Several children came in to my room. I knew two girls" (Enç 1991: 6). The indefinite NP *two girls* "has a covert partitive reading, and it introduces into the domain of discourse individuals from a previously given set" (*idem.*).

Enç's claims that "Specificity is a phenomenon distinct from definiteness, and while the definiteness of the NP can be determined from the determiner in languages like English, specificity cannot be so determined" (1991: 16). This is not the case in MC, where *la* is the morphological realization of the feature [+specific] of definite NPs. The [±specificity] contrast of indefinites, however, is not marked in MC, and in this respect the creole patterns like its lexifier.

On the basis of the above definitions, I equate Specificity with Referentiality both of which involve linking NP denotations to previous discourse.

4.5 Deixis

I argued that the specificity marker *la* is not equivalent to the definite article in English and French because it encodes the feature Deixis, and cannot, for example, be used with unique nouns, or in a generic context. Deixis is associated with demonstratives, which generally serve to 'referentially identify - as in *that* particular big primate, not *this* one' (Levinson 2004: 98). However, deictic expressions are used not only to point things out (exophoric use) but to track referents in discourse (anaphoric use). The morpheme *la* in MC performs both functions.

The demonstrative *sa ...la* is used when the item is present in the situational context, or for direct anaphora, in the case of a recently mentioned referent. It is not possible to use *la* on its own with a first mention of a discourse referent, even when accompanied by a pointing gesture, one must use *sa ... la*. The use of *la* on its own serves strictly to mark anaphoric definiteness.

Levinson points out that "Anaphora is so closely linked to deixis that it is not always separable, as in *I've been living in San Francisco for five years and I love it here* (where *here* is both anaphoric and deictic)" (2004: 103). The dual function of MC *la* may be a reflection on its dual origin, which has been argued to be the French demonstrative reinforcer *là*, which marks discourse deixis, and the homophonous locative adverb *là*, which marks situational deixis.

5. Syntactic framework

5.1 A Rationale for Minimalism

My syntactic analysis is within the framework of Chomsky's Minimalist Program (MP) (1995). The MP is a research program, developed from the earlier Principles and Parameters approach to generative grammar, which assumes that humans are biologically endowed with a Universal Grammar (UG), and that languages differ as a consequence of parametric variations. The goal of linguistic research within this framework is thus to seek both 'descriptive adequacy', i.e. achieve a description of the grammar of a particular language, and 'explanatory adequacy', i.e. "explain how knowledge of these facts arises in the mind of the speaker-hearer" (Chomsky 1995:3). In other words, it is a search for those universal principles of grammar that are manifested in natural language.

The driving principle behind the MP is the question of how to solve "the logical problem of language acquisition" (Chomsky 2002: 93). How can children acquire grammatical competence despite the impoverished nature of the primary linguistic data to which they are exposed? I take this question to be highly relevant to the study of creoles, given the increased poverty of the stimulus in a language contact situation. "No one doubts that grammatical competence is influenced by the nature of the primary linguistic data; Parisian children learn French and Cantonese children learn Chinese" (Epstein & Hornstein 1999: ix). Did the children of the slaves acquire a new language, or were the adults responsible for creating a new one?

A fundamental assumption of the MP is that language is a "perfect system", characterized by "simplicity, economy, symmetry, nonredundancy" (Chomsky 1995:1). Such an assumption is also highly relevant in the study of Creoles, which have been described as unmarked languages, closest to UG (Bickerton 1984; Seuren & Wekker 1986; McWhorter 2001). One would thus expect "descriptive adequacy" of a "radical" creole to facilitate "explanatory adequacy".

In the section that follows I summarize the assumptions of the MP that are relevant to this analysis, where I assume the reader's familiarity with generative syntax.[25]

5.2 Minimalist assumptions

The MP assumes that items that are selected from the lexicon enter a derivation fully inflected with their phonological, semantic and formal features. The lexicon comprises *substantive* items, such as verbs, nouns and adjectives, and *functional* items, such as complementizers, tense and determiners. Linguistic expressions are formed by the recursive application of the operations *Merge*, *Move* and *Agree*. The operation *Merge* concatenates two syntactic objects and projects the categorial feature of the head, e.g. the verb *love* merges with the noun *cats* to form the VP *love cats*.

Thus, syntactic structures are built up using general rules such that each phrase consists of a head (X), a complement (YP) and specifier (ZP) as in the schema below. The two basic relations are the *Spec(ifier)-head* relation of ZP to X, and the *head-complement* relation of X to YP:

(88)

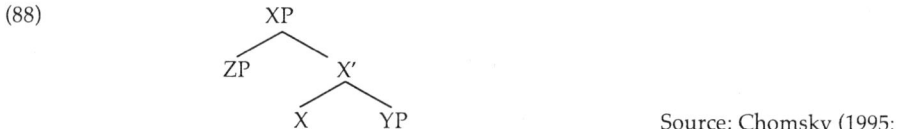

Source: Chomsky (1995: 172)

---

[25] This analysis forms part of a larger work on 'The form and function of the noun phrase in Mauritian Creole'. A more detailed syntactic analysis than that presented in Section 6 is beyond the scope of this article.

Items may be base generated in a head position or in a specifier position. Nouns, verbs and prepositions are heads. In the case of the determiner elements, some, like the definite determiner is a head,[26] while others, which are more adjectival in nature, such as demonstratives, occupy a specifier position (Giusti 1997).

The operation *Move* accounts for the phenomenon of displacement in language. In the MP framework, lexical (substantive) items are assumed to have interpretable features, while functional items have uninterpretable features, which must be checked by the matching features of a lexical item. The operation *Move* is triggered to satisfy the checking requirements of a lexical resource and, if conditions are satisfied, uninterpretable features delete. *Agree* is the operation that establishes a relation between lexical items. Movement can be head to head movement (e.g. raising of a noun into an empty determiner position) or phrasal movement, also referred to as XP movement, to a specifier position.

At any point in the derivation, Spell-Out can apply resulting in Phonetic Form (PF), which is the overt component, while the derivation continues yielding Logical Form (LF), which is the covert component. These are the only two interface levels, and account for the phenomena of language with sound and meaning respectively.

The point at which Spell Out occurs is language specific, as it is dependent on the strength of the features that must be eliminated. Feature strength is a parametric variation, and while strong features must be checked in the overt syntax (at PF), the checking of weak features can be delayed till after Spell-Out (at LF), and such movement is covert, it is "cheaper" than overt movement.

Notions of economy and optimality apply to both the derivations and the occurrence of features. Operations are driven strictly by necessity; they are defined as 'last resort', applied if they must, not otherwise. With regard to features, optimally, these occur on a head only to yield new scopal or discourse related properties.

6. The analysis

6.1 Functional projections within the MC noun phrase

I assume DP Hypothesis, whereby DP is the maximal category projected by the class of determiner elements, and heads the noun phrase (Abney 1987; Stowell 1989, 1991; Szabolcsi 1987). But what is D? Articles, demonstratives, quantifiers, have all been defined as determiners, heading their own projections. Following Lyons (1999), I refer to D as the head of the Definiteness Phrase (DefP). "In defining D as definiteness rather than determiner, I am implying that functional heads should be expected to correspond to grammatical categories rather than word classes" (Lyons 1999: 29-30).

Thus, I propose for MC a highly articulated noun phrase structure, where functional projections are instantiated in order to realize a semantic feature, such as Definiteness, Specificity, Deixis etc. Thus, the MC noun phrase comprises the following projections, in the order below:[27]

- The Specificity Phrase, SpP, is the highest projection. It is headed by *la*, which is the lexical realization of this feature for specific definites. It selects a DefP.
- The head of DefP is the phonologically null determiner represented as δ and is [+definite].
- The head of the Demonstrative Phrase, DemP, is specified for the feature [+deictic]. I follow Giusti (1997) in my assumption that demonstratives occupy specifier positions, thus *sa* is base generated in Spec,DemP.

---
[26] Lyons (1999) argues that the definite determiner occupies a specifier position.
[27] The Possessive Phrase is not included in this representation, as it does not form part of my analysis. It is in complementary distribution with DemP.

- The head of the Num(ber)P(hrase) is specified for the features [±plural]. The default is [−plural] and *bann* is the lexical realization of the feature [+plural]. It is in complementary distribution with cardinal numerals, and like numerals, it is base generated in SpecNumP. This projection is realized only for count nouns.
- The lowest projection is the NP.

(89)

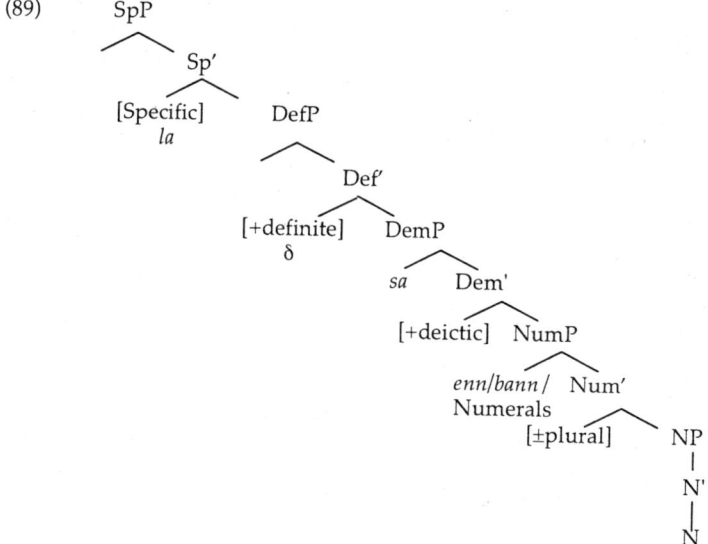

6.2 The role of Number

I claim that nouns come out of the lexicon as argumental, kind-denoting terms, with a default plural interpretation. Whenever a bare noun in MC has the feature [+definite] singular, the presence of null δ must be assumed.

Unlike mass nouns, count nouns have a Number argument which must be saturated. The count N raises to Num to check its Number feature. The default interpretation for N in Num is singular. In the case of plural nouns, *bann* is present in Spec,NumP and marks the NP accordingly.

While nouns in the N position denote kinds, nouns in Num denote instantiations of a kind; they represent a set of individuals of the kind denoted by the noun. NumPs are cardinality predicates that denote properties, and must combine with a determiner to form a referential expression, as illustrated in the schema below:

(90)

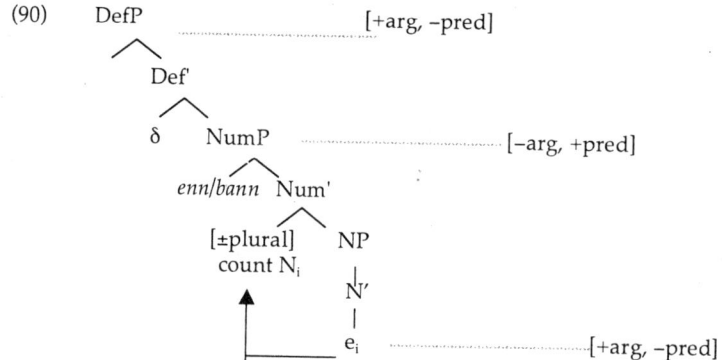

In the case of indefinite singular count nouns, the null definite determiner obviously does not project, and *enn* is present in Spec,NumP, marking both singularity and indefiniteness.

6.3 Licensing δ

Bare mass nouns can occur in any argument position irrespective of their [±referentiality] feature. While singular [+definite] count nouns are admitted in internal argument positions, they are barred in subject position, unless the noun can be interpreted as a proper name, or a generic noun. If such an interpretation is not possible, then the noun must be marked by *la*.

6.3.1 Singular count nouns

The ungrammaticality of bare singular common count nouns in subject position can be accounted for if null δ is analyzed as an empty category, whose occurrence is subject to certain licensing conditions, namely that they must be governed by an overt lexical head (Longobardi 1994; Rizzi 1990; Rizzi and Roberts 1989). When bare nouns are the direct object of a verb, or object of preposition, this condition is fulfilled, where null δ is licensed by a verbal or prepositional head, but there is no suitable head that can act as a licenser in subject position.

Thus, the occurrence of *la* to mark the singular count noun in subject position is a "last resort" operation, required to license null δ. The strong Specificity features of *la* force phrasal movement of DefP (including NP and modifiers) to its specifier, deriving its DP final position. In the following example, the clause final *la*, like *sa*, has scope over the NP headed by the noun *zom*, and not over the preceding NP headed by *lamer*, which is embedded in the relative clause:

(91) Sa   zom ki   okipp   partaz   delo lamer la (Maingard 2002: 81)
DEM man COMP look.after distribution water sea   SP
This man who looks after the distribution of sea water
Cet homme qui s'occupe du partage de l'eau de mer

6.3.2 Plural count nouns

Plural count nouns, i.e. *bann* + (unmodified) N also pattern differently from singular count nouns when in subject position, where their only possible interpretation is [+definite], evidence that null δ has projected. In this case, I propose that *bann* raises to Spec,DefP, where it is able to license the occurrence of null δ, assuming, like Giusti that "Once Spec,DP is filled with an element that has enough features to license the whole projection, no article needs to be inserted" (1997: 108). In this case, *la* does not need to surface to license null δ.

6.4 Mass nouns

In the case of mass nouns, the Number projection is not realized. I have claimed that nouns in the N position in MC have the parameters [+arg, −pred]. But a noun cannot in itself be [+definite] or [+specific]. These are semantic features of DPs, not NPs.

In order to account for the [+definite] feature of bare mass nouns, I resort to Longobardi's claim that "If N overtly moves to a phonetically empty D then it will be object referring" (2001: 595). This movement analogous to that proposed by Longobardi for proper names in Romance (1994, 2001). Such a move is possible given the argumental nature of mass nouns (unlike count nouns, they do not raise to Num). A similar operation is proposed for unique nouns, which, like proper names, are inherently referential. Hence their ability to occur in any argument position without a determiner.

"Failure to move in to the D position will result in a 'default' instance of existential interpretation" (Longobardi 1999:5). This is the case of bare mass nouns in subject position that have a [−definite] interpretation, as in example (31).

6.5 The demonstrative *sa*

In her analysis of the status of determiners, Giusti (1997) claims that demonstratives are inserted in a low specifier and subsequently raise to the highest position, where they check their referential features. Assuming this to be the case in MC, *sa* raises to Spec,DefP, where it is able to license null δ.[28] If both *sa* and *bann* are present, only *sa*, which is in a higher position than NumP, need raise to Spec,DefP to license δ.

6.6 The feature Specificity

I have argued that *la* surfaces as a 'last resort' when there is a need to license null δ in the case of singular count nouns in subject position. Does MC need an overt Specificity marker because the definite determiner is a phonologically null element? Given that French and English have overt definite determiners, there is no need for an overt Specificity marker to license these morphemes in subject position. In Minimalist terms, the Specificity feature in English and French is weak, and need only be checked at LF, hence no morphological realization. This is not the case in MC, where an overt Specificity marker is required to license null δ in subject position. This results in a strong Specificity feature for [+definite] NPs, which must be checked overtly. This analysis complies with the economy conditions of the MP, which stipulate that the occurrence of features is never gratuitous, but serves both to license grammatical elements and assign meaning.

The Specificity feature of indefinites however is not marked in MC, and in this respect the creole patterns like its lexifier. In both languages, the Specificity of indefinites is checked at LF, hence no morphological realization of the feature.

7. Conclusion

In summary, the determiner system of MC is quite different from that of its lexifier. Some of these differences are as follows:

- While nouns in French, with few exceptions, cannot occur in argument positions without a determiner, MC freely admits bare nouns in various syntactic configurations.
- While Specificity is not marked in French, [+definite] NPs in MC are marked by *la*.
- While all determiners in French are pre-nominal, MC *la* is post-nominal.

I have attempted to account for these differences both in terms of the different denotations of nouns in those two languages, and to the occurrence of a phonologically null [+definite] determiner in the creole. I have claimed that MC nouns come out of the lexicon as argumental, kind-denoting terms, with a default plural interpretation. If nouns in Romance are predicative, as claimed by Chierchia (1998), there must have been a shift in noun interpretation from French to Creole. This is not altogether inconceivable, given the fact that French determiners were not analyzed as separate functional items, but assumed to be an integral part of the nouns that they modified.

The catalyst for change was loss of the French determiners. Speakers of the early Creole would have interpreted common count nouns as occurring with a null determiner, i.e. δ + N, while mass nouns and unique nouns would have been interpreted like proper

---

[28] This analysis raises the question about the co-occurrence of Def and Dem, which is ungrammatical in French and English. Giusti (1997) compares the co-occurrence of Def and Dem to the doubly filled COMP filter. This is ungrammatical in English, but grammatical in MC, e.g.:
    Kisenla ki vini la?
    Who that come now
    Who's coming now? / Qui vient là? (*Kisenla* is derived from *qui celle-là*, lit. 'who that/this').

nouns in French, i.e. as N in the D position. In both instances, they were DPs, seemingly bare nouns that were grammatical in argument positions.

The ensuing grammaticalization of a Specificity marker and a plural marker may well be the manifestation of 'internal' language change, driven by universal principles of grammar. How else would the speakers of the new creole access the semantics associated with these morphemes? This work so far leaves open this question, but provides evidence that the new Creole strived for the means to express them.

Finally, a comparison of the determiner system of MC and its lexifier provides evidence that Definiteness and Specificity are universal and distinct categories of meaning.

8. References

Abney, Steven Paul 1987 The English noun phrase and its sentential aspect. PhD, Massachusetts Institute of Technology.
Ah-Vee, Alain 2002a Evolisyon dinamik lortograf kreol morisyen. Anon. (ed.) 2002: 37-41.
—— 2002b Lartik dan "Kwin syantifik" ki finn paret dan Lagazet *Lalit de Klas*. Anon. (ed.) 2002: 72-73.
Anderson, Samuel 1885 *L'Evangile selon S. Matthié (dan langaz créol Maurice). The Gospel according to St Matthew (in Mauritian creole)*. London: British and Foreign Bible Society.
Anon. 1980 [unidentified contributors to *Bord la mer*]. Anon. (ed.) 1980.
Anon. (ed.) 1980 *Bord la mer*. Port Louis: Port Louis Harbour and Docks Workers Union.
Anon. (ed.) 2002 *Langaz Kreol zordi: Papers on Kreol*. Port Louis: Ledikasyon pu Travayer.
Anon. 2004 *Diksyoner kreol angle*. Port Louis: Ledikasyon pu Travayer.
Arends, Jacques 1995 *The early stages of creolization*. Amsterdam: Benjamins.
Asgarally, Renée 1977 *Quand montagne prend difé*. Rose Hill, Mauritius: Mascarena University Publications.
Baissac, Charles 1880 *Étude sur le patois créole Mauricien*. Nancy: Imprimerie Berger Levrault.
—— 1888 *Le folk-lore de l'Île Maurice*. Paris: Maisonneuve & Larose.
Baker, Philip 1984 Agglutinated French articles in Creole French: their evolutionary significance. *Te Reo* 27: 89-129.
—— 2003 Quelques cas de réanalyse et de grammaticalisation dans l'évolution du créole mauricien. Kriegel, Sibylle (ed.) *Grammaticalisation et réanalyse: Approches de la variation créole et française*, Paris: CNRS Éditions, 111-41.
Baker, Philip & Hookoomsing, Vinesh Y 1987 *Diksyoner Kreol Morisyen*. Paris: L'Harmattan.
Bernstein, Judy B 1996 Demonstratives and reinforcers in Romance and Germanic languages. *Lingua* 102: 87-113.
Bickerton, Derek 1984 The Language Bioprogram Hypothesis. *Behavioral and Brain Sciences* 7: 173-88.
Bord la mer 1980 *See* Anon. (ed.) 1980.
Camle, George 1980 Lumpers. Anon. (ed.) 1980: 48-50.
Carlson, Gregory Norman 1978 *Reference to kinds in English*. Bloomington: Indiana University Linguistics Club.
Carpooran, Arnaud 2002 Konsep drwa langaz ek drwa lingwistik: propozisyon pou enn aplikasyon dan Moris. Anon. (ed.) 2002: 66-71.
—— 2005 *Diksioner Morisien: Version prototip Let A ziska E*. Quatre Bornes: Bartholdi.
Chaudenson, Robert 1981 *Textes créoles anciens: La Réunion et Île Maurice. Comparaison et essai d'analyse*. Hamburg: Buske.
Chierchia, Gennaro 1998 Reference to kinds across languages. *Natural Language Semantics* 6: 339-405.
Chiffone, Sydney 1980 Enn travayer angaze ki ti apel Georges Chiffone. Anon. (ed.) 1980: 82.

Chomsky, Noam 1995 *The Minimalist Program*. Cambridge, MA: MIT Press.
—— 2002 *On nature and language*. New York: Cambridge University Press.
Chrestien, François 1831 Les essais d'un bobre africain, Mauritius: Deroullède.
Christophersen, Paul 1939 *The articles: A study of their theory and use in English*. Copenhagen: Einar Munksgaard.
De Salle Essoo, Maya 2005 Ces métiers qui disparaissent. Port Louis: *L'Express* (daily newspaper).
Dholah, Veena 2002 Letid lor proporsyon lekritir an kreol dan *Revi Lalit* (1988-1992). Anon. (ed.) 2002: 79-80.
Donnellan, Keith S 1966 Reference and definite descriptions. *The Philosophical Review* 75: 281-304.
Elizier, Claude 1980 Anon. (ed.) 1980: 2.
Enç, Murvet 1991 The semantics of specificity. *Linguistic Inquiry* 22: 1-25.
Epstein, David & Hornstein, Norbert (eds) 1999 *Working Minimalism*. Cambridge, MA: MIT Press.
Federation of Preschool Playgroups 2002 Langaz Kreol dan preskoler. Ledikasyon pu Travayer, 119-24.
Fodor, Janet Dean & Sag, Ivan A 1982 Referential and quantificational indefinites. *Linguistics and Philosophy* 5: 355-98.
Giusti, Giuliana 1997 The categorial status of determiners. Haegeman, Liliane (ed.) *The new comparative syntax*, London: Longman, 95-123.
Grant, Anthony P 1995 Article agglutination in Creole French: a wider perspective. Baker, Philip (ed.) *From contact to creole and beyond*. London: University of Westminster Press, 149-76.
Haspelmath, M, Dryer, M S, Gil, D, & Comrie, B (eds) 2005 *The world atlas of language structures*. Oxford: Oxford University Press.
Hawkins, John 1978 *Definiteness and indefiniteness: A study in reference and grammaticality prediction*. London: Croom Helm.
Heim, Irene 1983 File change semantics and the familiarity theory of definiteness. Bauerle, Rainer, Schwarze, Christoph, & von Stechow, Arnim (eds) *Meaning, use and interpretation of language*, Berlin: de Gruyter, 164-89.
—— 1988 *The semantics of definite and indefinite noun phrases*. New York: Garland Publishing.
Himmelmann, Nikolaus P 2001 Articles. Haspelmath et al. (eds), 831-41.
Hookoomsing, Vinesh 2002 Kreol: Lang interfas an leritaz patrimwann et modernite. Anon. (ed.) 2002: 25-30.
Jespersen, Otto 1933 *Essentials of English grammar*. London: Allen & Unwin.
Karttunen, Lauri Juhani 1971 *Discourse referents*. Bloomington: Indiana University Linguistics Club.
Kearns, Kate 2000 *Semantics*. London: Macmillan.
Legallant, Georges 2002 Ver enn bibliografi: Sirvol liv an kreol morisyen depi lindependans. Anon. (ed.) 2002: 51-53.
Le Juge de Segrais, Xavier le 1939 *Vingt contes en patois mauricien imités des fables de La Fontaine*. Port Louis: M Gaud & Cie Ltd.
Levinson, Stephen C 2004 Deixis. Horn, Laurence R & Ward, Gregory (eds) *Handbook of pragmatics*, London: Blackwell, 97-121.
Longobardi, Giuseppe 1994 Reference and Proper Names: A Theory of N-Movement in Syntax and Logical Form [Fall]. *Linguistic Inquiry* 25: 609-65.
—— 2001 The structure of DPs. Baltin, Mark & Collins, Chris (eds) *The handbook of contemporary syntactic theory*, Oxford: Blackwell, 562-603.
Lyons, Christopher 1994 Movement in 'NP' and the DP Hypothesis. *Working Papers in Language and Linguistics* 8.
—— 1999 *Definiteness*. Cambridge: Cambridge University Press.

McWhorter, John 2001 The world's simplest grammars are creole grammars. *Linguistic Typology* 5: 125-56.
Maingard, Jan 2002 *Lagrin tambarin: 13 ti zistoires en kreol*. Baie du Tombeau, Mauritius: Editions Maurice.
Milsark, Gary 1979 *Existential sentences in English*. New York: Garland.
Partee, Barbara Hall 1970 Opacity, coreference, and pronouns. *Synthèse* 21: 359-85.
Pesetsky, David 1987 Wh-in-situ: Movement and unselective binding. Reuland, Eric J & ter Meulen, Alice G B (eds) *The representation of (in)definiteness*, Cambridge, MA: MIT Press, 98-129.
Quine, Willard V 1960 *Word and object*. Cambridge, MA: MIT Press.
Rizzi, Luigi 1990 *Relativized Minimality*. Cambridge, MA: MIT Press.
Rizzi, Luigi & Roberts, Ian 1989 Complex inversion in French. *Probus* 1.1: 1-30.
Romaine, Alain 2002 Itilizasyon langaz kreol dan domenn relizye. Anon. (ed.) 2002: 127-29.
Rungoo, Geerganand 2002 Within a state of linguistic anarchy. Anon. (ed.) 2002: 97-98.
Russell, Bertrand 1905 On denoting. *Mind* 14: 479-93.
Salamut, Rahim 1980 Arimer. Anon. (ed.) 1980: 18-20.
Seuren, Pieter A M & Wekker, Herman 1986 Semantic transparency as a factor in creole genesis. Muysken, Pieter & Smith, Norval (eds) *Substrata versus universals in creole genesis*, Amsterdam: Benjamins, 57-70.
Stowell, Tim 1989 Subjects, Specifiers, and X-Bar Theory. Baltin, M & Kroch, A S (eds) *Alternative conceptions of phrase structure*. Chicago: University of Chicago Press, 232-62.
—— 1991 Determiners in NP and DP. Leffel, K & Bouchard, D (eds) *Views on phrase structure*, Dordrecht: Kluwer, 232-62.
Strandquist, Rachel Eva 2005 Article incorporation in Mauritian Creole. Department of Linguistics, University of Victoria: MA.
Strawson, Peter Frederick 1950 On referring. *Mind* 59: 320-44.
Szabolcsi, A 1987 Functional categories in the noun phrase. Kenesei, I (ed.) *Approaches to Hungarian*, Szaged: JATE, 167-89.
Virahsawmy, Dev 1977 Lonbraz lavi / Lapo kabri. Retrieved 17 September 2007 from http://pages.intnet.mu/develog/polankporekLONBRAZ.html
—— 2003 Tizistwar 1. Retrieved 15 October 2007 from http://pages.intnet.mu/develog/polankTIZISTWAR1.html
—— 2004 *Aprann lir ek ekrir Morisien*. Rose-Hill, Mauritius: Cygnature Publications.
—— 2007 Trip sere lagorz amare. Retrieved 11 April 2007 from http://pages.intnet.mu/develog/poemtripsere.html
—— [n d] Jamouna-Ganga-Devi. Retrieved 14 September 2007 from http://pages.intnet.mu/develog/polanknovJAMOUNA.html
Von Heusinger, Klaus 2002 Specificity and definiteness in sentence and discourse structure. *Journal of Semantics* 19: 245-74.
Wiredu, Kwasi 2007 Toward decolonizing African philosophy and religion. *African Studies Quarterly: The Online Journal for African Studies* 9. Retrieved 14 September 2007 from http://www.africa.ufl.edu/asq/v1/4/3.htm.

After emigrating from Mauritius to Australia, Diana Guillemin's career alternated between academic publishing and librarianship.
While working at the University of Queensland, she developed an interest in linguistics, and is now in the process of completing her PhD on
The Mauritian Creole Noun Phrase: Its form and function.
d.guillemin@uq.edu.au

The development of the noun phrase in Mauritian Creole and the mechanisms of language development

Anand Syea

Introduction[1]

This article is concerned with three key developments inside the NP in MC: (a) the development of **la** (< Fr *là*) as a marker of definiteness and specificity, (b) the development of **ban** (< Fr *bande*) as a marker of plurality, and (c) the development of a Saxon-type genitive as an alternative to the Romance-type analytic possessive structure.[2] Each of these raises interesting questions from the perspective of Creole genesis, how and why these developments took place. The latter question is particularly pertinent given that neither the marking of definiteness and specificity nor the marking of plurality is a universal requirement. Languages such as Latin, Chinese and most of the Slavic languages have no articles at all, while Japanese, for example, has no plural markers.[3] As far as the development of the alternative possessive construction is concerned, this too is unexpected given that there was already a possessive structure in use. The motivation for these developments then cannot be explained in terms of communicative needs given that some languages do not have these markers. Rather, they must be viewed as being driven by the internal dynamics of an emerging grammatical system. As I will show, *là* developed into a marker of definiteness and specificity through its strong association with the demonstrative **sa** (< Fr '*ce*') in the early stage, while **ban** (< Fr *bande*) became a marker of plurality through changes in its s(emantic)-selection feature requirements. It came to be used with complements that were not only animate but also inanimate. And, finally, the Saxon-type genitive developed as a consequence of a possessive pronoun being used in the analytic possessive structure. The mechanisms that drive these changes, I argue, are precisely those that drive changes in other (i.e. non-Creole) languages, viz degrammaticalization, grammaticalization and independent principles of grammar. What is clear is that these changes may have come about without any particular effort on the part of the makers of MC. The changes, in my view, occurred as a consequence of whatever else was happening in the emerging system.

This article is organised as follows: Section 1 deals with **la**, the exponent of definiteness and specificity; it looks at the semantics and syntax of this word and discusses how it developed from the French enclitic *–là* through its association with the demonstrative **sa** (< Fr *ce*). Section 2 looks at the plural marker **ban** and how it developed from the French partitive noun *bande* (band/group/collection). Its development is linked to the loss of the semantic restriction on its use. Section 3 discusses the Saxon-type genitive construction and how it came about. I suggest that the position of the possessor NP changed as a consequence of the third person possessive pronoun occurring in the analytic possessive structure. Adopting the recent approach to case checking in Chomsky

---

[1] I am grateful to Philip Baker, Diana Guillemin, and Daniel Véronique for their comments on an earlier draft of this article.
[2] 'Saxon genitive' is a traditional term (see Adger 2003: 257).
[3] Japanese has the plural marker '-tati' with animate nouns. But some languages do lack the category number (see Foley 1997:38).

(1995), I suggest that the change in the position of the possessor NP was driven by the need to check its abstract case morphology. Section 4 analyses these developments in the context of the discussion of Creole genesis. Section 5 concludes the discussion.

1. The development of a marker of definiteness and specificity

In this section, I look briefly at the D(eterminer)-system in French before examining the D-system of MC. We will see that the D-system in MC is a much simplified system and I suggest that the simplification (including the loss of the French definite and partitive articles) was possible as a result of the loss of two morphosyntactic features, namely gender and number. I go on to show that the gap created in the system by the loss of the definite articles was subsequently filled by the development of the French enclitic -*là* into a marker of definiteness and specificity.

1.1 The French D-system

The D-system of French includes the following categories: articles (definite, indefinite and partitive; as in (1)-(2)), demonstratives, possessives, and quantifiers (as in (3)-(5), respectively).

(1a) la/une route
'the/a road'

(1b) le/un chemin
'the/a road'

(1c) les/des routes/chemins
'the/some roads'

(2a) de la biere
of the beer
'some beer'

(2b) du vin
of the wine
'some wine'

(3a) cette route
'this/that road'

(3b) ce chemin
'this/that road'

(3c) ces routes/chemins
'these roads'

(4a) ma plume
'my pen'

(4b) mon crayon
'my pencil'

(4c) mes plumes/crayons
'my pens/pencils'

(5a) tout le monde
all the world
'everybody'

(5b) toute la famille
'all the family'

(5c) tous les garcons
'all the boys'

(5d) toutes les filles
'all the girls'

As is clear from these examples, each category within the French D-system has members whose forms vary in terms of two morphosyntactic features namely, gender and number. These variations are displayed in the following table.

Table 1

	Masc.	Fem.	Plural
Articles	le	la	les
	un	une	des
	du	de la	des
Demonstratives	ce	cette	ces
Possessives	mon	ma	mes
	ton	ta	tes
	son	sa	ses
	notre	notre	nos
	votre	votre	vos
	leur	leur	leurs
Quantifiers	tout	toute	tous, toutes

French has a rather elaborate and complex D-system where the surface forms of the determiners encode the morphosyntactic information on the nouns that they occur with.

In other words, the gender and number of the referent denoted by the noun are overtly expressed by the different forms that the determiner displays.

1.2 The D-system of MC

The D-system in MC, as the table below shows, has, surprisingly, retained all the categories that exist in the French D-system even though the class of articles has only the indefinite article.

Table 2

		French D-system	MC D-system[4]
Articles		le, la, les; du, de la, des	Ø
		un, une	en
Demonstratives		ce(t), cette, ces	sa
Possessives		mon, ma, mes	mo
		ton, ta, tes	to
		son, sa, ses	so
		notre, nos	nu
		votre, vos [polite singular]	u
		votre, vos [plural]	zot
		leur(s)	zot
Quantifiers		tout, toute(s), tous	tu

The other important changes are: first, the loss of variant forms of the French determiners. In particular, the feminine and plural forms have disappeared while the masculine forms have been retained although in some cases in slightly altered forms. The French singular masculine possessive pronouns for instance occur in MC without nasalization.[5] The other change is that the French second and third plural possessive pronouns have been replaced by the new form of pronoun **zot** (from French *vous/eux autres*).

The most striking difference between the two D-systems however is the absence of the definite and partitive articles in the MC system. These articles have been lost in two ways: they have either become part of the nominal roots (agglutinated to the roots), as in the words in (6)-(7), or have been barred from occurring with the nouns with which they occur in French, as in the words in (8).

(6)a. **larut/*rut** (la route)   (6b) **lisyeń/*syeń** (le chien)   (6c) **zanimo/*animo** (les animaux)
    'road'   'dog'   'animal'

(7)a. **dilo/*o** (de l'eau)   (7b) **diveń/*veń** (du vin)   (7c) **dilwil/*wil** (de l'huile)
    'water'   'wine'   'oil'

(8)a. **simeń/*lesimeń** (le chemin)   (8b) **sez/*lasez** (la chaise)   (8c) **ańgi/*lańgi** (l'anguille)
    'road'   'chair'   'eel'

Without the French articles, the nouns in (6) and (7) are not well-formed and are not therefore part of the lexicon of MC. On the other hand, the nouns in (8) are ill-formed with the French articles prefixed to them. Note that where these articles do occur prefixed to the nouns, they have become an integral part of the root with no morpheme boundary to separate them from the original root. The agglutinated articles consequently have none

---

[4] MC examples in bold characters are written in the lortograf-linite orthography used in the Baker & Hookomsing dictionary of MC (1987).

[5] The forms that the determiners have derive from the masculine forms of the French determiners, but they do not encode gender. Interestingly, this form happens to be the unmarked form, as evidenced from studies on child language acquisition.

of the semantic functions they have in French and the newly formed nouns function in every respect as bare nouns.

What we then have in MC is a D-system that is comparable to the French system in terms of the range of categories it has but not in the number of determiner forms it allows. The D-system in MC is numerically a much simplified system, with each category containing a single member. This may well reflect an underlying principle governing D-systems in contact languages. An obvious question that arises here is what explains the changes that have resulted in the simplified D-system in MC.

A close examination of the two D-systems suggests that the changes can be seen as a direct consequence of the loss of the two morphosyntactic features, gender and number. Their loss provides a straightforward explanation for the loss of the feminine and plural forms of the determiners. However, as we saw earlier, with the definite and partitive articles, it is not just their feminine and plural forms that have been lost but their masculine forms too. The question then is what explains why the definite and partitive articles lost their masculine forms when the other determiners retained theirs.

1.3 French definite articles as expletive elements

The difference noted here between definite articles and the other members of the D-system, I suggest, can be explained by looking at the nature of the definite articles in French. As is well-known, the semantic function of definite articles is fundamentally to specify the reference of the noun they occur with. However, it has been suggested (see Harris 1978 and Foulet 1958) that the definite articles have in Modern French a semantically weakened specifying function and have as a result become mere grammatical markers of the noun's morphosyntax. In other words, they express the noun's gender and number and no longer have the same strong specifying role that they had in Old French for instance.

Some evidence for this historical change in the function of these articles comes from the observation that they occur in constructions in which they do not appear to have a 'specifying' role, as in the following (from Harris 1978).[6]

(9)a. J'aime les livres
    I love the books
    'I love books'

b. La haine provoque les guerres.
    the hate provoke the wars
    'Hate provokes wars.'

Similarly, the occurrence of the definite articles in (10) below also suggests that they do not have a 'specifying' role.

(10)a. tous les jours
     all the days
     'Everyday'

b. tout le monde
    all the world
    'Everyone'

According to Rickard (1978: 62), an example like (10a) was in Old French 'toz les jorz' and importantly meant 'for the whole of those days' and not 'every day'. The definite article in this phrase clearly had a specifying role. The change in the interpretation of this phrase provides additional evidence of the erosion of the semantic function of the definite articles in French. Foulet (1958: 49) notes that the French definite article has become a purely grammatical marker (of gender and number) that introduces the noun in much the same way that '-er' ending on verbs signals that they are in the infinitive.

If the definite articles in French have a weak semantic function and have become grammatical markers of gender and number, then their loss in MC is not at all unexpected. With a weakened semantic function, which I suggest was further eroded given the context-boundedness of Creoles in the early stages, the definite articles became expletive

---

[6] The use of the definite articles in such possessive structures as *Vas te laver les mains* ('Go wash your hands') also points to the definite articles not having a specifying function.

elements and therefore susceptible to loss, particularly in an emerging contact language where, for communicative reasons, only semantically valued items are useful.

The determiners that survived then did so because they, unlike the definite articles, retained their semantic function, 'specifying' in the case of the demonstrative and possessive pronouns and 'quantifying' in the case of the quantifiers (including perhaps the indefinite article/numeral 'en'). Thus the overall simplification of the D-system can be attributed to the loss of the two morphosyntactic features, gender and number.

The elimination of the French definite articles from the D-system in MC of course meant that there was no longer a way of expressing definiteness and specificity and plurality. As we will see below, MC went on to develop both a marker of definiteness and specificity and a marker of number, thus lexicalising the semantic concepts that that definite articles and plural markers grammaticalize. In what follows, I first look at the development of a marker of definiteness and specificity and then at the development of a marker of plurality.

1.4 Postnominal 'la' as a marker of definiteness and specificity

MC uses the independent postnominal morpheme **la** in order to specify the reference of a noun. Compare (11a) and (11b).

(11)a. liv   la ti lor latab   b. en liv   ti lor latab
        book D   T   on   table   a book T   on   table
        'The book was on the table'   'A book was on the table'

Note that the reference of the noun **liv** in (11a) is satisfied only if a specific book was on the table. By contrast, the reference of the noun **liv** in (11b) is satisfied if any book was on the table. The postnominal **la** then specifies a particular book, one that the hearer/reader must be familiar with.

Some independent evidence for the semantic function of the postnominal **la** as a marker of definiteness and specificity comes from its exclusion from the postverbal position of existential constructions, a position which, according to Milsark (1977), is only available to weak (e.g. indefinite) NPs.

(12)a. ena en zelev daṅ klas   b. *ena zelev la daṅ klas
        be   a   pupil in   classroom   be   pupil D   in   class
        'There is a pupil in the classroom'   'There is the pupil in the classroom'

1.4.1 Distribution of 'la'

As far as the distribution of **la** is concerned, it is unique among members of the D-system in that it alone occurs in a postnominal position. The other members are all prenominal, just like their French counterparts. Another important feature of the distribution of **la** is that it is restricted to the rightmost position inside the noun phrase. In other words, it follows not only the head noun but also all postnominal modifiers, whether they are APs (13a), PPs (13b) or TPs (i.e. clauses (13c)).

(13)a. liv   ruz la   b. liv ar li la   c. liv to ti lir la
        book red D   book with him D   book you T read D
        'The red book'   'The book that is with him'   'The book that you read'

Any attempt at reordering **la** and the postnominal modifiers in these examples results in ill-formed nominal phrases.

(14)a. * liv la ruz   b. * liv la ar li   c. * liv la to ti lir

However, if interpreted as clausal constructions, (14a-c) are grammatical, with **la** postposed to the noun **liv**, and they have the interpretations in (15a-c).

(15)a. The book is red   b. The book is with him   c. The/that book you read

The syntactic restriction on **la** to the rightmost position inside the noun phrase suggests that it, rather than the noun, is the head of the nominal expression. Evidence for the head status of **la** comes from the following considerations.

Nominal expressions like those in (13) can also occur without the noun while still retaining their nominal status. [7]

(16)a. (liv) ruz la   b. (liv) ar li la   c. (liv) to ti lir la
      book red D   book with him D   book you T read D
      'The red book/one'   'The book/one that is with him'   'The book/one you read'

Their nominal character can also be inferred from their distribution. As can be seen in the following examples, they occupy the same syntactic positions that they occupy when the noun is present.

(17)a. (liv) ruz la zoli   b. li ti praṅ (liv) ruz la   c. mo ti met li akote (liv) ruz la
      book red D pretty   he T take book red D   I   T put it beside book red D
      'The red book/one is pretty'   'He took the red book/one'   'I put it beside the red book/one'

Additionally, in (17b,c), the subcategorization requirements on the verb and the preposition are also met. Both require a nominal expression as their complement, and this requirement is satisfied with and without the noun.

Further evidence comes from their ability to undergo clefting and topicalization, processes which, in MC, affect only [-V] categories (i.e. NP and PP).

(18)a. ruz la ki   li ti praṅ   b. ar li   la ki mo ti lir
      red D that he T take   with him D that I   T   read
      'It was the red one that he took'   'It was the one that was with him that I read'

(19)a. ruz la li ti praṅ   b. ar li la mo ti lir
      red D he T take   with him D I   T   read
      'The red one he took'   'The one that was with him I read'

Note that adjectives or adjectival phrases cannot be clefted or topicalized in MC.

(20)a. * byeṅ graṅ (ki) Mari ete   b. *byeṅ move (ki) garsoṅ la ete
         very tall that Mary be   very naughty that boy   D   be

Note also that without **la** and the noun, the constructions in (16)-(19) are all ungrammatical.

(21)a. * ruz/*ar li   zoli   b. *li ti praṅ ruz/ar li   c.* mo ti met li akote ruz/ar   li
        red/with him pretty   he T take red/with him   I   T put it beside red/with him

It is clear from these examples that in the absence of a noun, the presence of **la** is obligatory for the expressions to retain a nominal character and have the distribution of NPs. From this it follows that such expressions must get their nominal status from **la** rather than the noun. In other words, **la** not only specifies the reference of the noun but also gives an expression its nominal character. The role that **la** plays and the distribution it has identify it as the head of the nominal expression. It is the source of both the semantic and distributional properties of the nominal expressions in which it occurs. This clearly makes it a head.

---

[7] (16c) is better as **seki to ti lir la**.

1.5 Development of 'la' as a marker of definiteness and specificity

Historically, the postnominal **la** in MC derives from the French nominal enclitic adverb -*là*, meaning 'there', rather than from the feminine definite article *la* or the independent adverbial locative *là*.[8] Unlike its source however, it does not express proximity but definiteness and specificity. In what follows I will look at how the enclitic -*là* developed into an autonomous morpheme with the function of specifying the reference of the noun to which it is postposed. The question here is, how did **la** come to acquire definiteness and specificity? To answer this question, we need to look at the context in which **la** occurred and how its distribution, status and meaning have changed. I will argue that through its association with **sa** (< Fr *ce(s)*), **la** acquired a 'specifying' role, in ways that are reminiscent of the development of *pas* as a negative marker in French.

1.5.1 'Sa' as the source of definiteness and specificity

The earliest examples of the postnominal **la** show that it occurred in the context of the accompanying prenominal demonstrative **sa** (< Fr *ce(s)*) just as in French. The following are a few of the earliest examples.

(30)a. *ça blanc là li beaucoup malin ...* **(1749)**   b. *Moi voulé baiser ça négresse là* **(1777)**
    D White he much clever   me want kiss D negress
    'This/That White man is very clever ..'   'I want to kiss this/that woman.'

  c. *... moy n'apa été batté ça Blanc là* **(1779)**
     me not T hit D White
     '... I didn't hit this/that White man.'

Although *là* in these examples has the French spelling, it is far from clear whether it has the proximity meaning that the French enclitic -*là* has. It appears that the proximity distinction expressed by the enclitics -*ci* (near) and -*là* (distant) in French did not survive in MC. Not surprisingly then, we find **la** co-existing with the adverb **isi** (here) without giving rise to any form of semantic incompatibility and with the adverb **laba** (there) without creating any redundancy.

(31)a. **sa liv isi la**   b. **sa liv laba la**
    D book here D   D book there D
    'this book here'   'that book there'

We are led to infer from these possibilities that **la** has no proximity meaning, unlike its source, and does not therefore express 'distance'.

Another difference to be noted between **la** and its historical source in the early texts is that, unlike its source, it can also occur independently of the demonstrative, as in the following.

(32)a. *... en montant piti la-ravine là !* **(1818a)**
       while climbing small ravine D   '... while climbing the small ravine'

  b. *mo trouve Marezanne, missie Desfontaines là.* **(1818a)**
     I see Marie-Jeanne mister Desfontaines D   'I saw Mr. Desfontaines' Marie-Jeanne'

  c. *La liberte la n'a pas va vini ...* (Nicolay 1835)
     freedom not FUT come   'That freedom will not come ...'

This represents a second significant development given that the French enclitic -*là* never occurs independently of the demonstrative in standard French, as the following makes clear.

---

[8] Although we cannot completely rule out the locative adverb *là* as the source of **la**, a question does arise as to why the locative adverb would have been preferred to the enclitic –*là*, which after all already occurred postposed to the noun.

(33)a. *(ce) chien-là a mordu mon chat
      D   dog   has bite   my cat   'That dog has bitten my cat'
   b. *(cette) fille –ci s' appelle Marie
      D   girl   REFL call   Mary   'This girl is called Mary'

A third difference between **la** and its historical source is that it has the status of a free standing morpheme as is evidenced from the fact that it does not have to be adjacent to the noun (see (34)). By contrast, *-là* stays suffixed to the noun in French.

(34) ... *cote ça grand pié di-bois piant Aughiste conné là* (**1818a**)
     by D tall   tree   smelly Aughiste know D '... by that tall smelly tree Aughiste knows'

The change in its status (from bound to free morpheme) is clear from the difference in its distribution if we compare (34) with the historical earlier examples in (35).

(35)a. *Li bon, ca bon Die-là qui dans vous paye, hein?* (**1805**)
    He good D god   who in   your country   'Is he good, the god that is in your country?'
   b. *vous per   ca bon Die là qui mauvais?* (**1805**)
     you afraid D god   who bad   'Are you afraid of the god that is bad?'

Whereas *là* stays postposed to the noun and therefore precedes the relative clause in (35), it is postposed to the relative clause in (34).

Together, these changes in the semantics and syntax of **la** in MC suggest that, although derived from the French enclitic *-là*, it has over time acquired a different status with a different meaning. It functions as a free morpheme and, as argued earlier, as the head of the nominal expression. The meaning it expresses is definiteness and specificity rather than proximity.

The question that remains to be answered is, how do we explain the changes in the meaning and distribution of **la**? As far as the change in meaning is concerned, it can be explained in the following way. The proximity meaning of the French *-là* was lost because the opposition between *-là* and *-ci* did not survive in MC. One reason why this opposition was lost is because it was not particularly communicatively useful in the early stages given the context-boundedness nature of the emerging language. At the same time, the acquisition of corresponding adverbs **laba** (there) and **isi** (here) may have made the opposition expressed by *-là* and *-ci* redundant.

It is important to note that the demonstrative **sa**, like its antecedent *ce(s)*, had no deictic meaning either even though it is classed as a demonstrative. The French demonstrative, as Harris (1978) argues, had long since lost its deictic meaning (which used to be expressed in Old French by *cest* (this) and *cel* (that)).[9] Any deictic meaning it expresses comes from the enclitics *-là* and *-ci*, which came into greater use once *cest* and *cel* coalesced as *ce* in Middle French. Now, although the demonstrative lost its deictic meaning, it retained and continues to have a specifying function. And it is this specifying function that **la** acquired through its early association with **sa**. It is tempting to draw a parallel here with the development of the negative marker *pas* in French. As has been shown (see Price 1969, Harris 1978), *pas* initially had a positive meaning and was used in Old French as a reinforcer of *ne*, then the only marker of negation. It is suggested that through frequent association with *ne*, *pas* came to shed its positive meaning and acquired its negative meaning. Not only that, once *pas* had replaced its positive meaning by the negative meaning associated with *ne*, it supplanted *ne* as the main marker of negation, as is evidenced by its optionality in popular spoken French. In fact, *ne* by itself can no longer express negation while *pas* can, as shown by the contrast between (35a) and (35b).

---

[9] The development of the 'démonstratif neutre' (neutral demonstrative) is seen as a consequence of the loss of the deictic meaning expressed by the demonstratives. But it retains a specifying role.

(36)a. *Elle ne fume.
      She   smoke
      'She doesn't smoke.'

b. Elle fume pas
   She smoke not
   'She doesn't smoke.'

A similar developmental pattern can be proposed for **la**. Thus having lost its proximity function, it acquired its specificity function through its constant association with the demonstrative **sa**. As a result, **sa** became redundant, hence optional. Interestingly, like *ne*, **sa** too has lost its original meaning or function and has become dependent on the new marker of 'specificity', as shown by the ungrammaticality of (37c).

(37)a. sa seval la ti tombe
     D horse D T fall
     'This/that horse fell.'

b. seval la ti tombe
   horse D T fall
   'This/that horse fell.'

c. * sa seval ti tombe
    D horse T fall

The parallel with the historical development of the French negative marker *pas* is therefore quite striking. In both cases, once the meaning/function has been transferred from the original exponent to the new one, the original then becomes redundant (almost an expletive), optional and crucially dependent on the new one. As is the case with the development of negation in French, the development of definiteness and specificity fits in well with what is known as Jespersen's cycle (see Jespersen 1917). The only difference is that whereas the development of *pas* as a negative marker is a case of grammaticalization, the development of *-là* as a marker of definiteness and specificity is a case of degrammaticalization, a potential problem for the unidirectionality hypothesis of Hopper & Traugott (1993).

As I have shown, the development of *la* as a marker of definiteness and specificity can be explained by linking it to the demonstrative, with which it co-existed in the early stages of the development of MC. The pattern of change seems to parallel that we find with the development of the negative marker *pas* in French. To that extent, this particular aspect of the development of the noun phrase is not unique and not restricted to Creole genesis.

2. Development of the plural marker 'ban'

2.1 Some basic facts about 'ban'

The plural of nouns is marked in MC by placing the free standing particle **ban** in front of the noun or in front of the noun and its modifier, as in the following.

(38)a. sa ban liv la
     D PLU book D
     'These/those books'

b. sa liv la
   D book D
   'This/That book'

(39)a. sa ban vye liv la
     D PLU old book D
     'These old books'

b. sa vye liv la
   D old book D
   'This old book'

The meaning difference between the (a) and (b) examples is readily attributable to the presence and absence of **ban**. Where it is present, the noun phrase has a plural interpretation.

The plural meaning that **ban** encodes is also clear from the agreement facts in the following.

(41)a. travayer la pe pini so/*zot lekor
     worker   D ASP punish his/their body
     'The worker is punishing himself'

b. ban travayer la pe pini   *so/zot lekor
   PLU worker   D ASP punish his/their body
   'The workers are punishing themselves'

(42)a. zelev la so/*zot mama fin vini
     pupil D his/their mother ASP come
     'The pupil's mother has come'

b. ban zelev la *so/zot   mama fin vini
   PLU pupil D his/their mother ASP come
   'The pupils' mothers/mother have/has come'

The string **pini so/zot lekor** is an idiomatic expression meaning 'to make oneself suffer' and the possessive pronoun in this string has to agree with the subject of the clause in number, as shown by the contrast in pronoun forms in (41). Likewise, the pronoun in the possessive expression in (42) shows number agreement with the possessor noun phrase (more on this later).

2.2 Distribution of the plural marker 'ban'

Not surprisingly, as a plural marker, **ban** occurs with common countable nouns.

(43)a. **ban liv/loto**   b. * **ban dilo/disab**
   PLU book/car   PLU water/sand
   'Books/Cars'

However, it is not restricted to such nouns. It can also occur with proper nouns (names of people and places) as in the following.

(44)a. **ban Zan pe rañz zot lakaz**
   PLU John ASP build their house   'John and his family are building their house'

   b. **ban Franse kontañ bwar diveñ**
   PLU French like drink wine   'The French like drinking wine'

   c. **ban Rose Hill fin perdi**
   PLU Rose Hill ASP lost   'The team from Rose Hill has lost'

The plural meaning of the subject NPs in (44) (where the heads are proper nouns) is again clear from the agreement facts in (45).

(45)a. **Zañ$_i$ pe rañz so$_{i/j}$ lakaz**   b. **ban Zañ$_i$ pe rañz zot/*so$_i$ lakaz**
   John ASP build his house   PLU John ASP build their/his house
   'John is building his house'   'John and his family are building their house'

Clearly, the presence of **ban** in (45b) rules out singular agreement.

As we saw earlier, the plural marker **ban** can also occur with the postnominal determiner **la** even though the head noun is absent. Consider (46a) and (46b).

(46)a. **ban zañfañ la move**   b. **ban la move**
   PLU child   D naughty   PLU D naughty
   'The children are naughty'   'They are naughty'

It might be argued here that since **la** is a determiner, **ban** may be functioning as a noun rather than a plural marker. This objection is pertinent given that **ban** (as we will see below) functions not only as a plural marker but also as a noun, as in the following.

(47)a. **mo ban   fin perdi**   b. **sak ban   bizeñ amen so bul**
   my team/group ASP lost   each team/group must bring its ball
   'My team/group has lost'   'Each team/group must bring their ball'

In these, **ban** co-exists with a prenominal determiner (possessive pronoun in (47a) and a quantifier in (47b)) and together they occupy a nominal (i.e. subject) position.

However, there is some evidence that suggests that when **ban** occurs with **la**, as in (46b), it functions not as a noun but as a plural marker. The evidence comes from the position that prenominal adjectives occupy in relation to **ban** in such examples. Adjectives such as **zoli** (beautiful) and **tipti** (small) for instance are in the unmarked cases restricted to prenominal position, as shown in the following.

(48)a. **ena buku zoli   lakaz   laba** (* **ena buku lakaz zoli laba**)
   have many beautiful house there   'There are many beautiful houses there'

b. buku grañ lakaz fin kase   dañ siklon (* buku lakaz grañ fin kase dañ siklon)
   many big   house ASP damaged in cyclone
                                             'Many big houses have been damaged in the cyclone'

(48a,b) are ungrammatical if the adjectives are placed after the noun **lakaz**. However, both these adjectives, which are characteristically prenominal, can follow **ban**, as shown in (49).

(49)a. **ban zoli**   **la fin kase**   b. **ban grañ la fin kase**
       ?   beautiful D ASP damaged   ? big   D ASP damaged
       'The beautiful ones have been damaged'   'The big ones have been damaged'

I take this to suggest that **ban** cannot be a noun in these examples. Instead it behaves as a plural marker, these (noun and number) being the only two categories to which it can be assigned.

Further evidence for treating **ban** in (49) as a plural marker and the adjectives that follow it as prenominal adjectives (with a following phonologically null nominal head; see below) comes from the contrast in the distribution of the different forms (contracted and non-contracted) of the adjective **piti** (small).

(50)a. **ban piti / ti lakaz la fin kase**   b. * **ban lakaz piti/ti la fin kase**
       PLU small   house D ASP damaged   PLU house small   D ASP damaged
       'The small houses have been damaged'

Neither the full form nor the contracted form of the adjective can occur postnominally, as shown in (50b). Now consider the contrast between (51a) and (51b).

(51)a. **ban piti   la fin kase**   b.* **ban ti   la fin kase**
       PLU small D has damaged   PLU small D ASP damaged
       'The small ones have been damaged.'

If we take **ban** to be a noun in (51), the contrast between (50b) and (51a) becomes mysterious. Likewise, the contrast between (51a) and (51b) does not make sense. Taking **ban** to be a plural marker on the other hand does not give rise to these problems. The adjective, we assume, precedes a phonologically null head noun, as shown in (52).

(52) [ban piti/ti [Ø] la]
                      N

The impossibility of (51b), with the contracted form, follows not from the categorial status of **ban** but from a constraint on Contraction in the context of a following empty element, which applies in both MC and English, as the contrast between (53a) and (53b) shows.

(53)a. I don't remember where the station is.   b. * I don't remember where the station's.

Constructions like (53) are assumed to have a representation like (54) where a wh-trace is linked to the moved Wh-phrase (Chomsky 1977). Crucially, the copula verb in (53) is immediately next to the Wh-trace (a phonologically null element).

(54) I don't remember [where$_i$ the station is t$_i$]

The contrast between (53a) and (53b), as the contrast between (51a) and (51b), then suggests that the contraction of the copula or the adjective (in our case) is sensitive to the form of the constituent that follows them, whether it is overt or null.

So, although **ban** can function as a noun, the evidence we have suggests that in an example like (46b), where it is followed by the determiner **la**, it functions as a plural marker, encoding the plurality of a phonologically null head noun.

It is also worth pointing out that **ban** also occurs in noun phrases with a range of prenominal determiners including the indefinite article **en** (a/an), quantifiers such as **tu** (all) and possessive pronouns but, interestingly, not with numerals.

(55) a. **en ban liv** b. **tu ban liv** c. **mo ban liv** d. * **de ban liv**
  D PLU book   D PLU book   my PLU book   two PLU book
  'many/a lot of books' 'all books'   'my books'   'two books'

Note here that (55d) is ungrammatical only if we interpret **ban** as a plural marker. If interpreted as a noun, in which case (55d) would translate as 'two lots of books', the phrase is well-formed (although marginally). It is better where the noun refers to people, as in the following.

(56) a. **de ban travayer**   b. **kat ban zwer**
    two band worker   four band player
    'two bands/teams of workers'   'four bands/teams of players'

The impossibility of (55d) suggests that numerals and the plural marker **ban** occupy the same position and are therefore mutually exclusive. Assuming that cardinal numbers head their own projection (i.e. NumP), we could take **ban** to belong to the category Number and to head a NumP, as shown in (57).

(57)

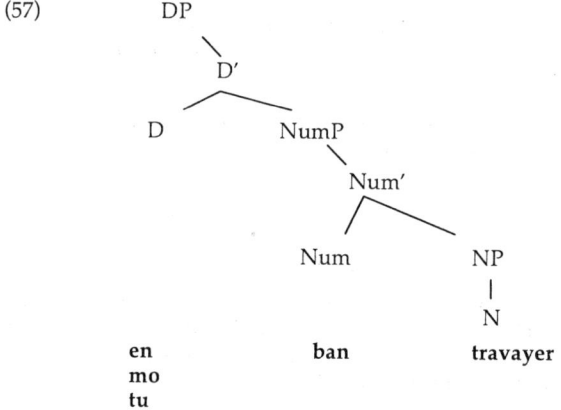

How then do we explain those cases where numerals and **ban** co-occur? In such cases, **ban** functions as a partitive noun and the structure we would assign to (56a) for instance would be (58).

(58)

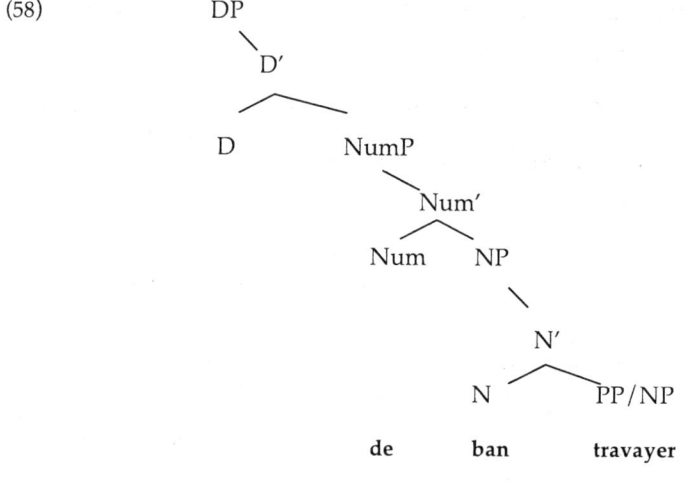

104

The determiner in this case is phonologically null, but the structure predicts cases such as those in (59) where the determiner is overt.

(59)a. sa de ban travayer la
    D two team worker D
    'those two teams of workers'

b. mo de ban travayer
    my two team worker
    'my two teams of workers'

Example (55a) is also interesting because the categorization of **ban** (whether it is a plural marker or a noun) depends on how **en** is interpreted. If it is interpreted as a numeral (one), then **ban** will of course function as a noun. If, on the other hand, it is interpreted as an indefinite article, then **ban** functions as a plural marker. An example like (60) can thus be read either as 'many/lots of workers' or 'one group/team of workers'.[10]

(60) **en ban travayer**
    a. a lot/many workers ('ban' is stressed)
    b. a team/group of workers ('en' is stressed)

On the first reading, **ban** has a non-partitive reading; on the second, it has a partitive reading and is therefore a partitive noun (just like 'bunch', 'load', etc,). The semantic difference can be structurally represented as in (61a) and (61b).

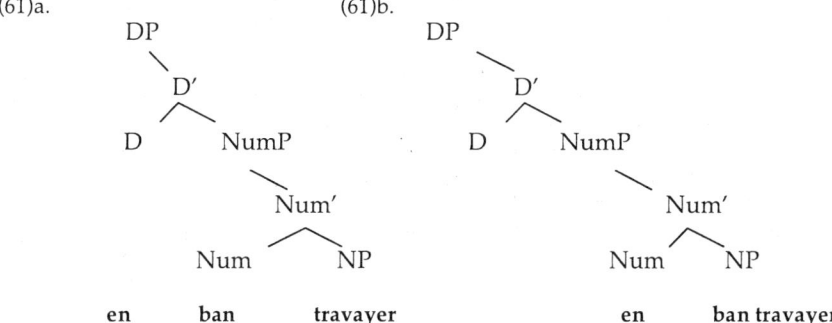

2.3 Development of 'ban' into a plural marker

Plurality in French is expressed by the articles *les* (definite) and *des* (indefinite). With the loss of these articles, MC had no way of expressing plurality until the French noun *bande* (group/bunch/company) began to be used as a plural marker.

The French etymon *bande* is of Middle French origin and is a partitive noun which selects a PP complement. Indeed the first occurrence of this word in MC is in the context of an immediately following PP.

(62) *la bande de son jensse* (Lambert 1828)
    group of his people   'a group of his people'

Subsequent examples show *bande* occurring either on its own (i.e. independently of its complement) or with a preposition-less complement.

(63)a. *et toi sivre la bande comment toujours* (1839d)
    and you follow D group as always   'and you follow the group as always'
   b. *enne gran bande apré casse maille* (1850)
    a large group ASP pick corn   'a large group was picking corn'

---

[10] The ambiguity does not arise in spoken MC given the role that stress plays (see (60)).

    c. *enne lotre bande noirs apré coupe canne* **(1850)**
       a   other group black ASP cut   cane   'another group of slaves was cutting sugar canes'

    d. *coman voar ça ban   dimoune là, ...*   (Anderson 1885)
       as   see D group people D   'on seeing these people, ...'

An interesting observation concerning the use of *bande/band/ban(ne)* is that in the early examples it occurs strictly with animate human nouns such as *jensse* (people), 'noirs' (slaves) and *dimune* (people) as in the examples above. Later examples (particularly those that are attested from 1885 onwards) show however that this partitive noun also occurs with non-human animate nouns as in (64) and inanimate nouns (both concrete and abstract) as in (65).

(64)a. *ein band' p'tits miletons*   (Lolliot 1855)
     a shoal little mullet   'a group of little mullets'
   b. *coman mouton dan milié éne band loulou*   (Anderson 1885)
     like   sheep in middle a   band wolf 'just like a sheep in the midst of a pack of wolves'

(65)a. *ça bande larzent là*   (Baissac 1888)
     D pile   money D   'this pile of money'
   b. *ça bande   lamisière qui li fine passé*   (Baissac 1888)
     D amount misery that he ASP pass   'All the suffering that he endured'

What these examples show is that the word *bande*, which in French selects animate complements as in 'une bande de voleurs' (a gang of thieves), 'une bande de pirates'(a band of pirates) and 'une bande d'oiseaux' (a flock of birds), was initially used with animate complements only, but it later came to be used with inanimate complements as well, as in (65). In other words, what we find here is an extension of the use of this partitive/quantifying noun (meaning 'a lot') to contexts in which it does not occur in French (i.e. with inanimate complements). This means that the semantic restrictions on *bande* were lifted and this enabled it to occur with inanimate complements, as in these examples.

(66)a. *donne li éne bande mauvés conseils* (Baissac 1888)
     give him a   lot   bad   advice   'gave him a lot of bad advice'
   b. *éne bande pitit   cimins*   (Baissac 1888)
     a   lot   narrow road   'many narrow roads'
   c. *ça bande léplats qui làhaut latabe*   (Baissac 1888)
     D lot   dishes that on   table   'those dishes that are on the table'

The change, I suggest, is a reflection of a change in its categorial status. The word *bande* now belongs to the functional category Number and encodes plurality.

Importantly, the categorial change that the French word *bande* underwent in MC fits in well with the traditional idea of grammaticalization, as a process whereby a lexical element becomes a grammatical element (Meillet 1921, Heine, Claudi & Hünnemeyer 1991) or a more independent element becomes less independent (Hopper & Traugott 1993). The change, as far as one can tell from the available historical texts, appears to have been gradual (and therefore a late development (Baker 1994)) and, unlike the development of the enclitic -*là* into a marker of definiteness and specificity, it lends strong support to the central idea of unidirectionality in the theory of grammaticalization, whereby a less grammatical item becomes more grammatical but not vice versa.

It is also worth noting that the categorial change also triggered a structural change in that the complement of *bande/band/ban(ne)* is no longer a PP but an NP. The reanalysis is illustrated in (67).

(67) DP => DP
      /\   /\
     D'   D'
    /\   /\
   D NP   D NumP
       \   \
        N'   Num'
       /\   /\
      N PP   Num NP

   une bande de voleurs   en ban voler
   labande de son jensse

3. Synthetic genitives

In this section I will look at the development of Saxon-type genitives. This is an unexpected development which suggests substrate influence (see Corne 1986, Baissac 1880). But as I argue here (but see Syea 1994 as well) this might have been the result of language-internal changes, but possibly reinforced by convergence.

3.1 Some data

MC, unlike French, has not only the French analytic possessive construction but also a type of possessive construction that closely resembles English Saxon genitives (e.g. John's book). In Syea (1994, 1995) I referred to this latter type as synthetic genitives (in contrast to the analytic possessive structure we find in French). The following illustrates these two types of genitive construction in MC.

(68) a. **liv   Zañ**   b. le livre de Jean
        book John   D book of John
        'John's book'   'John's book'

(69) a. **Zañ so liv**   b. * Jean son livre
        John his book   John his book
        'John's book'

The analytic type (68a) retains the surface word order of the French genitive construction (68b) but importantly lacks the functional words (i.e. the definite article and the preposition). The synthetic type (69a) by contrast has no parallel in French. It is closer at the surface to the English possessive except for the possessive pronoun that separates the two NPs. English possessives have a cliticized possessive marker instead of a possessive pronoun.

3.2 Properties and structure of synthetic genitives

The synthetic genitive construction in MC, like English Saxon genitives, has three basic constituents: the possessor NP (henceforth NP1) followed by the possessive pronoun (POSS) which in turn is followed by the possessee NP (henceforth NP2). This ordering is strict and any deviations result in ungrammatical structures.

Unlike the possessive marker in English genitives (i.e. the apostrophe –s), the free standing possessive pronoun that intervenes between the two NPs in MC is closer structurally to NP2 than to NP1. This is suggested by the fact that the string POSS and NP2 can be coordinated while NP1 and POSS can't.

(70) a. **Zañ so ser e so mama ti vini**   b. * **Zañ so e Mari so mama ti vini**
        John his sister and his mother T come   John his and Mary her mother T come
        'John's sister and his mother came'   'John's and Mary's mother came'

As the English translation of (70b) shows, coordinating NP1 and POSS is grammatical in English. This suggests that POSS is closer to NP1 in English and together they form a phonological/rhythmical unit.

Further evidence that POSS and NP1 do not form a constituent in MC, while they do in English (at least phonologically), comes from the following sentence-fragment examples.

(71)a. Whose mother came?   John's; John's mother

   b. **Kisenla so mama ti vini?**   *Zaṅ so; (Zaṅ) so mama.
      who   his mother T come   John his; John his mother
      'Whose mother came?'

The impossibility of **Zaṅ so** as a response to the question in (71b) and the failure of coordination shown in (70b) suggest that NP1 and POSS do not form a constituent in MC.

Another property of synthetic genitives in MC is that, just like in English genitives, NP1 can itself contain a complex genitive phrase. In fact what we find is embedded or recursive genitive phrases, as in the following.

(72)a. **Zaṅ so mama so ser so kamarad so   zaṅfaṅ**
      John his mother her sister her friend   his/her child   'John's mother's sister's friend's child'

   b. **Zaṅ so loto so laport**
      John his car its door   'John's car's door'

Note that in such constructions, each POSS morpheme takes its reference from the NP immediately to its left (i.e. the head of the possessor NP) and whether POSS should be translated (in English) as 'his', 'her' or 'its' depends on the contextually determined gender marking of the head of this NP.

Interestingly, NP1 can also be complex by virtue of modification of the head of the possessor phrase. It can for instance be relativized as shown in the following.

(73)a. **garsoṅ ki ti vini la so ser**   b. **liv ki to ti praṅ la so kuvertir**
      boy   who T come D his sister   book that you T take D its cover
      'The boy who came's sister'   'The book that you took's cover'

A third property that synthetic genitives in MC have is that NP1 can be not only definite as in the above examples, but also indefinite and generic

(74)a. **en garsoṅ so liv   lor latab**
      a   boy   his book on table   'A boy's book is on the table'

   b. **person so kamarad pa ti vini**
      no one   his friend   not T come   'Nobody's friend came'

   c. **lelefaṅ   so lake long**
      elephant its tail long   'An elephant's tail is long'

A fourth, and important, property of MC genitives is that POSS and NP1 must agree in number, as shown in the following.

(75)a. **tifi la so mama ti al bazar**   b. **ban tifi la *so/zot   mama ti al bazar**
      girl   D her mother T go market   PL   girl D her/their mother T go market
      'The girl's mother went to the market'   'The girls' mother went to the market'

The POSS pronoun, as we see in (75b), must be plural when the possessor NP (i.e. NP1) is plural.

As for the structure of synthetic genitives, I propose that POSS is the head of these constructions and, being a determiner, projects a DP, just like POSS in English and other languages. The specifier of this DP is NP1 while the complement is NP2, as shown in (76).

(76)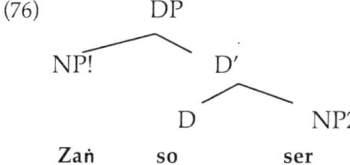

This structure for the synthetic genitives in MC appears to be both intuitively and empirically justified.

3.3 Development of synthetic genitives in MC

MC is not alone among Creole languages in having synthetic type genitive construction, as is clear from the following brief survey.[11]

(77) a. die kind se   trui   (Afrikaans)
       the child POSS jersey 'the child's jersey'

   b. Jan shi boek (Negerhollands)
      John his book 'John's book'

   c. ti   garson so pje   (Louisiana)
      little boy   his foot 'the little boy's feet'

   d. mo pitxit so fwa   (Karipuna)
      my child his liver 'my child's liver'

   e. Sami fi jerma   (Berbice Dutch)
      Sammy his wife   'Sammy's wife'

   f. mi tata   su buki   (Papiamentu)
      my father his book 'my father's book'

How this type of genitive constructions has ended up in French Creoles such as MC, Louisiana Creole and Karipuna for instance is an interesting question. Clearly, it is not derived from French (standard or regional or popular) and so must be attributed to either a substrate or universalist source. Corne (1986) and Baissac (1880) before him attributes this type of genitive to the Indic languages (in particular Bhojpuri and Hindi) of the Indian immigrants, which have exactly the structure that the synthetic genitives in MC have.

(78) a. ap-ki patni ki   sthiti (Hindi; Corne 1986)
        your wife her health 'Your wife's health'

   b. tor burhia ke hal   (Bhojpuri; Corne 1986)
      your wife   her health 'Your wife's health'

The Hindi and Bhojpuri genitives, like those in MC, have three constituents: the possessor NP followed by POSS, which in turn is followed by the possessee NP. So a substrate claim may be said to have some plausibility. Also, the first example of synthetic genitives appears in a text from 1867, three decades after the first Indian immigrants arrived in Mauritius.

(79) *grand Misie   son causé*   (Descroizilles 1867)
      big   master his words   'the chief's words'

This sequence of events could be seen to lend some credibility to the proposals of both Baissac and Corne that genitives of this type owe their existence in MC to the Indian languages. However, as I observed in Syea (1994), the same text also has examples of a type of genitive construction that subsequently became obsolete.

(80) a. *dans son lamain Governement*   (Descroizilles 1867)
        in   its hand   government   'in the hand of the government'

   b. *son lipie Nicolas*   (Descroizilles 1867)
      his foot Nicholas   'Nicholas's feet'

Similar examples also occur later in Baissac (1888):

---

[11] The Afrikaans example is from Taylor (2000); the other five are all from Holm (1988-89).

(81) a. so kat laru en kales   (Baissac 1888)
       its four wheels a carriage   'a carriage's four wheels'
    b. son fils leroi   (Baissac 1888)
       his son king   'The king's son'

It seems then that in the second half of the 19th century three different types of genitive construction were in use: the analytic, the synthetic and a third type that I refer to as the 'mixed' type in Syea (1994). Close examination of the third type shows that it shares properties of both the analytic and the synthetic. The possessor NP (for example *leroi* in (81b)) is on the right of the possessee NP *fils*, just like in the analytic structures, while the possessive morpheme POSS is to the left of the possessee NP, just as in synthetic genitives.

These 'mixed' genitives have no substrate basis and their occurrence only makes sense if we link them to synthetic genitives and look upon them as an intermediate stage in the development of synthetic genitives. Of course, if the presence of synthetic genitives were attributed to a substrate source, the existence of the 'mixed' genitives would remain inexplicable. This, together with the fact that other French Creoles with no access to an Indian substrate (e.g. Louisiana Creole) or African substrate (e.g. Karipuna) also have synthetic genitives, casts doubts on Corne's proposal that the synthetic genitives in MC had their origin in Hindi and Bhojpuri. However, it is conceivable that the development of the synthetic type was reinforced by the fact that an increasingly large group of speakers had a similar structure in their native languages. There is nothing to rule out the possibility of these two structures converging in order to produce synthetic genitives.

From a syntactic point of view, the mixed genitives could be argued to have been instrumental in the development of synthetic genitives. The presence of the POSS morpheme (which we could interpret as the realization of overt genitive case marking on the left of the possessee) means that the only way the possessor NP could have had its abstract genitive case checked was by raising to the spec of DP position where in a spec-head relation with POSS its case gets checked.[12] From this perspective, synthetic genitives can be treated as an independently motivated innovation.

4. Discussion

In the context of the discussion of Creole evolution, the three developments in the nominal phrase in MC raise interesting questions. One of these is this: what do they tell us about how Creoles develop? All three developments, as they are described here, suggest that they were gradual and may have been linked to other internal changes. The French enclitic -*là* lost its proximity meaning but survived because of its association with the demonstrative **sa**, from which it acquired its specifying function (and therefore its definiteness and specificity meaning). As pointed out earlier, there is a strong parallel here with the development of *pas* which, through its association with *ne*, became the new marker of negation in French. It is also clear from our discussion that the French enclitic was degrammaticalized, a process that is rather surprising in Creole development where the direction is, as generally assumed, from independent, less grammatical, lexical items to dependent, more grammatical and functional items. The general assumption that Creoles develop from pidgins predicts precisely this developmental path, and yet what we find in the case of the development of **la** as a marker of definiteness and specificity is just the reverse. This surprising development is at odds with all theories of Creole development with perhaps the exception of the superstratist theory (Chaudenson 1992). Here the development of the French enclitic into a free morpheme encoding definiteness and specificity is something that is expected as a further development from one language to its vernaculars.

---

[12] Given that the possessor NP occupies a spec position, I would suggest that the whole NP (a maximal projection) rather than an N moves to spec.

The development of French *bande* into a marker of plurality in MC is one that poses the least problem. It represents a good example of grammaticalization, where a lexical item becomes over time a grammatical item. Such a development is consistent with several of the theories of Creole genesis (for instance, the superstratist (Chaudenson 1992), the universalist (Bickerton 1981) and creativist (Baker 1994). However, it is also a type of change that affects not just Creoles but other natural languages as well.

The third and final development discussed here is one that cannot be accounted for particularly by the superstratist theory or the creativist theory. A convergent approach (as discussed in Bynon (1996) goes some way towards providing an explanation for the emergence of synthetic genitives in MC but it is equally explicable in terms of language internal developments.

5. Summary and conclusion

In this article I have discussed three key developments in the NP in MC. The development of a marker of definiteness and specificity, the development of a marker of plurality (number) and the development of a synthetic structure for expressing possession. These three developments together make the NP in MC significantly different from the NP of French. Definiteness, plurality and possession are expressed in different ways in MC. Interestingly, none of these developments can be said to have been triggered by the communicative needs of the makers of MC. Rather, they are developments that are driven by some of the mechanisms of language change (e.g. degrammaticalization, grammaticalization, etc.) that operate in other languages, not just Creoles.

References

Adger, David 2003 *Core Syntax*. Oxford: Oxford University Press.
Anderson, Samuel 1885 *L'Evangil sélon S Matthié (dan langaz créol Maurice)*. London: British and Foreign Bible Society.
Baker, Philip 1994 Creativity in creole genesis. Adone, Dany & Plag, Ingo (eds) *Creolization and language change*, Tübingen: Niemeyer, 65-84.
——— 2000 Theories of creolization and the degree and nature of restructuring. Neumann-Holzschuh, Ingrid & Schneider, Edgar (eds) *Degrees of restructuring in creole languages*. Amsterdam: Benjamins, 41-63.
Baker, Philip & Syea, Anand (eds) 1996 *Changing meanings, changing functions*. London: University of Westminster Press.
Baissac, Charles 1880 *Etude sur le patois créole mauricien*. Nancy: Imprimerie Berger-Levrault.
——— 1888 *Le folklore de l'île Maurice*. Paris: Maisonneuve & Larose.
Bickerton, Derek 1981 *Roots of language*. Ann Arbor: Karoma.
Bollée, Annegret 2004 Le développement du démonstratif dans les créoles de l'Océan Indien. http://www.creolica.net/article.php3?id_article=34.
Bynon, Thea 1996 Convergent change: some recent rethinking. Baker & Syea (eds), 47-52.
Chaudenson, Robert 1981 *Textes créoles anciens (La Réunion et Ile Maurice)*, Hamburg: Buske.
——— 1992 *Des îles, des hommes, des langues :essais sur la créolisation linguistique et culturelle*. Paris: L'Harmattan.
Chomsky, Noam 1995 *The minimalist program*. Cambridge, Mass.: MIT Press.
——— 1997 On Wh-movement. Culicover, P, Wasow, T & Akmajian, A (eds) *Formal Syntax*, New York: Academic Press, 71-132.
Chrestien, François 1831 *Les Essais d'un bobre Africain*. Port Louis: Déroullède.

Corne, Chris 1986 Possessive indexing, inalienable possession, and the Mauritian Creole genitive. *Te Reo* 29: 159-73.

Descroizilles, H C 1867 *Navire fin engazé : The «Mauritius» in danger*. Port Louis: Dupuy & Dubois.

Foley, William 1997 *Anthropological Linguistics*. Oxford: Blackwell.

Foulet, L 1958 *Petite syntaxe de l'ancien français*. Paris: Champion.

Freycinet, Louis C D de 1827 *Voyage autour du monde ...*, Paris: Pillet âiné, vol. 2(2).

Harris, Martin 1978 *The evolution of the French Language*. London: Longman

Heine, B, Claudi, U & Hünnemeyer, F 1991 *Grammaticalization: A conceptual framework*. Chicago: University of Chicago Press.

Holm, John 1988-89 *Pidgins and Creoles*. Cambridge: Cambridge University Press, 2 vols.

Hopper, Paul & Traugott, Elizabeth 1993 *Grammaticalization*. Cambridge: Cambridge University Press.

Jespersen, Otto 1917 *Negation in English and other languages*. Historisk-filologiske Meddeleser 1.

Lambert, Richard [1828] 1888-92 Catéchisme en créole de l'île Maurice en 1828. *Bulletin de la Société de Linguistique de Paris* 7: 122-32.

Lolliot, Pierre 1855 *Poésies créoles*. Port Louis : Imprimerie du Mauricien..

Meillet, Antoine 1921 *Linguistique historique et linguistique générale*. Paris: Champion.

Milsark, G L 1977 Toward an explanation of certain peculiarities in the existential construction. *Linguistic Analysis* 3: 1-29.

Nicolay, William 1835 Proclamation. Pour noirs esclaves dans Maurice. *Recueil des lois, ordonnances, proclamations, notes et avis du gouvernement publiés à l'Ile Maurice pendant l'année 1835*. Port Louis.

Philippi, Julia 1997 The rise of the article in the Germanic languages. van Kemenade, A & Vincent, N (eds) *Parameters of morphosyntactic change*. Cambridge: Cambridge University Press, 62-93.

Pitot, Thomy 1805 Quelques observations sur l'ouvrage intitulé Voyage à l'Ile de France par un officier du Roi. *Revue historique et littéraire de l'Ile Maurice* 2: 372-74.

Price, Glanvill 1969 La transformation du système français des demonstratifs. *Zeitschrift für Romanische Philologie* 85: 489-505.

Rickard, Peter 1974 *A history of the French language*. London: Hutchinson.

Syea, Anand 1994 The development of genitives in Mauritian Creole. Adone, D & Plag, I (eds) *Creolization and Language Change*. Tubingen: Niemeyer, 85-97.

—— 1995 Synthetic genitives in Mauritian Creole: Indo-Aryan influence or local innovation? Baker, Philip (ed.) *From contact to creole and beyond*. London: University of Westminster Press, 177-88.

—— 1996 The development of a marker of definiteness in Mauritian Creole. Baker & Syea (eds), 171-86.

Taylor, John 2000 *Possessives in English*. Oxford: Oxford University Press.

Anand Syea is Senior Lecturer in Linguistics in
the Department of English and Linguistics at the University of Westminster.
<syeaa@westminster.ac.uk>

Conjunction and ditransitives: Some functional domains covered by *avec, et,* and *ensemble*

Sibylle Kriegel
Susanne Michaelis[1]

1 Introduction

In Mauritian Creole (MC) the relators derived from the French lexemes *avec, et,* and *ensemble* cover a huge semantic area, partly overlap in use, and do not have the same distribution as in French (see Baker 1996 and Chaudenson 1974). In this paper, we will retrace their evolution drawing on the corpus of old texts[2] collected for this volume as well as on our own corpus of modern MC.[3]

Our approach will be functional, but given the confusing formal variation, we will start with an inventory of forms (see Baker 1996 for a detailed overview). Then, we will look more closely at the semantic relations which these forms express by introducing typological distinctions that go beyond the simple classical categorization as preposition or as conjunction.

Baker (1996: 50) gives a systematic table of the occurrence of these items in diachrony. The full form *avec*, as well as the forms *et* and *ensemble* in different spellings, are attested from 1818 (**1818a, 1818b**). From 1850 onwards, we find, alongside *avec*, the abbreviated form *av(e)*; *ec(que)* is attested from 1880, *ar(e)* from 1929.

In modern MC, we find the forms *avek, ek* and *ar* as well as *ansam* in different spellings and also the form *e*.

Table 1: Diachrony and synchrony of *avec, et,* and *ensemble*

diachrony (until 1929)	synchrony
avec (>1818)	*avek*
av(e) (>1850)	
ar(e) (>1929)	*ar*
ecque (>1880)	*ek*
ensemb(l)e (>1818)	*ansam*
et (>1818)	*e*

On the formal level, the main difference between modern and older varieties lies in the fact that the latter contain occurrences of a form written *av* or *ave*, very widely attested in

---

[1] The present study was carried out within the German-French PROCOPE program ("The evolution of Romance-based creole languages in language contact: syntactic aspects"). We gratefully acknowledge the financial suppport from the DAAD (German Academic Exchange Service), Egide, and the French Ministry of Foreign and European Affairs.
[2] We used the version of the corpus circulated in 2006. A few more texts were added to the corpus in 2007.
[3] Our corpus of modern MC contains the spoken, spontaneous texts in Kriegel (1996) and Ludwig et al. (2001) as well as a great variety of written texts of different genres. In line with the overall editorial policy, examples from texts reproduced in their entirety in this volume are referred to by date only (in bold characters). Bibliographical details for all other examples are given in the References at the end of this article.

texts between 1850[4] and 1929, date at which *av(e)* disappears and is replaced by the form *ar(e)*, which is the current form today.

In Xavier Le Juge de Segrais' *Quarante zolies Zistoires Missié Lafontaine'* ([1939], [1952], 1976) we find a metalinguistic observation which confirms exactly the data found in the corpora. In a passage titled *Remarques sur le créole* he writes:

> *Ave* (avec) est devenu *are*, qui signifie aussi la conjonction *et* (1976: 52).[5]

The formal variation in Seychelles Creole (SC) is less important (see Michaelis & Rosalie 2000). *Av(ek)* is used almost exclusively, but we also find some attestations of *e* in very specific functions. The forms *av(e)* and *ar(e)* are not attested.

The relators *avec*, *et*, and *ensemble* and their MC successors assume above all functions of conjunction[6], of encoding comitative and semantically related functions (for a typological approach, see Stolz et al. 2006; for SC, see Michaelis & Rosalie 2000). *Avec* and *ensemble* are also used as recipient markers in ditransitive constructions (see Michaelis & Haspelmath 2003). In §2 we will deal with conjunction, and in §3 we will focus on recipient marking with the ditransitive verbs *donne* and *dir*. We will not deal with their function in encoding comitative and related semantic domains given that there does not seem to be very much deviation from the situation in modern SC treated in Michaelis & Rosalie 2000 even if the situation in SC is less complex because all those functions are expressed by *av(ek)*.

In this article, we will compare the old MC data not only with those of modern MC, but also (though less systematically) with those of modern SC, as the latter can be viewed as a continuation of MC (see the end of §3.2).

2 Conjunction

2.1 Typology of conjunction: *The World Atlas of Language Structures* (WALS)

In this section, we will be mainly concerned with nominal conjunction (Haspelmath 2005: 262ff) or noun phrase conjunction (Stassen 2005: 258ff), the conjunction of two nominal phrases. Nominal conjunction is opposed to verbal conjunction (verb phrase conjunction in Stassen 2005):

nominal conjunction: Jean *et* Marie
verbal conjunction: Jean danse *et* Marie chante (conjunction of clauses)
                         Ils dansent *et* chantent (conjunction of verb phrases)

Typologically, there are two major differences between MC (and SC), on the one hand, and most European languages on the other. In order to point out these differences, we will

---

[4] As reproduced in Chaudenson (1981), the **1850** text contains a few examples of *are* but, as Baker (1996: 53) points out, "it seems more likely that the v of the original manuscript has in some instances been wrongly identified as an r rather than that the variant form *are* is as old as *ave*."
[5] Véronique (1996: 7) observes, with astonishment, the presence of the prononciation *av* used by a close relative of the author Xavier Le Juge de Segrais (see References) in the 1960s: "Originaire de Port-Louis, (...), j'ai été fort surpris, en arrivant dans le village sucrier de St Pierre (District de Moka), en 1964, à l'âge de 16 ans d'entendre le Père Le Juge de Segrais, curé de la paroisse, âgé alors d'une soixantaine d'années au moins, s'adresser à ses fidèles, lors de ses prônes en créole à la messe de 9 heures, messe des noirs disait-on, dans une langue suffisamment différente de celle que je pratiquais pour que j'en fusse surpris. Je me souviens qu'il employait [lao] à la place de [loː'] (sur) dans mon usage, [av] pour [aː'] dans mon ideolecte, ou encore [suː'ti] (sorti)." (Véronique 1996: 7ff)".
[6] "Three different semantic types of coordination are usually distinguished: conjunction (=conjunctive coordination, 'and' coordination (…)), disjunction (=disjunctive coordination, 'or coordination (…)), and adversative coordination ('but' coordination (…))" (Haspelmath 2004: 5).

refer to the features *Nominal and Verbal Conjunction* (map 64) and *Noun Phrase Conjunction* (map 63) in *WALS*:

nominal and verbal conjunction (*WALS* map 64):

According to Haspelmath, "in the European languages [surveyed by WALS], the same marker is used both for conjunction of noun phrases and for conjunction of verb phrases and clauses (...)" (2005: 262). In French for instance, the same marker *et* encodes nominal, verbal (and clause)[7] conjunction.

As we will try to show in §2.2, in old and modern MC there is a tendency to use different markers for nominal conjunction and verbal (and clause) conjunction. MC is a language that shows "category sensitivity of coordinating constructions" (Haspelmath 2004: 10ff). But we will see below that MC shows considerable variation of forms; we do not have a one-to-one relation: one form expresses one type of conjunction.

noun phrase conjunction (*WALS* map 63):

The second difference concerns noun phrase conjunction. Stassen (2000, 2005) introduces the distinction between AND-languages and WITH-languages:

> The basic distinction is between those languages which use a different marker for noun phrase conjunction and comitative phrases (so-called AND-languages; Stassen 2000) and those languages in which markers for noun phrase conjunction and comitative phrases are the same (WITH-languages) (Stassen 2005: 258).

In the European languages there exist different markers to encode conjunction (*et, and*) and comitative phrases (*avec, with*), they have to be qualified as AND-languages.[8] As we will show in §2.2.2.1, in MC the same marker (corresponding to WITH) may be used to encode both noun phrase conjunction and comitative phrases (and also in SC, see Michaelis & Rosalie 2000). So MC and SC can be considered WITH-languages.

In the sample of 234 languages analyzed according to this distinction, 131 are classified as being AND-languages, 103 languages as being WITH-languages (*World Atlas of Language Structures*, map 63: 260f). This distinction is very pertinent for accounting for the difference between most Creoles and the European languages to which they are related.[9] We will show that both old and modern MC function much like WITH-languages even if the markers have changed during the evolution of this language.

Theoretically, a combination of the features 63 and 64, available thanks to the interactive reference tool in WALS, leads to four major possibilities.[10]

1. *And* different from *with* AND identity of nominal and verbal conjunction
2. *And* identical to *with* AND differentiation of nominal and verbal conjunction
3. *And* different from *with* AND differentiation of nominal and verbal conjunction
4. *And* identical to *with* AND identity of nominal and verbal conjunction

All Indo-European languages surveyed for these two features are of type 1, while in Africa nine of the fifteen languages surveyed are of type 2. The nine African languages of type 2 include all three Bantu languages which were surveyed. MC also shows a tendency to belong to type 2.

---

[7] With Haspelmath (2005: 262) we will use the term 'verbal conjunction' for both verb phrase and clause conjunction given that clauses generally contain verb phrases.
[8] A language like English is a clear instance of an AND-language, French is, in our opinion, an AND-language showing a tendency to allow WITH-encoding in particular cases, see below.
[9] The only Creole language surveyed by WALS, Haitian Creole, is classified as a WITH-language.
[10] We did not take into account the possibility of juxtaposition given that it is not relevant for the languages we are interested in.

2.2 Conjunction in Mauritian Creole

In the diachrony and synchrony of MC, the forms *e(t)* (AND-word) and *avek* (and derived forms) and *ensemble* (and derived forms) (WITH-words) are attested in conjunction constructions. Verbal conjunction is in the majority of cases done by the AND-word *e(t)*. Nominal conjunction is almost always done by WITH-words.

We will retrace chronologically the occurrences of the items when used for verbal (§2.2.1) or nominal (§2.2.2) conjunction in the corpus.

2.2.1 Verbal conjunction

2.2.1.1 Dominant use of AND-word: e(t)

In the corpus of old texts (about 100.000 words), 2015[11] occurrences of the item *et*, written *et, e* or *é*, are attested. *Et* (in any spelling) is found in the vast majority of cases of verbal conjunction, corresponding to the use of *et* in French. It is attested for the first time in **1818b**,[12] and as might be expected, it is used in its prototypical function of verbal conjunction (1):

> (1) *Moi porté mon la-caze, et li rèd' mon li-pié ;*
> *Mais c'est égal, moi va parié,*
> *Moi connois comment va faire:* (**1818b**)
>
> 'Je porte ma maison [sur le dos] et mes pattes sont raides, mais cela m'est égal, je vais faire le pari, je sais comment faire'
> 'I carry my house [on my back] and my feet are stiff, but I don't care, I will take on the bet, I know what I will have to do'

A look at modern corpora confirms this tendency: in the great majority of cases the occurrences of *et*, mostly in the spelling *e*, relate to contexts of verbal conjunction, including turn initiation, a pragmatic function similar to verbal conjunction given that its function is to relate whole phrases/sentences.

> (2) **B [** *e lavi laburer/ rakont en ti-pe ki manyer lavi laburer* < li/ li <u>dir</u> > (Kriegel 1996)
> 'Et la vie de laboureur? Racontez un petit peu comment se passe la vie de laboureur! Elle est dûre?'
> 'And the life of a labourer? Say a few words about the labourer's way of life. It is hard?'

In conclusion, we can state that in old and modern texts *e(t)* is in the vast majority of cases used for verbal conjunction (including its use as a turn initiator).

2.2.1.2 Marginal use of WITH-word: ek

Ek in verbal conjunction is not attested in Le Juge de Segrais (1939, 1952) and older texts. As stated below, *ek* is becoming more and more widely used in modern texts, above all as a comitative marker and in nominal conjunction. But it seems to continue its functional expansion and in modern texts, we also find some attestations where *ek* encodes verbal conjunction, even if the most frequently used technique for verbal conjunction remains the use of *e(t)* (see above).

> (3) *bizen bril en azordi isi* **ek** *bril en lot kote* (Kriegel 1996)
> 'Il faut en brûler un ici aujourd'hui et en brûler un (autre) de l'autre côté'
> 'One has to be burned here today and another on the other side'

---

[11] This figure relates to the 2006 version of the corpus which contained a small number of comments or translations in French (eliminated from the 2007 version) which contained a few occurrences of *et*.

[12] This in no way implies that it did not exist before. We have very few earlier texts and most of them are very short.

The evolution from comitative via nominal conjunction (see §2.2.2.3) to verbal conjunction is considered to be a common grammaticalization path (Heine & Kuteva 2005: 16, 160). In their *World lexicon of grammaticalization* (Heine & Kuteva 2002: 82), these authors cite MC as being one example of languages grammaticalizing nominal conjunction markers into verbal conjunction markers. However, they add the remark "rarely used". In examining our data, we would like to underline the fact that it is indeed a marginal process. In this respect, MC becomes more like SC where *ek* is also attested in verbal conjunction.

Maybe the phonetical proximity to French *et* plays some role in the functional expansion/grammaticalization of *ek* in modern MC, even if the two forms are not etymologically related.

2.2.2 Nominal conjunction

Nominal conjunction in MC, in contrast to French, is expressed by different WITH-words that are also attested in comitative functions. Nevertheless, we also found some attestations of nominal conjunction expressed by *et*, examples of which we will discuss in §2.2.2.2.

2.2.2.1 Dominant use of different WITH-words

Ensemble and derived forms

In old MC texts, we find attestations of items derived from *ensemble* in different spellings in contexts of nominal conjunction, in comitative functions as well as in the same functions as the adverb *ensemble* in modern French. We do not find *ensemble* in contexts of verbal conjunction.

The first clear example of *ensemble* in nominal conjunction is found in **1850**:[13]

(4) *Eti y en a enne vié blan qui ti gagne troi piti; li ti y en a enne moulin, enne bourique* **ensemble** *enne satte.*
'Il y avait un vieux blanc qui avait trois enfants; il possédait un moulin, une bourrique et un chat'
'There was an old white man who had three children; he owned a mill, a donkey, and a cat'

Lolliot (1855) contains many examples of *ensemble*, written *semb* in nominal conjunction, particularly in the titles of his poems, e.g.:

(5) *La mort **semb**' couper' di bois.*
*Loulou **semb**' p'tit mouton.*
*Pié filao **semb**' pié fataque.*
*Ein vié blanc avare **semb**' so pitit*
*Mouce a miel **semb**' mouce zaune.*
*Milet **semb**' miltons.* (Lolliot 1855)

In each of the above titles, *semb* means 'and'. Four of these titles are translations of La Fontaine *Fables* and, in each case, the *et* in his title is replaced by *semb* in Lolliot's MC version. In later texts we find examples of *ensemble*, in nominal conjunction, mostly in abbreviated forms; in Baissac (1880), for instance, these are written *sembe* or *sambe*. In all those texts *ensemble*, when used in its full form, is equivalent to the French adverb *ensemble*. This distribution of *ensemble* versus its abbreviated forms may be an indication that the latter had begun to grammaticalize before it was replaced by forms of *avec* in nominal conjunction.

---

[13] In **1818a**, we find three occurrences of *ensemb*. Whereas two of them clearly relate to the expression of comitative, one example could also be interpreted as a nominal conjunction.

The latest instance of a form of *ensemble* in nominal conjunction, this time written *assambe* is found in Le Juge de Segrais (1939, 1952). In the corpus of modern MC, *ensemble* is no longer found in nominal conjunction but it continues to be employed with the same functions as the French adverb,[14] and if used in comitative contexts, mostly in combination with a form of *avek*: *ansam avek/ek/ar* (Chaudenson 2003: 326).

(Av)(ek) and *ar(e)*

In this paragraph, we deal with all the successors of the French preposition *avec*. In the 1734-1929 corpus the item occurs 959 times with the spellings: *are* (6 tokens),[15] *av* (426 tokens), *av'* (78 tokens), *ave* (59 tokens), *avée* (1 token), *avec* (379 tokens), *ec* (1 token), *éc* (2 tokens), *ecque* (2 tokens) et *vec* (5 tokens) (see concordance).

The reason why we treat all the forms of *avec* in the same section is because we could not find any systematic functional differences between *avec* and its shortened forms in the old texts. Before 1850, we only find instances of the full form *avec*; from 1850 onwards, both the full form and abbreviated forms are attested. In texts from the middle of the 20th century (Le Juge de Segrais 1939; 1952), nominal conjunction is one of the main functions of all the forms of *avec*.[16]

For our concern (see below, §2.3.1) it is most interesting to consider the fact that between 1850 and 1952, the abbreviated forms, *av'*, *av* and later *ar(e)* are very often attested in the encoding of nominal conjunction.

(7) *Ça magnière là qui Léléphant **av** Baleine blizé croire qui Ième plis fort qui zaute* (Baissac 1888)
'Ainsi, l'éléphant et la baleine devaient croire que le lièvre était plus fort qu'eux'
'And so Elephant and Whale had to accept that Hare was stronger than them'

(8) *Li ti mentionne-toi **are** mo soeir, li ti dire li bien content to zare figuire **are** to manières* (Le Juge de Segrais 1939/52: 36)
'Il t'évoqué auprès de ma sœur, il a dit qu'il aimait ton visage et tes manières'
'He mentioned you to my sister, saying that he liked your face and your manners'

In the modern texts the situation is not homogeneous but we observe a change:

1. *Are*, most often in the spelling *ar* appears to be rarely used in nominal conjunction today. In most cases *ar* is used in comitative or related functions, often it is part of verb valency (see the first occurrence of *are* in example (8)).

2. The form *ek*, rarely attested between its first mention in Baissac (1880)[17] and Le Juge de Segrais (1939, 1952) becomes more and more frequent in modern texts. *Ek* is today the dominant encoding technique for nominal conjunction and the encoding of comitative and related functions. *Ek* actually has eliminated the two concurrent forms attested until 1952 in nominal conjunction: *ensemble* (and derived forms) and *ar(e)*. This wide use of *ek* reminds us of the situation in SC (cf Michaelis & Rosalie 2000). In MC, this may be due to

---

[14] In modern French the adverb *ensemble* is not attested as a preposition, neither in nominal conjunction nor in comitative functions. But Chaudenson (2003: 326, also in 1974: 692) states that its prepositional use was current in Old French.

[15] See note 4.

[16] The following example from *Le Mauricien* 1855 is a perfect illustration of the lack of functional differences between the full form *avec* and the abbreviated form *av'*. In (6), both forms are used in a context of nominal conjunction:

(6) *Ein malbar fine donn' moi 4 poules avec ein coq pour faire ein lettre pour qui li dire merci zens qui vlé malbars gagne plein femmes. Rend' moi service dire moi comment faut faire ou plitôt mette li dans vous papié pour li arrivé. Mo croir qui li fine donne moi 4 poules av' ein cioq pour fair' voir qui malbars aussi doit gagne trois quatre femmes. (Le Mauricien 1855h)*

[17] Baissac mentions the existence of the form in his grammar but he only uses it very rarely in his texts: "Avec, avéque, le plus souvent av, quelquefois éc. C'est la plus usitée des prépositions créoles" (1880: 77).

an indirect influence of French: French *et* is phonetically – but not etymologically – close to *ek* (see also §2.2.1.2).

(9) [*mm*] papi *ek* mami pre pu ale zot usi (Kriegel 1996)
'Mmm. Papa et maman sont prêts pour s'en aller eux aussi'
'Mmm. Daddy and Mum are ready to go, them too'

2.2.2.2 Marginal use of AND-word: et/e

In the texts of Chrestien, where the vast majority of occurrences of *et* concern verbal conjunction (see §2.2.1.1 above), we nevertheless found two attestations of *et* in a function of nominal conjunction.

(10) *Où prêtres fair' planté son brède et son loignon* (Chrestien 1831)
'Où les prêtres font planter leurs 'brèdes' et leurs oignons'
'Where the priests have their greens and onions planted'

But a preliminary examination of all attestations of *et* up to 1850 reveals that, of some 110 attestations, only three cases of nominal conjunction are attested, that is less than 3%.[18] In the texts after 1850, our observation is confirmed: nominal conjunction expressed by *et* is a marginal technique (between 0% and 20% depending on the text). In a majority of cases (see (10)) it concerns conjunction of conventionalized wholes or conceptual units (see Stassen 2000, Haspelmath 2004: 12f, with a discussion of the relevant literature):

(11) *poivre et disel* (Descroizilles 1867)   'poivre et sel'/'pepper and salt'
     fain é soaf (Anderson 1885)   'faim et soif'/'hunger and thirst'
     karant zour é karant noui (Anderson 1885)   'quarante jours et quarante nuits'
     'forty days and forty nights'

Possibly, frequent, conventionalized conjunctions of this kind are directly copied from the base language into Creole.[19]

In modern corpora, *e* in nominal conjunction is very rarely used,[20] and often concerns the conjunction of conventionalized wholes just as in older texts. It can in most cases be interpreted as being due to French influence;[21] see also the examples from old texts in (10) and (11).

(13) *an mo nom e an nom mo de kolistye* (Ludwig et al. 2001: 244).
'en mon nom propre, et au nom des deux (autres) candidats de mon parti'
'on my behalf and on behalf of my two fellow candidates'

---

[18] With one exception, we find *e* for nominal conjunction in Lambert's 1828 catechism. But a careful analysis shows that this text is very acrolectal in many respects. For instance, it contains constructions of the type NP de NP: *la peine de mort, la colaire de Bon Dieu*. So the examples found in this text need to be interpreted with caution, especially if they correspond to the coding in French.

[19] For the notion of copying, see Johanson (2002) or Kriegel, Ludwig & Henri (forthcoming-a).

[20] Surprisingly, the *Bord la Mer* texts, known for their basilectal character, are an exception: out of a total of only six occurrences of *e*, two concern nominal conjunction and form part of a kind of epigraph, of which the following is one example:

(12) *Ar nu lafors*
E kudmé sindika osi,
Ki nu'nn gayn sa ameliorasion la zordi (Bord la Mer, 1980: 4)

Here *e* could be interpreted as an instance of euphony in a rhyme.

[21] Baker 1972: 93 writes in his grammar: "The conjunctions that may link together two NPs include: /e/ 'and' ; /ek/ or /avek/ 'and'/'together with'..." and he gives the following example: /nu ti promne Bel Mar e Blu Be/ (1972: 135). Our observations suggest that Baker's remark is not wrong but that such use of *e* is very limited.

(13) is the transcription of an election speech with frequent occurrences of code switching between French and MC. One might consider this as being an instance of code switching to French (see Kriegel, Ludwig & Henri, *forthcoming*-a).

2.2.2.3 The problem of ambiguity between nominal conjunction and comitative expression

After this brief survey of the forms and their functions of conjunction, we want to focus on the problem of the differentiation between nominal conjunction and comitative. The attestations of *avec* start in 1818a. (Abbreviated forms of *avec* do not occur at that time.)

> (14) Ein' Torti avec Lièvre été voulé parié (**1818b**)
> ?'La tortue voulait faire un pari avec le lièvre'
> ?'La tortue et le lièvre voulaient faire un pari'
> ?'A tortoise wanted to make a bet with a hare'
> ?'A tortoise and a hare wanted to make a bet with each other'

This example is ambiguous. It can be interpreted as a nominal conjunction but it also can be read as a comitative phrase given that we are dealing with a specific semantic area where two participants do something together.[22] In translating this, we have to choose between two possibilities: 'The tortoise **and** the hare make a bet' or 'The tortoise wanted to bet **with** the hare'.[23] The semantic-syntactic change from comitative to nominal conjunction is well described in the literature. Heine & Kuteva (2002: 82ff, 2005: 159f) claim the existence of a universal grammaticalization path. Haspelmath (2004: 15ff) gives a series of criteria allowing us to distinguish between comitative and conjunctive markers.

It is precisely with regard to this semantic area of ambiguity that Chaudenson (2003: 329f) criticizes Parkvall's (2000)[24] analysis, but from a much less theoretically-based standpoint. We will summarize this in a simplified manner: Parkvall (2000) argues that the Atlantic Creoles are instances of WITH-languages and that this encoding is a clear instance of substrate influence from West African languages. Chaudenson (2003) answers that the phenomenon can be explained by French influence by citing examples of the type (13). In this semantic area of transition between comitative and nominal conjunction in particular, spoken varieties of French allow encoding with *avec* as well as with *et*. Even if Chaudenson (2003) is right concerning the situation in French, his argumentation is not entirely valid for Indian Ocean Creoles: in MC and SC the encoding technique with a WITH-word concerns the whole domain of nominal conjunction, in French only the contexts of transition between comitative and nominal conjunction in which one of the participants clearly has control over the situation can be encoded by *avec*. We will come back to this problem in §2.3.2.

The first wholly unambiguous attestation of a nominal conjunction is found in **1850**:

> (15) *mon pauvre mètre Moucié Caraba qui té envoye touzou lièvre are*[25] *perdri la.*
> 'Mon pauvre maître M Caraba qui avait pris l'habitude de vous envoyer un lièvre et une perdrix'
> 'My poor master Mr Caraba who is in the habit of sending you [gifts such as] a hare and a partridge'

---

[22] This theoretical problem also concerns *ensemble*.

[23] We naturally checked La Fontaine's original with a view to establishing which was the author's intended meaning but it contains nothing corresponding to Chrestien's sentence.

[24] "Two things in particular seem to characterise West African conjunctions. Firstly, in the vast majority of Niger-Congo languages, as opposed to European languages, the conjunction that coordinate NPs cannot join VPs or clauses (Welmers 1976 : 129). Secondly, the NP co-ordination is frequently derived from and/or homophonous with a comitative preposition, i.e. a word meaning 'with'. It should come as no surprise, then, that both these phenomena are relatively frequent in Atlantic Creoles.'(....), it does seem fair to consider the phenomenon substrate-derived."

[25] See note 4.

Mr Caraba has sent gifts of a hare and a partridge to the king. A comitative reading of this – a hare with a partridge – would sound odd and be inappropriate because the two gifts were sent on separate occasions, not together. In post-1850 texts, clear examples of nominal conjunction with *avec* and its different shortened forms become more and more frequent, see examples (7) and (8).

2.2.2.4 Summary

The encoding of verbal conjunction by *et* corresponds exactly to the encoding of verbal conjunction in French and therefore is, in a way, not very striking. What is much more interesting for our interpretation of the data in the context of language contact (§2.3), is the fact that

1. in contrast to French, nominal conjunction is almost always encoded by a WITH-word (§2.3.2).
2. this WITH-word takes the form *av(e)* from 1850, and was gradually replaced by *ar(e)* from 1929 onwards.

We would like to summarize our findings concerning nominal and verbal conjunction in Table 2. This table does not take into account the exceptions treated in §2.2.1.2 and §2.2.2.2. It only reflects tendencies.

Table 2: Expression of nominal and verbal conjunction

	French	Old MC	Modern MC
nominal conjunction	AND-word: *et*	WITH-words: *avec* and derived forms *av(e')* (later *ar(e)*), *ek*	WITH-words: *avek* *ek*
verbal conjunction		AND-word: *e(t)*	AND-word: *e(t)*

2.3 Language contact as the driving force

2.3.1 *ar(e)* – Bhojpuri influence

As stated above, for the period between 1850 and 1952, *av(e)* and, since 1929, its successor *ar(e)* clearly dominate the field of nominal conjunction in the old MC texts (see examples (7) and (8)) whereas in modern texts *ar* is very rarely attested in nominal conjunction. Like Baker 1996, we think that at least the change from *av(e)* to *a(r)e* may be explained by an influence from speakers of languages from the Indian subcontinent, especially of Bhojpuri speakers.[26] The observation that between 1929 and 1952 *ar(e)* is attested as the dominant technique for nominal conjunction seems crucial to us and may constitute the missing structural link between Mauritian Bhojpuri (MB) and modern MC where *ar* is typically used in comitative and verb valency. Baker (1996: 53) indicates that the MB conjunction *aur* has a very common variant pronunciation /ar/, and discusses the possibility that Bhojpuri may have influenced the appearence of *ar(e)* in MC. Enlarging on this (p c), he says that "the *aur* variant is the form in Hindi which is used in broadcasting and films in Mauritius and is thus a very important influence on MB today. But when I worked on MB [1980s], /ar/ appeared to be more frequent than /awr/. In different Indian varieties of Bhojpuri /ar/, /a:/, and /awr/ are all found. The form /a:/ occurs in Madhesi, one of the three Indian varieties identified as having had the greatest influence on MB. This is of course closest phonetically to MC *ar*." In Baker & Ramnah 1988, the authors provide a text in both MB and the Madhesi variety of Bhojpuri from which we derive the following example :

---

[26] An even stronger hypothesis claiming Bhojpuri influence for the emergence of *av(e)* from 1850 onwards is in preparation (Kriegel, ms) but will not be discussed here.

(16a) MB *Dukh-dard   bhag   gal.   ar duno jana: khusi me rah-e   lag-lan-sa*
         grief-pain   run+away go+PF and both person glad in   live-IN begin-PN-PL
    Madhesi *Dukh-dalidar bha:g   gail.   a: du:no bekat   khusi sa:th rah-e   la:g-al*
         'Grief and pain had left them *and*   they both began to live in happiness'
                                                                    (Baker & Ramnah 1998: 55)

But Baker (1996: 53) concludes: "However, the point [MB influence, SK & SM] should not be exaggerated – first because [aur]/[ar] is not a preposition in MB, 'with' being expressed by a post-posed particle [se] (…)".[27] In fact, *aur/ar* is not a preposition in Bhojpuri but it is attested in verbal as well as in nominal conjunction[28], see examples (16a/b):

(16b) South African Bhojpuri[29] *ham aur hamār   bahini   ainī.*
                          I   and I.Gen sister   come.1pl.past
                          'My sister and I came' (Mesthrie 1991: 258)

The function of the marker *aur/ar* in MB only partly overlaps with the functions of MC *ar* in the texts between 1929 and 1952 (and *av(e)* between 1850 and 1929). *Aur/ar* in MB is a typical instance of an AND-word used in nominal and verbal conjunction whereas *av(e)/ar(e)* in MC is, in the present corpus, only used in nominal conjunction. This raises two questions:

11. Why has *ar(e)* never been used in verbal conjunction in MC as is the case for *aur/ar* in MB?

In MC, the area of verbal conjunction has always been expressed in a very stable manner, by the successor of French *et*. Therefore, functionally, there was no need to replace such a well established marker in this precise function. On the other hand, the area of nominal conjunction was much more unstable, expressed by a variety of forms of *avec* and *ensemble*, and from 1850, often by *av(e)*, phonetically close to *ar(e)*.

2. Why should we admit an influence of the MB AND-word if MC at this time used different WITH-words?

The marker *av(e)* was interpreted as *ar(e)* because both forms partially covered the same semantic area of nominal conjunction. This may seem paradoxical from a typological point of view but not if one considers the linguistic situation in Mauritius in the mid-19th century. Indian labourers were arriving at a phenomenal rate, forming 43% of the population by 1851, rising to 68% by 1871. Most of them were speakers of Bhojpuri or related Indic languages,[30] in which *aur/ar* is used in both nominal and verbal conjunction. They all needed to acquire MC as a second language and would quickly have identified *av(e)/avec* as the marker of nominal conjunction in MC. Given the partial functional overlap and phonetic proximity, *av(e)* could easily have become *ar(e)*.

The existence of *ar(e)* in nominal conjunction between 1929 to 1952 in our corpus may thus be the product of code copying (Johanson 2002) or replication (Heine & Kuteva 2005) on the level of meaning and also of form, given the phonetical similarity (Heine & Kuteva 2005: 244).

---

[27] On the functions of the postposed marker *se*, see Kriegel, Ludwig, & Henri *forthcoming-b*.
[28] "Conjoining of two or more nouns or adjectives is effected by the use of the particle *aur* or *au*, which occurs before the last of the conjoined elements, for example, *Mohan aur Sohan* 'Mohan and Sohan'. *Aur* 'and' and *baki* 'but' may also be used as sentence co-ordinators in much the same way." (Mesthrie 1991: 257, voir aussi Shukla 1981: 176)
[29] This is also the case in other varieties of Bhojpuri, for instance in the Northern Bhojpuri variety of India described in Shukla (1981) where the item has the spelling *ao* as well as in MB. Unfortunately, we do not have an example in our corpora.
[30] Up to 30% of them, i.e. less than a third of the Indians, came from areas where Dravidian languages are spoken.

Another argument corroborating our hypothesis of MB influence lies in the fact that *ar* does not exist in the Seychelles where we do not have any influence of Indic languages.

2.3.2 WITH-words in nominal conjunction – influence from Bantu languages and spoken French: a case of convergence[31]

In spite of the great variation, MC (as well as Seychelles Creole, Haitian Creole, and the majority of Atlantic Creoles) can be considered WITH-languages. Even if in the diachrony of MC the marker has changed and even if in synchrony we continue to have a lot of variation, it seems clear to us, that at all times, MC has used a WITH-word for nominal conjunction which is different from the marker of verbal conjunction. WITH-languages are predominant in Subsaharan Africa. Creolists such as Parkvall (2000: 67ff), Lefebvre (2004), and Lefebvre & Therrien (2007[32]) use this fact as an argument for their hypothesis of West African substrate in Atlantic Creoles. In sum, they say that the Creoles of this geographical area are WITH-languages. Given that the European "base" languages are AND-languages and that the West African substrate languages are WITH-languages, this example is interpreted as a clear instance of substrate influence. Even if Chaudenson (2003; see above) is right in pointing out the wide use of *avec* in spoken varieties of French, we find the argumentation of Parkvall (2000), Lefebvre (2004), and Lefebvre & Therrien (2007) for substrate influence in Atlantic Creoles in this semantic area convincing.

Let us now consider the situation in the Indian Ocean Creoles: the languages playing a substantial role in the contact situation are French, Malagasy, and several East African Bantu languages.[33] For MC we have also an influence from Indic languages later in the 19th century. We know that French and English and the Indic varieties like Bhojpuri are AND-languages. In Stassen's (2000, 2005) classification, Malagasy is also considered to be an AND-language. Therefore, the only WITH-languages which could have played a role in the evolution of MC and SC are Bantu languages.[34]

We also should consider the fact that French also uses the marker *avec* in contexts of nominal conjunction belonging to the semantic area of transition between comitative and nominal conjunction (see §2.2.2.3) even if nominal conjunction is dominantly marked by *et*. Bearing those facts in mind, we could hypothesize that the marking of nominal conjunction by a WITH-word is the product of convergence between a phenomenon known in French, the use of *avec* in the semantic area of transition, and the influence from Bantu languages using a WITH-word in nominal conjunction.

3 Ditransitive constructions in old MC texts

3.1 *Avec/av* in ditransitive constructions

In this section, we would like to discuss yet another use of *avec/av* in old MC texts: the use in ditransitive constructions, as shown in examples (17) and (18):

(17) *Lhére li arrive lacase, li donne léfoie **av** son bonhomme loulou.* (Baissac 1888)
'Lorsqu'elle rentra à la maison, elle donna les foies à son mari, le loup'
'When she came home, she gave the livers to her husbund, the wolf'

---

[31] Convergence defined in the sense of Bollée (1982) or Kriegel (2003).
[32] Lefebvre & Therrien 2007: 9ff.
[33] While, overall, the great majority of slaves introduced into Mauritius spoke either a variety of Malagasy or a Bantu language, two other languages merit investigation for the 18th century; Wolof (dominant 1730-35) and Tamil (represented from 1728 by both paid artisans as well as a small minority of slaves throughout the 18th century, and then by 30% of Indians who arrived in the 19th century) (Baker, p c).
[34] In WALS, the feature 'identity/differentiation of WITH and AND' is attested for languages belonging to the family of Niger-Congo languages of the Bantoid genus: Ciluba, Nkore-Kiga, Luganda, Shona, Swahili, and Zulu. All these languages are classified as being WITH-languages.

(18) *Ein zour pié filao té dir'* **av** *pié fataque: (...)* (Lolliot 1855)
    'One day the filao tree said **to** the fataque plant: (...)'
    'Un jour le *filao* disait au *fataque (...)*'³⁵

By ditransitive constructions, we mean constructions with verbs of transfer and communication such as 'give', 'send', 'say', and 'ask' which require two objects, a Recipient (or receiver) and a Theme (or patient), i.e. the entity that is transferred – either an object or a message. In examples (17) and (18) the Recipient is marked by the marker *av* (*av son bonhomme, av pié fataque*). We will call such constructions Indirect-Object constructions (IOC) because the Recipient is overtly marked by an adposition (*av*).

In this section, we will concentrate on the verbs 'give' and 'say', which seem to be by far the most frequent ditransitive verbs in all languages.

Before we go into the detailed analysis of the examples, let us summarize the most important generalizations:

(i) By far the most prominent ditransitive construction with the verbs *donne* 'give' and *dir* 'say' in the corpus of old MC texts is the so-called Double-Object construction, a construction in which neither the Recipient nor the Theme is overtly marked by a case or adposition, unlike examples (17) and (18). An example of such a construction is:

(19) *Mo va donne vous ca qui vous voulé* (**1818a**)
    'Je vais vous donner ce que vous voulez'
    'I will give you what you want'

The Indirect-Object Construction illustrated in examples (17) and (18) accounts for less than 5% of the ditransitive constructions, i.e. it is a very clear minority pattern within ditransitive marking. But as we will see, the study of these data turns out to be very interesting.

(ii) It is striking that the modern MC and SC Double Object pattern with the verb *donne* (and *dir* to a somewhat lesser extent) has obviously been established in old MC from quite early on, and thus it has been very stable. From the first occurrences of ditransitive constructions with *donne* in **1805** onwards, we see no significant contrast with the patterns of modern varieties of MC or SC, in contrast to other linguistic domains, e.g. TMA markers (cf Stein, *this volume*), where we can trace different stages of grammaticalization over the centuries.

3.2 Ditransitive *donne* in old MC

Let us first look at the most frequent ditransitive transfer verb *donne*. In a third of all occurrences of *donne* in the present corpus, neither Recipient nor Theme are expressed overtly. This is a widespread phenomenon which we know from text corpora in other languages: the Recipient and/or the Theme stay implicit because they are known to the speaker and to the hearer from the pragmatic context. Out of the total number of 371 ditransitive *donne* contexts, we have classified 251 as 'true' ditransitives, because here the Recipient is expressed. It is only at this point that one can decide whether we are dealing with an IOC (the Recipient is overtly marked) or DOC (Recipient is not overtly marked).

Out of the 251 ditransitive constructions with *donne*, 244 (97%) are Double-Object Constructions and only 7 (3%) are Indirect-Object Constructions marked by *avec* or *av*.³⁶ As for the distribution of the 7 Indirect Object Constructions, we find two examples in

---

[35] The filao tree (casuarina) flourishes by the seashore; fataque is a species of tall grass used for making brooms. Both words are of Malagasy origin. This example comes from a free translation of La Fontaine's *La chêne et le roseau*.
[36] We do not find Indirect-Object constructions marked by *ensemble* (or shortened forms), but see an example in Réunionnais cited by Chaudenson (1974: 692): *mèt la pay* **ansam** *zanimo* 'give hay to the animals'.

Lambert 1828, one in Descroizilles 1867, one in Anderson 1885, and three in Baissac 1888 (all marked by *av*). Here are the relevant examples:

(20) *Li été donné **avec** Juife ein la loi* (Lambert 1828)
'Il a donné une loi aux Juifs'
'He gave a law to the Jews'

(21) *Bon Dieû été donné son sainte parol **avec** Juife et **avec** Chrétien* (Lambert 1828)
'Dieu a donné sa parole sainte aux Juifs et aux Chrétiens'
'God gave his holy word to the Jews and to the Christians'

(22) *Dans ça grand paye au Cap, fine touyé eine gros Alphant. Son la peau, done morceau, **avec** son zofficiers* (...) (Descroizilles 1867)
'Dans ce grand pays au Cap, un gros éléphant a été tué. Des morceaux de sa peau ont été donnés aux officiers'
'In that large country at the Cape, a big elephant was killed. Pieces of its skin were given to the officers'

(23) ***Avec** éne, li donne ceinq talan l'arzan, éne lot dé, éne lot éne* (Anderson 1885)
'A l'un (d'entre eux), il donna cinq talents, à un autre deux, à une autre un (seul)'
'To one person, he gave five talents, to another, two, and yet to another, one'

(24) *Li donne éne boute **av** baleine* (Baissac 1888)
'Il a donné un bout à la baleine'
'He gave the whale a piece'

(25) *Paulin tire pitit là lamains Lida, donne li **av** Pauline* (Baissac 1888)
'Paulin retira le petit des mains de Lida et le donna à Pauline'
'Paulin took the child from Lida's hands and gave him to Pauline'

(26) *Lhére li arrive lacase, li donne léfoie **av** son bonhomme loulou.* (Baissac 1888) (=17)
'Lorsqu'elle rentra à la maison, elle donna les foies à son mari, le loup'
'when she came home, she gave the livers to her husbund, the wolf'

As has been argued extensively in Michaelis & Haspelmath 2003, 'give'-ditransitive constructions in creole languages overwhelmingly show the patterns of their substrate languages, *irrespectively* of the inherited superstrate patterns. French, like other Romance languages, shows the Indirect-Object construction:

(27) *Léa a donné une mangue à Pierre.*
'Léa gave Pierre a mango'

In contrast to this pattern, MC and SC, French-based Creoles, show the Double-Object construction. Here the two Creoles follow the pattern of the East African Bantu languages. Now it is interesting to see that in old MC, from the very beginning of written records, the proportion of the Double-Object construction within the ditransitive contexts is nearly 100%. Thus, these data strongly confirm the claim by Michaelis & Haspelmath (2003).

But let us look at the seven 'counter-examples' of Indirect Object patterns which are interesting in the context of the overall *avec*-marking in these old MC texts.

(i) The first two examples come from a heavily French-influenced religious text (Lambert 1828, see footnote 18 above). Interestingly, this text shows five more ditransitive constructions with *donne,* all of which are Double-Object constructions. These five Double-Object constructions all have at the same time pronominal Recipient arguments (*nous, vous*), whereas the two Indirect-Object constructions have nominal Recipient arguments. This pattern seems to have a more general application because it also holds for the rest of the instances of indirect object marking in examples (20-26) cited above. All Recipients marked by *avec* or *av* are nominal, and not pronominal arguments. So, the pattern is: Verb + Theme (pronominal/nominal) + *av* Recipient (nominal).

This leads us to a more general observation about ditransitive constructions in a typological perspective. In the most frequent pattern of 'give'-constructions, the Recipient, as the most topical argument, is pronominally expressed right after the verb with the

Theme as the pragmatically new entity following the Recipient: Verb + Recipient (pronominal) + Theme (nominal). If, on the other hand, the Recipient is newly introduced into the context and therefore very low on the topicality scale (and/or the Theme is topic), often special marking is required in different languages (e.g. serial verb constructions, see Lefebvre 1998, Malchukov et al. 2007). Could the present Indirect Object pattern be interpreted in this way, i.e. as a conventionalized strategy for marking non-topic Recipients? We do not think so because we find a lot of examples (30, i.e. 12% of all Double-Object Constructions) where the Recipient is nominal and where it follows the Theme (Verb + Theme + Recipient (nominal)), and where it is still not overtly marked, as in (28) *vou zanfan*. Instead we get a Double Object pattern:

> (28) *vou conné comman donne bon cado vou zanfan* (Anderson 1885)
> 'Vous savez comment donner de bonnes choses à vos enfants'
> 'You know how to give good things to your children'

(ii) Another special case of indirect object marking is example (29). Here, the Recipient is left-dislocated and therefore in focus position. It seems that a Recipient in focus position can – or maybe must – be marked by *avec*.

> (29) *Avec éne, li donne ceinq talan l'arzan, éne lot dé, éne lot éne* (Anderson 1885) (=23)
> 'A l'un (d'entre eux), il donna cinq talents, à un autre deux, à une autre un (seul)'
> 'To one person, he gave five talents, to another, two, and yet to another, one'

The direct continuation of this sentence shows two more Recipients unmarked, i.e. a Double-Object construction (*éne lot dé, éne lot éne*). This pattern of marking still holds for modern MC and SC: focused Recipients are marked by *ek* (Adone 2004: 196):

MC (Adone 2004: 196)
> (30) *Mo ti dir ek Gabriel, pa ek Zan.*
> 'Je l'ai dit à Gabriel, pas à Jean'
> 'I said (it) to Gabriel, not to John'

SC (Marcel Rosalie, p c)
> (31) *Ek ki ou'n donn larzan?*
> 'A qui as-tu donné l'argent?'
> 'To whom did you give the money?'[37]

(iii) The three examples of Indirect Object patterns from Baissac 1888 are the first instances of Recipient-marking with *av*, the shortened version of *avec*.[38] We will come back to the question of the first attestation of *avec* and *av* in ditransitive constructions, see Table 3 in §3.4.

After analyzing the very few instances of *avec*-marking (only 3%) in ditransitive constructions in the old MC texts, let us now come back to the dominant Double-Object Construction, which accounts for 97% of all *donne*-constructions in the present corpus. As already mentioned, we believe that the Eastern Bantu languages, which show the Double-

---

[37] In modern MC, this marking by *ek* or, alternatively *ar*, may be optional (Fabiola Henri, p c):
> (32) *(ar) kisannla to'nn donn kas la?* 'A qui as-tu donné l'argent?' 'To whom did you give the money?'

[38] It should be mentioned that we have encountered three cases of IOC in Baissac 1888 where the indirect argument is marked by *pou(r)*. But as *pour* also marks beneficiary arguments, there seems to be an ambiguous interpretation between 'to give to someone' or 'to give for someone'.

> (33) *tout ça qui Pauline gagné li donne la moquié **pour** Paulin* (Baissac 1888)
> 'half of everything Pauline got she gave to Paulin'
> 'tout ce que Pauline gagne, elle en donne la moitié à Paulin'

As mentioned before, the most frequent ditransitive construction in this long text (Baissac 1888) is the Double-Object Construction (103 instances) with three cases of Indirect-Object Constructions (*av*-marking). Adone (2004: 198) cites modern MC data of *donne*-constructions with *pu*-marked Recipient/beneficiary arguments.

Object pattern in 'give'-constructions, are the main source for the retention of Double-Object Construction in old MC. Another interesting point to be mentioned in this context is the fact that the syntax of French imperative constructions with pronominal Recipients may look like, or better – may sound like – Double-Object Constructions:

(34) *Donne-moi ça*   *Donne-lui ça*

and not **Donne-ça-à-moi*   **Donne-ça-à-lui* etc.

These imperative constructions, which slaves speaking Bantu languages may very often have heard, could have lent themselves to reinterpretation as Double-Object Constructions.[39] Such people made up the majority of slave arrivals from the 1770s onwards in Mauritius, and the Seychelles were settled mainly from Mauritius in that period.[40]

3.3 Ditransitive *dir* in old MC

The situation of the ditransitive verb of communication *dir* is in many respects similar to the observations made for the ditransitive verb *donne* in §3.2. Out of some 1450 occurrences of *dir* in the whole corpus of old MC texts, only half are constructed with an overt Recipient, i.e. a much smaller proportion than for the verb *donne*. Within these ca. 700 'true' ditransitive constructions, only 41 (= ca. 6%) show an overtly marked Recipient whereas the other 94% show the Double-Object Construction. Among the relatively few instances of Indirect-Object Constructions with *dir* (41 examples), one finds overwhelmingly *avec/av*-marking of the Recipient (39 examples = 95%).

(35) *dir' lièvre **avec** torti*   (1818b)
'dit le lièvre à la tortue'
'said the hare to the tortoise'

We have come across only two instances of marking by the preposition *sembe* (2 examples = 5%), which goes back to the French adverb *ensemble* 'together' (see above §2.2.2.1).

(36) *Zamais li dire ça **sembe** son maitresse* (Baissac 1888)
'He never told this to his lover'
'Il ne le dit jamais à sa maîtresse'

Again, as for the verb *donne*, we can observe that in nearly all cases of Indirect-Object Constructions, the marked Recipient is a nominal argument or a proper name (except for two instances where the Recipient is the pronoun *zaute* (2P/3P)). In both modern MC and SC, the Indirect-Object Construction with *dir* has survived, but there seem to be a clear difference between the two languages. While we find rare indirect object marking with the verb *dir* in SC, this marking seems to be absent in MC (Adone 2004: 196), or only restricted to certain rural varieties of the language. In both languages, the conditions under which the Indirect Object pattern with the verb *dir* occurs merit further study.

3.4 Occurrences of Indirect-Object Constructions in chronological order

In this section, we look at the first occurrences of Indirect Object patterns in the old MC texts of the present corpus. Beside the marking of the Recipient, we are also interested in the expression of the comitative function ('with') and noun phrase conjunction ('and'). One question is whether there are differences in marking of these functional domains.

---

[39] In the present corpus, imperative constructions account for ca. 10% of all Double-Object Constructions.
[40] See also Bruyn et al. 1999 for a similar argument; for the historical data see Michaelis *forthcoming*.

Table 3: Marking of Recipient, comitative, and NP conjunction

Text	Recipient		Comitative and/or Nominal Conjunction
	done	dir	
1818 (Chrestien)		avec (1)	avec
1822 (Chrestien)		avec (1)	avec
1828 (Lambert)	avec (2)		
1855 (Lolliot)		av (1) asamb (1)	av', avec ensemble
1867 (Descroizilles)	avec (1)		avec, ave
1880 (Baissac)		av (4)	av, ac (1)
1885 (Anderson)	avec (1)	avec (3) av (3)	avec (verbal arguments often marked by av/vec, very rare)
1888 (Baissac)	av (3)	av (23) ave (1) sembe (2)	av, ave, avec (in headline of a story), éc, semb'
1892 (Antelme)		av' (1)	av', avec

* The number in parentheses refer to the number of tokens in the texts

Up to the mid 19th century, all three functions (recipient, comitative and nominal conjunction) are expressed by the marker *avec*. It is only in Lolliot 1855a that we find for the first time a Recipient marked by *av*:

(37) *Ein zour pié filao té dir' av pié fataque: (...)* (Lolliot 1855a)   (=18)
'One day the casuarina tree said to the fataque plant: (...)'
'Un jour le filao disait au fataque'

Furthermore, we can see that Baissac (1880, 1888) contrasts with Anderson 1885 in that in Baissac we do not find the marking of either Recipient or nominal conjunction by *avec* anymore, only with the more strongly grammticalized form *av*.

Another generalization from the data in Table 3 is that the marking of the Recipient argument is either as complex as, or less complex than, the marking of nominal conjunction or comitative.

3.5 Diachronic perspective and semantic domains

Even though the Indirect Object pattern seems to be a very marginal phenomenon in old MC as well as in both modern MC and SC, it is a very interesting fact in itself that the marking of the recipient in an Indirect-Object Construction is carried out by a marker which at the same time has a comitative meaning. From a typological point of view, this development from COMITATIVE to RECIPIENT seems to be rare (cf Malchukov et al. 2007). In an unpublished paper by Malchukov et al. (2007), the following semantic domains are in direct vicinity of recipient-marking and thus possible sources for coding this semantic role: MALEFACTIVE, BENEFICIARY, GOAL, and PATIENT of 'hit' verbs. From what we observe in old MC, we would have expected to find COMITATIVE as well.

But is it really the COMITATIVE function which was the source of *avec*-recipient marking in old MC? We think that there is a different explanation. When looking at yet other uses of *avec*-marking in the old MC texts, we find contexts which may have served as the missing link for the interpretation of *avec* as recipient marker:

(38) *E kan la sézon fri ti fine pros, li ti anvoy so zans domestic avec tou ça planter là, pour gaïn so fri.* (Anderson 1885)
'Et quand le temps des fruits approcha, il envoya ses serviteurs aux vignerons pour recevoir les fruits qui lui revenaient'
'And when harvesting season was near, he sent his servants to these vine planters to collect the fruits that belonged to him'

In example (38), the interpretation is clearly *not* COMITATIVE: '*he sent his servants **with** these planters (...)', but 'to these planters'. *Avec* thus refers to a location: 'at the planters'. An example from modern SC illustrates this locational 'at'-interpretation of *avec/ek*:

(39) *Ou napa en kreyon ek ou?* (Bollée & Rosalie 1994: 124)
 'Don't you have a pencil on/with you?'
 'Tu n'as pas un crayon sur toi/avec toi ?'

The marker *avec* refers to the local region (or PLACE in Jackendoff's terms) of an object or a person: 'to be at/with something or someone'. Now when the verb which combines with *avec* expresses oriented movement or spatial orientation as in example (38), it might seem that *avec* has a different meaning ('to'), but in fact it still only marks the location 'at' (here: the planters). The dynamic interpretation of PATH (orientation towards an object/person) remains implicit and is only recoverable via the interpretation of the verb 'to send'. In MC and SC, we can see the same mechanism at work with intransitive and transitive motion verbs, e.g. 'to go', 'to push'. In these constructions, the notion of 'motion-to' is not expressed overtly, but has to be inferred from the semantics of the verb (cf Michaelis *forthcoming*).[41]

Our claim is thus that the marking of the recipient with *avec* in old MC (and its traces in its modern successors) can be analyzed in exactly the same way. *Avec* only refers to the local region of the recipient, whereas the dynamic interpretation 'motion-to', 'transfer-to' has to be taken from the semantics of the verb *donne* 'to give'. In this view, the old MC use of *avec* for recipients is not due so much to a surprising COMITATIVE-RECIPIENT polysemy, but to an unexpected distribution of the overall meaning between the verb *donne* and the preposition *avec*.

4 Conclusion

We have looked at the evolution of the French derived relators *avec-et-ensemble* in old MC, modern MC, and SC texts. These relators do not have the same distribution as in French, and they cover a huge semantic area encoding nominal and verbal conjunction, comitative and semantically related functions, and recipient marking in ditransitive constructions (even though this latter pattern is extremely rare in old MC and its successor varieties). In the present article, we have dealt with nominal and verbal conjunction (§2), and ditransitive constructions (§3). The results are the following:

 (i) In the domain of conjunction, there exist two main differences with the European base language French:
 – Verbal and nominal conjunction tend to be marked differently.
 – Nominal conjunction is encoded by a WITH-word.

 (ii) In the domain of the ditransitive constructions, the major pattern is the one in which neither recipient nor theme is marked, the Double-Object construction, whereas French shows the Indirect-Object pattern. Only a very small proportion of the ditransitive constructions with *donne* and *dir* show a recipient marked by *avec* and thus a more French-like pattern.

We have argued that these linguistic facts are due to complex language contact phenomena. What we already find in both construction domains in the old MC texts is the pattern of East Bantu substrate languages. The ditransitive construction with its Double-Object pattern still shows the Bantu structures in the modern creoles, and the *avec* patterns only occupy a few niches. In the case of WITH-marking of nominal conjunction, we

---

[41] In the following two examples from SC with intransitive motion verbs (*ale, sorti*), MOTION-TO and MOTION-FROM are not marked overtly: MOTION-TO *mon al dan bwa* 'I go into the forest'; MOTION-FROM *mon sorti dan bwa* 'I come out of the forest'. For a more detailed analysis of Seychelles Creole PATH-constructions, see Michaelis *forthcoming*.

hypothesize a case of convergence: French ambiguous constructions with *avec* referring either to nominal conjunction or to a comitative reading may have lent themselves to reinterpretation on the basis of the Bantu pattern. As for *ar(e)*-marking in MC from 1929 (and this may also apply to *av(e)*-marking from 1850 onwards), we claim Mauritian Bhojpuri (MB) influence. In MB, the conjunction *aur/ar* is used in both verbal and nominal conjunction. This statement becomes relevant if one takes a closer look at the pre-1952 MC data. *Ar(e)* which replaced the earlier form *av(e)* (1850-1929) is the dominant conjunction linking nominal entities in the period 1929–1952). The MB marker *aur/ar* may have been copied into the MC nominal conjunction pattern. Even today, the frequent use of *ar* (especially in comitative/verbal constructions) appears to be associated with MC speakers from an Indo-Mauritian background.

The corpus of old MC texts which form the rock-bed of this book, and the concordance elaborated by Guillaume Fong Sing, are invaluable tools for present and future fine-grained philological studies of the development of MC. Even bearing in mind that the present collection of texts is due in part to historical accidents of recording and preservation, and also admitting that these texts can at best only represent a small fraction of the range of variation which probably existed in the 18th and 19th centuries, we must not underestimate the value of such historical linguistic data. Our theories will have to be checked against these treasures of Creole studies.

References

Adone, Dany 1994 Double-Object constructions in two French-based creoles. Escure, Geneviève & Schwegler, Armin (eds) *Creoles, Contact, and Language Change. Linguistic and social implications*, Amsterdam: Benjamins, 189-208.

Anon. 1980 *Bord la mer*. Port Louis: Port Louis Harbour and Docks Workers Union.

Baissac, Charles 1880 *Etude sur le patois créole mauricien*. Nancy: Imprimerie Berger-Levrault

Baker, Philip 1972 *Kreol. A Description of Mauritian Creole*, London: C Hurst.

—— 1996 On the development of certain prepositional forms in Mauritian and other French Creoles. Véronique, Daniel (ed.), 41-59.

Baker, Philip & Ramnah, Amarnath 1988 Recognizing Mauritian Bhojpuri. Barz, R C & Siegel, J (eds) *Language transplanted. the development of overseas Hindi*. Wiesbaden: Harrassowitz.

Bollée, Annegret 1977 *Le créole français des Seychelles. Esquisse d'une grammaire - textes - vocabulaire*, Tübingen: Niemeyer.

—— 1982 Die Rolle der Konvergenz bei der Kreolisierung, Ureland, P S (ed.) *Die Leistung der Strataforschung und der Kreolistik. Typologische Aspekte der Sprachkontakte*. Tübingen: Niemeyer, 391-405.

Bollée, Annegret & Rosalie, Marcel 1994 *Parol ek memwar. Récits de vie des Seychelles*, Hamburg: Buske.

Bord la mer, see Anon. 1980.

Bruyn, Adrienne, Muysken, Pieter & Verrips, Maaike 1999 Double-Object Constructions in the Creole Languages: Development and Acquisition. DeGraff, Michel (ed.), *Language creation and language change*, Cambridge: MIT Press, 329-73.

Chaudenson, Robert 1974 *Le lexique du parler créole de la Réunion*, Paris: Champion, 2 vols.

—— 1981 *Textes créoles anciens (La Réunion et Ile Maurice)*. Hamburg: Buske.

—— 2003 *La créolisation: théorie, applications, implications*, Paris: L'Harmattan.

Fon Sing, Guillaume 2006 Naviguer dans les textes anciens en créole mauricien: présentation d'un projet de concordancier à usage scientifique et pédagogique. *Etudes Créoles*, 28.1-2: 191-207.

Furlong, Robert & Ramharai, Vicram 2006 *Panorama de la littérature mauricienne: la production créolophone. vol. 1: des origines à l'indépendance*, Mauritius: Collection TIMAM.

Haspelmath, Martin 2004 Coordinating constructions: an overview. Haspelmath, M (ed.), 3-40.
—— 2005 Nominal and Verbal Conjunction. Haspelmath et al. (eds), 262-65.
Haspelmath, Martin (ed.) 2004 *Coordinating Constructions*. Amsterdam: Benjamins.
Haspelmath, M, Dryer, M S, Gil, D & Comrie, B (eds) 2005 *The World Atlas of Language Structures*. Oxford: Oxford University Press.
Heine, Bernd & Kuteva, Tania 2002 *World Lexicon of Grammaticalization*, Cambridge: Cambridge University Press.
—— & —— 2005 *Language Contact and Grammatical Change*, Cambridge: Cambridge University Press
Jackendoff, Ray 1983 *Semantics and Cognition*, Cambridge, Mass.: MIT Press.
Johanson, Lars 2002 Contact-induced change in a code-copying framework. Jones, Mari C & Esch, Edith (eds) *Language Change. The Interplay of Internal, External and Extra-Linguistic Factors*, Berlin: Mouton de Gruyter, 285-313
Kriegel, Sibylle 1996 *Diathesen im Mauritius- und Seychellenkreol*. Tübingen: Narr.
—— 2003 *Grammaticalisation et réanalyse. Approches de la variation créole et française*. Paris: CNRS-Editions.
—— [*in preparation*] Conjonction nominale et contact de langues en créole mauricien. Ms.
Kriegel, Sibylle, Ludwig, Ralph & Henri, Fabiola [*forthcoming*-a] Les rapports entre créole et bhojpouri à Maurice. Hookoomsing, V, Ludwig, R & Schnepel, B (eds) *Multiple identities in action: Mauritius and the Antillean parallelism*. [provisional title].
Kriegel, Sibylle, Ludwig, Ralph & Henri, Fabiola [*forthcoming*-b] Encoding Path in Mauritian Creole and Bhojpuri: problems concerning language contact. Michaelis, Susanne (ed.).
Lefebvre, Claire 1998 *Creole genesis and the acquisition of grammar. the case of Haitian Creole.* Cambridge: Cambridge University Press.
Lefebvre, Claire 2004 Coordinating constructions in Fongbe with reference to Haitian Creole. Haspelmath, M (éd.) *Coordinating Constructions*, Amsterdam: Benjamins, 123-65.
Lefebvre Claire & Therrien Isabelle 2007 *The Multiple Facets of Papiamentu* ku *, Creolica INFO
Le Juge de Segrais, Xavier [1939, 1952] 1976 *Quarante contes en patois mauricien*. Port-Louis: The Mauritius Printing Cy. Ltd.
Ludwig, Ralph, Telchid, Sylviane & Bruneau-Ludwig, Florence (eds) 2001 *Corpus créole. Textes oraux dominicais, guadeloupéens, guyanais, haitiens, mauriciens et seychellois*. Hamburg: Buske.
Malchukov, Andrej, Haspelmath, Martin & Comrie, Bernard 2007 Ditransitive constructions: a typological overview. MPI Leipzig, unpublished paper.
Mesthrie, Rajend 1991 *Language in Indenture. A Sociolinguistic History of Bhojpuri-Hindi in South Africa.* : Johannesburg: Witwatersrand University Press.
Michaelis, Susanne, (ed.). [*forthcoming*] *Creole language structure between substrates and superstrates*. Amsterdam: Benjamins.
Michaelis, Susanne [*forthcoming*] Valency patterns in Seychelles Creole: Where do they come from? Michaelis, Susanne (ed.).
Michaelis, Susanne & Haspelmath, Martin 2003 Ditransitive constructions: Creole languages in a cross-linguistic perspective. *Creolica* 2003-04-23, http://www.creolica.net.
Michaelis, Susanne & Rosalie, Marcel 2000 Polysémie et cartes sémantiques: le relateur (av)ek en créole seychellois. *Etudes Créoles* 23.2: 79-100.
Parkvall, Mikael 2000 *Out of Africa. African influences in Atlantic Creoles*. London: Battlebridge.
Shukla, Shaligram 1981 *Bhojpuri Grammar*. Washington DC: Georgetown University Press.
Stassen, Leon 2000 AND-languages and WITH-Languages. *Linguistic Typology* 4: 1-54.

—— 2005 Noun Phrase Conjunction. Haspelmath et al. (eds) *The World Atlas of Language Structures*. Oxford: Oxford University Press, 258-61.

Stolz, Thomas, Stroh, Cornelia & Urdze, Aina 2006 *On Comitatives and Related Categories. A Typological Study with Special Focus on the Languages of Europe*, Berlin: Mouton de Gruyter.

Véronique, Daniel 1996 présentation. Véronique, Daniel (ed.), 5-15.

Véronique, Daniel (ed.) 1996 *Matériaux pour l'étude des classes grammaticales dans les langues creoles*, Aix-en-Provence: PUP.

Welmers, William 1976 *A grammar of Vai*. Berkeley: University of California Press.

Sibylle Kriegel, chargée de recherches CNRS, est affectée au Laboratoire "Parole et Langage" à l'Université de Provence (Aix-Marseille 1). Elle travaille sur le changement linguistique et le contact de langues, notamment dans les langues créoles à base romane.
<sibylle.kriegel@lpl-aix.fr>

Susanne Michaelis is affiliated to the Max Planck Institute for Evolutionary Anthropology in Leipzig. She specializes in Indian Ocean French Creoles, and has recently developed a special interest in comparative creole research. She is a co-editor of the ongoing collaborative project *Atlas of Pidgin and Creole Language Structures* (APiCS).
<michaelis@eva.mpg.de>

Ena et *gagne* : à propos de la genèse de l'expression de l'existence et de la possession / propriété en créole mauricien[1]

Guillaume Fon Sing
Georges Daniel Véronique

1. Introduction

Cette étude porte sur les fonctions syntaxiques et les valeurs sémantiques qu'*ena* et *gagne(r)* ont occupés à date ancienne en créole mauricien (CM) et sur leurs fonctionnements actuels. Si *gagne(r)* provient du verbe français *gagner*, *ena*, lui, est dérivé du présentatif français *(il) y en a*. Selon Creissels (1996, 2006), les verbes de *possession / propriété*[2] se développent souvent à partir de verbes dont le sens originel se réfère à un processus d'acquisition plus ou moins concret (*saisir, obtenir, gagner*) ou à un résultat (*tenir, porter*). Il rappelle également que lat. *habere* et fr. *avoir* sont issus d'une racine indo-européenne qui signifie 'saisir' (Creissels 2006, vol. 2 : 97). En CM, *ena* et *gagne(r)* constituent non seulement des prédicats de possession / propriété mais font également partie des impersonnels sémantiques, dont relèvent les verbes météorologiques et les existentiels.[3] Si l'on se réfère à la typologie établie par Stassen (2001), le créole mauricien a développé une double expression de la propriété / possession : à l'aide d'un verbe signifiant l'acquisition et d'un existentiel, ce qui le différencie de nombre de langues créoles.

À partir d'un cadre théorique où seront succinctement redéfinis les rôles de la réanalyse, de la grammaticalisation et de l'analogie dans l'émergence grammaticale, nous nous proposons d'examiner selon quels mécanismes sémantiques et syntaxiques, le créole mauricien s'est doté de verbes de possession / propriété, qui permettent également d'exprimer « [...] n'importe quelle relation de rattachement d'une entité (représentée par l'objet) à la sphère personnelle du référent du sujet » (Creissels 2006, vol. 2 : 98) et de construire des impersonnels sémantiques. Nous tenterons donc d'apporter des éléments de réponse aux questions suivantes :

- Pourquoi *ena* et *gagne(r)* ont-ils été retenus pour exprimer l'existence, la localisation, la possession et la propriété en CM? En quoi ce fonctionnement sémantaxique diverge-t-il de celui des étymons français correspondants ?
- Quels sont les rapports entre *ena* et *gagner* en diachronie?

---

[1] Nous remercions Philip Baker, Robert Chaudenson et Diana Guillemin pour leur lecture de ce texte et leurs commentaires. Les erreurs demeurent nôtres.
[2] *Ena* exprime la propriété inaliénable (*li ena en gro vant* = il a un gros ventre) tout autant que la propriété aliénable (*mo ena en loto* = j'ai une voiture). En CM contemporain, le verbe processif *gagne* n'est équivalent au verbe statif *ena* qu'accompagné d'un marqueur de perfectif (*li ena en gro vant* = *li fin gegn en gro vant* ou *mo ena loto* = *mo fin gegn en loto*). *Gegn* est surtout attesté dans des contextes d'expression de la propriété aliénable ou de la possession.
[3] Ce phénomène est courant comme l'indique Creissels (2006 : 325 et suiv.) et Duff (1993).

2. L'expression de la POSSESSION / PROPRIÉTÉ (P), de la LOCALISATION (L) et de l'EXISTENCE (E) : quelques considérations typologiques

2.1. L'espace sémantique et morphosyntaxique des relations de P, L et E

Selon Clark (1970, 1978), un certain nombre de langues du monde encode les constructions possessives (possession / propriété) (P) et existentielles (E) grâce à la même unité. Slobin (1985 : 1179), utilisant la distinction *Figure-Ground* de Talmy (1983), envisage le chevauchement de l'expression de la localisation et de la possession et ses conséquences pour l'acquisition du langage de la façon suivante : « Broadly conceived, possession is a locative state in which the Ground is an animate being and the Figure-Ground relation is of an enduring or socially-sanctionned nature »[4]. Il cite des exemples provenant de l'acquisition du langage par l'enfant où un fonctionnel locatif est employé pour signifier la possession, malgré l'existence de deux formes distinctes pour exprimer ces mêmes notions dans la langue des adultes. Cette solution est retenue, de fait, par de nombreuses langues du monde (voir Creissels 1996, 2006).

Dans la perspective de la grammaire cognitive de Langacker (1987), le linguiste He (1989) distingue les fonctions chevauchantes P / E du morphème *you* en chinois en termes de « participant » et de « cadre ». Lorsque le sujet de *you*, ainsi que son objet, sont des participants, alors la relation entre le sujet et l'objet est possessive. Mais lorsque le sujet fonctionne comme cadre (l'objet étant toujours un participant), la relation est existentielle ; Creissels (2006) défend un point de vue analogue.

Selon Jackendoff (1983 : 192), « être possédé de manière aliénable » constitue une relation de localisation ; ceci signifie que 'Y a / possède X' est le parallèle conceptuel de 'X est à Y' ». Se basant sur cette formulation, Pinker (1989 : 190) pose HAVE (*avoir*) et BE (*être*) comme des « prédicats sémantiques distincts » en anglais et considère que « cognitivement, l'état HAVE est simplement l'inverse de l'état BE, traitant la localisation, plutôt que le locatum, comme 'sujet logique' ».

2.2. La possession / propriété (P) et l'existence (E) dans les langues créoles

Les langues créoles tendent à employer une même unité pour les constructions possessive et existentielle ; le doublet *ena / gagne(r)* du CM présente une exception relative de ce point de vue. Selon Bickerton (1981: 66) :

> « ... over a wide range of creoles, the same lexical item is used to express existentials ('there is') and possessives ('have'), even though this is not true of any of the superstrates »[5]

Cette observation est illustrée par les exemples (1) et (2) du créole anglais d'Hawaï et du papiamento respectivement :

(1)　　*get* wan washini she *get* wan data
　　　　il y a une femme elle a une fille
(2)　　*tin* un muhe cu *tin* un yiu-muhe
　　　　il y a une femme qui a une fille

---

[4] Traduction : « Selon une conception élargie, la possession est un état locatif où la figure est un être animé et le rapport figure-fond une relation de nature durable ou susceptible de sanctions sociales ».
[5] Traduction : « Dans un nombre important de langues créoles, le même item lexical exprime des existentiels (il y a) et des possessifs (avoir), même si les superstrats ne présentent pas un cas de figure identique ».

Bickerton (1981 : 250) représente l'espace sémantique partagé par P, E et L à l'aide du schéma suivant :

(3)

Ownership (Propriété)	Location (Localisation)
Possession (Possession)	Existence (Existence)

En ce qui concerne le CM, nous pouvons schématiser nos interrogations ainsi :

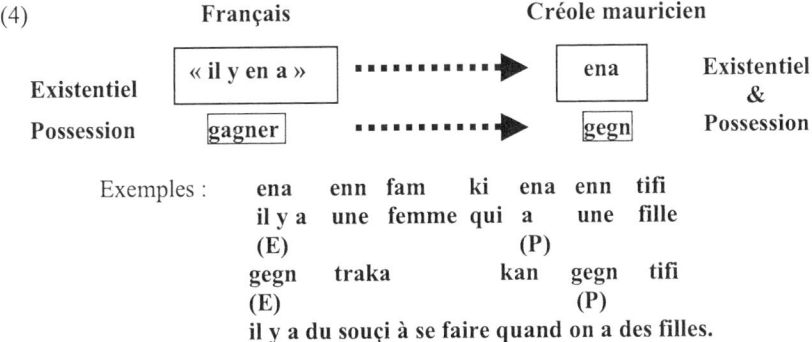

Exemples :   ena   enn fam   ki   ena enn tifi
                il y a   une femme qui a   une fille
                (E)   (P)
                gegn   traka   kan gegn tifi
                (E)   (P)
il y a du souçi à se faire quand on a des filles.

En d'autres termes, comment et pourquoi le présentatif français *il y a / il y en a* et le possessif *gagner* ont-ils conduit aux unités homophones du CM qui fonctionnent comme marqueurs d'existentiel et de relation de possession / propriété ?

3. Cadre théorique

3.1 Le changement linguistique

De Meillet (1912) à Lightfoot (1999), en passant par Hagège (1993), Bybee, Pagliuca & Perkins (1994) et Harris & Campbell (1995), on distingue, en règle générale, trois mécanismes du changement linguistique : l'« emprunt », l'« analogie » et la « grammaticalisation » (pour une présentation synthétique, voir Peyraube 2002). Selon les auteurs, la grammaticalisation est soit associée à un quatrième processus, non moins important, la « réanalyse », soit elle en est dissociée.[6] Dans ce qui suit, nous nous inspirerons du cadre théorique de Detges & Waltereit (1999) et Detges (2003) sur la réanalyse. Notre conceptualisation en diverge cependant car nous lions la réanalyse aux stratégies cognitives qui forment l'« analogie ». Tout comme Anttila (1977), pour qui tout changement linguistique présente, peu ou prou, un ingrédient analogique, nous posons que l'analogie est au cœur même du changement linguistique. Le *language builder* (Hagège 1993), à la fois auditeur et locuteur, met en œuvre des stratégies cognitives lors de la réception et de la production de messages, qui sont susceptibles d'être des facteurs de changement linguistique. C'est sur la base d'une différence événementielle entre la

---

[6] Nous avons ailleurs pu discuter des divergences théoriques sur ces deux mécanismes et de leur rôle dans la créolisation (cf Fon Sing 2004, 2005, 2006 [thèse en cours]). L'espace dont nous disposons ne nous permet pas de le faire ici.

réception et la production de messages que nous opposons non pas la « réanalyse » à « l'analogie », mais la « réanalyse analogique » à la « néologisation analogique », phénomène qui ne sera pas abordé ici.

3.2. La réanalyse, principal processus interne de la "créolisation"

3.2.1. La notion de réanalyse

Si l'on se fonde sur la définition classique de Langacker (1977 : 58),[7] la réanalyse entraîne :

- une restructuration de la construction syntaxique entière (*rebracketing*, Haspelmath 1998 : 330)
- une recatégorisation de l'élément réanalysé (*category relabelling*, Harris et Campbell 1995 : 63)

Pour ce qui est du « changement par réanalyse analogique », qui intervient au moment du traitement du message en réception, nous distinguerons, à la suite de Detges (2003).

- la réanalyse analogique par référence (analogie sémantico-référentielle)
- la réanalyse analogique par transparence (analogie formelle)

(5)

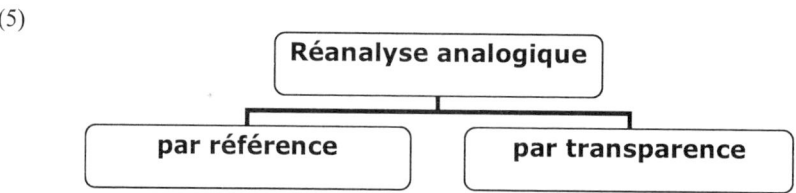

3.2.2.1. La réanalyse analogique par référence

Pour analyser une chaîne sonore X, donc pour la *comprendre*, l'auditeur a recours à un principe simple que Detges et Waltereit (1999) et Detges (2003) nomme le *principe de référence*, et qui est, selon ces auteurs, le plus important des deux principes sous-jacents aux opérations de réanalyse. Ce principe peut être résumé ainsi :

(6) *Le principe de référence*

Pour comprendre l'énoncé que tu entends, suppose que le signifié de la chaîne parlée correspond au type de référent auquel elle semble renvoyer.

Dans sa démonstration, Detges (2003 : 54-55) s'appuie sur l'exemple du SN arabe hispanique *al qâdí* « le maire » réanalysé en espagnol médiéval *alcade* « maire ». Selon cet auteur, les cas d'agglutination du déterminant – l'article défini arabe *al* y perd son statut de morphème – et du nom engendrent de nombreux substantifs de l'espagnol par réanalyse suivant le principe de référence,

(7) *aldea* « village », *alcohol* « alcohol », *almacén* « magasin », *algodón* « coton », *albañil* « maçon », *aduana* « douane », *aceite* « huile » etc.

---

[7] « [...] change in the structure of an expression or class of expressions that does not involve any immediate or intrisic modification of its surface manifestations » (changement dans la structure d'une expression ou d'une classe d'expression qui n'implique pas une modification intrinsèque ou immediate de sa manifestation en surface)

Selon Detges (2003 : 55), « les résultats des analyses de ce type sont donc *une survivance matérielle* en même temps qu'*une discontinuité fonctionnelle* ». Le principe de référence décrit une stratégie de l'*auditeur* qui cherche à attribuer un signifié à une chaîne sonore. Plus précisément, ce principe décrit une stratégie de *compréhension* et de *mémorisation* économique, basée sur la fréquence élevée de l'unité occurrente (*token*).

3.2.2.2 La réanalyse analogique par transparence

(8) *Le principe de transparence*

Pour comprendre l'énoncé que tu entends, compare la chaîne parlée avec d'autres chaînes parlées que tu connais déjà.

Ce deuxième principe est décrit par Lehmann (1995 : 1262) sous l'étiquette de « réanalyse analogique ». Tout comme le principe de référence, le principe de transparence décrit une stratégie de compréhension et de mémorisation économiques. Il s'applique dans tous les cas où les locuteurs sont peu familiers avec une expression donnée. À la différence du principe de référence dont l'application est favorisée par la fréquence élevée de la chaîne sonore en question, le principe de transparence s'applique surtout dans le cas d'unités (*tokens*) peu fréquentes. De ces deux principes, c'est le principe de référence qui prime : les réinterprétations analogiques ne sont légitimes que si elles garantissent que le principe de référence n'est pas violé.

4. L'émergence de *ena* et de *gagne(r)* en CM : graphiation et grammatisation

Dans ce qui suit, nous nous intéresserons aux emplois de *gagne(r)* comme marqueur d'existence et comme marqueur d'une relation de rattachement plutôt qu'à son emploi comme verbe transitif doté de la même signification que son étymon français. Nous étudierons également les modifications morphologiques, syntaxiques et sémantiques qui font de *ena*, un marqueur d'existence et de possession / propriété.

4.1. Premières attestations de *ena* et de *gagne(r)*

Les premières attestations d'un « marqueur de possession et de propriété » et d'un « marqueur existentiel » en CM datent de 1805 sous les formes *n'a pas, y en a* et *gagne* (9 à 12):

(9) «mô **gagne** posson, **gagne** sévrettes ; mô **n'a pas** zardin donc ? mô **gagne** ziromon, bananes» **(possession /propriété ; 1805)**

(10) «Mais, papa, vous **n'a pas** simise, donc, vous **n'a pas** kilotte ; n'a rien ? Si fait, dans mô case, **y en a**». **(possession / propriété ; 1805)**

(11) «Mais, papa, quand vous malade, qui soigné vous? Ah ! hé ! **n'a pas** l'optal, **n'a pas** sourzin ?» **(existence /localisation ; 1805)**

(12) «Papa, vous **y en a** femme, ou bien vous tout cèle ? Mo **y en a** femme» **(possession /propriété ; 1805)**

Les unités attestées en 9, 10 et 12 renvoient à des contextes de *possession* aliénable et la relation d'*existence / localisation* en 11 est strictement liée à la nature de lexèmes dépendants *l'optal, sourzin.*

4.2 La négation de *ena* et de *gagne(r)*

Bien que notre analyse ne soit pas centrée sur le marqueur de négation *n'a pas* (voir Véronique 2003 et Baker 2003), il est nécessaire d'aborder brièvement cette question. En effet, *n'a pas* apparaît tantôt en (9) et (10) comme « verbe marqueur de non possession » (comme semblent le suggérer les oppositions *n'a pas versus gagne* et *n'a pas versus y en a*), et en (11) comme « verbe marqueur de non existence » et, tantôt, comme « marqueur de négation » (négateur). Des attestations antérieures à 1805 (exemples 13 à 16) semblent indiquer un usage premier de *n'a pas* comme négateur. Dans le texte de **1805** où *gagne* est nié par *n'a pas* dans sa signification de « propriété/ possession », *gagne(r)* avec la signification d' « obtenir / recevoir » est, lui, nié par *n'a pas*, d'où *n'a pas gagné,*

(13) «*Vous **n'a pas** gagné coups de fouette ?*».

Il en est de même en (14),

(14) «*Si nous **n'a pas** gagné malheur*» (**1769**).

Dans ces premières attestations, la négation porte sur un prédicat, qui est tantôt un verbe, tantôt un nom ou un adjectif,

> S + Neg + V

(15)a. «*moi **n'a pas** vouler la guerre avec camarade*» (**1793**)
   b. «*Ça petit monde là **n'a pas** voulé palé pour **na pas** travail* » (**1802**)

> S + Neg. + Adj. ou Nom

(16) *ça **n'a pas** bon*» (**1769**)

(17)a. «*Hé ! Hé ! pourquoi mô **n'a pas** content ?*»
   b. *mô **n'a pas** volor, moi, mô **n'a pas** maron*
   c. *mô **n'a pas** saclave ?*
   d. *vous **n'a pas** libe donc ?* (**1805**)

Dans les exemples 13 à 17, l'analyse de *n'a pas* comme « marqueur de négation » (négateur) est justifiée par :

- l'occurrence de *n'a pas* dans le contexte de *gagné* en (14) comme en (13) alors que dans les exemples (9) et (10) *a* s'oppose à *gagne* (avec une différence de sens indéterminée) et à *y en a*. Le fait que *a* semble attesté uniquement dans un contexte négatif plaide en faveur de l'existence d'un verbe négatif.[8] Indice complémentaire : le scribe note tantôt *n'a pas* tantôt *na pas* (en 15) ;[9]

- dans les contextes (13-17) *n'a pas* ne peut signifier ni non-existence ni non-possession ;

---

[8] Il convient de noter une grammaticalisation ultérieure de *n'a pas* qui devient *napas / napa*, une forme longue de la négation – analysé par G Hazaël-Massieux comme *n'ailles pas* pour les Petites Antilles (voir Véronique 2003).

[9] A moins qu'il ne s'agisse d'erreurs typographiques (coquilles).

- *n'a pas* ou « *a* en contexte négatif » n'assume pas une fonction prédicative, comme en (9), mais détermine le prédicat.

De l'observation de la chronologie des attestations, on ne devrait pas en déduire, cependant, que *n'a pas* a d'abord été employé comme un négateur total avant de devenir un marqueur de « non existence » ou de « non possession ». Notre analyse rejoint plutôt celle de Baker qui relève que *napa* possédait encore au début de XIXe siècle une « force verbale » et qu'on peut supposer qu'il était « aussi bien une sorte de verbe négatif fossilisé qu'un marqueur de négation » (2003 : 123).

4.3 Les premières attestations graphiques de *ena*

4.3.1 Un recensement des occurrences

Comme le rappellent les éditeurs en introduction de cet ouvrage, les scripteurs/locuteurs présentent une certaine diversité d'usage graphique dans leur texte. On ne peut que conjecturer sur les évolutions phoniques, sachant que la grammaticalisation (selon la définition de Lehmann) inclut des phénomènes d'attrition phonétique. Reste que l'on souhaiterait identifier le moment du passage de [jãna] / [jena][10] à [ena] et de la chute du glide [j] ? On souhaiterait également comprendre l'évolution graphique de *y en a* et de *iéna*. Est-ce que « *y* » correspond à *li / i* (comme en CM contemporain li ena = [jena] ?) Autrement dit, est-ce que les scripteurs utilisent [jena] dans les textes anciens, comme le CM contemporain emploie [ena] ? Autre interrogation, les scripteurs du créole ont-ils tenté de distinguer graphiquement la suite *pronom + Verbe* « *y en a* » de l'existentiel *iéna* ? Les *scripta* du CM semblent recéler des questions d'évolution phonétique et de morphologisation.

Nous examinerons les premières attestations de chaque forme et nous tenterons de dégager une explication de ces attestations graphiques (qui sera sans doute approximative à cause de la diversité des usages). Nous essaierons d'entrevoir ce faisant les liens entre graphiation et grammatisation (dans le sens de « mise en grammaire », voir Auroux 1994, Véronique 2006) en fonction des auteurs analysés.

23 formes pour 399 occurrences (avec parfois des variantes écrites différentes chez un même auteur) sont attestées dans le relevé présenté dans le Tableau 1. Nous avons étiqueté les énoncés avec *ena* en fonction de la distinction entre 1) propriété / possession et 2) existence. Le critère de codage suivant a été retenu : *ena* est possessif quand son SN1 est un agent / contrôleur et son SN2 « *possessible* par un contrôleur». Au cas contraire, c'est un existentiel.

En répartissant toutes les formes de *ena* relevés en deux groupes – groupe 1 : [jena], groupe 2 : [ena], on obtient le Tableau 2 et son graphique correspondant. Ce tableau indique que le passage de [jena] à [ena] s'est fait de manière graduelle. Après s'être concurrencé, la forme [ena] l'a finalement emporté sur [jena] vers la fin du XIXe siècle.

---

[10] De quand date la dénasalisation du [ã] en [e]? La valeur phonique des graphèmes semble dans ce cas indécodable. Se pose un problème de scripta, rappelons nous par exemple qu'*étois* se prononçait [ete] en ancien français.

Tableau 1. Premières attestations graphiques des variantes de ENA par ordre chronologique

	Forme	Premières attestations		Nombre d'occurrences dans le corpus
1805	y en a	(…) vous n'a pas kilotte; n'a rien ? Si fait, dans mô case, **y en a**. **(1805)**	**(existence) ou (propriété/possession)?**	27
1822	y-en-a	Quand y **en-a** trou dans vou faitaze Dir'moi qui c'ella va boucé ? (Chrestien [1822] 1831 : 5-26)	(existence)	5
1823	en a	et si mon été **en a** couteau, moi va bien arrange toi, coquin **(1823)**	**(propriété/possession)**	3
1828	y-en a	Comment vous capable connéz qui vous **y-en a** un nâme dans vous le côr ? (Lambert 1828)	**(propriété/possession)**	14
1828	y-en à	Qui differance qui **y-en à** entre vous nâme et vous le côr ? (Lambert 1828)	(existence)	13
1828	y en à	(…) et tout sa mauvais mazination qui mo **y en à** dans mo la vie. (Lambert 1828)	**(propriété/possession)**	2
1831	y-en-a	Eté **y-en-a** ein' p'tit lé-Roi Qui fair' tout l'mond' bien aise n'a pas fier (…) (Chrestien 1831)	(existence)	16
1832	yen-a	Si vou **yen-a** l'ambition Si vous tendé la raison, (…) (1832a, in Chrestien 1838)	**(propriété/possession)**	1
1832	y enna	Combien bann' années vous **y enna** ? Quatorze Tété tombé, tété dibouté. **(1832b)**	**(propriété/possession)**	2
1839	y en ena	Y en **ena** dispite même : Myrtil qui fin trouvé son femme avec Philogène là haut grénier. **(1839a)**	(existence)	1
1839	yana	… Eh bien! figure, ou li ton sabre donc Mo na pas **yana**. **(1839c)**	**(propriété/possession)**	1
1855	ein-a	Li té saut' sauté la haut çaise, Comment dir' **ein-a** pinaise. (Lolliot 1855)	(existence)	1
1855	ein a	Entre nous dés **ein a** vingt pas ; (Lolliot 1855)	(existence)	1
1855	ein'a	Zens qui vantards Quand' même vous baiss' zot, **ein'a** touzours la langue ; (Lolliot 1855)	**(propriété/possession)**	8
1855	y-ein-a	Y-**ein-a** quiq' çose de pli Dans temps français, ma foi, ça n'a pas ein' zistoire **(1855b)**	(existence)	3
1860	yenna	Oui, Bondié faire tout, quand na pas Li, na pas té va **yenna** narien qui ti vivant. **(1860)**	**(propriété/possession)**	12
1867	yena	… et dans zot MAURICE, Tout dimal qui **yena**, zot va gagne SON MALICE. (Descroizilles 1867)	(existence)	20
1867	ena	Longtemps ty **ena** eine blanc, zot dire Bobre Africain (Descroizilles 1867)	(existence)	19
1880	iéna	Té **iéna** éne vié blanc qui té **éna** trois pitits (Baissac 1880)	(existence)	25
1880	éna	Té **iéna** éne vié blanc qui té **éna** trois pitits (Baissac 1880)	(existence)	177
1880	énan	Te **énan** éne vié bourique qui marce marcé dans lacour (Baissac 1880)	(existence)	37
1892	eina	Li mont'' la rie Rempart jousqu'à la rie Madam', la forc'' ne pi **eina**, li siz' lor macadam ([1892] Antelme 1923)	**(propriété/possession)**	3
1892	einan	Rés'ment dans mon lacour **einan** bon vetivert ([1892] Antelme 1923)	(existence)	1

Tableau 2. Répartition des occurrences de *ENA* dans le corpus
[jena] *vs* [ena] : chute du glide [j]

	1805	1818	1822	1823	1828	1831	1832	1835	1837	1839	1840	1850	1855	1860	1865	1867	1880	1885	1888	1892	1897	1925	1929
[jena]	5	1	7	0	29	19	6	4	1	8	1	7	0	2	10	20	10	0	15	0	0	0	0
[ena]	0	0	0	1	1	0	0	0	0	0	0	1	1	0	0	7	8	104	97	4	5	10	2

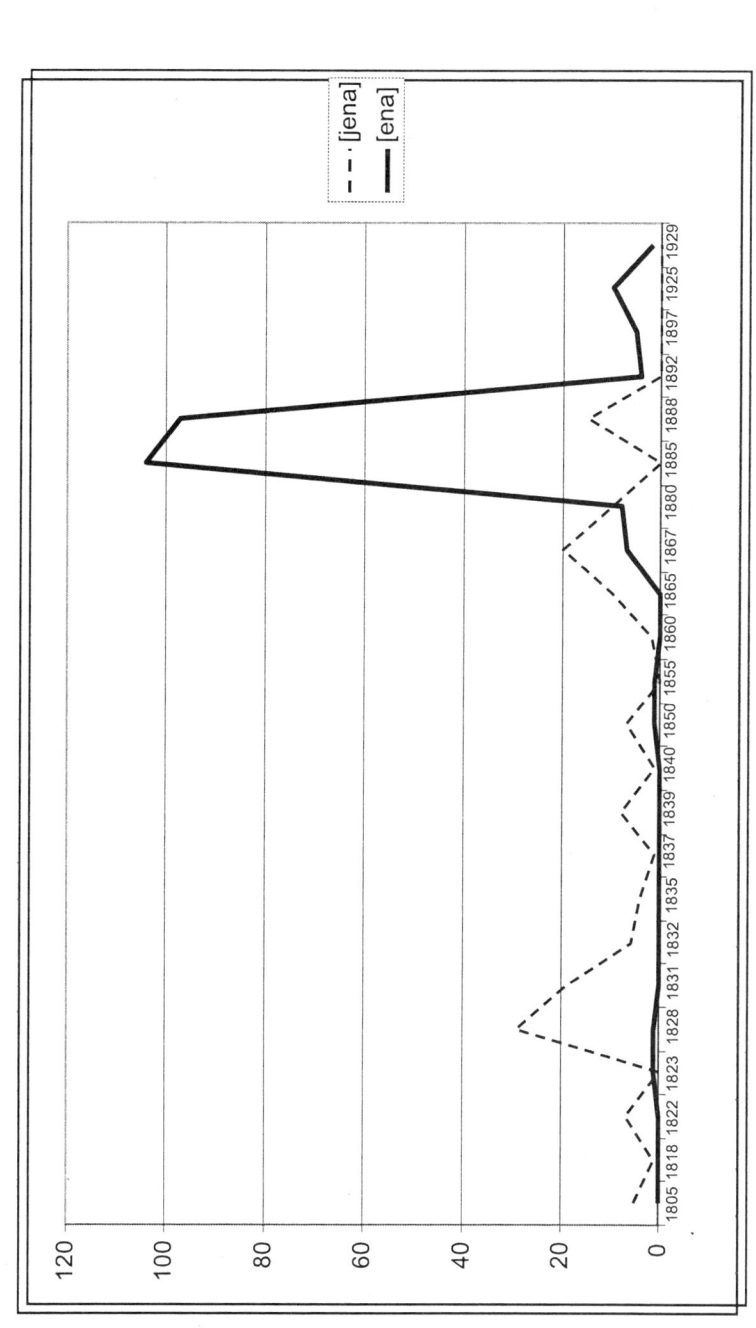

4.3.2. Un inventaire des pratiques de « graphiation » et de « grammatisation » de *ena*.

a) Chrestien ([1822] 1831 : 5-26)

La répartition des 7 instances de «*y en-a*» versus «*y en a*» relevées chez cet auteur ne semble pas être dictée par un souci de différencier l'existentiel du possessif.

(18) «**y en-a**» (4 occurrences)

a. Quand **y en-a** trou dans vou faitaze Dir'moi qui c'ella va boucé ? **(existence)**
b. Dir' moi comment vous vini gras Vous connais galoppé bien vite Quand **y en-a** bouillon couroupas? **(existence)**
c. Moi té commencé blié Vous té **y en-a** bonnet blanc Comment vous çarmant. **(propriété/ possession)**
d. Si vous **y en-a** sentiment Faut fair' comment blanc **(propriété/ possession)**

(19) «**y en a**» (3 occurrences)

a. Dimanç' quand moi gagné zournée Si moi **y en a** morceau tabac Pour fair' faro mon la-fimée **(propriété/ possession)**
b. Tout d'bon moi tout sèl rié Quand di-monde **y en a** malice Qui fair' li voulé sauvé **(propriété/ possession)**
c. Tout d'bon, maman Torti' vous **y en a** trop l'arzent Vou l'esprit li maron dans milié la savanne **(propriété/ possession)**

b) 1839b

La forme "*y ty ena*" s'y trouve attestée, ce qui conduit à s'interroger sur une éventuelle tentative de codage d'un clitique [i]. Malheureusement aucune autre attestation n'est disponible dans ce texte[1].

(20) **Y ty en a** partout, plein son la salle, plein son la varangue, plein son cabinet **(existence)**

c) Catéchisme en créole de l'Ile Maurice en 1828

Ce scripteur propose deux épellations de *a*: « sans accent grave » *versus* « avec accent grave ». Tout comme Chrestien, il a recours à un tiret de façon variable, cependant, l'alternance est ici entre *y-en a* et *y en a*. Ces variations graphiques ne semblent obéir à aucune règle de distribution particulière. Les différentes formes graphiques sont attestées dans des contextes similaires. Comme il s'agit d'un dialogue entre un évangéliste et un esclave, nous avons tenté d'observer s'il n'y avait pas une répartition des formes selon les interlocuteurs mais aucune règle de ce type n'a pu être relevée.

---

[1] Comme Diana Guillemin (DG) nous le fait remarquer, *y* ne remplit jamais une fonction adverbiale ou pronominale dans les anciens textes en CM. Le rattachement de *y* à l'élément subséquent, éventuellement à l'aide d'un tiret, puis la disparition du glide [j] de la langue pourraient être dus, selon DG, à l'absence de sujets explétifs en CM.

(21) **(P) = Propriété /Possession ; (E) = Existence**

en a	y-en a
1	14
Q. Comment vous capable connéz qui vous **y-en a** un nâme dans vous le côr ? (P)	
R. (…) et conné sa qui mo **y-en a** besoin,. (P)	
Q. Qui li montrée vous touts sa écritire qui **y-en a** parole Bon Dieû dans sa Livre là ? (P)	
R. Li été donné avec Juife ein la loi qui **y-en a** dix Commandement dans viée Testament (P)	
R. (…) et li **en a** deux dans Nouveau Testament. (P)	
R. (…) toi na pas vat **y-en a** l'autre Bon Dieû qui moi divant toi. (P)	
R. (…) ni auquine samblance de quique chose qui **y-en a** la haut dans le Ciele, (P)	
R. (…) mo dévrez conné son bonté avant tout quique chose qui **y-en a** la haut la terre, (P)	
R. Mo devrée quité tout sa pêchés qui mo **y-en a** dans mon licaire, (P)	
R. Bon Dieû li bien bon et li toujours **y-en a** pitié pour nous ; (P)	
Q. Par qui raison qui vous **y-en a**, pour croire que vous capabe sauvais ou évitée la colaire de Bon Dieû ? (P)	
Q. (…) vous **y-en a** asez [sic] la force et l'esprit pour vous repentir vous pêchés ? (P)	
R. Nous **y-en a** licaire qui na pas y-en a la force (P)	
R. Nous y-en a licaire qui na pas **y-en a** la force (P)	
Q. Mais dire nous, qui sa landroit là, qui **y-en a** l'Esprit, qui vous été dire qui nous nâme va allée quant nous mort ? (P)	
y-en à	**y en à**
13	2
Q. Qui differance qui **y-en à** entre vous nâme et vous le côr ? (E)	
R. (…) li ein Esprit, li partout, li na pas **y-en à** commencement, li n'a pas y-en à la fin (P)	
R. (…) li ein Esprit, li partout, li na pas y-en à commencement, li n'a pas **y-en à** la fin (P)	
R. (…) et qui moi vat **y-en à** l'esprit pour faire li contant. (P)	
R. (…) mo devréz demande li pour quique chose qui mo **y-en à** besoin, (P)	
R. (…) et tout sa mauvais mazination qui mo **y en à** dans mo la vie. (P)	
Q. Qui pêchés qui **y-en à** dans licaire ? (E)	
R. Pêchés qui **y-en à** dans licaire, sé quand moi oblie Bon Dieû, (E)	
Q. Qui ply grand pêché qui nous **y-en à** la haut la langue ? (P)	
R. Plus grand pêchés qui moi **y-en à** la haut la langue, c'est quand mo jourée, (P)	
Q. Qui mauvais chose qui **y-en à** la haut la terre ici qui vous devré quité ? (E)	
R. (…) pour sa même qui mo na pas **y-en à** auqu'in essquize [sic] qui raisonable pour faire divant Bon Dieû. (P)	
Q. (…) et pour li donné vous son Saint esprit ou l'autre bonté qui li **y-en à** ? (P)	
R. (…) même en didans li finie séparée, **y en à** un landroit pour Anges, un androit pour le dimons et un landroit pour nâmes (E)	

d) Descroizilles 1867

Chez ce scripteur, on relève 25 occurrences graphiques. Descroizilles commence par écrire *ti yena* pour passer ensuite à *ty ena*. Cette variation n'est pas liée aux significations assumées par *ena*. Par ailleurs, il écrit systématiquement *yena*. En voici quelques exemples,

(22) a. **Ti yena** morceau dibois, dipis lé temps Français (existence)

b. Vous bien conné, dans son pied Camisard, Coté **ti yena** l'angar compère César ; (existence)

c. a coté, **ti yena**, souvini, trois pieds jacq, Tout ça fini coupé, (existence)

(23) a. Longtemps **ty ena** eine blanc, zot dire Bobre Africain (existence)
   b. Mais Bobre Africain là, li **ty ena** drôle causé ; (possession)
   c. Eine jour qui son maitre, qui **ty ena** bon la bouce, **(possession)**

(24) a. Tout dimal qui **yena**, zot va gagne SON MALICE. (existence)
   b. Compère, mo ti toujours dire vous Blanc même qui **yena** toujours famé bagous.
   (propriété/ possession)
   c. Li oussi **yena** femme **(propriété/ possession)**

e) Baissac 1880

Dans les 16 instances de *ena* relevées chez cet auteur, on note un effort de régularisation : l'existentiel est graphié *té iéna* alors que le possessif est noté *té éna,* à une exception près. Cependant, *ti éna / té énan* et *ti énan* sont également attestés une fois, comme existentiel et comme possessif.

(25) *té iéna*
   a. **Té iéna** éne vié blanc qui té éna trois pitits (existence)
   b li allé, li allé zisqu'à li arive dans éne grand lapléne acote **té iéna** bon morceau iéves. (existence)
   c. li fére zautes assise dans éne grand lasalle àcote **té iéna** éne grand latabe (existence)

(26) *té éna*
   a. Té iéna éne vié blanc qui **té éna** trois pitits (propriété /possession)
   b. li **té éna** éne moulin, éne bourique ensembe éne çatte. (propriété /possession)
   c. to éne çatte coment zamés **té éna** çatte. (existence)
   d. So finition zhistoire çatte qui **té éna** botes (propriété /possession)

(27) *ti éna*
   ti éna éne divin, qui ti divin côment zamés divin ti divin ! (existence)

(28) *te énan*
   Te énan éne vié bourique qui marce marcé dans lacour ; (existence)

(29) *ti énan*
   Bourique couri, li alle dans térain éne grand moune qui **ti énan** maïe planté.
   (propriété /possession)

f) Anderson 1885.

Sur les 104 attestations, quatre « *ena* » étant des « *Ena* » qui comportent une majuscule à l'initiale, on peut sans risque de se tromper avancer qu'il s'agit de formes « *éna* » en début de phrase. Si l'on compare les 15 instances de *énan* avec 15 formes de *éna* prises au hasard (les 15 premières), on peut poser que la nasalisation de *énan* est due au contexte phonétique avec une assimilation régressive de la voyelle orale, donnant ainsi naissance à une variante [enã], encore attestée de nos jours.

Formes	éna	énan	ena
Nombre d'occurences	85	15	4

(30)

énan
- Bienhéré ça ki **énan bon** ker, parski zot va hérit la ter .
- Bienhéré ça ki **énan fain** é soaf la jistice, parski zot va rassazié.
- Bienhéré ça ki **énan** lé ker prop, parski zot va voar Bondié.
- parski li montré zot coman éne dimoune ki **énan** droa,
- **énan** éne la graine donne é çan,
- **énan** soass**ant**,
- **énan trant**.
- Parski **énan** dimoune ki unuk,
- ki ti né com ça ; **énan** ki dimoune fine fair vine unuk
- é **énan unuk** ki fine fair zot mem unuk,
- dir li : si to vlé vine parfé, al vand tou ça ki to **énan** ; é donne to l'arzan dimoune pov
- to va **énan** trézor dan le ciel ; apré ça, vini, sivré moa .
- PARSKI roayom lé ciel li coman éne cef **énan gran** la caz,
- Ça zour là mem, zans, ki dir ki na pa **énan** rézirekcion, vine pros li, é zot dimand li
- é coman li na pa ti **énan zanfan**, li ti lesse so fam pour so frer

éna
- li **éna** so vane dan so la main
- ça ki **éna** diab dan zot lé cor
- é **éna** boucou dimoune ki rantr par là .
- é **éna** pti guine dimoune ki trouv li .
- mo **éna** solda ki écout mo zordr
- là ki va **éna** ploré, avec greince lé dan .
- E dir li : Rénar **éna** zot trou, zozo dan l'air **éna** zot nic
- zozo dan l'air **éna** zot nic
- mé lé Fis de l'hom na pa **éna** éne l'androa, pour poz so la tét .
- E **éna** lot discip dir li, Sénier, lésse moa al anter mo papa avan.
- ki zaffair nou **éna** avec toa ?
- Loein zot, ti **éna** éne gran troupo coçon apré manzé.
- Mé pour ki vou conné, ki le Fis de l'hom **éna** droa laho la ter, pour pardonne pécé,
é zot tou fané, coman mouton ki na pa **éna** gardiein
- rodé ki bon dimoune **éna** làdan, é rest dan so la caz ziska vou all

g) Baissac 1888

Forme	éna	énan	iéna	ena
Nombre d'occurences	74	20	15	3

Les 20 occurrences de *énan*, avec des significations de propriété / possession et d'existence, ne sont pas toutes attestées dans un contexte de nasalisation diffuse.

(31) *énan*

    a. Li ti **énan** bon morceau larzent,

    b. li ti **énan** éne bande zanimaux

    c. Couin ! couin ! couin ! couin ! Napas **énan** zanimaux bête coument canard !

    d. moi qui **énan** lézailes mo va capabe envolé, mais to pour coule au fond, to coné !

    e. napas **énan** personne qui content toi coment li.

    f. Avlà li vine éne grand grand papa lïon coment napas **énan** dé dans paye Maurice.

iéna au contraire, attesté 15 fois dans ce texte, apparaît dans un contexte d'assimilation progressive ; *iéna* suit une voyelle d'avant, le plus souvent « é » [e] ou « i » [i] et se trouve parfois en position initiale.

(32) ***iéna***
   a. zofficier léroi vine dire li **qui iéna** éne doumounde qui dimande gardien bassin.
   b. éne coup là li lève so lézaile ; **iéna** quiqçose écrire en bas lézaile,
   c. **Té iéna** éne zécelle appiye dans miraille à côte zaute ;
   d. **Iéna** laçambes,

(33) ***ena***
   a. **Ena** gournouille làdans ?

L'alternance entre ***énan*** et ***ena*** semble être déterminée par un conditionnement phonique alors que l'alternance ***iéna / éna*** pourrait attester d'un changement grammatical en cours : i#ena vs Ø ena.

4.3.3. Bilan

L'examen détaillé de quelques graphiations permet de dégager trois constatations :
- comme souvent, les *scripta* utilisés par différents auteurs présentent une certaine inconsistance interne et une grande variation d'un scripteur à l'autre ;
- les *scripta* notent les variations phoniques les plus remarquables : *énan versus éna*, *iéna versus éna* ;
- les *scripta* grammatisent des évolutions linguistiques : le passage de *y-en a* ou *y en-a* à *iéna* et *éna / énan*.

L'analyse de ces pratiques scripturales, certes variables, permet de saisir les modifications phoniques et grammaticales qui conduisent du fr. *il y en a* au CM *ena*. On peut ainsi émettre des hypothèses quant au scénario de l'évolution phonétique du morphème : l'épellation 'y enna' (**1832**) suggère que la prononciation avec [e] était au moins une variante en ce temps. Ceci dit, la graphie 'yana' qu'on trouve en **1839** indique que les prononciations avec [ã] et [a] étaient toujours courantes durant cette période. Après **1850**, il n'y a pas d'indication claire que la prononciation [ã] était toujours courante. Les épellations très courantes 'ein' semblent destinées à indiquer que la première voyelle ne se prononçait ni [ã], ni [a] mais [e] ou [ẽ][2].

---

[2] Il est intéressant de noter qu'on entend encore de nos jours en français mauricien, même chez des locuteurs de langue maternelle française «il y en a» pour «il y a». Chaudenson (2003 : 378) analyse ce phénomène ainsi : « On se trouve en présence du cas classique où l'on ne sait pas si le français régional actuel est influencé par le créole; on stigmatise en français mauricien comme un créolisme « il y en a … » pour « il y a … » (comme dans « il y en a des mangues » pour « il y a des mangues » alors que rien ne prouve que n'était pas déjà présente, dans le français koïnèisé initial, la forme « il y en a » qui serait elle-même à l'origine du créole *éna* ».

4.4 *ena* vs *gagner*

	1769	1805	1818	1822	1823	1828	1830	1831	1832	1835	1837	1839	1840
Ena	0	5	1	7	1	30	0	19	6	4	1	8	1
gagner	1	12	2	3	0	8	2	8	13	9	1	8	2

	1850	1855	1860	1865	1867	1880	1885	1888	1892	1897	1920	1925	1929
	8	1	2	10	27	18	104	112	4	5	0	10	2
	8	77	1	7	37	8	116	149	2	4	1	21	0

Graphique : Répartition des occurrences de *ena* et *gagner* par année[3]

Si l'on compare les occurrences d'*ena* et de *gagne(r),* on peut noter qu'aucune forme ne supplante l'autre quantitativement sur la durée, hormis dans le texte de Lolliot (1855). Cela semble suggérer que ces deux morphèmes qui émergent de façon concomitante ne sont pas en concurrence et que le champ sémantique et fonctionnel propre à chacun a été déterminé dès leurs premières attestations. Reprenant le texte de **1850**, *Zistoire Moucié Caraba*, Baissac (1880) procède pourtant à la substitution suivante : il remplace *gagne* en 34a par *ena* en 34b.

(34) a) Eti y en a enne vié blan qui ti <u>gagne</u> troi piti (1850)
   b) Té iéna éne vié blanc qui té <u>éna</u> trois pitits (1880)

Il est possible qu'en 1850, le chevauchement sémantique entre les deux unités vecteurs de la signification de « propriété/ possession » ait été plus grand que par la suite. C'est ce que montre l'examen du texte de Lolliot (1855), qui emploie *gagne(r)* avec une valeur d'existenciel et comme marqueur de possession et de propriété. On pourrait imaginer qu'entre 1850 et 1880, l'usage d'*ena* se soit étendu au détriment de *gagne(r)* ; pourtant, les deux formes se sont maintenues. Rien ne permet de comprendre pourquoi le mauricien s'est doté des deux unités *ena* et *gagne*, là où le haïtien, par exemple, n'emploie que le seul *gegn* (voir aussi Chaudenson 2003 : 376-379).

5. Discussion

5.1. Evolution et fonctionnement de *(il) y en a / (il) y a* en français

5.1.1. Fonctionnements sémantico-syntaxiques de *il y a / il y en a* en français

On peut formuler trois observations à propos de *il y a / il y en a* en français :

- L'ordre *en y*, ayant été condamné par les grammairiens au XVIIe siècle, l'ordre *y en* s'impose ;
- Le pronom sujet *il* est souvent omis dans le langage populaire ;

(35) Faut pas t'en faire; n'empêche; y a. Faut le coucher, Monsieur, rien autre chose, il dormira, et d'main n'y paraîtra plus (Maupassant, *Contes et nouvelles,* t. 2, Masque, 1889 : 1162).

---

[3] Pour une meilleure visibilité, nous n'avons pas tenu compte des années où le nombre total d'occurrences était inférieur à 10.

- Le graphème *y*, qui dans la locution impersonnelle *il y a* peut s'interpréter comme l'équivalent à l'origine de *là* ou de *à cela*, est souvent utilisé comme notation de la prononciation populaire de *il*.

Exemples du *Trésor de la Langue Française* (TLF) :[4]

(36) a. J' fous ma démission, l' gouvernement s'arrangera comme y pourra!
(Courteline, *Train 8 h. 47*, 1888 : 70)

b. Y en a plus que du très bon [du vin blanc]. Y vaut cinq francs la bouteille...
(Céline, *Voyage*, 1932 : 50)

Le présentatif français *il y en a* est comme *il y a* un gallicisme qui sert à exprimer l'existence, la présence de quelqu'un ou de quelque chose, ou à exprimer une durée passée, un laps de temps écoulé. Exemples extraits du TLF :

(37) a. **Il y a** huit jours de cela; c'était **il y a** huit jours. Où allez-vous donc de si bonne heure

b. **Il y a** fête de congrégation, ce matin, à Saint-Louis de Gonzague (Estaunié, *Empreinte*, 1896 : 2)

c. Je m'enfonce dans mon opinion qu'**il n'y a** rien à faire, et me méfie de plus en plus des deux petites rides sur les coins de sa bouche (Gide, *Journal*, 1905 : 164).

A partir des études menées sur *il y a / il y en a* (voir Wagner 1964, Chevalier 1969, Jeanjean 1979, Giacomi & Véronique 1982),[5] on peut identifier trois fonctions de cette unité:

a) Morphème de présentation à valeur existentielle (à valeur de verbe recteur)

Il y a est un présentatif pur comme *voici* et *voilà* ; il peut être suivi d'un substantif précédé d'un article ou d'un adjectif indéfini, d'un adjectif possessif, d'un adjectif démonstratif, ou encore de l'article défini. *Il y a* opère un choix parmi tous les possibles : *il y a le facteur qui passe* (parmi tous ceux qui peuvent passer, le facteur est distingué). Le TLF cite les exemples suivants :

(38) a. Ce qu'**il y a eu** de jouissances et de poésie dans cette vie de troubadour, nul ne le saura jamais (Baudelaire, *Paradis artificiels*, 1860 : 331).

b. Au catéchisme, dit Poucette, **il y a** une petite fille qui est drôle, elle a les yeux pleins de larmes quand elle parle de Notre-Seigneur (Barrès, *Mes cahiers* t 11, 1914-17 : 144).

b) Support d'une rection temporelle (indication temporelle ponctuelle pour un intervalle temporel antérieur)

(39) **Il y a** à peu près deux mois que je me trouvai à dîner chez Madame d'Olmène. (Leclercq, *Proverbes dramatiques*, La Répétition d'un proverbe ou Il ne faut pas dire : Fontaine, je ne boirai pas de ton eau, 1835, 2, 369.

---

[4] Pour les références complètes des exemples (35) à (40), voir *TLF* : http://atilf.atilf.fr/tlf.htm
[5] Ces derniers indiquent la fréquence relativement faible de *y en a* en français parlé (Corpus D François).

c) Support d'autres rections

Il y a peut également servir de support à la restriction en *ne...que* (Blanche-Benveniste 1990)...

(40) **Il n'y a** qu'à moi qu'il ne veut pas parler (Blanche-Benveniste 1990, p. 65),

...ou à un pronom *en*, « indéfini, utilisé comme valence sujet d'un verbe qui suit »,

(41) **Il y en a** qui l'utilisent c'est vrai (Blanche-Benveniste 1990, p. 65).

Ces trois propriétés fonctionnelles de *il y a* en français (élément recteur de présentation, support introduisant un complément de temps et support d'autres rections) se retrouvent également en CM. Exemples :

(42) a. **Ena** zanfan (ki) pe zoue dan lakour (« Il y a des enfants qui jouent dans la cour »)
   b. **Ena** boukou letan avan li vini[6] (« Il y a beaucoup de temps avant qu'il vienne")
   c. **Ena** ki malad (« Il y en a qui sont malades»)

On doit noter, cependant, que les emplois d'*ena* en CM sont plus étendus que ces seuls contextes puisqu'il est également vecteur des significations de propriété/ possession et de localisation.

5.2. La réanalyse par référence et *il y a / il y en a*.

Le principe de référence qui constitue l'un des facteurs de la réanalyse fournit une explication possible du changement sémantique du français *il y en a* au créole mauricien *ena*. En effet, un locuteur qui énonce une suite comme *y en a* + N utilise cette structure pour PRESENTER N, INTRODUIRE N ou MANIFESTER L'EXISTENCE de N. La « fonction référentielle » de *il y a / il y en a* ou, plus précisément, la stratégie communicative que manifeste ce tour, est précisément celle de l'existentiel. L'esclave non-francophone exposé à cette forme n'en retient ni son signifié conventionnel ni sa structure morphosyntaxique mais son rôle référentiel. Il entend la forme phonique [jãna] et a accès à la *fonction référentielle* de la chaîne sonore, c'est-à-dire à la fonction présentative de ce morphème.

(43) (…) vous n'a pas kilotte; n'a rien ? Si fait, dans mô case, **y en a**. (**1805**)
(existence /propriété/ possession)

Le changement sémantique qui mène de *y en a* à *ena* « avoir » consiste à attribuer à la chaîne sonore le sens pragmatique de l'énoncé comme signifiant conventionnel. Ce phénomène de « délocutivité » (Benveniste 1958) est basé sur le fait que la formule *il y a / il y en a* et son sens pragmatique habituel se trouvent en relation de contiguïté.

---

[6] Autres exemples du web:
   "***Ena** sink sis mwa de sela, ti ena kolera dan Aden*".
   "*mo gran pere ti habitié batte li **ena** bien lontan de séla*".
   "***Ena** de semen de sela, mo ti rankontre Misie Macheath premie fwa dan lotel Octopus*".
   "*Mo finn assete avec enn dimounn Chamarel pour Rs 3 000, **ena** de semen de sela*".

5.3. La réanalyse par transparence : une hypothèse « substratiste » ?

5.3.1. Remarques préalables

Si l'on était absolument déterminé à trouver une origine de *ena* ailleurs qu'en français, on pourrait recourir au « principe de transparence » et proposer parmi les unités candidates à constituer la source de *ena* dans les langues serviles en contact avec le français :

a) le verbe *manana* (avoir) en malgache

(44) *manana trano   izy* (« Il a une maison »)
     avoir   maison 3sg

b) le verbe *kuwa na* (être avec, avoir) en swahili

(45)

Affirmatif	Traduction	négatif	Traduction
PANA	Il y a ici / là	HAPANA	Il n'y a pas ici / là
KUNA	Il y a par ici / par là	HAKUNA	Il n'y pas par ici / par là
MNA	il y a dedans	HAMNA	il n'y a pas dedans

5.3.2 Application

Suivant le principe de transparence, la stratégie adoptée par l'auditeur esclave malgachophone ou swahiliphone consiste à faire usage des proximités phoniques entre les unités de sa langue et celle du français. Ainsi, pour le swahiliphone par exemple, son savoir lui indique que lorsqu'une chaîne sonore en initiale de phrase se termine par le segment [na], il s'agit probablement du présentatif « il y a ». Au vu du fonctionnement sémantico-syntaxique de *manana* en malgache et de *kuwa na* en swahili, on ne peut exclure totalement que ces deux langues n'aient exercé une influence indirecte sur le CM ; ces locuteurs ont pu favoriser l'utilisation de l'élément français *(il) y (en) a* du fait qu'il présente des ressemblances à la fois fonctionnelles et formelles avec des unités de leur langue.

Pour ces locuteurs, leur langue première – si tant est que nous l'ayons bien identifiée – a pu jouer un rôle de *filtre*. On peut alors parler de *calque* et de *transfert*, qui sont à bien y regarder des applications du principe de transparence. Il s'agirait alors d'un cas de *convergence* (voir Bollée 1982).

5.3.3 Limites théoriques

Il convient toutefois de dire que ces scénarii hypothétiques présentent des faiblesses théoriques. Premièrement, comme nous le fait remarquer P Baker, le swahili n'est pas une langue « typiquement » bantoue en raison de l'influence extensive de l'arabe et il est très peu probable qu'il ait été une L1 des esclaves déportés à Maurice (ce n'est qu'après que le Kenya, l'Ouganda et la Tanzanie furent sous le gouvernement britannique que le swahili est devenu une langue importante et une L2 pour une grande partie des natifs de cette région. Deuxièmement, en ce qui concerne le malgache, bien que le verbe *manana* existe, il est plus naturel d'utiliser *misy* pour dire « il y a » et « avoir » (voir Chaudenson 2003 : 379).

Il serait utile de sonder les substrats potentiels du CM (malgache, fongbe, bengali, tamil, wolof, mandingue, indo-portugais, makhuwa, swahili, yao, nyanga, shona, bemba, maconde, sukuma, ...) et de voir parmi eux lesquels possèdent un seul et unique morphème faisant un *overlap* entre existence et possession, même si ce morphème n'a aucune ressemblance formelle avec [ena] (ce qui serait un cas de transfert uniquement fonctionnel) (voir Grant & Baker dans ce volume).

5.4 L'indication indirecte des études sur l'acquisition des langues étrangères

Giacomi & Véronique (1982) et Véronique (1983) constatent que des arabophones, en situation d'apprentissage informel du français, produisent des présentatifs « na/éna » - dont l'emploi est surgénéralisé pour la Possession et l'Existentiel ; ces phénomènes ne peuvent trouver leur origine dans la langue source. On peut penser que, dans l'appropriation du français, peut apparaître une alternance « il y a/ il y en a » et « il a/il en a », en raison de la saillance et de la fréquence des formes « il y en a » et « il en a ».

D'autres études longitudinales ont montré qu'une forme copulative (par exemple *is(a)* en anglais L2 ou /se/ en français L2) peut servir à plusieurs fonctions lors du développement précoce de L2, dont le marquage topical, la fonction d'identification, celles d'attribution, d'existence et de possession, avec des évolutions au cours de l'appropriation. Un sondage pratiqué dans les travaux sur l'appropriation de l'anglais langue seconde suggère que la production précoce de E en anglais L2 de la part d'apprenants de différents niveaux, de L1 différentes, à travers des modalités aussi bien orales qu'écrites est souvent réalisée avec quelques formes du verbe HAVE (au lieu de BE), qui est aussi utilisé pour P :[7]

(46) a. *Have* four man in my family 'There are four people in my family' (Duff 1988, Chinese L1)

b. THERE *HAVE* NOT DEAF FOR TEACHER [via Telecommunications Device for the Deaf)] 'There weren't any deaf teachers' (Cannon, 1985, Polish L1 and Polish Sign Language L1)

c. In Massachusetts *have* a man is bad, and he get the people (Andersen 1980, Spanish L1)

d. In the middle of the street here *has* a little … rock (Chesterfield & Levinson 1979, Portugese L1)

e. You *have* a clock on the wall (Lightbown 1987, French L1)

A partir de données longitudinales collectées auprès d'un Cambodgien apprenant l'anglais au Canada, Duff (1993) observe que le sujet utilise généralement la forme *has* (/haez/ ou /haeza/) pour signifier P et E, une forme qui alterne parfois avec un marquage zéro dans les constructions sans verbe. Contrairement à d'autres études, le sujet produit rarement /haev/ dans ces constructions mais plutôt – peut-être à cause de la saillance perceptuelle du morphème de troisième personne –s /z/ suivi de l'article indéfini (schwa) – il adopte et généralise la forme fléchie de troisième personne /haez(a)/.

Goglia (*à paraître*) discute de l'utilisation possessive de l'existentiel italien *c'è* « il y a » par des immigrants Igbo-Nigérians à Padova (nord de l'Italie). Il remarque que dans son corpus, la forme existentielle reflète l'usage de la langue-cible mais est aussi étendue à l'expression de la possession. Cet usage de l'existentiel comme possessif est persistent, même dans le parler des locuteurs immigrés ayant un niveau d'italien plus avancé. Il n'est donc pas exclusif aux premiers stages de l'acquisition, contrairement à ce que d'autres études sur l'italien des immigrants ont précédemment montré (Giagalone Ramat 2003).

---

[7] Pour les références complètes des exemples cités en (46), voir Duff (1993 : 8).

6. Conclusion

Des deux principes qui structurent la réanalyse, l'action du principe de référence semble la plus probable au vu de notre analyse. Nous serions en présence d'un cas de changement par réanalyse analogique par référence. L'influence des esclaves – apprenants – s'est donc surtout exercée à travers les stratégies d'appropriation qui, comme les travaux en acquisition non guidée d'une L2 le confirment, sont davantage liées à la perception de la langue-cible, en portant systématiquement au compte de la langue source – en invoquant le principe de calque ou de transfert – des phénomènes observés dans les interlangues des apprenants.

Le problème est le suivant : comment un locuteur s'y prend-il pour s'approprier une langue dont il ignore tout ? Ou comme le dit Véronique (1994 : 133) : il s'agit du problème de savoir ce que font les apprenants pour comprendre et employer l' « input » de la langue cible pour déchiffrer le code (« crack the code »). Nous pensons que la situation des esclaves peut être rapprochée, d'une certaine façon, de celui de l'ouvrier immigré qui apprend une nouvelle langue : ils ne réanalysent pas des structures dont ils connaissent déjà le sens et la fonction (réanalyse par transparence), mais ils analysent plutôt ce qui était, pour eux, jusqu'ici non analysé (réanalyse par référence). Lors de l'apprentissage non guidé, dans ses productions de la langue cible, l'esclave assigne à ce qu'il entend, à tort ou à raison, un sens et une fonction. De tels essais mènent forcément à des emplois « fautifs », comme par exemple à de fausses segmentations ou de fausses interprétations qui, elles, peuvent au cours du temps entraîner la surgénéralisation de certains éléments.

Toute acquisition engendre des innovations. Le processus que l'on désigne couramment sous le nom de créolisation est à concevoir comme un processus d'acquisition singulier en cela que « l'objet » a été modifié de façon définitive et dans des proportions inédites.

Le fait que le présentatif *(il) y (en) a* soit devenu le verbe plein *ena* en CM montre que les apprenants étaient en quête de formes « simples », et de leur point de vue [jāna] était certainement une forme simple. Une fois que cet élément a été saisi, il a subi un traitement cognitif et communicatif de réanalyse que nous avons tenté d'expliquer.

La présente étude sur l'émergence de *ena* en CM apporte des arguments soutenant l'idée que le processus de restructuration qu'est la réanalyse est responsable de l'autonomisation des créoles dont la grammaire suit, au moins en partie, d'autres principes que ceux de la langue de base. Bien que le matériau lexical des langues de base soit en général retenu, les fonctions spécifiques de certains éléments sont nouvelles. Il y a donc, comme le dit Detges, *continuité matérielle et discontinuité fonctionnelle*. Ceci n'exclut pas que des « processus auto-régulateurs » (Chaudenson 1992, 1999, 2003), aient joué un rôle dans ce processus, bien au contraire, mais c'est avant tout l'apprentissage non guidé qui produit, à travers un certain nombre de réanalyses, des structures qui n'ont pas de prédécesseurs directs dans les langues de base.

Bibliographie

Anderson, Samuel 1885 *L'Evangile selon S. Matthié (dan langaz créol Maurice). The Gospel according to St Matthew (in Mauritian creole)*. London: British and Foreign Bible Society.

Anttila, Raimo 1977 *Analogy*. The Hague : Mouton.

Auroux, Sylvain 1994 *La révolution technologique de la grammatisation*. Liège : Mardaga.

Baissac, Charles 1880 *Étude sur le patois créole Mauricien*. Nancy: Imprimerie Berger Levrault.

—— 1888 *Le folk-lore de l'Île Maurice*. Paris: Maisonneuve & Larose.

Baker, Philip 2001 Theories of creolization and the degree and nature of restructuring. Neumann-Holzschuh, Ingrid & Schneider, Edgar W (éds), *Degrees of Restructuring in Creole Languages*. Amsterdam: Benjamins, 41-63.

—— 2003 Quelques cas de la réanalyse et de la grammaticalisation dans l'évolution du créole mauricien. Kriegel, Sibylle (éd.), 111-41.

Benveniste, Émile 1958 Catégories de pensée et catégories de langue. In *Problèmes de linguistique générale*, I, Gallimard, pp 63-74.

Bickerton, Derek 1981 *Roots of Language*. Ann Arbor: Karoma.

Blanche-Benveniste, Claire 1990 *Le français parlé. Etudes grammaticales*, Paris : CNRS.

Bollée, Annegret 1977 *Le créole français des Seychelles*. Tübingen : Niemeyer.

—— 1982 Die Rolle der Konvergenz bei der Kreolisierung. Ureland, P S (éd.) : *Die Leistung der Strataforschung und der Kreolistik. Typologische Aspekte der Sprachkontakte. Akten des 5. Symposions über Sprachkontakt in Europa, Mannheim 1982*, Tübingen: Niemeyer, 391-405.

Bybee, J, Perkins, R, & Pagliuca, W 1994 *The evolution of grammar: Tense, aspect, and modality in the languages of the world*. Chicago; London: University of Chicago Press.

Chaudenson, Robert 1981 *Textes creoles anciens (La Réunion et Ile Maurice): Comparaison et essai d'analyse*. Hamburg: Buske.

—— 1992 *Des hommes, des îles, des langues*, Paris : L'Harmattan.

—— 2002 Une théorie de la créolisation : le cas des créoles français. *Etudes Créoles*, 25.1: 25-44.

—— 2003 *La créolisation : théorie, applications, implications*, Paris : L'Harmattan.

Chevalier, Jean-Claude 1969 Exercices portant sur le fonctionnement des présentatifs. *Langue Française* 1: 82-92.

Chrestien, François [1822] 1831 *Les essais d'un bobre africain*, Mauritius: Déroullède.

Clark, Eve V 1970 Locationals: A study of the relations between 'existential', 'locative' and 'possessive' constructions. *Working papers on language universals* Stanford, CA: Language Universals Project, Stanford University, n°3: L1-L26.

Clark, Eve 1978 Locationals: Existential, locative, and possessive constructions. Greenberg, J H (ed.) *Universals of human language:* vol. 4. *Syntax* Stanford, CA: Stanford University Press, 85-126.

Creissels, Denis 1996 Remarques sur l'émergence de verbes *avoir* au cours de l'histoire des langues. *Faits de Langues 7*, La relation d'appartenance, Paris : Ophrys, 149-58.

—— 2006 *Syntaxe générale. Une introduction typologique 1 et 2.* Paris : Lavoisier

Croft, William 2000 *Explaining language change : an evolutionary approach*. London : Longman.

Descroizilles, H C 1867 *Navire fin engazé : The «Mauritius» in danger*. Port Louis: Dupuy & Dubois.

Detges, Ulrich 2002 Créolisation et changement linguistique. *Etudes créoles* 15.1: 71-86.

—— 2003 La notion de reanalyse et son application à la description des langues creoles. Kriegel, Sibylle (éd.), 49-67.

Detges, Ulrich & Waltereit, Richard 1999 Grammaticalization vs reanalysis: a simplest systematics of functional change in grammar (manuscrit).

—— & —— 2002 Grammaticalization vs Reanalysis. A semantic-pragmatic account of functional change in grammar, *Zeitschrift für Sprachwissenschaft*.

Duff, Patricia 1993 Syntax, Semantics, and SLA: The Convergence of Possessive and Existential Constructions. *Studies in Second Language Acquisition* 15.1 : 1-34.

Fon Sing, Guillaume 2004 *Les phénomènes de grammaticalisation et de réanalyse dans le processus de créolisation : étude de la mise en place du système temps-mode-aspect et de l'évolution diachronique des particules préverbales en créole mauricien*. Mémoire pour le DEA de Sciences du langage et traductologie, Paris III.

——— 2005 Créolisation et grammaticalisation: le cas de *fin* en créole mauricien. *Actes des VIIIèmes Rencontres Jeunes chercheurs de l'Ecole Doctorale 268 'Langage et langues'*, Université de Paris 3, mai 2006, pp: 25-28

Francois, Denise 1974 *Français parlé*, Paris : SELAF.

Giacalone Ramat, Anna (ed.) 2003 *Verso l'italiana. Percosi e strategie di acquisizione*. Roma : Carocci editore.

Giacomi, Alain & Véronique, Daniel 1982 A propos de "il y a..."/ "il y en a ..." *Le français moderne*. 50e année, 3, pp 237-42.

Givòn, Talmy 1979 *On Understanding Grammar*. Academic Press.

Goglia, Francesco [*à paraître*] Language learners as agents of language change: the birth of a construction in immigrants' Italian. In *Lingua*.

Hagège, Claude 1993 *The Language Builder, An essay on the human signature in linguistic morphogenesis*. Amsterdam: Benjamins.

——— 2001 Les processus de grammaticalisation. Haspelmath et al (éds), 1609-23.

Harris, Alice C & Campbell, Lyle, (éds) 1995 *Historical syntax in a cross-linguistic perspective*, Cambridge: Cambridge University Press.

Haspelmath, M, Konig, E, Oesterreicher, W & Raible W, (éds) 2001 *Language Typology and Language Universals. An International Handbook*, vol. 1, Berlin: De Gruyter.

Haspelmath, Martin 1998 Does grammaticalization need reanalysis ? *Studies in Language* 22.2 : 315-51.

He, S 1989 Participant and setting in possessive and existential domain: A cognitive grammar approach to *you* in Mandarin Chinese. Carlson, R, S. Delancey, Gildea, S, Payne, D & Saxena, A (eds), *Proceedings of the Fourth Meeting of the Pacific Linguistics Conference*. Eugene: University of Oregon, 229-38.

Heine, B, Claudi, U & Hünnemeyer, F 1991 *Grammaticalization. A conceptual Framework*, Chicago: University of Chicago Press.

Hopper, Paul J 1991 On Some principle of Grammaticalization, Traugott & Heine (éds), 17-35.

Hopper, Paul J & Traugott, Elizabeth C 1993 *Grammaticalization*, Cambridge: Cambridge University Press.

Jackendoff, Ray 1983 *Semantics and cognition*. Cambridge, MA: MIT Press.

Jeanjean, Colette 1979 Soit y'avait le poisson soit y'avait ce rôti farci. Etude de la construction de *il y a* dans la syntaxe du français. *Recherches sur le français parlé* 2: 121-56.

Klein, W & Perdue, C 1997 The Basic Variety. *Second Language Research* 13.4: 301-47.

Kriegel, Sibylle (éd.) 2003 *Grammaticalisation et réanalyse : approches de la variation créole et française*. Paris : CNRS.

Lambert, Richard [1828] 1888-92 Catéchisme en créole de l'île Maurice en 1828. *Bulletin de la Société de Linguistique de Paris* 7: 122-32.

Langacker Ronald 1977 Syntactic reanalysis. In C. N. Li (Ed.), *Mechanisms of syntactic change*, Austin/London: University of Texas Press.

——— 1987 *Cognitive grammar*. vol. 1. Stanford, CA: Stanford University Press.

Lehmann, Christian [1982], 1995 *Thoughts on Grammaticalization*, Lincom Europa: München. (First published 1982 as akup 48, University of Cologne)

Lightfoot, David 1999 *The development of language: Acquisition, change, and evolution.* Blackwell.
Lolliot, Pierre 1855 *Poésies créoles.* Port Louis: Imprimerie du *Mauricien.*
Meillet, Antoine [1912] 1921 L'évolution des formes grammaticales. Meillet, Antoine *Linguistique historique et linguistique générale*, 2 vols, Paris : Champion, 130-49.
Peyraube, Alain 2002 L'évolution des structures grammaticales. *Langages* 146: 46-58.
Pinker, Steven 1989 *Learnability and cognition.* Cambridge, MA: MIT Press.
Slobin, Dan I 1985 Crosslinguistic evidence for the language-making capacity. Slobin, D I (ed.), *The crosslinguistic study of language acquisition.* vol. II: *Theoretical issues.* Hillsdale, NJ: Erlbaum, 219-29.
Stassen, L M H 2001 Predicative Possession. Martin Haspelmath & et al. (eds.), *Language Typology and Language Universals. An International Handbook.* Vol. 2: 954-60. Berlin: Walter De Gruyter.
Talmy, Leonard 1983 How language structures space. Pick, H L & Acredolo, L P (eds), *Spatial orientation: theory, research and application.* New York: Plenum, 225-82.
Thomason, Sarah & Kaufman, Terrence 1988 *Language Contact, Creolization and Genetic Linguistics.* Berkeley : University of California Press.
Traugott, Elizabeth C & Heine, Bernd (eds), 1991 *Approaches to grammaticalization,* Amsterdam : Benjamins.
Trésor de la Langue Française : http://atilf.atilf.fr/tlf.htm
Véronique, Daniel 1983 Observations préliminaires sur *li* dans l'interlangue d'Abdelmalek. *Acquisition du français par des travailleurs marocains. Papiers de travail* vol. 1, 155-80). Aix-en-Provence: Université de Provence.
Véronique, Daniel (éd.) 1996 Matériaux pour l'étude des classes grammaticales dans les langues créoles. Aix-en-Provence : Université de Provence.
—— 1999 L'émergence des catégories grammaticales dans les langues créoles : grammaticalisation et réanalyse. Lang, J & Neumann-Holzschuh, I (éds) *Reanalyse und Grammaticalisierung in den romanischen Sprachen.* Tübingen : Niemeyer, 19-29.
—— 2003 Le développement de l'expression de la négation dans les créoles français et dans l'acquisition du français langue étrangère. Kriegel, S (éd.) 87-109.
Véronique, Daniel (éd.) 1994 *Créolisation et Acquisition des langues.* Aix-en-Provence : Université de Provence.
Wagner, Robert-Léon [1964] 1980 *Essais de linguistique française,* Paris, Nathan.

Guillaume Fon Sing est actuellement Attaché Temporaire d'Enseignement
et de la Recherche (ATER) à l'Université de la Sorbonne Nouvelle (Paris 3).
Il achève sa thèse de doctorat sur les créoles français
et enseigne la linguistique française. <gfonsing@yahoo.fr>

Georges Daniel Véronique est Professeur de linguistique française
et d'études créoles à l'Université de Provence (Aix-Marseille 1).
Il a publié sur les créoles français et en SLA.
<georges.veronique@orange.fr>

L'absence de marqueurs préverbaux et les fonctions du marqueurs zéro

Peter Stein

Introduction

Des études sur la structure des créoles de l'Océan Indien et des grammaires qui leur sont consacrées, tout comme des études plus générales sur les créoles ressort que le marqueur préverbal zéro exprime le présent dans les créoles mauricien, seychellois, rodriguais et réunionnais. Plus rares sont les études qui attribuent au marqueur zéro une valeur plutôt neutre dont la fonction et la signification concrètes dépendent du contexte de l'énonciation, comme p. ex. Stein (1984: 79).[1]

Bollée (1989: 191s) observe le même phénomène, mais l'interprète un peu différemment, car, pour elle, la fonction principale de la forme non marquée reste le présent. Ce présent, appelé présent historique comme dans beaucoup de langues, peut être utilisé dans des contextes où il remplace un temps du passé :

> En créole seychellois, le marqueur du passé est *ti*. Dans les contes qui proviennent de la tradition orale, ce marqueur se trouve au début du récit, où le conteur décrit la situation, l'arrière-plan ou les antécédents de l'action (et très souvent aussi au début de nouveaux épisodes) [...] Au moment où l'action du conte commence, le conteur n'utilise plus le marqueur *ti*, mais la forme non-marquée du verbe, qui, dans ce cas, assume la fonction d'un "présent historique".

Cette règle ne semble cependant plus être appliquée dans la création littéraire récente où "le conteur ne cesse d'utiliser le marqueur *ti* et ce, du début jusqu'à la fin du petit livre" (Bollée 1989: 193). Apparemment, son auteur s'est laissé influencer par le français et les langues européennes en général, où chaque forme personnelle du verbe exige d'être marquée par rapport au temps et au mode.

En ce qui concerne l'état ancien de la langue, Chaudenson (1981), dans son étude des plus anciens textes, part de la forme (marqueur zéro vs marqueur *ti*), sans discuter la possibilité de l'absence du marqueur (*ti* ou autre) dans des énoncés situés dans le passé.

Comment l'emploi ou le non-emploi des marqueurs verbaux se présente-t-il dans les textes anciens ? Supposons que les auteurs aient eu la ferme intention d'écrire correctement le créole en tant que système linguistique distinct du français. Ils étaient néanmoins francophones – et *francoscribes* – et nous ignorons dans quelle mesure ils se sont éventuellement laissés influencer par le français pour attribuer un marqueur concret à chaque verbe qui exprime un temps autre que le présent (non progressif). N'oublions pas non plus que le créole était une langue orale, et que le langage oral suit d'autres règles que le langage écrit.

---

[1] "Wenn Tempus und Modus sich eindeutig aus dem Kontext ergeben, steht in bestimmten FKS - wir haben es vor allem im KrMau und im KrRod beobachten können - die partikellose Form, die in diesem Fall als neutrale, unmarkierte Form fungiert. Die grammatische Markierung erfolgt also hier, wie auch in anderen Fällen, nur dann, wenn sie sich nicht eindeutig aus dem Kontext ergibt".

L'étude des textes

Le corpus des textes créoles anciens de l'Ile Maurice, base des études de ce volume, réunit des textes très hétérogènes sous tous les aspects : dates et circonstances de la rédaction, les auteurs, les variétés du créole ... et finalement l'orthographe. Le même mot y connait donc des graphies bien variées. L'étude statistique, par laquelle nous voudrions commencé notre approche des textes, est donc confronté à certains inconvenients.[2]

L'étude de l'absence de marqueur verbal ou, autrement dit, du marqueur zéro, pose des problèmes pratiques, car il est matériellement absent. Par conséquent, notre approche, basée sur un traitement automatique et une étude quantitative de l'emploi, c'est-à-dire de la fréquence des marqueurs verbaux, doit commencer par une étude d'éléments qui ne nous intéressent que négativement. Comme nous ne pouvons pas compter la fréquence du marqueur zéro, il convient de commencer par une étude de la fréquence des principaux marqueurs autres que le marqueur zéro.

Le tableau 1 montre le nombre des occurrences des marqueurs verbaux *ti, fiṇ, va, pou, pe* ainsi que des combinaisons de *ti va, ti pou* et *ti pe*. Non seulement la fréquence des marqueurs dans les textes est importante pour une meilleure compréhension de l'emploi ou du non-emploi des marqueurs, mais également la date de leur première attestation. C'est pourquoi nous avons réuni ces dates dans le tableau 2. Le tableau 3 montre ensuite le nombre d'occurrences des 20 verbes les plus fréquents et la fréquence des marqueurs qui les accompagnent. Dans ce tableau, nous ne tenons compte ni de toute la variation orthographique, ni des formes courtes et longues des verbes.[3] Le tableau 4 complète la documentation. Il réunit les 60 verbes les plus fréquents en tenant compte de la variation orthographique.[4]

Tableau 1: La fréquence des marqueurs préverbaux et des combinaisons avec *ti/té*

	nombre total	combiné avec ...										non-combinés
		ti	té	été	fine /fin	fini	fin	va	a	pour	après	apré	
ti	1083	–	–	3	141	–	4	27	3	13	7	21	-215 = **877**
té	722	–	–	-	31	2	6	36	-	10	7	2	-88 = **634**
été	111	–	–	–									**111**
fine, fin'	943												**943**
va	1271												**1271**

Commentaires

- Nous ne donnons pas de chiffres totaux pour les marqueurs *pou (pour)* et *pe/ape (après, apré)* étant donné qu'en l'état actuel des recherches, les données ne distinguent pas encore les marqueurs des adverbes (*apre*) ou de la préposition (*pou*) devant infinitif.

---

[2] On y trouve, en outre, quelques phrases en langue française qui entrent dans la statistique. Leur volume est toutefois trop restreint pour pouvoir influencer l'image globale.

[3] Les données ont été obtenues sur la base des documents distribués et les concordances déjà préparées ainsi que par le traitement des documents à l'aide du programme AntConc 3.2.1w (Windows), Developed by Laurence Anthony, Faculty of Science and Engineering, Waseda University, Japan, anthony@waseda.jp.

[4] Les calculs ont été faits sur une version non-définitive du corpus des textes anciens, ce qui fait que les chiffres peuvent montrer certaines différences par rapport à des calculs faits sur des versions plus avancées. Les différences ne sont pas significatives pour notre argumentation; c'est pourquoi nous avons renoncé à refaire les comptes et calculs pour la version définitive des textes du corpus.

- Pour la même raison, nous ne tenons pas compte de *a*, étant donné que la grande majorité des 858 occurrences ne correspond pas au marqueur de futur *a*, forme raccourcie de *va*. Voir à ce propos les données pour *a* dans le tableau 4.
- Le tableau ne distingue pas les formes personnelles du verbe des formes impersonnelles qui n'admettent pas de marqueurs. Pour une statistique plus stricte il faudra exclure tous les verbes impersonnels. Nous reviendrons à ce problème par la suite (cf *infra*).

Tableau 2: Les dates de la première attestation des marqueurs

1734		fini		
1777			va	
1779	été			
1816	té, te			
1818			? pour[5]	
1822				après
1830			a[6]	
1839	ti	fine, fin'		
1850	té fine			
1855	té fin'		té va ti va	
1865	ti fin'			
1867			pour[7] ti a, ti pour	
1880			a	
1888				ti après

Les marqueurs apparaissent dès les premiers documents. Au départ, on les trouve encore sous une forme plus proche du français: **1734**: *fini*, **1777**: *va*, et, comme troisième seulement **1779** : *été*, qui est raccourci dès **1816** à *té, te* (ce dernier n'est qu'une variante graphique, attesté seulement trois fois dans le corpus entier). En 1839 *fini* devient *fine* ou *fin'*. *Après* suit seulement en 1822, sous la forme *apré* dès 1850, et *pour* comme marqueur du futur n'est attesté qu'en 1867, sa futurité n'étant pas assurée en 1818 et 1855. les combinaisons *té/ti* avec *fine/fin'*, *va/a*, *pour* ne sont attestées que depuis 1850. *Té* et *ti* coexistent assez longtemps et en 1888 encore, Baissac les utilise dans ses contes l'un à côté de l'autre. Il est aussi le premier à utiliser *ti après* (1888) et *a* (1880), dont une première attestation en 1830 reste isolée (cf note 6). Il faut toutefois voir les attestations tardives avec certaines

---

[5] Cf infra la discussion de la fonction de *pour* dans cette phrase.
[6] Selon toute probabilité, il s'agit en 1830 d'une erreur typographique, car à côté de cinq *va* il n'y a qu'un seul *a* dans ce texte.
[7] *Pour* représente un cas difficile, car il peut également introduire des constructions impersonnelles (finales surtout) ou simplement faire la connexion avec des verbes modaux ou autres. Un premier cas difficile à classifier entre les deux est celui de 1818 (voir note 4), quelques autres se trouvent chez Lolliot (1855). Ce n'est qu'en 1867 que la fonction du futur est univoque.

réserves, car comme nous l'avons montré dans Stein (1995) a propos des textes en negerhollands du 18e siècle, l'emploi d'une forme ou construction par voie orale est une chose, la prise de conscience de son existence et son emploi comme forme écrite en est une autre. En ce qui concerne les différences par rapport au tableau de Baker (1995 : 9), elles s'expliquent soit par une nouvelle base de données, soit par une interprétation différente de certaines formes.

Tableau 3

Les 20 verbes les plus fréquents du corpus et les marqueurs qui les précèdent immédiatement.[8]

		ti / té / été	fine / fini/fin	va / a	pour	après
dir	1461	24	11	50	6	2
fer	1075	51	42	131	6	10
vin/vini	589	33	55	49	11	1
al/alé	503	29	23	18	12	1
gagn / -é	484	66	57	63	2	-
donn / -é	334	35	17	40	5	2
éna	305	74	-	16	-	-
pran	280	11	21	20	1	-
(v)oulé	276	26	-	10	-	-
konn /-é	272	18	3	11	-	-
trouv / -é	265	19	21	19	3	-
kapav	265	16	-	29	2	-
met / -é	263	12	13	9	5	1
koz / -é	239	5	13	4	1	6
vwar	236	32	5	28	1	-
manz / -é	227	7	3	12	8	9
get / -é	215	2	9	18	2	2
bizwen	169	3	-	4	-	-
ariv / -é	19	8	26	8	2	-
mor	154	9	29	8	16	-
somme	7631	480	348	547	83	34
% des verbes		6,3%	4,6%	7,2%	1,1%	0,45%

---

[8] L'orthographe des verbes a été modernisée dans ce tableau. Nous avons exclu les 234 occurrences de *fo*, étant donné qu'il s'agit d'un verbe impersonnel qui n'accepte pas de marqueur ni de sujet personnel. *Fo* a été exclu également du tableau 4. *Fini* n'a pas été retenu pour le tableau parce qu'il apparait sous cette forme également comme marqueur, en partie synonyme de *fin(e)*.

Nous ne donnons pas de chiffres pour le nombre des verbes non-accompagnés de marqueur, étant donné que ce chiffre incluerait les verbes dans les constructions non-personnelles et serait donc sans valeur pour notre étude.

Tableau 4: Les verbes fréquents et leurs marqueurs

verbe	nombre		ti	té	été	fine	fini	fin	va	a	pour	après	apré
dire		812	9	20	3	9	2	-	13	2	5	2	-
dir	= 1461	649	12	8	-	10	1	-	35	-	1	-	-
faire		554	9	5	14	9	2	-	55	11	5	5	-
fair		475	21	15	1	28	1	-	53	1	1	1	3
fére	= 1075	46	1	-	-	2	-	-	-	11	-	1	-
vine		302	17	4	-	29	-	-	23	4	8	-	-
vini	= 589	287	8	2	2	22	4	-	22	-	3	1	-
allé		224	5	-	-	15	-	-	7	-	2	-	1
alle		178	9	5	-	5	-	-	6	-	9	-	-
al	= 503	101	10	-	-	2	1	-	5	-	1	-	-
gagne		192	11	24	-	35	-	-	17	1	1	-	-
gagné		136	5	8	-	6	2	-	18	-	-	-	-
gaïn		104	13	-	-	14	-	-	19	-	2	-	-
gagn	= 484	52	-	5	-	-	-	-	8	-	-	-	-
donne		275	16	8	1	14	1	1	31	2	4	2	-
donné	= 334	59	1	4	5	1	-	-	7	-	1	-	-
éna		172	54	7	-	-	-	-	12	-	-	-	-
ena		20	-	-	-	-	-	-	-	-	-	-	-
énan		37	8	-	-	-	-	-	1	-	-	-	-
(y) en a		44	2	1	1	-	-	-	2	-	-	-	-
yena		20	1	-	-	-	-	-	-	-	-	-	-
yenna	= 305	12	-	-	-	-	-	-	1	-	-	-	-
prend		206	1	3	-	18	-	-	12	2	1	-	-
pran	= 280	74	7	-	-	3	-	-	6	-	-	-	-
vlé		151	15	4	-	-	-	-	5	-	-	-	-
voulé	= 276	125	1	6	-	-	-	-	4	1	-	-	-
conné		129	4	2	-	-	-	-	2	-	-	-	-
coné		53	3	-	-	1	-	-	3	-	-	-	-
connais		48	-	-	1	-	-	-	3	-	-	-	-
conne	= 272	42	6	2	-	2	-	-	3	-	-	-	-

verbe	nombre		ti	té	été	fine	fini	fin	va	a	pour	après	apré
trouve		144	2	3	-	10	-	-	8	3	1	-	-
trouvé		77	2	3	3	5	-	1	3	-	2	-	-
trouv	= 265	44	6	-	-	5	-	-	5	-	-	-	-
capav		121	9	2	-	-	-	-	11	1	-	-	-
capave		64	-	1	-	-	-	-	5	3	1	-	-
capabe		63	1	3	-	-	-	-	5	1	-	-	-
capable	= 285	37	-	-	-	-	-	-	2	1	1	-	-
mette		111	1	3	-	5	-	-	3	-	4	-	1
met		66	4	1	-	8	-	-	5	-	-	-	-
metté		50	2	-	1	-	-	-	1	-	1	-	-
méte	= 263	36	-	-	-	-	-	-	-	-	-	-	-
causé		178	3	1	-	10	3	-	4	-	-	2	-
cause		39	-	1	-	-	-	-	-	-	1	1	-
coz	= 239	22	-	-	-	-	-	-	-	-	-	3	-
voir		166	1	16	-	1	2	-	17	2	1	-	-
voar	= 236	70	15	-	-	2	-	-	9	-	-	-	-
manzé		148	4	2	-	2	1	-	3	-	2	3	3
manze	= 227	79	1	-	-	-	-	-	9	-	8	3	-
guette		84	-	-	-	-	-	-	1	-	-	1	-
guetté		83	1	-	1	5	1	3	7	2	-	-	1
guété	= 215	48	-	-	-	-	-	-	7	1	2	-	-
bisoin		134	-	2	-	-	-	-	4	-	-	-	-
bizoein	= 169	35	1	-	-	-	-	-	-	-	-	-	-
arrive		102	-	-	-	14	-	-	2	-	-	-	-
arrivé	= 161	59	8	-	-	11	1	-	6	-	2	-	-
fini	= 156	156	-	2	-	12	-	1	7	-	2	-	-
mort		114	2	3	1	13	7	-	4	-	14	-	-
mor	= 154	40	3	-	-	9	-	-	4	-	2	-	-
croire		103	2	1	-	-	-	-	4	-	-	-	-
croir	= 148	45	-	3	-	-	-	-	5	-	-	-	-
tourne		90	-	-	-	8	-	-	1	-	2	-	-
tourné	= 147	57	1	1	-	1	1	-	6	-	2	-	-

verbe	nombre		ti	té	été	fine	fini	fin	va	a	pour	après	apré
passe	= 144	51	2	-	-	2	-	-	-	-	1	-	-
tendé		76	2	7	-	7	2	-	4	-	-	-	-
tende	= 142	66	1	1	-	4	-	-	-	-	-	-	-
sorti		69	4	1	-	3	1	-	3	-	-	-	-
sourti	= 136	67	-	-	-	1	1	-	-	-	2	-	-
tombé		58	1	-	-	5	-	-	7	-	1	-	-
tombe		42	1	-	-	-	-	-	1	-	-	1	-
tomb	= 135	35	-	1	-	-	-	-	5	-	2	-	-
appelle		76	8	6	-	-	-	-	-	-	-	-	-
appel	= 131	55	6	-	-	3	-	-	7	-	-	-	1
laisse		91	3	-	-	1	-	-	4	-	1	-	-
lésse	= 128	37	-	-	-	-	-	-	4	-	-	-	-
rente		43	-	-	-	2	-	-	-	-	1	-	-
rantr		36	3	-	-	8	-	-	2	-	-	-	-
rentré	= 115	36	-	1	1	-	-	-	2	1	2	-	-
lévé		76	2	-	-	7	-	-	5	-	-	-	-
lève	= 111	35	-	-	-	2	-	-	-	-	1	-	-
ploré	= 97	97	1	-	-	2	-	-	1	-	-	5	-
boire	= 92	92	-	1	-	3	1	-	-	-	-	2	-
tire	= 88	88	-	1	-	5	-	-	-	-	4	-	-
per		37	4	-	-	2	-	-	-	-	-	-	-
peir	= 83	46	-	-	-	-	-	-	-	-	-	-	-
dimande	= 80	80	1	-	-	2	-	-	1	-	-	-	-
marcé	= 80	80	-	1	-	-	-	-	1	-	-	-	-
marié	= 80	80	1	-	-	5	1	-	10	-	6	-	-
zette		46	1	-	-	3	-	-	-	-	1	-	-
zet	= 79	33	-	-	-	3	-	-	3	-	1	-	1
reste		43	3	2	-	2	-	-	-	1	3	-	-
resté	= 77	34	1	2	2	1	1	-	1	-	1	-	-
amène	= 75	75	3	-	-	3	-	-	2	-	1	-	-
crié	= 74	74	-	1	-	2	-	-	3	-	-	-	-

verbe	nombre		ti	té	été	fine	fini	fin	va	a	pour	après	apré
ouvert	• = 71	71	-	1	-	1	-	-	-	-	1	-	-
paye	= 71	71	-	-	-	-	-	-	1	-	1	-	-
blizé	= 70	70	-	5	-	-	-	-	4	1	-	-	-
maziné	= 68	68	2	2	-	1	-	-	-	-	1	1	-
dourmi	= 68	68	-	1	1	-	-	-	-	-	2	6	-
sivré	= 65	65	5	1	1	2	-	-	2	-	-	-	-
touye	= 65	65	2	-	-	3	-	-	8	-	7	-	-
répond	= 63	63	-	-	-	-	-	-	4	-	-	-	4
parlé	= 56	56	1	1	2	-	-	-	1	-	-	-	-
perdi	= 53	53	1	1	-	10	2	-	8	-	3	-	-
saute	= 50	50	-	1	-	-	-	-	1	-	1	-	-
senti	= 47	47	-	5	-	-	-	-	2	-	-	-	-
travaille	= 47	47	-	1	1	1	-	-	2	-	3	-	-
casse	= 46	46	1	1	-	4	-	-	2	-	-	1	1
çanté	= 45	45	-	1	-	-	-	-	1	-	1	1	-
quitte	= 41	41	-	3	-	2	-	-	3	-	-	-	-
pousse	= 40	40	3	-	-	1	-	-	1	-	-	-	-
comence	= 39	39	-	-	-	-	-	-	-	-	-	-	-
	11196	11196	382	235	42	458	41	6	632	54	140	42	17
% des verbes			3,4	2,1	0,4	4,5	<--	<--	6,1	<--	1,25	0,4	<--

Les données quantitatives réunies dans les tableaux permettent des observations qui ne seraient pas possibles sans la considération du nombre des occurrences et de la fréquence des phénomènes recherchés. Mais ils ne présentent que des données brutes qu'il convient d'interpréter.

Le tableau 1 est le point de départ de notre argumentation, mais le nombre des marqueurs ne nous dit rien tant que nous ne connaissons pas le nombre total des verbes et par conséquent le nombre de verbes non-précédés de marqueur. De plus, ce tableau est incomplet, car certains marqueurs ne pouvaient être pris en considération, étant donné que les programmes de l'ordinateur ne distingue pas entre la fonction de marqueur et celle d'adverbe ou de préposition. Toutefois, les deux principaux concernés (*pou, pe*) ne sont pas souvent utilisés, et ainsi l'absence de certaines données n'a pas d'importance dans notre contexte. Pour approfondir l'étude, il faudra y revenir et inclure les aspects sémantique et fonctionnel-syntaxique.

Le principal défaut du tableau est de ne pas fournir de données pour le nombre total des verbes dans le corpus, et il serait encore plus souhaitable de partir du nombre des verbes personnels seulement où la présence d'un marqueur peut se trouver en opposition à l'absence de marqueurs. Mais on n'arrive au nombre total de verbes personnels dans les textes qu'après une étude sémanto-syntaxique de la catégorie des mots en procédant phrase par phrase. Après avoir effectué plusieurs tests, nous estimons que la part des verbes dans des constructions non-personnelles varie entre 20% et 30% selon les verbes. Comme un examen exhaustif ne nous était pas possible, le tableau 3 tient compte de tous les occurrences des verbes; il convient donc de le lire tout en étant conscient de ce défaut. Nous y avons réuni les 20 verbes les plus fréquents dans les textes de notre corpus, avec l'indication du nombre de marqueurs qui les accompagnent: 1492 des 7631 verbes sont précédés immédiatement d'un des marqueurs mentionnés, ce qui fait un pourcentage de 19,6%. Si on réduit ce chiffre d'un quart, la proportion estimée de verbes de forme et fonction non-personnelle, on arrive à 5723 verbes finis, ce qui donne un pourcentage de 26,1% de verbes finis accompagnés de marqueurs. En répertoriant les 60 verbes les plus fréquents, représentés dans le tableau 4 et ayant une occurrence de 39 ou plus dans les textes du corpus, on arrive à 18,2% de verbes accompagnés d'un marqueur, ce qui confirme donc le premier résultat. Pour compléter le répertoire des données quantitatives, ce tableau 4 fournit des informations plus détaillées sur les verbes utilisés au moins 39 fois dans les textes, tout en tenant compte des variantes orthographiques et des formes longue et courte des verbes.[9]

Les résultats à retenir du tableau 1 sont la fréquence relativement élevée des marqueurs du futur et la fréquence relativement élevée de *fin* par rapport à *ti*. Celles-ci pourraient être la conséquence d'un emploi *économique* du marqueur du passé *ti/té*.

Environ trois quarts ou 75% des verbes finis ne sont donc pas précédés de marqueurs, ou, autrement dit, ils sont précédés du marqueur zéro. Nous sommes arrivé à ce résultat de façon indirecte en faisant le compte d'éléments qui, en fin de compte, ne nous intéressent que négativement, car, et c'est un des problèmes des études quantitatives, s'il est facile de compter des éléments *in praensentia*, qui se laissent définir et délimiter par le contexte, il est difficile sinon impossible de compter *in absentia* un élément zéro dans des contextes matériellement multiples et très variables sans une étude sémanto-syntaxique préalable qui permette d'insérer un élément comptable.

Environ 14% des verbes sont précédés des marqueurs du passé (*ti, fin*), 10% marquent le futur (*a/va, pou*) et 1% le progressif (*(a)pe*). Le chiffre de 10% de verbes marqués pour le futur dans des textes écrits qui, pour la plupart, sont des récits, semble plutôt élevé, mais n'oublions pas que les récits, bien qu'ils parlent surtout de ce qui s'est passé dans le passé, contiennent également de nombreux dialogues et des réflexions qui concernent l'avenir. En revanche il est étonnant que seulement 14% des verbes finis soient précédés d'un marqueur du passé, car la majorité de nos textes racontent des histoires et parlent donc d'événements passés. Pourtant, au regard des seuls verbes, trois quarts de nos textes, selon les grammaires et l'opinion des locuteurs, parleraient alors du présent – ou utilisent la forme non-marquée comme *présent historique*. Une autre interprétation serait de dire que les marqueurs du passé ne sont pas obligatoires et peuvent être omis (remplacés par le marqueur zéro), dès que le contexte est défini comme une situation du passé et les actions comme des actions passées, accomplies. Une troisième interprétation serait que le marqueur zéro est *neutre*, qu'il exprime aussi bien le présent que le passé, la signification concrète étant donnée alors par le seul contexte. Cette dernière interprétation aurait l'avantage de rapprocher les créoles de l'océan Indien de ceux de la Caraïbe.

Ce que nous venons de dire du passé pourrait également s'appliquer à l'avenir. Mais ici la situation est différente. La limite entre le présent et l'avenir, entre ce qui se passe au moment où le locuteur parle et ce qui va suivre après, est bien moins nette. Dans de nombreuses langues – nous ne citons que l'allemand, où la forme appelée futur a plutôt

---

[9] Les variantes avec une fréquence inférieure n'ont en général pas été retenu. Plusieurs tests ont montré que leur situation ne diffère pas du reste des variantes, de sorte que cette simplification de l'étude nous parait légitime.

une valeur modale que temporelle et où c'est avant tout l'adverbe qui exprime et précise le futur, et à un moindre degré seulement la forme du verbe – la forme morphologique du présent peut facilement inclure l'avenir.

Le dialogue de Pitot (**1805**) en donne l'exemple. Les questions concernent l'avenir, et nous avons donc le marqueur *va* devant le premier verbe de ce passage, mais les futurs sans marqueur prédominent et *va* n'apparait que quand le locuteur met l'accent sur ce qu'il dit:

> Q. Qui li **va donné** vous, ça bon Dié là qui bon ?
> R. Ah ! bé ! li **n'a pas donné** moi n'a rien ; li **empesse** moi gagné grand malher ; quand mo **mort** li **faire** moi arrive dans mo paye ?
> [...]
> Q. Mais, papa, quand vous **capave** quitte Maurice pour alle dans vous paye, vous **va allé** ?
> R. Hé ! hé ! mô n'a pas pense ça, moi, qui mô **va faire** dans mô paye ? mô **n'a pas saclave** ?
> Q. Ah ! bin ; quand vous **arrive** dans vous paye, vous **n'a pas libe** donc ?
> R. Non va ; mô **saclave** la guerre ; quand mô **arrive** là ; zotte **prend** moi encore pour vendé moi. Quand mô **fini mort**, mô **va allé** dans mon paye, à v'là tout.

Chez Baissac (1888: 21-23, 29), le marqueur du futur apparait plus souvent et apparemment avec une certaine régularité, mais toujours dans le discours direct. Voici deux brefs exemples:

> Quand même léroi çagrin, li blizé rié : « Et toi, commère, mais quand ça qui **to pour tourné** ? — Mo **va tourné** quand mo **va tourné**, mon roi ; mais quand mo **va tourné** vous **va gagne** vous réponse. » Léroi laisse li allé.

> Li donne éne boute av baleine, li dire li: « Amarre bien séré. Lheire mo **va crïe** vous : Avlà mo **fine paré**, hissé ! nous dé nous **va hisse** ensemble. »

Est-ce le style de Baissac ou est-ce que le marqueur du futur est devenu plus obligatoire au cours du temps? Nous verrons par la suite qu'à la différence du futur, Baissac restera fidèle au marqueur zéro pour le passé.

Après ce bref regard sur le futur, retournons à l'examen du passé et regardons les textes et les interprétations que nous pouvons donner à la forme non-marquée de la forme personnelle des verbes.

Le premier document où la forme non-marquée exprime nettement le passé date de **1784** (Chaudenson 1981:78) : Des trois phrases du bref texte, la première exprime le présent: *Moi vieux, Monsieur, Moi malade, vendez moi*, la deuxième peut aussi bien se référer à une action passée qu'à un fait présent: *Moi faire bien et vous battez mon corps*. Le premier verbe de la troisième phrase est marqué par *fini*, le deuxième, dont le premier est la conséquence, est sans marqueur: *Papa, votre femme fini mort, moi tué ly*. Il s'agit donc nettement d'un passé qui est exprimé par le marqueur zéro.

Le texte de **1802** donne la deuxième attestation, et ici, il n'y a aucun marqueur pour indiquer *matériellement* qu'il s'agit d'un événement du passé: *Ah ! moi voir comme li venir dans mon li qui ; quand maître avez zoté chimise, vous laissé si chaise, moi asisé, disi, remué comme ça disi chaise, bouton li veni dans mon li qui*. L'esclave invente une petite histoire pour expliquer ce qui s'est passé. Il y a alors cinq verbes dont aucun n'est précédé d'un marqueur du passé: *venir, laissé, asisé, remué, veni*. La forme francisante et peu créole *avez zoté* exprime l'antériorité par rapport à ce que l'esclave raconte.

Le texte de **1818a** raconte une partie de chasse: *Le chasseur. Conte en langage créole de l'Ile-de-France*. Dans le texte d'une certaine longueur (610 mots), on ne trouve que cinq verbes qui soient précédés du marqueur du passé *té*, dont quatre se réfèrent à un fait antérieur à ce qui se passe dans le récit. Après la phrase introductive *Enne zour ça nous té la sasse cerf Grand-Rivière*, les verbes non-marqués se suivent dans le récit. Les quatre *té* qui suivent encore ont une autre fonction, à savoir celle de marquer un fait comme antérieur au récit. Voici la suite du conte: *L'her solé lévé, mo pour alle prend mon poste au pavé; mo passe drète cote ça grand pié di-bois piant Aughiste conné là* [présent ou passé, les deux sont possibles ici] ; *à v'la mo **sive** la rivière pour saute l'aut' coté: mo **ramasse** enne tondre, mo **guette** li; li encor **fimé**. Ah ah! Qui dou-monde qui **té pass'** là!* ...

La phrase *L'her solé lévé mo pour alle prend mon poste* est à situer au passé et signifie "Quand le soleil s'est levé, j'ai été pour = j'ai dû aller prendre mon poste".[10]

Dans une des poésies de son petit volume, Chrestien ([1822] 1831: 17-19) utilise le verbe sans et avec marqueur pour caractériser les deux personnes : Monsieur et Madame Denis se souviennent de leur jeunesse et parlent du passé. Mais alors que Monsieur utilise le verbe sans marqueur, Madame le fait assez souvent précéder de *té*:[11] Cette différence caractérise l'attitude des deux personnes et donne l'impression pour le lecteur, que les souvenirs de Monsieur Denis sont beaucoup plus vivants que ceux de sa femme. Lui il vit dans les souvenirs de sa jeunesse et de ses amours, alors que sa femme prend de la distance et ne s'y intéresse plus: c'est du passé pour elle.

I. Monsieur Denis.
Mon coco vous <u>souvini</u>
Dans lé temps la Compagni
Vous **mett'** condé paliaca !
Vous **zoli** comme ça !.. *(bis.)*
Tout blancs **guetté** nous passé
Et zaut' tout **crêvé rié**.. *(bis.)*

II. Madame Denis.
Tout d'bon vous <u>faire</u> moi pensé
Moi **té commencé** blié
Vous **té y en-a** bonnet blanc
Comment vous **çarmant**.. *(bis.)*
Et derrière ein' p'tit la-qué
Qui **té donn'** vous l'air fronté.. *(bis.)*

III. Monsieur Denis.
Quand vous **sorti** tous lé-soir
Vous **mett'** ein' grand mant'let noir.
Zipon **amar'** dans lé-rein
Comment vous **té bien**.. *(bis.)*
Et dé grands poss' la toil' blanc
Pour mett' tout qui-qu'soz' là dans.
(bis.)

IV. Madame Denis.
Nous **mett'** balein' dans corsêt
Nous **té rêd'** comment piquêt
Et zaut quilotte à-goussêt
Moi **té bien connais**.. *(bis.)*
La-clé là-dans **fair'** clin-clin !
Quand moi pens'-ça, moi sagrin.. *(bis.)*

V. Monsieur Denis.
Quand zaut' **appell'** moi *Zanot*
Si-fais va moi **té** faro !
Fill' **fair'** moi signe - dans çimin
Moi **fair'** mon faquin *(bis.)*
V'là zaut' **dir'** moi *Papa Zean* !
Moi foi Dié moi **mal - content**. *(bis.)*

VI, Madame Denis.
Quand di mond' <u>commencé</u> vié
Si-pas pourquoi zaut' <u>sanzé</u> ?
Vous **té zoué** tromp' la zournè
Pour fair' moi dansé.. *(bis.)*
A-s'ter là ma foi **tiéga**
(Avec un soupir.)
Quand mêm' zour' sam'di.. <u>n'a pas</u>.. *(bis.)*

VII. Monsieu Denis.
Mon femm' <u>faut tendé</u> raison
Quand <u>vié</u>, dansé n'a pas bon :
Si vous <u>y en-a</u> sentiment
Faut <u>fair'</u> comment blanc.. *(bis.)*
Quand la-têt' <u>commenc'</u> branlé
(avec gravité)
Dé ç'tems là <u>prié</u> bon Dié.. *(bis.)*

Le texte de **1839a**, du journal *Le Cernéen* (du premier janvier 1839), est un texte parodique ou satyrique. Là encore, ce sont les verbes non-précédés de marqueur qui dominent, bien que le texte rapporte des faits qui se sont passés quelques jours auparavant. Les quelques *ti* situent le texte au passé, mais dès que l'on raconte les événements, il n'y a plus de marqueurs, sauf dans des cas d'antériorité:

---

[10] D'après notre interprétation, il ne s'agit pas (encore) du marqueur du futur *pour*, qui n'est attesté qu'en 1867.
[11] Dans le texte qui suit, les verbes et adjectifs attributs sont mis en gras; les verbes qui se réfèrent au présent sont soulignés.

Moussié La Gazette,

Vous **ti dire** Moussié Sirandale **fin' donne** nous boire zour Noël di vin, la bierre ensemble la liquère. Laut' zour vous **ti dire** Gouvernère **bête** à cause li **causé** quiqu' çose qui li n'a pas **coné**: à c't'hère vous même qui <u>bête</u>, vous <u>parle</u> ça qu'vous n'a pas <u>coné</u>. M. Sirandale ça même qui <u>zize</u> pour nous, li **ti donne** ene grand bal dans son la case. Coument nous **ti hérés** !

Assise dans fauteuils; **boire** dans verre zize ; domestiques na pas **manqué**, zendarmes!!. **y en a** di vin, **y en a** la bierre, **y en a** la liquère; tout madame **si** l'eau cologne dans moussoir. Mo même **la misique** avec Prosper. Moussié Sirandale **dire** nous comme ça moutié français, moutié anglais: amisez mo z'enfants, badinez; ça même nous banne année azourdi. A v'la tout la nouit nous **dansé**, zisqu'à viélon na pas **capabe** marcé; colophane **na pas**. Sitôt la LIBERTÉ **finie**, nous **tire** galop zisqu'à nous **fine soûlé**! Moussié Sirandale même **toné**.

Y en ena dispite même: Myrtil qui **fin trouvé** son femme avec Philogène là haut grénier.

L'hère nous **maziné** pour quitte bal, a v'la camrades **saut'** dans parc cabris, ça povre moussié Sirandale pour dire li merci, **prend** trois cabris, **coupe** son la tête, f..... la haut l'épaule; la tête même **quitte** divant la porte. La zoie aussi **gagne** malhor; quatre **fine saboulé**. Pauvre Moussié Sirandale! Son zendarme où li? Après **donne** la liquère tout zènes filles la Rivière Grampant . l'hère pour TIOMBO PIOSSE, COURAZE NA PAS li zié **bourlé** coument piment, li **plié** raide, **reinté** qui n'a pas pelle **reinté** même, pa la moutié **all'** l'hôpital. A soir **vini** cabris la zoie, tout ça dans marmite.

A v'la Moussié la Gazette, ça qu'vous na pas **ti coné**; Si vous na pas voulé croire moi donne di l'eau béni : mo boire !

ZEAN ENSEMBLE PROSPER,
MISICIENS LA RIVIERE GRAMPART

Avec *Zistoire Moucie Caraba* (1850), nous passons au genre littéraire du conte, dont le grand maître a été 30 ans plus tard Charles Baissac; ce dernier ayant d'ailleurs repris, modestement retravaillé et élargi le présent texte, l'histoire du Chat Botté (Baissac 1880: 121-41). Nous présentons les deux versions l'une à côté de l'autre.[12]

Pour placer l'histoire dans le passé, nous trouvons plusieurs *ti* au début du conte. Ensuite, abstraction faite des discours directs et de quelques informations sur des événements antérieurs, nous ne trouvons plus que des verbes non-précédés de marqueurs:

Zistoire Moucié Caraba (1850)	*Zistoire éne çatte qui té éna botes* (1880)
E **ti y en** a enne vié blan qui **ti gagne** troi piti; li **ti y en a** enne moulin, enne bourique ensemble enne satte. Enne zour, sa vié bonome la, **li gagne** gran malade, pour mor même, **li appelle** son troi piti, **li dire**, « mon piti, mon piti, avla mo **va mor**, [...]	**Té iéna** éne vié blanc qui **té éna** trois pitits : li **té éna** éne moulin, éne bourique ensemble éne çatte. Éne zour ça vié bonhomme là li **gagne** grand malade pour môrt méme. Li **apéle** so trois pitits, li **dire** zautes : « Mo pitits, avlà mo pour mort ; [...]
Avla astore satte **metté** son botte dans son li pié, li **amarre** son sac dans son lé rin, astore li **allé**, li **allé**, li **allé** zousqua li **arrive** dans enne gran carré doublé, astore li **ouvri** bien la bouce son sac, li **mette** la dan bon morceau laceron, li **té amare** [action antérieure] enne pti la corde bien longue, astore li **arquillé**, li **cacié** dans fon boursaille, rien que son li zié même **té** dohore, mo dire vou, un poti moman, arla enne gran B... lièvre **vini** cri, cri, cri, cri, avla li **voir** la lasseron, li **antre** dan son sac pour li manzé; manami! satte **trouve** sa, li **halle** son piti lacorde tou din	**Çatte méte** so botes, li **prend** so sac, li **amare** li dans so léreins, aprés li **allé**, li **allé** zisqu'à li **arive** dans éne grand lapléne acote **té iéna** bon morceau iéves. Li **prend** so sac, li **méte** làdans bon morceau lastrons, li **ouvert** labouce ça sac là li **amare** éne ptit lacorde bien longue ; aprés li **arquilé**, li **caciéte** enbas feilles, so liziés tout séle dohors, mo dire vous. Avlà éne papa iève **vini**, cri, cri, cri, cri. Li **arive** drète av lacorde éne coup : li **làdans**, manami ! Iéve **crié** : grâce, papa çatte, mo napas fére encore ! Çatte napas **acoute** li, li **touye** li. Aprés, li **amare** so lipiéds, li **ouvert**

---

[12] Les versions complètes du conte se trouve aux pages 35-40.

cou, avla lièvre **fini pri** [voix passive]. Avla lièvre li **dire**: grasse papa satte, grasse papa satte, mo napa faire encore. Satte na pas **coute** tou sa. Li **touille**, apré li **mette** li dans son sac.

Avla astore li **allé**, li **allé**, li **allé**. Li **arrive** cote la caze lé roi, li **voulé** entré, soldat qui **té** la garde la porte lé roi napa **voulé** lésse li entré. Avla lé Roi qui **tende** dou monde barbouille barbouille dan son la porte, li **dire**: [...]

so vente, li **foure** éne ptit dibois làdans, li **méte** li dans so boursac,

li **alle** drétte lacase léRoi. Çatte **vlé** entré, avlà soldat qui **té** monte lagarde dans laporte léRoi, li **barre** li cimin. Més çatte **entété**. Avlà léRoi qui **tende** doumoune cause fort dans so la porte li **dire** : [...]

Perrault, lui, dont le conte a sûrement servi de modèle, raconte le tout au passé simple. L'emploi du marqueur zéro n'est donc pas dû au français, mais représente une structure propre au créole (mauricien). Fait étonnant: Baissac, qui utilise couramment le marqueur zéro pour exprimer le passé, n'en fait aucune mention dans sa grammaire: "Présent. C'est le thème verbal" (1880: 23). Si lui déjà se laisse tant influencer par le français dans sa façon d'interpréter les structures du créole, que dire alors en général de la fiabilité des ouvrages écrits par des francophones?

Nous disposons toutefois également de quelques textes où la présence du marqueur *ti* contredit nos observations préalables. Le premier texte est de Lolliot (1855: 1) et c'est la dédicace de ses poésies. Le *té* y est très fréquent, sans que nous puissions l'expliquer. Ce n'est qu'au milieu que l'on trouve quelques verbes non marqués. Ces constructions ne nous semblent pas spécialement expressives, plutôt lourdes.

A MM A de Rochecouste et E de Chazal

Zot dé là zot voir bien, mo dir' ça sans menti,
Tout sels **fin' conn' gardé** touzours zot zenr' créole ;
Zot léquer là zamais **té donn'** nous démenti ;
Zot **té touzours zot mêm'** sans zamais zoué rôle,
Et **té marcé** tout dret' sans zamais zot çanzé,
Sans baiss' à droite à gauce et sans fair' la poussière,
Sans qui zamais personn' **té par zot écrasé**.
Mo conné pouquoi ça ! zot **té tourné** derrière
Pour guet ein pé cimin qui Créoles l'aut' fois
Té touzours conné sivre, et zot léquer **té dire**
Qui ça la route là, quand mêm' cimin dans bois,
Fin' marqué par l'honner comment là haut la cire ;
Aussi, zot **na pas hont'** met' zilet la toil' blé
Et quand mêm' pour sourti **met** zot çapeau la paille,
A cauz' qui zot **conné** qui zilet là doublé
Semb' ein léquer qui bon et qu'en bas son p'tit maille
L'aut la **couvri** zot front qui zamais **té courbé**.
Si mo **té çoisi** zot pour parrains mo l'ouvraze,
Na pas à cauz' zot riç' et qui mo per tombé ;
Non, personne mo croir' va tini ça langaze,
Car zamais **mo té conn'** ni flatté, ni menti.
Ça qui dans mo papié **mo té faire** comm' ça même ;
Mais pourtant **mo té v'lé** pour parrains mo pitit,
Dé vrais Mauriciens, Créol' comment li même.

Le deuxième texte de Lolliot (1855: 37-39), une fable, contient plusieurs *té* au départ, mais dès que l'action commence, les verbes ne sont plus précédés de marqueur. Un seul *té* revient au milieu du texte quand un nouvel acteur entre en scène. Lolliot connait donc bien la signification du marqueur zéro, ce qui ne l'empêche d'avoir plus souvent recours au marqueur *té* que les auteurs des textes étudiés avant le sien.

EIN VIÉ BLANC AVARE SEMB' SO PITIT

Ein' zour, mo na pas conné comment,
Ein' blanc qui **té gagné** plein plein gros sacs l'arzent,
Mais qui **té plis avare** encor' qui li **té rice**,
Té si tant bon l'himer
Qui li **té dir'** ma foi, faut mo pass' mo caprice
Et pour mo l'estomac faut mo morceau bon quer.
Avla li **prend** so parasol la toile,
Ein' ptit panier couvert semb' la voile
Et **fair'** exprès arriv' ein pé tard
Dans bazar,
Pour gagné bon marcé quiques mangues Fizet.
En tournant qui li **fair'** ? Li **met** zot dans l'armoire,
Divant zot tous les zours **dire** son çapelet,
Vous capav' croire,
Et contenté manzé ça qui fin' gât' gâté.
So garçon ein brigand, ein p'tit mauvais sizé
Qui **té senti** l'oder, nous conné l'oder mangue
Li **monté** dans nénez, pez' ein zour so la clé,
Invit' dé so zamis qui li **conn'** sans la langue
Et sans mo bisoin dir', zot trois là zot **raflé**
Si pas qui quantité. Zot à peine **fini**,
Qui bonhomm' là, papa, li **rentré** dans la case ;
So léquer li **manqué**, so li zié li **tourdi**.
Ah ! Coquins qui li **dir'**, ça mêm' qui zot l'ouvraze !
Faut qui zot rend' mo mang' ou sans ça zot va voir
Si mo na pas va coup' zot li cou semb' razoir.
Papa, **dire** so pitit, na pas bisoin la peine,
Ni bisoin tant çagrin :
Nous **té nèque manzé**, guetté plitòt la graine
Ca qui té gagn' farçin.

Le dernier texte que nous présentons, paru dans *Le Mauricien* du 27 juillet 1855, est difficile à classer. Il s'agit apparemment de la critique d'une mauvaise pièce représentée récemment au théâtre - ou de sa parodie. Le fait de trouver un tel texte dans *Le Mauricien* surprend, si ce n'est une parodie, peut-être avec un arrière-fond de critique politique.

L'emploi conséquent de *té* dans ce texte va à l'encontre de nos expériences précédentes, mais avalise ce que l'on trouvera plus tard dans les grammaires et descriptions du créole, et ce que les locuteurs eux-mêmes pensent apparemment du fonctionnement de leur créole. Le texte semble peu authentique, plutôt artificiel. Faut-il y voir une volonté particulière de la part de l'auteur ou peut-on en déduire qu'il maîtrise mal le créole ? Est-il peut-être francophone et suit-il des règles qu'il croit correctes, comme font les auteurs modernes du seychellois mentionnés par Bollée 1989 (cf *supra*) ?

Mais tout ça là na rien. La Comédie là qui li! Vous vlé mo racont' vous li.
Ein Missié **té baiss'** ein l'autre, l'autre là **té rend'** li, après zot **té boir'** ensemb', zot **té rié**, rié zisqu'à n'a pas bon. Après ça zot **té la guerr'** ensemb' encor'; zot **té tomb'** par ein la fenêtre; après ça ein' Missié qui **té rice té fine vine** domestique; l'autre so camrade **té cacié** dans la cave et pis tous sortes quiq' çoses. Primier pièce là mo **té bien cout'** ; mais les zaut' ma foi **mo té voir** tout di monde rié tant, qui mo **té tant rié** voir zot rié qui mo **té malade** mo côté.

Tout de bon vous là, zamais quand vous voir Anglais dans la rie, vous capav' qui zot' mêmes qui faire la Comédie qui farce comme ça.

Conclusion

Dans notre étude, nous sommes partis de la constation suivante: dans les créoles de l'océan Indien le verbe non-précédé de marqueur du passé est souvent employé dans des contextes relatifs au passé. Cela est possible dès que le contexte indique qu'il s'agit du passé et non du présent. L'étude quantitative des textes du corpus a montré qu'environ trois quarts des verbes dans des constructions personnelles ou finies ne sont pas précédés de marqueur et seulement environ 13% sont précédés d'un marqueur du passé. Selon toute probabilité, la part des verbes au passé devrait être beaucoup plus élevée, et cela davantage encore puisqu'il s'agit de textes écrits. L'étude de quelques textes particulièrement intéressants pour notre propos, commençant vers la fin du 18e siècle, a confirmé que les verbes non-précédés de marqueur ou - autrement dit - précédés du marqueur zéro, sont très fréquents pour exprimer le passé. La langue actuelle ne semble pas beaucoup avoir changé sous cet aspect, comme le montreront les deux textes modernes que nous avons ajoutés en annexe.

Afin d'expliquer ce phénomène, deux hypothèses ont été proposées : ou bien il s'agit d'un présent historique, ou bien c'est le principe de l'économie qui autorise à omettre le marqueur dès que le contexte est clair et qu'il ne prête pas à de fausses interprétations. Nous proposons une troisième explication: la forme non-marquée du verbe en mauricien et probablement aussi dans les autres créoles de l'océan Indien n'est pas un présent, mais elle exprime le passé aussi bien que le présent. Sa signification précise dépend du contexte. En acceptant cette interprétation, on peut rapprocher les créoles de l'océan Indien des créoles des Antilles, à la différence qu'il ne faut pas mettre le marqueur du progressif pour exprimer le présent, mais que le marqueur zéro peut aussi bien exprimer le passé que le présent. Il n'y aurait donc pas de différence entre les verbes statifs et les verbes non-statifs, ce qui est le cas pour les Antilles. Cette observation n'est cependant pas tout à fait valable, car, sur un autre plan, les verbes statifs n'acceptent pas le marqueur *fin*, et ceux qui l'acceptent changent de signification pour exprimer un développement ou une action.[13]

Annexe moderne

Pour terminer, nous présentons deux textes modernes où l'emploi de *ti* respectivement du marqueur zéro pour exprimer des faits du passé n'a pas changé depuis les premiers texte du corpus des textes créoles mauriciens. Le premier texte est tiré de *Bord la mer* ([1980]: 54), le deuxième est tiré d'un enregistrement que nous avons effectué à Rodrigues en 1975 avec un homme âgé de plus de 93 ans, que l'on trouve également dans Stein (1984: 130):

I. Renga

Mo **ti ena** enn frer **travay** isi, ti frer. Zot **ti apel** li 'Latet-Latet', enn nom badinaz, me **li apel** Renga. Me, li **ti'nn travay** anfin bien lontan dan dok. Ziska li **kit** lekol, li **travay** dan batlaz. Li **ti travay** kum regilié, après li'**nn kité**, li'**nn alé**, li'**nn revini**, li'**nn travay** kum zurnalyé.

Li'**nn travay, travay, travay**. Alors, enn zur li **ti pe al** abor, enn dimans sa. Travay abor enn Olandé. Abé, ant 9 er, li **al manzé**. Avan 10 er Palané **sorti**. Kan palanké **sorti**, li **lev** latet, li **get** lao. Li **truv** palanké la. Li **dir** so bann kamarad: "Buré!" Kuma dir "Buré!" la, li pa **gayn** letan sa palanké la, ners la **kasé** lao.

Letan li **alé**, so lipié **may** ek enn lakord palanké la, **k-kraz** li net, **krazé** net. So latet **eklaté**, laservel **tom** dan delo partu.

Lerla bato **donn** alarm partu. **Degaze, ramase**. Ler **ramas** li, ondiré enn butey kasé, **pran** li, **met** li dan enn sak plastik, alors, motobot **kosté, pran** li **met** dan motobot, **amenn** li ater. Lerla zot **dir** mwa, "To frer **finn mor**'."

---

[13] Cf à ce propos les chiffres des tableaux pour la fréquence de *fin*, en tenant compte du caractère sémantique des verbes en question.

II. Per Kayo

Per Kayo **mor**. Kan per Kayo **ti mor**, mo mem ki **ti** avek li isi. [..] Ler [mo] **ariv** isi tanto, senker dan lapremidi, ler kouzinyen **in prepar** so dinen. Alor kouzinyen **ale**, **dir** [ki] mwa byé **servi** per so manze. [Mo] **pran** manze dan lasal-a-manze, **pran** manze dan isi, [..] **met** lor so latab. Ler **in fini met** sa lor so latab, avan li **manze** li **pran** en manng. Ti ann-ete sa, sezon annoktob. Li **pran** enn manng, li **manze**. Ler **fini manz** sa manng la, li **rantre** dan so lasam. Mo **sorti**, mo **ale**, mo **debrouy-debrouye** la. En ti moman, mo **tan** en ronfleman lor lili. Mo **dir** li: "Mon per, ou pa pou dine?" Li pa **koze**. Alor mo **dir**: "Me ki ou gagné?" Li **dir** mwa: "Mo **fin tom** malad, mo **fini tom** malad". Ler li **fini tom** malad, li pa **koze**, so lizye **fermé**. Mo **marse**. An galoupan mo **met** demi er pou sort Sen Gabriel pou ariv o Por Matiren. Demi er mo **marse**, mo **taye**, mo **al** an-vil. Mo **al zwenn** per Simeon. Per Simeon **apre asize** apre fer so brevier. Li **diman** mwa: "Kot to ale?" Mo **dir** li: "Mon per **fin tom** malad, gravman malad".

Alor **ti ena** enn seval an-vil. Li **kit** sa seval la. Nou pa **kapav** met an seval parski seval, pandan lanw,it koum sa, li **abriti**. Kikfwa li **tann** enn tapaz, li **abriti**, e li **vepa** marse. Li **kit** seval, li **taye** depi laba, **vin** isi. Ler nou **ariv** isi, per **lor lili** an long, pa ankor **mor**. Alor per Simeon **dir** li: "Mon per!" Per Simeon **dir** li: "Mon per, ou kontan mo donn ou lestromoksyon?" Li **dir**: "Non!"

Alor **ti ena** enn dokter ki **apel** dokter Rousel, **ti** enn franse. Li **ti abit** Moulibé, so madam **ti** enn fransez. Alor [per Simeon] **dir** mwa: "Al laba, al sers, al apel soz; to kapav ale, minwu". **Se** minwi ler la. Mo **sorti**, mo **taye**, mo **ale**. Ler mo **ariv** laba, mo **tap** laport dokter. Dokter **dir**: "Ki sa? Ki malad?" Mo **dir** li ki per **in tom** gravman malad. Alor li, li **abiye**, so madam **abiye**, zot tou-le-de **marse-vini**. Ler **ariv** isi, **tat** per, **tat** so de pou. Per **in mor**, enn ti moman per **tonbe mor**.

Références[14]

Anon. 1980 *Bord la mer.* Port Louis : Port Louis Harbour and Docks Workers Union.
Baissac, Charles 1880 *Étude sur le patois créole mauricien.* Nancy: Berger-Levrault.
—— 1888. *Le folk-lore de l'Île Maurice.* Paris: Maisonneuve & Larose.
Baker, Philip 1995 Motivation in Creole genesis. Baker, Philip (ed.) *From contact to Creole and beyond.* London: University of Westminster Press, 3-15.
Bollée, Annegret 1989 Le développement du créole écrit aux Seychelles. Ludwig, Ralph (éd.) *Les créoles français entre l'oral et l'écrit.* Tübingen: Narr 183-97.
Bord la mer v. Anon. 1980.
Chaudenson, Robert 1981 *Textes créoles anciens (La Réunion et Ile Maurice). Comparaison et essai d'analyse.* Hamburg: Buske.
Chrestien, François [1822] 1831 Les essais d'un bobre africain, Mauritius: Déroullède.
Lolliot, Pierre 1855 *Poésies créoles.* Port Louis : Imprimerie du *Mauricien.*
Stein, Peter 1984 *Kreolisch und Französisch.* Tübingen: Niemeyer.
—— 1995 Early Creole writing and its effects on the discovery of Creole language structure. The case of eighteenth century Negerhollands. Arends, Jacques (ed.) *The early stages of creolization.* Amsterdam: Benjamins, 43-61.

Peter Stein, romaniste et créoliste. Principaux domaines de recherche créolistique: l'Ile Maurice et les anciens documents en créole à base néerlandaise des Iles Vierges. Thèse sur la situation linguistique de l'Ile Maurice; co-éditeur de la *Missionsgeschichte* d'Oldendorp et éditeur de son dictionnaire du *negerhollands*. La communauté des romanistes allemands ne lui ayant pas accordé le droit d'un poste permanent, il s'est spécialisé dans les remplacements de chaires, depuis 2004 à l'Université Humboldt de Berlin.
<p.stein@t-online.de> et <peter.stein@rz.hu-berlin.de>.

---

[14] Les textes ci-dessus mentionnés ou cités avec la référence **1805, 1818a, 1839a, 1850** se trouvent parmi **The Corpus of MC texts** (ce volume, pages 1-60). On y trouve toutes les informations bibliographiques.

The resumptive pronoun *li* in Mauritian Creole

Diana Guillemin

1. Introduction[1]

The focus of this article is on the morpheme *li* in early and modern Mauritian Creole (MC). It is derived from the French *lui* ('him'), and is by far the most frequently occurring morpheme in the concordance.[2] It occurs as subject, object and, very importantly, as a resumptive pronoun in Topic/Comment constructions, whose frequency has been attributed to Bantu influence. The aim of my analysis is to determine if the function of *li* has always been strictly pronominal or whether it is gradually being reanalyzed as an inflectional element, either an agreement marker or a copula.[3] This proposal is somewhat controversial, given that predicative constructions with a phonologically null (zero) copula have always been grammatical in MC. I compare *li* to another copula *se*, a recent borrowing from French, which is in complementary distribution with *li*.[4]

In current MC dictionaries, *li* is defined strictly as a 3rd singular pronoun (Baker & Hookoomsing 1987, Ledikasyon pu Travayer 2004). In his grammar of MC, Virahsawmy (2004) also defines *li* as a pronoun, though he does concede that, in some instances, it seems to function as a copula (p c). The copulative use of *se* is relatively recent in MC, and is not acknowledged by Baker & Hookoomsing (1987). The more recent dictionary by Ledikasyon pu Travayer (2004) define it as follows: 'v. is, *lide se pu uver li pu tu dimunn* = the idea is to open it to all'.[5]

1.1 *Li* in early MC

From the first instantiations of MC, *li* occurs between the subject and the predicate in non-tensed copulative like clauses, as shown:

(1) a. *ça li nègre blanc* (**1802**)   b. *bibass' li goût!* (Chrestien 1822)
        this *li* negro white   loquat *li* tasty
        That's a white slave   That loquat is tasty!
        Sa (li) ênn esklav blan (modern MC)   *Bibass la dan gu!* (modern MC)

The occurrence of *li* was by no means mandatory, as zero copula was grammatical in early MC, as it is today. In the modern MC equivalents, where the nominal predicate is modified by the indefinite singular determiner *enn* as in (1a), *li* is optional. When the

---

[1] I thank the editors of this volume for their constructive feedback on an earlier draft of this article, and assume responsibility for all inconsistencies.
[2] There are 5659 occurrences of *li* in the 100,000 word Concordance (Baker p c).
[3] The editors of this volume maintain that *li* only functions as a resumptive pronoun in modern MC.
[4] In this article I use the term 'copula' for both *li* and *se*, although they perform different functions. My analysis is based on the definition of 'copula' as: 'The verb 'be' and its equivalent in other languages, seen simply as a link or mark of relationship between one element and another. E.g. *am* is a copula in *I am cold* or *I am a doctor*, where it links the subject (*I*) and the predicative element (*cold, a doctor*). Distinguished from, in particular, the existential use of 'be', e.g. in *There is a solution* ('A solution exists') (Matthews 1997: 77). For existential 'be', MC uses *ena*. See Fon Sing & Véronique, *this volume*, for a detailed analysis.
[5] A list of abbreviations appears at the end of this article.

subject is marked by the Specificity marker *la* as in (1b), *li* is not required. These determiners were lacking in very early MC. The first instantiations of the indefinite article *enn*, and the first instance of the use of *la* to mark anaphoric definiteness are both dated 1818.[6] From the time that it is first used, *enn* unambiguously marks the NP as singular and [–definite], but the grammaticalization of *la* into a Specificity marker was a more gradual process.[7]

Corne (1974) argued that the emergence of *li* was a direct consequence of the loss of the copula, where the notion of copula is strictly understood as the link between the subject and the predicate, equivalent to the verb 'to be'. In the absence of an overt copula, *li* serves to indicate that what precedes it is the subject and what follows is the predicate.

1.2 The loss of the French determiners

Another significant change from French to MC was the loss of the determiners, which, in French, serve to mark the semantic contrasts of [±definite] and singular versus plural.[8] An immediate consequence of article incorporation was the occurrence of bare nouns in various syntactic configurations, with ambiguous interpretations between [±definite] and singular versus plural interpretations.

This represented a significant divergence from the lexifier, which does not admit bare nouns, bar few exceptions.[9] The occurrence of bare nouns in argument positions in early MC triggered a shift in noun interpretation from French to MC (Guillemin, *in preparation*). Such a claim is based on Chierchia's (1998) analysis of 'Kinds across languages', where he postulates that nouns vary with respect to the parameters ±argumental or ±predicative. In Romance, nouns are predicative, hence the need for them to occur with a determiner in argument positions. Nouns in Chinese and Japanese are argumental, hence the occurrence of bare nouns in argument positions in these languages. In some languages like English, nouns can be [+arg, +pred]. Singular count nouns require a determiner, but bare mass nouns and bare plurals can occur as arguments. MC nouns are also [+arg, +pred]. While bare mass nouns can occur in any argument position yielding [±definite] interpretations, count nouns require a determiner when they are [+definite].

In existential constructions, which admit only indefinites (Milsark 1979) bare MC nouns have a default plural interpretation, as with *dodo* in (2):

---

[6] There are no occurrences of the indefinite article in Pitot (1805), where one would expect such use, e.g.:

(1) *Papa,   vous   y en a   femme,   ou bien   vous   tout cèle?   Mo   y en a   femme.*
     father 2.SG.F have   wife   or   2.SG.F all alone   1.SG have   wife
     Father do you have a wife or are you all alone? I have a wife.
     Papa, est-ce que vous avez une femme, ou est-ce que vous êtes tout seul. J'ai une femme.
     Papa, u ena enn fam ubyen u tu sel? Mo ena enn fam.   (modern MC)

(2) *mô   saclave la guerre;*
     1.SG slave   war
     I am a slave of the war / Je suis un esclave de la guerre
     Mo enn esklav lager   (modern MC)

[7] The grammaticalization of *la* was not complete until it was used to mark mass nouns as well as plural count nouns, and this did not occur until the late 19th century. One of the first occurrences of *la* with a mass noun is in Baissac (1880):

(1) *Qui fére   ente   dans dileau   frés   là!*
     why   enter   into cold   water   SP
     Why get into that cold water! / Pourquoi entrer dans cette eau froide!

[8] French determiners also mark Gender, but this feature is not grammaticalized in MC and consequently it is not relevant to this analysis. For more details on Article incorporation, or agglutination, see Chaudenson (1981), Baker (1984), Grant (1995) and Strandquist (2005).

[9] Some of the exceptions include the predicative use of bare nouns that denote a role or profession, with coordinated nouns, *Père et fils* ("Father and son"), and in fused expressions, such as proverbs.

(2) Ena   dodo dan mize
    have   dodo in museum
    There are dodos in (the) museum(s) / Il y a des dodos dans des musées/ le musée

The above sentence ambiguous between a 'habitual' or 'generic' statement, e.g. 'Normally there are dodos in museums', in which case *mize* is [–definite] plural. If reference is being made to a specific museum, then *mize* is [+definite] singular. When a bare noun in MC has a [+definite] singular interpretation, the presence of a phonologically null definite determiner is assumed. It is a null element, which, like other 'empty categories' needs licensing in ungoverned positions, e.g. in subject position, where there is no lexical head (verb or preposition) to act as a governor (Rizzi 1990). In modern MC, when a bare singular common count noun occurs in subject position, the Specificity marker *la* surfaces as a 'last resort' (Chomsky 1995) to license the null determiner.

(3) Dodo la dan mize
    dodo SP in museum
    The dodo is in the museum / Le dodo est dans le musée

The Specificity Marker *la* forces a singular interpretation of the count noun, just like *li* in very early MC. Further evidence that these morphemes were, at one stage, performing similar functions comes from the two versions of 'The hare and the tortoise', the one collected by Freycinet in 1818 and the one published by Chrestien in 1822, where *li* and *la* are interchangeable:

(4) Mais   son   nation   là   trop tourdi   (1818a)
    but   3.SG.POSS   race   SP   too scatterbrain
    But those of his race are too stupid / Mais sa race est trop abrutie

(5) Mais   son   nation   li   trop tourdi   (Chrestien 1822)

Both *li* and *la* initially occurred only with singular count nouns.[10] The use of *li* to mark the subject as referential subsided following the grammaticalization of *la*, but its use as a resumptive pronoun, co-referential to a topicalized subject, never ceased. However, just as in English and French, a Topic/Comment construction, where the Topic is left dislocated, represents a marked construction.

1.3 The reanalysis of *li*

I put forward the tentative proposal that the resumptive pronoun *li* may be in the early stages of reanalysis into an inflectional element, and that its path to grammaticalization may be linked to that of *la*. Such a claim is based on a comparison of MC and Seychellois Creole (SC), which does not have a Specificity Marker, but where the morpheme *i*, a cognate of *li*, occurs in all affirmative present tense clauses.

The morphemes *li* and *la* seemed to have had equal status when the creoles diverged in the mid 1830's. The paths to grammaticalization of these morphemes in those two creoles obviously diverged at some point - in SC *la* is only a locative adverb, not a determiner. On the basis of sociohistorical factors, it would be reasonable to assume that substrate influence played a more significant role in the development of SC than in that of MC during the second half of the 19th century.[11] In early MC, both morphemes functioned as operators assigning quantificational force to NP variables in subject position. The

---

[10] There are very few occurrences (about 4) of *li* with plural subjects in the concordance, thus the claim that it only occurs with singular subjects.
[11] Following the abolition of slavery in 1835, a large contingent of Creole speaking slaves moved from Mauritius to the Seychelles, and the British continued to dump a large number of new, 'rescued slaves' there right up to the 1860s. This colony then remained in relative isolation, and the substrate languages were likely to have had a far greater influence in the development of SC than in that of MC, (Bollée 1977, Baker, p c). See Section 8.1.1 for discussion.

Specificity Marker *la* now fulfils this role in modern MC, but this morpheme did not grammaticalize into a determiner in SC. The precise function of SC *i* is still the subject of much debate, which is summarized in Section 8.

Although this article does not include a detailed syntactic analysis, I abide by Chomsky's (1995) Minimalist assumption that language is a perfect system that strives for economy of derivation and representation, with no superfluous steps in derivation. The occurrence of any morpheme is assumed to entail a grammatical function. My semantic assumptions are within the framework of Truth Conditional Semantics, where a sentence is analyzed as a proposition which has a Truth value, which is either true or false. A proposition with a free variable is an 'open proposition'; it is incomplete in that it cannot have a truth value.

The organization of this article is as follows: In Section, I look at the many uses of the verb *être*, 'to be', and how these transferred into MC. Section 3 comprises brief syntactic and semantic definitions of Predication. In Section 4, I look at the distribution of *li* in early MC, and in Section 5, I look at the distribution of *li* in modern MC. Section 6 comprises a discussion of the new copula *se* where I compare its function to that of *li*. Section 7 is my analysis, where I provide typological evidence of pronouns and demonstratives that have grammaticalized into copulas. Section 8 summarizes the debate on Seychellois *i*, a cognate of MC *li*, where my aim is to shed light on the function of *li*. Section 9 is my conclusion.

2. The verb 'to be' in MC

2.1 The loss of the French copula

In his *Étude sur le patois créole mauricien*, Baissac bemoans the loss of verb 'to be', claiming that 'le verbe abstrait par excellence, le verbe essential *être* n'existe pas en créole, où il est impossible de dire: Dieu est. Descartes fut heureux d'avoir une autre langue à son service' (1880: viii-ix). [12]

The verb *être*, like English 'be', can be:
- A full verb meaning 'to exist'
- An auxiliary bearing Tense and Agreement in predicative constructions
- A copula which functions as a full verb, also referred to as 'equative be' or 'identity be'

Stowell refers to the auxiliary and the copula as the predicative and referential uses of the verb *be* (1989: 255), giving as examples: 'John is a fool" and 'The morning star is the evening star', respectively.

Baissac would have been referring to all three meanings, for the verb *existe* does not figure in the early corpus, and both predicative and copulative constructions appeared to be lacking the verb 'to be' in early MC. But when Baker & Corne claim that 'The fact of the matter is that IdeFC (Isle de France Creole) does not have an underlying copula, and that no useful purpose is achieved by postulating one' (1982: 35), they are referring to both the auxiliary and copulative uses of 'be', for the full verb *existe* has found its way back into the modern MC lexicon.[13]

The loss of the copula represented a significant change from French to Creole, accompanied as it was by the loss of inflectional morphology on nouns and verbs. MC has

---

[12] 'The verb of abstraction *par excellence*, the essential verb 'to be' does not exist in creole, where it is impossible to say: God exists. Descartes was fortunate to a have access to another language'.
[13] 'Isle de France Creole' refers to the creole of Mauritius, the Seychelles, Rodrigues and the Chagos Archipelago. It is a French based creole that originated in Mauritius in the eighteenth century, when the island was known as Isle de France. The Creoles spoken in Mauritius and the Seychelles are also referred to as Mauritian Creole and Seychellois Creole (or Seselwa) respectively. There are some minor differences between them, but they are mutually intelligible. IdeFC does not include Réunion Creole.

retained the SVO word order of its lexifier, and Tense, Mood and Aspect are marked by preverbal morphemes, which occur in strict TMA order.[14]

2.1.1 Auxiliary

The verb *être*, like 'be' functions as an auxiliary bearing tense and agreement in predicative constructions, as shown:

(6) a. Tu **es** triste   b. Tu **étais** triste   French
       You **are** sad   You **were** sad   English
       To sagren   To **ti** sagren   MC

(7) a. Serge **est** maçon   b. Serge **était** maçon   French
       Serge is a bricklayer   Serge was a bricklayer   English
       Serz mason / Serz (**li**) enn mason   Serz **ti** mason/Serz **ti** enn mason   MC

(8) a. Paul **est** mon copain   b. Paul **était** mon copain   French
       Paul is my friend   Paul was my friend   English
       Pol (**se**) mo kamwad   Pol **ti** mo kamwad   MC

In (6), the predicate is an adjective, and, when the clause is in the present tense, the subject and predicate are string adjacent in MC. When the clause is in the past tense, *ti* occurs between the subject and the predicate.

In (7) the predicate is a noun denoting a profession or role. When a bare noun is used, the subject and predicate are string adjacent. When the predicate is an indefinite NP, the use of *li* is optional. A resumptive pronoun can be used with TMA markers, but it is a marked construction, where the Topic is left dislocated and contrastive focus is implied, as in:

(9) Serz, li ti enn mason, pa enn sarpantye
    Serge, he was a bricklayer, not a carpenter

In (8), the predicate is a common noun and MC has the optional morpheme *se* when the clause is in the present tense. The use of *se* in a tensed clause would be ungrammatical:

(10) *Pol   se   ti   mo   kamwad
     Paul   COP PST 1.SG.POSS   friend

2.1.2 Equative 'se'

The morphemes *li* and *se* are in complementary distribution. A significant difference between sentences with *li* and those with *se* is that in the case of the latter, predicate inversion is possible, but not so in the case of the former:

(11) a. MC. *Mo kamwad se Pol* / My friend is Paul /   Fr. Mon copain c'est Paul
     b. MC. **Enn mason li Serz* / *A bricklayer is Serge / Fr. *Maçon est Serge

Unlike *li* which functions like an auxiliary in English (which bears tense and agreement), *se* functions like a full verb; it takes a subject and a complement and assigns to each one a theta role. However, unlike other full verbs in MC, *se* is in complementary distribution with TMA markers (see example (10)).

---

[14] The TMA markers are:
  Tense: *ti* – Past, derived from Fr. *était* ('was') 3sg imperfect tense, and the past participle *été*: *était* / *été* → *té* → *ti*.
  Mood: *pu*- Irrealis, derived from Fr. *pour* (*Être pour* (et l'infinitif): *être sur le point de*.
    ava → *va* → *a* – Irrealis, derived from Fr. *va* ('will') 3sg present indicative of the verb *aller* 'to go'.
  Aspect: *ape* → *pe* – Progressive, derived from Fr. *après* (adv.): *en train de*.
    finn → *inn* → *'n*- Completive derived from Fr. *finir* (finish), 3sg perfect tense.

2.1.3 Presentational 'se'

Baker & Hookoomsing (1987) do not acknowledge the copulative use of *se*, but they do include an entry for this morpheme, which they define as: 'That's, it's (clause-initially)', derived from French *c'est*. There are a few occurrences of *c'est* in the concordance (12 to be precise). In all instances it only occurs sentence-initially, as shown:

(12) *C'est   moi tout s'el   qui   çéf   ici.*   (Chrestien 1822)
     be   1.SG all alone   COMP   chief   here
     It's me alone who's in charge here / C'et moi seul qui suis chef ici

(13) *c'est   quand   mo   jourée,* (Lambert 1828)
     be   when   1.SG   swear
     That's when I swear / C'est quand je jure

In the above examples, *c'est* is glossed simply as 'be', in spite of the fact that it translates as 'that's' or 'it's' respectively. The verbs 'to be' (*se*) and 'to have' (*ena*) do not take expletive subjects. Despite being relatively rare in early MC, the use of *se* sentence initially is common in modern MC texts, e.g.:[15]

(14) *se   laspe   semantik   ki   determinn   nu   konpreansyon* (Nadal 2002:108)
     be   aspect   semantic   COMP   determine   1.PLU.POSS understanding
     It's the semantic aspect which determines our understanding
     C'est l'aspect sémantique qui détermine notre compréhension

(15) *Se   parski   lekritir   enn zafer   nouvo   pou kreol* (Carpooran 2005: xv)
     That's because   writing   a thing   new   for creole
     That's because writing is a new thing for the creole
     C'est parceque l'écriture est quelque chose de nouveau pour le créole

2.1.4 Copula 'ete'

The present tense of the verb *être* does not survive in MC, but the past participle *été* assumes the role of marking past tense. It has the form *ti* in modern MC:

(16) *moy n'apa   été   batté   ça   Blanc   là*   **(1779)**
     1.SG NEG   PST   hit   DEM   white   DEM
     I did not hit this white man / Je n'ai pas frappé ce blanc
     Mo pas ti bat sa blan la   modern MC

(17) *Qui dou-monde   qui   té   pass' là!*   **(1818a)**
     what person   COMP   PST   pass here
     Who passed by here! / Qui est passé par là!
     Kisenla ki ti pas par la!   modern MC

In the 1880's, once the process of change from *té* → *ti* was well advanced, the form *été* was reintroduced in MC, but is used only sentence finally. Ete is defined as follows:

- Baker & Hookoomsing (1987): 'The copula corresponding to a form of 'be'. ('This occurs only sentence-finally and results from 'wh movement' e.g. *kot li ete?* 'where is he?' *ki li ete?* 'what is he?' etc.'
- Carpooran (2005): 'v. Mo ki servi pou etablir lien ki ena ant size enn fraz ek so bann konpleman dan enn kestion' Fr. être; ang. to be.'[16]
- Ledikasyon pu Travayer (2004): 'v. is, are, *ti ete* = was, were, *pu ete* = will be.'

---

[15] Albeit in a high register, by speakers who are also fluent in French. However, one of my informants, a fisherman from the north coast frequently uses *Se sa* (Fr. *C'est ça*, 'That's it') to confirm a statement.
[16] Word which is used to establish the link between the subject of a sentence and its complements in a question.'

Baker notes that 'The essential utility of the overt copula is to enable copulative sentences to participate in the same set of movement rules as sentences containing verbs' (1997: 103-04). Like other full verbs in MC, *ete* can combine with tense markers or modals:

(18) *Parfois   mo   maginer, Hier   ki   mo ti   ete,*
sometimes 1SG wonder yesterday what 1.SG PST be
Zordi ki mo ete, Demain ki mo pou ete (Anon. 2007)
today what 1.SG be, tomorrow what 1.SG MOD be
Sometimes I wonder, what I was yesterday, what I am today, what I will be tomorrow
Des fois j'imagine, ce que j'étais hier, ce que je suis aujourd'hui, ce que je serai demain

In the next section I briefly define what I understand by Predication.

3. Predication

"There could hardly be a relation more fundamental to grammar than predication. Indeed, it could be argued that predication is, in a certain sense, *the* most fundamental relation in both syntax and semantics" (Bowers 2003: 328, emphasis in original).

3.1 The syntax of predication

A requirement of Chomsky's Extended Projection Principle (1993) is that clauses must have a subject. This principle is defined by the phrase structure rule:

(19) S → NP INFL VP

A clause thus comprises minimally, a subject, an inflectional element, and a predicate. Predicates can be of the category A, N, P or V. Furthermore, predicates fall into two categories, those that describe enduring properties of an individual, e.g. 'Paul is tall' and those that describe temporary properties of individual, e.g. 'Paul is drunk'.[17]

Frege (1997) defines a predicate as a polyadic function which takes n arguments to form a sentential expression. A function in the Fregean sense is incomplete, or "unsaturated", and in order that it be closed, or "saturated", the empty place must be filled by an argument. In other words, predicates are one place functions, and the subject of a predicate is the argument which saturates that function. The act of predication consists of saturating or completing structures that are inherently unsaturated or incomplete

In a similar vein, Rothstein (1985) defines a predicate as "an open one-placed syntactic function requiring SATURATION, or closure by an argument" (1985:7, emphasis in original). She postulates the 'predicate linking rule', which states that every predicate must be closed by being linked to an appropriate syntactic argument to be called its formal subject' (1985: 3).

However, a restriction on this condition is that a predicate can be linked only to something which itself does not require linking i.e. to something which is internally closed, or quantified, such as a DP with a strong determiner.

3.1.1   Weak and strong determiners

Determiners fall into two categories, weak and strong (Milsark 1979; Barwise & Cooper 1981). Strong determiners are quantificational devices, analyzed as operators that want a

---

[17] Milsark uses the terms 'Property' and 'state' to differentiate between the permanent and temporary characteristics of individuals, respectively: 'Properties are those facts about entities which are assumed to be, even if they are not in fact, permanent, unalterable, and in some sense possessed by the entity, while states are conditions which are, at least in principle, transitory, not possessed by the entity of which they are predicated, and the removal of which cause no change in the essential qualities of the entity.' (1979: 212).

restriction, i.e. a predicate (Longobardi 1994, Stowell 1991). Thus, DPs with strong determiners are internally closed or quantified, and they can function as arguments of any predicate. Strong determiners in MC include the phonologically null definite determiner and the Specificity Marker *la*.

Nouns that are modified by weak determiners, such as the indefinite *enn* and the plural marker *bann* in MC, are cardinality predicates that are not internally closed, and in order to be licensed, they must be quantified by an external element. These external elements are sentential operators that typically include, amongst others, Tense, Modals, adverbs of quantification, propositional attitude verbs, and other quantificational NPs.

3.2 The semantics of Predication

Aristotle's definition of 'predicate' is a semantic one. In his *De Interpretatione* he defines a verb as 'a sign of something said of something else, i.e. of something either predicable of or present in some other thing' (Ch. 3). The 'thing' which it is said of or predicated of is the 'subject'. A subject and its predicate together form a 'proposition'.

Aristotle defines a proposition as a type of sentence that has a truth value – it is either true or false. However, a subject and a predicate are not sufficient to yield a proposition with a True or False value. 'A simple proposition is a statement, with meaning, as to the presence of something in a subject or its absence, in the present, past, or future, according to the divisions of time' (Ch 5). Thus, the semantic definition of a proposition complies with the syntactic definition expressed by the phrase structure rule: S → NP INFL VP.

INFL stands for any of the categories Tense, Mood or Aspect, which are morphologically realized in MC as separate functional heads that precede the verb. Besides marking 'divisions of time', these inflectional elements also function as operators, binding variables and assigning scope.

A formula with no free variable stands for a 'closed proposition', which is complete and has a Truth value. In Chomsky's terminology, a closed proposition is '*complete function complex*' which can stand alone as a complete 'thought' or 'information unit' (1986: 15). "In short, language does not permit free variables" (Chomsky 1995: 153).

Typically, variables that get introduced in a sentence are indefinite NPs that lack quantificational force, and the 'event' variable of activity sentences. Traditionally sentences have been divided into categories: <u>Activities</u> (which include 'events' and 'processes'), and <u>States</u>. Davidson (1997), Higginbotham (1985) and Parsons (1990) are of the view that the event variable is present in the argument structures of *all* predicates, whether verbal, adjectival or nominal, and irrespective of both the state versus event distinction of sentences. Others like Adger & Ramchand (2003) claim that the event variable is present only in activity sentences, not states.

4. *Li* and *la* in early MC

On the basis of the above definitions, one must assume the presence of INFL in all sentences. The occurrence of *li* in predicative constructions in early MC can be analyzed either as a resumptive pronoun in a Topic-Comment construction where the copula is phonologically null (represented as ∅), as in (20a), or as an inflectional element in a simpler copulative structure as in (20b). In a Topic-Comment structure, the Topic is left-dislocated, and binds a resumptive pronoun, which functions as the subject of the predicate:

(20) a. *maisMadagascar li ∅ là* (1749)
but Madagascar 3.SG COP there
But Madagascar it's (over) there / Mais Madagascar c'est là-(bas)
b. *maisMadagascar li là* (1749)
but Madagascar COP there
But Madagascar is (over) there /Mais Madagascar est là-(bas)

In early MC, *li* served to mark the subject as singular and referential, as in the following example, where *satte* has a discourse antecedent:

(21) Satte **li** alle dan son la-sambre pour **li** dourmi. (1850)
cat *li* go in 3.SG.POSS bedroom for 3.SG sleep
The cat went in its bedroom to sleep / Le chat alla dans sa chambre pour dormir

Li was in complementary distribution with the Specificity marker *la*, which also started marking anaphoric definiteness on singular NPs around 1820:

(22) Et torti **là** touzours marcé. (1818b)
and tortoise *la* still walk
And the tortoise was still walking / Et la tortue marchait toujours

Both morphemes served to disambiguate the interpretation of bare count nouns in subject position by forcing a singular, referential interpretation of the subject. If neither *li* nor *la* was used, the subject NPs in (21) and (22) would be ambiguous between a [–definite] plural or [+definite] singular interpretation, as shown:

(23) Satte alle dan son la-sambre pour li dourmi.[18]
Cat went in his/its room to sleep / Cats went into his bedroom to sleep
Chat alla dans sa chambre pour dormir / Des chats allèrent dans sa chambre pour dormir

(24) Et torti touzours marcé
And Tortoise was still walking / And tortoises were still walking
Et Tortue marchait toujours / Et des tortues marchaient toujours

In modern MC, a bare common count noun can only occur in subject position when it functions as a unique noun or a proper noun, e.g. as the name of the character in the story (except in generic sentences). Otherwise, it must be marked by *la* as in example (22).

4.1 Where *li* does not occur in early MC

The environment in which a morpheme occurs gives an insight into its function. Similarly, its non-occurrence in certain environments can shed light on its function. We have already seen that it is in complementary distribution with *la*. In the next section, I look at other predicative constructions without *li*.

4.1.1 No 'li' with pronominal subjects

When the subject is a personal pronoun, which is inherently referential, subject and predicate are string adjacent, as shown:

(25) Moi vieux, Monsieur, Moi malade, vendez moi. (1784)
1.SG old mister 1.SG sick sell 1.SG
I am old, Mister, I am sick, sell me / Je suis vieux, monsieur, je suis malade, vendez moi.

4.1.2 'Li' and TMA markers

In the concordance, there is one occurrence of *li* as a resumptive pronoun in a tensed clause:

(26) Qui Jésus-Christ **li** après faire apprésant la haut dans le Ciele? (Lambert 1828)
what Jesus Christ 3.SG ASP do now above in heaven
What is Jesus Christ doing now in heaven above?
Jésus-Christ que fait-Il à présent là haut dans le ciel?

---

[18] Despite the absence or pre-verbal markers, there is evidence that the sentence is in the past tense. See Stein, *this volume*.

The fact that the above example is a question may or may not be significant. Otherwise, *li* and TMA markers do not appear to co-occur. Examples follow :

(27) *votre   femme **fini**   mort*,   **(1784)**
     2.SG.F.POSS wife   ASP   dead
     your wife has died / Votre femme est morte

(28) *Quand mon   femm' **pour** fair' badinaze* (Chrestien [1822] 1831)
     when   1.SG.POSS wife   MOD   make   teasing
     When my wife will play up / Quand ma femme va faire des tours

(29) *Ein' torti avec lièvre **été** voulé parié* **(1818b)**
     a   tortoise with hare PST   want bet
     A tortoise wanted to bet with the hare / Une tortue voulait parier avec le lièvre

(30) *enne gran bande   **apré** casse   maille* **(1850)**
     a   big   group   ASP   thresh   corn
     A large group (of people who were) threshing corn
     Une grande quantité (de gens) qui battaient du maïs

The absence of *li* in tensed clauses suggests that this morpheme may have been functioning as a sentential operator, perhaps marking present tense. However, it must be pointed out that the use of TMA markers in early MC was by no means as frequent as it is today. Furthermore, the use of a resumptive pronoun with these markers is grammatical in modern MC.

5. *Li* in modern MC

5.1 Where '*li*' occurs in modern MC

In modern MC, *li* is frequently used between the subject and the predicate, when the latter is an AP, NP, PP or VP, as in the following examples:

(31) *formasion teorik   ek   pratik   li   indispansab* (Virahsawmy 2004)
     training theoretical and   practical   li   essential
     Theoretical and practical training is essential
     La formation en théorie et en pratique est indispensable

If *li* was left out of the above <u>written</u> example, *indispansab* could be taken as a modifier of the preceding NP *pratik*, yielding the interpretation *pratik indispansab* = 'essential practice'. I stress <u>written</u> because intonation and a pause between *pratik* and *indispansab* would dispel such ambiguity in spoken creole.

(32) *nu   lalinn, li   enn espes but   ros*   (Ah-Vee 2002b: 73)
     1.PLU.POSS   moon   li   a   type piece   rock
     Our moon is like a piece of rock / Notre lune est comme une espèce de rocher

(33) *Deziem laspe   li an rapor   avek   lang   la limem*   (Carpooran 2003: 13)
     second aspect   li in keeping with   language SP itself
     The second aspect is in keeping with the language itself
     Le deuxième aspect est en rapport avec la langue elle-même

Without *li*, the above word string would yield a noun phrase, where the predicate *an raport avek lang la limem* would be interpreted as a relative clause, modifying *Deziem laspe*, thus, the meaning would be: 'The second aspect that is in keeping with the language itself'.

(34) *form 'plin' enn verb li fonksionn   inpe kouman so   infinitif* (Carpooran 2005: xxiii)
     form full a   verb *li* function   a bit like   3.SG.POSS infinitive
     the 'full' form of a verb functions a bit like the infinitive
     la forme 'pleine' d'un verbe fonctionne un peu comme l'infinitif

If *li* was analyzed strictly as a resumptive pronoun in the above 4 sentences, one would need to translate them as Topic/Comment constructions, where the subject is left dislocated and *li* is subject of the predicate, with zero copula:

(35) a.　　Theoretical and practical training **it's** essential
　　 b.　　Our moon is like **it's** a piece of rock
　　 c.　　The second aspect **it's** in keeping with the language itself
　　 d.　　The 'full' form of a verb *it* functions a bit like the infinitive

5.2 Co-occurrence of '*li*' and TMA markers

In early MC, *li* appeared to be in complementary distribution with TMA markers. In modern MC, when they do co-occur, *li* can only be analyzed as a 3sg resumptive pronoun as in the following examples:

(36) a.　　*Mo　　frer　　ki　　travay　　'Air France'　li　　Moris　　zordi*
　　　　　1.SG.POSS brother COMP　work　　Air France　3.SG　Mauritius　today
　　　　　My brother who works for 'Air France' he's in Mauritius today
　　　　　Mon frère qui travaille pour 'Air France' il est à Maurice aujourd'hui

　　 b.　　*Mo　　frer . li　　ti　　Moris　　yer/　　li　　pu　　Moris　　demen*
　　　　　1.SG.POSS frer ...3.SG PST Mauritius yesterday /3.SG MOD Mauritius tomorrow
　　　　　My brother ...he was in Mauritius yesterday, he will be in Mauritius tomorrow
　　　　　Mon frère ... il était à Maurice hier, il sera à Maurice demain

These are clearly marked Topic/Comment constructions, where contrastive focus is implied, as in: *Mo frer .. li pu Moris demen, pa Langleter* ('My brother ... he will be in Mauritius tomorrow, not England').

In the following example, the use of a comma clearly marks the Topic as left dislocated; the resumptive pronoun *li* is the subject of the Comment, and *enn kreol* is the predicate:

(37) *li　ousi, li　ti　enn kreol*　　(Cheung 2002 : 21)
　　 3.SG too 3.SG PST a　creole
　　 He too, he was a Creole / Lui aussi, il était un créole

When there are two occurrences of *li*, one may assume that the first is a resumptive pronoun and the second serves to link the subject and the predicate, giving support to the claim that *li* may be undergoing reanalysis:

(38) *Kolo li　　li　dir　so　　bisiklett　ki　　admirab* (Maingard 2002: 101)
　　 Kolo 3.SG　li　say 3.SG.POSS bicycle COMP fantastic
　　 As for Kolo, he says it's his bicycle which is fantastic
　　 Kolo il dit que c'est son vélo qui est admirable

The occurrence of a resumptive pronoun with TMA markers clearly grammatical, but it by no means essential, as shown in (39) to (41):

(39) *Premye　gran Reform　Konstitisyonel　dan　　Moris, ...*
　　 first　　big reform　constitutional　in　　Mauritius
　　 ti　　fer　　an　　1947　　(Hookoomsing 2002 :26)
　　 PST　make　in　　1947
　　 The first important constitutional reform in Mauritius, ... was made in 1947
　　 La première grande réforme consitutionelle à Maurice ... eut lieu en 1947

(40) *Sa　　mazorite-　la　　pe　　grandi　sak　　lane* (Ah-Vee 2002a: 39)
　　 DEM　majorite　SP　　ASP　grow　　each　year
　　 This majority is increasing each year
　　 Cette majorité augmente chaque année

(41) *Tel langaz finn fer pu servi dan lasyans ek teknolozi* (Hookoomsing 2002: 29)
such language ASP make for use in science and technology
Such a language was designed for use in science and technology
Telle langue a été conçue pour être utilisée dans les domaines de la science et de la technologie

5.2.1 No' li' with plural subjects

A strong argument against the analysis of *li* as a copula is the fact that it does not occur with plural subjects. The use of a resumptive pronoun is a discourse strategy in MC, just as in English and French, where the pronoun agrees in Number with the subject, as in:

(42) *bann langaz Kreol zot sirtu bann nuvo langaz ki* ... (Ah-Vee 2002a: 37)
PLU language creole 3.PLU mostly PLU new language COMP ...
Creole languages they are mostly new languages that ...
Les langues créoles ce sont de nouvelles langues qui ...

(43) *Sa bann desandan esklav la zot bann dimoun ki* ... (Virahsawmy 2005)
DEM PLU descendant slave SP 3.PLU PLU person COMP ....
Those/these descendants of the slaves they are people who ...
Ces descendants des esclaves ce sont des gens qui ...

5.2.2 'Li' and se and Negation

Another argument against the analysis of *li* as an element of the verbal inflectional system relates to its position within the clause. If *li* was an operator marking present tense, one would expect it to occupy the same position in the clause as the TMA markers, but while the latter follow Negation, *li* precedes Negation, as shown:

(44) *Me personn pa ti koir li* (Virahsawmy, 2005)
but no.one NEG PST believe 3.SG
But no one believed him
Mais personne ne le croyait

(45) *Me literesi li pa zis difisil pou aprann* (Virahsawmy, 2005)
but literacy COP NEG just difficult to learn
But literacy is not just difficult to learn
Mais l'alphabétisation n'est pas seulement difficile à apprendre

One explanation for the position of *li* above Negation could be accounted for in terms of feature strength. If *li* is functioning as an auxiliary, it may be that it patterns like English auxiliaries 'be' and 'have' which precede Negation, while full verbs follow Negation. In French, all verbs can raise above Negation, not just auxiliaries (Pollock 1989):

(46) Paul fume pas
Paul doesn't smoke / *Paul smokes not
Pol pa fime / *Pol fime pa* MC

Chomsky attributes this differential behaviour of French and English verbs to the strength of the Agreement feature in these languages. Agreement is strong in French and weak in English; 'weak Agr is unable to 'attract' true verbs such as *kiss* or *lose*, though it can attract auxiliaries, whereas strong Agr attracts all verbs' (Chomsky 1995: 136-37).

The fact that a resumptive pronoun and a copula appear to occupy a similar position in the clause, and the fact that they are homophonous, makes it difficult to thresh out their precise function, but a strong argument in support of the claim that *li* is being reanalyzed is the fact that it is in complementary distribution with the new copula *se*.

6. The new copula 'se'

In the last 30 years or so, we find the increasing use of *se* occurring between the subject and the predicate in identity statements, or 'equative be' type constructions. Some speakers suggest that *se* is a more elegant alternative to *li*, possibly because of the fact that it is homophonous with the French *c'est* ('it is'), but there is evidence that these two morphemes have clearly distinct functions.

While *li* functions like auxiliary 'be', *se* functions like 'equative be'. It is a full verb that takes two arguments, assigning each of them a theta role, and identifying them as having the same reference. The predicate is either a noun phrase or an infinitival VP, as shown:

(47) *Enn adverb se enn mo   ki   modifie enn fraz* (Virahsawmy 2004)
     an adverb COP a word   COMP modifies a   clause
     An adverb is a word that modifies a clause
     Un adverbe c'est un mot qui modifie une phrase

(48) *Deziem tes se konpar sintax   Morisien ek   Franse* (Virahsawmy 2004)
     second test COP compare syntax   Mauritian and French
     The second test is to compare the syntax of Mauritian and French
     Le deuxième test c'est de comparer la syntaxe du mauricien et du français

Predicate inversion is possible with the above sentences:

(49) *enn mo ki modifie enn   fraz se enn   adverb*
     A word that modifies a clause is an adverb

(50) *Konpar sintax Morisien ek Franse se deziem tes*
     To compare the syntax of Mauritian and French is (that's) the second test

In the following example, we have a plural subject with *se*; as with other full verbs in MC, there is no Number agreement between subject and *se*:

(51) *Angola ek Benin, ... se de pei   Afriken kot ...* (Carpooran 2002: 68)
     Angola and Benin ... se two country African where ...
     Angola and Benin ... are two African countries where ...
     L'Angola et le Bénin ... sont deux pays africains où ...

However, unlike full verbs, *se* is in complementary distribution with TMA markers. Its complement can be an NP or an infinitival VP, but never a tensed VP.

The copulative use of *se* (as opposed to 'presentational *se* which occurs only sentence initially) is a recent development in MC. In 19th century MC, *li* was used with all types of predicates, including identity predicates, but such use in modern MC is ungrammatical, as shown:

(52) *Son   nom   li Emanuel* (Lambert, 1828)
     3.SG.POSS name   li Emanuel
     His name is Emanuel
     Son nom c'est Emmanuel
     *So nom se Emanuel   / *So nom li Emanuel*   modern MC

While the reanalysis of *li* is a relatively slow process of the grammaticalization of a lexical item into a functional item, the emergence of *se* is a case of lexical borrowing and subsequent relabelling, a process defined by Langacker as 'a change in the structure of an expression or class of expressions that does not involve any immediate or intrinsic modification of its surface manifestation (1977:59).

The use of *se* is viewed by some as a 'stylistic gimmick', an endeavour to sound more learned. Baker (p c) attributes the copulative use of *se* directly to French *c'est* translated as *se* instead of zero copula. The corpus from which most of the above examples of *se* derive comprises articles and conference papers written and delivered in MC by native speakers who would most likely also be fluent in French. The formal framework of a conference, aimed at an educated target audience, would no doubt have been motivation (albeit subconscious) for adopting a more 'elegant' style, copied on French constructions. The point must also be made that these documents were prepared for publication; they are not transcripts of spontaneous speech. As pointed out in Section 5.1, constructions with a complex predicate and zero copula may give rise to ambiguous interpretations in the written creole, as there is no clear demarcation between the subject and the predicate. Such ambiguities are dispelled by intonation in the spoken language. The use of *se* where zero copula would have been equally grammatical may be a consequence of the fact that MC had transcended its primarily oral tradition.

7. The analysis

7.1 Why new copulas ?

Given that zero copula is grammatical in modern MC, what nuances of meanings do *li* and *se* introduce in predicative constructions? In the following examples with nominal, adjectival, and prepositional predicates, subject and predicate are string adjacent:

(53) Pol   solda   /   malad   /   deor
     Paul   soldier /   sick   /   outside
     Paul is a soldier/ is sick/ is outside
     Paul est soldat/est malade/est dehors

However, bare NP predicates are barred in MC, except for the categories of nouns that designate roles or professions, irrespective of whether *li* is present or not[19]:

(54) a.   *Pol zanfan   b.   *Pol   li   zanfan
         Paul child/ ≠Paul is a child   Paul   li   child / ≠ Paul is a child

When the predicate is a bare NP, or an indefinite NP denoting a role or profession, the occurrence of *li* is optional:

(55) a.   Pol (li) solda   b.   Pol (li)   enn solda
         Paul li   soldier   Paul li   a   soldier
         Paul is a soldier/Paul est soldat   Paul is a soldier/Paul est un soldat

If *li* is interpreted as a resumptive pronoun, contrastive focus is implied, as in the following sentence, where the copula is represented as a null element (Ø):

(56) Pol,   li   Ø   (enn)   solda,   li   pa   (enn)   maren
     Paul   3.SG   COP   a   soldier   3.SG   NEG   a   sailor
     Paul, he's a soldier, he's not a sailor / Paul, il est soldat, il n'est pas marin

If *li* is interpreted as a copula, there is a slight difference in meaning between *Pol enn solda* and *Pol li enn solda*. The former means that 'Paul has the property of being a soldier', it is an enduring characteristic of Paul. When *li* is present, there is the implication that the predicate is a temporary predicate; it yields an 'activity sentence, with the meaning 'Paul works as a soldier'. The presence of *li* can justified if it is analyzed as an operator which surfaces to bind the event variable of the activity sentence.

Copula *se* can be used with DP or infinitival VP predicates, never with adjectival or prepositional predicates, or tensed VPs. When the predicate is a noun phrase, it must be

---

[19] Interestingly, names of professions are the only nouns that can occur without a determiner in predicative constructions in French.

referential, as in the following examples, where the indefinite NP is modified by a relative clause:

(57) Enn Leta ki   pa pran tou dispozisyon pou ki .... se-t-enn Leta ki   pe kondann...[20]
(Carpooran 2002: 70)
a   state COMP NEG take all disposition for COMP... COP a state COMP ASP condemn ..
A State which does not take all the necessary steps to ... is a State which is condemning ...
Un Etat qui ne prend pas toutes les dispositions pour ... c'est un état qui est en train de condamner ...

If *se* was not used, in modern MC, the demonstrative *sa* would be used, as in: *Enn Leta ki pa pran tou dispozisyon pou ki ...., **sa**, enn Leta ki pe kondann ..*, literally 'A State which does not take all the necessary steps to ... **that's** a State which is condemning ...'

In sum, copula *se* functions more like a lexical verb, expressing identity between the subject and the predicate, while *li* functions more like an operator, or an auxiliary, bearing a present tense feature. Interestingly, the use of the morpheme *se* in copulative constructions in Haitian Creole (HC) presents an interesting comparison. Its precise function is still subject of debate.

7.2 *Se* in Haitian Creole

To quote DeGraff: 'At first glance, the pattern of Haitian predicative constructions is puzzling. The puzzle manifests itself most clearly in simple affirmative sentences that are unmarked for tense' (1992: 103). With an AdjP, NP or PP predicate, the subject is adjacent to the predicate:

(58) Bouki   malad   /   dokter   /   anba tab la
     Bouki   is sick /   is a doctor /   is under the table

When the predicate is a DP (as opposed to a bare noun), the morpheme *se* must surface between the subject and the predicate:

(59) Bouki *se* enn malad

DeGraff claims that '*se* is a resumptive nominal element which functions as a 'last resort' to circumvent ECP violation.[21] The potentially-offending trace occupies the base-subject position inside a Small Clause and results from movement of the subject to Spec(IP)' (1992: 105).

Déprez & Vinet analyze *se* in Haitian Creole as a 'predicate forming aspectual head' (1997: 203) which always occurs with DP predicates, not with any other type of predicate. It is obligatory in present affirmative constructions, as shown:

(60) Jan/   li   *(se)   yon dokte/ pwesidan   an /   fre   m.
     John /   3ps   SE   a   doctor/ president the / brother   Poss
     John he is a doctor/ the president/my brother   (Déprez & Vinet 2003: 204)

But *se* need not be realized if a tense marker like *te* or a negation is present:

(61) a.   Jan   te   yon dokte/ pwesidan   an /   fre   m.
          John   Past   a   doctor/ president the / brother   Poss
          John was a doctor/ the president/my brother

     b.   Jan   pa   yon dokte/ pwesidan   an /   fre   m.
          John   Neg   a   doctor/ president the / brother   Poss
          John is not a doctor/ the president/my brother (Déprez & Vinet 2003: 205)

---

[20] The *t* in *se-t-enn* is an epenthetic consonant.
[21] ECP stands for the 'Empty Category Principle' which stipulates that all empty categories, which include traces, must be governed.

The morpheme *se* can co-occur with tense markers or negation 'only if the subject is an NP or an emphatic third person pronoun. In this respect HC *se* seems to pattern like the resumptive pronoun *li* in MC:

(62) *Pye/   li-mem   se   te   fre   m*
     Peter / him   SE   Past   brother   Poss
     Peter/ him, he was my brother   (Déprez & Vinet 2003:206)
     Pyer / li, li ti mo frer   (modern MC)

While recognizing the pronominal function of *se* in HC, Déprez & Vinet also analyze this morpheme as an aspectual head which surfaces when the movement of a lexical predicate to the functional projection Pred° is blocked by the presence of any intervening (functional) head (cf the Head Movement Constraint).[22] In example (60), the heads that block movement are the determiners *yon* and *an*, and the possessive *m*. These determiners are not present in DeGraff's example (58) and there is no requirement for *se* to surface.

7.3 Why two different morphemes?

Assuming that *li* was functioning as an auxiliary, why would a distinct morpheme *se* be required for equative 'be' constructions? English has the verb 'to be' functioning both as an auxiliary and as a full verb ('be of identity').

The processes involves in the reanalysis of *li* are quite different from those that brought about the use of *se* in modern MC. The process of grammaticalization, as documented by Haspelmath (1999), Hopper & Traugott (2003), Heine et al. (1991) and van Gelderen (2004) amongst others, is a 'unidirectional' process, whereby contentful morphemes become gradually bleached of their original meaning. The change from functional element back to lexical item is not attested. To quote Haspelmath: "Grammaticalization, the change by which lexical categories become functional categories, is overwhelmingly irreversible. Prototypical functional categories never become prototypical lexical categories and less radical changes against the general directionality of grammaticalization are extremely rare' (1999:1043).

The introduction of se as a copula in modern MC is a case of direct borrowing from French, followed by relabelling of an already existing morpheme in MC. Its use as a copula would involve broadening of its semantics and argument structure, for while presentational *se* does not take a subject, copula *se* has a subject and a complement, and assigns a theta role to each one.

Furthermore, the occurrence of two distinct copulas in a language, one marking 'identity' and the other marking 'predication' is not an isolated phenomenon. Ewe makes such a distinction, for example between the equative and the locative: *É-nye fia* 'I am the chief', and *Me-lè xo me* 'I am in the house (McWhorter 1994:57). Swahili uses *ni* for the equative, and zero copula for the locative:

(63) a. *Hamissi ni mpishi*   b. *Hamisi yu -ko   nyumba-ni*
         Hamisi COP cook   Hamisi AGR-LOC house-LOC
         Hamishi is a cook   *Hamisi is in the house* (McWhorter 1994:57)

---

[22] The 'Head Movement Constraint' (HMC) was proposed by Lisa Travis in 1984. It is a strict condition that applies to head movement and stipulates that a moved head can only move into the lexical head position in the next highest phrase immediately containing it, and cannot cross over another lexical head.

7.4 The rise of INFL

7.4.1 *From pronoun to Agreement marker*

Both syntactic and semantic definitions of predication comply with the phrase structure rule S → NP INFL VP. INFL can encompass either Tense, or Agreement (Agr), or both. These features have been shown by Pollock (1989) to be separate syntactic entities, though they can be conflated in the auxiliary, as in English and French. However, there is morphological evidence that, in a number of languages, 'the agreement element is "outside" the tensed element in the verbal morphology' (Chomsky 1995: 146). As a resumptive pronoun, *li* already encodes the Number feature of the subject. Its position "outside" the verbal morphology, above Negation and TMA markers would be justified if it was analyzed as an agreement marker.

Givon proposes that the process by which subject agreement arises may be called 'de-marking', and occurs when a marked construction is over-used in a weaker context. 'Speakers eventually recognize the context as being much too weak to justify a marked status for the TS (Topic Shift) construction. Thus they re-analyze it as the neutral syntax. The erstwhile topic-subject gets re-analyzed as "mere" subject, while the topic-agreement anaphoric pronoun gets re-analyzed as subject-agreement':

(64) TS ("MARKED")   NEUTRAL (RE-ANALYZED)
     The man,   he came   ⇒   The man   he-came
     TOP   PRO   SUBJ   AGR   (Givon 1975: 154-55)

Givon claims that 'The morphological binding of the pronoun to the verb is an inevitable natural phenomenon, cliticization, having to do with the unstressed status of pronouns, their decreased information load and the subsequent loss of resistance to phonological attrition' (1975: 155). If MC *li* were to be overused in a unmarked context, this resumptive pronoun would be an obvious candidate for reanalysis as an agreement marker.

7.4.2 *From pronoun to copula*

The topicalization mechanism as a source for copula constructions is justified for Mandarin by Li & Thompson (1977), who claim that copula *shi* is derived from a demonstrative in archaic Chinese (11th – 3rd century BC). This language did not originally have a copula in equational sentences:

(65) Wáng-Tái   wù   zhě   yě
     Wang-Tai   outsantding person   declarative particle
     Wang-Tai is an outstanding person.
     (Zhuáng-z   4th century BC)   (Li & Thompson 1977: 421)

But in modern Mandarin, the copula, *shì*, occurs regularly in equational sentences:

(66) nèi -   ge   rén   shì   xuésheng
     that   classifier   man   be   student
     That man is a student   (Li & Thompson 1977: 422)

The copula *shi* was a demonstrative in archaic Chinese, as shown in the following example, where the topic is clause initial and the comment is the clause consisting of the demonstrative pronoun subject *shi* and the predicate NP:

(67) jì   yù   qí   shēng   yòu yù   qí   sǐ,   **shi** huò   ye
     already   wish   him   live   also wish   him die,   **this** indecision   decl. particle
     Wishing him to live while wishing him to die, that is indecision.
     (Analect 5th c. B.C.) (Li & Thompson 1977: 424)

Li & Thompson (1977) describe similar processes in other languages, as evidence that the reanalysis of a subject resumptive pronoun as a copula is a well attested phenomenon in other languages of the world.[23]

7.4.3 A simpler structure

An attractive argument in favour of the reanalysis of resumptive pronoun into an agreement marker or a copula as proposed by Givon (1975) and Li & Thompson (1977) respectively is that the end result is a simpler structure. Example (20) is repeated here, with two interpretations, the first a Topic-Comment construction with a resumptive pronoun in (68a), and a simplified copulative structure in (68b):

(68) a. [$_{TopP}$ Madagascar   [$_{IP}$ li   [$_{I'}$ ∅   [$_{PP}$ là]]]]
        TOPIC   SUBJECT   COP   PREDICATE

     b. [$_{IP}$ Madagascar   [$_{I'}$ li   [$_{PP}$ là]]]
        SUBJECT   COP   PREDICATE

This process of simplification would comply with Chomsky's Minimalist claim that language is a perfect system that strives for economy of derivation and representation, with no superfluous steps in derivation (1995). The very principle of economy, which is a basic assumption in this analysis, is compelling motivation to assign a grammatical function to every morpheme, though the precise function of many may defy categorization. Such is the case of *i* in Seychellois Creole (SC), which is derived from MC.

In the section that follows, I summarize the debate on SC *i*, a cognate of MC *li*, where my aim is to shed light on the function of *li* in MC.

8. The mysterious '*i*' in Seychellois Creole[24]

8.1 SC *i* and MC *la*

"There is in SC an element *i* which has been at the centre of an on-going debate ... It has so far resisted all attempts at an adequate explanation, although there is little doubt about the facts of its occurrence." (Corne 1974: 68). The use of *i* between the subject and the predicate in all affirmative, present tense clauses, and the lack of the Specificity Marker *la* in SC represent the most significant differences between the two Creoles.

In Section 4 I argued that *li* and *la* were performing a similar function in early MC, namely that of marking a count noun in subject position as singular and referential. Such use of *li* subsided following the grammaticalization of *la*. Could the paths to the grammaticalization of these morphemes be linked?

8.1.1 Socio-historical factors

On the basis of the sociohistorical factors that prevailed in the second half of the 19th century, it would be reasonable to assume that substrate influence played a more significant role in the development of SC than in that of MC. Baker (p c) attributes the use of *i* in SC directly to substrate influence. All count nouns in Bantu languages belong to two noun classes, one singular and one plural, which, identified by different prefixes which must be attached to the nouns. A requirement of the Bantu 'concordial' agreement system is that the same prefix which identifies class membership of the noun must also

---

[23] These languages include Hebrew, Palestinian Arabic, Wappo (a Californian Indian language) and Zway (an Ethopian language).
[24] Subtitle borrowed from Corne (1974).

occur on the first element of the predicate. In the following examples from Swahili, the word for 'cup' takes the prefix and concord marker *ki* for singular and *vi* for plural:[25]

(69) a. *Kikombe ki- moja   ki- li- anguka*
        7-cup   7SM-one   7SM-PST- fall
        One cup fell
    b. *Vikombe   vi- tatu   vi- li- anguka*
        8-cups   8SM-three   8SM-PST- fall
        Three cups fell   (Adapted from Mchombo 1993:10)

The Bantu concordial system would have favoured the use of a morpheme between the subject and predicate in SC. The situation would have been different in Mauritius, where the greater presence of French would have promoted the use of the demonstrative particle *là*, and the homophonous locative adverb, which eventually grammaticalized into a Specificity marker.

8.2 Analysis of SC *i*

8.2.1 Subject clitic – The '*i*' insertion rule

In his description of SC, Papen notes that 'the status of this element (*i*) is somewhat controversial among those scholars who have attempted a description of Seychellois Creole'(1975: 27). He defines *i* as a 'subject clitic' which must be inserted whenever the subject is <u>nominal</u> (common noun or proper noun) and the verb is in the present tense:

(70) *Torti   i   kom ros*   (Papen 1975: 27) SC
     tortoise *i*   like rock
     Tortoises are like rocks
     Torti kuma ros   modern MC
(71) *Ler   dimun   seselua   i bat   triang,   zot   dāse* (Corne, 1974: 68) SC
     when   people   Seychellois *i* beat   triangle 3.PLU   dance
     When Seychellois people play the triangle, they dance
     Kan dimun Sesel bat triang, zot danse   modern MC
(72) *ki   en   zanfan i bezwen   avan   e   apre son   nesans* (Anon 1989) SC
     COMP   a   child *i* need   before   and   after 3.SG.POSS birth
     that a child needs before and after his/her birth
     ki enn zanfan bizin avan e apre so nesans   modern MC
(73) *Sa prefas   i   osi reaffirm sa   bezwen   legal ...* (Anon 1989)   SC
     DEF preface *i*   also reaffirm DEF need   legal...
     This preface also reaffirms the legal requirement ...
     Sa prefas la (li) osi reafirm bezwen legal ...   modern MC

The above SC examples suggest that, unlike with *li* in MC, the occurrence of *i* in SC does not depend on the interpretation of the subject NP with regard to the features [±definite] and [±plural]. The subject is:

- [+definite] in (70). It is a generic sentence, where MC uses bare nouns.
- [+definite] plural in (71), where *dimun seselua* is co-referential with the plural pronoun *zot* in the subordinate clause.
- [–definite] singular in (72)
- [+definite] singular in (73)

Papen notes that this '*i* insertion rule' holds even when there is no lexical verb, as in (74):

---

[25] In somewhat oversimplified terms, it is as if every verb requires a preceding pronoun regardless of whether there is a preceding NP or not. But because of the noun class systems of Bantu languages, there are as many '3rd person pronouns' as noun classes (usually between 12 and 20) (Baker, p c).

(74) *Sa   i   bon*   (Papen 1975: 27) SC
    that i   good
    That's what's really good!
    Sa ki bon sa![26]   modern MC

Corne suggests that this subject clitic 'has no extra-linguistic reference and its function is deictic, simply marking what follows as the predicate' (1977: 66).

8.2.2   Resumptive pronoun

Bollée (1977), on the other hand, identifies *i* as a resumptive pronoun, claiming that "l'emploi du pronom personnel de la troisième personne, *i*, est obligatoire au présent" (the use of the 3rd pronoun *i* is mandatory in the present tense), as shown :

(75) *ler   sō   ban servant i al sers delo* (Bollée 1977:62) SC
    when   3.SG.POSS PLU servant *i* go fetch water
    when his servants go fetch water
    ler so bann servant al rod dilo   modern MC

I refute Bollée's analysis on the grounds that if *i* was a resumptive pronoun, it would agree in number with the subject, and the well established form *zot* would be used with plural subjects, as in the next example:

(76) *nenen   ek   msje   zot al dā lakaz Sūgula   e   Zako* (Bollée 1977: 62) SC
    maid   and master 3.PLU go in house Soungoula and Monkey
    the maid and the master they go into the house of Soungoula and Monkey
    nenenn ek missye zot al dan lakaz Sangula et Zako   modern MC

However, Bollée argues that '*i* est nettement préféré à *zot*; quelques locuteurs semblent éviter *zot* complètement' (*i* is much preferred to *zot*; some speakers avoid the latter completely). She quotes one of her informants: 'I prefer *i*, it makes the sentence flow more easily' (1977: 62). Corne also notes that when a plural resumptive pronoun is used 'there is either a pause of an intonational equivalent thereof, and ... such sentences should be written "NP, *zot* ..."' (1974: 89 n.31).

The predicative use of *i/li* may be blurred by the fact that these morphemes are homophonous with the 3sg pronoun, and also by the fact that the use of resumptive pronouns is a common discourse strategy in both creoles, as in English and French.

8.2.3   Non-future tense marker

The fact that in SC *i* is in complementary distribution with past tense markers has also prompted Papen (1975) to analyze this morpheme as a 'non-future tense' marker. Interestingly, MC when *li* is analyzed as an inflectional element (as opposed to a resumptive pronoun) it is in complementary distribution with **all** TMA markers, not just tense markers. In the SC sentences below, *i* is used with an Aspect marker in (77) and with a modal in (78):

(77) *tu   dimun   i ape dāse*   (Corne 1974 : 69) SC
    all person *i* ASP dance
    everyone is dancing
    tu dimun ape danse   modern MC

(78) *i   pa   i   pu   maze   tato?* (Corne 1974: 59) SC
    3.SG NEG *i* MOD eat   afternoon
    he will not eat this afternoon?
    Li pa pu manze tanto?   modern MC

---

[26] 'Sa ki bon sa!' Direct quote from an advertisement for 'Chantecler' chicken, dated 2004..

In their analysis of SC *i*, both Corne and Papen clump this morpheme with TMA markers, suggesting that it is part of the verbal inflectional system, perhaps a present Tense marker. This analysis comes closest to what I propose for MC *li*, which, in its copulative function, is in complementary distribution with TMA markers.

9. Conclusion

Li & Thompson (1977) noted that some languages 'seem to "go out of their way" to develop a copula. That is, given that it seems to be so easy to get rid of or do without a copula, at least in the present tense, what motivates some languages to redevelop one?' (1977: 437). Thirty years after the publication of their article, this question is still very relevant.

Haspelmath suggests that 'Grammaticalization is a side effect of the maxim of extravagance, that is, speakers' use of unusually explicit formulations in order to attract attention. As these are adopted more widely in the speech community, they become more frequent and are reduced phonologically' (1999: 1043). This view is in agreement with Givon's (1975) claim that when marked constructions are overused, they become reanalyzed as 'neutral' syntax, with simpler structures.

In the case of Mandarin Chinese, the change from pronoun to copula is complete and documentation of this change is possible because of several thousand years of written literature. It is not possible in the case of such new languages as Creoles to make invincible claims about the function of morphemes which may be at very early stages of reanalysis. The problem is further compounded by the fact that there is an overlap of function and phonological form between the new functional item and its lexical source, and also because they occupy the same surface structure.

Despite such a claim, Givon maintains that the status both the subject and object agreement still retain their original <u>anaphoric-pronoun</u> functions in Bantu (1975: 168, emphasis in original). Mchombo, on the other hand, claims that the subject argument of the verb is 'functionally ambiguous as a pronominal or an agreement marker' (1993: 185).

With regard to *se*, a direct borrowing from French *c'est*, it too may be a 'maxim of extravagance', used initially by francophones, either as a consequence of 'lazy translation' or in an endeavour to sound 'more elegant', but such use may gradually percolate through the broader speech community, and become an alternative to the zero copula in equative sentences. The emergence of *se* is a relatively fast process, and quite different from that of *li* which involves the grammaticalization of a lexical item into a functional item.

This analysis of the morphemes *li* and *se* in MC has probably raised more questions than what it has answered, but may hopefully point to future research on the precise function of these morphemes in MC.

References

Adger, David & Ramchand, Gillian 2003 Predication and equation. *Linguistic Inquiry* 34: 325-59.

Ah-Vee, Alain 2002a Evolisyon dinamik lortograf kreol morisyen. Ledikasyon pu Travayer (eds), 37-41.

—— 2002b Lartik dan 'Kwin syantifik' ki finn paret dan Lagazet Lalit de Klas. Ledikasyon pu Travayer (eds), 72-73.

Anon. 1989 Konvansyon lo drwa zanfan. Adopte par Lasanble Zeneral Nasyon Ini le 20 novanm 1989. Retrieved on May 5 2006 from: http://www.seychelles.net/ncc/crc-cre.htm.

Anon. 2007 Parfois mo maginer. Retrieved on October 7 2007 from: http://pages.intnet.mu/yoga/parfois_mo_maginer.htm

Baissac, Charles   1880   *Étude sur le patois créole mauricien*. Nancy: Imprimerie Berger Levrault.
—— 1888 *Le folk-lore de l'Ile Maurice*. Paris: G P Maisonneuve & Larose.
Baker, Philip   1984   Agglutinated French articles in Creole French: their evolutionary significance. *Te Reo* 27: 89-129.
—— 1997 Directionality in pidginization and creolization. Spears, Arthur K & Winford, Donald (eds) *The structure and status of pidgins and creoles*. Amsterdam: Benjamins, 91-109.
Baker, Philip & Corne, Chris   1982   *Isle de France Creole: affinities and origins*. Ann Arbor: Karoma.
Baker, Philip & Hookoomsing, Vinesh Y   1987   *Diksyoner Kreol Morisyen; Dictionary of Mauritian Creole; Dictionnaire du créole mauricien*. Paris: L'Harmattan.
Baltin, Mark & Collins, Chris (eds)   2003   *The handbook of contemporary syntactic theory*. Oxford: Blackwell.
Barwise, Jon & Cooper, Robin   1981   Generalized quantifiers and natural language. *Linguistics and Philosophy* 4: 159-219.
Bollée, Annegret   1977   *Le créole français des Seychelles : esquisse d'une grammaire - textes – vocabulaire*. Tubingen: Niemeyer.
Bowers, John   2003   *The syntax of predication*. Baltin & Collins (eds), 299-333.
Carpooran, Arnaud   2002   Konsep drwa langaz ek drwa lingwistik: propozisyon pou enn aplikasyon dan Moris. Ledikasyon pu Travayer (eds), 66-71.
—— 2003 Lang kreol ant oralit ek lekritir. *Revi Kiltir Kreol* 3:13-24.
—— 2005 *Diksioner Morisien: version prototip Let A ziska E*. Quatre Bornes: Bartholdi.
Chaudenson, Robert   1981   *Textes créoles anciens: La Réunion et Ile Maurice. Comparaison et essai d'analyse*. Hamburg: Buske.
Cheung, Georges   2002   *Fos temoin letan margoz: Novela otobio-gra-fiktif*. Port Louis: Mauritius.
Chierchia, Gennaro   1998   Reference to kinds across languages. *Natural Language Semantics* 6: 339-405.
Chomsky, Noam   1986   *Barriers*. Cambridge, Mass.: MIT Press.
—— 1993 *Lectures on government and binding*. New York: Mouton de Gruyter.
—— 1995 *The Minimalist Program*. Cambridge, Mass.: MIT Press.
Corne, Chris   1974   Tense, Aspect and the Mysterious *i* in Seychelles and Réunion Creole. *Te Reo* 17: 53-93.
Davidson, Donald   1997   The logical form of action sentences. Ludlow, Peter (ed.) *Readings in the philosophy of language*, Cambridge, Mass., MIT Press, 217-32.
DeGraff, Michel   1992   The syntax of predication in Haitian. *NELS 22, Proceedings of the 22nd Meeting of the North-Eastern Linguistics Society* 22: 103-117.
Déprez, Viviane & Vinet, Marie-Thérèse   1997   Predicative constructions and functional categories in Haitian Creole. *Journal of Pidgin and Creole Languages* 12: 203-35.
Fon Sing, Guillaume & Véronique, Georges Daniel   2007   'Ena' et 'gagne': à propos de la genèse de l'expression de l'existence et de la possession / propriété en créole mauricien. *This volume*.
Frege, Gottlob   1997   Function and concept (translated by Peter Greach). Beaney, Michael (ed.) *The Frege reader*, Oxford: Blackwell, 130-48.
Givon, Talmy   1975   Topic, pronoun and grammatical agreement. Li, Charles N. (ed.) *Subject and topic*. New York: Academic Press, 149-88.
Grant, Anthony P   1995   Article agglutination in Creole French: a wider perspective. Baker, Philip (ed.) *From contact to creole and beyond*, London: University of Westminster Press, 149-76.
Guillemin, Diana   2007   Definiteness and Specificity in Mauritian Creole: a syntax semantics mapping. *This volume*.
—— [*in preparation*] Noun interpretation and function of determiners in Mauritian Creole.

Haspelmath, Martin 1999 Why is grammaticalization irreversible? *Linguistics* 37: 1043-68.
Heine, Bernd, Claudi, Ulrike & Hünnemeyer, Friederike 1991 *Grammaticalization : a conceptual framework*. Chicago: University of Chicago Press.
Higginbotham, J 1985 On semantics. *Linguistic Inquiry* 16: 547-93.

Hookoomsing, Vinesh 2002 Kreol: lang interfas an leritaz patrimwann et modernite. Ledikasyon pu Travayer (eds), 25-30.
Hopper, Paul J & Traugott, Elizabeth C 2003 *Grammaticalization*. Cambridge: Cambridge University Press.
Langacker, Ronald 1977 Syntactic reanalysis. Li, Charles N (ed.) *Mechanisms of syntactic change*, Austin: University of Texas Press, 57-193.
Ledikasyon pu Travayer (eds). 2002 Langaz kreol zordi. Port Louis: Ledikasyon pu Travayer.
—— (eds.) 2004 *Diksyoner Kreol Angle*. Port Louis : Ledikasyon pu Travayer.
Li, Charles N (ed.) 1977 *Mechanisms of syntactic change*, Austin: University of Texas Press.
Li, Charles N & Thompson, Sandra A 1977 A mechanism for the development of copula morphemes. Li, Charles N (ed.), 419-44.
Longobardi, Giuseppe 1994 Reference and proper names: a theory of N-Movement in syntax and Logical Form. *Linguistic Inquiry* 25: 609-65.
—— 2003 *The structure of DPs*. Baltin & Collins (eds), 562-603.
Maingard, Jan 2002 *Lagrin tambarin: 13 ti zistoires en kreol*. Baie du Tombeau, Mauritius: Editions Maurice.
Matthews, Peter H 1997 *The Concise Oxford Dictionary of Linguistics*. Oxford: Oxford University Press.
Mchombo, Sam A 1993 Introduction. Mchombo, Sam A (ed.) *Theoretical aspects of Bantu grammar*. Stanford, CA: Center for the Study of Language and Information, 1-16.
McWhorter, John 1994 From focus marker to copula in Swahili. *Proceedings of the Meeting of the Berkeley Linguistics Society: Special session on Historical Issues in Linguistics*, 57-66.
Milsark, Gary 1979 *Existential sentences in English*. New York: Garland.
Nadal, Pascal 2002 Problematik langaz kreol parle et langaz kreol ekri kuma azan leksplikasyon sinplifye. Ledikasyon pu Travayer (eds), 108-09.
Papen, Robert A 1975 *A short grammar of Seychellois Creole*. Ms.
Parsons, Terence 1990 *Events in the semantics of English: a study in subatomic semantics*. Cambridge, Mass.: MIT Press.
Pollock, Jean Yves 1989 Verb movement, Universal Grammar, and the structure of IP. *Linguistic Inquiry* 20: 365-424.
Rizzi, Luigi 1990 *Relativized Minimality*. Cambridge, Mass.: MIT Press.
Rothstein, Susan D 1985 *The syntactic forms of predication*. Bloomington: Indiana University Linguistics Club.
Stein Peter 2007 L'absence de marqueurs préverbaux. *This volume*.
Stowell, Tim 1989 Subjects, Specifiers, and X-Bar Theory. Baltin, Mark & Kroch, Anthony S (eds) *Alternative conceptions of phrase structure*, Chicago: University of Chicago Press, 232-62.
—— 1991 Determiners in NP and DP. Leffel, Katherine & Bouchard, Denis (eds), *Views on phrase structure*, Dordrecht: Kluwer, 37-56.
Strandquist, Rachel Eva 2005 *Article incorporation in Mauritian Creole*, Department of Linguistics, University of Victoria: MA.
Travis, Lisa 1984 Parameters and effects of word order variation. PhD thesis, MIT.
Van Gelderen, Elly 2004 *Grammaticalization as economy*. Amsterdam; Benjamins.
Virahsawmy Dev 2003 Literesi an Morisien. Retrieved on April 24 2003 from: http://pages.intnet.mu/develog/dev0802.htm.
—— 2004 *Aprann lir ek ekrir Morisien*. Rose-Hill, Mauritius: Cygnature Publications.
—— 2005 Detrwa lartik. Retrieved on August 28 2007 from: http://pages.intnet.mu/develog/ polankvaryeLARTIK.html

—— 2006 Ti-Prins: tradiksion-adaptasion 'Le Petit Prince' par Antoine de Saint-Exupéry. Retrieved on August 28 2007 from: http://www.kiltir.com/kreol/b0009/dev-virahsawmy-ti-prins-intro.shtml

Abbreviations

A: Adjective
AdjP: Adjectival Phrase
AGR: Agreement; **arg:** argument
ASP: Aspect
COMP: Complementizer
COP: Copula
decl: declarative
DEM: Demonstrative
DP: Determiner Phrase
ECP: Empty Category principle
F: Formal form of address used with the 2nd singular French pronoun
HC: Haitian Creole
HMC: Head Movement Constraint
INFL: Inflection
IP: Inflectional Phrase
LOC: Locative
MC: Mauritian Creole
MOD: Modal
N: Noun
NEG: Negation
NP: Noun Phrase
P: Preposition
PLU: Plural
POSS: Possessive
PP: Prepositional Phrase
Pred: Predicate
PredP: Predicate Phrase
PST: Past Tense
S: Sentence
SC: Seychellois Creole
SG: Singular;
Spec: Specifier
TMA: Tense, Mood, Aspect
TP: Tense Phrase
V: Verb
VP: Verb Phrase

After emigrating from Mauritius to Australia, Diana Guillemin's career alternated between academic publishing and librarianship.
While working at the University of Queensland, she developed an interest in linguistics, and is now in the process of completing her PhD on
The Mauritian Creole Noun Phrase: Its form and function.
<d.guillemin@uq.edu.au>

Comparative Creole typology and the search for the sources of Mauritian Creole features[1]

Anthony P Grant & Philip Baker

1. Introduction

This paper has three objectives. Firstly it examines structural data from Mauritian Creole (henceforth MC), to see how typical they are of Creoles in general and of Atlantic Creoles in particular. Secondly, it lists 24 MC features which appear to be at least partly of non-French origin and considers evidence for possible sources of these in seven (groups of) languages spoken in the island in the 18th and/or 19th centuries.. Thirdly, it looks at one distinctive feature of MC, and of Creole French in general, and examines the distribution of syllabic and consonantal agglutinated nominals in MC compared with Seselwa and other French Creoles spoken further afield.

2. How typical a Creole is MC?

Many features employed for typological purposes and for cross-Creole and cross-lexifier comparison in previous studies were drawn up by linguists whose speciality was the study of one or more of the Atlantic Creoles. The latest, and by far the most detailed and thoroughly researched of these, is Holm & Patrick (2007) who list and discuss the presence or absence of 97 such features in a carefully chosen selection of 18 Creoles. Two of the many questions of interest raised by this publication are whether the chosen features are in some way "biased" towards Atlantic Creoles, and how does MC compare with Caribbean area Creoles, especially those with a mainly French-derived lexicon? Before addressing these questions, a brief summary of the non-francophone ethnolinguistic groups in Mauritius in the 18th century would be useful.

After more than a century of Dutch ownership, Mauritius was once again uninhabited when the French took control at the end of 1721. In the following 15 years, non-francophones were brought to the island from the following places: Madagascar, southern India, northeastern India, Whydah (Benin), Gorée (Senegal), and Mozambique. The southern Indians were mainly and perhaps exclusively Tamils. Those from northeastern India were described as "Bengali" but this may mean simply that they were brought from the Bengal presidency rather than that they were necessarily been speakers of Bengali. They are nevertheless bound to have been speakers of related Indic languages. Note that both groups of Indians, but especially those from southern India, included a proportion of skilled artisans who were paid for their work, as well as slaves. Slaves from Benin are likely to have been speakers of Gbe languages but it is not known which one(s). Most of those from Senegal are described as "Yolof" but a significant minority, generally described as "Bambara" were probably speakers of Mandinka. Slaves from Mozambique are likely to have been speakers of Makhuwa, the dominant language of the northern half of that country, as well as other East African Bantu languages. From at least 1740,

---

[1] We gratefully acknowledge the assistance and support of Diana Guillemin, Tasleem Shakur, Ian Smith and Sunyog Soogumbur in the production of this paper.

speakers of Malagasy and Bantu languages were numerically dominant. No arrivals from West Africa are known after 1765 and it was in approximately the same year that arrivals from East Africa began to overtake those from Madagascar by a significant margin. Small numbers of Indians continued to arrive throughout the 18th century, both as slaves and paid artisans. (For further information on everything in this paragraph, see Baker (*this volume*, 1982a, 1982b).

All but one of the above mentioned (groups of) languages are represented in the MC lexicon. Baker (1982b) identified a total of 1535 words of non-metropolitan French origin in MC representing about 10% of its vocabulary,[2] but more than a third of these are of English origin and it is thus unlikely that any of these became established in MC prior to the 19th century.[3] Of the 1535 words, 94 are classed as "Indian Ocean French" (IOF) but include items of ultimate Indic, Tamil, Malagasy, and even Bantu origin believed to have become established in local French earlier than in MC.[4] There are also 50 items thought to result from convergence between two or more non-european words (totalling 114 etyma for the 50 items). If account is taken of the ultimate sources of IOF words and convergences, there are 662 non-European words in MC. 333 of these are of Indic origin, 102 of Tamil or other Dravidian origin, 96 from Malagasy, 60 from Bantu languages, 15 from Chinese, 16 from Mandinka and other Manding languages, 17 from Wolof, and 23 from other sources. The great majority of words of Asian origin will undoubtedly have come into MC following the abolition of slavery.[5] Too much should not be made of the ratio of the number of words from Malagasy to those from Bantu languages because whereas there are several good Malagasy dictionaries, only short word lists exist for several of the relevant Bantu languages.

The preceding two paragraphs demonstrate that MC has potentially rather more in common with Atlantic Creoles than might have been supposed. Not only were the West African languages taken to Mauritius also influential in many Atlantic Creoles but massive numbers of speakers of Bantu languages were taken to the Americas as well as to Mauritius. And while there are many different Bantu languages, they all have a great deal grammatically in common while some lexical items are shared by these languages across central and southern Africa.[6] Having established that, let us now turn Holm & Patrick (2007).

Holm & Patrick' authors'[7] list, discuss, and exemplify a total of 97 features under 20 headings for 18 Creoles. Each feature is marked in one of four ways: as being present (+), absent (0), present but rare (R), or of uncertain status because of the lack of relevant data (?). It is important to note that not all features which they mark with + can to be regarded as being especially typical of Creoles although many of them are. A few show the opposite tendency. For instance, 11.1 asks whether the language in question uses a passive construction. Here a + response would indicate that the language was *less* typically Creole since most Creoles lack overt passive constructions. The same is true for case-marking on personal pronouns. Logic further dictates that all such "untypically Creole" items marked with zero should actually be assessed positively. Thus we have

---

[2] Baker & Hookoomsing (1987) includes approximately 18,000 entries of which about 15,000 are for individual words, the rest being combinations of two or more words.

[3] The majority are almost certainly 20th century adoptions.

[4] For example, many species of flora were introduced from Madagascar and India by the French and some of these have phonetic forms in MC which suggest they came via local French rather than directly from Malagasy or an Indian language.

[5] But not all. Words of Tamil origin include some relating to building construction. Since Tamil artisans were brought to mauritius specifically for such work from the 1720s onwards, these probably became established in MC in the 18th century.

[6] For example, the MC word of Bantu origin, *sega*, applied to a musical form and a dance, comes from a widespread root meaning 'play' (in all senses). Forms of this with s/ʃ/č as the first segment, *e* or *i* as the second, *k* or *g* as the third and always *a* as the final vowel occur right across bantu Africa. *Sega* is cognate with "chica", attested as the name of an African dance in both Brazil and Martinique.

[7] The individual chapters are written by specialists in each of the languages covered.

switched the ratings around, 0 instead of + and + instead of 0, for all such 'pseudo-negative' features in the table below.

The table includes all 18 of the languages assessed in Holm & Patrick, to which Grant has added MC.

Table 1
Categorization of 97 features associated with Creoles (Holm & Patrick 2007)

Creole	Positive Creole features (+)	Negative Creole features (-)	Number of R	Number of ?
Haitian	78	19	0	0
Jamaican	76	17	4	0
Ndyuka	71	21	5	0
Tok Pisin	71	21	5	0
Krio	71	25	1	0
Angolar	69	24	4	0
Papiamentu	69	27	1	0
Mauritian	**69**	**28**	**0**	**0**
Negerhollands	68	23	5	1
Seselwa	67	29	1	0
Cape Verdean	66	31	0	0
Berbice Dutch	64	26	6	1
Dominican Cr Fr	64	30	3	0
Guinea-Bissau	63	30	3	1
Palenquero	58	37	2	0
Nubi	53	43	1	0
Zamboangueño	51	45	1	0
Korlai Portuguese	45.5	49.5	2	0
Nagamese	44	49	4	0

Insofar as Tok Pisin (of Papua New Guinea) occupies joint third place in the table, and Mauritian scores only two positive points fewer, Holm & Patrick features cannot be accused of being excessively "Atlantocentric". However, the average score for all Atlantic Creoles in the table is 68 whereas the average for all the others, which we can term "Indo-Pacific", is significantly less, 58. A possibly more informative set of averages can be calculated according to the main lexical source language. The average score for English Creoles is 72, that for French is 70, Dutch averages 66, while the Iberian Creoles score 60. Arabic-based Nubi and Assamese-based Nagamese score even less, 53 and 44, respectively. If, on the basis of these figures, we accept that creolization operates slightly differently according to the nature of the main lexical source language, then the latter is the main reason why the Indo-Pacific average score is less than the average Atlantic score. We should probably also allow that, as more becomes known of Creoles not related to European languages, additional "typical Creole features" may be identified.

In an earlier and far more limited study, Baker (2001) examined the degree to which 24 structural features typical of pidgins were attested, currently or formerly, in 16 Creoles. The word "formerly" is important here because some of the pidgin features attested in the early data, such as zero copula in equative and locative structures, were no longer current in some of the languages. Somewhat similarly, the range of bimorphemic interrogatives found in the early texts was sometimes greater than found in modern data.

Baker argued that the greater the number of these pidgin features which were attested in a particular Creole at any time, the likelier it was that it had its origins in a pidgin. His findings are set out in Table 2.[8] The features are listed in Appendix A. (Holm & Patrick (2007) provide information on most of these insofar as they remain current in the 18 languages they cover.)

Table 2

Number of pidgin features (out of 24) attested, formerly or currently, in the languages listed below

Language	Number of pidgin features
Réunionnais	12
Pitcairnese	13
Korlai Indo-Portuguese	14
Zamboangueño	15
Hawai'i Creole English	16
Tayo	17
Louisianais	18
Average	19.1
Guyanais	20
Papiamentu	20
Sãotomense	20
Caribbean ECs including Jamaican	23
Haitian	23
MC	23
Sranan	23
Antillean Creole French	24
Tok Pisin	24

Baker's conclusions can be summarized as follows:

The two languages in which the fewest pidgin features are attested, Réunionnais and Pitcairnese, have in common that the first European males arrived with, or acquired soon after, non-European consorts. In such circumstances it seems likely that both parties would have been keen for the non-Europeans to acquire the European language as such, thus limiting the potential for pidginized features to become established.[9]

Korlai Indo-Portuguese and Zamboangueño have only slightly more pidgin features. A factor here is that the only available data are recent; some formerly current pidgin features may since have been lost. It is also likely that in both cases the first male Europeans had non-European consorts, as in Réunion and Pitcairn.

Two other languages lacking more than the average number of pidgin features are Hawai'i Creole English and Tayo Creole French. A factor common to just these two is that in both locations children received formal education in the European language.

Four languages which score close to the average are Louisianais, Guyanais, Papiamentu, and Sãotomense. Few early data exist for any of these which leaves open the possibility that they may formerly have had more pidgin features than they currently have.

At least 23 of the 24 pidgin features are attested in the remaining six languages even though not all of these are necessarily in current use. One factor common to them is that a good deal of early data exist for all six. Interim conclusions which can be drawn from this small survey are:

---

[8] As published in *Te Reo*, the equivalent table listed the number of pidgin features NOT attested in these languages.

[9] A much clearer view of Réunionnais in the 18th century is now available in the study of two previously unknown and substantial texts analysed by Bollée (2007).

- where initial contact between people of different ethnolinguistic backgrounds took place in a domestic setting, fewer pidgin features were likely to become established;
- where formal education in the European language, this too would tend to result in the retention of fewer pidgin features;
- but in slave plantation societies where neither of the above conditions applied, all 24 pidgin features probably existed in the past even if not all of these survive today.

3. MC and potential sources of its non-French features

We must acknowledge at the outset that the idea for this section arose rather late in the history of the preparation of this book, mainly as the result of requests for information from fellow contributors. It is, therefore, somewhat tentative in nature. The basic intention has been to compile a list of non-lexical MC features which do not appear to be attributable to varieties of French, for which the influence of one or more of the other languages formerly or currently spoken in the island might be suspected, and to explore the latter possibility. The findings are summarized in Table 3

Table 3 lists 24 numbered features of MC and comments on their presence or absence in the following languages: French, Wolof, Mandinka, Fongbe, Hindustani, Makhuwa, Tamil, and Malagasy. A few remarks on this selection of languages are needed.

Since the chosen MC features are those which cannot (wholly) be ascribed to French, the purpose of including this is to indicate how French differs from MC.

Slaves from Senegal, generally described in the parish registers as Yolof (the majority) and Bambara (the minority), were brought to Mauritius in the period 1730-65. They formed the largest group of slaves for the first five years of that period but the proportion dininished thereafter. Yolof is the ethnonym of Wolof-speakers. In the 18th century, the French tended to apply the word "Bambara" to the Manding peoples in general. It is far more likely that the "Bambara" taken to Mauritius came from the lower Gambia area where Mandinka predominates, rather than from Mali where the Bambara (Bamana) language is actually spoken.

Only one group of slaves is definitely known to have come from Whydah (Ouidah, Juda) in 1729, in what is now Benin, but there may have been others. These people are described in the early parish registers as "Guinée".[10] Neither Fon nor any other ethnic name is used from them there. As Enoch Eboh (p c) has suggested to another contributor to this book, if the Fon were the dominant group in Benin at that time, those sold to European slave traders would almost certainly have belonged to a different ethnolinguistic group. Nevertheless, speakers of Gbe languages are numerically dominant in that area. It thus seems important to look at one such language for possible influence and Fon is by far the best described of these.

Indic is the current collective term for the languages formerly known as Indo-Aryan. The only Indic language name attested in Mauritius in the 18th century is Bengali but this seems to have been applied indiscriminately to slaves (and some paid artisans) who embarked at the French enclave of Chandernagor surrounded what was the Bengal Presidency under the British and these may well have spoken eastern varieties of Hindustani. In the absence of any MC words known to be specifically of Bengali rather than Hindustani origin, we have taken the latter as the most appropriate representative of Indic languages. (The term 'Hindustani' in the 19th century also embracedc the Bihari dialects such as Bhojpuri which was to be dominant among indentured labourers following abolition.) In 18th century Mauritus, slaves described as "Bengali" appear to have worked exclusively as domestics.

Makhuwa is today spoken by about 40% of the population of Mozambique located in the northern half of that country. In various spellings (Macoua, Macoa, etc.), this is the

---

[10] In the second half of the 18th century, this word was generally applied to all slaves of West African origin.

most frequent East African ethnonym encountered in 18th century documents from Mauritius but at least a dozen other Bantu groups were represented among the slaves so occasional reference will be made to these. Speakers of Bantu languages are known to have been present in Mauritius from at least 1736 and accounted for the great majority of slave arrivals from about 1765 until the abolition of the slave trade.

The arrival of Tamils is recorded from the late 1720s. While their numbers were never very large, their presence may have been more influential than their proportion of the population alone would suggest because they included paid artisans as well as slaves and the latter, like those from northeast India, worked as domestics rather than as labourers.

There were Malagasy slaves in Mauritius from 1722 until abolition. They were at all times well represented and consistently the numerically dominant group from 1740 until at least 1765.

3.1 The selected features[11]

The features selected for examination range over various **phonological, morphological** and **syntactic** properties. In § 3.2 we will use an admittedly crude points system to obtain some measure of the potential for each language (or group of languages) to influence MC. In general, 1 = 'same as MC', 0 = 'different from MC', as will be obvious from Table 3. Only in dubious cases or where half a point is awarded will this be mentioned here.

The first four features (hereafter F) are **phonological**. MC differs from Caribbean French Creoles is having five rather than seven peripheral oral vowels (vowel length contrasts are ignored. While the West African languages in the table each have seven, the three of the Indian Ocean languages have five and thus score 1 point each. With traditionally only four vowels, we consider that Malagasy would also have contributed to the loss of the mid-high vs mid-low vowel distinctions of French so it too scores 1 point.

F2 concerns the absence of the French phonemes /š/ and /ž/ in MC (replaced by /s/ and /z/, respectively). Of the other languages, Hindustani has only /š/, and scores 0,5.[12] All the other languages lack both /š/ and /ž/ and score 1 point each.

The scoring for F3 will be obvious except for Malagasy. Since /ts/ and /dz/ of the latter appear to be regularly assimilated to MC /s/ and /z/, respectively, we do not see these as having contributed to the establishment of /č/ and /ǰ/ in MC so we score Malagasy as 0 here.

None of the languages in the table has F4.[13]

F5, F6 and F7 relate to the agglutination of French articles to noun stems which were then analysed as consisting of a single morpheme whose first segment happen to be derived from a French article. (See § 4 for more details.) F5 and F6 are thus irrelevant for languages which lack extensive contact with French. None of the (groups of) languages has agglutinated French articles to and great extent but those showing some tendency to do so score 0,5.[14] All cases of agglutination in MC result in nouns with an initial

---

[11] Data in Table 3 come from a number of sources. Typological data for French and Hindustani are from Grant's knowledge of these languages. Schmidt (2002a, 2002b) provides further Hindi and Urdu data, while structural observations on Bengali are from Dasgupta (2003) and Tasleem Shakur (P C). Sources for (Merina) Malagasy information were Rasoloson (1999, 2000). The structural sketches of Wolof by Sauvageot (1981) and of Bambara by Tersis (1981) were consulted for those languages, while material was also available for Wolof from Dem (1995 a, b) and for another Manding language, Gambian Mandinka, from Colley (1995 a, b). Fongbe data come from Lefebvre & Brousseau (2002). Annamalai & Steever (1998), Asher (1985) and Victor (2004) are the sources for Indian Tamil data. Makhuwa data are from Kisseberth (2003) and Maples (1879).
[12] Bhojpuri also lacks both /š/ and /ž/.
[13] This is also a feature of Réunionnais (Chaudenson 1974: xxxvii) so French regional or dialectal origin for this cannot be excluded.
[14] Bantu is scored 0,5 because such languages in Central Africa typically include some examples of syllabic agglutination, the most widespread items are probably those deriving from French *du pain* and *du vin*.

consonant. This process might therefore have been encouraged by languages in which most or all nouns have initial consonants, the subject of F7.

F8: The diminutive MC noun-prefix *ti-* derives from French *petit* but is a separate morpheme, in the same way as many Bantu languages have special diminutive noun class markers which can be added to normal stems in order to create a sense of diminution. *Ti-* is a bound morpheme which cannot occur alone ('small' in MC is *piti*, 'tiny' is *tipti*.[15])

F9: As a single morpheme preposed marker of plurality, *bann* is first recorded as such in the 1880s. (It is attested earlier as part of the phrase *éne bande* 'a group of', see Baker (2003: 135-39).

F10 concerns the postposed marker of definiteness and/or specificity *la*; see Guillemin (*this volume*) and Syea (*this volume*) for contrasting analyses.

F11. Speakers of MC can if they wish distinguish between inclusive ('you and I': MC *nutu*) and exclusive ('s/he and I but not you': MC *nuzot*) 1st person plural pronouns, a distinction which is also made in Tamil and Malagasy.

F12. *Zot* does service as both the 2pl and 3pl personal pronouns.

F13. The use of an expression meaning '(my) body' as a means of expressing '(my)self' is widespread in Creoles, including MC, and is also found in various other languages.

F14 concerned the position of morphemes indication tense, modality, and aspect.

It has proved somewhat problematic to find an adequate way of comparing TMA distinctions (F15). Part of the problem is that available grammatical descriptions tend to assume, not necessarily wrongly, that tense is comparable to that in European languages. We feel that the most important distinction is whether systems mark anterior or past and, for that reason have scored positively only languages known to mark anterior rather than past.

F16 and F17 are concerned with whether languages have zero copula for equatives and/or locatives. Wolof, Fongbe, and Tamil all have the former but only Wolof has the latter.

F18: Most MC verbs have two forms, the used of which is determined entirely by syntactic criteria. Nothing similar was found in any of the other languages.

F19: Reduplication has four different roles in MC. Wolof, Indic languages, and Tamil each have just one of these but Malagasy has three. However, to augment the meaning of an adjective, the two copies of the adjective have to be linked by another morpheme (see footnote 26). Since this is somewhat different from what is ordinarily understood by 'reduplication', we have scored this as 0.5.

F20, F 21: The use of a single word meaning both 'with' and 'and' to link two or more noun groups is well attested in MC, though less frequently today than in the past. The same word is also used to mark the indirect object of a ditransitive verb (see Kriegel & Michaelis, *this volume*, for more details).

F22: MC verbs are negated using preverbal *pa*. This contrasts with colloquial French where *pas* follows the first part of the verb group.

F23: The senses of MC *depi* 'since' and *ziska* 'until', both of which can have spatial as well as temporal senses, are often confused in speech, and this feature may have its roots in Hindustani or another Indic language in which the periods of time before and after an event are sometimes labelled with the same word, e.g. Hindustani *kal* could refer to 'yesterday' or 'tomorrow'. Somewhat similarly, MC *lot* 'other' can mean 'the one before last' or 'the one after next', e.g. *lot samdi* 'the Saturday before last', 'the Saturday after next'.

F24: Finally, MC, like many other languages, uses the word literally meaning '(it) has', *ena*, to express the idea of 'there is' (cf Véronique & Fon Sing, *this volume*). While this is unquestionably from French, the use of the verb 'have' to express 'there is' may have been reinforced by similar structures in other languages.

---

[15] Reasons for considering MC *ti-* to be a diminutive prefix rather than an adjective are set out in Baker (1994: 80-81)

Table 3: MC features of potentially non-French origin compared with their presence or absence in eight other languages currently or formerly spoken in Mauritius

	MC	French	Wolof	Mandinka	Fongbe
1. No. of peripheral oral vowel positions	5	8 (tending toward 7)[16]	7	7	7
2. /š/, /ž/	No	Yes	No	No	No
3. /č/ /ǰ/	Yes but almost only in non-French items	Only in loans	Yes	Yes	No
4. Light affrication /palatalization of /t/ and /d/ before /i/.	Yes	No	No	No	No?
5. Syllabic agglutination	Yes	No	No	No	Yes
6. Consonantal agglutination	Yes	No	Some examples in French loans	A few examples in French loans	No
7. Consonant-initial nouns markedly pre-dominant in core lexis?	Yes	No	To some extent	Yes	No
8. Diminutive prefix?	Yes	No	No	No	No
9. Pluralisation marker precedes the noun stem	Yes, preposed /ban/ (optional but frequent)	None as such, but preceding plural articles les and des.	Yes (class prefixes are used)	None	Yes
10. Principal means of marking definiteness / specificity	Postposed la[17]	Preposed definite, articles	Postposed classifiers	Low tone marks definite status	Postposed determiner
11. Exclus/inclus 1pl	Yes (but rare)	No	No	No	No
12. 2pl=3pl pronoun?	Yes	No	Yes (but only in object position)	No	No[18]
13. 'My body' = 'myself'	Yes	No	No	No	No

[16] The traditional contrast between [a] and [ɑ], as in patte and pâte, respectively, appears to be coming increasingly rare.
[17] Note that Guillemin and Syea differ in their analysis of the role of postposed la. See their respective articles in this volume.
[18] But note that 1 pl = 2 pl in this language.

	MC	Indic (Hindustani)	Bantu (Makhuwa)	Tamil	Malagasy
1. No. of positions of articulation of peripheral oral vowels	5	5	5	5	4 /u i. e a/[19]
2. /š/, /ž/	No	/š/ only	No	No	No[20]
3. /č/ /ǰ/	Yes (mainly in non-French items)	Yes	Yes	Yes (complementary distribution)[21]	No (but it has /ts/ and /dz/)
4. Light affrication /palatalization of /t/ and /d/ before /i/.	Yes	No	Not so far as we are aware	No	No (/ts/ and /dz/ can be followed by any vowel)
5. Syllabic agglutination	Yes	Irrelevant	Irrelevant	Irrelevant	c. 20 French loans
6. Consonantal agglutination	Yes	Irrelevant	Irrelevant	Irrelevant	No
7. consonant-initial nouns predominant in core lexis?	Yes	Many nouns with a- initially but few with other vowels.	Yes, if noun-class prefixes are excluded[22]	Yes, to some extent	No
8. Diminutive prefix?	Yes	No	Yes, diminutive noun class	No	No
9. Pluralisation marker precedes noun stem	Yes	No (suffixes)	Yes (noun class prefixes)	No (suffixes)	No
10. Principal means of marking definiteness / specificity	Postposed la	None	No overt determiners	No (definiteness unmarked)	Preposed
11. Exclusive/ inclusive 1 pl distinction	Yes (but rare)	No	No	Yes	Yes
12. 2pl=3pl pronoun?	Yes	No	No	No	No
13. 'my body' = 'myself'?	Yes	No	No	No	Yes

---

[19] Continuing contact with French has resulted in words adopted from the latter in which /o/ is distinguished from /u/ but no minimal pairs have been reported.

[20] Word-finally, graphic <sy> and <zy>, representing in principle [si] and [zi], may be realised as /š/ and /ž/, respectively.

[21] In romanized transcriptions of Tamil, <c> represents /č/ word-initially. Between vowels, <c> is pronounced /ǰ/ but <cc> represents /č/. This system has been somewhat complicated by the adoption from Hindustani and English of words with initial /ǰ/ in those languages.

[22] Most nouns in Bantu languages occur with a pair of class prefixes, e.g. mu-ntu 'person, ba-ntu 'people'. In most and perhaps all Bantu languages, the noun root has an initial consonant, in this case n. Most noun class prefixes also have an initial consonant but noun class prefixes with an initial vowel do occur. the largest noun class in Makhuwa, for example has the prefixes e- (singular) and i- (plural).

	MC	French	Wolof	Mandinka	Fongbe
14. Pre- or post verb (stem) TMA marking	Preposed	Mainly postposed	Essentially preposed[23]	Preposed	Preposed
15. TMA distinctions	Anterior;[24] progressive; completive; definite and indefinite future	Past, present, future, perfect, imperfect, conditional	Present continuous, future, 2 pasts and a non-past; also an iterative completive	Progressive, continuous, future, past, habitual, imperfect, perfect, hortative	Anterior, definite and indefinite future, subjunctive, habitual, imperfective
16. Equative Ø copula?	Yes	No	Yes	No	Yes
17. Locative Ø copula	Yes	No	Yes	No	No
18. Short versus long verbs syntactically determined?	Yes	No	No	No	No
19. Reduplication for....	(a) Attenuation; (b) Augmentation; (c) Iteration, (d) Distributive numerals	(Little used outside children's speech registers)	(c) Iteration	Deverbative nouns	Deverbal adjectives, deverbative nouns, participles, gerunds
20. 'with' = 'and' in NPs?	Yes, getting rarer	No	Yes	No	No
21. 'with' = 'and" marks indirect object in ditransitives?	Yes	No	No	No	No
22. Negation is preverbal?	Yes	Vestigial; postverbal in spoken French	No (postverbal suffix)	No (postverbal suffix)	Yes
23. Confusion between 'time before now' and 'time after now'	Yes	No	No	No	No
24. 'there is' = 'it has'	Yes	= 'it has there'	Yes	Yes	No

[23] Wolof has just one postposed marker, -aan, which is a kind of "iterative completive".
[24] The anterior marker can occur with each of the others. Anterior + progressive 'imperfect'; anterior + completive 'pluperfect'; anterior + future 'conditional'. The glosses in quotes are somewhat misleading in that, once anterior is established, it is not repeated. thus, for example, the progressive marker alone can indicate 'imperfect'. See Stein (*this volume*).

206

	MC	Indic (Hindustani)	Bantu (Makhuwa)	Tamil	Malagasy
14. Predominantly pre- or post verb (stem) TMA marking	Preposed	Postposed	Mainly preposed (mood postposed)	Postposed	Initial consonant of present prefix changed for past and future.[25]
15. TMA distinctions	Anterior; progressive; completive; definite and indefinite future	Tenses and perfective expressed with auxiliaries	Numerous tenses, aspects, and moods	Tense-based	Present, past, future tenses and completive aspect.
16. Equative Ø copula?	Yes	No	No	Yes	No
17. Locative Ø copula?	Yes	No	No	No	No
18. Short versus long verbs syntactically determined?	Yes	No	No	No	No
19. Reduplication used for….	(a) Attenuation; (b) Augmentation; (c) Iteration, (d) Distributive numerals	(d) Distributive numerals	No evidence found	(d) Distributive numerals	(a) Attenuation; (b) Augmentation?;[26] (d) Distributive numerals
20. 'with' = 'and' in NPs?	Yes (getting rarer)	No	Yes	No	No ('and': *sy*, 'with': *misy*)
21. 'with' = 'and' marks indirect object in ditransitives?	Yes	No	Yes	No	No
22. Negation is preverbal?	Yes	No	Yes (prefixal and bound preverbal form)	No	Yes
23. Some confusion between 'time before now' and 'time after now'	Yes	Yes: same word for '(day before) yesterday' and '(day after) tomorrow'.	No	No	No
24. 'there is' = 'it has'	Yes	No	Yes	Yes	Yes

[25] According to Richardson (1885), active verbs in Malagasy belong to two groups. One makes no distinction between present and past but future is indicated by preposed *ho*. The others all have *m-* initially in the present tense prefix which changes to initial *n-* for past, and to initial *h-* for future. There is also a preposed completive marker.

[26] Reduplicated adjectives are attenuative, but if *dia* is positioned between the two forms, the interpretation is augmentative, e.g. *tsara* 'good', *tsaratsara* 'somewhat good', *tsara dia tsara* 'intensely good' (Richardson 1885).

3.2 Summary

As indicated at the start of the previous section, we fully acknowledge that our points system is rather crude. Our immediate aim is very modest: to gain a first impression of the relative non-lexical contribution of languages other than French to MC. In the longer term, we hope to devise a more sophisticated system covering a wider range of features.

An obvious limitation of Table 3 is that the features we have considered are not of equal significance but, in the absence of any obvious simple way of grading their relative importance it seems preferable to score one point for all those which are broadly "the same as MC". We have to admit that even this somewhat imprecise wording is not suited to categorizing all the features and has led us to use 0,5 as the score for 'partially resembling MC' in some cases. In addition, we have paid little attention to the third of the Bickertonian requirements that we need to show that the right slaves were in the right place at the right time. However, if we allow that all languages brought to the island were liable to remain in continuing if diminishing use for 40 years or so after the ending of the arrivals of slaves who spoke those languages, only features attributed to West African source which are not attested by 1805 can be considered dubious. Furthermore, the discussion of the texts in the Corpus (Fon Sing, *this volume*, 1-62) provides abundant evidence that the Franco-Mauritians who were responsible for writing most of these texts were slow to accept what they saw as slave innovations. Thus some feature may have been well established in slave usage a decade or two before they appeared in print. These reservations having been indicated, let us turn our attention to Table 4.

Table 4
Number of features in Table 3 which resemble MC

Bantu (Makhuwa)	12
Wolof	10,5
Malagasy	10
Tamil	7,5
Fongbe	6,5
Mandinka	5,5
Indic (Hindustani)	4,5

That Bantu (Makhuwa) scores the most points is not particularly surprising. Although the the arrival of the first slaves speaking Bantu languages began marginally later (1736) than all the other groups listed above, they almost immediately became the second most important source after Malagasies. They overtook Malagasy arrivals from about 1765 and in the 20 years from 1770, arrivals from East Africa outnumbered those from Madagascar by about ten to one (Baker, *this volume*). Overall, they probably account for half of all the slaves introduced in the 18th century. However, that Wolof scores marginally more than Malagasy is altogether unexpected. Malagasy was the language of the first slaves brought to Mauritius and they were at all times well represented. Their known contribution to the MC lexicon is also greater than that of Bantu languages or Wolof. One would, therefore, have expected Malagasy to occupy at least second place in this table.

Wolof-speaking slaves were numerically important for several years in the 1730s and were dominant among the slaves belonging to the Compagnie des Indes for a much longer period. The number of slaves belonging to the Compagnie – already well over 100 in 1735 and as many as 1674 in 1758 (Baker, *this volume*) – was always very considerably greater than those attached to any individual plantation. With little opportunity of access to French as spoken by francophone families, Compagnie slaves might have formed something of an avant-garde in the development of MC. That, at least, would seem a possibility worthy of consideration.

The middle-of-the-range Tamil score is not a surprise since they were represented from the 1720s both as paid artisans (with slaves working under them) and as slaves. Though their numbers were relatively small, their presence was continuous throughout the 18th century, and they were subsequently to account for about 30% of the Indian labours introduced after the abolition of slavery in 1835 (Baker *this volume*).

The only slightly smaller score for Fongbe is unexpected, especially since we cannot even be sure that the slaves from Whydah were Fongbe-speakers and only one shipment from this port (in 1729) is definitely known! However, these slaves are very likely to have been speakers of a related Gbe language sharing many of the same features. Many of them worked for the Companie des Indes which may also have added something to their potential to influence the early development of MC.

The score for Mandinka, never the language of more than a very small majority, is also better than expected. They, too, worked mainly for the Companie.

The lowest score for the Indic languages is not surprising, at least for the 18th century, since they worked exclusively as domestics, thus having far more access to French and fewer close contacts with field slaves than other groups.

It is perhaps also interesting to list features in the order of the number of languages scoring positively for them, as is done in Table 5.

Table 5

Features listed in order of the number of positive scores obtained

6,5   F2 (lack of /š/ and /ž/)
5   F3 (presence of /č/ and /ǰ/), F14 (preverbal TMA markers), F24 (have = there is)
4   F1 (5 or fewer peripheral vowels)
3,5   F7 (consonant initial nouns predominant in core lexis)
3   F9 (pre-posed plural marker), F16 zero equative copula, F19d (reduplication for distributive numerals, F22 (preverbal mark of negation)
2   F10 (postposed marker of definiteness), F11 (exclusive/inclusive 1st pl pronoun distinction), F20 (with = and)
1,5   F6 (consonantal agglutination)
1   F8 (diminutive prefix), F13 (my body = myself), F15 (anterior rather than past marker), F17 (zero locative copula), F19a (reduplication for attenuation), F19c (reduplication for iteration), F21 (word meaning 'with', 'and' marks indirect object), F23 (confusion between time before and time past now)
0,5   F5 (syllabic agglutination of French article to noun), F12 (2 pl = 3 pl pronoun), F19b (reduplication for augmentation)
0   F4 (palatalization, slight affrication of /t/ and /d/ before /i/), F18 (short vs long forms of verbs determined syntactically)

Languages which are the only source noted for a particular feature are Bantu (Makhuwa) F8, F21; Malagasy F13, F19a; Wolof F17, F19c; Fongbe F15, Hindustani (Indic) F23. Of the two features for which no potential source is indicated in the table, it seems most improbable that F4 could have developed locally yet its origin remains to be determined. By contrast, the data in the corpus strongly suggest that F18 is indeed a purely local development and not a feature transferred from another language.

We have drawn attention to three factors, all of them rather obvious, which seem to have affected the extent to which the languages of non-Francophones influenced MC. These are: the number of their speakers, the timing of their arrival and duration of their presence, and their roles in society. This list may not be complete. Baker has argued, in connection with his "constructive approach", that a possible fourth factor is that features of particular language with the potential to assist the development of an emergent contact language were likely to find acceptance in it independently of the other three factors. A good example is reduplication, which has four distinct roles in MC. He sees reduplication has having provided MC with an effective means of increasing its vocabulary without requiring the acquisition of additional morphemes. But we must end this section by emphasizing the tentative nature of this exercise so far: there are undoubtedly more features to be added, and a more sophisticated scoring system needs to be developed.

4. Agglutinated nominals

In this section we concentrate on one feature of the MC lexicon which distinguishes it sharply from French: agglutinated nominals. As indicated in section 3 (F5 and F6 of Table 3), they are of two kinds: consonantal and syllabic. Consonantal agglutinated nominals derive from French nouns with an initial vowel which have become established in MC, and in Creole French in general, with an initial consonant deriving from (a trace of) a French article, e.g. /lekors/ 'bark (of a tree)'(< Fr. *l'écorce*), /zãfã/ 'child' (< Fr. *les enfants*), /nam/ 'soul' (< Fr. *une âme*). Such initial consonants are an integral, non-deletable part of these nouns in Creole French. Syllabic agglutinated nominals are the historically more distinctive type. These have an initial syllable wholly derived from French *la, le, les, du, de l'*, or *des*. Some MC examples are:

/lasan/	'ash'	< Fr. *la cendre*	/lapo/	'skin'	< Fr. *la peau*
/leker/	'heart'	< Fr. *le coeur*	/liku/	'neck'	< Fr. *le cou*
/lezo/	'bone'	< Fr. *les os*	/lizye/	'eye'	< Fr. *les yeux*
/disã/	'blood'	< Fr. *du sang*	/dimun/	'person'	< Fr. *du monde*
/dilo/	'water'	< Fr. *de l'eau*	/dilwil/	'oil'	< Fr. *de l'huile*
/dizef/	'egg'	< Fr. *des oeufs*			

As with consonantal agglutinated nominals, these agglutinated syllables are an integral, non-deletable part of the MC nouns. However, whereas large numbers of consonantal agglutinated nominals occur in all French Creoles, syllabic agglutinated nominals are far more numerous in MC, and its derivative Seselwa (SC), than in other French Creoles, as indicated in the upper part of Table 6.

Table 6
Statistics on agglutinated article in five French Creoles

Syllabic agglutinated nominals	Haitian	St Lucian	Guyanais	MC	Seselwa
La-		168	101	724[27]	565
Le-/lez- etc	154	9	2	72	52
di-/dil- etc.	6	6	10	36	35
TOTAL	160	183	113	832	652
Consonantal agglutinated nominals					
n-	1	2	2	4	2
z-	56	63	56	169[28]	85

The table above includes some statistics on agglutinated nominals from Haitian (for which the data from Grant 1995b have been amplified by those in Targète & Urciolo 1993), and also from St Lucian (Mondesir 1992, Crosbie et al 2001), Guyanais (Barthelemi 1995), MC (Baker & Hookoomsing 1987) and Seselwa (St Jorre & Lionnet 1999). l- consonantal nominals are excluded from the table but are very numerous in all these French Creoles.

---

[27] Of which 195 can be considered archaic. Many of these occur in translations of biblical texts and are not attested elsewhere. Some have simply become obsolete.

[28] Of which 45 are archaic.

There can be no doubt that a prerequisite for French articles to be analysed as part of the following noun by non-francophones immigrants is what may be termed 'frequency of collocation'. For example, in spoken French the words *lune* 'moon', and *fumée* almost always follow the feminine definite article *la*. These two occur as syllabic agglutinated nominals, /lalin/ and /lafime/, in seemingly all French Creoles apart from Réunionnais. But an explanation is needed to account for the far greater number of such syllabic agglutinated forms in MC than in any French Creole of the Caribbean area.

Baker (1982b: 800-02; 1984) proposed that the cause of this could be the influence of Bantu languages. All Bantu languages have a dozen or more noun classes, each with its particular prefixes (singular and plural). The distribution of nouns among the classes is very unequal. The largest class can encompass a third or more of all nouns while some classes only have a handful of members. Since nouns do not occur without their prefixes, the result is that large numbers of nouns in these languages are pronounced with the same initial syllable. For example, of the 54 nouns in Makhuwa on the Swadesh 100 list, 20 belong to the class which has singular prefix *ni-* and, usually, the plural prefix *ma-*.[29] A further 16 belong to the class which has *e-* and *i-* as its singular prefixes. Thus two thirds of the most basic nouns in this language (36/54) belong to just two classes. This led Baker to suggest that speakers of Bantu languages would not consider it unusual that the language they encountered in Mauritius should also have large numbers of nouns with the same initial syllable. (Of the 54 nouns on the Swadesh 100 list, MC has 16 beginning with *la-*, 10 with *li-* or *le-*,[30] and 5 with *di-*. Thus more than half of these basic nouns could be seen as belonging to one of just three "noun classes".)

This hypothesis still required an explanation of why e.g. Haitian Creole had far fewer examples of syllabic agglutinated nominals than MC. Baker attributed this to timing. In Mauritius, the presence of slaves speaking Bantu languages dates from just 15 years from the start of settlement and their proportion increased steadily thereafter, reaching almost 90% of slave arrivals from ca. 1765. In Haiti, the numbers of slaves speaking Bantu languages also peaked in the latter part of the 18th century, although their proportion of arrivals never rivalled the level in Mauritius. Even more importantly, the settlement of the territory by the French had begun fully half a century earlier. Therefore, he suggested, most nouns would probably have acquired their definitive form before speakers of Bantu languages became an important proportion of the slave population.

While this hypothesis may be less than perfect, those who have rejected it have so far failed to find a convincing alternative explanation for the much greater number of syllabic agglutinated nominals in MC than in other French Creoles. Furthermore, Grant (1995a, 1995b), using a significantly larger database, and, more recently, Strandquist (2005) have also concluded that the influence of Bantu languages was the decisive factor. While neither of the authors of this article have changed their views about that, work on section 3 has brought to our attention two additional factors which may have contributed to both consonantal and syllabic agglutination in MC.

First of all, Malagasy is the only language (other than French) in Table 3 which has preposed articles. Thus, for speakers of all the other languages, anything immediately preceding a French noun, not intonationally separated from it, and not identifiable as belonging to another word-class might be liable to interpretation as part of the following noun. Secondly, since one overall impact of both consonantal and syllabic agglutination is to greatly increase the proportion of consonant-initial words, it may be worthwhile comparing the proportion of such words both in the lexicon as a whole and among the nouns in the Swadesh lists in a number of relevant languages, as is done in Table 7 (overleaf). (We have generally used the 70 nouns on the Swadesh 207 list but some cases, indicated in footnotes, only data on the 54 nouns in the 100 list were readily available.)

---

[29] In this and several other classes, there are a few exceptions which take a different plural prefix.
[30] Almost all MC nouns with an initial syllable derived from Fr. *le* or *les* are variably attested in early data with both *li-* and *le-* although in most cases only one of these variants remains current.

Figures for total lexicon are based on page counts in the dictionaries indicated in the footnotes. The first four languages in the table are not relevant for MC but are frequently cited as major influences on Caribbean-area Creoles.[31] For that reason, we have not calculated the proportion of vowel-initial nouns in the Swadesh lists but, in each case, more than 40% of the total lexicon is vowel-initial.

Fongbe, Tamil, and French occupy the next three positions; in each of these more than 20% of the total vocabulary is vowel-initial and only Tamil has a much lower proportion among the Swadesh nouns.

The names of all the French Creoles in the table are in italics to distinguish them from languages taken to Mauritius by slaves and indentured labourers. As can be seen, the proportion of vowel-initial words is every case far less than in French in the total lexicon, and either very small or non-existent among the Swadesh nouns. The main cause of this undoubtedly results from article agglutination.[32]

Tamil and all the remaining languages in the table were spoken by immigrants in Mauritius in the 18th and/or 19th centuries. The proportion of vowel-initial words in their total lexicons varies from 22.2% (Tamil) to 4.1% (Wolof) and averages 11%, a little more than the figure for MC (9.5%). Among the Swadesh nouns, the average falls to 6.5% compared with 0.0% in MC.

Table 7
Proportion of total lexicon and of nouns on the Swadesh lists with initial vowel

Language	Total lexicon	Swadesh lists nouns[33]
Bini/Edo[34]	54.5%	
Yoruba[35]	48%	
Akan (Fante)[36]	42%	
Igbo[37]	42%	
Fongbe[38]	23.6%	32.9%
Tamil	22.2%	8.6%
French[39]	21.2%	24.3%
St Lucian French Creole	15.5%	0.0%
Malagasy[40]	14.8%	15.7%
Haitian Creole	14.5%	4.3%
Seselwa	13%	0.0%*
Guyanais	11.0%	1.4%
(Indic) Hindustani[41]	11.2%	9.3%*
Mauritian Creole	9.5%	0.0%
Mandinka[42]	9.5%	0.0%
Réunionnais Creole	8.7[43]	0.0%*
Bantu (Makhuwa)	4.5%	0.0%
Wolof	4.1%	5.7%

---

[31] Albeit, more often for English- rather than French-based Creoles.
[32] It is, however, not the only cause. All these French Creoles also have some consonant-initial verbs which have lost the initial vowel of the French verb from which they derive.
[33] Asterisked figures are based on the 54 nouns in the 100 Swadesh list. All other figures are based on the 70 nouns in the 207 Swadesh list.
[34] Derived from Melzian (1937).
[35] Derived from Anon. (ca. 1950).
[36] Derived from Russell (1910).
[37] Derived from Echeruo (1998).
[38] Derived from Höftmann (2002). The Swadesh figure is based on 69 of the 70 nouns in that list.
[39] Derived from *Petit Robert*.
[40] Derived from Richardson (1885).
[41] Derived from Forbes (1859).
[42] Derived from Colley (1995).
[43] Result obtained by averaging the figures for Armand (1987; 8.8%) and Baggioni (1987; 8.6%)

With regard to Bantu languages, the figures in Table 7 are those for Makhuwa and only the basic forms of nouns are taken into account, i.e. class prefixes are ignored. Noun class prefixes in the relevant East African Bantu languages are mainly consonant-initial but, as mentioned above, a major noun class in Makhuwa has e- for singulars and i- for plurals. Thus, if noun class prefixes are considered to be the initial elements of nouns in Bantu languages, the proportion of vowel-initial words in Makhuwa in this table would be very much larger.

Overall, it is clear that French Creoles have a much larger proportion of consonant-initial words than French. Contributory factors in this are the absence of anything resembling a preposed definite article in many of the immigrants' languages and, in the Indian Ocean Creoles in particular, a much smaller proportion of vowel-initial nouns than in French. However, no alternative explanation to the Bantu hypothesis has emerged to explain the much greater proportion of syllabic agglutination in MC and Seselwa than in other French Creoles.

There is one additional factor which has not been mentioned so far. MC has fewer phonemic contrasts than Caribbean area French Creoles (five rather than seven oral vowels; lack of ʃ and ʒ). Thus there was a greater potential for agglutinated articles to maintain distinctions between nouns which would otherwise have become homophones in MC than in Haitian or St Lucian Creole. A few illustrate this:

/lafwa/ 'faith' (< Fr. *la foi*)   /lefwa/ 'liver' (< Fr. *le foie*)   /fwa/ 'time(s)' (< Fr.*fois*)
/latur/ 'tower' (< Fr. *la tour*)   /letur/ 'circuit' (< Fr. *le tour*)   /tur/ 'turn' [n] (<Fr. *tour*)

/lasãte/ 'health' (< Fr. *la santé*)   /sãte/ 'song' (< Fr. *chanter* [v.])
/laswa/ 'silk' (< Fr. *la soie*)   /swa/ 'choice' (< Fr. *choix*)
/lever/ 'worm' (< Fr. *le ver*)   /ver/ 'glass' (< Fr *verre*)
/lisu/ 'cabbage' (< Fr. *le chou*)   /su/ 'cent' (< Fr *sou*)
/diber/ 'butter' (< Fr. *du beurre*)   /ber/ 'cot' (< Fr. *ber*

The implication is that the population of Mauritius (unconsciously) found the contrasts provided by agglutination alone useful and retained them. If it could be demonstrated that any of the French Creoles of the Americas formerly had considerably more examples of syllabic agglutination than at present, this might provide an alternative to the hypothesis of Bantu influence. But no such evidence has yet emerged.

5. Summary and conclusions

In section 2, we showed that MC's share of the Creole features identified by Holm & Patrick (2007) was similar to that of Atlantic Creoles. We also demonstrated that this is not as surprising as MC's location in the Indian Ocean might suggest because several West African and Bantu languages were spoken there in the 18th century as well as in the territories where Atlantic Creoles arose. That said, there remain certain features which typify Atlantic Creoles to the exclusion of those located in the Indo-Pacific such as the serial use of verbs for 'give', 'say' and 'pass' with the meanings 'to, for', 'that', and 'more than'.

Section 3 is the most original part of our article but, for that reason, the methodology adopted requires considerable refinement. While there is now abundant evidence that Creole languages developed much more slowly than had once been thought, higher than expected scores for the West African languages which were best represented in Mauritius in the first half of the 18th century seems to suggest that many grammatical features became established rather early. But, as we acknowledge, our approach needs a great deal of further development before any firm conclusions can be drawn. In additional, there are undoubtedly more features to be added to those currently in Table 3.

In section 4, we have revisited article agglutination, a major characteristic of the French Creoles which is only found to a limited extent in Creoles based on other languages.[44] In view of the preliminary, tentative findings of section 3, we sought to examine possible alternatives to the hypothesis that such agglutination was due primarily to the influence of Bantu languages. While we found evidence indicating that the proportion of words in general, and basic nouns in particular, which have initial consonants is a good deal higher in most of the immigrant languages of Mauritius than in French, and while the utility of retaining agglutinated articles as a means of avoiding homophones was demonstrated, we nevertheless conclude that syllabic agglutination is as yet best accounted for by influence from Bantu languages. This is an unusual and subtle case of what Grant (2002) calls *transfer of pattern* (as opposed to *transfer of fabric*, which refers to the more straightforward borrowing of structural or lexical morphemes).

References

Annamalai, E & Steever, S 1998 Modern Tamil. Steever S B (ed.) *The Dravidian languages*, London: Routledge, 100-28.
Anon. [ca. 1950] *A dictionary of the Yoruba language*. Oxford: Oxford University Press.
Armand, Alain 1987 *Dictionnaire Kréol rénioné Français*. Réunion: Océan Editions.
Asher, R E 1985 *Tamil*. London: Croom Helm.
Baggioni, Daniel 1987 *Petit Dictionnaire Créole réunionnais / Français*. Réunion: Université de la Réunion.
Baker, Philip 1982a On the origins of the first Mauritians and of the Creole language of their descendants. Baker & Corne (eds.) 131-259.
—— 1982b the contribution of non-francophone immigrants to the lexicon of Mauritian Creole. PhD thesis, School of Oriental and African Studies, University of London.
—— 1984 Agglutinated French articles in Creole French: their evolutionary significance. *Te Reo* 27: 89-129.
—— 2001 No creolisation without prior pidginisation? *Te Reo* 44: 31-50.
—— 2003 Quelques cas de réanalyse et de grammaticalisation dans l'évolution du créole mauricien. Kriegel (ed.), 111-41.
—— 2007 Elements for a sociolinguistic history of Mauritius and its Creole. *This volume*.
Baker, Philip & Corne, Chris 1982 *Isle de France Creole: origins and affinities*. Ann Arbor: Karoma.
Baker Philip, Fon Sing, Guillaume & Hookoomsing, Vinesh Y 2007 The Corpus of Mauritian Creole texts. *This volume*, 1-62.
Baker Philip & Hookoomsing, Vinesh Y 1987 *Diskyoner kreol morisyen Dictionary of Mauritian Creole Dictionnaire du créole mauricien*. Paris: L'Harmattan.
Barthelemi G 1995 *Dictionnaire créole guyanais-français*. Matoury: Ibis Rouge.
Bollée, Annegret 2007 *Deux textes religieux de Bourbon du 18e siècle et l'histoire du créole réunionnais*. London: Battlebridge.
Bollée, Annegret (ed.) 1999, *see* St Jorre & Lionnet.
Cardona G R & Jain, D (eds). 2003 *The Indo-Aryan Languages*. London: Routledge / Curzon.
Chaudenson, Robert 1974 *Le lexique du parler créole de la Réunion*. Paris: Champion.
Colley, E 1995a *Mandinka grammar manual*. Washington: Peace Corps.
—— 1995b *Mandinka dictionary*. Washington: Peace Corps.
Crosbie, P, Frank, D, Leon, E & Samuel, D 2001 *Kwéyòl Dictionary*: Castries: Summer Institute of Linguistics/St Lucia Ministry of Education.
Dasgupta, P 2003 Bengali. Cardona G R & Jain, D (eds), 351-90.
Dem, S 1995a *Wolof grammar manual*. Washington: Peace Corps.

---

[44] Most notably, the Gulf of Guinea Portuguese Creoles; see Ladhams (2007).

―― 1995b *Wollof* [sic] - *English dictionary*. Washington: Peace Corps.
Echeruo, M J C 1998. *Igbo-English dictionary: a comprehensive dictionary of the Igbo language, with an English-Igbo index*. New Haven: Yale University Press.
Fal, A, Santos, R & Doneux, J-L 1990 *Dictionnaire wolof-français suivi d'un index français-wolof*. Paris: Karthala.
Fon Sing, Guillaume & Véronique, Daniel 2007 *Ena* et *gagne* : à propos de la genèse de l'expression de l'existence et de la possession / propriété en créole mauricien. *This volume*, 133-56.
Forbes, Duncan 1859 *A dictionary of the Hindustani language*. London: Wm H Allen & Co.
Grant, A P 1995a. *Agglutinated nominals in Creole French: synchronic and diachronic aspects*. Unpublished PhD dissertation, University of Bradford.
―― 1995b Article agglutination in Creole French: a wider perspective' in P. Baker (ed.) *From contact to creole and beyond*, 149-76. London: University of Westminster Press.
―― 2002. Fabric, pattern, shift and diffusion: What change in Oregon Penutian languages can tell historical linguists.' *Proceedings of the Meeting of the Hokan-Penutian Workshop, June 17-18, 2000, U. of California at Berkeley. Report 11, Survey of California and Other Indian Languages*, 33-56, Laura Buszard-Welcher, L (ed.). Dept of Linguistics, University of California at Berkeley.
Guillemin, D 2007 Definiteness and specificity in Mauritian Creole: A syntactic and semantic overview. *This volume*, 63-91.
Höftmann, H (with the help of M Ahohounkpanzon) 2002 *Dictionnaire fon-français*. Köln: Rüdiger Köppe.
Holm, John 2007 Creole typology and substrate typology. Paper presented at the Symposium on Language Contact and the Dynamics of Language Theory, 10-13 May 2007, Max-Planck Institute for Evolutionary Anthropology, Leipzig.
Holm, John & Patrick, Peter L 2007 *Comparative Creole Syntax*. London: Battlebridge.
Kisseberth C 2003 Makhuwa Nurse, D & Philippson, G (eds) *The Bantu languages*, London: Routledge / Curzon, 546-65.
Kriegel, Sibylle & Michaelis, Susanne 2007 Conjunction and ditransitives: Some functional domains covered by *avec, et,* and *ensemble. This volume*, 113-32.
Ladhams, John 2007 Article agglutination and the African contribution to the Portuguese-based Creoles. www.battlebridge.com/blackwhite/ladhams.pdf
Lefebvre, C & Brousseau, A-M 2002 *A grammar of Fongbe*. Berlin: Mouton de Gruyter.
Maples, C 1879 *Collections for a handbook of the Makua language*. London: Society for Promoting Christian Knowledge.
Melzian H 1937. *A concise dictionary of the Bini language of southern Nigeria*. London: Kegan Paul, Trench, Trübner & Co.
Mondesir, J (ed.) 1992 *Dictionary of St Lucian Creole*. The Hague: Mouton.
Perrot, J (ed.) 1981 *Les langues dans le monde ancient et moderne, vol I*. Paris: Editions du Centre National de recherché scientifique.
Petit Robert 2007 *Le nouveau Petit Robert: dictionnaire alphabetique et analogique de la langue française*. London: Collins.
Rasoloson, J N 1999 *Lehrbuch der madagassischen Sprache*. Hamburg: Buske.
―― 2000 *Sprachführer Madagassisch*. Hamburg: Helmut Buske.
Richardson, J [1885] 1967 *A new Malagasy-English dictionary*. Farnborough: Gregg.
Russell, J D 1910 *English-Fanti, Fanti-English dictionary*. London: Methodist Printing House.
Saint Jorre, Danielle de & Lionnet, Guy 1999 *Diksyonner kreol – franse. Dictionnaire créole seychellois – français*. Bamberg & Mahé: Impr. Difo-Druck (edited by Annégret Bollée).
Sauvageot S 1981 Le wolof. Perrot J (ed), 33-53.
Schmidt, R L 2003a Hindi. Cardona & Jain (eds), 250-85.
―― 2003b Urdu. Cardona & Jain (eds), 286-350.
Stein, Peter 2007 L'absence de marqueurs préverbaux et les fonctions du marqueurs zéro. *This volume*, 157-72.

Strandquist, Rachel Eva 2005 Article incorporation in Mauritian Creole. Department of Linguistics, University of Victoria: MA.

Syea, Anand 2007 The development of the noun phrase in Mauritian Creole and the mechanisms of language development. *This volume*, 93-112.

Targète, J & Urciolo, R G 1993 *Haitian Creole-English dictionary.* Wheaton, Maryland: Dunwoody Press.

Tersis, N 1981 Le bambara. Perrot (ed), 75-83.

Victor, C J 2004 *Tamil-English dictionary and phrasebook, romanized.* New York: Hippocrene.

APPENDIX A. The pidgin features examined in Baker (2001: 38-41), renumbered consecutively

1. Gender: nouns are undivided into masculine and feminine or broadly comparable categories.
2. Adjectives invariant for gender.
3. Verbs invariant for gender.
4. Definite articles inherently marked in the source language for gender no longer serve as articles.
5. No gender distinction in pronouns.
6. Major word classes are unmarked for number (which can only be determined by context or use of quantifiers).
7. Pronouns which can be either singular or plural in the source language are exclusively singular in the pidgin.
8. Tense, modality and aspect are expressed by independent ('free') morphemes.
9. Major word classes lack case inflection.
10. Where subject and object distinctions are represented in pronouns in the source language, only the form used in pointing to the person or persons is found in the pidgin.
11. Zero copula in declarative equative sentences.
12. Zero copula in declarative locative sentences.
13. The definite article in the source language is replaced by the demonstrative in the latter.
14. If the source language distinguishes between an indefinite article and the numeral 'one', the latter is adopted as the indefinite article in the pidgin.
15. If the usual adjectival quantifier in the source language does not mean 'a large quantity' then it is replaced by a term meaning the latter.
16. Negator can only occur predicate-initially.
17. Monomorphemic interrogatives are replaced by bimorphemic forms with literal meanings as follows: "who" = "what/which person/body"?
18. "What" = "what/which thing".
19. "Where" = "which/what side/place/part".
20. "When" = "which/what hour/time".
21. "how" = "which/what manner/way".
22. "why" = "what make/cause".
23. Absence of the most basic locative preposition in the source language as an independent morpheme.
24. Absence of the most basic genitive preposition in the source language as an independent morpheme.

Philip Baker worked in Mauritius for MBC TV and L'Express newspaper 1965-67 but the interest in MC which this aroused led him to study linguistics formally and many publications have resulted. He is currently Professor of Linguistics at the University of Westminster, <phildbaker@yahoo.co.uk>.

Anthony Grant is Reader in Historical Linguistics and Language Contact at Edge Hill University. Pidgins and Creoles, Romani, Native American and Austronesian languages are his special interests. He conducted fieldwork on Mauritian Creole in 1992-4 for his PhD thesis. <granta@edgehill.ac.uk>

La concordance

Guillaume Fon Sing

1. Constitution du corpus et méthodologie

Comme nous l'expliquons en début d'ouvrage, le corpus regroupe une soixantaine de textes anciens en créole, écrits entre 1721 (date du début de la colonisation française à Maurice) et 1929. Cet ensemble comprend entre autres des extraits de récits de voyage, des témoignages de procès judiciaires, des contes, des poèmes, des proverbes, des devinettes ritualisées (sirandanes), des chansons, des annonces de journaux (*Le Mauricien, Le Cernéen, L'Albion, L'Essor*, etc.). Contrairement à d'autres territoires, la grande majorité des textes ont été écrits par des locaux qui auraient acquis le créole dans leur enfance, que cette langue fut ou non celle qu'ils utilisaient pour s'adresser à leurs parents. En enlevant les caractères numéraux et les éléments de ponctuation, l'ensemble du corpus totalise en tout 99209 occurrences/mots.

Ci-après la liste des dix mots les plus fréquents du corpus de textes anciens comparée aux dix mots les plus fréquents en français et en anglais.

	Mots les plus fréquents du corpus créole	Mots les plus fréquents en français[1]	Mots les plus fréquents en anglais[2]
1	li	le (déterminant)	the
2	qui	de	be
3	mo	un	of
4	ça	être	and
5	dans	et	a
6	pour	à	in
7	là	il	to (marqueur de l'infinitif)
8	so	avoir	have
9	va	ne	it
10	éne	je	to (préposition)

La concordance que nous avons effectuée pour ce projet est un travail philologique qui n'a jamais été réalisé auparavant dans le domaine de la créolistique. Cette oeuvre, dont la nomenclature a été obtenue à l'aide du logiciel *Lexico 3*[3], fournit l'ensemble des mots de notre corpus de textes anciens en créole mauricien, leurs étymons, leurs différentes graphies attestées ainsi que le nombre d'occurrences de ces dernières.

---

[1] Source : http:eduscol.education.fr/D0102/liste-mots-frequents.htm.
[2] Source : Parkvall (2006: 170).
[3] Réalisé par l'équipe universitaire SYLED-CLA2T de Paris 3 :
  http:www.cavi.univ-paris3.fr/Ilpga/tal/lexicoWWW/lexico3.htm

A plus long terme, la suite de ce projet sur lequel nous travaillons consistera à éditer un concordancier informatique qui fournira pour chaque occurrence l'ensemble précis de ses contextes[4].

2. Règles de présentation

La description linguistique des textes nous semblant prioritaire sur un usage pédagogique contingent, nous n'avons pas procédé à la normalisation du corpus et conservé la transcription originelle des mots selon les auteurs. Notons cependant que lorsque les textes publiés présentaient visiblement des erreurs d'impression, nous les avons corrigées dans le corpus mais la graphie d'origine a été conservée dans les textes publiés dans ce volume.

Les mots sont rangés dans l'ordre alphabétique et les principales règles peuvent être résumées ainsi :

- les formes créoles sont en lettres *minuscules italiques* ;
- les étymons français sont en lettres CAPITALES ;
- les étymons non-français sont en lettres **CAPITALES GRASSES** et leur origine est indiquée à la suite entre crochets ;
- les formes créoles proprement créées (ou construites[5]) sont en ***CAPITALES GRASSES ITALIQUES***. Par exemple, le morphème -er du français « -eur » est noté ***+ER***
 Ex : *bagoutère* v BAGOU(T)***+ER*** ;

Concernant l'étymologie, il est important que nous soyons clairs sur plusieurs points. Notre concordance n'est AUCUNEMENT un dictionnaire étymologique. Tous les lecteurs qui souhaitent en savoir plus sur l'origine des mots du corpus devraient, en premier lieu, consulter Bollée (1993-2007). Cet important ouvrage non seulement réunit les informations recueillies par les publications de référence de ceux qui se sont spécialisés dans l'étude des créoles de l'Océan indien (incluant Chaudenson 1974, Baker & Hookoomsing 1987, St Jorre & Lionnet 1999, etc.), mais l'auteur elle-même y a apporté les fruits de sa propre recherche menée sur plusieurs années.

Pour les mots d'origine française (au sens large), la forme donnée en CAPITALES est généralement le mot correspondant en français standard car nous croyons que cela est plus commode pour les lecteurs, même si parfois une forme dialectale légèrement différente s'avère être la source immédiate. Lorsqu'il n'y a pas de forme standard correspondante, ou lorsque la forme dialectale est très différente de la forme standard, les mots dialectaux sont donnés en capitales.

Pour les mots d'origine non-française, il y a souvent plus d'un étymon possible. Nous n'avons pas de place ou d'inclination pour discuter de ces cas problématiques ici et nous avons simplement indiqué l'étymon que nous considérons comme le plus important ou le plus probable. (Dans les cas controversés ou particulièrement douteux, un astérisque précède l'étymon.) Pour plus d'information, nous renvoyons une nouvelle fois les lecteurs à Bollée (1993-2007).

---

[4] Voir Fon Sing (2006).
[5] Voir la théorie constructiviste de Baker (2001).

En ce qui concerne les formes créoles proprement créées, nous souhaitons mettre l'accent sur le fait que les mots identifiés ainsi sont ceux que nous considérons comme étant plus probablement des mots forgés localement que des mots d'origine dialectale, mais il n'y a pas, et ne peut y avoir, de distinction claire et nette entre ces deux possibilités.

Pour toutes épellations créoles, qu'elles diffèrent ou non de leur étymon, il y a une référence à l'étymon ;

- à droite de chaque étymon, le nombre total d'occurrences est donné. S'il y a deux ou plus de deux épellations attestées en créole, ces épellations sont données entre parenthèses avec le nombre d'attestations de chacune d'elles. Voir par ex : FAIBLE, FAIRE, etc. ;

- l'agglutination de mots a été prise en compte et nous l'avons rendue visible en la marquant avec le symbole + dans l'étymon.
    Ex :   PETIT+FILLE (*pti fi, pti fiye, ptit fill', ptit fille, p'tit fille, ptitfille*)
           PETIT+GUIGNE (*piti guine, pitiguine, pti guine*)
           GRAND+MATIN (*gran matein, grand matin, grands matins*) ;

- le + en initiale d'étymon signale l'agglutination d'un déterminant (l', la, le, les, du, etc.) ou d'une partie phonique du déterminant qui s'est liée ([n] de un, [z] de les ou des, etc.).
    Ex :   +ÂME (*l'âme, nâme, etc.*)
           +HOMME (*l'hom, lé zom, zhom, etc.*)
           +RIZ (*di-riz, douriz, du riz, etc.*) ;

Cette convention, proposée par Baker, possède l'important avantage de réunir ensemble alphabétiquement les formes agglutinées et non-agglutinées dérivant du même nom français.
    Ex :   NUIT (*nouit, nouite, nuit, etc.*)
           +NUIT (*la nouite, lanouit, la nuit, etc.*)

- lorsqu'il y a plusieurs épellations qui pourraient dériver de plus d'un étymon, nous avons vérifié toutes ces occurrences présentes dans les textes afin d'enlever toute ambiguïté. Par exemple, '*fer*' réfère aussi bien FER qu'à FAIRE. '*famé*' est AFFAMÉ ou FAMEUX. '*ferm*' est le nom FERME ou le verbe FERMER ;

- lorsque l'auteur a orthographiquement joint deux mots en les attachant ou en les liant par un tiret, nous l'avons marqué par une virgule.
    Ex :   *aubout, auboute* v AU, BOUT
           antan v EN, TANT
           boidebène v BOIS, +ÉBENNE
           laffe-laboue v **LÁFA,** +BOUE

Liste des abréviations utilisées

[adj] : adjectif
[adv] : adverbe
[angl.] : anglais
[anglo-ind.] : anglo-indien
[ar.] : arabe
[bant.] : bantou
[bret.] : breton
[chin.] : chinois
[dial.] : dialectal
[esp.] : espagnol
[fr. dial.] : français dialectal
[hind.] : hindoustani
[indo-port.] : indo-portugais
[interj.] : interjection
[mak.] : makua (makhuwa)
[malg.] : malgache
[n] : nom
[neg] : négation
[onomat.] : onomatopée
[port.] : portugais
[prép] : préposition
[tam.] : tamoul
[v] : verbe
v : voir

Références

Baker, Philip 2001 Theories of creolization and the degree and nature of restructuring. Neumann-Holzschuh, Ingrid & Schneider, Edgar W (éds), *Degrees of Restructuring in Creole Languages*, 41-63.

Baker, Philip & Hookoomsing, Vinesh Y 1987 *Diksyoner kreol morisyen, Dictionary of Mauritian Creole. Dictionnaire du créole mauricien*. Paris : L'Harmattan.

Bollée, Annegret 1993-2007 *Dictionnaire étymologique des créoles français de l'Océan Indien. Première partie. Mots d'origine française. Deuxième partie. Mots d'origine non-française ou inconnue.* Hamburg: Buske, 4 vols.

Chaudenson, Robert 1974 *Le lexique du parler créole de La Réunion*. Paris : Champion.

Fon Sing, Guillaume 2006 Naviguer dans les textes anciens mauriciens : présentation d'un concordancier à usage scientifique et pédagogique. *Etudes Créoles,* vol. XXVIII, n°1, 2006 : 191-207.

Parkvall, Mikael 2006 *Limits of Language. Almost everything you didn't know you didn't know about language and languages.* London : Battlebridge.

St Jorre, Danièle de & Lionnet, Guy 1999 *Diksyonner kreol – franse. Dictionnaire créole seychellois – français*. Bamberg & Mahé: Impr. Difo-Druck (édité par Annegret Bollée).

Guillaume Fon Sing est actuellement Attaché Temporaire d'Enseignement et de Recherche (ATER) à l'Université de la Sorbonne Nouvelle (Paris 3). Il achève sa thèse de doctorat sur les créoles français et enseigne la linguistique française, <gfonsing@yahoo.fr>.

A

a_1 v VA$_1$
$a_2, à_1$ v À
$à_2$ v VA$_1$
À 6 (a_2 2, $à_1$ 4)
abandonne v ABANDONNER
ABANDONNER
　　1 (*abandonne*)
ab beh v AH+BIEN
+ABBÉ 5 (*l'abbé* 4, *z'abé* 1)
abé v AH+BIEN
ABÓBORA 11 (*bobre*)
　　[mot port.]
+ABOMINATION
　　1 (*l'abominacion*)
à bou v À+BOUT
À+BOUT 1 (*à bou*)
à bord v À+BORD
À+BORD 3
　　(*à bord* 2, *à-bord* 1)
à-bord v À+BORD
aborde v ABORDER
ABORDER 1 (*aborde*)
+ABSINTHE 3 (*l'absinthe*)
ac v AVEC
a çaqu' instant
　　v À+CHAQUE+INSTANT
À+CAUSE 80 (*a cause* 5,
　　acause 3, *à cause* 25,
　　àcause 2, *a cauz'* 4,
　　à cauz', 3, *à cauze* 1,
　　a cose 1, *acôse* 3, *àcôse* 2,
　　a coz 9, *à coz* 8, *a coze* 1,
　　acoz 13)
*a cause, à cause, acause,
àcause, a cauz', à cauz',
à cauze* v À+CAUSE
accepté v ACCEPTER
ACCEPTER 2 (*accepté*)
accompli v ACCOMPLIR
ACCOMPLIR 2 (*accompli*)
accord v ACCORDER
ACCORDER 1 (*accord*)
accouce, accoucé
　　v ACCOUCHER
ACCOUCHER 9 (*accouce* 5,
　　accoucé 4)
accuz v ACCUSER
ACCUSER 2 (*accuz*)
*acete, acéte, acète, aceté, acété,
aceter, acetez* v ACHETER

À+CETTE+HEURE(+LÀ) 155
　　(*à c't'heire* 3, *a c't'hère* 3,
　　à c't'hère 2, *à c't-heire* 1,
　　a s'ter 1, *à s'ter* 3, *à s'tér*
　　4, *a s'tèr* 1, *à s'tèr* 6,
　　à s'tère 1, *a s'ter-la* 1,
　　à s'ter-la 1, *à s'ter-là* 1,
　　à s'tér-là 1, *à s'tèr-là* 1,
　　a'ce terre 1, *a'sterè-la* 1,
　　a'sterè-là 1, *à ster* 6, *à
stér* 2, *a ster* 1, *a ster-là* 1,
　　à ster-là 1, *à stèr-là* 2,
　　ac'te hère 1, *acthére* 4,
　　açthére 3, *àçthéra* 3,
　　açthère 8, *a-s'ter* 2,
　　à-s'tèr 1, *aster* 44,
　　astèr 5, *aster'* 1, *astère* 1,
　　asterla 4, *asterlà* 2,
　　astheire 8, *asthére* 4,
　　asthère 3, *astore* 15)
À+CHAQUE+INSTANT
　　1 (*a çaqu' instant*)
acheté v ACHETER
ACHETER 48 (*acete* 1,
　　acéte 6, *acète* 11,
　　aceté 16, *acété* 2,
　　aceter 1, *acetez* 1, *acheté*
　　3, *achetté* 1, *asseté* 1,
　　asseté 1, *asséter* 1, ***asté* 3**)
achetté v ACHETER
à confesse v À+CONFESSE
À+CONFESSE 1 (*à confesse*)
a cose, acôse, àcôse
　　v À+CAUSE
*à côt, à cot', à côt', a cote,
à cote, a côte, à côte, a coté,
a côté, à côté, acot, acôt, acot',
acote, àcote, acôte, àcôte,* **âcôte**
　　v À+CÔTÉ
À+CÔTÉ 179 (*à côt* 1,
　　à cot' 1, *a côt'* 4, *a **cote** 8*,
　　à cote 19, *a côte* 4,
　　à côte 46, *a coté* 1,
　　a côté 2, *à côté* 10,
　　a cotte 1, *acot* 59, *acôt* 1,
　　acot' 1, *acote* 13, **àcote 9**,
　　acôte 2, *àcôte* 5, **âcôte 1**)
a cotte v À+CÔTÉ
a coup d'pieds
　　v À+COUP+DE+PIED
À+COUP+DE+PIED
　　4 (*a coup d'pieds*)

*a coup d'poings,
a coup de poings*
　　v À+COUP+DE+ POING
À+COUP+DE+POING
　　2 (*a coup d'poings* 1,
　　a coup de poings 1)
acout, acoute, acouté
　　v ÉCOUTER
ACQUITTER 1 (*akitté*)
*acthére, açthére, àçthére,
açthère, à c't'heire, a c't'hère,
à c't'hère, a c't'hère, à c't-
heire, ac'te hère* v À+CETTE+
　　HEURE(+LÀ)
ACTION 1 (*akcion*)
a coz, à coz, a coze, acoz
　　v À+CAUSE
Adam v ADAM
ADAM 1 (*Adam*) [nom de
　　personnage]
+ADDITION 1 (*ladition*)
adié v ADIEU
ADIEU 1 (*adié*)
adilter v ADULTÈRE
ador, adoré, adorée
　　v ADORER
ADORER 13 (*ador* 8, *adoré* 2,
　　adorée 2, *dor* 1)
Adrien v ADRIEN
ADRIEN 1 (*Adrien*) [prénom]
à droite v À+DROITE
À+DROITE 1 (*à droite*)
ADULTÈRE 10 (*adilter*)
+AFFAIRE 84 (*za fère* 2,
　　zafère 7, *zafère* 1, *zaffair* 10,
　　zaffair' 1, *zaffaire* 50,
　　z'affaire 5, *zaffaires* 4,
　　zaffairs 2, *zaffer* 2)
affranchi v AFFRANCHI
AFFRANCHI 1 (*affranchi*)
affreise v AFFREUX
AFFREUX 1 (*affreise*)
AFFÛTER 1 (*fitter*)
afin v AFIN
AFIN 1 (*afin*)
*à fôce, a forç', a force, à force,
aforce, àforce, afôrce*
　　v À+FORCE
À+FORCE 65 (*à fôce* 1, *a forç'*
　　2, *a force* 13, *à force* 25,
　　a fors 4, *à fors* 1, *aforce*
　　4, *àforce* 4, *afôrce* 1)

a fors, *à fors* v À+FORCE
+AFFRONT 1 (*zaffront*)
africain v AFRICAIN
AFRICAIN 3 (*africain*)
+AFRICAIN 1 (*l'africain*)
agace v AGACER
AGACER 2 (*agace*)
à gauce v À+GAUCHE
À+GAUCHE 3 (*à gauce* 2, *à gosse* 1)
+ÂGE 13 (*l'aze* 4, *laze* 1, *lâze* 8)
À+GENOUX 4 (*à zénoux* 1, *a zounou* 1, *à zounoux* 2, *azounou* 4)
agile v AGILE
AGILE 2 (*agile* 1, *azile* 1)
à gosse v À+GAUCHE
à-goussêt v À+GOUSSET
À+GOUSSET 1 (*à-goussêt*)
ah v AH
AH+BIEN (*ab beh* 1, *abé* 39, *ah-bin* 1)
AH 118 (*ah* 117)
ah-bin v AH+BIEN
AH+VOILÀ 396 (*ala* 1,*a la* 1, *alà* 23, *arla* 44,[6] *a vela* 1, *avelas* 1, *a v'la* 4, *à v'la* 4, *a v'là* 6, *à v'là* 1, *a vla* 3, *a vlà* 2, *a'vlà* 1, *av'la*6, *a-v'la* 3, *av'là* 2, *a-v'là* 2, *avla* 117, *avlà* 173, *a-vlà* 1)
aïa v AÏA
AÏA 2 (*aïa*) [interj.]
aid v AIDER
aide v AIDER
aidée v AIDER
AIDER 10 (*aid* 1, *aide* 1, *aidée* 4, *éd* 1, *ide* 3)
+AIGLE 1 (*zégl*)
AIGUILLE 3 (*gouïe* 2, *gouïes* 1)
+AIGUILLE 6 (*zégouie* 1, *zaigouïes* 1, *zégouïes* 3, *zégui*₁1)
+AILE 22 (*lé zaile* 1, *lézaile* 4, *lé-zaile* 1, *lézailes* 15, *lézél* 1)
AIMABLE 1 (*aimables*)
+AIMABLE 1 (*l'aimable*)

aimables v AIMABLE
aimé v AIMER
AIMER 1 (*aimé*)
ainsi v AINSI
AINSI 5 (*ainsi*)
aio, aïo, aïoh v **AYO**
air v AIR
AIR 3 (*air*)
+AIR 26 (*l'air* 14, *lair* 22)
aise v AISE
AISE 4 (*aise*)
AJOUTER 3 (*azout* 1, *azoute* 1, *azouté* 1)
ajourd'hui , ajourdhi
v AUJOURD'HUI
akcion v ACTION
akitté v ACQUITTER
al, al' v ALLER
a la, ala, alà v AH+VOILÀ
albatr v ALBÂTRE
ALBÂTRE 1 (*albatr*)
Albert v ALBERT
ALBERT 1 (*Albert*) [prénom]
à l'entour v À+L'ENTOUR
À+L'ENTOUR 1 (*à l'entour*)
a la fein, a la fin , à la fin
v À+LA+FIN
À+LA+FIN 11 (*a la fein* 1, *a la fin* 5, *à la fin* 5)
à la fois v À+LA+FOIS
À+LA+FOIS 5 (*à la fois*)
à la hât v À+LA+HÂTE
À+LA+HÂTE 1 (*à la hât*)
a la Quaisin
v À+LA+QUAISIN
À+LA+QUAISIN 1 (*a la Quaisin*)
à l'infini v À+L'INFINI
À+L'INFINI 1 (*à l'infini*)
all, all', allait, alle , allé , allè , allée, allent, aller v ALLER
ALLER 569 (*al* 100, *al'* 1, *all* 1, *all'* 12, *allait* 1, *alle* 188, *allé* 230, *allè* 1, *allée* 3, *allent* 1, *aller* 4, *alles* 1, *allez* 6, *allons* 20)
allelouya v ALLELUIA
ALLELUIA 1 (*allelouya*)
allez v ALLER
alliance v ALLIANCE
ALLIANCE 2 (*alliance*)
+ALLIANCE 1 (*l'allians*)

allim, allime, allimé
v ALLUMER
ALLONGER 16 (*alonze* 2, *alonzé* 2, *allonze* 9, *allonzé* 2, *lonzé* 1)
allons v ALLER
allonze, allonzé
v ALLONGER
ALLUMER 14 (*allim* 3, *allime* 11, *allimé* 6)
+ALLUMETTE 1 (*zallimettes*)
+ALOËS 1 (*l'aloi*)
alonze, alonzé v ALLONGER
alor, alors v ALORS
ALORS 32 (*alor* 8, *alors* 20, *alorse* 3, *alorsse* 1)
alorse, alorsse v ALORS
alphan, alphant v ÉLÉPHANT
+AMANDE 1 (*zamandes*)
amar, amar', amare, amarr', amarre, amarré v AMARRER
AMARGOSO 9 (*margause* 1, *margauze* 1, *margose* 1, *margoz* 1, *margoze* 5) [mot port.]
AMARRER 51 (*amar* 3, *amar'* 3, *amare* 7, *amarr'* 2, *amarre* 32, *amarré* 4)
amas v AMAS
AMAS 3 (*amas*)
+AMBITION 4 (*l'ambition*)
AMBÉRIVÁTRY 3 (*barvades* 1, *barvat* 1, *barvatte* 1)[mot malg.(betsileo)]
+AMBERIVATRY
1 (*zambrevatte*)
ambras, ambrassé
v EMBRASSER
âme v ÂME
ÂME 1 (*âme* 1,)
+ÂME 40 (*l'am* 2, *l'àme* 1, *l'âme* 1, *nam* 4, *nâm* 4, *nâm'* 2, *name* 10, *nàme* 1, *nâme* 14, *nâmes* 1)
à même temps
v EN+MÊME+TEMPS
amen v AMEN
AMEN 2 (*amen*)
amene, améne, amène, améné, amêné, améné
v AMENER/EMMENER

---

[6] v p 35.

AMENER/EMMENER 122
  (*amene* 2, *améne* 32,
  amène 78, *améné* 2,
  amèné 1, *aménée* 2,
  emmen' 1, *emmèn'* 1,
  emmène 1, *enméné* 1,
  méné 1)
amer   v AMER
AMER   7 (*amer* 4, *amère* 3)
Amère   v AMER
À+MESURE 3 (*a misire* 1,
  à misire 2)
+AMI   35 (*zami* 28, *z'ami* 1,
  zamis 6, *zamie* 2, *zamies*
  1) v aussi MON+AMI
à minoui v À+MINUIT
À+MINUIT 1 (*à minoui*)
+AMIRAL 3 (*zamiral*)
amise, amisé, amisez
            v AMUSER
a misire, à misire
            v À+MESURE
+AMITIÉ 3 (*l'amitié* 2,
  z'amitié 1)
amizé   v AMUSER
a moein v À+MOINS
a moi   v À+MOI
À+MOI 5 (*a moi* 3, *à mouan* 2)
a moins v À+MOINS
À+MOINS 2 (*a moein* 1,
  a moins 1)
à mor, à mort v À+MORT
À+MORT 2 (*à mor* 1, *à mort* 1)
à mouan v À+MOI
+AMOUR 18 (*l'amour*)
amouré   v AMOUREUX
AMOUREUX 1 (*amouré*)
+AMOUREUX 1 (*zamoureix*)
ampéce   v EMPÊCHER
amporté   v EMPORTER
ampreint v EMPRUNTER
AMUSER 14 (*amise* 3, *amisé* 9,
  amisez 1, *amizé* 1)
+AMUSEMENT 1 (*l'amiz'ment*)
an$_1$ v UN
an$_2$ v AN
an$_3$ v EN
AN   8 (*an$_2$* 3, *ans* 5)
+AN   1 (*l'an*)
+ANANAS   1 (*zanana*)
an ba, anba v EN+BAS
anceint v ENCEINTE

+ANCÊTRE 1 (*zancétr*)
anciein, ancien v ANCIEN
ANCIEN   3 (*anciein* 1,
  ancien 2)
+ANCIEN 13 (*l'anciein* 2,
  lé zanciein 2, *zanciein* 9,
  zanciens 4)
ancor   v ENCORE
+ANCRE 5 (*l'ancre*)
andan   v EN+DEDANS
andéhor v EN, DEHORS
Anderson v ANDERSON
ANDERSON 1 (*Anderson*)
  [nom de famille]
+ANDOUILLE 1 (*z'andouille*)
androit v ENDROIT
+ANETH 1 (*l'anet*)
anfoncé v ENFONCER
angaz   v ENGAGER
ANGE   24 (*anges* 5, *anz* 19)
+ANGE   2 (*zanges*)
anges   v ANGE
anglais v ANGLAIS
ANGLAIS 35 (*anglais* 24,
  anglé 10, *anglés* 1)
+ANGLAIS 8 (*zanglais* 5,
  z'anglais 2, *zanglé* 1)
anglé, anglés v ANGLAIS
Anglétère, Angleterre
            v ANGLETERRE
ANGLETERRE 4 (*Anglétère* 1,
  Angleterre 2, *Angliterre* 1)
+ANGLETERRE
  1 (*l'angleterre*)
angliterre v ANGLETERRE
anguïes, anguille v ANGUILLE
ANGUILLE 3 (*anguïes* 1,
  anguille 2, *anguy* 1)
+ANGUILLE 2 (*zangui* 1,
  zanguïe 1)
anguy   v ANGUILLE
+ANIMAUX 32 (*zanimau* 3,
  z'animau 1, *zanimaux* 27,
  zanimo 1)
anlev, anlév. anlévé
            v ENLEVER
année   v ANNÉE
ANNÉE   1 (*année*)
+ANNÉE 4 (*l'anné* 2,
  l'année 2, *nané* 1,
  nanné 2, *nannées* 1)

annonce, annoncé, annoncée
            v ANNONCER
ANNONCER 11 (*annonce* 1,
  annoncé 7, *annoncée* 1,
  anoncé 2)
ano   v À+NOUS
ânon   v ÂNON
ÂNON   1 (*ânon*)
anoncé   v ANNONCER
anons, a nous, à nous. anous
            v À+NOUS
À+NOUS 38 (*ano* 3, *anons* 29,
  a nous 2, *à nous* 2,
  anous 2)
an péne v EN+PEINE
ans   v AN
ansam, ansamb v ENSEMBLE
antan   v EN, TANT
anter   v ENTERRER
Antoine v ANTOINE
ANTOINE 1 (*Antoine*)
antour   v ENTOURER
antr$_1$ v ENTRE
antr$_2$, antre v ENTRER
anvé   v ENVIER
anvelop v ENVELOPPE
an verté v EN+VÉRITÉ
anvi   v ENVIE
anvoy, anvoye, anvoyé
            v ENVOYER
anz   v ANGE
aouah   1 [interj.]
APAISER 1 (*apéz*)
à part   v À+PART
À+PART 1 (*à part*)
a pein', à peine v À+PEINE
À+PEINE 2 (*a pein'* 1, *à peine* 1)
*apel, apele, apéle, apélé, apelle,
  apélle* v APPELER
a pé   v APRÈS
a pendant v À+PENDANT
À+PENDANT 1 (*a pendant*)
à pé pré, apépré, à pé-près
            v À+PEU+PRÈS
apercevoar v APERCEVOIR
APERCEVOIR 1 (*apercevoar*)
À+PEU+PRÈS 2 (*à pé pré* 1,
  à pé-près 1, *apépré* 2)
apéz   v APAISER
à pic   v À+PIC
À+PIC   1 (*à pic*)
a pié   v À+PIED

À+PIED   1 (*a pié*)
aplati   v APLATIR
APLATIR 1 (*aplati*)
aporte   v APPORTER
apotr   v APÔTRE
APÔTRE   1 (*apotr*)
appel, appel', appele, appéle,
appèle, appelé, appélé, appell',
appelle, appellé, appellés
   v APPELER
(AP)PARÂITRE 13 (*paraîte* 1,
   paraître 1, *parét* 11)
+APPARENCE 3 (*l'apparence*
   1, *l'apparans* 2)
+APPEL   2 (*l'appel*)
APPELER 196 (*apel* 2, *apele* 1,
   apéle 7, *apélé* 4, *apelle* 2,
   apélle 1, *appel* 51,
   appel' 3, *appele* 1,
   appéle 4, *appèle* 2,
   appelé 11, *appélé* 6,
   appell' 8, *appelle* 74,
   appellé 9, *appellés* 1,
   péle 2, *pèle* 2, *pelle* 5)
appiye, appiyé v APPUYER
apport, apport', apporte
   v APPORTER
APPORTER 15 (*aporte* 1,
   apport 7, *apport'* 2,
   apporte 5)
APPUYER 6 (*appiye* 4,
   appiyé 2)
apprand, apprende, apprendre
   v APPRENDRE
APPRENDRE 6 (*apprand* 3,
   apprende 1, *apprendre* 2)
+APPRENTIS 7 (*zapprenti* 1,
   zapprentis 6)
appresant, appresent, appresént
   v À+PRÉSENT
approçant v APPROCHANT
approce, approcé
   v APPROCHER
APPROCHANT 5
   (*approçant* 4, *aproçant* 1)
APPROCHER 12 (*approce* 9,
   approcé 3)
a pré, apré, aprè, apres, aprés,
après   v APRÈS
APRÈS   296 (*apé* 1,
   apré 112, *a pré* 1, *aprè* 1,
   apres 3, *aprés* 16,

   après 162)
aprésant, à present, a présent,
à présent   v À+PRÉSENT
À+PRÉSENT 64 (*à present* 1, *a*
   présent 22, *à présent* 27,
   a prézan 4, *aprésant* 1,
   appresent 1, *apprésent* 1,
   aprésant 3, *aprézan* 4)
a prézan, aprézan
   v À+PRÉSENT
aproçant v APPROCHER
arabe   v ARABE
ARABE   1 (*arabe*)
+ARAIGNÉE   20 (*zairignée* 1,
   zéreigné 1, *zergnée* 18)
aranze   v ARRANGER
+'ARAQ   4 (*l'arack* 2, *larac* 2)
   [mot ar.]
+ARBRE   25 (*zarb* 3, *zarbe* 7,
   zarbes 10, *zarbre* 1,
   zarbres 4)
+ARC-EN-CIEL
   1 (*l'arc-en-ciel*)
+ARCHE   1 (*l'arsh*)
are   v AVEC
à rebours   v À+REBOURS
À+REBOURS 1 (*à rebours*)
aréte, arête, arété
   v ARRETER
+ARGAMASSA 3
   (*largamasse*) [mot port.]
+ARGENT 94 (*l'argent* 21,
   l'arzan 17, *larzan* 3,
   l'arzen 1, *l'arzent* 25,
   larzent 27)
Argovie   v ARGOVIE
ARGOVIE 1 (*Argovie*)
   [toponyme]
à rien   v N'A+RIEN
arive, arivé   v ARRIVER
arla   v AH+VOILÀ
+ARME   1 (*zarmes*)
armasse   v RAMASSER
+ARMOIRE 5 (*l'armoire* 2,
   larmoire 1, *larmoires* 1,
   lormoire 1)
arose   v ARROSER
arqilé, arquilé, arquiler,
arquillé   v RECULER
arraç', arrace, arracé
   v ARRACHER

ARRACHER 16 (*arraç'* 1,
   arrace 10, *arracé* 1,
   race₂ 2, *racé* 2)
arrange, arrangé
   v ARRANGER
+ARRANGEMENT
   1 (*l'aranz'mens*)
ARRANGER 50 (*aranze* 3,
   arrange 1, *arrangé* 1,
   arranz 7, *arranze* 28,
   arranzé 6, *ranze* 1,
   ranzé 3)
arranz, arranze, arranzé
   v ARRANGER
arrêt', arréte, arrète, arrête,
arreté, arrété, arrêté, arrêtée
   v ARRÊTER
ARRÊTER 48 (*aréte* 2, *arête* 2,
   arété 1, *arrêt'* 2, *arréte* 3,
   arrète 1, *arrête* 20,
   arreté 1, *arrété* 7,
   arrêté 8, *arrêtée* 1)
arriv, arriv', arrive, arrivé
arrivée, arriver v ARRIVER
ARRIVER 187 (*arive* 6,
   arivé 1, *arriv* 17, *arriv'* 2,
   arrive 99, *arrivé* 59,
   arrivée 2, *arriver* 1)
ARROSER 1 (*arose*)
+ARROSOIR 1 (*larrosoir*)
a-s'ter   v
   À+CETTE+HEURE(+LÀ)
à-s'tèr   v
   À+CETTE+HEURE(+LÀ)
asamb, asambe, asembe
   v ENSEMBLE
asez   v ASSEZ
a soar, à soar, a soir, à soir,
asoir, a-soir, àsoir, à-soir
   v À+SOIR
À+SOIR 71 (*a soar* 5, *à soar* 2,
   a soir 21, *à soir* 25,
   asoir 9, *asoirs* 1, *a-soir* 1,
   àsoir 6, *à-soir* 2)
asper, aspére, aspère, aspéré
   v ESPÉRER
assamb, assamb', assambe,
assame   v ENSEMBLE
+ASSASSIN 1 (*zassasein*)
ASSASSINER 1 (*sazinée* 1)
assé   v ASSEZ
assembe   v ENSEMBLE

224

assemblé v ASSEMBLER
ASSEMBLER 1 (*assemblé*)
asseté, assété , asséter
　　　　v ACHETER
assez v ASSEZ
ASSEZ 39 (*asez* 1, *assé* 7,
　　　　assez 31)
assise, assisé, assiz, assize,
assizé v ASSEOIR
assoar v À+SOIR
+ASSIETTE 15 (*l'assiète* 1,
　　　l'assiette 2, *lassiette* 10,
　　　lassiétes 1, *zassiettes* 1)
ASSEOIR 103 (*assise* 17,
　　　assisé, 23, *assiz* 4,
　　　assize 1, *assizé* 4, *cizsé* 1,
　　　sise 3, *sisé* 4, *siz* 22,
　　　siz' 1, *size* 7, *sizé*₁ 16)
+ASSOCIÉ 3 (*zassociés*)
assom, assomme
　　　　v ASSOMMER
ASSOMMER 5 (*assom* 1,
　　　assomme 4)
+ASSOMOIR 1 (*l'assommoir*)
asté v ACHETER
a s'ter, à s'ter, à s'tér,
a s'tèr, à s'tér, à s'tère
a s'ter-la à s'ter-la à s'ter-là,
à s'tér-là, à s'tèr-là, à ster,
à stér, a ster-là, a ster-là,
à stèr-là, a'ce terre, a'sterè-la,
a'sterè-là, aster, astèr, aster',
astère, asterla, asterlà, astheire,
asthére, asthère, astore v
　　　À+CETTE+HEURE(+LÀ)
a tab, à tab, à tabe, a tabl,
a table, à table v À+TABLE
À+TABLE 15 (*a tab* 2, *à tab* 2,
　　　à tabe 4, *a tabl* 1,
　　　a table 4, *à table* 2)
a ter, à ter, à terre v À+TERRE
À+TERRE 9 (*a ter* 1, *à ter* 1,
　　　à terre 7)
à tout moment
　　　　v À+TOUT+MOMENT
À+TOUT+MOMENT
　　　2 (*à tout moment*)
attace, attacé v ATTACHER
ATTACHER 22 (*attace* 5,
　　　attacé 6, *tace* 4,
　　　tacé 6, *tâcé* 1)
attancion v ATTENTION

attandi v ATTENDRE
+ATTAQUE 1 (*z'attaque*)
ATTAQUER 3 (*taque* 1,
　　　taqué 2)
+ATTE 2 (*zatte* 1, *z'attes* 1)
+ATTELIER 1 (*zatteliers*)
attendant v ATTENDANT
ATTENDANT 1 (*attendant*)
attende v ATTENDRE
ATTENDRE 6 (*attandi* 4,
　　　attende 2)
attention v ATTENTION
ATTENTION 7 (*attancion* 4,
　　　attention 3)
attitré v ATTITRÉ
attrap, attrap', attrape, attrapé
　　　　v ATTRAPER
ATTRAPER 24 (*attrap* 8,
　　　attrap' 2, *attrape* 5,
　　　attrapé 2, *trape* 2,
　　　trappé 4, *trapper* 1)
au v AU
AU 49 (*au* 48, *aux* 1)
au jour d'huit
　　　　v AUJOURD'HUI
au lieu v AU+LIEU
AU+LIEU 7 (*au lieu* 2, *aulié*
　　　2, *aulier* 1, *auliére*
　　　1, *aulière* 1)
aubout, auboute v AU, BOUT
aucaine v AUCUN
AU+CONTRAIRE
　　　1 (*o contrér*)
AUCUN 15 (*aucaine* 3,
　　　auqu'in 1, *auqu'ine* 1,
　　　auqueine 1, *auquine* 2,
　　　okéne 7)
Aughiste v AUGUSTE
augmenté v AUGMENTER
AUGMENTER 6 (*augmenté* 4,
　　　ogmanté 2)
AUGUSTE 1 (*Aughiste*)
aujordhi v AUJOURD'HUI
AUJOURD'HUI 40
　　　(*ajourd'hui* 3, *ajourdhi* 1,
　　　au jour d'huit 1,
　　　auzourdi 2, *azourd'hi* 1,
　　　azourdhi 2, *azourdi* 6,
　　　ozourdi 3, *zoudi* 1,
　　　zourdhi 1, *zourd'hi* 4,
　　　zordi 1, *zourdi* 15)

aulié, aulier, auliére, aulière
　　　v AU+LIEU
AUPARAVANT 1 (*oparavan*)
auqu'in, auqu'ine, auqueine
auquine v AUCUN
+AURORE 1 (*l'aurore*)
AU+SECOURS 2 (*o sicours*)
aussi v AUSSI
AUSSI 158 (*aussi* 50,
　　　ossi 47, *oussi* 61)
AUSSITÔT 17 (*ossito* 3,
　　　sitot 4, *sitôt* 10)
AUTANT 3 (*otan*)
+AUTEL 9 (*l'autel* 1, *l'otel* 8)
+AUTO 5 (*l'auto*)
autour v AUTOUR
AUTOUR 4 (*autour* 3, *otour* 1)
autre v AUTRE
AUTRE 3 (*autre* 1, *autres* 1,
　　　ot' 1)
+AUTRE₁ 195 (*l'aut* 4,
　　　l'aut' 18, *laut'* 2, *l'aute* 4,
　　　laute 39, *lautes* 1,
　　　l'autre 59, *l'ot* 1, *lot* 63,
　　　lote 1, *lotre* 3)
+AUTRE₂ 15 (*les autres* 1, *lé*
　　　zot 12, *les zaut'* 1, *lezot* 1)
+AUTRE₃ 2035 (*sautres* 3,
　　　zaut 16, *zaut'* 50, *zaute*
　　　539, *zautes* 57, *zautre* 7,
　　　z'autre 1, *zautres* 72,
　　　z'autres 1, *zot* 1137,
　　　zot' 12, *zote* 31, *zotre* 15,
　　　zotres 1, *zott* 29, *zotte* 62,
　　　zout 1, *zoute* 1)
autrefois v AUTREFOIS
AUTREFOIS 2 (*autrefois* 1,
　　　autréfois 1)
+AUTREFOIS 8 (*lautefois* 1,
　　　l'autfois 1, *l'aut'fois* 2,
　　　l'autrefois 4)
autréfois v AUTREFOIS
autrement v AUTREMENT
AUTREMENT 1 (*autrement*)
+AUTREMENT 3 (*l'autrement*)
autres v AUTRE
aux v AU
auzourdi v AUJOURD'HUI
av, av' v AVEC
a vela, av'la, a-v'la, av'là,
a-v'là v AH+VOILÀ
aval, avale, avalé v AVALER

AVALER 12 (*aval* 1, *avale* 6,
   avalé 5)
avan v AVANT
avance, avancé v AVANCER
AVANCER 5 (*avance* 1,
   avancé 4)
avant v AVANT
AVANT 78 (*avan* 22,
   avant 56)
+AVANTAGE 1 (*l'avantaze*)
avare v AVARE
AVARE 3 (*avare*)
+AVARIÉS 1 (*zavaries*)
ave, avec v AVEC
AVEC 998 (*ac* 1, *are* 6, *av* 448,
  av' 78, *ave* 59, *avec* 385,
  avéc 1, *ec* 7, *éc* 2,
  ecque 3, *èque* 5, *vec* 5)
avéc v AVEC
aveg, avég v AVEUGLE
avelas v AH+VOILÀ
averti v AVERTIR
AVERTIR 5 (*averti*)
avez v AVOIR
AVEUGLE 15 (*aveg* 9, *avég* 6)
a v'la, à v'la, a v'là, à v'là,
a vla, a vlà, a'vlà, avla, avlà
a-vlà v AH+VOILÀ
+AVOCAT₂ 1 (*zavocat*)[7]
avoih 1 [interj.]
avoir v AVOIR
AVOIR 2 (*avez* 1, *avoir* 1)
awoa 2 [interj.]
+AVRIL 1 (*d'avril*)
awouah 1 [interj.]
aye 6 [interj.]
ayo 2 [interj.]
AYO 32 (*aio* 1, *aïo* 30,
   aïoh 1) [mot tam.]
à zénoux, a zounou, à zounoux,
azile v AGILE
azounou v À+GENOUX
azourd'hi, azourdhi, azourdi
   v AUJOURD'HUI
azout, azoute, azouté
   v AJOUTER

B

bâ v BA2
BA 2 (*bâ*)
  [mot fr. dial.?]
baba v **BABA**
BABA 8 (*baba*) [mot tam.]
babillé v BABILLER
BABILLER 1 (*babillé*)
babylone v BABYLONE
BABYLONE 3 (*babylone*)
Bacoa v BACOA
BACOA 1 (*Bacoa*) [nom de
   personnage]
bacoua v **VAKOA**
badabam 1 [onomat.]
badamier v BADAMIER
BADAMIER 6 (*badamier* 4,
   badamiers 2)
badamiers v BADAMIER
badinage v BADINAGE
BADINAGE 27 (*badinage* 1,
   badinaze 26)
badinant v BADINANT
BADINANT 2 (*badinant*)
badinaze v BADINAGE
badine, badiné, badiner
   v BADINER
BADINER 34 (*badiné* 26,
  badine 7, *badiner* 1,
  badinez 2)
badinez v BADINER
bagasse v BAGASSE
BAGASSE 4 (*bagasse*)
bagaze v BAGAGE
BAGAGE 1 (*bagaze*)
bagne v BAGNE
BAGNE 1 (*bagne*)
bagou v BAGOU(T)
BAGOU(T) 19 (*bagou* 6,
  bagous 1, *bagoût* 4,
  bagout 8)
bagous, bagoût, bagout
   v BAGOU(T)
bagoutère v BAGOU(T)+*ER*
BAGOU(T)+*ER* 1 (*bagoutère*)
bague v BAGUE
BAGUE 15 (*bague*)
baguétte, baguette
   v BAGUETTE

BAGUETTE 4 (*baguétte* 1,
   baguette 3)
bah v BAH
BAH 7 (*bah*) [interj.]
baigne, baigné v BAIGNER
BAIGNER 32 (*baigne* 3,
  baigné 4, *baingne* 16,
  baingné 5, *bègne* 1,
  bégné 3)
bain v BAIN
BAIN 2 (*bain*)
baingne, baingné v BAIGNER
baïonétte v BAÏONNETTE
BAÏONNETTE 1 (*baïonétte*)
baise, baiser v BAISER
BAISER 5 (*baise* 3, *baiser* 2)
baiss', baisse, baissé v BAISSER
BAISSER 25 (*baiss'* 7,
  baisse 7, *baissé* 6,
  bésse 2, *béssé* 2)
bal v BAL
BAL 22 (*bal*)
BALAI 11 (*balié*₁)
BALAYER 16 (*balié*₂)
Balam v **BALAM**
BALAM 1 (*Balam*) [mot
   hind.]
balance, balancé v BALANCER
BALANCER 8 (*balance* 2,
   balancé 6)
balançoire v BALANÇOIRE
BALANÇOIRE 1 (*balançoire*)
balein', baleine v BALEINE
BALEINE 16 (*balein'* 1,
   baleine 15)
*balié*₁ v BALAI
*balié*₂ v BALAYER
balizaze v BALISAGE
BALISAGE 5 (*balizaze*)
ball's, balle v BALLE
BALLE 11 (*ball's* 1, *balle* 10)
ballotté v BALLOTER
BALLOTER 1 (*ballotté*)
bam 3 [onomat.]
bambou v BAMBOU
BAMBOU 9 (*bambou* 5,
   bambous 4)
bambous v BAMBOU
ban v BANDE
banané v BONNE+ANNÉE
banane v BANANE

---

[7] Homme de loi.

BANANE 20 (*banane* 13, *bananes* 7)
bananée, bananées, bananés
    v BONNE+ANNÉE
bananes   v BANANE
banc   v BANC
BANC   2 (*banc*)
+BANC   1 (*lébanc*)
bancal   v BANCAL
BANCAL 2 (*bancal*)
band, band', bande v BANDE
BANDE   91 (*ban* 1, *band* 25, *band'* 3, *bande* 34, *bane* 12, *banes* 2, *banne* 14)
+BANDE   3 (*la bande* 2, *labande* 1)
bane, banes   v BANDE
bangue   1 [onomat.]
banme   1 [onomat.]
bann'années
    v BONNE+ANNÉE
banne   v BANDE
banoir, banoirs v BOIS+NOIR
banque   v BANQUE
BANQUE 1 (*banque* 1)
+BANQUE 2 (*la banq* 1, *la banque* 1)
baouw   2 [onomat.]
baptême, baptême v BAPTÊME
BAPTÊME 9 (*baptême* 1, *baptême* 6, *bâtem* 1, *batême* 1)
+BAPTÊME 1 (*le baptême*)
baptisé, baptise v BAPTISER
BAPTISER 13 (*baptisé* 1, *baptise* 2, *baptisez* 2, *batiz* 7, *batizé* 1)
baptisez   v BAPTISER
Bara   1 (*Bara*)[8]
barachoix v BARACHOIX
BARACHOIX 1 (*barachoix*)
+BARBE 7 (*la barbe* 1, *labarbe* 6)
barbouille v BARBOUILLER
BARBOUILLER 3 (*barbouille*)
bardeau v BARDEAU

BARDEAU 5 (*bardeau* 1, *bardeaux* 3, *bardo* 1)
bardeaux, bardo v BARDEAU
barique, bariques v BARRIQUE
BARRAGE 1 (*barraze*)
barraze   v BARRAGE
barre, barré v BARRER
BARRER 4 (*barre* 2, *barré* 2)
barreau   v BARREAU
BARREAU 3 (*barreau* 2, *barreaux* 1)
barreaux   v BARREAU
barriqu', barrique
    v BARRIQUE
BARRIQUE 13 (*barique* 8, *bariques* 1, *barriqu'* 1, *barrique* 3)
barsaque v HABRESAC
barvades, barvat, barvatte
    v **AMBÉRIVÁTRY**
bas   v BAS
BAS   5 (*bas* 4, *basse* 1)
+BAS   2 (*lébas* 1, *lé bas* 1)
BASILE   1 (*Bazile*) [prénom]
basse   v BAS
basse cour v BASSE-COUR
BASSE-COUR 1 (*basse cour*)
bassein, bassin bassins
    v BASSIN
BASSIN 45 (*bassein* 1, *bassin* 42, *bassins* 2)
bat   v BATTRE
bataille   v BATAILLE
BATAILLE 2 (*bataille*)
+BATAILLE 1 (*la bataille*)
BÂTARD 1 (*bâtards*)
bâtards   v BÂTARD
batate, batates v PATATE
batatran   v **BATATRANA**
BATATRANA (*batatran* 1) [mot port.]
baté   v BATTRE
bateau   v BATEAU
BATEAU 23 (*bateau* 10, *bato* 13)
bâtem, batême v BAPTÊME
batiman, batiment, bâtiment
    v BÂTIMENT
BÂTIMENT 5 (*batiman* 1, *batiment* 1, *bâtiment* 3)
batir, bâtir v BÂTIR

BÂTIR   2 (*batir*1, *bâtir*1)
batisse v BATISSE
BATISSE 2 (*batisse*)
batiz, batizé v BAPTISER
bato   v BATEAU
battoir   v BATTOIR
BATTOIR 2 (*battoir*)
bâton   v BÂTON
BÂTON 29 (*bâton* 23, *baton* 4, *batons*1, *bâtons* 1)
baton, batons, bâtons v BÂTON
batt'   v BATTRE
battant   v BATTANT
BATTANT 2 (*battant*)
batté, batte, battez v BATTRE
battoir   v BATTOIR
BATTOIR 2 (*battoir*)
battre   v BATTRE
BATTRE 77 (*bat* 8, *baté* 7, *batt'* 3, *batté* 24, *batte* 29, *battez* 1, *battre* 3)
bavardaze v BAVARDAGE
BAVARDAGE 1 (*bavardaze*)
+BAVE 1 (*la bave*)
bavé   v BAVER
BAVER 8 (*bavé*)
bazar   v BAZAR
BAZAR 16 (*bazar* 13, *bazard* 3)
bazard   v BAZAR
Bazile   v BASILE
beau   v BEAU
BEAU 82 (*beau* 19, *bel* 17, *bel'* 1, *belbel* 5, *bélébéle* 2, *bell'* 3, *belle* 27, *bellebelle* 2, *belles* 4, *bo* 3)
beaucoup v BEAUCOUP
BEAUCOUP 92 (*beaucoup* 8, *boucou* 44, *boucoup* 40)
beau-frère v BEAU-FRÈRE
BEAU-FRÈRE 2 (*beau-frère*)
Beau-li-ton v BEAU-LI-TON
BEAU-LI-TON [nom de personnage]
beau-père v BEAU-PÈRE
BEAU-PÈRE 6 (*beau-père* 5, *beauperes* 1)
Beauperes v BEAU-PÈRE
beauté   v BEAUTÉ
BEAUTÉ 1 (*beauté*)

---

[8] Mot indien pour 'grand, important', utilisé ici, semble-t-il, comme partie d'un titre respectueux pour la reine Victoria [PB].

Beau Vallon v BEAU+VALLON
BEAU+VALLON 1 (*Beau Vallon*)
Béber v BÉBER
BÉBER 1 (*Béber*) [nom de personnage]
bébêt', bébétes, bébète, bébête, bébètes, bébette v BÊTE
+BEC 9 (*labec* 6, *la bec* 3)
bédeau v BÉDEAU
BÉDEAU 1 (*bédeau*)
bef, béf, befs, béfs v BŒUF
bègne, bégné v BAIGNER
béguèle v BÉGUEULE
BÉGUEULE 1 (*béguèle*)
beif, beifs v BŒUF
bein v BIEN
beirée, beirré v *BEURÉE
bel, bel', belbel, bélebéle, bell', belle, bellebelle v BEAU
bel fiye v BELLE-FILLE
bel mer v BELLE-MÈRE
belle-fille v BELLE-FILLE
BELLE-FILLE 2 (*bel fiye* 1, *belle-fille* 1)
belle mère, bellemère v BELLE-MÈRE
BELLE-MÈRE 3 (*bel mer* 1, *belle mère* 1, *bellemère* 1)
belles v BEAU
Bellone v BELLONE
BELLONE 1 (*Bellone*) [nom de navire]
ben v BEIN
BEIN 46 (*ben* 36, *bin* 7, *bé* 3) [interj.]
bénédiction v BÉNÉDICTION
BÉNÉDICTION 2 (*bénédiction*)
+BÉNÉDICTION 1 (*la bénédiction*)
bénéfice v BÉNÉFICE
BÉNÉFICE 1 (*bénéfice*)
bengali v BENGALI
BENGALI 6 (*bengali*)
béni, bénie, bénit v BÉNIR
BÉNIR 14 (*béni* 9, *bénie* 1, *bénit* 4)
benoiton, bénoiton, bénoit-ton v BENOÎTON
BENOÎTON 3 (*benoiton* 1, *bénoiton* 1, *bénoit-ton* 1)

bénosayres v BUENOS AIRES
BENJOIN 1 (*benzoin*)
benzoin v BENJOIN
bergé v BERGER
BERGER 1 (*bergé*)
berloque v BRELOQUE
besogne v BESOGNE
BESOGNE 1 (*besogne*)
besoin v BESOIN
BESOIN 210 (*besoin* 24, *bésoin* 1, *bisoin* 143, *bizen* 1, *bizin* 1, *bizoein* 36, *bizoin* 4, *bizouin* 1)
bésoin v BESOIN
bésse, béssé v BAISSER
bet, bêt, bêt', béte, bète, bête v BÊTE
BÊTE 75 (*bébêt'* 1, *bébétes* 1, *bébète* 3, *bébête* 1, *bébètes* 1, *bébette* 1, *bet* 5, *bêt* 1, *bêt'* 1, *béte* 4, *bète* 2, *bête* 51, *bête-bête* 1, *bêtes* 1)
+BÊTE 1 (*la bête*)
bête-bête, bêtes v BÊTE
betise, bétise, bêtise v BÊTISE
BÊTISE 6 (*betise* 1, *bétise* 1, *bêtise* 4)
+BEURRE 9 (*dibeirre* 7, *diber* 1, *diberre* 1)
*BEURÉE 2 (*beirée* 1, *beirré* 1)
biais v BIAIS
BIAIS 1 (*biais*)
bibass', bibasse v BIBASSE
BIBASSE 4 (*bibass'* 2, *bibasse* 2)
bibi v **BIBI**
BIBI 6 (*bibi* 4, *bibis* 2) [mot hind.]
bibis v **BIBI**
+BIBLE 1 (*la bible*)
bice, bices, biche v BICHE
BICHE 7 (*bice* 4, *bices* 1, *biche* 2)
biein v BIEN
bieinaimé v BIEN-AIMÉ
bieinhéré v BIENHEUREUX
bien v BIEN
BIEN 501 (*bein* 2, *biein* 37, *bien* 470, *bienbien* 1)

+BIEN 15 (*di biein* 3, *di bien* 4, *dibien* 7, *di-bien* 1; *le biein* 1)
BIEN-AIMÉ 2 (*bieinaimé*)
bien-aise v BIEN+AISE
BIEN+AISE 2 (*bien-aise*)
bienbien v BIEN
BIEN+FAIRE 1 (*bienfét*)
bienfét v BIEN+FAIRE
bienhéré v BIENHEUREUX
BIENHEUREUX 14 (*bieinhéré* 4, *bienhéré* 10)
bientot, bientôt v BIENTÔT
BIENTÔT 16 (*bientot* 1, *bientôt* 15)
+BIERRE 2 (*la bierre*)
big v BIG
BIG 4 (*big*) [mot angl.]
bigarade v BIGARADE
BIGARADE 1 (*bigarade*)
bigorneau v BIGORNEAU
BIGORNEAU 5 (*bigorneau* 2, *bigorneaux* 3)
bigorneaux v BIGORNEAU
bigoud 1 [interj.]
bigre v BIGRE
BIGRE 1 (*bigre*)
+BILE 1 (*la bile*)
billet v BILLET
BILLET 11 (*billet* 4, *biyet* 7)
billot v BILLOT
BILLOT 3 (*billot*)
bin v BEIN
bing 1 [onomat.]
bingali v **BINGALI**
BINGALI 1 (*bingali*) [mot hind.]
bireau, bireaux v BUREAU
biscouits, biscuit v BISCUIT
BISCUIT 4 (*biscouits* 2, *biscuit* 2)
bisoin v BESOIN
bisqué v BISQUER
BISQUER 1 (*bisqué*)
bit v BUT
bite v *BUTER
bitation v HABITATION
bitte v BUT
biter, bitté v *BUTER
biver v BUVEUR
biyet v BILLET

bizen, bizin, bizoein, bizoin,
bizouin v BESOIN
blague, blagué v BLAGUER
BLAGUER 6 (*blague* 1,
 blagué 5)
blan, blanc v BLANC
BLANC 158 (*blan* 6, *blanc* 104,
 blancblanc 1, *blancs* 49)
blancblanc v BLANC
BLANCHIR 1 (*blanci*)
blanci v BLANCHIR
blancs v BLANC
blasféme v BLASPHÈME
blasfémé v BLASPHÈMER
BLASPHÈME 4 (*blasfém* 3,
 blasféme 1)
BLASPHÈMER 1 (*blasfémé*)
+BLÉ 15 (*di blé* 7, *diblé* 7,
 di-blé 1)
blé, blei v BLEU
blesse, blessé v BLESSER
BLESSER 7 (*blesse* 1, *blessé* 6)
bleu v BLEU
BLEU 9 (*blé* 5, *blei* 3, *bleu* 1)
blie, blié, bliie, bliye, bliyé
 v OUBLIER
blize, blizé v OBLIGER
bloc v BLOC
BLOC 2 (*bloc*)
blye, blyié v OUBLIER
bo v BEAU
boar v BOIRE
boaté v BOÎTER
bobre v ABÓBORA
+BOËTE 3 (*la boëte* 2,
 la bouette 1)
boeuf v BŒUF
BŒUF 35 (*bef* 12, *béf* 5,
 bèfe 1, *befs* 2, *béfs* 2,
 beif 9, *beifs* 3, *boeuf* 1)
boidebène v BOIS, +ÉBENNE
boidenatte v BOIS+DE+**NATO**
boir, boir', boire v BOIRE
BOIRE 144 (*boar* 19, *boir* 3,
 boir' 15, *boire* 106,
 boiré 1)
boiré v BOIRE
bois v BOIS
BOIS 35 (*boi* 1, *bois* 34)
bois de natte v
 BOIS+DE+**NATO**

BOIS+DE+**NATO** 2
 (*boidenatte* 1, *bois
 de natte* 1) [*nato* est
 d'origine malg.]
+BOIS 72 (*di bois* 12, *diboi*
 1, *dibois* 46, *di-bois* 13)
bois-blanc v BOIS-BLANC
BOIS-BLANC 1 (*bois-blanc*)
boisdebène v BOIS, +ÉBENNE
boisdfer v BOIS+DE+FER
BOIS+DE+FER 1 (*boisdfer*)
bois de ronde v BOIS+DE+
 HARÓNGANA
BOIS+NOIR 8 (*banoir* 6,
 banoirs 2)
BOIS+DE+**HARÓNGANA** 1
 (*bois de ronde*)[9]
Bois des Amourettes v BOIS-
 DES-AMOURETTES
BOIS-DES-AMOURETTES 1
 (*Bois des Amourettes*)
Bois d'oiseaux v
 BOIS+D'OISEAUX
 [toponyme]
+BOISSON 1 (*la boisson*)
boit', boite, boîte v BOÎTE
BOÎTE 4 (*boit'* 1, *boite* 1,
 boîte 2)
boité v BOÎTER
BOÎTER 6 (*boaté* 5, *boité* 1)
bol v BOL
BOL 2 (*bol*)
bôm 1 [onomat.]
*bo matin, bomatin, bômatin,
 bomatins* v BON+MATIN
bombance v BOMBANCE
BOMBANCE 2 (*bombance*)
bombarbe, bombarde
 v BOMBARDE
BOMBARDE 5 (*bombarbe* 1,
 bombarde 4)
bon v BON
BON 438 (*bon* 419,
 bonne 2, *bons* 17)
bon à rien v BON+À+RIEN
BON+À+RIEN 1 (*bon à rien*)
bon à vini, bonavini
 v *BON+À+VENIR

*BON+À+VENIR 9 (*bon à vini*
 1, *bonavini* 8)
bonbom', bonbon v BONBON
BONBON 8 (*bonbom'* 2,
 bonbon 4, *bon-bon*
 1, *bonbons* 1)
bon-bon, bonbons v BONBON
bon caire v BON+CŒUR
bon cœur v BON+CŒUR
BON+CŒUR 18 (*bon caire* 1,
 bon cœur 1, *bon keir* 8,
 bon ker 3, *bonquér* 1,
 bon quer 3, *bon quér* 1)
+BONDE 1 (*la bonde*)
*bondié, bon-dié, bon dié, bon
 dieu* v BON+DIEU
BON+DIEU 249 (*bondié* 97,
 bon-dié 12, *bon dié* 65,
 bon dieu 75)
boné, bonéts v BONNET
*bonheir, bonher, bonhèr,
 bonhère, bonheur* v BONHEUR
BONHEUR 15 (*bonheir* 2,
 bonher 6, *bonhèr* 1,
 bonhère 4, *bonheur* 2)
*bonhom', bonhome, bonhomes,
 bonhomm', bonhomme*
 v BONHOMME
BONHOMME 113 (*bonhom'* 2,
 bonhome 6, *bonhomes* 3,
 bonhomm' 4,
 bonhomme 96, *bonome* 1,
 bonshomes 1)
Boniface v BONIFACE
BONIFACE 1 (*Boniface*)
 [nom de personnage]
bonjour v BONJOUR
BONJOUR 21 (*bonjour* 2,
 bonzour 18, *bozour* 1)
bon keir, bon ker
 v BON+CŒUR
BON+MATIN 49 (*bomatin* 36,
 bômatin 4, *bomatins* 2,
 bon matein 2, *bon matin* 5)
BON+MATIN 5 (*bomatin* 2,
 bomatins 2, *bomatin* 1)
bonne v BON

---
[9] Arbre connu à la Réunion sous le nom de [bwa d rõg].

BONNE+ANNÉE 40 (banané 14, bananée 3, bananées 10, bananés 3, bann'années 1, bonne années 4, bonne-anné 1, bonne-année 2, bonne-années 2)
bonne années
  v BONNE+ANNÉE
bonnefanme, bonne femme
  v BONNE+FEMME
BONNE+FEMME 119 (bonnefanme 1, bonne femme 30, bonnefemme 89)
bonne-anné, bonne année, bonne- années
  v BONNE+ANNÉE
bonnefemme
  v BONNE+FEMME
+BONNE NOUVELLE 1 (la bonn nouvel)
bonnet   v BONNET
BONNET 6 (boné 1, bonéts 1, bonnet 4)
bonome   v BONHOMME
bonquér, bon quer, bon quér
  v BON+COEUR
bons   v BON
bonshomes v BONHOMME
bonsoir   v BONSOIR
BONSOIR 11 (bonsoir 10, bonzoir 1)
bonté   v BONTÉ
BONTÉ 7 (bonté)
+BONTÉ 5 (la bonté)
bontemps, bon-tems
  v BON+TEMPS
BON+TEMPS 4 (bontemps 3, bon-tems 1)
bon-vivant v BON+VIVANT
BON+VIVANT 1 (bon-vivant)
bonzoir   v BONSOIR
bonzour   v BONJOUR
bor, bord   v BORD
BORD 89 (bor 12, bord 69, bôrd 8)
bôrd   v BORD
bordé   v BORDER
BORDER 2 (bordé)
borer   v **BORER**
BORER 1 (borer) [mot angl.]

borgn', borgne v BORGNE
BORGNE 2 (borgn' 1, borgne 1)
borrim borré
  v *BORIM BORE
*BORIM BORE 1 (borim boré) [cri de porteurs de palanquins; origine inconnue]
bosco   v BOSCOT
BOSCOT 1 (bosco)
bosse   v BOSSE
BOSSE 3 (bosse)
bossé   v BOSSER
BOSSER 1 (bossé)
bote, botes, botte v BOTTE
BOTTE 13 (bote 1, botes 6, botte 6)
bottine   v BOTTINE
BOTTINE 2 (bottine 1, bottines 1)
bottines   v BOTTINE
boucan   v BOUCAN
BOUCAN 1 (boucan)
bouce, boucé, boucer, boucés
  v BOUCHER
+BOUCHE 89 (la bouç 1, la bouç' 1, la bouce 15, labouce 44, la-bouce 2, la-bouçe 2, la bous 14, la bouss' 2, la-bouss' 4, la bousse 2, la-bousse 2)
BOUCHER 15 (bouce 5, boucé 5, boucer 4, boucés 1)
+BOUCHERIE 1 (la boucerie)
BOUCLE 1 (bouque)
bouçon   v BOUCHON
BOUCHON 2 (bouçon)
boucou, boucoup v BEAUCOUP
boudé   v BOUDER
BOUDER 1 (boudé)
Boudet   v BOUDET
BOUDET 1 (Boudet) [nom de famille]
boudin   v BOUDIN
BOUDIN 1 (boudin)
boudoum 1 [onomat.]
+BOUE 26 (la boue 7, laboue 19)
bouf 1 [onomat.]
boufé   v BOUFFER
BOUFFER 1 (boufé)

BOUGER 38 (bouz 1, bouz' 1, bouze 11, bouzé 25)
+BOUGIE 3 (la bouzie 2, labouzie 1)
bougonné v BOUGONNER
BOUGONNER 1 (bougonné)
bougr', bougre v BOUGRE
BOUGRE 7 (bougr' 1, bougre 1, bougue 5)
bougue   v BOUGRE
boui, bouï v BOUILLIR
bouillante v BOUILLANT
BOUILLANT 2 (bouillante)
bouilli   v BOUILLIR
bouillon   v BOUILLON
BOUILLON 11 (bouillon)
BOUILLIR 20 (boui 1, bouï 16, bouï 1, bouir 1, bouilli 1)
bouir   v BOUILLIR
boul', boule   v BOULE
BOULE 7 (boul' 1, boule 6)
boulet   v BOULET
BOULET 1 (boulet)
boum 5 [onomat.]
boumm 1 [onomat.]
bouque   v BOUCLE
bouquet   v BOUQUET
BOUQUET 10 (bouquet 7, bouquets 3)
bouquets   v BOUQUET
bour'   v BOURRER
bourade   v BOURADE
BOURADE 1 (bourade)
bourbac   v HABRESAC
bourbon   v BOURBON
BOURBON 3 (bourbon)
bouré   v BOURRER
BOURGEOIS 5 (bourzeois)
bourik, bourique
  v BOURRIQUE
bourl, bourl', bourle, bourlé
  v BRÛLER
bourloque v BRELOQUE
bouro   v BOURREAU
BOURREAU 1 (bouro)
bourre, bourré, bourrer
  v BOURRER
BOURRER 21 (bour' 1, bouré 1, bourre 7, bourré 11, bourrer 1)
bourrié   v BRÛLER

bourriqu', bourrique
    v BOURRIQUE
BOURRIQUE 60 (*bourik* 5, *bourique* 31, *bourriqu'* 9, *bourrique* 15)
boursac   v HABRESAC
boursaille, boursailles
    v BROUSSAILLE
boursaqu', boursaque
    v HABRESAC
bourse   v BOURSE
BOURSE 1 (*bourse*)
bourzeois v BOURGEOIS
BOUSCULER 2 (*bousquile*)
BOUSIN 1 (*bouzin*)
bousquile v BOUSCULER
bout   v BOUT
BOUT   37 (*bout* 5, *boute* 32)
boute   v BOUT
bouteille v BOUTEILLE
BOUTEILLE 12 (*bouteille* 2, *bouteilles* 3, *boutey* 1, *bouteye* 2, *boutéye* 4)
+BOUTEILLE 1 (*la bouteille*)
bouteilles, boutey, bouteye,
boutéye   v BOUTEILLE
boutiq', boutique v BOUTIQUE
BOUTIQUE 2 (*boutiq'* 1, *boutique* 1)
+BOUTIQUE 14 (*la boutique* 6, *laboutik* 1, *laboutique* 6, *laboutiques* 1)
bouton   v BOUTON
BOUTON 1 (*bouton*)
boutonnière v BOUTONNIÈRE
BOUTONNIÈRE
    1 (*boutonnière*)
Bouvet   v BOUVET
BOUVET 2 (*Bouvet*) [nom de personnage]
bouz, bouz', bouze, bouzé
    v BOUGER
bouzin   v BOUSIN
BOYAU 1 (*bôyau*)
bôyau   v BOYAU
bozour   v BONJOUR
BRACONNIER
    1 (*braconniers*)
braconniers v BRACONNIER
+BRAI 3 (*labrai*)
brancard v BRANCARD
BRANCARD 2 (*brancard*)

brançaze v BRANCHAGE
brance, brances v BRANCHE
BRANCHAGE 2 (*brançaze*)
BRANCHE 18 (*brance* 11, *brances* 3, *brans* 4)
brandy   v **BRANDY**
BRANDY 1 (*brandy*) [mot angl.]
brané, branlé v BRANLER
BRANLER 8 (*brané* 3, *branlé* 3, *branné* 2)
branné   v BRANLER
brans   v BRANCHE
+BRAS 29 (*l'bras* 1, *lé bras* 6, *lebras* 1, *le-bras* 1, *lébras* 19, *les bras* 1)
brave   v BRAVE
BRAVE 5 (*brave*)
bravo   v BRAVO
BRAVO 3 (*bravo*)
bred', bréd', brèd', bréde, brède
    v BRÈDE
BRÈDE 18 (*bred'* 1, *bréd'* 1, *brèd'* 1, *bréde* 3, *brède* 5, *brédes* 3, *brèdes* 4)
brédes, brèdes   v BRÈDE
BRELOQUE 2 (*berloque* 1, *bourloque* 1)
+BRELOQUE 1 (*la berloq'*)
BRETELLE 1 (*bretelles*)
bretelles   v BRETELLE
BREUVAGE 1 (*brévaz*)
brévaz   v BREUVAGE
bric-à-brac v BRIC-À-BRAC
BRIC-À-BRAC 1 (*bric-à-brac*)
+BRIDE 6 (*labride*)
brigan, brigand v BRIGAND
BRIGAND 64 (*brigan* 1, *brigand* 63)
BRIGANDAGE 1 (*brigandazes*)
brigandazes v BRIGANDAGE
brilant   v BRÛLANT
brill'   v BRÛLER
brillant   v BRILLANT
BRILLANT 1 (*brillant*)
bringelle   v BRINGELLE
BRINGELLE 3 (*bringelle* 1, *brinzelle* 1, *brinzelles* 1)
brinzelle, brinzelles
    v BRINGELLE
BRIOCHE 1 (*brioces*)
brioces   v BRIOCHE

BRISANT 1 (*brizants*)
+BRISE 1 (*la brise*)
brise, brisé v BRISER
BRISER 3 (*brise* 1, *brisé* 2)
brizants   v BRISANT
brodé   v BRODER
BRODER 1 (*brodé*)
bross', brosse v BROSSE
BROSSE 4 (*bross'* 1, *brosse* 2, *brôsse* 1)
brôsse   v BROSSE
brouill'   v BROUILLER
BROUILLAGE 1 (*brouillaze*)
brouillaze v BROUILLAGE
brouille, brouillé
    v BROUILLER
BROUILLER 20 (*brouill'* 1, *brouille* 12, *brouillé* 7)
broul   v BRÛLER
BROUSSAILLE 2 (*boursaille* 1, *boursailles* 1)
brousses   v BROUSSE
BROUSSE 3 (*brousses*)
brrrt   1 [onomat.]
+BRUIT 2 (*di-brit* 1, *dibruit* 1)
BRÛLANT 1 (*brilant*)
BRÛLER 37 (*bourl* 2, *bourl'* 1, *bourle* 8, *bourlé* 23, *bourrié* 1, *broul* 1, *brill'* 1)
+BRUNE 1 (*la brine*)
Brutus   v BRUTUS
BRUTUS 1 (*Brutus*) [nom de personnage]
BUENOS AIRES 1 (*bénosayres*) [toponyme]
Bulbul   v **BULBUL**
BULBUL 1 (*Bulbul*) [mot hind.]
bureau   v BUREAU
BUREAU 6 (*bireau* 3, *bireaux* 2, *bureau* 1)
BUT 5 (*bit* 1, *bitte* 4)
*BUTER 3 (*bite* 1, *biter* 1, *bitté* 1)
BUVEUR 1 (*biver*)
bzinne   3 [onomat.]

C

c'ella	v CELUI-LÀ					

c'ella   v CELUI-LÀ
c'est   v C'EST
C'EST   15 (c'est 12, sé 1, cé 2)
c't'hère   v À+CETTE+HEURE
ca, ça, cà, çà v ÇA
ÇA   2074 (ca 18, ça 1881, cà 5, çà 42, çaça 6, sa 120, sà 2)
ça va   v ÇA+VA
ÇA+VA   12 (ça va 5, cava 5, ça-va 1, sava 1)
cabar   v **KABAR**
cabardar   v ***KABORDAR**
cabine   v CABINE
CABINE   1 (cabine)
cabinet   v CABINET
CABINET   5 (cabinet 2, cabinêt 1, cabinéts 2)
cabinêt, cabinéts   v CABINET
cabo   v CABOT
cabotin, cabotine   v CABOTIN
CABOTIN   4 (cabotin 2, cabotine 2)
CABOT   4 (cabo 2, cabots 2)
cabo   v CABOT
cabots   v CABOT
cabri   v CABRI
CABRI   18 (cabri 9, cabris 3, cabrit 5, cabrits 1)
cabris, cabrit, cabrits v CABRI
caca   v CACA
CACA   13 (caca)
çaça   v ÇA
çacaine   v CHACUN
ça caine   v CHACUN
cace   v **KAS**
çace, çacé   v CHASSER
caces   v **KAS**
CACHER   23 (cacié 21, caçié 2, cassié 1)
CACHETTE   29 (caciet 8, caciét 6, caciéte 4, caciette 10, caciétte 1)
cacié, caçié   v CACHER
caciet, caciét, caciéte, caciette
caciétte   v CACHETTE
cadeau   v CADEAU
CADEAU   17 (cadeau 12, cado 5)

cado   v CADEAU
café   v CAFÉ
CAFÉ   14 (café)
café au lait v CAFÉ+AU+LAIT
CAFÉ+AU+LAIT
    2 (café au lait)
*CAGNARD   1 (gnangnan)
çagrein, cagrin, çagrin, çagrine, çagrins   v CHAGRIN
cahier   v CAHIER
CAHIER   2 (cahier)
caille   v CAILLE
CAILLE   1 (caille)
+CAILLE   1 (la-caille)
CAILLOU 1 (calou)
caïman   v CAÏMAN
CAÏMAN   32 (caïman 31, caïmans 1)
caïmans   v CAÏMAN
caise, caises   v CHAISE
caisse   v CAISSE
CAISSE   1 (caisse)
çak   v CHAQUE
çakéne   v CHACUN
cal'basse   v CALEBASSE
çala   v CELUI LA
calçon   v CALEÇON
CALCULER 1 (calquilé 1)
Calcutta   v CALCUTTA
CALCUTTA 1 (Calcutta) [toponyme]
cale   v CALER
CALER   3 (cale)
çale   v CHALE
calebasse   v CALEBASSE
CALEBASSE 11 (cal'basse 1, calebasse 10)
+CALEBASSE 2 (la calbasse 1, la callebasse 1)
caléce, calèce   v CALÈCHE
CALÈCHE 15 (caléce 2, calèce 12, calesse 1)
caleçon   v CALEÇON
CALEÇON 5 (calçon 1, caleçon 2, caneçon 2)
calesse   v CALÈCHE
Calfat   v CALFAT
CALFAT   1 (Calfat) [nom de famille]
calm   v CALME
CALME   1 (calm)
calmé   v CALMER

CALMER 1 (calmé)
calomelas v CALOMELAS
CALOMELAS 1 (calomelas)
calou   v CAILLOU (?)[10]
CALOUCHE 2 (caye louce)
calquilé   v CALCULER
cam'rad, cam'rad', cam'rade, camarad', camarade
    v CAMARADE
CAMARADE 89 (cam'rad 1, cam'rad' 1, cam'rade 2, camarad' 3, camarade 6, camarades 6, camela 1,[11] camerade 3, camerades 2, cammarade 7, camila 2, camilas 1, cammarades 1, cammrade 1, camrad 13, camrad' 1, camrade 17, camrades 24, cramouade 1)
camarades v CAMARÃO
camaron   v **CAMARÃO**
CAMARÃO 2 (camaron) [mot port.]
cambare   v **KAMBARA**
camela, camerade, camerades
    v CAMARADE
cami   v CAMUS
camila, camilas
    v CAMARADE
camis   v CAMUS
camisard   v CAMISARD
CAMISARD 1 (camisard)
cammarade, cammarades, cammrade v CAMARADE
çamo   v CHAMEAU
camp   v CAMP
CAMP   5 (camp)
+CAMP   3 (l'camp 1, le camp 2)
campagne   v CAMPAGNE
CAMPAGNE 1 (campagne)
+CAMPAGNE 3 (la campagne 2, lacampagne 1)
CAMPETEKE 1 (sirampeck 1) [mot bant.]
çampion   v CHAMPIGNON

---
[10] Le contexte suggère une faute d'impression pour « caillou ».
[11] Les formes camela et camila(s) sont attribuées aux immigrés chinois.

camrad, camrad', camrade,		
camrades	v CAMARADE	
CAMUS 3 (*cami* 1, *camis* 2)		
can	v CANNE	
çan	v CHAMP	
canaille	v CANAILLE	
CANAILLE 3 (*canaille*)		
canal	v CANAL	
CANAL 6 (*canal*)		
canana	v *CANANA	
*CANANA 1 (*canana*) [origine inconnue]		
canapé	v CANAPÉ	
CANAPÉ 4 (*canapé*)		
canard	v CANARD	
CANARD 15 (*canard* 14, *canards* 1)		
canards	v CANARD	
cancarla, cancarlat, çancarlat	v CANCRELAT	
çancé	v SENSE	
CANCRELAT 7 (*cancarla* 3, *cancarlat* 1, *çancarlat* 1, *cancrélas* 1, *carcala* 1)		
cancrélas	v CANCRELAT	
çandélié	v CHANDELIER	
candioc 2 [origine inconnue]		
caneçon	v CALEÇON	
cang'	v **KANCI**	
çangé	v CHANGER	
canne	v CANNE	
CANNE 24 (*can* 1, *canne* 17, *cannes* 6)		
cannes	v CANNE	
canon	v CANON	
CANON 7 (*canon*)		
CANOT 5 (*canote* 1, *canotes* 1, *canotte* 3)		
canote, canotes, canotte	v CANOT	
çanpéc	v **TCAMPETEKE**	
çanson, çansons	v CHANSON	
çant, çant', cante, çante, canté,		
çanté	v CHANTER	
çantenié	v CENTENIER	
çanter	v CHANTER	
cantharides	v CANTHARIDE	
CANTHARIDE 1 (*cantharides*)		
cantic	v CANTIQUE	
+CANTINE 7 (*la cantine* 4, *la-cantin'* 1, *la-cantine* 2)		
cantique	v CANTIQUE	
CANTIQUE 2 (*cantic* 1, *cantique* 1)		
çanz, çanze, canzé, çanzé,		
canzer	v CHANGER	
cap	v CAP	
CAP 5 (*cap*)		
capab, capab', capabe, capabl',		
capable	v CAPABLE	
CAPABLE 140 (*capab* 17, *capab'* 1, *capabe* 71, *capabl'* 6, *capable* 38, *capables* 7, *capav* 76, *capav'* 47, *capave* 77)		
capables, capav, capav',		
capave	v CAPABLE	
çape, çapé	v ÉCHAPPER	
cape	v CAPER	
çapeau	v CHAPEAU	
çapelet	v CHAPELET	
CAPER 1 (*cape*)		
capitaine	v CAPITAINE	
CAPITAINE 21 (*capitaine* 14, *capitaines* 4, *captain* 1, *captain'* 1, *captaine* 1)		
capitaines	v CAPITAINE	
capon	v CAPON	
CAPON 2 (*capon*)		
CAPORAL 1 (*caporals*)		
caporals	v CAPORAL	
capores	v **KAPORO**	
cappe, çappe, çappé	v ÉCHAPPER	
capra	v **KAPRA**	
caprice	v CAPRICE	
CAPRICE 5 (*caprice*)		
capricorne	v CAPRICORNE	
CAPRICORNE 1 (*capricorne*)		
captain, captain', captaine	v CAPITAINE	
caqu'ein, caqu'einne	v CHACUN	
caque, çaque	v CHAQUE	
çaquein, caquein', çaquein', çaqueine, çaquéne, çaquenne	v CHACUN	
car	v CAR	
CAR 27 (*car*)		
Caraba, Carabas	v CARABAS	
CARABAS 29 (*Caraba* 15, *Carabas* 14) [nom de personnage]		
carabes	v CRABE	
carabine	v CARABINE
CARABINE 1 (*carabine*)	
caractère	v CARACTÈRE
CARACTÈRE 2 (*caractère*)	
carafon	v CARAFON
CARAFON 1 (*carafon*)	
CARAMBOLE 3 (*caramboles* 1, *carambolle* 2)	
caramboles, carambolle	v CARAMBOLE
carangue	v CARANGUE
CARANGUE 12 (*carangue*)	
CARAPATE 1 (*carapattes*)	
carapattes	v CARAPATE
cararaca 1 [onomat.]	
caraye	v **KARAHI**
çarbon, carbons	v CHARBON
carcala	v CANCRELAT
Car-Car	v CAR-CAR
CAR-CAR 1 (*Car-Car*) [nom de personnage]	
carcas	v CARCASSE
carcassaile 1 [origine inconnue]	
CARCASSE 1 (*carcas*)	
cardinal	v CARDINAL
CARDINAL 1 (*cardinal*)	
carêm', carême	v CARÊME
CARÊME 2 (*carêm'* 1, *carême* 1)	
caress', caresse, carèsse, caressé	v CARESSER
CARESSER 9 (*caress'* 1, *caresse* 6, *carèsse* 1, *caressé* 1)	
çarête	v CHARRETTE
çaretier	v CHARRETIER
çarette	v CHARRETTE
cari	v **KARI**
caria, carias	v **KARAIYAN**
çarié	v CHARRIER
caris	v **KARI**
çaritable	v CHARITABLE
çarite, çarité	v CHARITÉ
çarmant	v CHARMANT
CARNACIER 2 (*carnacière*)	
carnacière	v CARNACIER
carnage	v CARNAGE
CARNAGE 2 (*carnage* 1, *carnaze* 1)	
carnaval	v CARNAVAL 1
CARNAVAL 1 (*carnaval*)	
carnaze	v CARNAGE

Caroline v CAROLINE	*Cassetout, Casse-tout*	*çausette* v CHAUSSETTE
CAROLINE 1 (*Caroline*) [prénom]	v CASSE-TOUT	*causez* v CAUSER
	CASSE-TOUT 8 (*Cassetout* 1,	*çaussire* v CHAUSSURE
carosse v CARROSSE	*Casse-tout* 7) [nom de	*cauz', cauzé* v CAUSER
carotté v CAROTTER	personnage]	*çava, ça-va* v ÇA+VA
CAROTTER 2 (*carotté*)	*cassette* v CASSETTE	+CAVE 4 (*la cav* 1,
çarpentier v CHARPENTIER	CASSETTE 1 (*cassette*)	*la cave* 1, *lacave* 2)
carquille v ÉCARQUILLER	*cassié* v CACHER	*caverne* v CAVERNE
carré v CARRE	*cassis* v CASSIS	CAVERNE 8 (*caverne*)
CARRÉ 1 (*carré*)	CASSIS 1 (*cassis*)	*çavir, çavire, çaviré, çavirer*
carreau v CARREAU	*castor* v CASTOR	v CHAVIRER
CARREAU 9 (*carreau*)	CASTOR 1 (*castor*)	*caya caya* v *KAYAYA
carrément v CARRÉMENT	*çat* v CHAT	*caye louce* v CALOUCHE
CARRÉMENT 1 (*carrément*)	CATAU 1 (*cateau*)	*cayes* 1 [étymon non
çarretier v CHARRETIER	*cat-cat, cat-catte* v **KATEKATÉ**	établi ; cf *caye louce*]
carri v **KARI**	*çate* v CHAT	*caz* v CASE
çarrié v CHARRIER	*cate* v CHAT	*cazavëcks* v CAZAVEK
carrière v CARRIÈRE	*cateau* v CATAU	CAZAVEK 1 (*cazavëcks*) [mot
CARRIÈRE 1 (*carrière*)	*cate-cate* v **KATEKATÉ**	wallon]
carrosse v CARROSSE	*catéra* v **KATTĒRU**	*caze* v CASE
CARROSSE 22 (*carosse* 15,	**CATNI** 1 (*çat'ni*) [mot hind.]	*ce* v CE
carrosse 7)	*çat'ni* v **CATNI**	CE 14 (*ce* 12, *cé* 2)
cartier v QUARTIER	*çatouille* v CHATOUILLER	*cé* v CE
çarze, çarzé v CHARGER	*çats, catte, çatte* v CHAT	*ceci* v CECI
cas v CAS	*çaud* v CHAUD	CECI 1 (*ceci*)
CAS 1 (*cas*)	*çaudière* v CHAUDIÈRE	*cef, çef, céf, çéf, cefs* v CHEF
case v CASE	*çauffe, çauffé* v CHAUFFER	**CEGA** 13 (*céga* 2, *chéga* 5,
CASE 4 (*case* 2, *caz* 1,	ÇA+UN[12] 3 (*cein'* 1, *cène* 1,	*tchéga* 2, *tiéga* 1,
caze 1)	*çenne* 1)	*sega* 1, *séga* 2) [mot
+CASE 375 (*la case* 35,	*caus'* v CAUSER	bantou]
la caz 52, *la caz'* 2,	*causant* v CAUSANT	*céga* v **CEGA**
la caze 40, *lacas'* 2,	CAUSANT 1 (*causant*)	*cein'* v ÇA+UN
lacase 216, *la-case* 5,	*cause* v CAUSER	*ceine là* v CELUI-LÀ
lacases 3, *la-caz'* 1,	CAUSE 1 (*coz*$_1$)	*ceinq* v CINQ
lacaze 4, *la-caze* 15)	+CAUSE 13 (*la cause* 10,	*ceintir* v CEINTURE
CASH 6 (*casse*)	*la cauz'* 1, *la coz* 1,	CEINTURE 2 (*ceintir*)
casquette v CASQUETTE	*lacause* 1)	*cel' là* v CELUI-LÀ
CASQUETTE 1 (*casquette*)	*causé, causecausé, causée,*	*cela* v CELA
cass', casse v CASSER	*causer* v CAUSER	CELA 1 (*cela*)
casse v **CASH**	CAUSER 282 (*caus'* 1,	*célébrer* v CÉLÉBRER
çasse v CHASSER	*cause* 40, *causé* 181,	CÉLÉBRER 1 (*célébrer*)
cassé v CASSER	*causecausé* 1, *causée* 1,	*cella, célla, celle là, celles là*
çassé v CHASSER	*causer* 2, *causez* 1, *cauz'* 6,	v CELUI-LÀ
casse cou v CASSER+COU	*cauzé* 4, *cos'* 11, *cose* 7,	CELUI-LÀ 34 (*c'ella* 5, *çala* 1,
cassée, cassées v CASSER	*cosé* 2, *coz*$_2$ 12, *cozé* 16)	*ceine là* 1, *cel' là* 5, *cella*
çasseir, çasser v CHASSEUR		1, *célla* 1, *celle là* 3,
CASSER 88 (*cass'* 5, *casse* 44,		*celles là* 1, *céne là* 8, *céne*
cassé 33, *cassée* 4,		*la* 3, *cenne là* 5)
cassées 2, *cassés* 1)		+CENDRE 5 (*la çand* 1,
CASSER+COU 1 (*casse cou*)		*la cendre* 1, *lacende* 2,
cassés v CASSER		*la cende* 1)
		+CÈNE 1 (*la cène*)

---

[12] L'étymologie impliquée ici est presque certainement fausse. *Cein'* (tout comme ses variantes) est probablement une abréviation de *céne là* (et de ses variantes) qui dérive en fait de Fr. *celle-là* (due à la variation [l]/[n] ; v CELUI-LÀ).

cène v ÇA+UN
céne là, céne la, cenne là v CELUI-LÀ
çenne v ÇA+UN
cent v CENT
CENT 14 (cent 10, cents 4)
CENTENIER 2 (çantenié)
centpieds v CENT+PIED
CENT+PIED 1 (centpieds)
cents v CENT
cependant v CEPENDANT
CEPENDANT 1 (cependant)
cépourkoa v C'EST, POURQUOI
cepté v EXCEPTÉ
cer v CHER
cerç', çerç', cerce, cercé, cerçé, çerçé v CHERCHER
cérémonie v CÉRÉMONIE
CÉRÉMONIE 1 (cérémonie)
cerf v CERF
CERF 28 (cerf 24, cerfe 3, cerfs 1)
cerfe, cerfs v CERF
cerf-volant v CERF-VOLANT
CERF-VOLANT 1 (cerf-volant 1, cervolant 2)
cerne v CERNER
Cernéen v CERNÉEN
CERNÉEN 1 (Cernéen) [nom d'un journal]
CERNER 1 (cerne)
cerpentier v CHARPENTIER
cerpie v CHARPIE
certain v CERTAIN
CERTAIN 1 (certain)
cerveau v CERVEAU
CERVEAU 1 (cerveau)
cervolant v CERF-VOLANT
César v CÉSAR
CÉSAR 5 (César)
cése, cèse v CHAISE
cet, cett' v CET/CETTE
CET 15 (cet)
cèv' v CHÈVRE
cévé v CHEVEU
cèvr', cevre v CHÈVRE
cévrette v CHEVRETTE
Ceylan v CEYLAN
CEYLAN 1 (Ceylan) [nom de navire]

Cézaré Philip v CÉZARÉ PHILIP
CÉZARÉ PHILIP 1 (Cézaré Philip 1) [nom de personnage]
çéze v CHAISE
CHACUN 52 (çacaine 2, ça caine 1, çakéne 7, caqu'ein 1, caqu'einne 2, çaquein 2, caquein' 1, çaquein' 8, çaqueine 1, çaquéne 12, çaquenne 1, chaq'in 1, chaqène 1, chaquein' 1, chaqu'ein 1, chaquèn 2, chaquén' 1, chaquèn' 1, chaquéne 1, chaquène 2, sa caine 1, sa quène 1, saquène 1)
chagrin v CHAGRIN
CHAGRIN 57 (çagrein 9, cagrin 3, çagrin 3, çagrine 1, çagrins 1, chagrin 3, sagrin 1, sagrinne 2)
+CHAÎNE 3 (la caine 1, la chaine 1, la-çaine 1)
+CHAIR 4 (la çair 1, la çér 2, la chair 1)
chaise v CHAISE
CHAISE 19 (çaise 6, çaises 2, chaise 4, cése 2, cèse 1, çéze 2, chéze 2)
CHÂLE 1 (çale)
+CHALEUR 2 (la çaler 1, laçaleir 1)
+CHAMBRE 50 (la çambe 1, la çambr 1, la chambr 1, laçambe 43, laçambes 3, la sambre 1)
CHAMEAU 3 (çamo)
CHAMP 7 (çan)
CHAMPIGNON 1 (çampion)
CHANDELIER 1 (çandélié)
CHANDELLE 1 (sandèles)
changé, changès v CHANGER
CHANGER 29 (çangé 1, çanz 3, çanze 4, canzé 1, çanzé 9, canzer 1, changé 1, changès 1, sanzé 7, senger 1)
chanson v CHANSON

CHANSON 19 (çanson 13, çansons 1, chanson 5)
chanté, chanter v CHANTER
CHANTER 62 (çant 1, çant' 3, cante 1, çante 1, canté 3, çanté 49, çanter 1, chanté 2, chanter 1)
chapeau v CHAPEAU
CHAPEAU 21 (çapeau 15, chapeau 4, sapeau 1, sapo 1)
CHAPELET 2 (çapelet 1, saplé 1)
chaq'in, chaqène v CHACUN
chaque v CHAQUE
CHAQUE 12 (çak 1, caque 1, çaque 9, chaque 1)
chaquein', chaqu'ein, chaquèn, chaquén', chaquèn', chaquéne, chaquène v CHACUN
charbon v CHARBON
CHARBON 7 (çarbon 4, carbons 1, charbon 2)
charette v CHARRETTE
chargé v CHARGER
CHARGER 1 (çarze 8, çarzé 2, chargé 1)
charitable v CHARITABLE
CHARITABLE 2 (çaritable 1, charitable 2)
CHARITÉ 3 (çarite 1, çarité 2)
+CHARITÉ 3 (la çarité)
charpantié v CHARPENTIER
CHARMANT 2 (çarmant)
CHARPENTIER 4 (çarpentier 2, cerpentier 1 charpantié 1)
CHARPIE 1 (cerpie)
CHARRETTE 34 (çarête 1, çarette 31, charrette 1, sarette 1)
CHARRETIER 6 (çarretier 2, çaretier 4, sarretier 1, sartié 1)
chassé v CHASSÉ
CHARRIER 6 (çarié 2, çarrié 3, sarrié 1)
CHARRON 1 (sarron)
CHASSÉ 1 (chassé)

+CHASSE 47 (*la çass'* 1, *la çasse* 21, *la chasse* 2, *la-cass'* 1, *laçasse* 10, *la-çasse* 1, *la sasse* 1, *la-sasse* 1, *là-sasse* 1)
CHASSER 29 (*çace* 20, *çacé* 2, *çasse* 4, *çassé* 1, *sasse* 1, *sassé* 1)[13]
CHASSEUR 5 (*çasseir* 4, *çasser* 1)
CHAT 116 (*çat* 7, *cate* 1, *çate* 6, *çats* 1, *catte* 2, *çatte* 49, *satte* 40)
CHATOUILLER 2 (*çatouille*)
Chassepct v CHASSEPCT
CHASSEPCT 1 (*Chassepct*) [nom de personnage]
Chatte-Chatte v CHATTE-CHATTE
CHATTE-CHATTE 1 (*Chatte-Chatte*) [nom de personnage]
chaud v CHAUD
CHAUD 10 (*çaud* 5, *chaud* 3, *seau* 1, *so*^{2} 1)
CHAUDIÈRE 5 (*çaudière*)
CHAUFFER 4 (*çauffe* 2, *çauffé* 1, *soffé* 1)
CHAUSSETTE 1 (*çausette*)
CHAUSSURE 1 (*çaussire*)
CHAUVE-SOURIS 5 (*soursouri* 1, *soursouris* 4)
+CHAUX 3 (*la chaux, la-chaux* 1)
CHAVIRER 12 (*çavir* 1, *çavire* 5, *çaviré* 5, *çavirer* 1)
chef v CHEF
CHEF 35 (*cef* 29, *çef* 1, *céf* 1, *céf* 1, *cefs* 1, *chef* 2)
chéga v SÉGA
CHEMIN 140 (*chimin* 1, *cimein* 25, *cimin* 103, *çimin* 19, *cimins* 2)
CHEMISE 11 (*chimise* 3, *cimise* 5, *cimises* 1, *cimize* 1, *simise* 1)
CHENILLE 2 (*chini* 1, *cinille* 1)
cher v CHER

CHER 10 (*cer* 7, *cher* 2, *sère* 1)
cherché v CHERCHER
CHERCHER 24 (*cerç'* 4, *çerç'* 2, *cerce* 7, *cercé* 6, *çerçé* 2, *çerçé* 1, *cherché* 1, *serce* 1)
CHEVAL 33 (*chouval* 3, *çouval* 19, *çouvals* 8, *souval* 3)
CHEVEU 31 (*cévé* 1, *chivé* 1, *civé* 15, *civés* 14)
CHÈVRE 4 (*cèv'* 1, *cèvr'* 1, *cevre* 2)
CHEVRETTE 4 (*cévrette* 3, *sévrettes* 1) [mot fr. dial.]
CHEZ 1 (*sez* 1)
chéze v CHAISE
chimère v CHIMÈRE
CHICANER 3 (*cicane*)
CHICANEUR 1 (*sicanair*)
CHICANER 1 (*sicané*)
CHICOT 3 (*cicot*)
+CHIEN 84 (*li ciein* 3, *li cien* 13, *licien* 52, *li-cien* 3, *li-çien* 2, *li ciens* 2, *liciens* 6, *li-ciens* 1, *li sien* 2)
CHIENDENT 1 (*ciendent*)
CHIFFON 2 (*ciffon*)
CHIMÈRE 1 (*chimère*)
chimin v CHEMIN
chimise v CHEMISE
china grass v CHINA+ GRASS
CHINA+GRASS 1 (*china grass*) [mot angl.]
chini v CHENILLE
chinois v CHINOIS
CHINOIS 41 (*chinois* 2, *cinois* 38, *çinois* 1)
CHIPOTER 3 (*cipote* 1, *cipoté* 2)
CHIQUER 1 (*cique*)
CHIROUTE 1 (*sirouttes*)[14]
CHIRURGIEN 2 (*çiruzien* 1, *sourzin* 1)
chivé v CHEVEU
CHOCOLAT 1 (*çocolat*)

CHOISIR 18 (*çoazir* 3, *çoisi* 7, *çoisir* 1, *cosiré* 1, *çosiré* 3, *soizir* 1, *sosir* 1, *sozir* 1)
choléra v CHOLÉRA
CHOLÉRA 4 (*choléra*)
CHOPINE 2 (*çopine*)
chose v CHOSE
CHOSE 108 (*chose* 37, *choses* 3, *choze* 22, *çose* 9, *çoses* 2, *coz*$_3$ 1, *çoz* 29, *coz'* 1, *çoz'* 2)
choses v CHOSE
chouval v CHEVAL
choze v CHOSE
chrétien v CHRÉTIEN
CHRÉTIEN 9 (*chrétien* 5, *chretiens* 3, *chrétiens* 1)
chretiens, chrétiens v CHRÉTIEN
Christ v CHRIST
CHRIST 2 (*Christ*)
ci v CI
CI 2 (*ci*)
cicane v CHICANER
cicot v CHICOT
ciel v CIEL
CIEL 12 (*ciel* 9, *ciele* 3)
+CIEL 98 (*le ciel* 21, *lé ciel* 62, *le ciél* 3, *lé ciél* 2, *le ciele* 6, *léciel* 3, *léciél* 1)
ciele v CIEL
ciendent v CHIENDENT
cierge v CIERGE
CIERGE 1 (*cierge*)
ciffon v CHIFFON
cilindres v CYLINDRE
cim'tière v CIMETIÈRE
CIMARRÓN 19 ([adj] *marron* 5; [n] *marron* 3, *marrons* 1, *marron* 4, *marrons* 2; [adv] *maron* 1, *marron* 2; [v] *maron* 1) [mot esp.].
cimein v CHEMIN
cimetière v CIMETIÈRE
CIMETIÈRE 10 (*cim'tière* 1, *cimetière* 2, *cimiquière* 4, *cimitière* 3)
cimin, çimin, cimins v CHEMIN
cimiquière v CIMETIÈRE
cimise, cimises v CHEMISE
cimitière v CIMETIÈRE

---

[13] Certains de ces exemples donnent l'impression que la distinction entre *chasser* et *chercher* a été perdue.

[14] Forme francisée du tamoul *curuttu*, dont un seul exemple est connu (1782).

cimize	v CHEMISE	
cinille	v CHENILLE	
cinois, çinois	v CHINOIS	
cinq	v CINQ	
CINQ	28 (*ceinq* 14, *cinq* 9, *cinque* 5)	
CINQUANTE 5 (*cinquante*)		
cinquante	v CINQUANTE	
cinque	v CINQ	
cinquième	v CINQUIÈME	
CINQUIÈME 1 (*cinquième*)		
ci pas	v SAIS+PAS	
ciplique	v EXPLIQUER	
cipote, cipoté	v CHIPOTER	
cique	v CHIQUER	
cirandane	v **CIRANDANI**	
CIRANDANI	6 (*cirandane* 1, *sirandane* 1, *sirandanne* 4) [mot bant.]	
cire	v SÛR	
+CIRE	3 (*la cire* 2, *lacire* 1)	
Cirepipe	v CUREPIPE	
cironquelle	v *CIRONQUELLE	
*CIRONQUELLE	1 (*cironquelle*) [mot d'origine inconnue]	
ciroutes	v **CURUTTU**	
CIRQUE	1 (*cirques*)	
cirques	v CIRQUE	
Cirtis	v CIRTIS	
CIRTIS	1 (*Cirtis*) [prénom]	
çiruzien	v CHIRURGIEN	
CISEAU	2 (*ciseaux*)	
ciseaux	v CISEAU	
cîte	1[15]	
citoyen	v CITOYEN	
CITOYEN 1 (*citoyen*)		
citron	v CITRON	
CITRON	3 (*citron* 2, *citrons* 1)	
citronelle	v CITRONELLE	
CITRONELLE 1 (*citronelle*)		
citrons	v CITRON	
civé, civés	v CHEVEU	
cizsé	v ASSEOIR	
clac	1 [onomat.]	
clair	v CLAIR	

[15] Mot utilisé par Pitot (1865) dont nous n'avons pu déterminer ni le sens, ni l'étymon.

CLAIR	27 (*clair* 14, *claire* 8, *clairs* 2, *cler* 2, *clér* 1)	
claire	v CLAIR	
clairé	v ÉCLAIRER	
clairs	v CLAIR	
clairté	v CLARTÉ	
+CLARTÉ	5 (*la clarté* 1, *laclairté* 4)	
claqué	v CLAQUER	
CLAQUER 1 (*claqué*)		
clarté	v CLARTÉ	
CLARTÉ	6 (*clairté* 4, *clarté* 2)	
clate, claté	v ÉCLATER	
Claude	v CLAUDE	
CLAUDE 5 (*Claude*)		
+CLÉ	7 (*la clé* 4, *laclé* 2, *la-clé* 1)	
cler, clér	v CLAIR	
clian	v CLIENT	
clic	2 [onomat.]	
CLIENT 1 (*clian*)		
clin-clin	1 [onomat.]	
+CLOCHE	37 (*la cloce* 4, *lacloce* 30, *lacloces* 3)	
cloison	v CLOISON	
CLOISON	4 (*cloison* 3, *cloisons* 1)	
cloisons	v CLOISON	
CLOU	6 (*clou* 1, *coulou* 2, *coulous* 3)	
CLOUTER	3 (*coulout* 2, *couloute* 1)	
coa	4 [onomat.]	
çoazir	v CHOISIR	
cocé, cocher	v COCHER	
COCHER	6 (*cocé* 5, *cocher* 1)	
COCHON	18 (*coçon* 17, *côçon* 1)	
coco	v COCO	
COCO	52 (*coco* 49, *cocos* 3)	
Cocodès	v COCODÈS	
COCODÈS	3 (*Cocodès*) [nom de personnage]	
çocolat	v CHOCOLAT	
cocombe	v CONCOMBRE	
CONCOMBRE 3 (*cocombe*)		
COCHON	21 (*coçon* 18, *côçon* 1, *cosson* 2)	
coçon, côçon	v COCHON	
cocos	v COCO	
COCU	2 (*coqui*)	
coein	v COIN	

coeur	v CŒUR	
CŒUR	2 (*cœur* 1, *kère* 1) v aussi BON+COEUR	
+CŒUR	139 (*lé ker* 22, *le kère* 2, *lékère* 1, *lé queir* 4, *lé·quér* 1, *lè·quèr* 1, *léqueir* 6, *lequer* 2, *léquer* 23, *lé-quer* 5, *léquér* 4, *léquèr* 3, *lé-quèr* 1, *léquére* 1, *léquère* 1, *lékeir* 18, *licaire* 13, *li quer* 1, *liquer* 23, *liquèr* 2, *liquère* 1, *liquerre* 2, *liquierre* 2)	
coffe, coffre	v COFFRE	
COFFRE	10 (*coffe* 7, *coffre* 2, *coffres* 1)	
coffres	v COFFRE	
cogne, cogné	v COGNER	
COGNER	7 (*cogne* 1, *cogné* 3, *coïn* 1, *coïnié* 2)	
coin	v COIN	
COIN	16 (*coein* 2, *coin* 13, *coins* 1)	
coïn, coïnié	v COGNER	
coins	v COIN	
çoisi, çoisir	v CHOISIR	
Colas	v NICOLAS	
côle, colé, côlé, coler	v COLLER	
colèr', coléré, colère	v COLÈRE	
COLÈRE	55 (*coler* 5, *colèr'* 2, *coléré* 1, *colère* 47)	
+COLÈRE	7 (*la colaire* 5, *la coler* 1, *la-colère* 1)	
colidor, colidors	v CORRIDOR	
colier	v COLLIER	
colique	v COLIQUE	
COLIQUE 2 (*colique*)		
+COLLE	5 (*la cole* 2, *la colle* 1, *lacolle* 2)	
colle, collé	v COLLER	
COLLER	16 (*côle* 1, *colé* 1, *côlé* 2, *colle* 8, *collé* 4)	
collecter	v COLLECTER	
COLLECTER 1 (*collecter*)		
colle-des-keirs	v COLLE-DES-KEIRS	

COLLE-DES-KEIRS 32 (*colle-des-keirs* 32) [nom de personnage]
collége, collège v COLLÈGE
COLLÈGE 2 (*collége* 1, *collège* 1)
colier v COLLIER
COLLIER 4 (*colier* 2, *colier* 2)
colomb, colombe v COLOMBE
COLOMBE 2 (*colomb* 1, *colombe* 1)
colon' v COLONNE
COLONEL
1 (*quhaullxllhauxnhaillent*) [mot angl.]
colonial v COLONIAL
COLONIAL 1 (*colonial*)
+COLONIE 2 (*la colonie*)
colonnades v COLONNADE
COLONNADE 1 (*colonnades*)
COLONNE 3 (*colon'* 1, *colonne* 1, *colonnes* 1)
colonne, colonnes v COLONNE
colophane v COLOPHANE
COLOPHANE 10 (*colophane* 8, *colophanes* 2)
colophanes v COLOPHANE
com v COMME
com'ça v COMME+ÇA
coma, côma, comâ v COMMENT
comacé, comacè
v COMMENCER
coman, côman v COMMENT
comance v COMMENCER
comanceman
v COMMENCEMENT
comand, comande, comandé, co-mandé v COMMANDER
comandeir v COMMANDEUR
comandman
v COMMANDEMENT
cômant, comas v COMMENT
combiein, combien
v COMBIEN
COMBIEN 16 (*combiein* 11, *combien* 5)
comça v COMME+ÇA
come v COMME
começa v COMME+ÇA
COMÉDIE 1 (*comédies*)
+COMÉDIE 5 (*la comédie*)
comédies v COMÉDIE

comenc'ment
v COMMENCEMENT
comence, cômence, comencé
v COMMENCER
coment, côment v COMMENT
coméré, comère v COMMÈRE
COMMÈRE 29 (*coméré* 3, *comère* 2, *commer'* 2, *commér'* 1, *commèr'* 1, *commère* 20)
comission v COMMISSION
COMMISSION 1 (*comission*)
comm' v COMME
comm'ça v COMME+ÇA
comman v COMMENT
commance v COMMENCER
command v COMMANDER
commandant v COMMANDANT
COMMANDANT
8 (*commandant*)
commande, commandé, commandée v COMMANDER
commandemant, commandement
v COMMANDEMENT
COMMANDEMENT 25 (*comandman* 6, *commandemant* 2, *commandement* 16, *commandman* 1)
commander$_{1,2}$
v COMMANDER, COMMANDEUR
COMMANDER 51 (*comand* 9, *comande* 10, *comandé* 5, *co-mandé* 1, *command* 3, *commande* 7, *commandé* 11, *commandée* 1, *commander$_1$* 1, *commandér* 1, *commandèr* 2)
commandér, commandèr
v COMMANDEUR
COMMANDEUR 7 (*comandeir* 2, *commander$_2$* 1, *commandér* 1, *commandèr* 2, *comandére* 1)
commandman
v COMMANDEMENT
comme v COMME

COMME 132 (*com* 22, *come* 9, *comm'* 26, *comme* 76, *coume* 9)
COMME+ÇA 36 (*com'ça* 1, *comça* 28, *começa* 1, *comm'ça* 6)
commenc', commenç', commence, commencé
v COMMENCER
commencement
v COMMENCEMENT
COMMENCEMENT 7 (*comanceman* 3, *comenc'ment* 1, *commencement* 3)
+COMMENCEMENT 1 (*le comanceman*)
COMMENCER 103 (*comacé* 1, *comacè* 1, *comance* 8, *comence* 40, *cômence* 2, *comencé* 3, *commance* 8, *commenc'* 1, *commenç'* 3, *commence* 15, *commencé* 15, *coumence* 5, *coumencé* 1)
comment v COMMENT
COMMENT 835 (*coma* 81, *côma* 12, *comâ* 1, *coman* 170, *côman* 2, *cômant* 1, *comas* 1, *coment* 213, *côment* 50, *comman* 19, *comment* 254, *common* 1, *conmment* 1, *couma* 5, *coumâ* 1, *couman* 6, *coument* 17)
commer', commér', commèr'
v COMMÈRE
commerce v COMMERCE
COMMERCE 1 (*commerce*)
commercial v COMMERCIAL
COMMERCIAL
3 (*commercial*)
commère v COMMÈRE
COMMÈRE 29 (*coméré* 3, *comère* 2, *commer'* 2, *commér'* 1, *commèr'* 1, *commère* 20)
commi, commis v COMMIS
COMMIS 2 (*commi* 1, *commis* 2)
commis-caca
v COMMIS, CACA

commission v COMMISSION
COMMISSION 12
   (*commission* 5, *commissions* 7)
commissionnaire v
   COMMISSIONNAIRE
COMMISSIONNAIRE 1
   (*commissionnaire*)
commissions v COMMISSION
common v COMMENT
compagné v COMPAGNIE
+COMPAGNIE 2 (*la compagni*
   1, *la-compagni* 1)
COMPAGNIE 1 (*compagné*)
compagnon v COMPAGNON
COMPAGNON 1 (*compagnon*)
compar v COMPARER
comparét v COMPARAITRE
COMPARAITRE 1 (*comparét*)
COMPARER 1 (*compar*)
compas v COMPAS
COMPAS 1 (*compas* 1)
compèr, *comper'*, *compere*,
compère, *compère* v COMPÈRE
COMPÈRE 64 (*compèr* 2,
   comper' 4, *compère* 1,
   compére 3, *compère* 53,
   compères 1)
compères v COMPÈRE
complaisance
   v COMPLAISANCE
COMPLAISANCE
   2 (*complaisance*)
compliment v COMPLIMENT
COMPLIMENT 3 (*compliment*
   2, *compliments* 1)
compliments v COMPLIMENT
comploté v COMPLOTER
COMPLOTER 1 (*comploté*)
compran, *comprend*,
comprend', *comprende*,
comprendre v COMPRENDRE
COMPRENDRE 46 (*compran*
   20, *comprend* 20,
   comprend' 1, *comprende*
   1, *comprendre* 4)
compte₁ v COMPTE
compte₂ v COMPTER
COMPTE 12 (*compte₁* 4,
   cont 7, *cont'₁* 1)
compté, *comptez* v COMPTER

COMPTER₂ 11 (*compte* 1,
   compté 3, *comptez* 1,
   cont'₂ 1. *conte₁* 1. *conté₁* 4)
con' v CONNAÎTRE
concert v CONCERT
CONCERT 1 (*concert*)
condamn' v CONDAMNER
CONDAMNATION
   1 (*condanacion*)
condamne, *condamnés*
   v CONDAMNER
CONDAMNER 13 (*condamn'*
   1, *condamne* 3,
   condamnés 1, *condane* 5,
   condané 2, *condanée* 1)
condanacion
   v CONDAMNATION
condane, *condané*, *condanée*
   v CONDAMNER
condé v **KONTAI**
condicion v CONDITION
condicter, *condictér*
   v CONDUCTEUR
condir, *condir'*, *condire*,
condiré v CONDUIRE
condit v CONDUITE
condition v CONDITION
CONDITION 11 (*condicion* 2,
   condition 9)
CONDUCTEUR 4 (*condicter* 2,
   condictér 2)
conduir' v CONDUIRE
CONDUIRE 15 (*condir* 7,
   condir' 1, *condire* 5,
   condiré 1, *conduir'* 1)
conduit, *conduite* v CONDUITE
CONDUITE 4 (*condit* 1,
   conduit 1, *conduite* 2)
cone, *cône*, *coné*, *côné*
   v CONNAÎTRE
confes, *confess*, *confessé*
   v CONFESSER
CONFESSER 5 (*confes* 2,
   confess 1, *confessé* 2)
confession v CONFESSION
CONFESSION 1 (*confession*)
confessionnal
   v CONFESSIONAL
CONFESSIONAL
   1 (*confessionnal*)
CONFIANCE (*confians* 2)
confians v CONFIANCE

confié v CONFIER
CONFIER 1 (*confié*)
confitire v CONFITURE
CONFITURE 2 (*confitire*)
confonde v CONFONDRE
CONFONDRE 1 (*confonde*)
CONGÉ 1 (*conzé*)
conmment v COMMENT
conn', *connai*, *connaie*, *connais*
   v CONNAÎTRE
connaissance
   v CONNAISSANCE
CONNAISSANCE
   1 (*connaissance*)
connait, *connaît*
   v CONNAÎTRE
CONNAÎTRE 364 (*con'* 1,
   cone 16, *cône* 7, *coné* 57,
   côné 28, *conn'* 13, *connai*
   5, *connaie* 1, *connais* 48,
   connaît 1, *connaît* 3
   conne 44, *conné* 131,
   connée 1, *connent* 1,
   connét 1, *connéz* 2,
   connois 9, *connoit* 1)
CONN(AÎTRE)+*ER* 1
   (*conneir*)
conne, *conné*, *connée*
   v CONNAÎTRE
conneir v
   CONN(AÎTRE)+*ER*
connent, *connét*, *connéz*,
connois, *connoit*
   v CONNAÎTRE
conseil v CONSEIL
CONSEIL 16 (*conseil* 7,
   conseils 3, *consey* 3,
   conséy 3)
conseillère v CONSEILLEUR
CONSEILLEUR 1 (*conseillère*)
conseils v CONSEIL
consèns v CONSENTIR
CONSENTIR 1 (*consèns*)
conserv v CONSERVER
CONSERVE 1 (*conserves*)
conservé v CONSERVER 1
CONSERVER 2 (*conserv* 1,
   conservé 1)
conserves v CONSERVE
consey, *conséy* v CONSEIL
consider v CONSIDÉRER
CONSIDÉRER 1 (*consider*)

consilt v CONSULTER
consolateur v CONSOLATEUR
CONSOLATEUR 1 (*consolateur*)
console, consolé v CONSOLER
CONSOLER 8 (*console* 3, *consolé* 5)
constant v CONSTANT
CONSTANT 2 (*constant*)
Constantin v CONSTANTIN
CONSTANTIN 1 (*Constantin*) [nom de personnage]
constricter v CONSTRUCTEUR
constrikcion v CONSTRUCTION
CONSTRUCTEUR 1 (*constricter*)
CONSTRUCTION 1 (*constrikcion*)
CONSULTER 2 (*consilt*)
cont, cont'$_1$ v COMPTE
cont'$_2$ v COMPTER
contan, contant v CONTENT
contantman v CONTENTEMENT
conte$_1$ v COMPTER
conte$_2$ v CONTER
conte$_3$ v CONTRE
conté$_1$ v COMPTER
conté$_2$ v CONTER
conten, contens, content v CONTENT
CONTENT 277 (*contan* 23, *contant* 13, *conten* 1, *contens* 2, *content* 220, *contént* 1, *contente* 1, *contents* 16)
contént v CONTENT
contenté v CONTENTER
CONTENTER 1 (*contenté*)
contentement v CONTENTEMENT
CONTENTEMENT 2 (*contantman* 1, *contentement* 1)·
contents v CONTENT
CONTER 3 (*conte*$_2$ 1, *conté*$_2$ 2)
continié v CONTINUER
CONTINUER 2 (*continié*)

contr v CONTRE
contraire v CONTRAIRE
CONTRAIRE 4 (*contraire* 3, *contraires* 1, *contrér* 1)
contraires v CONTRAIRE
contre v CONTRE
CONTRE 34 (*conte*$_3$ 3, *contr* 24, *contre* 7)
contredance, contredanse v CONTREDANSE
CONTREDANSE 4 (*contredance* 1, *contredanse* 3)
contrér v CONTRAIRE
CONVENIR 3 (*convini*)
converti v CONVERTIR
CONVERTIR 1 (*converti*)
convini v CONVENIR
CONVOITER 1 (*convoat* 1)
convoat v CONVOITER
conzé v CONGÉ
copié v COPIER
COPIER 1 (*copié*)
çopine v CHOPINE
coq, côq v COQ
COQ 37 (*coq* 34, *côq* 1, *coq-di-bois* 1, *coqs* 1)
coq-di-bois v COQ
coqs v COQ
+COQUE 9 (*la coque* 2, *la coques* 1, *lacoque* 6)
coquette v COQUETTE
COQUETTE 3 (*coquette* 2, *coquettes* 1)
coquettes v COQUETTE
coqui v COCU
coquin v COQUIN$_1$
coquin v COQUIN$_2$
COQUIN$_1$ 14 (*coquin* 9, *coquins* 5) [nom]
COQUIN$_2$ 6 (*coquin*) [vb.]
+COQUINE 1 (*la coquine*)
coquins v COQUIN
corail v CORAIL
CORAIL 1 (*corail*)
Corazin v CORAZIN
CORAZIN 1 (*Corazin*) [nom de personnage]
CORBEILLE 1 (*corbéy*)
corbéy v CORBEILLE
corce v ÉCORCHER

+CORDE 46 (*laccord'* 1, *la corde* 10, *la côrde* 1, *lacorde* 30, *lacôrde* 4)
cordon v CORDON
CORDON 3 (*cordon*)
CORIACE 1 (*corriace*)
coricoco 1 [onomat.]
cornard v CORNARD
CORNARD 1 (*cornard*)
CORNE 5 (*corne* 2, *cornes* 3)
corne, cornes v CORNE
cornet v CORNET
CORNET 1 (*cornet*)
corps v CORPS
CORPS 5 (*corps*)
+CORPS 117 (*le cor* 2, *lé cor* 26, *le côr* 11, *lé corps* 5, *lécor* 1, *lé-cor* 1, *lécorps* 66, *lé-corps* 5)
corps-sans-âme v CORPS-SANS-ÂME
CORPS-SANS-ÂME 4 (*corps-sans-âme*) [nom de personnage]
corriace v CORIACE
CORRIDOR 2 (*colidor* 1, *colidors* 1)
corset v CORSET
CORSET 3 (*corset* 2, *corsèt* 1)
corsêt v CORSET
corvé, corvée v CORVÉE
CORVÉE 2 (*corvé* 1, *corvée* 1)
corvette v CORVETTE
CORVETTE 2 (*corvette*)
cos', cose v CAUSER
çose, çoses v CHOSE
cosiré, çosiré v CHOISIR
cosson v COCHON
costime, costimé v COSTUME
COSTUME 5 (*costime* 4, *costimé* 1)
cot, cot', cote, côte, coté, côté v CÔTÉ
CÔTÉ 120 (*cot* 9, *cot'* 3, *cote* 9, *côte* 6, *coté* 36, *côté* 35, *côtés* 3, *cotte* 9, *cotté* 10)
côtés v CÔTÉ
cothurne v COTHURNE
COTHURNE 1 (*cothurne*)
côtier v CÔTIER
CÔTIER 1 (*côtier*)
cotillon v COTILLON

COTILLON 1 (*cotillon* 1)
coto maïe v COTON+MAÏS
coton v COTON
COTON 5 (*coton*)
COTON+MAÏS 2 (*coto maïe*)
cotte, cotté v CÔTÉ
cou$_1$ v COU
cou$_2$ v COUP
COU 1 (*cou$_1$*) [interj.]
+COU 13 (*lécou* 1, *licou* 12)
cou d'vent v COUP+DE+VENT
cou de pié v COUP+DE+PIED
couac 1 [onomat.]
couc v **KOUG**
coucé v COUCHER
COUCHER 10 (*coucé*)
coud v COUP+DE
coud poein
　　v COUP+DE+POING
coude$_1$ v COUDRE
coude$_2$ v COUP+DE
coudé v COUDÉE
COUDÉE 1 (*coudé*)
coudebâton
　　v COUP+DE+BÂTON
coudefisil
　　v COUP+DE+FUSIL
coude pié v COUP+DE+PIED
coudepied v COUP+DE+PIED
coudesipion
　　v COUP+DE+SCIPION
coudre v COUDRE
COUDRE 7 (*coude$_1$* 6, *coudre* 1)
couderoce, coudroce
　　v COUP+DE+ROCHE
coudvan v COUP+DE+VENT
+COUENNE 2 (*la couen'* 1,
　　la couénne 1)
couh 2 [interj.]
coui v CUIRE
couillers v CUILLÈRE
COUILLON 2 (*couyon*)
couin 8 [onomat.]
couit v CUIRE
couive, couivre v CUIVRE
coul, coul', coule, coulé
　　v COULER
couleir v COULEUR
couler$_1$ v COULER
couler$_2$ v COULEUR

COULER 35 (*coul* 1, *coul'* 2,
　　coule 5, *coulé* 26,
　　couler$_1$ 1)
coulère v COULEUR
COULEUR 10 (*couleir* 6,
　　couler$_2$ 3, *coulère* 1)
coulou v CLOU
coulous v CLOU
coulout, couloute v CLOUTER
couma, coumâ, couman
　　v COMMENT
coume v COMME
coumence, coumencé
　　v COMMENCER
coument v COMMENT
coup v COUP
COUP 154 (*cou$_2$* 7,
　　coup 142, *coups* 5)
coup' v COUPER
coupab v COUPABLE
COUPABLE 2 (*coupab* 1,
　　coupables 1)
coupables v COUPABLE
coup à boire v COUP+À+BOIRE
COUP+À+BOIRE
　　1 (*coup à boire*)
coup d'çapeau
　　v COUP+DE+CHAPEAU
coup de v COUP+DE
COUP+DE 10 (*coud* 1, *coude$_2$*
　　4, *coup de* 6)
COUP+DE+BÂTON
　　2 (*coudebâton* 1,
　　coupdebâtons 1)
coupdebâtons
　　v COUP+DE+BÂTON
COUP+DE+CHAPEAU
　　1 (*coup d'çapeau*)
coupdefisil
　　v COUP+DE+FUSIL
COUP+DE+FUSIL 4
　　(*coudefisil* 1, *coupdefisil* 3)
COUP+DE+MAIN
　　1 (*coup d'main*)
COUP+DE+PATTE
　　1 (*coups d'patt'*)
coupdepied, coup de pied
　　v COUP+DE+PIED

COUP+DE+PIED 10 (*cou de
　　pié* 1, *coude pié* 1,
　　coudepied 1, *coup de pied*
　　4, *coupdepied* 2,
　　coupdepieds 1)
coupdepieds v COUP+DE+PIED
coup de poing
　　v COUP+DE+POING
COUP+DE+POING 3 (*coud
　　poein* 1, *coup de poing* 1,
　　coupdepoings 1)
coupdepoings
　　v COUP+DE+POING
COUP+DE+ROCHE 2
　　(*couderoce* 1 *coudroce* 1)
coup de vent
　　v COUP+DE+VENT
COUP+DE+VENT 17 (*cou
　　d'vent* 1, *coudvan* 1, *coup
　　d'vent* 3, *coup de vent* 10,
　　coups 'd'vent 1, *coups-de-
　　vent* 1)
coup d'main v COUP+DE+MAIN
coup d'vent v COUP+DE+VENT
*coupe, coupé, coupecoupe,
coupe-coupe* v COUPER
COUPER 66 (*coup'* 1,
　　coupecoupe 1,
　　coupe-coupe 1,
　　coupe 42, *coupé* 21)
couper' v COUPEUR
COUPEUR 3 (*couper'*)
couplé, couplet v COUPLET
COUPLET 4 (*couplé* 1,
　　couplet 3)
coups v COUP
coups d'patt'
　　v COUP+DE+PATTE
coups 'd'vent, coups-de-vent
　　v COUP+DE+VENT
+COUR 46 (*la cour* 12,
　　lacour 34)
cour' v COURIR
courage v COURAGE
COURAGE 1 (*courage* 1,
　　couraz 3, *couraz'* 1,
　　couraze 11)
courant d'air
　　v COURANT+D'+AIR
COURANT+D'+AIR
　　1 (*courant d'air*)
couraz, couraz' v COURAGE

couraze v COURAGE
courbé v COURBER
COURBER 2 (*courbé*)
couri, courir v COURIR
COURIR 42 (*cour'* 1, *couri* 36, *courir* 2, *courri* 3)
courone, couronne v COURONNE
COURONNE 2 (*courone* 1, *couronne* 1)
couroupa, couroupas v **EKHOROPA**
courri v COURIR
+COURSE 6 (*la course* 4, *lacourse* 2)
court v COURT
COURT 9 (*court* 1, *courte* 6, *courtecourte* 2)
courte, courtecourte v COURT
cousin v COUSIN
COUSIN 9 (*cousin* 2, *cousines* 7)
cousines v COUSIN
cousinier v CUISINIER
cousins v COUSIN
cousparvani 1[16]
cout, coute$_2$ v COÛTER
cout'$_1$, coute$_1$ v ÉCOUTER
couté$_1$ v COÛTER
couté$_2$ v ÉCOUTER
couteau v COUTEAU
COUTEAU 12 (*couteau* 7, *couto* 5)
COÛTER 4 (*cout* 1, *coute$_2$* 1, *couté$_1$* 2)
coutirières v COUTURIÈRE
COUTURIÈRE 1 (*coutirières*)
çouval, çouvals v CHEVAL
couve, couvé, couver, couvér v COUVRIR
couvert v COUVERT
COUVERT 5 (*couvert* 4, *couverte* 1)
couverte v COUVERT
couvertire, couvertires v COUVERTURE
couverts v COUVERTS

COUVERTS 2 (*couverts*)
COUVERTURE 5 (*couvertire* 4, *couvertires* 1)
couvri v COUVRIR
COUVRIR 11 (*couve* 1, *couvé* 3, *couver* 3, *couvér* 1, *couvri* 4)
couyère v CUILLÈRE
couyon v COUILLON
couzoupa[17] v **EKHOROPA**
coz$_1$ v CAUSE
coz$_2$ v CAUSER
coz$_3$ v CHOSE
çoz, coz', çoz' v CHOSE
cozé v CAUSER
CRABE 1 (*carabes*)
+CRACHE 1 (*lacrace*)
CRACHER 4 (*crace*)
crace v CRACHER
crainte v CRAINTE
CRAINTE 2 (*crainte*)
+CRAINTE 2 (*lé crainte*)
cramouade v CAMARADE
+CRAMPE 1 (*la crampe*)
crâne v CRÂNE
CRÂNE 1 (*crâne*)
crase, crasé, craz, crazé v ÉCRASER
+CRÉATION 1 (*la créacion*)
CRÉATURE 2 (*criatire*)
crécoquin v SACRÉ+COQUIN
créol, créol', créole v CRÉOLE
CRÉOLE 17 (*créol* 1, *créol'* 2, *créole* 6, *créoles* 3, *criole* 5, *crool'* 1)
créoles v CRÉOLE
cresson v CRESSON
CRESSON 1 (*cresson*)
+CRÊTE 1 (*la crêt'*)
crétin v CRÉTIN
CRÉTIN 2 (*crétin*)
crève, crévé, crêvé v CREVER
CREVER 9 (*crève* 2, *crévé* 5, *crêvé* 2)

---

[17] Bien que *couzoupa* puisse être une erreur pour *couroupa* dans ce texte, il faut noter que /kuzupa/ est aussi attesté en CM pour le nom d'un personnage animal dans les contes. Ce dernier est d'origine bantoue et signifie « hyène » en ngulu et en makua.

cri v CRI
CRI 10 (*cri*)
criatire v CRÉATURE
cricifié v CRUCIFIER
crid v CRU
crie, crïe, crié, crïé, crië v CRIER
CRIER 143 (*crie* 12, *crïe* 23, *crié* 82, *crïé* 1, *crië* 4, *crire$_2$* 3, *criye* 5, *criyé* 13)
criminel v CRIMINEL
CRIMINEL 1 (*criminel*)
+CRIN 1 (*dicrin*)
criole v CRÉOLE
crire$_1$ v ÉCRIRE
crire$_2$ v CRIER
CRISE 2 (*criz*)
criye, criyé v CRIER
criz v CRISE
croar v CROIRE
croazé v CROISER
croc v CROC
CROC 1 (*croc*)
crocée, crocet, crocher v CROCHER
CROCHET 2 (*crocée* 1, *crocet* 1)
CROCHER 1 (*crocher*)
croir, croir', croire v CROIRE
CROIRE 172 (*croar* 20, *croir* 8, *croir'* 37, *croire* 107)
CROIRE+PAS 1 (*crois pas*)
CROISER 1 (*croazé*)
crois pas v CROIRE+PAS
+CROIX 11 (*la croa* 7, *la croix* 4)
crool' v CRÉOLE
Croolc v CROOLC
CROOLC 2 (*Croolc*) [nom de personnage]
crouc-crouc 1 [onomat.]
+CROUPIÈRE 1 (*la-croupière*)
CRU 1 (*crid*)
CRUCIFIER 9 (*cricifié*)
Cuba v CUBA
CUBA 1 (*Cuba*) [toponyme]
CUILLÈRE 3 (*couillers* 1, *couyère* 2)
CUIRE 26 (*coui* 5, *couit* 20, *cui* 1)

---

[16] Mot indien utilisé par Descroizilles (1867) dont le sens et l'étymon n'ont pas été identifiés. Pour le contexte, v p 54 ci-dessus.

+CUISINE 24 (*la cousine* 9, *lacousine* 15)
CUISINIER 26 (*cousinier* 26)
CUIVRE 7 (*couive* 6, *couivre* 1)
+CUL 1 (*li qui*)
CULER v (RE)CULER
CULOTTE 11 (*kilotte* 1, *quilote* 1, *quilotte* 9)
cumin v CUMIN
CUMIN 1 (*cumin*)
Cure pipe v CUREPIPE
CUREPIPE 4 (*Cirepipe* 1, *Cure pipe* 1, *qirpip'* 1, *quirpipe* 1) [nom de ville]
CURUTTU 1 (*ciroutes*) [mot tam.]
CUVETTE 1 (*quivettes*)
cyclone v CYCLONE
CYCLONE 1 (*cyclone*)
cylindes v CYLINDRE
CYLINDRE 2 (*cilindres* 1, *cylindes* 1)

D

d'abord v D'ABORD
D'ABORD 1 (*d'abord* 1)
d'accor, d'accord v D'ACCORD
D'ACCORD 3 (*d'accor* 1, *d'accord* 1, *dacord* 1)
d'ant, d'antr v D'ENTRE
D'AVANCE 3 (*d'avans* 1, *davance* 2)
d'avans v D'AVANCE
d'avantage v D'AVANTAGE
D'AVANTAGE 5 (*d'avantage* 2, *d'avantaze* 3)
d'avantaze v D'AVANTAGE
dacord v D'ACCORD
D'ENTRE 2 (*d'ant* 1, *d'antr* 1)
DAL 2 (*dholl*) [mot hind.]
Dalais v DALAIS
DALAIS 1 (*Dalais*) [nom de famille]
dames Céré v MADAME+SÊRÉ
dan v DANS
dance v DANS, CE
Dandin v DANDIN

DANDIN 2 (*Dandin*) [nom de personnage]
DANGER 1 (*danzer*)
dangue 2 [onomat.]
dans v DANS
DANS 1982 (*dan* 501, *dans* 1481)
+DANSE 3 (*la danse*)
danse, dansé, danser v DANSER
DANSER 48 (*danse* 2, *dansé* 43, *danser* 1, *dansez* 2)
dansez v DANSER
danzer v DANGER
davance v D'AVANCE
de v DE
DE 91 (*de* 85, *dé₁* 6)
dé₁ v DE
dé₂, dè v DEUX
+DÉ 2 (*lédé*)
débarque, débarqué, débarquer v DÉBARQUER
DEBARQUER 5 (*débarque* 3, *débarqué* 1, *débarquer* 1)
débatté v DÉBATTRE
DÉBATTRE 1 (*débatté*)
débordé v DÉBORDER
DÉBORDEMENT 1 (*débordements*)
débordements v DÉBORDEMENT
DÉBORDER 2 (*débordé*)
DEBOUT 58 (*dibout* 17, *diboute* 15, *dibouté* 23, *diboutte* 1, *dibouttè* 1, *doubouté* 1)
déboutône v DÉBOUTONNER
DÉBOUTONNER 1 (*déboutône*)
débrouille v DÉBROUILLER
DÉBROUILLER 3 (*débrouille*)
décacétte v DÉCACHETER
DÉCACHETER 1 (*décacétte*)
Decaen v DECAEN
DECAEN 2 (*Decaen*) [nom de famille]
décembre v DÉCEMBRE
DÉCEMBRE 1 (*décembre* 1)
décendant v DESCENDANT
décents v DEUX-CENT
DE+CE+TEMPS 4 (*dé c'tems* 1, *dé ç'tems* 2, *destemps* 1)

déchirée v DÉCHIRER
DÉCHIRER 15 (*déchirée* 1, *décir* 4, *désiré* 2, *dicire* 6, *diciré* 4)
décid', décidé v DÉCIDER
DÉCIDER 4 (*décid'* 1, *décidé* 2, *dicidé* 1)
décir v DECHIRER
déclaré v DECLARER
DÉCLARER 1 (*déclaré*)
décolle v DÉCOLLER
DÉCOLLER 1 (*décolle*)
décor v DÉCOR
DÉCOR 1 (*décor*)
décoré v DECORER
DÉCORER 2 (*décoré*)
découver, découvert v DÉCOUVRIR
DÉCOUVRIR 4 (*découver* 1, *découvert* 3)
dé c'tems, dé ç'tems v DE+CE+TEMPS
DEDANS 6 (*didans*)
défaire v DÉFAIRE
DÉFAIRE 4 (*défaire*)
défend', défendé v DÉFENDRE
défendie v DÉFENDU
DÉFENDRE 2 (*défend'* 1, *défendé* 1)
DÉFENDU 1 (*défendie*)
défié v DÉFIER
DÉFIER 1 (*défié*)
défiguir v DÉFIGURER
DÉFIGURER 1 (*défiguir*)
défin, défint v DÉFUNT
défonç', défoncée v DÉFONCER
DÉFONCER 2 (*défonç'* 1, *défoncée* 1)
défunt v DÉFUNT
DÉFUNT 11 (*défin* 3, *défint* 7, *défunt* 1)
dégàt v DÉGÂT
DÉGAGER 11 (*dégaze* 3, *dégazé* 8)
DÉGÂT 2 (*dégàt* 1, *dégats* 1)
dégats v DÉGÂT
dégaze, dégazé v DÉGAGER
déhor, dehors v DEHORS
DEHORS 50 (*déhor* 22, *dehors* 3, *déhors* 3, *dohore* 1, *dohors* 21)
déhors v DEHORS

deix v DEUX
déja, déjà v DÉJÀ
DÉJÀ 15 (*déjà* 1, *déjà* 5, *déza* 6, *dézà* 3)
DÉJEÛNER 12 (*dez'né* 1, *dézeiner* 1, *dézéné* 1, *dijné* 3, *dizné* 6)
dé l'eau v +EAU
dé l'eau de mer v +EAU+DE+MER
délire v DÉLIRE
DÉLIRE 1 (*délire*)
délivré v DÉLIVRER
DÉLIVRER 1 (*délivré*)
déliz v DÉLUGE
DÉLUGE 2 (*déliz*)
demain v DEMAIN
DEMAIN 33 (*demain* 1, *dimain* 24, *diméin* 3, *dimen* 1, *dimin* 4)
démancé v DÉMANCHER
DÉMANCHER 4 (*démancé* 4, *dimancé* 3)
demande, demandé, demandée v DEMANDER
DEMANDER 141 (*demande* 5, *demandé* 4, *demandée* 1, *dimand* 19, *dimand'* 2, *dimande* 81, *dimandé* 29)
démenti v DÉMENTIR
DÉMENTIR 1 (*démenti*)
démére v DÉMEURRER
DÉMEURRER 1 (*démére*)
demi v DEMI
DEMI 9 (*demi* 1, *dimi* 8)
démon v DÉMON
DÉMON 8 (*démon* 8)
+DÉMON 2 (*le démon* 1, *le dimons* 1)
démoniac v DÉMONIAQUE
DÉMONIAQUE 1 (*démoniac*)
dénié v DENIÉ
DENIÉ 1 (*dénié*)
denier₁ v DÉNIER
denier₂ v DERNIER
DÉNIER 1 (*denier₁*)
+DENT 32 (*lé dan* 8, *lé den* 1, *lé dent* 6, *lédent* 1, *lé-dent* 2, *lédents* 11, *lé-dents* 3)
dentelle v DENTELLE
DENTELLE 2 (*dentelle*)
dépassé v DÉPASSER

DÉPASSER 1 (*dépassé*)
dépécé, dépéçé v DÉPÊCHER
DÉPÊCHER 4 (*dépécé* 3, *dépéçé* 1)
DÉPENDANCE 1 (*dépendances*)
dépendances v DÉPENDANCE
dépensé v DÉPENSER
DÉPENSER 1 (*dépensé*)
dépis v DEPUIS
DÉPOSER 4 (*dépoz*)
dépoz v DÉPOSER
depuis v DEPUIS
DEPUIS 71 (*dépis* 5, *depuis* 4, *dépuis* 1, *di'pi* 1, *dipi* 28, *dipis* 32)
dépuis v DEPUIS
déracine, déraciné v DÉRACINER
DÉRACINER 2 (*déracine* 1, *déraciné* 1)
dérange v DÉRANGER
DÉRANGER 3 (*dérange* 1, *déranze* 1, *déranzé* 1)
déranze, déranzé v DÉRANGER
dériére v DERRIÈRE
dernié, dernier v DERNIER
DERNIER 24 (*denier₂*1, *dernié* 10, *dernier* 12, *dernière* 1)
dernière v DERNIER
dérobe, dérobé v DÉROBER
DÉROBER 4 (*dérobé* 1, *dérobé* 3)
derrier, derriere, derrière v DERRIÈRE
DERRIÈRE 54 (*dériére* 7, *derrier* 2, *derriere* 1, *derrière* 43, *derrîère* 1)
derrière v DERRIÈRE
des v DES
DES 2 (*des*)
dés v DEUX
désabille v DÉSHABILLER
desçand, désçand v DESCENDRE
désçandan, descendant v DESCENDANT
DESCENDANT 2 (*décendant* 1, *désçandan*1, *descendant* 1)

descend, descende, descendé, descendez v DESCENDRE
DESCENDRE 48 (*desçand* 3, *désçand* 5, *descend* 1, *descende* 1, *descendé* 1, *descendez* 1, *dessande* 1, *dicende* 13, *dicendé* 18, *discende* 1, *dissandé* 3)
dés-cents v DEUX-CENT
Desfontaines v DESFONTAINES
DESFONTAINES 1 (*Desfontaines*) [nom de famille]
DÉSERT 8 (*dézer*)
DÉSHABILLER 1 (*désabille*)
désiré v DÉCHIRER
+DÉSOLATION 1 (*la désolacion*)
DÉSOLÉ 1 (*désolés*)
désolés v DÉSOLÉ
désorde v DÉSORDRE
DÉSORDRE 1 (*désorde*)
de sort, dé sort v DE+SORTE
DE+SORTE 5 (*de sort* 3, *dé sort* 2)
dessande v DESCENDRE
dessert v DESSERT
DESSERT 2 (*dessert*)
dessin v DESSIN
DESSIN 1 (*dessin*)
DESSUS 2 (*disi*)
destemps v DE+CE+TEMPS
det v DETTE
détachement v DÉTACHMENT
DÉTACHMENT 3 (*détachement* 1, *tach'ment* 2)
DÉTACHEMENT 2 (*tach'ment*)
deterrer v DÉTERRER
DÉTERRER 1 (*deterrer*)
détrir v DÉTRUIRE
DÉTRUIRE 8 (*détrir*)
DETTE 4 (*det* 4)
deux v DEUX
DEUX 272 (*dé₂* 235, *dè* 3, *deix* 15, *dés* 16, *deux* 2)
DEUX-CENT 2 (*décents* 1, *dés-cents* 1)
DEUX+AN 1 (*dé zan*)
deuxième v DEUXIÈME
DEUXIÈME 4 (*deuxième*)

DEVANT 109 (*divan* 56, *divant* 53)
dévé, dévè v DEVOIR
(DE)VENIR 645 (*divini* 1, *divinie* 3, *divinis* 1, *venez* 1, *veni* 1, *venir* 2, *vin'* 18, *vine* 306, *vini* 299, *vini'* 1, *vinie* 12, *vinne* 1)
DEVIN 21 (*divin$_1$*)
déviné v DEVINER
DEVINER 1 (*déviné*)
dévoar, devoir v DEVOIR
DEVOIR 91 (*dévé* 4, *dévè* 1, *dévoar* 1, *devoir* 2, *devrait* 2, *devré* 2, *dévré* 2, *devrée* 17, *dévrée* 1, *devrez* 3, *dévrez* 2, *devréz* 1, *doa* 6, *doat* 9, *doit* 27, *doit'* 1, *doite* 10)
dévor v DÉVORER
DÉVORER 1 (*dévor*)
devrait, devré, dévré, devrée, dévrée, devrez, dévrez, devréz v DEVOIR
déza, dézà v DÉJÀ
dé zan v DEUX+AN
dézeiner, dézéné v DÉJEÛNER
dézer v DÉSERT
dez'né v DÉJEÛNER
dholl v **DAL**
diab, diab', diabe, diabl, diable v DIABLE
DIABLE 49 (*diab* 21, *diab'* 3, *diabe* 3, *diabl* 1, *diable* 16, *diables* 2, *diabre* 2)
+DIABLE 1 (*le diable*)
diables, diabre v DIABLE
diamant v DIAMANT
DIAMANT 13 (*diamant*)
d'ibainne v +ÉBENNE
dibeirre, diber, diberre v +BEURRE
di biein, di bien, dibien, di-bien v +BIEN
di blé, diblé, di-blé v +BLÉ
diboi, di bois, dibois, di-bois v +BOIS
dibout, diboute, dibouté, diboutte, dibouttè v DEBOUT
di brit, di brit', di-brit, dibruit v +BRUIT
diçan v +SANG

dicende, dicendé v DESCENDRE
dicidé v DÉCIDER
dicire, diciré v DÉCHIRER
dicrin v +CRIN
dictionnaire v DICTIONNAIRE
DICTIONNAIRE 1 (*dictionnaire*)
didans v DEDANS
dié, dieu v DIEU
DIEU 15 (*dié* 12, *dieu* 3), voir aussi BON+DIEU, MON+DIEU
dife, di fé, difé, difeu, diffé v +FEU
di fer v +FER
differance, différence v DIFFÉRENCE
DIFFÉRENCE 2 (*differance* 1, *différence* 1)
différé v DIFFÉRER
DIFFÉRER 1 (*différé*)
difficil', difficile v DIFFICILE
DIFFICILE 13 (*difficil'* 4, *difficile* 7, *dificil* 2)
dificil v DIFFICILE
di fiel v +FIEL
di fil, difil, difile v +FIL
di fils v DU+FILS
Diflo v DIFLO
DIFLO 1 (*Diflo*) [nom de personnage]
Dihazier v DIHAZIER
DIHAZIER 2 (*Dihazier*) [nom de famille]
di-i-i-i-i 1 [onomat.]
DIGNE 3 (*diine*)
diine v DIGNE
dijné v DÉJEUNER
dilait, di lait, dilé v +LAIT
di-lau, dileau, di l'eau, di leau,
di-l'eau, di-leau v +EAU
dilhouile v +HUILE
DILIGENCE 2 (*dilizence*)
+DILIGENCE 2 (*la dilizence*)
dilizence v DILIGENCE
di l'eau cologne v +EAU+COLOGNE
dilo, di lo v +EAU
diloseau v +EAU, CHAUD

di louil, di louïl, dilouil, dilouile, di luile v +HUILE
dimain v DEMAIN
dimal, di mal v +MAL
dimanç, dimanç', dimance, dimançe v DIMANCHE
dimancé v DÉMANCHER
dimanche v DIMANCHE
DIMANCHE 10 (*dimanç* 1, *dimanç'* 1, *dimance* 5, *dimançe* 1, *dimanche* 1, *dimanse* 1)
dimand, dimand', dimande, dimandé v DEMANDER
dimanse v DIMANCHE
+DÎME 1 (*la dim*)
diméin, dimen v DEMAIN
dimi v DEMI
di miel, di miél, dimiel, di-miel v +MIEL
dimin v DEMAIN
di-mini, diminié v DIMINUER
DIMINUER 3 (*diminié* 2, *di-mini* 1)
di mond, di mond', di monde, di mound', di mounde, di-mond, dimond', di-mond', di'mond', dimonde, di-monde, dimound, dimound', dimounde, di moune, dimoune v +MONDE$_1$
dinde v DINDE
DINDE 5 (*dinde* 4, *dindes* 1)
dindes v DINDE
dine, diné, dîné, diner, dîner v DÎNER
DÎNER 27 (*dine* 2, *diné* 12, *dîné* 3, *diner* 7, *dîner* 3)
dingue v DINGUE
DINGUE 2 (*dingue*)
di pain, dipain v +PAIN
di père v DU+PÈRE
di'pi, dipi v DEPUIS
dipici v DEPUIS, ICI
dipis v DEPUIS
diplomb v +PLOMB
dipoive v +POIVRE
dir, dir', dire v DIRE
DIRE 1469 (*dir* 482, *dir'* 167, *dire* 819, *diré* 2, *dit* 2)
diré v DIRE

directer v DIRECTEUR
DIRECTEUR 2 (*directer*)
di-riz v +RIZ
dis v DIX
di sab, di sabe , di sable
    v +SABLE
di san, disan, di sang, disang
    v +SANG
di saint-esprit
    v DU+SAINT-ESPRIT
discende v DESCENDRE
discip v DISCIPLE
DISCIPLE 78 (*discip*)
+DISCORDE 1 (*la discord*)
discours v DISCOURS
DISCOURS 1 (*discours*)
DISCUTER 2 (*disquité*)
di sel, disel v +SEL
di sen v +SANG
disi v DESSUS
disic, di sicre v +SUCRE
di sic' d'orze v
    +SUCRE+D'ORGE
dis-mil v DIX MILLE
di son v +SON$_2$
DISPARAÎTRE 2 (*disparét*)
disparét v DISPARAÎTRE
dispite, dispité, dispitté
    v DISPUTER
disposé v DISPOSER
DISPOSER 1 (*disposé*)
DISPUTER 11 (*dispite* 6,
    dispité 3, *dispitté* 1,
    sipite 1)
disquité v DISCUTER
dissandé v DESCENDRE
disse v DIX
disson v +SON$_2$
distance v DISTANCE
DISTANCE 2 (*distance*)
disuif v +SUIF
dit v DIRE
dit tout v DU+TOUT
dité, di thé v +THÉ
di tort v +TORT
di tou, di tout, ditout
    v DU+TOUT
divain v DU+VIN
di van v +VENT
divan, divant v DEVANT
di vein v +VIN

divent, di-vent, di vent, di vents
    v +VENT
divin$_1$ v DEVIN
di vin, divin$_2$ v +VIN
divini, divinie, divinis
    v DEVENIR
DIVISER 3 (*divizé*)
divizé v DIVISER
DIVORCE 2 (*divors*)
divors v DIVORCE
dix v DIX
DIX 20 (*dis* 3, *disse* 1, *dix* 17)
DIX MILLE 1 (*dis-mil*)
dixième v DIXIÈME
DIXIÈME 1 (*dixième*)
di zef, dizef, di-zef, dizéf, di zèfe,
dizefs, di-zefs, dizéfs, di-zéfs,
dizeif, dizéifs, di zoeuf
    v +ŒUF
dizné v DÉJEUNER
di zouitre v +HUÎTRE
di-zus v +JUS
djan foutte, djanfoute
    v JEAN-FOUT(R)E
doa, doat v DEVOIR
docteir, docteirs, docter ,
doctèr, doctèr' v DOCTEUR
DOCTEUR 19 (*docteir* 5,
    docteirs 3, *docter* 6,
    doctèr 1, *doctèr'* 1,
    doquitaire 3)
dohore, dohors v DEHORS
+DOIGT 13 (*lé doa* 1,
    lé doigt 1, *lédoigt* 7,
    lédoigts 1 *lédoit* 3)
doit, doit', doite v DEVOIR
dolive v +OLIVE
domaze v DOMMAGE
domestic, domestique,
doméstique, domestiques
    v DOMESTIQUE
DOMESTIQUE 60
    (*domestic* 17, *domestique* 27,
    doméstique 1, *domestiques* 12,
    doumestique 1, *doumistique* 2)
dommage v DOMMAGE
DOMMAGE 17 (*domaze* 8,
    dommage 1, *dommaz'* 1,
    dommaze 7)
dommaz', dommaze
    v DOMMAGE
dompté v DOMPTER

DOMPTER 1 (*dompté*)
don$_1$ v DONC
don$_2$, don' v DONNER
donc v DONC
DONC 93 (*don$_1$* 12,
    donc 81)
done v DONNER
dongue 6 [onomat.]
donn, donn', donne, donné
    v DONNER
DONNER 375 (*don$_2$* 1, *don'* 1,
    done 10, *donn* 1,
    donn' 29, *donne* 274,
    donné 56, *donnez* 3)
donnère v DONNEUR
DONNEUR 2 (*donnère*)
donnez v DONNER
doquitaire v DOCTEUR
d'or v D'OR
D'OR 1 (*d'or*)[18]
dor v ADORER
doré v DORÉ
DORÉ 3 (*doré*)
dormi v DORMIR
DORMIR 98 (*dormi* 19,
    dourmi 79)
+DOS 32 (*lé do* 1, *lédo* 2,
    lé dos 3, *lédos* 26)
+DOSE 2 (*la dose*)
+DOUANE 2 (*la douane*)
dou v DOUX
doublé$_1$ v DOUBLÉ
doublé$_2$ v DOUBLER
DOUBLÉ 4 (*doublé$_1$*)
DOUBLER 1 (*doublé$_2$*)
doubouté v DEBOUT
douç'ment v DOUCEMENT
douce v DOUX
doucement v DOUCEMENT
DOUCEMENT 57 (*douç'ment*
    1, *doucement* 56)
Doudy v DOUDY
DOUDY 1 (*Doudy*) [prénom
    malg.]
Douglas v DOUGLAS
DOUGLAS 2 (*Douglas*) [nom
    de famille]
douler v DOULEUR
DOULEUR 3 (*douler* 2,
    doulère 1)

---

[18] Pris ici de *zaune-d'or* (jaune d'or).

+DOULEUR 5 (*la douleir* 1, *ladouleir* 3, *ladoulére* 1)
doumestique, doumistique v DOMESTIQUE
doumonde, dou-monde, dou monde, doumondes, doumone, doumonnde, doumoumde, doumoun, doumoun', doumounde, dou mounde, doumoundes, doumoune, doumounne, doumounnes v +MONDE₁
douri, douriz, dou riz v +RIZ
dourmi v DORMIR
doutance v DOUTANCE
DOUTANCE 3 (*doutance*)
+DOUTANCE 2 (*ladoutance*)
douté v DOUTER
DOUTER 3 (*douté*)
doux v DOUX
DOUX 15 (*dou* 1, *douce* 3, *doux* 11)
douz v DOUZE
douzaine v DOUZAINE
DOUZAINE 1 (*douzaine*)
douze v DOUZE
DOUZE 15 (*douz* 13, *douze* 2)
dram v DRAME
DRAME 3 (*dram*)
DRAP 1 (*draps*)
draps v DRAP
dreite v DROIT
dress', dresse, dressé v DRESSER
DRESSER 6 (*dress'* 1, *dresse* 3, *dressé* 2)
dret', dréte, drète, drett, drétt, drette, drétte, droa, droat v DROIT
drogue v DROGUE
DROGUE 1 (*drogue*)
droit v DROIT
DROIT 61 (*dreite* 1, *dret'* 1, *dréte* 5, *drète* 2, *drett* 1, *drétt'* 1, *drette* 8, *drétte* 3, *droa* 16, *droat* 13, *droit* 6, *droite* 3, *droits* 1)
+DROIT 1 (*lé droit*)
droite, droits v DROIT
+DROITURE 1 (*la droatir*)
drol, drole, drôle v DRÔLE

DRÔLE 10 (*drol* 1, *drole* 5, *drôle* 4)
du riz v +RIZ
DU+FILS 3 (*di fils*)
DU+PÈRE 4 (*de père* 1, *di père* 3)
DU+SAINT-ESPRIT 3 (*de sainte-esprit* 1, *di saint-esprit* 2)
du seigneur v DU+SEIGNEUR
DU+SEIGNEUR 1 (*du seigneur*)
DU+TOUT 8 (*di tou* 2, *di tout* 3, *dit tout* 1, *ditout* 2)
Duperré v DUPERRÉ
DUPERRÉ 2 (*Duperré*) [nom de famille]
Dynamite v DYNAMITE
DYNAMITE 1 (*dynamite*)
DYSENTRIE 1 (*dyssenterie*)
dyssenterie v DYSENTRIE

E

e, é v ET
+EAU 216 (*dé l'eau* 2, *di l'eau*, 23, *di leau* 3, *di lo* 19, *di-l'eau* 3, *di-lau* 2, *dileau* 151, *di-leau* 2, *dilo* 11)
+EAU+COLOGNE 3 (*di l'eau cologne* 2, *l'eau cologne* 1)
+EAU+DE+MER 1 (*dé l'eau de mer*)
ébenne v ÉBENNE
ÉBENNE 1 (*ébenne*)
+ÉBENNE 4 (*debène* 2, *débène* 1, *d'ibainne* 1)
ec, éc v AVEC
écarlat v ÉCARLATE
ÉCARLATE 1 (*écarlat*)
ÉCARQUILLER 5 (*carquille*)
ÉCHAPPER 25 (*çape* 5, *çapé* 3, *cappe* 1, *çappe* 4, *çappé* 2, *sap* 3, *sape* 5, *sapé* 2)
+ÉCHASSE 1 (*zécasse*)
+ÉCHELLE 3 (*lécelle* 1, *léchelle* 1, *zécelle*)
+ÉCHO 6 (*zéco*)
+ÉCLAIR 3 (*zéclair*)
éclairé v ÉCLAIRER

ÉCLAIRER 4 (*éclairé* 2, *écléré* 1, *clairé* 1)
ÉCLATER 4 (*clate* 2, *claté* 2)
écléré v ÉCLAIRER
+ÉCOLE 8 (*l'écol'* 1, *l'école* 3, *lécole* 4)
+ÉCOLIER 10 (*zécolier*)
+ÉCONOMIE 2 (*l'économie* 1, *zéconomie* 1)
ÉCORCHER 3 (*corce*)
ecout, écout, écoute, écouté, écouté, ecouter, écouter v ÉCOUTER
ÉCOUTER 138 (*acout* 2, *acoute* 12, *acouté* 18, *cout'*₁ 5, *coute* 31, *couté*₂ 42, *ecout* 1, *ecout* 9, *écoute* 4, *ecouté* 5, *écouté* 5, *ecouter* 1, *écouter* 1, *ecoutez* 1, *écoutez* 1)
ecoutez, écoutez v ÉCOUTER
ecque v AVEC
écrasé v ÉCRASER
ÉCRASER 14 (*crase* 3, *crasé* 6, *craz* 1, *crazé* 1, *écrasé* 2, *écraz* 1)
écraz v ÉCRASER
écrir, écrir', écrire v ÉCRIRE
ÉCRIRE 24 (*crire* 6, *écrir* 9, *écrir'* 2, *écrire* 6)
ecritire, écritire v ÉCRITURE
ÉCRITURE 3 (*ecritire* 2, *écritire* 1)
+ÉCRITURE 10 (*l'écritir* 1, *lécritir'* 1, *l'écritire* 1, *lecritire* 1, *lécritire* 2, *lé zécritir* 2, *zécritir* 2)
ÉCRITEAU 1 (*écrito*)
écrito v ÉCRITEAU
ÉCUMER 5 (*kimé* 2, *quime* 1, *quimé* 2)
+ÉCURIE 5 (*léquérie* 1, *l'équirie* 1, *léquirie* 3)
éd v AIDER
+ÉDUCATION 1 (*zédication*)
+EFFET 2 (*léffet* 1, *zefféts* 1)
+EFFORT 1 (*zeffort*)
EFFRONTÉ 8 (*front'* 1, *fronté* 6, *frontés* 1)
égal v ÉGAL
ÉGAL 7 (*égal* 6, *gal'* 1)

+ÉGLISE 23 (*l'eglise 2, l'église 4, l'egliz 1, l'égliz 2, l'égliz' 1, l'eglize 1, l'églize 1, léglise 9, légliz 1, léglize 1*)
ÉGRENER 1 (*égrenné*)
égrenné v ÉGRENER
+EGYPTE 4 (*l'egypt*)
eh v EH
EH 80 (*eh 79, eh' 1*)
eh' v EH
ein, ein', eine, einne v UN
eina, ein a , ein'a, ein-a, einan v IL+Y+EN+A
einfirm v INFIRME
einkié v INQUIET
ein pé, ein pè, ein-pé, ein' pé v UN+PEU
einsilt v INSULTER
einstrir v INSTRUIRE
eintellizan v INTELLIGENT
einvit, einvité v INVITER
EKHOROPA 43 (*couroupa 36, couroupas 6, couzoupa 1*) [mot mak.]
ÉLASTIQUE 3 (*lastique*)
electrique v ÉLECTRIQUE
ÉLECTRIQUE 1 (*electrique*)
ÉLEPHANT 3 (*alphan 1, alphant 2*)
+ÉLÉPHANT 40 (*l'éléphant 5, leléphant 1, léléphant 1, léléphant 32, zalphant 1*)
élève, elevé, élevés v ÉLEVER
ÉLEVER 4 (*élève 1, élevé 2, élevés 1*)
Elise v ELISE
ELISE 1 (*Elise 1*) [prénom]
Emanuel v EMMANUEL
emballe v EMBALLER
EMBALLER 1 (*emballe*)
+EMBARRAS 5 (*l'ambara 1, l'embaras 2, l'embarras 2*)
embas v EN+BAS
embêtant v EMBÊTANT
EMBÊTANT 2 (*embêtant*)
embéte, embète, embête, embété, embêté v EMBÊTER

EMBÊTER 16 (*embéte 7, embète 1, embête 2, embété 4, embêté 2*)
embrace, embras, embrasse, embrassé v EMBRASSER
EMBRASSER 45 (*ambras 1, ambrassé 1, embrace 1, embras 1, embrasse 31, embrassé 10*)
+ÉMETTEUR 1 (*lémétère*)
emmance v EMMANCHER
EMMANCHER 6 (*emmance*)
EMMANUEL 1 (*Emanuel*) [prénom]
emmen', emmèn', emmène v AMENER/EMMENER
EMMENER v AMENER/EMMENER
emmerdé v EMMERDER
EMMERDER 2 (*emmerdé*)
empaille v EMPAILLER
EMPAILLER 1 (*empaille*)
emparqué v EMPARQUER
EMPARQUER 1 (*emparqué*)
empéce. empèce, empêce, empêçe, empêce, empécé, empêcé, empèçé, empècer , empêcer, empèche, empéché v EMPÊCHER
EMPÊCHER 27 (*ampéce 1, empéce 5, empèce 7, empêce 2, empêçe 1, empécé 3, empêcé 1, empèçé 1, empècer 1, empêcer 1, empèche 1, empéché 1, empesse 2*)
empesse v EMPÊCHER
+EMPLOYÉ 8 (*zamployé 8, z'employés 1*)
empigne v EMPOIGNER
EMPOIGNER 1 (*empigne*)
emporté v EMPORTER
EMPORTER 2 (*amporté 1, emporté 1*)
EMPRUNTER 1 (*ampreint*)
en₁ v EN
en₂, èn v UN
EN 231 (*an₃ 35, en₁ 196*)
en a, ena, éna, èna, énan v IL+Y+EN+A
enbande v EN, BANDE
en ba, en bas v EN+BAS

EN+BAS 141 (*an ba 1, anba 6, embas 1, en ba 4, en bas 62, enbas 66, en-bas 1*)
en d'dans v EN+DEDANS
en éçanz v EN+ÉCHANGE
EN+ÉCHANGE 1 (*en éçanz*)
enbas, en-bas v EN+BAS
enceinte v ENCEINTE
ENCEINTE 5 (*anceint 4, enceinte 1*)
+ENCENS 1 (*l'ançan*)
+ENCLUME 2 (*l'enclime 1, lenclime 1*)
encolère v EN+COLÈRE
EN+COLÈRE 4 (*encolère*)
encor, encor', encore v ENCORE
ENCORE 280 (*ancor 57, encor 34, encor' 13, encore 173, encôre 4*)
encôre v ENCORE
+ENCRE 5 (*lenque*)
EN+DEDANS 17 (*andan 9, endans 5, en d'dans 1, endidans 1, en didans 1*)
endans, endidans, en didans v EN+DEDANS
+ENDORMI 1 (*lendourmi*)
ENDROIT 1 (*androit*)
+ENDROIT 30 (*l'androa 22, lendroit 1, l'endroit 3, landroit 4*)
ene, éne, èné, éné v UN
énée v NAÎTRE
+ENFANT 168 (*zanfan 45, zanfant 1, zanfants 3, zenfan 2, zenfans 8, z'enfans 2, zenfant 39, z'enfant 2, zenfants 60, z'enfants 6*)
ENFANT DE CHIEN 4 (*fant-d'çien 1, fant-d'cien 3*)
ENFANT DE GARCE 2 (*fanegace 1, fanigasse 1*)
enfer v ENFER
ENFER 1 (*enfer*)
+ENFER 14 (*l'anfer 9, l'enfer 5*)
enfermé v ENFERMER
ENFERMER 2 (*enfermé*)
enfilé v ENFILER
ENFILER 1 (*enfilé*)

enfin, en fin v ENFIN
ENFIN 18 (*enfin* 13, *en fin* 5)
enfonce, enfoncé, enfoncés
    v ENFONCER
ENFONCER 7 (*anfoncé* 1
    enfonce 1, *enfoncé* 3,
    enfoncés 2)
enfoutant v ENFOUTANT
ENFOUTANT 2 (*enfoutant*)
ENGAGER 22 (*angaz* 2,
    engaze 5, *engazé* 10,
    engazés 1, *enguèse* 2,
    enguéz' 1, *enguéze* 1)
*engaze, engazé, engazés,
enguèse, enguéz', enguéze*
    v ENGAGER
enhaut v EN+HAUT
EN+HAUT 2 (*enhaut*)
enlair v EN+L'AIR
EN+L'AIR 13 (*enlair* 7, *enlére* 2,
    en lére 3, *en lère* 1)
ENLEVER 3 (*anlev* 1, *anlév* 1,
    anlévé 1)
enlére, en lére, en lère
    v EN+L'AIR
en même temps v
    EN+MÊME+TEMPS
EN+MÊME+TEMPS 2
    (*à même temps* 1,
    en même temps 1)
enméné v AMENER/
    EMMENER
enne v UN
ennemi v ENNEMI
ENNEMI 3 (*ennemi* 3)
+ENNEMI 7 (*l'ennemi* 1,
    zenemi 1, *zénemie* 1,
    zennemi 4)
ennouyant v ENNUYANT
ennouye, ennouyé, ennuyé
    v ENNUYER
ENNUYANT 1 (*ennouyant*)
ENNUYER 13 (*ennouye* 1,
    ennouyé 9, *ennuyé* 2)
en pé v UN+PEU
en peine v EN+PEINE
EN+PEINE 9 (*an péne* 2, *en
    peine* 7)
EN+PENDANT 3 (*en pendant* 3)
en pendant v EN+PENDANT
ENRAGER 4 (*enrazé*)
enrazé v ENRAGER

enroule v ENROULER
ENROULER 1 (*enroule*)
ensambe, ensame
    v ENSEMBLE
+ENSEIGNEMENT
    1 (*l'anseïnman*)
*ensemb, ensemb', ensembe,
ensemble* v ENSEMBLE
ENSEMBLE 212 (*ansam* 2,
    ansamb 10, *asamb* 11,
    asambe 1, *asembe* 2,
    assamb 4, *assamb'* 4,
    assambe 1, *assame* 1,
    assembe 10, *ensambe* 1,
    ensame 2, *ensemb* 1,
    ensemb' 16, *ensembe* 23,
    ensemble 16, *ensembre* 3,
    sambe 7, *same* 5, *semb* 1,
    semb' 39, *sembe* 49,
    sembl' 2, *semble* 1)
ensembre v ENSEMBLE
ente v ENTRER
entende, entendre v ENTENDRE
ENTENDRE 219 (*entende* 2,
    entendre 1, *tand* 30,
    tandé 24, *tend* 1,
    tend' 10, *tende* 67,
    tendé 78, *tendent* 1,
    tendez 1, *tendre*$_1$ 4)
*entére, entère, enterre, enterré,
enterrer* v ENTERRER
ENTERRER 12 (*anter* 4,
    entére 1, *entère* 1,
    enterre 2, *enterré* 1,
    enterrer 3)
+ENTERREMENT
    4 (*l'anterman* 1,
    l'enterrement 2,
    lenterrement 1)
entété, entêté, entétée, entêtés
    v ENTÊTÉ
ENTÊTÉ 6 (*entété* 3, *entêté* 1,
    entétée 1, *entêtés* 1)
entier v ENTIER
ENTIER 3 (*entier* 1, *entière* 2)
entière v ENTIER
en tour EN+TOUR
EN+TOUR 1 (*en tour*)
+ENTOURAGE 7 (*l'antouraz*
    1, *l'entourage* 1,
    l'entouraze 4,
    lentouraze 1)

entoure, entouré v ENTOURER
ENTOURER 5 (*antour* 1,
    entoure 3, *entouré* 1)
entre$_1$ v ENTRE
entre$_2$ v ENTRER
ENTRE 18 (*antr*$_1$ 9, *entre*$_1$ 9)
    [prép.]
entré, entrer v ENTRER
ENTRER 45 (*antr*$_2$ 4, *antre* 1,
    ente 7, *entre*$_2$ 6,
    entré 26, *entrer* 1)
    v aussi RENTRER
enver v ENVERS
ENVERS 2 (*enver*)
en verté, en-verté, en vérité
    v EN+VÉRITÉ
EN+VÉRITÉ 9 (*an verté* 1,
    en verté 3, *en-verté*
    2, *en vérité* 3)
envi, envie v ENVIE
ENVIE 11 (*anvi* 2, *envi* 1,
    envie 8)
+ENVIE 2 (*l'envie* 1, *lenvie* 1)
ENVIER 1 (*anvé*)
ENVELOPPE 1 (*anvelop*)
envil' v EN+VILLE
EN+VILLE 1 (*envil'*)[19]
envole, envolé, envolés
    v ENVOLER
ENVOLER 14 (*envole* 4,
    envolé 9, *envolés* 1)
*envoy', envoye, envôye, envoyé,
envoyée* v ENVOYER
ENVOYER 81 (*anvoy* 29,
    anvoye 1, *anvoyé* 1,
    envoy' 1, *envoye* 14,
    envôye 23, *envoyé* 12)
épais v EPAIS
ÉPAIS 2 (*épais* 1, *épaisse* 1)
épaisse v EPAIS
+ÉPAULE 5 (*l'épaule* 2,
    zépaules 1, *zépol* 1,
    zépole 1)
ÉPÉE 1 (*népée*)
+ÉPÉE 1 (*lépé*)
+ÉPERON 1 (*zéprons*)
+ÉPI 1 (*zépi*)
épis v ET+PUIS
ÉPLUCHER 2 (*plice* 1, *plicé* 1)

---

[19] Sens = « Port-Louis » en général.

+ÉPONGE 2 (*l'éponz* 1, *l'éponze* 1)
èque v AVEC
+ÉQUINOXE 2 (*l'équinoxe*)
ÉREINTER 4 (*reinté* 3, *rinté* 1)
ergot v ERGOT
ERGOT 1 (*ergot*)
+ERMITE 3 (*l'ermit'* 1, *l'ermite* 1, *l'hermit'* 1)
+ERRATA 2 (*zerrata*)
escalier v ESCALIER
ESCALIER 2 (*escalier* 1, *sacalié* 1)
+ESCALIER 7 (*l'escalier* 2, *lescalier* 3, *léscalier* 1, *lescaliers* 1)
+ESCLAVAGE 1 (*l'esclavaze*)
ESCLAVE 5 (*esclaves* 1, *saclave* 2, *séclâv'* 1, *séclaves* 1)
+ESCLAVE 2 (*zesclav* 1, *z'esclav'* 1)
esclaves v ESCLAVE
eski v EST-CE-QUE
espèce v ESPÈCE
ESPÈCE 1 (*espèce* 1)
+ESPÈCE 7 (*zespèce* 6, *n'espèce* 1)
esper, espère, espéré, espérée, espérer v ESPÉRER
+ESPÉRANCE 1 (*l'espérance*)
ESPÉRER 40 (*asper* 2, *aspère* 3, *aspère* 20, *aspéré* 7, *esper* 1, *espère* 1, *espéré* 2, *espérée* 2, *espérer* 1, *spère* 1)
+ESPOIR 1 (*lespoir*)
esprès v EXPRES
esprit v ESPRIT
ESPRIT 25 (*esprit* 4, *sipri* 12, *siprit* 7, *siprits* 2)
+ESPRIT 85 (*l'espri* 29, *lespri* 1, *l'espris* 1, *l'esprit* 52, *lesprit* 1, *lésprit* 1)
esqui v EST-CE-QUE
essaye v ESSAYER
ESSAYER 35 (*essaye* 1, *esséye* 1, *saye* 18, *sayé* 14, *seyé* 1)
+ESSENCE 3 (*l'essans*)
esséye v ESSAYER
essquize v EXCUSE

ESSUYER 6 (*souye* 5, *souyé* 1)
est v ÊTRE
EST-CE-QUE 63 (*eski* 48, *esqui* 3, *est ce qui* 1, *est-c' qui* 2, *est-ce qui* 18)
est ce qui, est-c' qui, est-ce qui v EST-CE-QUE
estimé v ESTIMER
ESTIMER 2 (*estimé*)
+ESTOMAC 4 (*l'estomac* 1, *lostoma* 1, *lostomac* 2)
estropié v ESTROPIÉ
ESTROPIÉ 2 (*estropié*)
et v ET
ET 2009 (*e* 359, *é* 1006, *et* 644)
éta v ÉTAT
établis v ÉTABLIR
ÉTABLIR 1 (*établis*)
ÉTABLISSEMENT 2 (*tablissement* 1, *tablissemment* 1)
était v ÊTRE
étal v ÉTAL
ÉTAL 1 (*étal*)
+ÉTALAGE 2 (*l'étalaze*)
ÉTALER 1 (*tale*)
etand, étand, étandi v ÉTENDRE
ÉTAT 1 (*éta*)
+ETAT 2 (*l'état*)
ÉTEINDRE 4 (*teïn* 2, *teingné* 1, *teinié* 1)
ÉTENDRE 6 (*etand* 1, *étand* 4, *étandi* 1)
eté, été$_1$ v ÉTÉ$_1$
été$_2$ v ÉTÉ$_2$
ÉTÉ$_1$ 1987 (*te* 10, *té* 734, *tè* 1, *ti*$_1$ 1120, *eté* 14, *été*$_1$ 108)
ÉTÉ$_2$ 4 (*été*$_2$)
+ÉTÉ 1 (*l'été*)
éternel v ÉTERNEL
ÉTERNEL 5 (*éternel*)
éternelment v ETERNELLEMENT
ÉTERNELLEMENT 1 (*éternelment*)
+ÉTOFFE 1 (*l'étof*)
+ÉTOILE 16 (*zétoal* 6, *zétoile* 1, *zétoiles* 8, *zétoille* 1)
étoné v ÉTONNER

étonnant v ÉTONNANT
ÉTONNANT 1 (*étonnant*)
étonne, étonné v ÉTONNER
ÉTONNER 27 (*étoné* 2, *étonne* 1, *étonné* 8, *toné* 8, *tôné* 1, *tonné* 6, *tonnés* 1)
étouf v ÉTOUFFER
ÉTOUFFER 7 (*étouf* 1, *touf* 1, *touffe* 4, *touffé* 1)
ÉTOURDI 2 (*tourdi*$_1$ 1, *tourdis* 1)
ÉTOURDIR 11 (*tourdi*$_2$)
ÉTOURDISSEMENT 1 (*tourdissement*)
et pis v ET+PUIS
ET+PUIS 14 (*épis* 1, *et pis* 13)
étrangé v ETRANGER
ÉTRANGER 6 (*étrangé* 1, *étranzé* 5)
+ÉTRANGER 2 (*zétranzé*)
étranzé v ÉTRANGER
ÉTRANGLER 4 (*tanguélé* 1, *tranglé* 3)
ÊTRE v EST+CE+QUE, ÉTÉ$_1$, ÉTÉ$_2$
ÊTRE 2 (*est* 1, *était* 1)
etroat, étroat v ÉTROIT
ÉTROIT 2 (*etroat* 1, *étroat* 1)
EUNUQUE 4 (*unuk*)
evangile v ÉVANGILE
ÉVANGILE 2 (*evangile*)
+ÉVANGILE 4 (*l'évangil* 2, *l'evangile* 2)
+ÉVEILLÉ 2 (*l'eveillé* 1, *l'éveillé* 1)
+ÉVENTAIL 9 (*léventail*)
évit, évitée v ÉVITER
ÉVITER 3 (*évit* 1, *évitée* 2)
excepté v EXCEPTÉ
EXCEPTÉ 8 (*cepté* 1, *excepté* 7, *xepté* 1)
EXCUSE 1 (*essquize*)
exemple v EXEMPLE
EXEMPLE 4 (*exemple*)
+EXEMPLE 2 (*l'exemp* 1, *legzamp* 1)
expédié v EXPÉDIER
EXPÉDIER 1 (*expédié*)
+EXPLICATION 2 (*l'explicacion* 1, *l'explication* 1)

EXPLIQUER 3 (*ciplique* 1, *explik* 2)
explik v EXPLIQUER
exprès v EXPRÈS
EXPRÈS 5 (*esprès* 1, *exprès* 4)

F

FABLE 1 (*fable*)
fable v FABLE
facé, façé v FÂCHÉ
FÂCHÉ 18 (*façé* 2, *facé* 15, *fâchée* 1)
fâchée v FÂCHÉ
facil v FACILE
FACILE 3 (*facil*)
FAÇON 2 (*façon*)
façon v FAÇON
facteir v FACTEUR
FACTEUR 1 (*facteir*)
FAGOTER 3 (*fagoté*)
fagoté v FAGOTER
FAHAMO 1 (*faham*) [mot malg.]
faham v **FAHAMO**
faibe v FAIBLE
FAIBLE 7 (*faibe* 4, *faible* 1, *feb* 1, *fébe* 1)
FAIBLESSE 1 (*faiblesse*)
faibli v FAIBLIR
FAIBLIR 1 (*faibli*)
fail, fail', fail'fail, faill', faille v FAILLIR
FAILLIR 31 (*fail* 1, *fail'* 3, *fail'fail* 1, *faill'* 1, *faille* 8, *faye* 17)
faim v FAIM
FAIM 22 (*faim* 22, *fain* 9, *fin* 3)
+FAIM 1 (*la faim*)
fain v FAIM
faique v FAIRE+QUE
fair, fair' v FAIRE
FAIRE 1115 (*fair* 267, *fair'* 203, *faire* 557, *fére* 51, *fère* 24, *feir* 3, *faisant* 1, *fait* 6, *fé* 3)
FAIRE+QUE 20 (*faique* 2, *fait que* 1, *fec* 4, *fecque* 1, *feq'* 1, *féque* 3, *fèque* 8)

fais v *si fais*
faisant v FAIRE
fait v FAIRE, v *si fait*
FAÎTAGE 7 (*faitaze* 6, *fétaze* 1)
faitaze v FAÎTAGE
faite v FAIRE
fallait, fallé v FALLOIR
fallait pas v FALLAIT+PAS
FALLAIT PAS 2 (*fallait pas*)
FALLOIR 231 (*fallait* 8, *fallé* 1, *fau* 1, *faudrait* 8, *faut* 188, *fo₂* 25)
fam, fam', fame v FEMME
famé, fameix v FAMEUX
FAMEUX 28 (*famé* 25, *fameix* 3)
fami, famie, famiie v FAMILLE
FAMILLE 17 (*fami* 4, *famie* 2, *famiie* 1, *famille* 10)
+FAMINE 1 (*la famine*)
famme v FEMME
fan v FAON
FANAL 2 (*fanal*)
fanal v FANAL
fand v FENDRE
fâné, fane, fané v FANER
fanegace v ENFANT+DE+ GARCE
FANER 52 (*fane* 15, *fâné* 1, *fané* 19, *fanné* 2, *fane* 15)
+FANER+*ER* 1 (*lé fanor*)
FANFARON 1 (*fanfaron*)
fanfaron v FANFARON
***FANGOHANA** 2 (*fangouni*) [mot malg.]
fangouni v ***FANGOHANA**
FANGORIÑANA 2 (*flangourin*) [mot malg. (betsileo)]
fanigasse v ENFANT+DE+ GARCE
fanme v FEMME
fanné v FANER
fant-d'çien v ENFANT+DE+ CHIEN
FAON 1 (*fan*)
fan v FAON
FAQUIN 1 (*faquin* 1)
faquin v FAQUIN
farau v FARAUD

FARAUD 16 (*farau* 1, *faraud* 1, *farauds* 1, *faro* 13)
farauds v FARAUD
FARCE 9 (*farce* 5, *farces* 4)
farce, farces v FARCE
FARCIN 1 (*farçin*)
farçin v FARCIN
FARDEAU 1 (*fardo*)
fardo v FARDEAU
+FARINE 13 (*la farine* 7, *lafarine* 6)
faro v FARAUD
farouce v FAROUCHE
FAROUCHE 2 (*farouce*)
FARQUHAR 1 (*Farquhar*) [nom de famille]
FATAKA 12 (*fataqu'* 1, *fataque* 11) [mot malg.]
fataqu', fataque v **FATAKA**
+FATIGUE 1 (*la fatig*)
fatigue, fatigué v FATIGUER
FATIGUER 7 (*fatigue* 1, *fatigué* 6)
fau, faudrait v FALLOIR
fausse v FAUX
faut v FALLOIR
FAUTE 1 (*fot*)
+FAUTE 2 (*la faut'* 1, *lafaute* 1)
fauteil, fauteuil, fauteuils, fautéyes v FAUTEUIL
FAUTEUIL 4 (*fauteil* 1, *fauteuil* 1, *fauteuils* 1, *fautéyes* 1)
faut pas v FAUT+PAS
FAUT+PAS 13 (*faut pas* 7, *fo pa* 6)
FAUX 8 (*fausse* 1, *fo₁* 7)
FAUX-COL 1 (*faux-col*)
faux-col v FAUX-COL
faye v FAILLIR
fé v FAIRE
feb, fébe v FAIBLE
fec, fecque v FAIRE+QUE
+FÉE 3 (*laféé*)
feillaze v FEUILLAGE
feille, feilles v FEUILLE
FEINTE 1 (*feinte*)
FEIR v FAIRE
félé v FÊLER
FÊLER 1 (*félé*)

FELLOW 1 (*fellows* 1) [mot angl.]
fellows v **FELLOW**
femél, fémél v FEMELLE
FEMELLE 2 (*femél* 1, *fémél* 1)
femm' v FEMME
FEMME 247 (*fam* 44, *fam'* 1, *fame* 4, *famme* 3, *fanme* 9, *femm'* 11, *femme* 165, *femme'* 2, *femmes* 8)
femme', femmes v FEMME
+FEMME 1 (*lé femme*)
fende v FENDRE
FENDRE 2 (*fand* 1, *fende* 1)
+FENÊTRE 20 (*la fenète* 1, *la fenêtre* 2, *la fnête* 1, *la fnêtre* 2, *lafenéte* 4, *lafenète* 4, *lafenête* 4, *lafenètes* 1, *lafenétes* 1)
FENTE 2 (*fente*)
fente v FENTE
feq', féque, fèque v FAIRE+QUE
FER 31 (*fer*)
fer v FER
fer, fére, fère v FAIRE
+FER 1 (*di fer*)
ferm, ferm', ferme, férme, fermé v FERMER
FERMER 38 (*ferm* 4, *ferm'* 1, *ferme* 1, *férme* 2, *fermé* 12, *fréme* 11, *frème* 2, *frémé* 5)
FERMIER 1 (*firmier*)
ferrire v FERRURE
FERRURE 1 (*ferrire*)
FESSE 1 (*fesses*)
fesses v FESSE
FESTON 1 (*festons* 1)
festons v *FESTON
fét, fet, fêt', fête v FÊTE
fétaze v FAÎTAGE
FÊTE 10 (*fét* 2, *fet* 4, *fêt'* 1, *féte* 1, *fête* 2)
+FÊTE 4 (*la fet* 1, *la fête* 3)
+FEU 66 (*di fé* 15, *dife* 1, *difé* 44, *difeu* 1, *diffé* 5)
FEUILLAGE 5 (*feillaze* 4, *féyaze* 1)
FEUILLE 28 (*feille* 7, *feilles* 19, *féy* 2)
FÉVRIER 2 (*février*)
février v FÉVRIER
féy v FEUILLE

féyaze v FEUILLAGE
fi v FILLE
fiancé v FIANCE
FIANCÉ 2 (*fiancé*)
+FICELLE 1 (*la ficel'*)
fichant v FICHANT
FICHANT 1 (*fichant*)
fiché v FICHER
FICHER 1 (*fiché*)
fidel, fidél v FIDÈLE
FIDÈLE 7 (*fidél* 1, *fidel* 5, *fidélle* 1)
fidélle 1 v FIDÈLE
fié, fiée v FIER₂
fiel v FIEL
FIEL 1 (*fiel*)
+FIEL 1 (*di fiel*)
fier v FIER₁
FIER₁ 5 (*fier* 3, *fière* 2) [adj]
FIER₂ 3 (*fié* 1, *fiée* 1, *fiez* 1) [v].
+FIER 3 (*la fière*)
fière v FIER₁
+FIÈVRE 12 (*la fiévr* 2, *la fievre* 2, *la fièvre* 8)
fiez v FIER₂
Fifi v FIFI
FIFI 2 (*Fifi*) [nom de personnage]
fig v FIGUE
FIGETTE 3 (*fizet* 2, *fizète* 1) [nom de famille]
FIGUE 6 (*fig*)
figuir, figuir', figuire v FIGURE
FIGURE 36 (*figuir* 7, *figuir'* 1, *figuire* 27, *figure* 1)
+FIL 11 (*di fil* 3, *difil* 7, *difile* 1)
filacter v PHYLACTÈRE
FILAO 7 (*filao*) [mot malg.]
file, filé v FILER
FILER 11 (*file* 5, *filé* 6)
fill', fille v FILLE
FILLE 66 (*fill'* 2, *fille* 52, *filles* 7, *fiy* 1, *fiye* 5), v aussi BELLE+FILLE, PETIT+FILLE
+FILLE 12 (*la fille* 3, *la fiy* 1, *la fiye* 1, *lafille* 5, *lé-fille* 1, *les filles* 1)
filles v FILLE
FILOU 1 (*filous*)

filous v FILOU
fils v FILS
FILS 8 (*fils* 4, *fis* 3)
+FILS 6 (*le fis* 5, *lé fis* 1)
+FILS+DE+DIEU 1 (*fis de dieu*)
+FILS+DE+DIEU 7 (*le fis de dié* 5, *le fis de dieu* 2)
+FILS+DE+L'HOMME 31 (*le fis de l'hom* 26, *lé fis de l'hom* 2, *le fis de lhom* 2, *lé fis de lhom* 1)
filtr v FILTRE
FILTRE 1 (*filtr*)
fime, fimé v FUMER
fimié v FUMIER
fin₁ v FINIR
fin₂ v FIN
fin₃ v FAIM
FIN₁ 6 (*fin* 5, *fins* 1) [adj]
+FIN 14 (*la fein* 9, *la fin* 4, *lafin* 1)
fin', fine v FINIR
finesse v FINESSE
FINESSE 1 (*finesse*)
fini, finie v FINIR
finition v FINITION
FINITION 4 (*finition*)
FINIR 1168 (*fin* 14, *fin'* 43, *fine* 938, *fini* 154, *finie* 15, *finn'* 1, *finne* 3)
finn', finne v FINIR
Finniss v FINNISS
FINNISS 1 (*Finniss*) [nom de personnage]
fins v FIN₁
fiou 6 [onomat.]
firié v FURIEUX
firmier v FERMIER
fis v FILS
fis de dieu v FILS+DE+DIEU
Fisher v FISHER
FISHER 2 (*Fisher*) [nom de famille anglais]
fisi, fisil v FUSIL
FIT 1 (*fite*) [mot angl.]
fite v **FIT**
fitter v AFFUTER
fiy, fiye v FILLE
fizet, fizète v FIGETTE
fizi, fizil v FUSIL
flacon v FLACON

FLACON 2 (*flacon*)	FONCLAIR 5 (*Fonclair*) [nom de personnage]	FOUET 14 (*fouéte* 9, *fouète* 1, *fouette*₁ 4)
Flacq v **VLAKT**		
flambe, flambé v FLAMBER	*fond* v FOND	*fouét* v FOUETTER
flambeau v FLAMBEAU	FOND 29 (*fon* 2, *fond* 27)	*fouéte, fouète* v FOUET
FLAMBEAU 1 (*flambeau*)	*fondacion* v FONDATION	*fouété* v FOUETTER
FLAMBER 6 (*flambe* 1, *flambé* 5)	FONDATION 1 (*fondacion* 1)	*fouette*₁ v FOUET
	+FONDATION 1 (*la fondacion*)	*fouette*₂ v FOUETTER
+FLAMME 2 (*laflamme*)		FOUETTER 7 (*fouet* 2, *fouét* 1, *fouété* 1, *fouette*₂ 3)
flangourin v **FANGORIÑANA**	*fonde, fondre* v FONDRE	
flanqué, flanque v FLANQUER	FONDRE 11 (*fonde* 8, *fondre* 3)	*fou fou* v FOU
FLANQUER 8 (*flanque* 7, *flanqué* 1)	+FONTAINE 1 (*la fontaine*)	FOUGÈRE 3 (*fougère* 1, *fouzère* 1, *fouzères* 1)
flanquére, flanquère v FLANQUEUR	*fo pa* v FAUT+PAS	+FOUGÈRE 4 (*la fouzère*)
	for v FORT	*fouill', fouille, fouillé* v FOUILLER
FLANQUEUR 30 (*flanquére* 1, *flanquère* 29) [nom de personnage]	*forçat* 1 v FORÇAT	
	FORÇAT 1 (*forçat*)	FOUILLER 16 (*fouill'* 1, *fouille* 5, *fouillé* 9, *fouye* 1)
flatté v FLATTER	*forcé, force* v FORCER	
FLATTER 1 (*flatté*)	FORCE 1 (*fors*₁)	+FOUINE 1 (*la fouine*)
FLÈCHE 11 (*flèce*)	+FORCE 22 (*la forc'* 1, *la force* 8, *la fors* 5, *laforce* 7, *lafôrce* 1)	*fouka fouka* v **FOKA**
flèce v FLÈCHE		+FOULE 49 (*la foul*)
fleir, fleirs, fler, flère, flers v FLEUR		*fou pas mal* v FOUTRE+PAS+MAL
	FORCER 12 (*forcé* 3, *force* 8, *fors*₂ 1)	
FLEUR 7 (*fleir* 1, *fleirs* 2, *fler* 2, *flère* 1, *flers* 1)		*fouqué* v FOUQUET
	forêt v FORÊT	FOUQUET 1 (*fouqué*)
floter v FLOTTER	FORÊT 1 (*forêt*)	FOUR 1 (*fours*)
flotte v FLOTTE	+FORÊT 7 (*la forêt* 3, *laforêt* 4)	*four, four', foure* v FOURRER
FLOTTE 2 (*flotte*)		*fours* v FOUR
FLOTTER 1 (*floter*)	+FORGE 1 (*laforze*)	FOURMI 6 (*formi* 1, *fourmi* 5)
+FLÛTE 3 (*la flit* 2, *la flîte* 1)	FORGERON 9 (*forzeron* 9)	FOURNAISE 2 (*fournéz*)
*fo*₁ v FAUX	*forme*₁ v FORME	*fournéz* v FOURNAISE
*fo*₂ v FALLOIR	*forme*₂ v FORMER	*fourni* v FOURNIR
foa, fois v FOIS	FORME 1 (*forme*)	FOURNIMENT 1 (*fourniment*)
FODY 2 (*foude*) [mot malg.]	FORMER 1 (*forme*)	FOURNIR 4 (*fourni*)
fofère v FALLOIR, FAIRE	*formi* v FOURMI	*fourre, fourrefourre* v FOURRER
FOIS 97 (*foa* 16, *fois* 81)	FORNICATION 1 (*fornication*)	
FOKA 4 (*fouca* 3, *foucafouca* 1, *fouka fouka* 1) [mot malg.]	*fors*₁ v FORCE	FOURRER 8 (*four* 2, *four'* 2, *foure* 1, *fourre* 2, *fourrefourre* 1)
	*fors*₂ v FORCER	
	fort v FORT	
+FOI 12 (*la foa*)	FORT 44 (*for* 10, *fort* 33, *forts* 1)	*fous* v FOU
+FOIE 3 (*léfoie*)		*fout, foutant, fouti* v FOUTRE
+FOIRE 1 (*la fouarre*)	*forts* v FORT	*fout pas mal* v FOUTRE+PAS+MAL
foli v FOLIE	*forzeron* v FORGERON	
FOLIE 2 (*foli* 1, *folies* 1)	+FOSSE 1 (*lafosse*)	FOUTRE 23 (*fout* 14, *foutant* 1, *fouti* 7)
folies v FOLIE	*fossé* v FOSSÉ	
FOLKLORE 1 (*folk-lore*)	FOSSÉ 4 (*fossé*)	FOUTRE+PAS+MAL 4 (*fou pas mal* 2, *fout pas mal* 2)
folk-lore v FOLKLORE	*fot* v FAUTE	
fon v FOND	FOU 40 (*fou* 30, *fou fou* 1, *fous* 9)	*foutte* v FOUTRE
fonce, foncé v FONCER		*fouye* v FOUILLER
FONCER 21 (*fonce* 18, *foncé* 3)	*fouca* v **FOKA**	*fouzère, fouzères* v FOUGÈRE
	fouca-fouca v **FOKA**	+FRAICHEUR 1 (*lafraiceir*)
Fonclair v FONCLAIR	*foude* v **FODY**	FRAIS 25 (*frais* 14, *fré* 5, *frès* 1, *frés* 5)
	fouet v FOUETTER	

FRAMBOISE 2 (*framboises* 1, *frambouése* 1)
framboises, frambouése
　　　　　v FRAMBOISE
francais v FRANÇAIS
FRANÇAIS 27 (*francais* 2, *français* 21, *française* 1, *francé* 2, *françois* 1)
française, francé v FRANÇAIS
FRANCE 3 (*France*)
françois v FRANÇAIS
François v FRANÇOIS
FRANÇOIS 1 (*François*) [prénom]
FRANGE 1 (*franz*)
franz v FRANGE
frap, frappe v FRAPPER
FRAPPER 2 (*frap* 1, *frappe* 1)
+FRAYEUR 2 (*lafrayeir*)
fré v FRAIS
fréme, frème, frémé v FERMER
frér, frer, frèr', frére, fréres, frères v FRÈRE
FRÈRE 107 (*frér* 2, *frer* 38, *frèr'* 1, *frère* 45, *fréreé* 8, *fréres* 2, *frères* 11)
frès, frés v FRAIS
fri v FRUIT
FRINGANT 1 (*fringant*)
FRIRE 1 (*fris*)
fris v FRIRE
FRISÉ 1 (*frisée*)
frisée v FRISÉ
frit v FRUIT
FROMAGE 7 (*fromaze*)
fromaze v FROMAGE
fron v FRONT
fronce v FRONCER
FRONCER 1 (*fronce*)
front v FRONT
FRONT 7 (*fron* 1, *front* 6)
front', fronté, frontés
　　　　　v EFFRONTÉ
frôté, frotte, frotté v FROTTER
FROTTER 22 (*frôté* 1, *frotte* 18, *frotté* 3)
FRUIT 24 (*fri* 22, *frit* 1, *fruits* 1)
fruits v FRUIT
fuir v FUIR
FUIR 2 (*fuir*)

+FUMÉE 20 (*la fimé* 3, *la fimée* 1, *lafimée* 15, *la-fimée* 1)
FUMER 9 (*fime* 4, *fimé* 5)
FUMIER 4 (*fimié*)
FURIEUX 10 (*firié*)
fusil 1 v FUSIL
FUSIL 20 (*fisi* 3, *fisil* 13, *fizi* 2, *fizil* 1, *fusil* 1)

G

gacette v GACHETTE
GACHETTE 1 (*gacette*)
gaga v GAGA
GAGA 9 (*gaga*)
gagn, gagn', gagne, gagné
gagnè, gagnée, gagner
　　　　　v GAGNER
GAGNER 518 (*gagn* 1, *gagn'* 51, *gagne* 207, *gagné* 137, *gagnè* 1, *gagnée* 1, *gagner* 2, *gaigne* 2, *gain* 3, *gaïn* 104, *ganié* 9)
gaillard v GAILLARD
GAILLARD 1 (*gaillard*)
gaigne, gain, gaïn v GAGNER
GAI 5 (*gais*)
gais v GAI
gal' v ÉGAL
galant v GALANT
GALANT 17 (*galant* 16, *galants* 1)
galants v GALANT
Galatea v GALATEA
GALATEA 1 (*Galatea*) [nom de navire]
+GALE 13 (*lagale* 9, *la gale* 4)
galé v GALET
GALÈRE 2 (*galére* 1, *galère* 1)
galère v GALÈRE
GALET 2 (*galé*)
gallon v GALLON
GALLON 1 (*gallon*)
galon v GALON
GALON 3 (*galon* 1, *galons* 2)
galonné v GALONNE
GALONNE 1 (*galonné*)
galons v GALON
galop v GALOP
GALOP 3 (*galop*)

GALOPER 54 (*galopp'* 1, *galoppé* 9, *galoupe* 2, *galoupé* 14, *galouppe* 2, *galouppé* 4, *galpé* 22)
galopp', galoppé, galoupe, galoupé, galouppe, galouppé, galpé v GALOPER
GAMELLE 2 (*gamelle, gamelles*)
gamelle, gamelles
　　　　　v GAMELLE
GANDOLA 3 (*gandaule*) [mot malais]
gandaule v **GANDOLA**
gandia v **GANJA**
GANJA 1 (*gandia*) [mot hind.]
gandin v GANDIN
GANDIN 2 (*gandin*)
gangrené v GANGRENER
GANGRENER 1 (*gangrené*)
ganié v GAGNER
+GANT 2 (*lé gants* 1, *légants* 1)
garçon v GARÇON
GARÇON 104 (*garçon* 94, *garçons* 10)
garçons v GARÇON
gard$_1$ v GARDE
gard$_2$ v GARDER
gard'$_1$ v GARDE
gard'$_2$ v GARDER
garde$_1$ v GARDE
garde$_2$ v GARDER
GARDE 17 (*gard$_1$* 2, *gard'$_1$* 1, *garde$_1$* 8, *gardes* 6)
　　　　　v aussi PRENDRE+GARDE
+GARDE 4 (*la gard* 2, *la garde* 1, *lagarde* 1)
gardé v GARDER
garde-çasse v GARDE+CHASSE
GARDE+CHASSE
　　　　　1 (*garde-çasse* 1)
gardée v GARDER
garde-la-police
　　　　　v GARDE+LA+POLICE
GARDE+LA+POLICE
　　　　　1 (*garde-la-police*)
garde-manzé
　　　　　v GARDER+MANGER

GARDER+MANGER 2 (*garde-manzé*)
GARDER 24 (*gard₂* 3, *gard'₂* 1, *garde₂* 7, *gardé* 10, *gardée* 1, *gardez* 1)
gardes v GARDE
gardez v GARDER
gardiein, gardien v GARDIEN
GARDIEN 47 (*gardiein* 4, *gardien* 43)
gare v GARE
GARE 2 (*gare*)
gargouille, gargouillé v GARGOUILLER
GARGOUILLER 2 (*gargouille* 1, *gargouillé* 1)
gargoulett', gargoulétte, gargoulettes v GARGOULETTE
GARGOULETTE 3 (*gargoulett'* 1, *gargoulétte* 1, *gargoulettes* 1)
garni v GARNI
GARNI 1 (*garni*)
GASPILLER 1 (*gaspiyé*)
gaspiyé v GASPILLER
gat, gât', gàté, gâté v GATER
gateau, gàteau, gâteau v GÂTEAU
GÂTEAU 21 (*gateau* 2, *gàteau* 1, *gâteau* 17, *gâteaux* 1)
gâteaux v GÂTEAU
GÂTER 19 (*gat* 2, *gât'* 1, *gate* 1, *gaté* 1, *gàté* 1, *gâté* 12, *gâtés* 1)
gâtés v GÂTER
gauce v GAUCHE
GAUCHE 7 (*gauce* 1, *gos* 6)
GAULETTE 3 (*gaulett's* 1, *golet'* 1, *golette* 1)
gaulett's v GAULETTE
gaz v GAZ
GAZ 1 (*gaz*)
+GAZETTE 31 (*l'agazet'* 1, *la gazett'* 2, *la gazette* 24, *la gazettte* 1, *lagazet* 1, *lagazette* 2)
gazon v GAZON
GAZON 3 (*gazon*)
GAZOUILLAGE 1 (*gazouillaze*)
gazouillaze v GAZOUILLAGE

GENDARME 10 (*zendarm'* 1, *zendarme* 7, *zendarmes* 2)
GÊNER 7 (*zên'* 2, *zêne* 1, *zéné₁* 3, *zèné* 1)
général v GÉNÉRAL
GÉNÉRAL 4 (*général* 1, *zénéral* 3)
GÉNIE 2 (*zénie*)
GENOU 1 (*zénoux*)
GENRE 6 (*zanre* 3, *zenr'* 2, *zenre* 1)
gens v GENS
GENS 147 (*gens* 7, *jensse* 6, *zans* 77, *zanse* 1, *zence* 1, *zences* 3, *zens* 37, *zense* 17)
v aussi JEUNE+GENS
GENTIL 1 (*zentille*)
+GENTIL 1 (*la zentille*)
GENTILLESSE 1 (*zentillesse*)
GEORGES 1 (*Zeorz'*)
getté v GUETTER
gibier v GIBIER
GIBIER 5 (*gibier* 1, *zibié* 2, *zibier* 2)
GILET 3 (*zilet*)
GINGELY 1 (*zinzelis*)
zinzembe v GINGEMBRE
GINGEMBRE 1 (*zinzembe*)
GINGHAMS 1 (*guingan* 1) [mot anglo-ind.]
giroffle v GIROFFLE
GIROFFLE 2 (*giroffle* 1, *ziroffle* 1)
+GLACE 6 (*la glace* 3, *laglace* 3)
glisé, glisse, glissé v GLISSER
GLISSER 9 (*glisé* 1, *glisse* 4, *glissé* 4)
glissère v GLISSER –*ER*
GLISSER –*ER* 1 (*glissère*)
GLOBE 1 (*globes*)
globes v GLOBE
+GLOIRE 10 (*la gloar* 9, *la gloire* 1)
gnangnan v *CAGNARD
gobe v GOBER
GOBEUR 2 (*gobère*)
GOBER 1 (*gobe*)
gobère v GOBEUR
GOD-DAMN 2 (*god dem* 1, *goddam* 1)

god dem, goddam v GOD-DAMN
godon v GODON
GODON 4 (*godon*) [mot malais]
golet', golette v GAULETTE
gomon v **GOMON**
GOMON 1 (*gomon*) [mot breton]
gondole v GONDOLE
GONDOLE 1 (*gondole*)
gonflé, gonflées v GONFLER
GONFLER 5 (*gonflé* 4, *gonflées* 1)
GONI 3 (*gouni*) [mot hind.]
+GORGE 12 (*la gorg* 1, *la gorge* 1, *la gorz* 1, *la gorze* 2, *lagorze* 1, *lagôrze* 5, *lagôze* 1)
GORGÉE 2 (*gorzée*)
gorzée v GORGÉE
gos v GAUCHE
gou v GOÛT
goudron v GOUDRON
GOUDRON 3 (*goudron*)
gouïe, gouïes v AIGUILLE
gouni v GONI
gounn v ***GUN**
*GOURAMIE 2 (*gouramié* 1, *gouramis* 1)
gouramié, gouramis v *GOURAMIE
gourman, gourmand v GOURMAND
GOURMAND 5 (*gourman* 2, *gourmand* 3)
gournouies, gournoüies, gournouille, gournoye v GRENOUILLE
gout, goût v GOÛT
GOÛT 19 (*gou* 4, *gout* 13, *goût* 2)
GOÛTER 15 (*gout'* 1, *goute* 9, *gouté* 5)
goutt', goutte v GOUTTE
GOUTTE 2 (*goutt'* 1, *goutte* 1)
gouvener v GOUVERNEUR
gouvernail v GOUVERNAIL
GOUVERNAIL 1 (*gouvernail*)
gouverné v GOUVERNER
gouverneir v GOUVERNEUR

gouvern'ment, gouvernement
    v GOUVERNEMENT
GOUVERNEMENT 15
    (*gouvern'ment* 3,
    gouvernement 12)
gouverner   v GOUVERNEUR
GOUVERNER 2 (*gouverné*)
gouvernèr, gouverner',
gouvernère, gouverneur
    v GOUVERNEUR
GOUVERNEUR 34 (*gouvener* 1,
    gouverneir 2, *gouverner* 22,
    gouvernèr 3, *gouverner'* 1,
    gouvernère 2, *gouverneur*
    2, *governer* 1)
gouyaves   v GOYAVE
gouyavier   v GOYAVIER
governer   v GOUVERNEUR
goyave   v GOYAVE
GOYAVE 3 (*gouyaves* 2,
    goyave 1)
GOYAVIER 1 (*gouyavier*)
gra   v GRAS
grace, grâce v GRACE
GRACE   20 (*grace* 8,
    grâce 12)
+GRÂCE   1 (*lagrace*)
gracié   v GRACIER
GRACIER 1 (*gracié*)
grain   v GRAIN
GRAIN   5 (*grain*)
+GRAIN   6 (*lagrain* 1,
    la grain 1, *lagrains* 4)
GRAINE   1 (*grène*)
+GRAINE 19 (*la graine*)
+GRAISSE 1 (*la gresse*)
gram   v **GRÃO**
grampant, grampart
    v REMPART
gran, grand, grand', grande,
grandgrand   v GRAND
granbois   v GRAND, BOIS
GRAND   620 (*gran* 87,
    grand 515, *grand'* 3,
    grande 2, *grandgrand* 4,
    grands 9)
grandbois   v GRAND, BOIS
+GRAND+CHEMIN
    1 (*la gran soumin*)
grander, grandeur
    v GRANDEUR

GRANDEUR 2 (*grander* 1,
    grandeur 1)
GRAND+JOUR 1 (*grandzour*)
Grand-Louis v GRAND-LOUIS
GRAND-LOUIS
    1 (*Grand-Louis*) [nom de
    personnage]
GRAND+MAMAN 8
    (*grandmaman* 1,
    grand-maman 1,
    grandmanman 5,
    grandmanmân 1)
grandmaman, grand-maman,
grandmanman
    v GRAND+MAMAN
GRAND+MATIN 10
    (*gran matein* 3, *grand*
    matin 7, *grands matins* 1)
GRAND+MONDE 8
    (*grand monde* 1, *grand*
    mounde 4, *grand moune*
    1, *grand'moune* 1,
    grandmoune 1)
grand monde, grand mounde,
grand moune, grand'moune,
grandmoune
    v GRAND+MONDE
GRAND+NOIR 1 (*grand noir*)
GRAND+PAPA 7
    (*grandpapa* 1, *grand-*
    papa 3, *grandppâ* 3)
grandpapa, grand-papa,
grandppâ
    v GRAND+PAPA
grand père v GRAND+PÈRE
GRAND+PÈRE 2 (*grand père*)
granpretr, granprétr
    v GRAND+PRÊTRE
GRAND+PRÊTRE 2
    (*granpretr* 1, *granprétr* 1)
Grandrivière, Grand-Rivière
    v GRAND-RIVIÈRE
GRAND-RIVIÈRE 2
    (*Grandrivière* 1, *Grand-*
    Rivière 1) [toponyme]
grands   v GRAND
grands matins
    v GRAND+MATIN
grandterre v GRAND+TERRE
GRAND+TERRE
    3 (*grand'terre* 1, *grand'-*
    terre 1, *grandterre* 1)

GRAND+TRAIN   2
    (*gran train* 1, *gran trin* 1)
gran train, gran trin
    v GRAND+TRAIN
grand'terre , grand'-terre
    v GRAND+TERRE
grandzour v GRAND+JOUR
GRÃO   1 (*gram*) [mot port.]
gras   v GRAS
GRAS   21 (*gra* 1, *gras* 17,
    grasse 2)
grasse   v GRAS
graté, gratt', gratte, gratté
    v GRATTER
GRATTER 24 (*graté* 3, *gratt'*
    1, *gratte* 16, *gratté* 4)
gredin   v GREDIN
GREDIN   2 (*gredin* 1, *grédins* 1)
grédins   v GREDIN
Grégoire   v GRÉGOIRE
GRÉGOIRE 3 (*Grégoire*)
greince   v GRINCER
GRENADE 1 (*grénade*)
grénade   v GRENADE
GRENADIER 1 (*guernadié*)
grène   v GRAINE
grénié, grenier v GRENIER
GRENIER 10 (*grénié* 2, *grenier*
    1, *grénier* 6, *grinié* 1)
grénier   v GRENIER
GRENOUILLE 14
    (*gournouies* 1, *gournouïes* 2,
    gournouille 9, *gournoye* 1,
    grounouille 1)
gri gri, gri-gri v GRI-GRI
GRI-GRI   3 (*gri gri* 1, *gri-gri*
    1, *gris-gri* 1)
grillé   v GRILLER
GRILLER 4 (*grillé*)
grillot   v GRILLOT
GRILLOT 1 (*grillot*)
grimace   v GRIMACE
GRIMACE 5 (*grimace*)
+GRIMACE 2 (*la grimace*)
GRINCER 6 (*greince*)
grinié   v GRENIER
gri, gris   v GRIS
GRIS   2 (*gri* 1, *gris* 1)
gris-gri   v GRI-GRI
gro   v GROS
grog   v **GROG**
GROG   1 (*grog*) [mot angl.]

grogne, grogné v GROGNER
GROGNER 6 (*grogne* 1, *grogné* 4, *groïnié* 1)
groïnié, grond, gronde, grondé v GRONDER
GRONDER 7 (*grond* 2, *gronde* 2, *grondé* 3)
gros v GROS
GROS 108 (*gro* 2, *gros* 106)
grosseir v GROSSEUR
GROSSEUR 1 (*grosseir* 1)
grounouille v GRENOUILLE
guéle v GUEULE
gueilé, guéle, guèle, guélé, guêlé v GUEULER
guéri v GUERIR
GUERIR 36 (*guéri*)
guernadié v GRENADIER
+GUERRE 50 (*la guer* 3, *la guer'* 2, *la guère* 1, *la guerr'* 3, *la guerre* 23, *laguer* 1, *laguer'* 2, *laguerre* 13, *la-guerre* 2)
guet, guet', guéte, gueté, guété, guett, guett', guette, guétte, guetté, guetter v GUETTER
GUETTER 283 (*getté* 1, *guet* 19, *guet'* 1, *guéte* 9, *guète* 9, *guête* 4, *gueté* 1, *guété* 50, *guett* 1, *guett'* 11, *guette* 85, *guétte* 8, *guetté* 82, *guetter* 2)
GUEULE 2 (*guéle*)
+GUEULE 11 (*la-guél* 2, *laguéle* 5, *la guéle* 1, *la guèle* 1, *la guêle* 1, *la guelle* 1)
GUEULER 16 (*gueilé* 2, *guéle* 1, *guèle* 1, *guélé* 10, *guêlé* 2)
guingan v **GINGHAMS**
GUIGNE v PETIT+GUIGNE
GUIGNON 1 (*guignon*)
guine v GUIGNE
guinée v GUINÉE
GUINÉE 2 (*guinée*)
+GUITARE 1 (*la guitar*)
*GUN 1 (*gounn*) [not d'origine inconnue]

H

habi v HABIT
habille, habillé, habillée v HABILLER
HABILLER 13 (*habille* 6, *habillé* 3, *habillée* 1, *habiye* 3)
HABIT 1 (*habi*)
+HABIT 5 (*l'habit* 1, *nabi* 1, *nhabit* 1, *nhabits* 1, *zabit* 1, *z'habits* 1)
+HABITANT 15 (*zabitant* 1, *zabitants* 2, *z'bitant* 1, *zhabitans* 1, *z'habitans* 2, *z'habitant* 4, *z'habitants* 4)
HABITATION 17 (*bitation*)
+HABITATION 13 (*l'abitacion* 2, *l'habitation* 10, *l'habitations* 1)
habitié v HABITUER
+HABITUDE 1 (*l'abitid*)
HABITUER 1 (*habitié* 1)
habiye v HABILLER
HABRESAC 8 (*barsaque* 1, *bourbac* 2, *boursac* 3, *boursaqu'* 1, *boursaque* 1)
+HACHE 9 (*la hace* 1, *la hache* 1, *lahace* 7)
haï, haïe, haïè, haïr v HAÏR
HAÏR 16 (*haï* 4, *haïe* 1, *haïè* 6, *haïr* 3, *hayir* 2)
+HALEINE 1 (*l'haleine*)
HALER 3 (*halle* 3)
halle v HALER
+HAMEÇON 7 (*l'amçon* 1, *l'ham'çon* 1, *lhamçon* 1, *lhameçon* 3, *l'hameçon* 1)
Hamelin v HAMELIN
HAMELIN 1 (*Hamelin* 1) [nom de famille]
han 2 [interj.]
+HANGAR 3 (*l'angar* 1, *l'angard* 1, *l'hangard* 1)
hanté v HANTER
HANTER 1 (*hanté* 1)
+HARDE 13 (*la harde* 7, *la hardes* 2, *la-hard'* 1, *laharde* 1, *lahardes* 2)
+HARICOT 1 (*zaricots*)

harnais v HARNAIS
HARNAIS 1 (*harnais* 1)
harro v HARRO
HARRO 1 (*harro* 1)
HASARD 2 (*hazard* 2)
haut v HAUT
HAUT 34 (*haut* 31, *hot* 3)
hayir v HAÏR
hazard v HASARD
hé v HÉ
HÉ 26 (*hé* 26)
hein v HEIN
HEIN 9 (*hein* 9)
heire, heires v HEURE
hem 1 [interj.]
Henri v HENRI/HENRY
Henry v HENRI/HENRY
HENRI/HENRY 2 (*Henri* 1, *Henry* 1) [nom de famille]
+HERBAGE 1 (*z'herbaze*)
+HERBE 29 (*l'erbe* 1, *l'heirbe* 1, *l'herb* 3, *l'herb'* 1, *l'herbe* 7, *lherbe* 14, *lhérbe* 2)
héré v HEUREUX
héres v HEURE
hérés v HEUREUX
hérit v HÉRITER
+HÉRITAGE 1 (*l'héritaz*)
HÉRITER 2 (*hérit* 2)
héritié v HÉRITIER
HÉRITIER 1 (*héritié* 1)
+HÉRITIER 1 (*l'héritié*)
heun 1 [interj.]
HEURE 22 (*heires* 10, *héres* 12)
+HEURE 327 (*ler* 4, *lèr* 2, *lère* 3, *l'heire* 16, *lheire* 64, *l'her* 5, *lher* 45, *l'hére* 2, *l'hère* 3, *lhere* 1, *lhére* 74, *lhère* 15, *lherla* 82, *lherlà* 9, *l'herla* 1, *l'hères* 1)
heureuse, heureux v HEUREUX
HEUREUSEMENT 2 (*rés'ment* 1, *rheisement* 1)
HEUREUX 18 (*héré* 2, *héres* 12, *hérés* 2, *heureuse* 1, *heureux* 1)
hier v HIER
HIER 3 (*hier*)
hihan 3 [onomat.]
hi-i-i-i-i 1 [onomat.]

himilié v HUMILIER
hip 2 [interj.]
hipocrit v HYPOCRITE
+HIRONDELLE 8 (*zirondelle* 6, *z'hirondelle* 1, *zirondelles* 1)
hisse, hissé v HISSER
HISSER 33 (*hisse* 22, *hissé* 10, *risse*₂ 1)
+HISTOIRE 77 (*z'histoir* 1, *z'histoir'* 1, *zhistoire* 3, *z'histoire* 10, *zistoire* 61, *z'istoire* 1)
historique v HISTORIQUE
HISTORIQUE 1 (*historique* 1)
+HIVER 2 (*l'hiver*)
holà v HOLÀ
HOLÀ 1 (*holà* 1)
hom v HOMME
homard v HOMARD
HOMARD 3 (*homar* 1, *homard* 2)
homme v HOMME
HOMME 65 (*hom* 53, *homme* 12)
+HOMME 24 (*l'hom* 1, *lé zhom* 5, *lé zom* 4, *les z'homm'* 1, *zhom* 6, *zhomme* 1, *z'homm'* 1, *zom* 4, *zomme* 1)
honéte, honnet, honnète, honnête v HONNÈTE
HONNÈTE 5 (*honéte* 1, *honnet* 1, *honnète* 1, *honnête* 1, *honnêtes* 1)
honnêtes v HONNÈTE
+HONNÊTETÉ 1 (*l'honnêté*)
+HONNEUR 10 (*l'honner* 9, *l'honnér* 1, *lonère* 1)
honor v HONORER
HONORER 1 (*honor* 1)
hont', honte v HONTE
HONTE 16 (*hont'* 1, *honte* 2, *honté* 13)
+HONTE 1 (*la hônte*)
honté v HONTE
+HÔPITAL 10 (*l'hôpital* 3, *lhcptal* 4, *l'optal* 1, *zhopital* 1, *zopital* 1)
HORITA 1 (*houritte*) [mot malg.]

+HORITA 3 (*zourite* 1, *zouritte* 1, *z'ouritte* 1)
+HORREUR 2 (*lhorreir*)
hot v HAUT
+HÔTEL 1 (*l'hôtel*)
houhah 1 [interj.]
houhahouah 1 [interj.]
houillère v HOUILLÈRE
HOUILLÈRE 1 (*houillère*)
houit, houite v HUIT
+HOULE 1 (*la houle*)
houn 6 [interj.]
hourah v HOURAH
HOURAH 5 (*hourah* 2, *hourrah* 2, *hurrah* 1) [interj.]
houritte v HORITA
hourrah v HOURAH
+HUILE 17 (*di louil* 1, *di louïl* 1, *dilhouile* 7, *dilouil* 1, *dilouile* 1, *di luile* 5, *l'houile* 1)
huit v HUIT
HUIT 11 (*houit* 3, *houite* 5, *huit* 3)
huitième v HUITIÈME
HUITIÈME 1 (*huitième* 1)
+HUITRE 10 (*di zouitre* 6, *zhuître* 1, *z'huître* 3)
hum 2 [interj.]
+HUMEUR 2 (*l'himer*)
HUMILIER 1 (*himilié* 1)
hurrah v HOURAH
+HYPOCRISIE 1 (*lipocrizi*)
hypocrit v HYPOCRITE
HYPOCRITE 3 (*hipocrit* 2, *hypocrit* 1)
+HYPOCRITE 11 (*zipocrit*)

I

ici v ICI
ICI 85 (*ici*)
ide v AIDER
+IDÉE 3 (*l'idé* 1, *lidé* 1, *lidée* 1)
iéna v IL+Y+EN+A
iéve, ième, iéves v LIÈVRE
IGNORANT 1 (*ingnorans*)
il v IL
IL 6 (*il*)
+ÎLE 5 (*l'ile* 1, *l'île* 3, *lil'* 1)

IL+FAUT 12 (*y faut*)
+ILOT 10 (*l'illote* 2, *l'illotte* 3, *lilote* 1, *l'ilote* 1, *l'ilotte* 1, *zilots* 2)
ILOT 1 (*ilots*)
ilots v ILOT
IL+Y+EN+A 470 (*ein a* 1, *ein'a* 8, *eina* 3, *ein-a* 1, *einan* 1, *en a* 3, *ena* 22, *éna* 218, *èna* 8, *énan* 37, *iéna* 28, *yana* 19, *yanna* 1, *y-ein-a* 3, *yena* 20, *y en a* 27, *yen-a* 1, *y-en a* 15, *y en-a* 5, *yenà* 2, *y-en à* 13, *y-en-a* 20, *yenna* 12, *y enna* 2)
+IMAGE 2 (*zimage* 1, *zimages* 1)
IMAGINATION 2 (*mazination*)
IMAGINER 93 (*mazine* 24, *maziné* 68, *maziner* 1)
impé v UN+PEU
imposer v IMPOSER
IMPOSER 1 (*imposer*)
+IMPÔT 21 (*zeimpo* 1, *zimpot* 4, *zimpots* 14, *zimpôts* 1, *z'impots* 1)
imprimé v IMPRIMER
IMPRIMER 1 (*imprimé*)
in v UN
+INDE 4 (*l'inde*)
+INDÉPENDANT 1 (*zindépendants*)
+INDIENNE 1 (*zindiennes*)
+INDIGNITÉ 1 (*l'indignité*)
+INDIGO 1 (*l'indigo*)
+INFECTION 1 (*linféction*)
INFIRME 1 (*einfirm*)
+INFIRMITÉ 5 (*zeinfirmité* 4, *zéinfirmité* 1)
ingnorans v IGNORANT
INJUSTE 1 (*inziste*)
innoçan v INNOCENT
INNOCENT 3 (*innoçan*)
inpé, in-pé v UN+PEU
INQUIET 1 (*einkié*)
+INSTINCT 1 (*linstinct*)
instruire v INSTRUIRE
INSTRUIRE 2 (*einstrir* 1, *instruire* 1)

INSULTE 3 (*einsilt*)
INTELLIGENT 1 (*eintellizan*)
+INTÉRÊT 5 (*zeintéré* 1, *zintéré* 1, *zintérê* 1, *zintérêts* 2)
+INVALIDE 1 (*z'invalide*)
+INVITATION 3 (*l'invitation*)
+INVITÉ 1 (*zinvités*)
invit', *invite*, *invité*, *invités*   v INVITER
INVITER 11 (*einvit* 1, *einvité* 4, *invit'* 1, *invite* 1, *invité* 3, *invités* 1)
inziste   v INJUSTE
Iphizénie 1
+IRLANDAIS 1 (*zirlandais*)
isés   v USÉ
ivrogne   v IVROGNE
IVROGNE 1 (*ivrogne*)
+IVROGNE 1 (*zivroïn*)
IRAVĀṆAM 1 (*ravanne*) [mot tam.]

J

JABOT 2 (*zabot*)
JACONAS 2 (*zaconat* 1, *zaconat* 1)
jacot   v *JAKO
jacq   v CHAKKA
CHAKKA 2 (*jacq* 1, *zacques* 1) [nom du fruit ; mot dravidien]
JAGAN-NATH 3 (*zangarna* 1, *zangarna* 1, *zanguerna* 1) [mot hind.]
*JAKO 93 (*jacot* 1, *zaco* 13, *zacot* 80, *zacots* 1) [mot bantou]
jalou   v JALOUX
JALOUX 11 (*jalou* 2, *zaloux* 9)
Jamaïque   v JAMAÏQUE
JAMAÏQUE 1 (*Jamaïque*) [toponyme]
jamais   v JAMAIS
JAMAIS 181 (*jamais* 12, *zamais* 117, *zamé* 30, *zamés* 22)

+JAMBE 10 (*la jambe* 1, *la zamb'* 1, *la zambe* 1, *la-zamb'* 1, *lazambe* 3, *lazambes* 3)
JAMBOLÕES 2 (*zanblongue* 1, *zanblongues* 1) [mot port.]
JAMBON 4 (*zambon*)
JAMBO-ROSA 1 (*zambourzois*) [mot indo-port.]
Jan   v JEAN(NE)
JAPPER 15 (*zape* 1, *zapé* 6, *zappe* 3, *zappé* 5)
jardin   v JARDIN
JARDIN 20 (*jardin* 2, *zardein* 10, *zardin* 6, *zardins* 2)
jaune   v JAUNE
JAUNE 7 (*jaune* 1, *zaune* 5, *zon'* 1)
Jean   v JEAN(NE)
JEAN(NE) 160 (*Jan* 3, *Jean* 2, *Jeanne* 1, *Zan$_1$* 3, *Zane* 4, *Zeanne* 45, *Zean* 102)
JEAN-FOUT(R)E 3 (*djan foutte* 1, *djanfoute* 1, *Zanf...* 1)
JEAN+LA+GUERITE 1 (*Zean-la-Guérite*) [nom de personnage]
JEAN-MARIE 1 (*Zan marie*) [prénom]
Jeanne   v JEAN(NE)
JEANNOT 2 (*Zanot*)
jensse   v GENS
JÉRÉMIE 1 (*Zérémi*) [nom de famille]
Jérôme   v JÉRÔME
JÉRÔME 1 (*Jérôme*)
jésuit   v JÉSUITE
JÉSUITE 1 (*jésuit*)
Jesus, *Jésus*   v JÉSUS(-CHRIST)
Jesus-Christ, *Jésus-Christ*   v JÉSUS(-CHRIST)
JÉSUS(-CHRIST) 38 (*Jesus* 1, *Jésus* 1, *Jesus-Christ* 1, *Jésus-Christ* 33, *Jésus-Crist* 1, *zési* 1)
Jésus-Crist   v JÉSUS(-CHRIST)
jetté   v JETER

JETER 95 (*jetté* 1, *zet* 32, *zet'* 1, *zète* 2, *zété* 6, *zette* 47, *zétte* 5, *zetté* 1)
JEUDI 2 (*zédi*)
jeune   v JEÛNE
JEUNE 90 (*zeine* 5, *zeines* 1, *zéne* 16, *zène* 53, *zenes* 2, *zènes* 13)
JEÛNE 4 (*jeune*)
jeuné   v JEÛNER
JEUNE+GENS 2 (*zênes-zens* 1, *zênes-zens* 1)
JEÛNER 5 (*jeuné* 4, *zéné$_2$* 1)
JEUNESSE 2 (*zênesse*)
jigée   v JUGER
jigement   v JUGEMENT
jillet   v JUILLET
JIRUMUN 13 (*ziraumon* 7, *ziromon* 6) [mot tupi]
jisqu', *jisqu'à*   v JUSQUE
jisqu'à soir
   v JUSQU'À, À+SOIR
jist, *jiste*   v JUSTE
jize, *jizé*   v JUGER
JOCKEY 1 (*jockey*)
jockey   v JOCKEY
+JOIE 1 (*la joie*)
joindre   v JOINDRE
JOINDRE 41 (*joindre* 3, *zoinde* 31, *zouinde* 3, *zouindre* 1, *zoine* 3)
JOINT 1 (*joint*)
joint   v JOINT
JOLI 65 (*jolie* 3, *zoli* 52, *zolie* 5, *zolies* 2, *zolis* 3, *zouli* 4)
jolie   v JOLI
jolly   v JOLLY
JOLLY 1 (*jolly*) [mot angl.]
JOSEPH 4 (*Zozef*) [prénom]
+JOUE 5 (*la zou* 1, *lazoue* 1, *lazoues* 3)
joué   v JOUER
JOUER 23 (*joué* 4, *zoué* 18, *zouyé* 1)
JOUEUR 1 (*zouères*)
JOUJOU 2 (*zouzou*)
jour   v JOUR
JOUR 250 (*jour* 26, *jours* 6, *zor* 1, *zour* 183, *zour'* 1, *zours* 33)

+JOUR 13 (*le jour* 1, *lé zour* 1, *lézour* 1, *li zour* 2, *lizour* 4, *li-zour* 4)
jourée   v JURER
JOUR-EN-JOUR 1 (*zour-en-zour*)
JOURNÉE1 (*zournée*)
+JOURNÉE 21 (*la zourné* 10, *la zournée* 5, *lazournée* 5, *la-zournée* 1)
jours   v JOUR
jousqu'a, jousqu'à v JUSQUE
JUGE   26 (*zige* 1, *ziz*₁ 4, *zize* 17, *zizes* 4)
+JUGE   1 (*lézize*)
jugement v JUGEMENT
JUGEMENT 9 (*jigement* 1, *jugement* 1, *zizman* 7)
JUGER 17 (*jigée* 2, *jize* 1, *jizé* 1, *ziz*₂ 4, *zizé* 8, *zizer* 1)
juif   v JUIF
JUIF   7 (*juif* 5, *juife* 2)
juife   v JUIF
JUILLET   1 (*jillet*)
JUMENT   6 (*ziment*)
JUPE   2 (*zipe* 1, *zipes* 1)
Jupiter   v JUPITER
JUPITER   1 (*Jupiter*)
JUPON   1 (*zipon*)
jurer   v JURER
JURER   9 (*jourée* 1, *jurer* 1, *jurez* 1, *zoure* 4, *zouré* 2)
jurez   v JURER
jusqu'à   v JUSQUE
JUSQUE/ JUSQU'À   135 (*jisqu'* 1,   *jisqu'à* 13, *jousqu'a* 2, *jousqu'à* 4, *jusqu'à* 2, *ziska* 53, *zisqu'* 1, *zisqua* 1, *zisquà* 4, *zisqu'à* 26, *zisqué* 3, *zousqua* 1, *zousqu'à* 14)
+JUS   1 (*di-zus*)
JUSTE   39 (*jist* 1, *jiste* 7, *zis* 1, *zisse* 5, *zist* 12, *ziste* 13)
+JUSTE   1 (*lé zist*)
JUSTICE   4 (*zistice*)
+JUSTICE 6 (*la jistice* 1, *la zistice* 4, *la zistis* 1)

K

KABAR   1 (*cabar*) [mot ar.]
*KABORDAR 1 (*cabardar*) [origine inconnue]
KAMBARA 1 (*cambare*) [mot malg.]
KANCI 1 (*cang'*) [mot tam.]
kalité   v QUALITÉ
kan   v QUAND
KAPORO 1 (*capores*) [mot bant.]
KAPRA   2 (*capra*) [mot hind.]
kar   v QUART
KARAHI 1 (*caraye*) [mot hind.]
KA<u>R</u>AIYA<u>N</u> 2 (*caria* 1, *carias* 1) [mot tam.]
karant   v QUARANTE
KARI   25 (*cari* 23, *caris* 1, *carri* 1) [mot tam.]
Karikal   v KARIKAL
KARIKAL 1 (*Karikal*) [toponyme tam.]
kartié   v QUARTIER
KAS   4 (*cace* 1, *caces* 3) [mot hind.]
kat   v QUATRE
KATEKATÉ 3 (*cat-cat* 1, *cat-catte* 1, *cate-cate* 1) [mot malg.]
KATTĒRU 1 (*catéra*) [mot tam.]
katorz   v QUARTORZE
katr   v QUATRE
katriem   v QUATRIÈME
katro-vein-diz-nef v QUATRE-VINGT-DIX-NEUF
*KAYAKAYA 1 (*caya caya*) [mot bant.]
kek   v QUELQUE
Kerr   v KERR
KERR   1 (*Kerr*) [nom de famille]
kestion   v QUESTION
kestionne v QUESTIONNER
ki   v QUI
ki ci ça, ki-ci-ça v QU'EST-CE+QUE+C'EST+ÇA
kik   v QUELQUE
kikçoz   v QUELQUE+ CHOSE

kikéne, kikène v QUELQU'UN
kikfoa   v QUELQUE FOIS
kilotte   v CULOTTE
kimé   v ÉCUMER
KISS   2 (*kissekisse*) [mot ar.]
kissekisse v KISS
kit   v QUITTER
koa   v QUOI
KONTAI 2 (*condé*) [mot tam.]
KOUG 2 (*couc*) [mot bret.]

L

la, là   v LÀ
LÀ   1478 (*la* 79, *là* 1398, *la'* 1)
la'   v LÀ
laba, la ba, là ba v LÀ-BAS
labande, la bande v +BANDE
la banq, la banque
    v +BANQUE
labarbe, la barbe v +BARBE
làbas, là bas, là-bas v LÀ-BAS
LÀ-BAS   22 (*la ba* 1, *là ba* 4, *là bas* 2, *laba* 1, *làbas* 3, *là-bas* 11)
la bataille v +BATAILLE
la bave   v +BAVE
l'abavent v+ABAT-VENT
+ABAT-VENT 1 (*l'abavent*)
l'abbé   v +ABBÉ
labec, la bec v +BEC
la bénédiction
    v +BÉNÉDICTION
la berloq' v +BRELOQUE
la bête   v +BÊTE
la bible   v +BIBLE
la bierre   v +BIERRE
la bile   v +BILE
l'abitacion v +HABITATION
l'abitid   v +HABITUDE
la boëte   v +BOËTE
la boisson v +BOISSON
la bonde   v +BONDE
la bonn nouvel
    v +BONNE NOUVELLE
la bonté   v +BONTÉ
la bouç, la bouç', labouce, la-bouce, la-bouçe, la bouce
    v +BOUCHE
la boucerie v +BOUCHERIE

laboue, la boue v +BOUE
la bouette v +BOËTE
LABOURDONNAIS 1
    (*Labourdonné*) [nom
    de famille]
Labourdonné
    v LABOURDONNAIS
labourer v LABOUREUR
LABOUREUR 2 (*labourer*)

*la bous, la bouss', la-bouss',
la-bousse, la bousse*
    v +BOUCHE
la bouteille v +BOUTEILLE
la boutique v +BOUTIQUE
la bouzie v +BOUGIE
l'abominacion v
    +ABOMINATION
laboutik, laboutique, laboutiques
    v +BOUTIQUE
labouzie v +BOUGIE
labrai v +BRAI
labride v +BRIDE
la brine v +BRUNE
la brise v +BRISE
l'absinthe v +ABSINTHE
la-caille v +CAILLE
la çaine, la-çaine v +CHAÎNE
la cair v +CHAIR
la calbasse, la callebasse
    v +CALEBASSE
laçaleir, la çaler v +CHALEUR
*laçambe, la çambe, laçambes,
la çambr* v +CHAMBRE
lacampagne, la campagne
    v +CAMPAGNE
la çand v +CENDRE
*la-cantin', la cantine,
la-cantine* v +CANTINE
la çarité v +CHARITÉ
*lacas', lacase, la case, la-case,
lacases* v +CASE
*la-çass', la çass', laçasse,
la çasse, la-çasse* v +CHASSE
lacause, la cause, la cauz'
    v +CAUSE
la cav, lacave, la cave v +CAVE
la cayane 1 [origine inconnue]
*la caz', la-caz', la caz, lacaze,
la-caze, la caze* v +CASE
laccord' v +CORDE

lace v LÂCHE
lacende, la cende, la cendre
    v +CENDRE
la cène v +CÈNE
la çér v +CHAIR
laceron v LACERON
LACERON 4 (*laceron* 1,
    l'astron 1, *lastrons* 1,
    lastrou 1) [mot fr. dial.]
+LACERON (*la lasseron* 1)
LÂCHE 1 (*lace*)
la chaine v +CHAÎNE
la chair v +CHAIR
la chambr v +CHAMBRE
la chasse v +CHASSE
la chaux v +CHAUX
lacire, la cire v +CIRE
laclairté, la clarté v +CLARTÉ
laclé, la clé , la-clé v +CLÉ
lacloce, la cloce, lacloces
    v +CLOCHE
la colaire, la coler, la-colère
    v +COLÈRE
la colle, lacolle, lacolle
    v +COLLE
la colonie v +COLONIE
la comédie v +COMÉDIE
la compagni v +COMPAGNIE
la coque, la coques, lacoque
    v +COQUE
la coquine v +COQUINE
*lacorde, lacôrde, la corde,
la côrde* v +CORDE
la couen', la couénne
    v +COUENNE
lacour, la cour v +COUR
lacourse, la course
    v +COURSE
lacousine v +CUISINE
la cousine v +COUSINE
la coz v +CAUSE
lacrace v +CRACHE
la crampe v +CRAMPE
la créacion v +CRÉATION
la crêt' v +CRÊTE
la croa, la croix v +CROIX
la-croupière v +CROUPIÈRE
*ladan, làdan, ladans, làdans,
la dans, là dans, là-dans*
    v LÀ+DEDANS
la danse v +DANSE
ladaube, la daube v +DAUBE

LÀ+DEDANS 59 (*ladan* 4,
    làdan 1, *la dan* 7, *ladans*
    3, *la dans* 1, *làdans* 35, *là
    dans* 3, *là-dans* 5)
la désolacion v +DÉSOLATION
la dilizence v +DILIGENCE
la dim v +DÎME
la discord v +DISCORDE
ladition v +ADDITION
la dose v +DOSE
la douane v +DOUANE
ladouleir, la douleir, ladoulére
    v +DOULEUR
ladoutance v +DOUTANCE
la droatir v +DROITURE
LÁFA 14 (*laffe*) [mot
    malg.]
la faim v +FAIM
la famine v +FAMINE
lafarine, la farine v +FARINE
la fatig v +FATIGUE
lafaute, la faut' v +FAUTE
lafée v +FÉE
la fein v +FIN
*lafenéte, lafenète, lafenête,
lafenètes, lafenéte, la fenète,
la fenêtre* v +FENÊTRE
la fet , la fête v +FÊTE
laffe v **LÁFA**
laffe-laboue v **LÁFA**, +BOUE
la ficel' v +FICELLE
la fière v +FIER
la fiévr, la fievre, la fièvre
    v +FIÈVRE
lafille, la fille v +FILLE
*la fimé, lafimée, la fimée,
la-fimée* v +FUMÉE
lafin, la fin v +FIN
la fiy, la fiye v +FILLE
laflamme v +FLAMME
la flit, la flîte v +FLÛTE
la fnête, la fnêtre v +FENÊTRE
la foa v +FOI
la fondacion v +FONDATION
la fontaine v +FONTAINE
*laforce, lafôrce, la forc',
la force* v +FORCE
laforêt, la forêt v +FORÊT
la fors v +FORCE
laforze v +FORGE
lafosse v +FOSSE
la fouarre v +FOIRE

la fouine	v +FOUINE	
la foul	v +FOULE	
la fouzère	v +FOUGÈRE	
lafraiceir	v +FRAICHEUR	
lafrayeir	v +FRAYEUR	
l'africain	v +AFRICAIN	
lagale	v +GALE	

la gard, lagarde, la garde v +GARDE
lagazet, l'agazet', la gazett', lagazette, la gazette, la gazettte v +GAZETTE
laglace, la glace v +GLACE
la gloar, la gloire v +GLOIRE
la gorg, la gorge, la gorz, lagorze, lagórze, la gorze, lagôze v +GORGE
lagrace v +GRÂCE
lagrain, la grain v +GRAIN
la graine v +GRAINE
lagrains v +GRAIN
la gran soumin v +GRAND+CHEMIN
la gresse v +GRAISSE
la grimace v +GRIMACE
la-guél, laguéle, la guéle, la guèle, la guêle, la guelle v +GUEULE
laguer, la guer, laguer', la guer', la guère, la guerr', laguerre, la guerre, la-guerre v +GUERRE
la guitar v +GUITARE
lahace, la hace, la hache v +HACHE
la-hard', laharde, la harde, lahardes, la hardes v +HARDE
la hau, lahaut, làhaut, la haut, là haut, la-haut, là-haut v LÀ-HAUT

LÀ-HAUT 452 (*l'haut* 1, *la hau* 3, *la haut* 50, *là haut* 4, *lahaut* 14, *la-haut* 2, *làhaut* 154, *là-haut* 16, *laho* 150, *lao* 10, *la o* 1, *lhaut* 24, *lhaute* 1, *lor*$_2$ 4, *or* 18[20])
laho v LÀ-HAUT

---

[20] L'épellation *or* pour *lor* en CM moderne est uniquement trouvée chez Soulsobontemps (1925).

la hônte v +HONTE
la houle v +HOULE
l'aimable v +AIMABLE
lair, l'air v +AIR
laiss', laisse, laissé, laissée v LAISSER

LAISSER 149 (*laiss'* 11, *laisse* 89, *laissé* 3, *laissée* 1, *lesse* 4, *lésse* 40, *léssé* 1)
+LAIT 6 (*dilait* 3, *di lait* 2, *dilé* 1)
la jambe v +JAMBE
la jistice v +JUSTICE
la joie v +JOIE
la lasseron v +LACERON
la lamp, lalampe, la lampe, lalampes v +LAMPE
la-langu', lalangue, la langue, lalangues v +LANGUE
la lépr v +LÈPRE
la lev, la lèv' v +LÈVRE
laliane, lalianne v +LIANNE
la liberté v +LIBERTÉ
laligne, la ligne v +LIGNE
la limier, la limiér, lalimière, la limière v +LUMIÈRE
la lin', laline, la line, la-line v +LUNE
laliqueir, laliqueir, la liquère, laliqueur, laliquier v +LIQUEUR
lalitière v LITIÈRE
l'allians v +ALLIANCE
lalo v *LALU
*LALU 1 (*lalo*)
la loa, laloi, la loi v +LOI
l'aloi v +ALOËS
la louanz v +LOUANGE
l'am v +ÂME
la maille v +MAILLE
lamain, la main, la-main, lamains v +MAIN
la maliç', lamalice, la malice v +MALICE
la malidiction v +MALÉDICTION
lamalle, la malle v +MALLE
lamance, la mance v +MANCHE
la manière, la-manière v +MANIÈRE
la mant v +MENTHE
la marce v +MARCHE
la mare v +MARE

lamarée v +MARÉE
lamariée, la mariée v +MARIÉE
la marre v +MARE
la masse v +MASSE
l'ambara v +EMBARRAS
Lambert v LAMBERT
LAMBERT 1 (*Lambert*) [nom de famille]
l'ambition v +AMBITION
l'amçon v +HAMEÇON
l'àme, l'âme v +ÂME
la méçanceté v +MÉCHANCETÉ
la mel v +MEULE
lamélasse v +MÉLASSE
la même, la-même, là-même v LÀ+MÊME
LÀ+MÊME 10 (*la même* 6, *la-même* 1, *là-même* 3)
LA+MÊME+CHOSE 7 (*la mem çoz* 5, *la même çose* 1, *la même çoze* 1)
la même çose, la mem çoz, la même çoze v LA+MÊME+CHOSE
lamer, la mer v +MER
la mésh v +MÈCHE
la mésire v +MESURE
la messe, la-messe v +MESSE
la mézir v +MESURE
lamigraine v +MIGRAINE
la mine v +MINE
la minicipalité v +MUNICIPALITÉ
la mir v +MYRRHE
lamiraille v +MURAILLE
la misaire, la misèr', lamisère, la-misère, la misère, lamisères v +MISÈRE
lamisique, la misique v +MUSIQUE
l'amitié v +AMITIÉ
la mizique, la-mizique v +MUSIQUE
l'amiz'ment v +AMUSEMENT
la mod', la mode v +MODE
la moitié v +MOITIÉ
lamonaie, la moné, la monnaie, la monné v +MONNAIE
lamontagne, la montagne, la montaïn v +MONTAGNE

lamontée v +MONTÉE	lao, la o v LÀ-HAUT	lapoude, la poude, la poudre
lamoquié, la moquié v +MOITIÉ	lapaill', lapaille, la paille	v +POUDRE
la mor, la more v +MORT	v +PAILLE	la poudre d'or
la mori, lamorie v +MORUE	lapaix v +PAIX	v +POUDRE D'OR
la mort v +MORT	la pâk v +PÂQUES	la pouissans v +PUISSANCE
la mousse v +MOUSSE	la parol v +PAROLE	la poussier, la poussière
la moutard v +MOUTARDE	lapartaze, la partaze	v +POUSSIÈRE
la moutié v +MOITIÉ	v +PARTAGE	l'apparance, l'apparans
l'amour v +AMOUR	la passe v +PASSE	v +APPARENCE
+LAMPE 17 (la lamp 7, la	la passion v +PASSION	l'appel v +APPEL
lampe 7, lalampe 2,	la pât v +PÂTE	la pride v +PRUDE
lalampes 1)	lapatte, la patte, lapattes	la-priér, lapriére, laprière
l'an v +AN	v +PATTE	la prière, la-prière v +PRIÈRE
l'ançan v +ENCENS	la paye v +PAILLE	la preuve, la prév v +PREUVE
lance v LANCER	la pé v +PAIX	la princesse v +PRINCESSE
LANCER 1 (lance)	lapeau, la-peau, la peau	la prise v +PRISE
l'anciein v +ANCIEN	v +PEAU	la prison v +PRISON
l'ancre v +ANCRE	lapéce, lapèce, la pèce, la-pèce	la priyer, la priyér v +PRIÈRE
landimain v LENDEMAIN	v +PÊCHE	la prom'nade v +PROMENADE
l'androa, landroit	la pein', lapeine, la peine	la qué, la-qué, laqué, laquée,
v +ENDROIT	v +PEINE	laquèe, laquées v +QUEUE
la neiz v +NEIGE	la peintire v +PEINTURE	larac, l'arack v +'ARAQ
la néssans v +NAISSANCE	lapéne, la pène v +PEINE	la rade, la rades v +RADE
l'anet v +ANETH	la per v +PEUR	la raie v +RAIE
l'anfer v +ENFER	laperte v +PERTE	la raison v +RAISON
langage v LANGAGE	la pesse v +PÊCHE	l'aranz'mens
LANGAGE 14 (langage 6,	la pharmacie v +PHARMACIE	v +ARRANGEMENT
langaz 3, langaz' 1,	lapin v LAPIN	la-ravine v +RAVINE
langaze 4)	LAPIN 2 (lapin)	la raz, la raze v +RAGE
langaz, langaz', langaze	la pince v +PINCE	l'arc-en-ciel v +ARC-EN-CIEL
v LANGAGE	la pioce v +PIOCHE	la recerce v +RECHERCHE
LANGOUTI 10 (langouti 8,	la pipie v +PÉPIE	la récolt v +RÉCOLTE
langoutis 1, langouty 1)	laplace, la place v +PLACE	la règle v +RÈGLE
langouti, langoutis, langouty	laplaine, la plaine, la-plaine,	lareine, la reine v +REINE
v LANGOUTI	lapléne, la pléne v +PLAINE	la religion v +RELIGION
+LANGUE 24 (la langue 11,	la plaine line v	la rente v +RENTE
la-langu' 2, lalangue 10,	+PLEINE+LUNE	la réponse, laréponse,
lalangues 1)	la Plaine Wilainne	laréponses v +RÉPONSE
langui v LANGUIR	v +PLAINE WILHELMS	la république
LANGUIR 1 (langui)	lapli, la pli, laplie, la plie	v +RÉPUBLIQUE
l'angar, l'angard v +HANGAR	v +PLUIE	la rézirekcion, la rézirékcion
l'angleterre v +ANGLETERRE	la plime v +PLUME	v +RÉSURRECTION
l'anné, l'année v +ANNÉE	la plipar v +PLUPART	larestant v +RESTANT
la noce v +NOCE	la po v +PEAU	larg v LARGUER
la noui, la nouit, lanouite,	la pointe v +POINTE	largamasse v +**ARGAMASSA**
la nouite, la nouy v +NUIT	lapolice, la police v +POLICE	large v LARGE
l'anseïnman	lapommade, la pommade	LARGE 3 (large 2, larz 1)
v +ENSEIGNEMENT	v +POMMADE	l'argent v +ARGENT
l'anterman	lapompe v +POMPE	largu', largue, largué
v +ENTERREMENT	la port, la port', laporte,	v LARGUER
l'antouraz v +ENTOURAGE	la porte, la-porte, lapôrte,	LARGUER 58 (larg 2, largu' 2,
la nuit, la nuit' v +NUIT	laportes v +PORTE	largue 29, largué 25)

larhime, la rhim' v +RHUME	lasoie, la soie v +SOIE	lautefois v +AUTREFOIS
la ri, larie, la rie, laries v +RUE	lasoif, la soif v +SOIF	l'autel v +AUTEL
la rivier, la riviér, la rivièr',	lasoupe, la soupe v +SOUPE	lautes v +AUTRE₁
larivière, larivière, la-rivière,	la source v +SOURCE	l'autfois, l'aut'fois
la riviere, la rivière v +RIVIÈRE	lasse v LAS	v +AUTREFOIS
la riz v +RUSE	lassé v LASSER	l'auto v +AUTO
la r'lizion v +RELIGION	LASSER 30 (lassé)	l'autre v +AUTRE₁
larmoire, l'armoire, larmoires	l'assiète, lassiette, l'assiette,	l'autrefois v +AUTREFOIS
v +ARMOIRE	lassiétes v +ASSIÈTE	l'autrement v +AUTREMENT
larobe v +ROBE	l'assommoir v +ASSOMMOIR	lav v LAVER
laroce v +ROCHE	lastique v ÉLASTIQUE	la valer v +VALEUR
laronde, la ronde, la-ronde	l'astron v LACERON	l'avantaze v +AVANTAGE
v +RONDE	lastrons, lastrou²¹	lavarangue, la varangue
la rose v +ROSE	v LACERON	v +VARANGUE
laroue, laroues v +ROUE	la tab, latabe, la tabe, latable	lave, lavé v LAVER
la rout', la route v +ROUTE	v +TABLE	la veine v +VEINE
larouille, la rouy v +ROUILLE	la tace v +TÂCHE	lavente, la vente v +VENTE
la rouzeole v +ROUGEOLE	la taill' v +TAILLE	laver v LAVER
larrosoir v +ARROSOIR	la tangaze v +TANGAGE	LAVER 18 (lav 5, lave 4,
l'arsh v +ARCHE	la tant v +TENTE	lavé 8, laver 1)
la ruche v +RUCHE	la tarace v +TRACE	la vérèt', la vérette
larz v LARGE	la tendresse v +TENDRESSE	v +VAIRETTE
larzan, l'arzan, larzent, l'arzen,	la ter, la ter', la tère, latère, la	la vériol v +VARIOLE
l'arzent v +ARGENT	terr', laterre, la terre	la vérité, la verté v +VÉRITÉ
las v LAS	v +TERRE	la vi v +VIE
LAS 8 (las 1, lasse 7)	latêt, la tet, la tét, la têt',	la viand', laviande, la viande,
lasabe v +SABLE	la-têt', la téte, la tète, latète,	la-viande, lavianne v +VIANDE
la sagesse v +SAGESSE	latéte, latête, la tête, la-tête,	lavie, la vie v +VIE
la sainte cène, la sainte-cène	latêtes v +TÊTE	la vierge v +VIERGE
v +SAINTE CÈNE	la tisane v +TISANE	la vil, laville, la ville v +VILLE
lasaison, la-saison v +SAISON	latoéle, la toil', la toile, latouéle	lavoile v +VOILE
la sal v +SALLE	v +TOILE	lavoix, la-voix v +VOIX
la saline v +SALINE	la toilette v +TOILETTE	la vill'bague
la sall', lasalle, la salle	latrine v LATRINE	v +VILLE-BAGUE
v +SALLE	LATRINE 2 (latrine)	la ville noire v +VILLE+NOIR
la sambre v +CHAMBRE	la tour v +TOUR	la voa, la voi v +VOIX
la santé v +SANTÉ	la traces v +TRACE	la voile v +VOILE
la sasse, la-sasse, là-sasse	la treille v +TREILLE	la voix v +VOIX
v +CHASSE	latripe v +TRIPE	la volonté v +VOLONTÉ
la sauce v +SAUCE	la trompette v +TROMPETTE	la-zamb', la zamb', lazambe,
la savanne v +SAVANNE	Laurette v LAURETTE	la zambe, lazambes v +JAMBE
lascar v **LASHKAR**	LAURETTE 9 (Laurette) [nom	Lazare, Lazarre v LAZARRE
lascie, la scie v +SCIE	de personnage]	LAZARRE 4 (Lazare 3,
laseine, la seine v +SEINE	laurier v LAURIER	Lazarre 1) [nom de
la semaine v +SEMAINE	LAURIER 1 (laurier)	personnage]
la semence v +SEMENCE	l'aurore v +AURORE	laze, lâze, l'aze v +ÂGE
laséne, la séne v +SEINE	laut', l'aut, l'aut', laute, l'aute	la zentille v +GENTIL
la sézon v +SAISON	v +AUTRE₁	la zistice, la zistis v +JUSTICE
LASHKAR 7 (lascar) [mot		lazoie, la zoie, lazoies, lazois
hind.]		v +OIE
la site v +SITE	²¹ Cette épellation est probablement	la zou, lazoue, lazoues
la s'maine v +SEMAINE	un erreur typographique (u au lieu de n).	v +JOUE

la zourné, lazournée,
la zournée , la-zournée
        v +JOURNÉE
l'bras   v +BRAS
l'camp   v +CAMP
lé$_1$ v VOULOIR
lé$_2$ v LE
LE   1 (*lé$_2$*)
l'eau cologne
        v +EAU+COLOGNE
lébanc   v +BANC
le baptême   v +BAPTÊME
lébas, lé bas   v +BAS
le bien   v +BIEN
lebras, lébras , le-bras , lé bras
        v +BRAS
le camp   v +CAMP
lécelle, léchelle   v +ÉCHELLE
léciel, léciél, le ciel, lé ciel, le ciél,lé ciél, le ciele   v +CIEL
l'écol', lécole , l'école
        v +ÉCOLE
le comanceman
        v +COMMENCEMENT
LEÇON   1 (*leçons*)
l'économie   v +ÉCONOMIE
leçons   v LEÇON
lécor, le cor, lé cor, le côr , lé-cor, lécorps, lé-corps, lé corps   v +CORPS
lécou   v +COU
lé crainte   v +CRAINTE
lécritr', l'écritir, l'écritire, lecritire, lécritire
        v +ÉCRITURE
lé dan   v +DENT
lédé   v +DÉ
le démon   v +DÉMON
lé den, lé dent, lédent, lé-dent, lédents, lé-dents   v +DENT
le diable   v +DIABLE
le dimons   v +DÉMON
lé do, lédo   v +DOS
lé doa, lédoigt, lédoigts, lé doigt, lédoit   v +DOIGT
lédos, lé dos   v +DOS
lé droit   v +DROIT
lé fanor   v +FANEUR-**ER**
lé femme   v +FEMME
léffet   v +EFFET
lé-fille   v +FILLE
le fis, lé fis   v +FILS

le fis de dié, le fis de dieu
        v +FILS+DE+DIEU
le fis de l'hom, lé fis de l'hom, le fis de lhom , lé fis de lhom
        v +FILS+DE+L'HOMME
léfoie   v +FOIE
légants, lé gants   v +GANT
léger   v LÉGER
LÉGER   3 (*léger* 1, *légère* 1, *lézé* 1)
légère   v LÉGER
léglise, l'eglise, l'église, légliz l'egliz, l'égliz, l'égliz', léglize l'eglize, l'églize   v +ÉGLISE
léguime, léguimes, légume
        v LÉGUME
LÉGUME   5 (*léguime* 1, *léguimes* 3, *légume* 1)
l'egypt   v +EGYPTE
legzamp   v +EXEMPLE
l'einne   v +UN
leinz   v LINGE
le jour   v +JOUR
lékel   v +LEQUEL
lé ker, le kère, lékère, lékeir
        v +CŒUR
leléphant , léléphant, léléphant, l'éléphant   v +ÉLÉPHANT
l'embaras, l'embarras
        v +EMBARRAS
lémétère   v +ÉMETTEUR
lémoi   v +MOIS
le mond   v +MONDE$_2$
lémots   v +MOT
l'enclime, lenclime
        v +ENCLUME
lendemain   v LENDEMAIN
LENDEMAIN   35 (*landimain* 1, *lendemain* 4, *lendimain* 28, *lendimé* 1, *lendimin* 1)
lendimain, lendimé, lendimin
        v LENDEMAIN
lendourmi   v +ENDORMI
lendroit, l'endroit
        v +ENDROIT
l'éne   v +UN
lénerfs   v +NERF
l'enfer   v +ENFER
l'ennemi   v +ENNEMI
le nom   v +NOM
lenque   v +ENCRE

lenterrement, l'enterrement
        v +ENTERREMENT
lentii   v LENTILLE
LENTILLE   10 (*lentii* 9, *lentis* 1)
lentis   v LENTILLE
lentouraze, l'entourage l'entouraze   v +ENTOURAGE
lenvie, l'envie   v +ENVIE
l'épaule   v +ÉPAULE
lé payère   v +PAYEUR
lépé   v +ÉPÉE
le pêchés   v +PÊCHÉ
le per   v +PÈRE
léplats   v +PLAT
l'éponz, l'éponze   v +ÉPONGE
+LÈPRE   1 (*la lépr*)
lépré   v +PRÉ
le profét   v +PROPHÈTE
léqueir, lé queir   v +CŒUR
LEQUEL   1 (*lékel*)
lequer, léquer, léquér, léquèr, lé quér, lè quèr, lé-quer, lé-quèr, léquère, lèquère
        v +CŒUR
l'équinoxe   v +ÉQUINOXE
léquérie, léquirie, l'équirie
        v +ÉCURIE
ler, lèr, lère v +HEURE
le ra, lé ra, lérat , lé rat, lé-rat, lérats , lé-rats   v +RAT
lérails   v +RAIL
l'erbe   v +HERBE
lérein, lé rein   v +REIN
le reïn   v +RÈGNE
lé-rein, léreins, lé reins
        v +REIN
le réziman   v +RÉGIMENT
lerest   v +RESTE
lérin, lé rin   v +REIN
l'ermit', l'ermite   v +ERMITE
lé roa   v +ROI
le roayom , lé roayom
        v +ROYAUME
léroi, lèroi, lé roi, lè roi, le roi, lé-roi, lérois   v +ROI
lérond   v +ROND
lé-roy   v +ROI
le saint-ecritire
        v +SAINTE ÉCRITURE
le salue   v +SALUT
les autres   v +AUTRE$_2$

les bras v +BRAS	l'évangil, l'evangile	l'herbe v +HERBE
lescalier, léscalier, l'escalier,	v +ÉVANGILE	lhere, lhére, lhère, l'hére,
lescaliers v +ESCALIER	léve, lève, lêve, levé, lévé, lèvè,	l'hèrel'hères v +HEURE
l'esclavaze v +ESCLAVAGE	levée, lévée v LEVER	l'héritaz v +HÉRITAGE
le seigneur, le sénier,	Léveillé v LÉVEILLÉ	l'héritié v +HÉRITIER
lé séniér v +SEIGNEUR	LÉVEILLÉ 2 (Léveillé) [nom	lherla, lherlà, l'herla
les filles v +FILLE	de personnage]	v +HEURE, LÀ
les morts v +MORT	l'eveillé, l'éveillé v +ÉVEILLÉ	l'hermit' v +ERMITE
lé-soir, lésoirs v +SOIR	léventail v +ÉVENTAIL	l'himer v +HUMEUR
lé son, léson v +SON$_1$	LEVER 162 (lev 13, lév 4,	l'hiver v +HIVER
les ordres v +ORDRE	lév' 1, lèv' 2, léve 10,	l'hom v +HOMME
lé sou v LE+SOU	lève 38, lêve 1, levé 5,	l'honner, l'honnér
LE+SOU 1 (lé sou)	lévé 84, lèvè 1, levée 1,	v +HONNEUR
les pauvres v +PAUVRE	lévée 2)	l'honnêtê v +HONNÊTETÉ
l'éspérance v +ESPÉRANCE	léver v +VER	l'hôpital, lhoptal v +HÔPITAL
lespoir v +ESPOIR	lé ver v +VERRE	lhorreir v +HORREUR
les pots v +POT	lé voix v +VOIX	l'hôtel v +HÔTEL
l'espri, lespri, l'espris, l'esprit,	+LÈVRE 2 (la lev 1, la lèv' 1)	l'houile v +HUILE
lesprit, lésprit	l'exemp v +EXEMPLE	li v LUI
v +ESPRIT	l'explicacion, l'explication	LIANNE 3 (laliane 1,
l'essans v +ESSENCE	v +EXPLICATION	lalianne 2)
lesse, lésse, léssé v LAISSER	lézaile, lé zaile, lé-zaile,	lib, libe v LIBRE
lessive v LESSIVE	lézailes v +AILE	liberté v LIBERTÉ
LESSIVE 1 (lessive)	lé zanciein v +ANCIEN	LIBERTÉ 1 (liberté)
les soirs v +SOIR	LÉZARD 2 (lézard 1, lézards 1)	+LIBERTÉ 13 (la liberté)
l'estomac v +ESTOMAC	Lézard, lézards v LÉZARD	libr, libr', libre v LIBRE
les trois v +TROIS	lézé v LÉGER	LIBRE 20 (lib 2, libe 1,
les z'homm' v +HOMME	lé zécritir v +ÉCRITURE	libr 1, libr' 1,
les zaut' v +AUTRE$_2$	lézél v +AILE	libre 5, libres 10)
l'étalaze v +ÉTALAGE	lé zélu v +ÉLU	libres v LIBRE
le tampl, lé tampl v +TEMPLE	lé zhom v +HOMME	licaire v +CŒUR
le tan, lé tan v +TEMPS	léziés v +YEUX	lice v LISSER
l'état v +ETAT	lé zist v +JUSTE	**LI CHI** 1 (letcis) [mot chin.]
letcis v **LI CHI**	lézize v +JUGE	li ciein, licien, li cien, li-cien,
l'été v +ÉTÉ	lezo, lézo v +OS	li-çien, liciens, li ciens, li-ciens
le templ v +TEMPLE	lézoie v +OIE	v +CHIEN
letemps, létemps, le temps,	lé zom v +HOMME	licou, li cou v +COU
lé temps, lé-temps, lé tems,	lézos v +OS	lidé, l'idé, lidée v +IDÉE
lé-tems v +TEMPS	lezot, lé zot v +AUTRE$_2$	liétenant v LIEUTENANT
lé toa v +TOIT	lézour, lé zour v +JOUR	LIEUTENANT 19 (liétenant)
l'étof v +ÉTOFFE	l'habit v +HABIT	liéve, lièvr', lièvre v LIÈVRE
létoit v +TOIT	l'habitation, l'habitations	LIÈVRE 72 (ieve 3, ieve 49,
letr v LETTRE	v +HABITATION	ieves 1, liéve 1, lièvr' 2,
létroncs v +TRONC	l'haleine v +HALEINE	lièvre 14, yève 64, yévre 1)
lé troubl v +TROUBLE	l'ham'çon, lhamçon, lhameçon,	LIGNE 2 (la ligne 1,
lette, lettre v LETTRE	l'hameçon v +HAMEÇON	laligne 1)
LETTRE 25 (letr 2, lette 21,	l'hangard v +HANGAR	lil', l'ile, l'île v +ÎLE
lettre 2)	lhaut, l'haut, lhaute v LÀ-HAUT	lili, lilit, li-lit, lilits v LIT
lev, lév, lév', lèv' v LEVER	l'heirbe v +HERBE	l'illote, l'illotte, lilote, l'ilote,
levain v LEVAIN	lheire, l'heire, lher, l'her	l'ilotte v +ÎLOT
LEVAIN 5 (levain 4, lévain 1)	v +HEURE	lime v LIME
lévain v LEVAIN	l'herb, l'herb', lherbe, lhérbe,	LIME 1 (lime)

limon	v LIMON	
LIMON	1 (*limon*)	
l'Inde	v +INDE	
lindi	v LUNDI	
l'indignité	v +INDIGNITÉ	
l'indigo	v +INDIGO	
linette	v LUNETTE	
linféction	v +INFECTION	
linge	v LINGE	
LINGE	57 (*leinz* 30, *linge* 1, *linze* 26)	
lingue, lingué	v LINGUER	
LINGUER	3 (*lingue* 1, *lingué* 2)	
linstinct	v +INSTINCT	
l'invitation	v +INVITATION	
linze	v LINGE	
lion	v LION	
LION	34 (*lion* 11, *lïon* 21, *lions* 2)	
lïon, lions	v LION	
lipié, li-pié$_1$, li pied$_1$, lipied$_1$, lipieds, lipiéds, li-pieds, li-piés	v +PIED$_1$	
li-pié$_2$, li pied$_2$, lipied$_2$	v +PIED$_2$	
lipocrizi	v +HYPOCRISIE	
li pou, lipoux	v +POUX	
lipou-poule	v +POUX, POULE	
liquer, liquèr, li quer	v +CŒUR	
liquère, liquerre	v +CŒUR	
li qui	v +CUL	
liquierre	v +CŒUR	
+LIQUEUR	9 (*la liqueur* 2, *la liquère* 3, *laliqueur* 2, *laliqueur* 1, *laliquier* 1)	
lir, lir'	v LIRE	
lira	v +RAT	
lire	v LIRE	
LIRE	25 (*lir* 8, *lir.'* 1, *lire* 15, *lisez* 1)	
lis	v LIS	
LIS	1 (*lis*)	
lisez	v LIRE	
li sien	v +CHIEN	
lisiés	v +YEUX	
LISSER	5 (*lice*)	
Lissir	v LISSIR	
LISSIR	1 (*Lissir*) [nom de personnage]	
LIT	65 (*lili* 4, *lilit* 52, *li-lit* 4, *lilits* 4, *lit* 1)	
lité	v LUTTER	
litemps	v +TEMPS	
litière	v LITIÈRE	
LITIÈRE	1 (*litière*)	
+LITIÈRE	1 (*lalitière*)	
litt', litté	v LUTTER	
liv, live, lives, livre	v LIVRE	
LIVRE	10 (*liv* 4, *live* 1, *lives* 3, *livre* 1, *livres* 1)	
livré	v LIVRER	
LIVRER	1 (*livré* 1)	
livres	v LIVRE	
li zié, lizié, li-zié, liziées, liziés, li-ziés, liziès	v +YEUX	
li zour, lizour, li-zour	v +JOUR	
lo	v LOT	
l'observatoire	v +OBSERVATOIRE	
l'obskirité	v +OBSCURITÉ	
locataire	v LOCATAIRE	
LOCATAIRE	5 (*locataire*)	
l'ocazion	v +OCCASION	
lodeir, lodéir, l'odeir, l'oder, l'odér, l'odère, lodère	v +ODEUR	
loein	v LOIN	
lofé, lôfé	v LOFER	
LOFER	5 (*lofé* 4, *lôfé* 1)	
l'office	v +OFFICE	
l'offrand	v +OFFRANDE	
l'offre	v +OFFRE	
LOGE	3 (*loze* 2, *lozes* 1)	
lognon	v +OIGNON	
+LOI	27 (*la loa* 10, *la loi* 16, *laloi* 1)	
loignon	v +OIGNON	
loin	v LOIN	
LOIN	64 (*loein* 13, *loin* 50, *loinloin* 1)	
loinloin	v LOIN	
lombe, l'ombr	v +OMBRE	
l'ombraze	v +OMBRAGE	
l'ombrelle	v +OMBRELLE	
lombri	v NOMBRIL	
lomelette	v +OMELETTE	
lon lan la	4 [interj.]	
London	v **LONDON**	
LONDON	1 (*London*)	
Lonère	v +HONNEUR	
long	v LONG	
LONG	30 (*long* 4, *long'* 1, *longue* 25)	
long'	v LONG	
longaille	v LONGAILLE	
LONGAILLE	1 (*longaille*)	
longtemps	v LONGTEMPS	
LONGTEMPS	60 (*longtemps* 42, *long-temps* 1, *long-tems* 12, *lontan* 2, *lontant* 1, *lon-tems* 2)	
long-tems, long-tems	v LONGTEMPS	
longue	v LONG	
longuére, longuère	v LONGUEUR	
LONGUEUR	2 (*longuére* 1, *longuère* 1)	
lontan, lontant, lon-tems	v LONGTEMPS	
lonzé	v ALLONGER	
l'optal	v +HÔPITAL	
lor$_1$	v +OR	
lor$_2$	v LÀ-HAUT	
l'or	v +OR	
l'oragan	v +OURAGAN	
loranzé	v +ORANGER	
lorateir	v +ORATEUR	
l'oraze	v +ORAGE	
lorde	v +ORDRE	
Lord Moïra	v LORD MOIRA	
LORD MOIRA	1 (*Lord Moïra*)	
l'ordr, l'ordre	v +ORDRE	
l'oreiller	v +OREILLER	
lorgnon	v LORGNON	
LORGNON	1 (*lorgnon*)	
lorguéye	v +ORGUEIL	
l'orian	v +ORIENT	
LOT	1 (*lo*)	
l'ot	v +AUTRE$_1$	
l'otel	v +AUTEL	
l'ouragan	v +OURAGAN	
l'ouvertir	v +OUVERTURE	
l'ouvrage, l'ouvraz, l'ouvraz', l'ouvraze, l'ouvrazes	v +OUVRAGE	
lormoire	v +ARMOIRE	
lostoma, lostomac	v +ESTOMAC	
lot, lote, lotre	v +AUTRE$_1$	
+LOUANGE	1 (*la louanz*)	
loucé	v LOUCHER	
LOUCHER	1 (*loucé*)	
loué	v LOUER	

LOUER   8 (*loué*)
loulou, louloup, loulous
    v LOUP/ **LOLO**
LOUP/**LOLO**   239 (*loulou* 160, *louloup* 43, *loulous* 36) [*lolo* est un mot malg.]
loup-garou   v LOUP-GAROU
LOUP-GAROU 1 (*loup-garou*)
lour, lourd   v LOURD
LOURD   11 (*lour* 2, *lourd* 5, *lourde* 4)
lourde   v LOURD
louvrage, louvraze
    v +OUVRAGE
Lovart   v LOVART
LOVART 1 (*Lovart*) [nom de personnage]
loyan   v NOYAU
loze, lozes v LOGE
lui   v LUI
LUI   5659 (*li* 5652, *lui* 3, *ly* 4)
+LUMIÈRE 13 (*la limier* 4, *la limiér* 4, *la limière* 2, *lalimière* 3)
LUNDI   1 (*lindi*)
+LUNE   10 (*la lin'* 3, *la line* 1, *laline* 5, *la-line* 1)
LUNETTE   2 (*linette* 2)
LUTTER   7 (*lité* 2, *litt'* 1, *litté* 4)
ly   v LUI

M

M, *m'sié, m'sier, m'sye*
    v MONSIEUR
ma   v *ma fille, ma fiye, ma foi, ma foi dié, ma foi-dié*
macadam v MACADAM
MACADAM   2 (*macadam*)
macatia   v **MKATTHE**
MACHOIRE 2 (*maçoire*)
Macoa   v **MAKHUWA**
maçoire   v MACHOIRE
maçon   v MAÇON
MAÇON   6 (*maçon* 1, *maçons* 5)
maçons   v MAÇON
macote, macotte
    v **MAKOTA**

Macpherson v MACPHERSON
MACPHERSON 1 (*Macpherson*) [nom de famille]
Madagascar v MADAGASCAR
MADAGASCAR 3 (*Madagascar*)
madam, madam', madame, madames v MADAME

madameséré, madam serré
    v MADAME+CÊRÉ
madam-céré
    v MADAME+CÊRÉ
MADAME   63 (*madam* 7, *madam'* 6, *madame* 44, *madames* 4, *médame* 1)
MADAME+CÊRÉ 5 (*madam-céré* 2, *madameséré* 1, *dames Céré* 1, *madam serré* 1)
MADEMOISELLE 87 (*mamezelle* 1, *mamzel* 2, *mamzel'* 4, *mamzéle* 2, *mamzell'* 3, *mam'zell* 2, *mam'zell'* 7, *mamzelle* 41, *mamz'elle* 1, *mam'zelle* 7, *mamzélle* 2, *mamzelles* 12, *mam'zelles* 1, *mamzélles* 2)
MADURAI-VIRAN 1 (*mardé virin*) [mot tam.]
ma fille   v MA+FILLE
MA+FILLE   2 (*ma fille* 1, *ma fiye* 1)
ma fiye   v MA+FILLE
ma foi, ma-foi v MA+FOI
MA+FOI   25 (*ma foi* 23, *ma-foi* 2)
ma foi dié, ma foi-dié
    v MA+FOI+DIEU
MA+FOI+DIEU 5 (*ma foi dié* 3, *ma foi-dié* 1, *moi foi dié* 1)
magasin   v MAGASIN
MAGASIN 11 (*magasin* 9, *magazein* 1, *magazin* 1)
magazein, magazin v MAGASIN
mage   v MAGE
MAGE   4 (*mage*)
MAGICIENNE 2 (*Mazicienne*) [nom d'un bateau].

magnère, magniére, magnière
    v MANIÈRE
magnioc, magnoc v MANIOC
Magon   v MAGON
MAGON 1 (*Magon*) [nom de personnage]
MAHA-RANI 2 (*marani*) [mot hind]
Mahebourg, Mahébourg
    v MAHEBOURG
MAHEBOURG 9 (*Mahebourg* 2, *Mahébourg* 7)
malhonête v MALHONNÊTE
maï, maïe, maïë v MAÏS
maigre   v MAIGRE
MAIGRE   4 (*maigre* 1, *maigue* 3)
maigri   v MAIGRIR
MAIGRIR 1 (*maigri*)
maigue   v MAIGRE
maille$_1$ v MAILLE
MAILLE   1 (*maille$_1$*)
+MAILLE 4 (*la maille*)
maille$_2$ v MAILLER
maille$_3$ v MAÏS
maillé   v MAILLER
MAILLER 12 (*maille$_2$* 4, *maillé* 8)
maillet   v MAILLET
MAILLET 1 (*maillet*)
+MAIN   154 (*la main* 74, *lamain* 55, *la-main* 2, *lamains* 23)
mais   v MAIS
MAIS   735 (*mais* 464, *me* 3, *mé* 254, *més* 14)
maïs   v MAÏS
MAÏS   38 (*maï* 2, *maïe* 17, *maïë* 2, *maille$_3$* 6, *maïs* 2, *maiz* 1, *maye* 7, *mayë* 1)
maît', maite, maîte, maîtr', maitre, maître v MAÎTRE
MAÎTRE 119 (*maît'* 1, *maite* 2, *maîte* 9, *maîtr'* 1, *maitre* 2, *maître* 22, *maîtres* 19, *mète$_1$* 1, *mètr* 39, *mêtr* 1, *mètre* 22)
maîtres   v MAÎTRE
maitresse v MAÎTRESSE
MAÎTRESSE 2 (*maitresse*)
maiz   v MAÏS
MÁKA   2 (*maque*) [mot malg.]

MAKHUWA1 (*Macoa*) [mot bantou]
MAKOTA 3 (*macote* 2, *macotte* 1) [mot malg.]
mal v MAL
MAL 20 (*mal*)
+MAL 25 (*di mal* 14, *dimal* 11)
mâl v MÂLE
MALABAR 30 (*malabars* 2, *malbar* 17, *malbare* 2, *malbars* 9) [mot tam.]
malabars v **MALABAR**
malad$_1$ v MALADE$_1$
malad$_2$ v MALADE$_2$
malad'$_1$ v MALADE$_1$
malad'$_2$ v MALADE$_2$
malade$_1$ v MALADE$_1$
malade$_2$ v MALADIE
MALADE$_1$ 36 (*malad*$_1$ 17, *malad'*$_1$ 1, *malade* 17, *malades* 1) [malade]
MALADE$_2$ 10 (*malade*$_2$) [maladie]
malades v MALADE
maladi v MALADIE
MALADIE 18 (*malad*$_2$ 1, *malad'*$_2$ 3, *maladi* 4)
malappris v MALAPPRIS
MALAPPRIS1 (*malappris*)
Malartic v MALARTIC
MALARTIC 1 (*Malartic*)
malbar, malbare, malbars
   v **MALABAR**
mal dé mer v MAL+DE+MER
MAL+DE+MER 1 (*mal dé mer*)
mâle v MÂLE
MÂLE 3 (*mâl* 1, *mâle* 1, *males* 1)
MALÉDICTION 1 (*malédikcion*)
+MALÉDICTION 1 (*la malidiction*)
malédikcion v MALÉDICTION
males v MÂLE
malère v MALHEUR
malgaç', malgace, malgache
   v **MALGACHE**
MALGACHE 10 (*malgaç'* 1, *malgace* 4, *malgache* 5)
malgré v MALGRÉ

MALGRÉ 1 (*malgré*)
malheir, malher, malhèr
   v MALHEUR
Malherb' v MALHERBE(S)
MALHERBE(S) 1 (*malherb'*) [nom de famille].
malhére v MALHEUR
malhéré, malhéreise, malhérés, malhérése, malhérèse
   v MALHEUREUX
malheur v MALHEUR
MALHEUR 40 (*malère* 1, *malheir* 6, *malher* 23, *malhèr* 1, *malhére* 3, *malheur* 1, *malhor* 5)
MALHEUREUX 22 (*malhéré* 12, *malhéreise* 2, *malhérés* 2, *malhérése* 4, *malhérèse* 2)
malhonnête v MALHONNÊTE
MALHONNÊTE 3 (*malhonnête* 2, *malhonête* 1)
malhor v MALHEUR
malice v MALICE
MALICE 21 (*malice* 19, *malices* 2)
+MALICE 4 (*la maliç'* 1, *la malice* 2, *lamalice* 1)
malices v MALICE
malin v MALIN
MALIN 31 (*malin* 29, *malins* 2)
malinbougue
   v MALIN+BOUGRE
MALIN+BOUGRE 3 (*malinbougue*)
malins v MALIN
+MALLE 3 (*la malle* 2, *lamalle* 1)
malprop, malprôpe
   v MALPROPRE
malprôpetés v MALPROPRETÉ
malpropre v MALPROPRE
MALPROPRE 4 (*malprop* 1, *malprôpe* 1, *malpropre* 2)
MALPROPRETÉ 1 (*malprôpetés*)
mama, maman$_1$ v MAMAN$_1$
maman$_2$ v MAMAN$_2$
MAMAN$_1$ 203 (*mama* 4, *maman* 82, *mamans* 1, *manman* 116)

MAMAN$_2$ 1 (*maman*$_2$) [très grand]
mamans v MAMAN
MAMBOLO 1 (*mambolos*) [mot philippin]
mambolos v **MAMBOLO**
mambr v MEMBRE
mament v MOMENT
mamezelle
   v MADEMOISELLE
mami v *MAMI
*MAMI 1 (*mami*) [fr. dial. ou de l'angl.]
mamzel, mamzel', mamzéle, mamzell', mam'zell, mam'zell', mamzelle, mam'zelle, mamz'elle, mamzélle, mamzelles, mam'zelles, mamzélles
   v MADEMOISELLE
manami v MON+AMI
+MANCHE 4 (*la mance* 1, *lamance* 3)
mang' v MANGUE
mange, mangé v MANGER
MANGER 282 (*mange* 1, *mangé* 2, *manz* 8, *manz'* 7, *manze* 102, *manzé* 159, *manzer* 3)
MANGEUR 1 (*manzère*)
mangue v MANGUE
MANGUE 11 (*mang'* 2, *mangue* 7, *mangues* 2)
mangues v MANGUE
manié v MANIER
MANIER 1 (*manié*)
manier, maniér, maniér', maniére, manière v MANIÈRE
MANIÈRE 69 (*magnère* 7, *magniére* 1, *magnière* 20, *manier* 2, *maniér* 1, *maniér'* 1, *maniére* 1, *manière* 37)
+MANIÈRE 2 (*la manière* 1, *la-manière* 1)
Manille v MANILLE
MANILLE1 (*Manille*) [toponyme].
manimani, mani mani
   v *MANIMANI
*MANIMANI 8 (*manimani* 2, *mani mani* 6) [mot bant.]

269

manioc   v MANIOC
MANIOC   21 (*magnioc* 8,
    magnoc 1, *manioc* 12)
manman   v MAMAN
manoeuvré, manœuvré,
manoeuvreé v MANOEUVRER
MANOEUVRER   4
    (*manoeuvré* 2, *manœuvré*
    1, *manoeuvreé* 1)
manq', manque, manqué,
manquée   v MANQUER
MANQUER 41 (*manq'* 1,
    manque 16, *manqué* 23,
    manquée 1)
mansonz   v MENSONGE
mant'let   v MANTELET
MANTELET 1 (*mant'let*)
mantère   v MENTEUR
mantie   v MENTIR
manto   v MANTEAU
MANTEAU 1 (*manto*)
manz, manz', manze, manzé,
manzer   v MANGER
Mapou   v MAPOU
MAPOU 2 (*Mapou*)[22]
maque   v **MÁKA**
marani   v **MAHA-RANI**
marbre   v MARBRE
MARBRE 1 (*marbre*)
març'   v MARCHER
marçan, marçand
             v MARCHAND
marçandise, marçandises,
marçandiz, marçandize
             v MARCHANDISE
marce, marcé, marçé
             v MARCHER
MARCHAND   21 (*marçan* 1,
    marçand 20)
marchandise
             v MARCHANDISE
MARCHANDISE
    14 (*marçandise* 7,
    marçandises 2, *marçandiz*
    1, *marçandize* 2,
    marchandise 1,
    marsandises 1)
+MARCHE 1 (*la marce*)
marche   v MARCHER

MARCHEPIED   1 (*marspié*)
MARCHER 124 (*març'* 1,
    marce 29, *marcé* 89,
    marçé 3, *marche* 1,
    marçons 1)
marçons   v MARCHER
mardé virin v
    MADURAI-VIRAN
mardi   v MARDI
MARDI   1 (*mardi*)
+MARE   6 (*la mare* 2, *la*
    marre 4)
marée   v MARÉE
MARÉE   2 (*marée*)
marée noire v MARÉE+NOIRE
MARÉE+NOIRE 2 (*marée*
    noire 1, *marées noires* 1)
+MARÉE+NOIRE
    1(*lamarée noire*)
marées noires v MARÉE+NOIRE
Mare Vacoa v MARE+**VAKOA**
MARE+**VAKOA**
    1 (*Mare Vacoa*)
Marezanne v MARIE-JEANNE
margause, margauze, margose,
margoz, margoze
             v **AMARGOSO**
mari   v MARI
MARI   80 (*mari* 76, *maris* 4)
mariage   v MARIAGE
MARIAGE 34 (*mariage* 3,
    mariaz 10, *mariaze* 21)
mariaz, mariaze v MARIAGE
Marie Zane v MARIE-JEANNE
MARIE-JEANNE
    18 (*Marezanne* 1, *Marie*
    Zane 16, *Marijeanne* 1)
Marie Zozé v MARIE-JOSÉ
MARIE-JOSÉ 16 (*Marie Zozé*)
marié   v MARIER
+MARIÉE 2 (*la mariée* 1,
    lamariée 1)
marier   v MARIER
MARIER 85 (*marié* 82,
    marier 1, *mariés* 1,
    mariez 1)
mariés, mariez v MARIER
Marijeanne v MARIE-JEANNE
maris   v MARI
mark   v MARQUE
marmaille v MARMAILLE
MARMAILLE 7 (*marmaille*)

marmit', marmite v MARMITE
MARMITE 57 (*marmit'* 2,
    marmite 45, *marmites* 2,
    marmitte 8)
marmites, marmitte
             v MARMITE
maron, marons v **CIMARRÓN**
MÁROVÁNY 1 (*marvanne*)
    [mot malg.]
marque₁   v MARQUE
marque₂   v MARQUER
MARQUE 2 (*mark* 1,
    marque₁ 1)
marqué, marquer v MARQUER
MARQUER 13 (*marque₂* 1,
    marqué 10, *marquer* 2)
marraine   v MARRAINE
MARRAINE 9 (*marraine*)
marron, marrons
             v **CIMARRÓN**
marsandises
             v MARCHANDISE
marseillaise
             v MARSEILLAISE
MARSEILLAISE
    1 (*marseillaise*)
marspié   v MARCHEPIED
marteau   v MARTEAU
MARTEAU 1 (*marteau*)
martin₁   v MÂTIN
martin₂   v **MARTINHO**
MARTINHO 8 (*martin₂* 7,
    martins 1) [mot indo-
    port.]
martins   v **MARTINHO**
marvanne   v **MÁROVÁNY**
MASALAH 3 (*massala*) [mot
    hind.]
maseirs   v MA+SOEUR
MA+SOEUR 1 (*maseirs*)
massala   v **MASALAH**
+MASSE 2 (*la masse*)
mastic   v MASTIC
MASTIC 1 (*mastic*)
MATAR 1 (*mâté*) [port.]
mâté   v **MATAR**
MATELAS   4 (*matelas* 3,
    matelat 1)
matelas, matelat v MATELAS
matelot   v MATELOT
MATELOT 7 (*matelot* 5,
    matelots 2)

---

[22] Nom de lieu qui porte le nom caraïbe d'une espèce d'arbre.

matelots v MATELOT
matiapa v **MCHAPA**
MATIN v BON+MATIN, GRAND+MATIN
mâtin v MÂTIN
MÂTIN 7 (*martin*₁ 6, *mâtin* 1) [interj.]
matirité v MATURITÉ
MATURITÉ 1 (*matirité*)
MAUDIRE 2 (*modi* 1, *modie* 1)
Maurel v MAUREL
MAUREL 1 (*Maurel*) [nom de famille]
*Maurice*₁ v MAURICE₁
*Maurice*₂ v MAURICE₂
MAURICE₁ 36 (*Maurice*₁ 34, *Mauris* 2) [= île Maurice]
MAURICE₂ 3 (*Maurice*₂) [prénom masculin]
mauricien v MAURICIEN
MAURICIEN 2 (*mauricien* 1, *mauriciens* 1)
mauriciens v MAURICIEN
Mauris v MAURICE¹
mauvais v MAUVAIS
MAUVAIS 100 (*mauvais* 66, *mauvaise* 2, *mauvé* 1, *mauvés* 3, *movais* 1, *mové* 27)
mauvaise v MAUVAIS
MAUVAIS+VIE 1 (*movéz vi*)
mauvé, mauvés v MAUVAIS
maye, mayë v MAÏS
mazambique, mazambiques v MOZAMBIQUE
mazicienne v MAGICIENNE
mazination v IMAGINATION
mazine, maziné, maziner v IMAGINER
mazĭzĭ v **MAZIZI**
MAZIZI 2 (*mazizi*) [mot bant.]
MCHAPA 1 (*matiapa*) [mot bant.]
me, mé v MAIS
méblé v MEUBLER
méçan v MÉCHANT
méçanceté v MÉCHANCETÉ
méçant, méçants v MÉCHANT
MÉCHANCETÉ 4 (*méçanceté* 3, *missanceté* 1)
+MÉCHANCETÉ 1 (*la méçanceté*)

méchant v MÉCHANT
MÉCHANT 23 (*méçan* 8, *méçant* 3, *méçants* 2, *méchant* 1, *missant* 8, *missants* 1)
+MÈCHE 1 (*la mésh*)
médaille v MÉDAILLE
MÉDAILLE 3 (*médaille*)
médame v MADAME
médecine v MÉDECINE
MÉDECINE 10 (*médecine* 6, *médecines* 4)
médecines v MÉDECINE
medisant v MÉDISANT
MÉDISANT 1 (*medisant*)
meibes v MEUBLE
MEILLEUR 1 (*meyer*)
mêl' v MÊLER
+MÉLASSE 2 (*lamélasse*)
mèle, mélé, mêlé v MÊLER
MÊLER 6 (*mêl'* 1, *mèle* 1, *mélé* 1, *mêlé* 3) v aussi S'EN+MÊLER
MELON D'EAU 1 (*moulondeau*)
mem, mem', mèm', mêm' v MÊME
MEMBRE 3 (*mambr*)
meme, méme, mème, même v MÊME
MÊME 739 (*mem* 218, *mem'* 3, *mèm'* 1, *mêm'* 63, *meme* 6, *méme* 33, *mème* 4, *même* 408, *mêmes* 3)
mêmes v MÊME
mémoire v MÉMOIRE
MÉMOIRE 3 (*mémoire*)
ménace v MENACER
MENACER 2 (*ménace*)
MÉNAGE 4 (*ménaze*)
MÉNAGÈRE 1 (*ménazère*)
ménaze v MÉNAGE
ménazère v MÉNAGÈRE
méné v AMENER / EMMENER
MENSONGE 4 (*mansonz* 2, *mensonze* 2)
mensonze v MENSONGE
+MENTHE 1 (*la mant*)
MENTEUR 16 (*mantère* 1, *mentor* 14, *mentore* 1)
menti, mentir v MENTIR

MENTIR 21 (*mantie* 1, *menti* 19, *mentir* 1)
mentor, mentore v MENTEUR
MENUISIER 2 (*minisier*)
méprisée v MÉPRISER
MÉPRISER 3 (*méprisée* 1, *mépriz* 2)
mépriz v MÉPRISER 3
+MER 54 (*la mer* 45, *lamer* 9)
mér v MÈRE
merci v MERCI
MERCI 55 (*merci* 54, *merçi* 1)
merçi v MERCI
mère v MÈRE
MÈRE 2 (*mér* 1, *mère* 1)
mérit, mérite, mérité, meritéa, méritée v MÉRITER
MÉRITER 20 (*mérit* 7, *mérite* 1, *mérité* 7, *meritéa* 1, *méritée* 4)
merle v MERLE
MERLE 1 (*merle*)
mertr v MEURTRE
més v MAIS
mes zenfants v MES+ENFANTS
MES+ENFANTS 1 (*mes zenfants*)
Mesnil v MESNIL
MESNIL 1 (*Mesnil*) [toponyme]
MESSAGÉ 1 (*messazé*)
messazé v MESSAGÉ
+MESSE 6 (*la messe* 5, *la-messe* 1)
MESURE 2 (*mézir*₁)
+MESURE 3 (*la mésire* 1, *la mézir* 2)
mesuré, mésuré v MESURER
MESURER 12 (*mesuré* 3, *mésuré* 1, *mézir*₂ 2, *misire* 6, *misiré* 4, *mizoure* 1)
*mète*₁ v MAÎTRE
*met, met', méte, mète*₂, *mété* v METTRE
metère v METTRE–*ER*
métié, métier v MÉTÏER
MÉTIER 18 (*métié* 3, *métier* 11, *métiers* 1, *mitié* 2, *mitier* 1)

métiers v MÉTIER	millions v MILLION	mitié, mitier v MÉTIER
métr, mêtr, mètre v MAÎTRE	milon v MEULON	mizer v MISÈRE
mett', métt', mette, métte, metté,	miltons v MULLETIN	mizérab v MISÉRABLE
métté, mettre v METTRE	mince v MINCE	mizoure v MESURER
METTRE 306 (met 51, met' 14,	MINCE 1 (mince)	**MKATTHE** 2 (macatia)
méte 37, mète₂ 7, mété 8,	+MINE 7 (la mine)	[mot bant.]
mett'20, métt' 1, mette115,	*MINE+GUEULE 1 (miguelle)	mo, mô, moa, môa, moan
métte 5, metté 51, métté 2,	Minerve v MINERVE	v MOI(+MON)
mettre 1, mi 1)	MINERVE 1 (Minerve) [nom	moassonner, moassonnèr
METTRE–*ER* 1 (metère)	d'un bateau]	v MOISSONNEUR
MEUBLE 2 (meibes)	minisier v MENUISIER	mobile v MOBILE
MEUBLER 1 (méblé)	minition v MUNITION	MOBILE 1 (mobile) [nom de
+MEULE 2 (la mel)	minouite v MINUIT	personnage]
MEULON 1 (milon) [mot dial.]	MINUIT 3 (minouite)	MOCHE 3 (moss 2, mosse₁ 1)
MEURTRE 1 (mertr)	mir₁ v MÛR	+MODE 5 (la mod' 1,
meyer v MEILLEUR	mir₂ v la mir	la mode 4)
mézamis v MON+AMI	mîr v MÛR	modi, modie v MAUDIRE
mézir₁ v MESURE	mirac, mirâcle v MIRACLE	mofine v **MOFINO**
mézir₂ v MESURER	MIRACLE 21 (mirac 16,	**MOFINO** 7 (mofine 6,
mi v METTRE	mirâcle 1, miraque 4)	mophine 1) [port.]
midi v MIDI	miraill', miraille, mirailles	moi v MOI(+MON)
MIDI 6 (midi)	v MURAILLE	MOI(+MON) 2968 (mo 1897,
mié₁ v MIEUX, v aussi	miraque v MIRACLE	mô 26, moa 131, môa 3,
vaut/vo mié	mire v MÛR	moan 4, moi 900,
mié₂ v MUET	mirte v MYRTE	mos 1, mouan 3, moy 3)
+MIEL 30 (di miel 7, di miél	misaire v MISÈRE	moi foi dié v MA-FOI+DIEU
1, dimiel 20, di-miel 2)	miscadine v MUSCADINE	moins v MOINS
mieux v vaut/vaux mieux	miseau v MUSEAU	MOINS 6 (moins)
MIEUX 4 (mié₁), v aussi	miser' v MISÈRE	mois v MOIS
VAUT MIEUX	misérable v MISÉRABLE	MOIS 30 (mois)
miguelle v *MINE+GUEULE	MISÉRABLE 2 (misérable 1,	+MOIS 1 (lémoi)
+MIGRAINE 1 (lamigraine)	mizérab 1)	MOISSONNEUR
mil v MILLE	misère v MISÈRE	2 (moassonner 1,
MIḶAKU-T-TAṆṆĪR	MISÈRE 35 (misaire 1,	moassonnèr 1)
1 (moulouctani)	miser' 1, misère 31,	moitié v MOITIÉ
[mot tam.]	mizer 2)	MOITIÉ 3 (moitié 1, moutié 2)
milate v MULÂTRE	+MISÈRE 24 (la misaire 1,	+MOITIÉ 10 (la moitié 3,
milatresse v MULÂTRESSE	la misèr' 1, la misère 13	la moquié 2, la moutié 1,
milé, milet₁ v MULET₁	lamisère 6, la-misère 2,	lamoquié 4)
milet₂ v MULET₂	lamisères 1)	mok v MOQUER
miletons v *MULLETIN	misicien, misiciens v MUSICIEN	Moka v MOKA
milice v MILICE	misié v MONSIEUR	MOKA 4 (Moka) [toponyme]
MILICE 1 (milice)	misire, misiré v MESURER	moké v MOQUER
milié, miliè, milieix v MILIEU	miské, misqué v MUSQUÉ	moman, moment v MOMENT
MILIEU 51 (milié 49, miliè 1,	missanceté v MÉCHANCETÉ	MOMENT 27 (mament 2,
milieix 1)	missant, missants v MÉCHANT	moman 3, moment 22)
mille v MILLE	missié, missiers, missiés	mon v MON
MILLE 18 (mil 5, mille 13)	v MONSIEUR	MON 339 (mon), v aussi
millepattes v MILLE-PATTES	mistère v MYSTÈRE	MOI(+MON),
MILLE-PATTES	misyé v MONSIEUR	MON+AMI,
1 (millepattes)	mitan v MITAN	MON+DIEU,
MILLION 1 (millions)	MITAN 1 (mitan) [mot dial.]	MON+NOIR

mon ami, monami v MON+AMI
MON+AMI 19 (*manami* 10, *mézamis* 1, *mon ami* 3, *monami* 4, *monanmi* 1)
monanmi v MON+AMI
monde v MONDE
MONDE 6 (*monde*), v aussi GRAND+MONDE, VIEUX+MONDE
+MONDE$_1$ 442 (*di mond* 7, *di mond'* 2, *di monde* 6, *di-mond* 2, *dimond'* 1, *di'mond'* 1, *di-mond'* 10, *dimonde* 17, *di-monde* 16, *dimound* 26, *dimound'* 5, *di mound'* 3, *di mounde* 3, *dimounde* 35, *di moune* 1, *dimoune* 178, *doumonde* 1, *dou monde* 1, *dou-monde* 4, *doumondes* 1, *doumone* 1, *doumonnde* 2, *doumoumde* 1, *doumoun* 7, *doumoun'* 1, *doumounde* 80, *doumoundes* 3, *doumoune* 23, *doumounne* 2, *doumounnes* 1, *dou mounde* 1)
+MONDE$_2$ 3 (*le mond*)
mon dié, mondieu v MON+DIEU
MON+DIEU 12 (*mon dié* 10, *mondieu* 1, *moundié* 1)
+MONNAIE 11 (*la moné* 5, *la monnaie* 2, *la monné* 1, *lamonaie* 3)
mon noir v MON+NOIR
MON+NOIR 5 (*mo noir* 1, *monoir* 1, *mon noir* 3)
mo noir, monoir v MON+NOIR
monqué v MOQUER
monsié, monsieur v MONSIEUR
MONSIEUR 271 (*M* 13, *misié* 49, *missié* 35, *missiers* 1, *missiés* 2, *misyé* 1, *monsié* 2, *monsieur* 3, *moucié* 16, *mousié* 14, *moussié* 48, *Mr* 35, *msié* 30, *m'sié* 32, *m'sier* 1, *m'sye* 1, *mushee* 1)
monstr v MONSTRE
MONSTRE 1 (*monstr*)

mont$_1$ v MONTER
mont$_2$ v MONTRER
mont' v MONTER
montagne, montagnes, montaïn v MONTAGNE
MONTAGNE 27 (*montagne* 14, *montagnes* 1, *montaïn* 12)
+MONTAGNE 16 (*la montagne* 5, *la montaïn* 4, *lamontagne* 7)
montant v MONTANT
MONTANT 1 (*montant*)
monte$_1$, monté v MONTER
monte$_2$ v MONTRER
monte$_3$ v MONTRE
montée v MONTÉE
MONTÉE 1 (*montée*)
+MONTÉE 1 (*lamontée*)
montent, monter v MONTER
MONTER 80 (*mont$_1$* 4, *mont'* 3, *monte$_1$* 39, *monté* 31, *montent* 1, *monter* 2)
montre$_1$ v MONTRE
montre$_2$ v MONTRER
MONTRE 4 (*monte$_3$* 2, *montre$_1$* 2)
montré, montrée, montrer v MONTRER
MONTRER 49 (*mont$_2$* 1, *monte$_2$* 1, *montre$_2$* 6, *montré* 38, *montrée* 2, *montrer* 1)
mophine v **MOFINO**
moq', moque, moqué v MOQUER
MOQUER 13 (*mok* 5, *moké* 1, *monqué* 3, *moq'* 2, *moque* 1, *moqué* 1)
mor v MORT
morceau v MORCEAU
MORCEAU 165 (*morceau* 150, *morceaux* 6, *morço* 9)
morceaux, morço v MORCEAU
mord', morde, mordé v MORDER
MORDER 5 (*mord'* 1, *morde* 3, *mordé* 1)
more, mort v MORT
mors v MORS
MORS 1 (*mors*)

MORT 157 (*mor* 33, *more* 1, *môrs* 1, *mort* 108, *môrt* 12, *morts* 2)[23]
+MORT 19 (*la mor* 6, *la more* 1, *la mort* 11, *les morts* 1)
môrs, môrt, morts v MORT
+MORUE 2 (*la mori* 1, *lamorie* 1)
mos v MOI(+MON)
moss, mosse$_1$ v MOCHE
mosse$_2$ v MOSSE
MOSSE 1 (*mosse$_2$*) [nom de personnage]
mot v MOT
MOT 4 (*mot* 1, *mots* 3)
+MOT 1 (*lémots*)
mots v MOT
mou v MOU
MOU 3 (*mou*)
mouan v MOI(+MON)
mouç-à-miel v MOUCHE+À+MIEL
mouce v MOUCHE
mouce a miel, mouce à miel v MOUCHE+À+MIEL
mouces v MOUCHE
mouce zaun', mouce zaune, mouce zone, mousse zone v MOUCHE+JAUNE
MOUCHE 28 (*mouce* 13, *mouces* 11, *moush* 1, *mousse* 3) v aussi MOUCHE+À+MIEL, MOUCHE+JAUNE
MOUCHE+À+MIEL 4 (*mouç-à-miel* 1, *mouce a miel* 2, *mouce à miel* 1)
MOUCHE+DU+MIEL 1 (*mous' dimiel*)
MOUCHE+JAUNE 7 (*mouce zaun'* 1, *mouce zaune* 3, *mouce zone* 1, *mous' zon'* 1, *mousse zone* 1)
mouchoir v MOUCHOIR
MOUCHOIR 7 (*mouchoir* 2, *mouçoir* 4, *moussoir* 1)
moucié v MONSIEUR
mouçoir v MOUCHOIR
moudiawa v **MUCAWA**

---

[23] Adjectifs et verbes sont ici compris.

moudre v MOUDRE
MOUDRE 2 (*moudre*)
MOUILLAGE 2 (*mouillage* 1, *mouillaze* 1)
mouillage, mouillaze v MOUILLAGE
mouille, mouillé v MOUILLER
MOUILLER 8 (*mouille* 2, *mouillé* 6)
moule, moulé v MOULER
moulein v MOULIN
MOULER 3 (*moule* 1, *moulé* 2)
mouli v MOULU
MOULU 1 (*mouli*)
moulin v MOULIN
MOULIN 18 (*moulin* 17, *moulein* 1)
moulondeau v MELON D'EAU
moulouctani v MIḶAKU-T-TAṆṆĪR
mounde v GRAND+MONDE
moundié v MON+DIEU
moune v GRAND+MONDE
mouri v MOURIR
MOURIR 1 (*mouri*)
mous' dimiel v MOUCHE+DU+MIEL
moush v MOUCHE
mousié v MONSIEUR
moussana v *MUSANNA
mousse v MOUCHE
+MOUSSE 2 (*la mousse*)
MOUSSELINE 1 (*mousselines*)
mousselines v MOUSSELINE
moussié v MONSIEUR
moussoir v MOUCHOIR
moustaç', moustace v MOUSTACHE
MOUSTACHE 2 (*moustaç'* 1, *moustace* 1)
moustiquaire v MOUSTIQUAIRE
MOUSTIQUAIRE 2 (*moustiquaire* 1, *moustiquaires* 1)
moustiquaires v MOUSTIQUAIRE
moustique v MOUSTIQUE
MOUSTIQUE 5 (*moustique* 4, *moustiques* 1)
moustiques v MOUSTIQUE
+MOUTARDE 2 (*la moutard*)

moutié v MOITIÉ
mouton v MOUTON
MOUTON 40 (*mouton* 29, *moutons* 11)
moutons v MOUTON
moutouc, moutoucs v *MUTUK
MOUVEMENT 1 (*mouvman*)
mouvman v MOUVEMENT
movais, mové v MAUVAIS
movéz vi v MAUVAIS+VIE
moy v MOI
moyen v MOYEN
MOYEN 17 (*moyen* 2, *môyen* 15)
môyen v MOYEN
mozambique v MOZAMBIQUE
MOZAMBIQUE 11 (*mazambique* 1, *mazambiques* 3, *mozambique* 6, *mozambiques* 1)
mozambiques v MOZAMBIQUE
Mr, msié v MONSIEUR
MUCAWA 1 (*moudiawa*) [mot bant.].
MUET 5 (*mié₂*)
MULÂTRE 1 (*milate*)
MULÂTRESSE 1 (*milatresse*)
MULET₁ 3 (*milé* 2, *milet₁* 1) [mammifère]
MULET₂ 3 (*milet₂*) [poisson]
*MULLETIN 3 (*miletons* 1, *miltons* 2)
+MUNICIPALITÉ 1 (*la minicipalité*)
MUNITION 1 (*minition*)
MÛR 11 (*mir₁* 4, *mîr* 4, *mire* 3)
MURAILLE 4 (*miraill'* 1, *miraille* 2, *mirailles* 1)
+MURAILLE 7 (*lamiraille*)
*MUSANNA 2 (*moussana*) [mot hind.]
MUSCADINE 1 (*miscadine*)
MUSEAU 1 (*miseau*)
mushee v MONSIEUR
MUSICIEN 2 (*misicien* 1, *misiciens* 1)

+MUSIQUE 10 (*la misique* 1, *la mizique* 5, *lamisique* 2, *la-mizique* 2)
MUSQUÉ 2 (*miské* 1, *misqué* 1)
*MUTUK 4 (*moutouc* 3, *moutoucs* 1) [mot d'origine inconnue]
+MYRRHE 1 (*la mir*)
MYRTE 1 (*mirte*)
myrtil v MYRTILLE
MYRTILLE 1 (*myrtil*)
myster, mystère v MYSTÈRE
MYSTÈRE 3 (*mistère* 1, *myster* 1, *mystère* 1)

N

nabi v HABIT
nacion v NATION
NAGER 5 (*naze* 1, *nazé* 4)
+NAISSANCE 1 (*la néssans*)
naître v NAÎTRE
NAÎTRE 9 (*énée* 1, *naître* 1, *né* 7)
nam, nâm, nâm' v +ÂME
namcame 1 [origine inconnue]
Namcouticouti v NAMCOUTICOUTI
NAMCOUTICOUTI 36 (*Namcouticouti*)
name, nàme, nâme, nâmes v +ÂME
nana v NANA
NANA 1 (*nana*)
nané, nanné, nannées v +ANNÉE
nanque, nanqui v N'A+QUE
napa, n'apa, na pa, napas, na pas, nà pas, n'a pas v N'A+PAS
N'A+PAS 1502 (*n'a pas* 396, *n'apa* 1, *n'as pas* 1, *na pa* 254, *na pas* 304, *nà pas* 1, *napa* 96, *napas* 449)
N'A+PAS+EN+A 3 (*na péna* 1, *n'a péna* 2)
na péna, n'a péna v N'A+PAS+EN+A
n'a pi, na pis, n'a pis, na pli, na plis, n'a pli, naplis, n'a plis v N'A+PLUS

N'A+PLUS 81 (*n'a pi* 3, *na pis* 1, *n'a pis* 3, *na pli* 16, *naplis* 29, *n'a pli* 2, *na plis* 18, *n'a plis* 9)
N'A+QUE 2 (*nanque* 1, *nanqui* 1) v aussi N'EST+QUE
nariein, na riein, nariéin, narien, na rien, narién, n'a rien v N'A+RIEN
N'A+RIEN 128 (*à rien* 2, *nariein* 14, *na rien* 6, *nariéin* 1, *narien* 82, *narién* 1, *na rien* 16, *n'a rien* 16)
n'as pas v N'A+PAS
Natal v NATAL
NATAL 1 (*Natal*) [province de l'Afrique du Sud]
nates v NATTE
nation v NATION
NATION 36 (*nacion* 25, *nation* 10, *nations* 1)
nations v NATION
natire v NATURE
natt', natte$_1$*, nattes* v NATTE
natte$_2$ v NATTER
natte$_3$ v bois de natte
NATTE 12 (*nates* 1, *natt'* 1, *natte*$_1$ 9, *nattes* 1)
natté v NATTER
NATTER 2 (*natté*$_2$ 1, *natté* 1)
NATURE 1 (*natire*)
NAUFRAGE 1 (*naufraze*)
naufraze v NAUFRAGE
navigué v NAVIGUER
NAVIGUER 1 (*navigué*)
navir, navir', navire v NAVIRE
NAVIRE 31 (*navir* 1, *navir'* 2, *navire* 28)
naze, nazé v NAGER
né v NAÎTRE
ne pi, né pi, né pli v N'EST+PLUS
nec, necque v N'EST+QUE
nef, néf, nèfe v NEUF$_1$
NÉGLIGÉ 1 (*négligée*)
négligée v NÉGLIGÉ
NÉGLIGER 1 (*négliz*)
négliz v NÉGLIGER

negre, nègre v NÈGRE
NÈGRE 2 (*negre* 1, *nègre* 1)
négresse v NÉGRESSE
NÉGRESSE 21 (*négresse* 5, *neingresses* 1, *ningresse* 15)
neif v NEUF$_2$
+NEIGE 1 (*la neiz*)
neimport v N'IMPORTE
neingresses v NÉGRESSE
neinque v N'EST+QUE
nénaine v NÉNAINE
NÉNAINE 2 (*nénaine* 1, *nénène* 1) [fr. dial.]
néné v +NEZ
nénène v NÉNAINE
nénez v +NEZ
népée v ÉPÉE
néq, nèq, neq', néq', nèq', néqu, néqu', né qu', neque, néque, nèque
v N'EST+QUE
Néréide v NÉRÉIDE
NÉRÉIDE 1 (*Néréide*) [nom d'un bateau]
+NERF 1 (*lénerfs*)
n'espèce v +ESPÈCE
n'est pas v N'EST+PAS
N'EST+PAS 1 (*n'est pas*)
N'EST+PLUS 7 (*ne pi* 1, *né pi* 5, *né pli* 1)
N'EST+QUE 159 (*nec* 11, *necque* 1, *neinque* 1, *néq* 2, *nèq* 1, *neq'* 5, *néq'* 5, *nèq'* 1, *néqu* 1, *néqu'* 2, *né qu'* 1, *neque* 8, *néque* 21, *nèque* 91, *ninq'* 3, *ninqu'* 1, *ninque* 2)
nétoye, nétoyé v NETTOYER
nette v NETTE
NETTE 1 (*nette*)
nettoy, nettoyé v NETTOYER
NETTOYER 8 (*nétoye* 1, *nétoyé* 2, *nettoy* 3, *nettoyé* 2)
NEUF$_1$ 6 (*nef* 4, *néf* 1, *nèfe* 1) [adj]
NEUF$_2$ 3 (*neif*) [chiffre]
neuvième v NEUVIÈME
NEUVIÈME 4 (*neuvième* 1, *néviem* 3)
neveix v NEVEU

NEVEU 1 (*neveix* 1, *névit'* [24]1)
néviem v NEUVIÈME
névit' v *NEVEU
+NEZ 21 (*néné* 4, *nénez* 17)[25]
nhabit, nhabits v +HABIT
ni$_1$ v NI
NI 38 (*ni*$_1$)
ni$_2$ v TOUT+NU
niaz, niaze v NUAGE
nic v NIC
NIC 8 (*nic* 2, *nique* 6) [mot dial. fr. pour *nid*]
Nicolas v NICOLAS
NICOLAS 2 (*Colas* 1, *Nicolas* 1) [prénom masculin]
Nicole v NICOLE
NICOLE 1 (*Nicole*) [prénom féminin]
*NICULI 1 (*nitçoulis*) [mot dravidien]
nié v NIER
NIER 4 (*nié* 2, *niyé* 2)
nigaud v NIGAUD
NIGAUD 1 (*nigaud*)
N'IMPORTE 42 (*neimport*)
ningresse v NÉGRESSE
Nini v NINI
NINI 3 (*Nini*) [prénom diminutif féminin]
ninq', ninqu', ninque
v N'EST+QUE
nique v NIC
nitçoulis v *NICULI
niveau v NIVEAU
NIVEAU 1 (*niveau*)
niyé v NIER
no v NON
noar v NOIR$_{2,3}$
noaye v NOYER
noble v NOBLE
NOBLE 2 (*noble*)
+NOCE 2 (*la noce*)
noel, noël v NOËL

---

[24] Peut-être un mot dial.
[25] PB considère qu'il est très peu vraisemblable que /nene/ résulte de la réduplication de Fr. *nez*. Une origine plus probable est le nez avec le changement de [l] à [n] résultant d'une variation répandue entre ces deux phones en CM.

NOËL 4 (*noel* 1, *noël* 3)
noir v NOIR$_{1,2,3}$
NOIR$_1$ 79 (*noir* 55, *noirs* 24) [n = 'esclave'], v aussi GRAND+NOIR, MON+NOIR
NOIR$_2$ 8 (*noar* 1, *noir* 5, *noirnoir* 2) [n = 'noirceur, obscurité']
NOIR$_3$ 49 (*noar* 5, *noir* 31, *noire* 6, *noirs* 7) [adj.]
noire v NOIR$_3$
noirnoir v NOIR$_2$
noirs v NOIR$_{1,3}$
noix v NOIX
NOIX 1 (*noix*)
nom v NOM
NOM 37 (*nom* 35, *noms* 1, *non* 1)
+NOM 1 (*le nom*)
NOMBRIL 1 (*lombri*)
nomé, nommé v NOMMER
NOMMER 8 (*nomé* 1, *nommé* 7)
noms v NOM
non$_1$ v NON
non$_2$ v NOM
NON 48 (*non*$_1$, *no* 1)
non pli, non plus v NON+PLUS
NON+PLUS 12 (*non pli* 11, *non plus* 1)
non va v NON+VA
NON+VA 2 (*non va*)
nos v NOS
NOS 2 (*nos*)
note, notr, notre v NOTRE
NOTRE 5 (*note* 1, *notr* 1, *notre* 3)
nou v NOUS
noui v NUIT
nouri, nouris v NOURRIR
nouritire v NOURRITURE
nourri v NOURRIR
nourriç', nourrice v NOURRICE
NOURRICE 2 (*nourriç'* 1, *nourrice* 1)
NOURRIR 14 (*nouri* 1, *nouris* 1, *nourri* 12)
nourritire v NOURRITURE
NOURRITURE 2 (*nouritire* 1, *nourritire* 1)

nous v NOUS
NOUS 755 (*nou* 112, *nous* 643)
nouveau v NOUVEAU
NOUVEAU 17 (*nouveau* 5, *nouvo* 10, *nouvel*$_1$ 1, *nouvelle*$_1$ 1) [adj]
Nouveau-Testament v NOUVEAU-TESTAMENT
NOUVEAU-TESTAMENT 2 (*Nouveau-Testament*)
nouvel$_1$ v NOUVEAU
nouvel$_2$, *nouvelle*$_1$ v NOUVEAU
nouvelle$_2$ v NOUVELLE
NOUVELLE 16 (*nouvel*$_2$ 7, *nouvelle*$_2$ 5, *nouvelles* 4) [nom]
nouvelles v NOUVELLE
nouvo v NOUVEAU
NOYAU 1 (*loyan*)
NOYER 4 (*noaye* 1, *nôyé* 3)
nôyé v NOYER
NUAGE 26 (*niaz* 4, *niaze* 22)
NUIT 3 (*noui*)
+NUIT 36 (*la noui* 4, *la nouit* 2, *la nouite* 3, *la nuit* 4, *la nuit'* 1, *lanouite* 20, *la nouy* 2)
*NYANG 1 (*yang*) [mot bant.]

O

o v O
O 11 (*o*) [interj.]
obeïe, obéïe v OBÉIR
OBÉIR 3 (*obeïe* 2, *obéïe* 1)
oblie v OUBLIER
obligé, obligée v OBLIGER
OBLIGER 5 (*obligé* 2, *obligée* 2, *obliz* 1, *oblize* 1)
obliz, oblize v OBLIGER
OBSCUR 5 (*sicour*$_1$ 4, *sicours*$_1$ 1)
+OBSCURITÉ 4 (*l'obskirité* 4)
+OBSERVATOIRE 1 (*l'observatoire*)
OCCASION 1 (*ocazion*)
+OCCASION 2 (*l'ocazion* 2)
ocazion v OCCASION
occipe v OCCUPER

OCCUPER 6 (*occipe* 1, *oquipe* 5)
o contrér v AU+CONTRAIRE
Odier v ODIER
ODIER 1 (*Odier*) [nom de famille]
+ODEUR 15 (*lodeir* 4, *lodéir* 1, *l'odeir* 2, *l'oder* 4, *l'odér* 1, *l'odère* 1, *lodère* 1, *zoder* 1)
+ŒUF 54 (*di zef* 1, *dizef* 30, *di-zef* 3, *dizéf* 4, *di zèfe* 1, *dizefs* 3, *di-zefs* 1, *dizéfs* 2, *di-zéfs* 1, *dizeif* 6, *dizéifs* 1, *di zoeuf* 1)
offancé, offans, offensé v OFFENSER
+OFFICE 1 (*l'office*)
+OFFICIER 18 (*zofficié* 3, *zofficier* 4, *zofficiers* 7, *z'officiers* 1, *zoficié* 3)
+OFFENSE 2 (*zoffans*)
OFFENSER 4 (*offancé* 2, *offans* 1, *offensé* 1)
offer, offert v OFFRIR
+OFFRANDE 6 (*l'offrand* 3, *zoffrand* 3)
offre v OFFRIR
+OFFRE 1 (*l'offre*)
OFFRIR 5 (*offer* 1, *offert* 3, *offre* 1)
ogmanté v AUGMENTER
oh! v OH !
OH ! 28 (*oh!*)
+OIE 8 (*la zoie* 2, *lézoie* 2, *lazoie* 1, *lazoies* 2, *lazois* 1)
+OIGNON 3 (*lognon* 1, *loignon* 1, *zonions* 1)
+OISEAU 73 (*zozeau* 1, *zozeaux* 1, *zozo* 64, *zozos* 7)
okéne v AUCUN
+OLIVE 1 (*dolive*)
+OLIVIERS 3 (*zolivié*)
+OMBRAGE 1 (*l'ombraze*)
+OMBRE 4 (*lombe* 3, *l'ombr* 1)
+OMBRELLE 1 (*l'ombrelle*)
+OMELETTE 1 (*lomelette*)
Omer-Paça v OMER-PASHA

OMER-PASHA	1 (*Omer-Paça*) [nom de personnage[26]]	ou_1	v OU	*pacequi*	v PARCE+QUE
+ONGLE	1 (*zongues*)	OU	42 (*ou₁*) v aussi OU BIEN	*pacians*	v PATIENCE
onz, onze	v ONZE	ou_2	v OÙ	PAGAÏE	1 (*pagaye*)
ONZE	3 (*onz* 1, *onze* 2)	OÙ	19 (*ou²*)	PAGAILLER	2 (*pagaille* 1, *pagayé* 1)
onziem	v ONZIÈME	ou_3	v VOUS	*pagaille, pagayé*	v PAGAILLER
ONZIÈME	2 (*onziem*)	*ouah !*	v OUAH !	*pagaye*	v PAGAÏE
oparavan	v AUPARAVANT	OUAH !	5 (*ouah !*)	*Paganini*	1 [nom propre]
oquipe	v OCCUPER	*ou biein, oubiein, ou bien,*		PAGE	1 (*paz*)
or	v LÀ-HAUT	*oubien*	v OU+BIEN	*pagla*	v **PAGLA**
+OR	33 (*l'or* 11, *lor₁* 20)	OU+BIEN	101 (*ou biein* 18, *oubiein* 24, *ou bien* 58, *oubien* 1)	**PAGLA**	1 (*pagla*) [mot hind.]
ORANG-OUTAN	1 (*ourangue-outan*)	OUBLIER	32 (*blie* 1, *blié* 27, *bliie* 1, *bliye* 1, *bliyé* 1, *oblie* 1)	*pagné, pagnier*	v PANIER
+ORAGE	5 (*l'oraze*)			*paie*	v PAYS
+ORANGE	1 (*zoranges*)			PAÏEN	8 (*payein* 1, *payeins* 6, *payens* 1)
+ORANGER	1 (*loranzé*)				
+ORATEUR	1 (*lorateir*)	*oui*	v OUI	*paille*	v PAILLE
ordonne, ordonné	v ORDONNER	OUI	103 (*oui*)	PAILLE	1 (*paille*)[27]
ORDONNER	2 (*ordonne* 1, *ordonné* 1)	*oulé*	v VOULOIR	+PAILLE	25 (*la paille* 6, *la paye* 5, *lapaill'* 1, *lapaille* 13)
+ORDRE	27 (*les ordres* 1, *l'ordr* 12, *l'ordre* 5, *lorde* 1, *zordes* 4, *zordr* 1, *zordre* 1, *zordres* 2)	+OURAGAN	3 (*l'oragan* 1, *l'ouragan* 2)		
		ourangue-outan	v ORANG-OUTAN	*paille-en-queie*	v PAILLE-EN-QUEUE
		our-r-r-r-r	1 [onomat.]	PAILLE-EN-QUEUE	10 (*paille-en-queie* 2, *paille-en-qui* 1, *paye-en-qui* 1, *payenqui* 6)
+OREILLE	29 (*zoreill'* 1, *zoreille* 9, *zoreilles* 1, *zorey* 2, *zoréy* 8, *zoreye* 1, *zoréye* 2, *zoréyes* 4, *zorèyes* 1)	*ous*	v VOUS		
		oussi	v AUSSI		
		+OUTIL	1 (*zoutils*)		
		ouv'lé	1 [sens douteux]	*paille-en-qui*	v PAILLE-EN-QUEUE
		ouver, ouvert, ouvért	v OUVRIR	+PAIN	32 (*di pain* 22, *dipain* 10)
+OREILLER	3 (*l'oreiller* 1, *zoriés* 2)	+OUVERTURE	1 (*l'ouvertir*)	*paire*	v PAIRE
+ORGUEIL	1 (*lorguéye*)	+OUVRAGE	62 (*l'ouvrage* 5, *l'ouvraz* 3, *l'ouvraz'* 1, *l'ouvraze* 14, *l'ouvrazes* 1, *louvrage* 1, *louvraze* 36, *zouvraze* 1)	PAIRE	1 (*paire*)
+ORIENT	3 (*l'orian*)			*paix*	v PAIX
+OS	8 (*lezo* 1, *lézo* 4, *lézos* 3)			PAIX	1 (*paix*)
				+PAIX	7 (*la pé* 6, *lapaix* 1)
osé, oser	v OSER	*ouvre, ouvri*	v OUVRIR	*Pak, Pâk*	v PÂQUES
OSER	7 (*osé* 3, *oser* 1, *oz* 2, *oze* 1)	+OUVRIER	8 (*zouvrié* 5, *zouvrières* 1, *zouvriers* 2)	*paké*	v PAQUET
		OUVRIR	95 (*ouver* 11, *ouvert* 74, *ouvért* 3, *ouvre* 1, *ouvri* 6)	*palais*	v PALAIS
o sicours	v AU+SECOURS			PALAIS	2 (*palais* 1, *palé₁* 1)
ossi	v AUSSI			*palan*	v PALAN
ossito	v AUSSITÔT			PALAN	2 (*palan*)
ot'	v AUTRE	*oz, oze*	v OSER	*palanquin*	v PALANQUIN
otan	v AUTANT	*ozourdi*	v AUJOURD'HUI	PALANQUIN	2 (*palanquin*)
+ÔTER	1 (*zoté*)			*palé₁*	v PALAIS
		# P		*palé₂*	v PARLER
otour	v AUTOUR			*paleto, paletot*	v PALETOT
		p'tit, p'tit', p'tits	v PETIT	PALETOT	2 (*paleto* 1, *paletot* 1)
		P'tit Sabe	v PETIT+SABLE	*palfrémier*	v PALFRENIER
		pa_1	v PAS_1	PALFRENIER	1 (*palfrémier*)
		pa_2	v PAPA		
		pa'	v PAS_1		

---

[26] Nom adopté par un Serbe qui adopta la nationalité turque et qui connut un succès phénoménal comme stratège militaire au milieu du XIXe siècle.

[27] Forme attestée suivant *en*.

paliaca v **PALIAKATE**
palidéenne v PALUDÉENNE
PALIAKATE 5 (*paliaca* 2,
　　pariaca 2, *pariaka* 1)
　　[toponyme]
palmisses, palmiste
　　v PALMISTE
PALMISTE 3 (*palmisses* 2,
　　palmiste 1)
PALUDÉENNE 1 (*palidéenne*)
pamé v PAMÉ
PAMÉ 1 (*pamé*)
Pamplemousse, Pamplemousses
　　v PAMPLEMOUSSES
PAMPLEMOUSSES 5
　　(*Pamplemousse* 1,
　　Pamplemousses 4)
pandan v PENDANT
pandi v PENDRE
PANELA 7 (*panell'* 1,
　　panelle 6) [mot port.]
panell', panelle v **PANELA**
pangar, pangard
　　v PRENDRE+GARDE
panié, panier v PANIER
PANIER 28 (*pagné* 1,
　　pagnier 11, *panié* 3,
　　panier 13, *paniers* 1)
paniers v PANIER
pans, pansé v PENSER
pantouffe v PANTOUFLE
PANTOUFLE 1 (*pantouffe*)
papa v PAPA
PAPA 294 (*pa* 1, *papa* 289,
　　papas 4)
pa-pa-pa-pa-pa 1 [onomat.]
papas v PAPA
papaye v PAPAYE
PAPAYE 6 (*papaye* 5,
　　papayes 1)
papayes v PAPAYE
papié, papier v PAPIER
PAPIER 25 (*papié* 7,
　　papier 18)
papillon, papions v PAPILLON
PAPILLON 4 (*papillon* 3,
　　papions 1)
+PÂQUES 1 (*la pâk*)
paqués, paquet, paquét, paquêt,
　　paquets v PAQUET

PAQUET 29 (*paké* 2, *paqués*
　　1, *paquet* 8, *paquét* 6,
　　paquêt 3, *paquets* 9)
PÂQUES 4 (*Pak* 1, *Pâk* 3)
par₁ v PAR
par₂ v PART
PAR 149 (*par₁*)
parabol v PARABOLE
PARABOLE 17 (*parabol*)
paradis v PARADIS
PARADIS 1 (*paradis*)
PARAGES 4 (*paraz* 2,
　　paraze 2)
parain v PARRAIN
paraîte, paraître
　　v (AP)PARAÎTRE
paralizé v PARALYSÉ
paralizi v PARALYSIE
PARALYSÉ 1 (*paralizé*)
PARALYSIE 4 (*paralizi*)
paran v PARENT
parasol v PARASOL
PARASOL 4 (*parasol*)
paraz, paraze v PARAGES
parc v PARC
PARC 1 (*parc*)
parce que, parce qui, parcé qui
　　v PARCE+QUE
PARCE+QUE 216 (*pacequi* 1,
　　parce que 1, *parce qui* 8,
　　parcequé 3, *parcé qui* 5,
　　parcequi 2, *parski* 172,
　　passequi 3, *pass'qué* 6,
　　pass qui 14, *pass'qui* 1)
parcequé, parcequi
　　v PARCE+QUE
pardon₁ v PARDON
PARDON 10 (*pardon₁*)
pardon₂, pardonée, pardonne,
　　pardonné v PARDONNER
PARDONNER 17 (*pardon₂* 1,
　　pardonée 1, *pardonne* 10,
　　pardonné 5)
paré v PARER
pare à virer
　　v PARER+À+VIRER
pareil v PAREIL
PAREIL 5 (*pareil* 2, *pareille*
　　1, *parey* 1, *paréy* 1)
pareille v PAREIL
parent v PARENT

PARENT 6 (*paran* 1, *parent* 2,
　　parents 3)
parents v PARENT
PARER 11 (*paré*)
PARER+À+VIRER 1 (pare à
　　virer) [expression
　　nautique]
pares, paresse v PARESSE
PARESSE 6 (*pares* 1,
　　paresse 5)
parét v (AP)PARAÎTRE
parey, paréy v PAREIL
PARFAIT 4 (*parfé*)
parfé v PARFAIT
pari v PARI
PARI 2 (*pari*)
pariaca, pariaka
　　v **PALIAKATE**
PARIAGE 1 (*pariaze*)
pariaze v PARIAGE
parié v PARIER
PARIER 14 (*parié*)
Paris v PARIS
PARIS 1 (*Paris*)
parjur v PARJURE
PARJURE 1 (*parjur*)
parl, parl', parle, parlé, parlée,
　　parler v PARLER
PARLER 95 (*palé₂* 1, *parl* 28,
　　parl' 3, *parle* 9,
　　parlé 49, *parlée* 2,
　　parler 1, *parlez* 2)
parlez v PARLER
parmi v PARMI
PARMI 14 (*parmi*)
parol, parol', parole
　　v PAROLE
PAROLE 54 (*parol* 28,
　　parol' 5, *parole* 17,
　　paroles 4)
+PAROLE 12 (*la parol*)
paroles v PAROLE
PARRAIN 3 (*parain* 1,
　　parrains 2)
parrains v PARRAIN
parski v PARCEQUE
PART 7 (*par₂* 1, *part* 6) [n]
PARTAGE 4 (*partaze₁*)
+PARTAGE 4 (*la partaze* 3,
　　lapartaze̦ 1)

PARTAGER 8 (*partaz* 2, *partaze*₂ 4, *partazé* 1, *partazer* 1)
partaz v PARTAGER
*partaze*₁ v PARTAGE
*partaze*₂, *partazé*, *partazer* v PARTAGER
par ter, par ter', par tère, par terre, partére, parterre v PAR+TERRE
PAR+TERRE 31 (*partére* 2, *parterre* 1, *par ter* 7, *par ter'* 1, *par tère* 1, *par terre* 19)
*parti*₁ v PARTIE
*parti*₂ v PARTIR
*partie*₁ v PARTIE
*partie*₂ v PARTIR
PARTIE 8 (*parti*₁ 7, *partie*₁ 1)
PARTIR 15 (*parti*₂ 13, *partie*₂ 1, *partis* 1)
partis v PARTIR
partou, par tou, partout v PARTOUT
PARTOUT 78 (*partou* 9, *par tou* 1, *partout* 66, *par tout* 2)
par tout v PARTOUT
*pas*₁ v PAS₁
PAS₁ 50 (*pa*₁ 12, *pa'* 1, *pas*₁ 37) [neg]
*pas*₂ v PAS₂
PAS₂ 6 (*pas*₂) [n]
pass' v PASSER
PASSAGE 1 (*passaze*)
passager v PASSAGER
PASSAGER 2 (*passager* 1, *passagers* 1)
passagers v PASSAGER
passant v PASSANT
PASSANT 2 (*passant*)
passaze v PASSAGE
+PASSE 3 (*la passe*)
*passe, passé*₁ v PASSER
*passé*₂ v *s'en passé*
passée v PASSER
passequi v PARCEQUE
passer v PASSER
PASSER 155 (*pass'* 4, *passe* 51, *passé*₁ 96, *passée* 1, *passer* 1, *passés* 2)

PASSEREAU 2 (*passero*)
passero v PASSEREAU
passés v PASSER
passion v PASSION
PASSION 2 (*passion*)
+PASSION 1 (*la passion*)
pass'qué, pass qui, pass'qui v PARCEQUE
pastor v PASTOR
PASTOR 1 (*pastor*)
pataracque v PATRAQUE
patate v PATATE
PATATE 7 (*batate* 3, *batates* 1, *patate* 2, *patates* 1)
patates v PATATE
+PÂTE 1 (*la pât*)
paté v PÂTÉ
PÂTÉ 3 (*paté* 2, *pâtés* 1)
patente v PATENTE
PATENTE 1 (*patente*)
pâtés v PÂTÉ
patience v PATIENCE
PATIENCE 4 (*pacians* 2, *patience* 2)
patraque v PATRAQUE
PATRAQUE 2 (*pataracque* 1, *patraque* 1)
patron v PATRON
PATRON 1 (*patron*)
PATTE 22 (*pattes*)
+PATTE 21 (*la patte* 3, *lapatte* 15, *lapattes* 3)
pattes v PATTE
Paul v PAUL
PAUL 1 (*Paul*) [prénom]
Paulin v PAULIN
PAULIN 26 (*Paulin*) [prénom]
Pauline v PAULINE
PAULINE 72 (*Pauline*) [prénom]
paupière v PAUPIÈRE
PAUPIÈRE 1 (*paupière*)
PAUSER/(RE)POSER 28 (*pose*₂ 2, *posé* 18, *poz*₂ 3, *poz'* 1, *poze* 1, *pozé* 3)
pauv, pauv', pauve, pauvre v PAUVRE

PAUVRE 115 (*pauv* 2, *pauv'* 13, *pauve* 35, *pauvre* 48, *pauvres* 6, *pov* 4, *pov'* 1, *pôve* 4, *povre* 2)
+PAUVRE 1 (*les pauvres*)
pauvres v PAUVRE
pavé v PAVÉ
PAVÉ 3 (*pavé*)
pavillon v PAVILLON
PAVILLON 13 (*pavillon* 8, *pavillons* 3, *pavion* 2)
pavillons, pavion v PAVILLON
pay' v PAYS
*paye*₁ v PAYER
*paye*₂ v PAYS
payé v PAYER
paye-en-qui v PAILLE-EN-QUEUE
payein, payeins v PAÏEN
payenqui v PAILLE-EN-QUEUE
payens v PAÏEN
payer v PAYER
PAYER 43 (*paye*₁ 11, *payé* 15, *payer* 1, *péye*₁ 15, *péyé* 1)
+PAYEUR 1 (*lé payère*)
payi, pays v PAYS
PAYS 125 (*paie* 4, *pay'* 5, *paye*₂ 54, *payi* 1, *pays* 8, *péye* 3, *péyi* 54)
paz v PAGE
+PEAU 45 (*la peau* 16, *la po* 5, *lapeau* 23, *la-peau* 1)
Peau d'âne v PEAU+D'ÂNE
PEAU+D'ÂNE 12 (*Peau d'âne* 11, *Peau-d'âne* 1) [nom de personnage]
Peau-d'âne v PEAU+D'ÂNE
PÉAGER 4 (*peazé* 2, *péazé* 2)
peazé, péazé v PÉAGER
pécé, péçé v PÉCHÉ
péceirs, pécer v PÊCHEUR
pécés v PÉCHÉ
+PÊCHE 8 (*la pèce* 2, *la pesse* 2, *lapéce* 2, *lapèce* 1, *la-pèce* 1)
PÉCHÉ 54 (*pécé* 20, *péçé* 1, *pécés* 1, *pêché*₁ 2, *péchés* 2, *pêchés*₁ 28) [n]
+PÉCHÉ 1 (*le péchés*)

pêché$_1$ v PÉCHÉ
pêché$_2$ v PÉCHER
pêcheir   v PÊCHEUR
PÉCHER   6 (*pêché*$_2$ 4,
   pêchés$_2$ 2)
pêchés, pêchés$_1$ v PÉCHÉ
pêchés$_2$ v PÉCHER
PÊCHEUR 2 (*pêcheur* 1,
   pecheurs 1)
pêcheur   v PÊCHEUR
PÊCHEUR 5 (*péceirs* 1,
   pécer 2, *pécheir* 2)
pecheurs   v PÊCHEUR
pécore   v PÉCORE
PÉCORE   1 (*pécore* 1)
peign', peigné   v PEIGNER
PEIGNER 3 (*peign'* 1, *peigné* 2)
peignoir   v PEIGNOIR
PEIGNOIR 3 (*peignoir* 1,
   peinoir 1, *peinoirs* 1)
PEINE   v EN+PEINE,
   SANS+PEINE
+PEINE   33 (*la pein'* 1, *la
   peine* 19, *lapeine* 10,
   lapéne 2, *la pène* 1)
peinoir, peinoirs v PEIGNOIR
PEINT 1 (*peinte*)
peinte   v PEINT
peintire, peintiré
   v PEINTURER
+PEINTURE 1 (*la peintire* 1)
PEINTURER 6 (*peintire* 5,
   peintiré 1)
peir$_1$ v PEUR$_1$
peir$_2$ v PEUR$_2$
Peir-Narien   v PEIR-NARIEN
PEIR-NARIEN 38 (*Peir-
   Narien*) [nom de
   personnage]
péle, pèle, pelle   v APPELER
pelote   v PELOTER
PELOTER 2 (*pelote*)
pence, pencée, pencées
   v PENSER
pendan, pendant v PENDANT
PENDANT 11 (*pandan* 1,
   pendan 2, *pendant* 8) v
   aussi À+PENDANT et
   EN+PENDANT
pendgare
   v PRENDRE+GARDE
pendi   v PENDRE

pendile   v PENDULE
PENDRE   5 (*pandi* 1, *pendi* 4)
pends gar'
   v PRENDRE+GARDE
PENDULE 2 (*pendile*)
pengare v PRENDRE+GARDE
pénice   v PÉNICHE
PÉNICHE 12 (*pénice*)
pens', pense, pensé v PENSER
PENSER 50 (*pans* 1, *pansé* 3,
   pence 1, *pencée* 11,
   pencées 1, *pens'* 4, *pense*
   8, *pensé* 20, *pensez* 1)
pensez   v PENSER
+PÉPIE 1 (*la pipie*)
peppermint v **PEPPERMINT**
PEPPERMINT 1 (*peppermint*)
   [mot angl.]
per$_1$ v PEUR$_1$
per$_2$ v PEUR$_2$
per$_3$ v PÈRE
pér   v PEUR$_1$
pèr$_2$ v PEUR$_2$
pèr$_3$ v PÈRE
per'$_1$ v PEUR$_1$
per'$_2$ v PEUR$_2$
perce, percé   v PERCER
PERCER   4 (*perce* 1, *percé* 3)
perdé, perdi   v PERDRE
perdicion   v PERDITION
PERDITION 1 (*perdicion*)
perdie   v PERDRE
PERDRE   56 (*perdé* 2,
   perdi 53, *perdie* 1)
perdri, perdrix   v PERDRIX
PERDRIX 10 (*perdri* 4,
   perdrix 6)
pére$_1$ v PEUR$_1$
pére$_2$ v PEUR$_2$
père$_1$ v PEUR$_1$
père$_2$ v PEUR$_2$
père$_3$ v PÈRE
PÈRE   11 (*per*$_3$ 5, *pèr*$_3$ 1,
   père$_3$ 5)
+PÈRE   4 (*le per*)
Périne   v PÉRINE
PÉRINE   1 (*Périne*) [nom de
   famille]
perl, perle   v PERLE
PERLE   4 (*perl* 3, *perle* 1)
permet   v PERMETTRE
PERMETTRE 3 (*permet*)

permission v PERMISSION
PERMISSION 1 (*permission*)
peron   v PERRON
péroquet   v PERROQUET
PERRON 1 (*peron*)
PERROQUET 21 (*péroquet*)
PERSÉCUTER 4 (*persékit*)
PERSÉCUTION
   2 (*persékicion*)
persékicion v PERSÉCUTION
persékit   v PERSÉCUTER
person, person', personn'
personne   v PERSONNE
PERSONNE 81 (*person* 2,
   person' 1, *personn'* 2,
   personne 75,
   personnne 1)
personnne v PERSONNE
+PERTE   1 (*laperte*)
pése, pèse, pésé   v PESER
PESER   36 (*pése* 2, *pèse* 4,
   pésé 30, *pez'* 2, *pèz'* 2)
pétard   v PÉTARD
PÉTARD   3 (*pétard* 1,
   pétards 2)
pétards   v PÉTARD
péte, pété   v PÉTER
PÉTER   6 (*péte* 1, *pété* 1,
   pette 4)
PETER BOTH 1 (*piterbote*)
pèt-être   v PEUT-ÊTRE
petit   v PETIT$_1$
PETIT$_1$ 460 (*petit* 13, *piti*$_1$ 43,
   pitit$_1$ 86, *pitits*$_1$ 1, *poti* 1,
   pti 29, *ptit* 175, *p'tit*$_1$ 87,
   p'tit' 1, *ptits* 11, *p'tits* 13,
   ti$_3$)[28] [adj.]
PETIT$_2$ 159 (*piti*$_2$ 53, *pitis* 1,
   pitit$_2$ 80, *pitits*$_2$ 22,
   p'tit$_2$ 3) [n]
PETIT+FILLE 27 (*pti fi* 1, *pti
   fiye* 1, *ptit fill'* 1, *ptit fille*
   16, *p'tit fille* 7, *ptitfille* 1)
PETIT+GUIGNE 12 (*piti guine*
   4, *pitiguine* 1, *pti guine* 7)

---

[28] Au moment où nous mettons ce livre sous presse, nous avons découvert que les données pour les attestations (relativement peu nombreuses) de *ti* < PETIT manquent. Nous nous excusons pour cette omission.

pétition v PÉTITION
PÉTITION 3 (*pétition*)
PETIT+MOKA 1 (*pitit moka*) [toponyme]
PETIT+POIS 3 (*pitit pois* 1, *p'tit pois* 1, *pitits pois* 1)
PETIT+POUCET 44 (*ptit poucet*)
PETIT+RIVIÈRE 1 (*Pitit Rivière*) [toponyme]
PETIT+SABLE 1 (*P'tit Sabe*) [nom d'un village]
pétrole v PÉTROLE
PÉTROLE 3 (*pétrole*)
pette v PÉTER
peu v PEU
PEU 1 (*peu*)
peur$_1$ v PEUR$_1$
peur$_2$ v PEUR$_2$
PEUR$_1$ 17 (*peir*$_1$ 8, *per*$_1$ 5, *per'*$_1$ 1, *pére*$_1$ 1, *père*$_1$ 1, *peur*$_1$ 1) [n]
PEUR$_2$ 101 (*peir*$_2$ 39, *per*$_2$ 35, *pér* 1, *pèr* 10, *per'*$_2$ 1, *pére*$_2$ 6, *père*$_2$ 8, *peur*$_2$ 1) [v]
+PEUR 2 (*la per*)
peut-êtr', peut-être v PEUT-ÊTRE
PEUT-ÊTRE 23 (*pèt-être* 2, *peut-êtr'* 1, *peut-être* 5, *pitêt* 1, *pitêt'* 1, *pit'êt'* 1, *pit-êt'* 1, *pitêtre* 1, *pit-être* 10)
péye$_1$ v PAYER
péye$_2$ v PAYS
péyé v PAYER
péyi v PAYS
pez, 'pèz' v PESER
+PHARMACIE 1 (*la pharmacie*)
Philippe v PHILIPPE
PHILIPPE 1 (*Philippe*) [nom de famille]
Philogène v PHILOGÈNE
PHILOGÈNE 1 (*Philogène*) [prénom]
PHYLACTÈRE 1 (*filacter*)
pi$_1$ v PUER
pi$_2$ v PLUS
piano v PIANO
PIANO 1 (*piano*)
piant v PUANT
piasses, piastes , piastre v PIASTRE
PIASTRE 16 (*piasses* 6, *piastes* 2, *piastre* 4, *piastres* 4)
piastres v PIASTRE
piblicain v PUBLICAIN
piblik v PUBLIC$_1$
piblique v PUBLIC$_2$
pic v PIQUER
pic' v PIQUE
pices v PUCE
pié v PIED
piéce, pièce v PIÈCE
PIÈCE 15 (*piéce* 11, *pièce* 2, *pièces* 2)
pièces v PIÈCE
pied$_1$ v PIED$_1$
pied$_2$ v PIED$_2$
PIED$_1$ 91 (*pié* 38, *pied*$_1$ 43, *pieds*$_1$ 10) [arbre]
PIED$_2$ 4 (*pied*$_1$ 1, *pieds*$_2$ 3) [unité de mesure]
+PIED$_1$ 72 (*li pié* 19, *lipié* 5, *li-pié*$_1$ 5, *li pied*$_1$ 4, *lipied*$_1$ 12, *li pieds* 1, *lipieds* 19, *li-pieds* 3, *lipiéds* 1, *li piés* 2, *li-piés* 1)
+PIED$_2$ (*li-pié*$_2$ 2, *li pied*$_2$ 1, *lipied*$_2$ 2)
pieds$_1$ v PIED$_1$
pieds$_2$ v PIED$_2$
Pierre v PIERRE
PIERRE 19 (*Pierre*) [prénom et nom de famille]
PIERRE+À+L'HUILE 2 (*pierre à l'huile* 1, *pierre à l'uile* 1)
pierre à l'huile, pierre à l'uile v PIERRE+À+L'HUILE
Pierrot v PIERROT
PIERROT 12 (*Pierrot*) [prénom]
PIGEON 29 (*pizon* 26, *pizons* 3)
Pignard v PIGNARD
PIGNARD 1 (*Pignard*) [nom de famille]
pignon v PIGNON
PIGNON 1 (*pignon*)
pikan v PIQUANT
***PIKUNKAI** 2 (*pipengaille*) [mot tam.]
pile$_1$ v PILE
PILE 1 (*pile*$_1$)
pile$_2$*, pilé* v PILER
PILER 7 (*pile*$_2$ 3, *pilé* 4)
pilié v PILIER
PILIER 1 (*pilié*)
pilil' v PILULE
pilime v PLUME
pilon v PILON
PILON 4 (*pilon*)
PILULE 1 (*pilil'*)
piman, piment v PIMENT
PIMENT 13 (*piman* 3, *piment* 8, *piments* 3)
piments v PIMENT
pinaise, pinaises v PUNAISE
PINCE 1 (*pinces*)
+PINCE 4 (*la pince*)
pinceau v PINCEAU
PINCEAU 1 (*pinceau* 1)
pinces v PINCE
pini v PUNIR
pinicion v PUNITION
pinie v PUNIR
pintad', pintade v PINTADE
PINTADE 4 (*pintad'* 1, *pintade* 2, *pintades* 1)
pintades v PINTADE
pioce$_1$ v PIOCHE
pioce$_2$ v PIOCHER
PIOCHE 19 (*pioce*$_1$ 18, *piosse* 1)
+PIOCHE 1 (*la pioce*)
piocher v PIOCHER
PIOCHER 4 (*pioce*$_2$ 1, *piocher* 1, *piossé* 2)
pion v PION
PION 1 (*pion*)
piosse v PIOCHE
piossé v PIOCHER
pip', pipe v PIPE
PIPE 4 (*pip'* 1, *pipe* 3)
pipengaille v ***PIKUNKAI**
piquant v PIQUANT
PIQUANT 20 (*pikan* 14, *piquant* 4, *piquants* 2)
piquant-pioce v PIQUANT+ PIOCHE

PIQUANT+PIOCHE		place	v PLACE	PLANTER	32 (*plant* 2, *plante* 6,
	2 (*piquant-pioce*)	PLACE	63 (*place* 62,		*planté* 22, *planter*₂ 2)
piquants	v PIQUANT		*places* 1)	PLANTEUR	6 (*planter*₁)
pique	v PIQUER	+PLACE	3 (*la place* 2,	*plaque*	v PLAQUE
PIQUE	1 (*pic'*)		*laplace* 1)	PLAQUE	5 (*plaque* 4,
piqué	v PIQUER	*placé, placée* v PLACER			*plaques* 1)
PIQUER	34 (*pic* 1, *pique* 23,	PLACER	2 (*placé* 1, *placée* 1)	*plaques*	v PLAQUE
	piqué 10)	*places*	v PLACE	*plat*₁	v PLAT₁
piquet	v PIQUET	*plack !*	v PLACK !	*plat*₂	v PLAT₂
PIQUET	2 (*piquet* 1, *piquêt* 1)	PLACK !	1 (*plack !*) [onomat.]	PLAT₁	3 (*plat*₁ 1, *plate* 2)
piquêt	v PIQUET	PLAIDER	1 (*pléd*)		[adj]
pir	v PIRE	*plaign', plaigné* v PLAINDRE		PLAT₂	7 (*pla* 5, *plat*₂ 2,
pirate	v PIRATE	+PLAINE	46 (*la plaine* 20,		*plats* 1) [n]
PIRATE	2 (*pirate* 1, *pirates* 1)		*la pléne* 1, *laplaine* 19,	+PLAT	1 (*léplats*)
pirates	v PIRATE		*la-plaine* 1, *lapléne* 4)	*plate*	v PLAT₁
PIRE	2 (*pir*)	*Plain' Wilhems*		*plats*	v PLAT₂
pirogue	v PIROGUE		v PLAINE WILHEMS	*pléd*	v PLAIDER
PIROGUE 12 (*pirogue* 7,		PLAINE WILHEMS		*plein*	v PLEIN
	pirogues 5)		1 (*Plain' Wilhems*)	PLEIN	90 (*plein* 86,
pirogues	v PIROGUE	+PLAINE WILHELM			*pleins* 3, *plin* 1)
pirzé	v PURGER		1 (*la Plaine Wilainne*)	+PLEINE+LUNE 1	
pis	v PIS	PLAINDRE	18 (*plaign'* 2,		(*la plaine line*)
PIS	2 (*pis*)		*plaigné* 12, *plaine* 1,	*pleine mer* v PLEINE+MER	
pisqué	v PUISQUE		*plaingné* 2, *plainié* 1)	PLEINE+MER 1 (*pleine mer*)	
PISTACHE 1 (*pistace*)		*plaine, plaingné, plainié*		*pleins*	v PLEIN
pistace	v PISTACHE		v PLAINDRE	PLEURER 114 (*plor* 2, *plor'* 1,
pit	v **PIT**	*plaint', plainte* v PLAINTE			*plore* 9, *ploré* 101,
PIT	2 (*pit*) [mot angl.]	PLAINTE	5 (*plaint'* 1,		*plorè* 1) [forme dial.]
pit...	v PUTAIN		*plainte* 4)	PLEUREUR 1 (*plorère*)	
piterbote	v PETER BOTH	*plair'*	v PLAIRE	*pli*	v PLUS
pit'êt', pitêt', pitêt', pit-êt',		PLAIRE	1 (*plair'* 1)	*plice, plicé* v ÉPLUCHER
pitêtre, pit-être v PEUT-ÊTRE		*plaisir*	v PLAISIR	*plié, pliés* v PLIER
*piti*₁	v PETIT₁	PLAISIR	9 (*plaisir* 7,	PLIER	3 (*plié* 2, *pliés* 1)
*piti*₂	v PETIT₂		*plaisire* 1, *plaizir* 1)	*plime, plimes* v PLUME
pitié	v PITIÉ	*plaisire, plaizir* v PLAISIR		*plin*	v PLEIN
PITIÉ	17 (*pitié* [n 3, v 14])	*plan*	v PLAN	*plis*	v PLUS
*pitis*₁,₂, *pitit*₁,₂, *pitits*₁,₂		PLAN	10 (*plan*)	*plisiers*	v PLUSIEURS
	v PETIT₁,₂	*plance*	v PLANCHE	*plisse*	v PLUS
piti guine, pitiguine, pti guine		*plancé*	v PLANCHER	*plissé*	v PLISSER
	v PETIT+GUIGNE	*plances*	v PLANCHE	PLISSER 1 (*plissé*)	
Pitit Moka v PETIT+MOKA		PLANCHE	3 (*plance* 1,	*plito, plitot, plitôt* v PLUTÔT
pitit pois, p'tit pois, pitits pois			*plances* 2)	*plizier*	v PLUSIEURS
	v PETIT+POIS	*planché*	v PLANCHER	*plomb*	v PLOMB
Pitit Rivière v PETIT+RIVIÈRE		PLANCHER 2 (*plancé* 1,		PLOMB	1 (*plomb*)
pito	v PLUTÔT		*planché* 1)	+PLOMB	3 (*diplomb*)
Piton	v PITON	*plant*	v PLANTER	PLONGER	7 (*plonze* 4,
PITON	2 (*Piton*) [toponyme]	PLANTAGE 1 (*plantaze*)			*plonzé* 3)
pizon, pizons v PIGEON		*plantaze*	v PLANTAGE	*plonze, plonzé* v PLONGER
pla	v PLAT₂	*plante, planté* v PLANTER		*plor, plor', plore, ploré, plorè*
placata	v PLACATA	*planter*₁	v PLANTEUR		v PLEURER
PLACATA 2 (*placata*)		*planter*₂	v PLANTER	*plorère*	v PLEUREUR
	[onomat.]			*plôyé*	v PLOYER

PLOYER 1 (*plôyé*)
+PLUIE 22 (*la pli* 16, *la plie* 1, *lapli* 2, *laplie* 3)
PLUME 39 (*pilime* 2, *plime* 30, *plimes* 7)
+PLUME 3 (*la plime*)
+PLUPART 1 (*la plipar*)
plus v PLUS
PLUS 173 (*pi₂* 1, *pli* 50, *plis* 114, *plisse* 1, *plus* 6, *ply* 1)
PLUSIEURS 3 (*plisiers* 1, *plizier* 2)
plutôt v PLUTÔT
PLUTÔT 16 (*pito* 2, *plito* 5, *plitot* 2, *plitôt* 5, *plutôt* 2)
ply v PLUS
poa v POIDS
poal v POIL
poasson v POISSON
poce, poçe v POCHE
POCHE 17 (*poce* 15, *poçe* 1, *poss'* 1)
pôdeçambe v POT+DE+CHAMBRE
poêlon, poëlon v POÊLON
POÊLON 3 (*poêlon* 1, *poëlon* 1, *poilon* 1)
pognée, pognés v POIGNÉE
poids v POIDS
POIDS 2 (*poa* 1, *poids* 1)
poignée v POIGNÉE
POIGNÉE 7 (*pognée* 2, *pognés* 3, *poignée* 1)
poignées de main v POIGNÉE+DE+MAIN
POIGNÉE+DE+MAIN 1 (*poignées de main*)
poil v POIL
POIL 3 (*poal* 1, *poil* 1, *poils* 1)
poils v POIL
pointe v POINTE
POINTE 3 (*pointe*)
+POINTE 2 (*la pointe*)
pointères v POINTEUR
POINTEUR 1 (*pointères*)
POIRE 1 (*poires*)
poires v POIRE
pois di cap v POIS+DU+CAP
POIS+DU+CAP 1 (*pois di cap*)
Poisson v POISSON

POISSON 36 (*poasson* 1, *poisson* 2, *posson* 24, *pôsson* 6, *possons* 3)
poivre v POIVRE
POIVRE 1 (*poivre*)
+POIVRE 1 (*dipoive*)
police v POLICE
POLICE 3 (*police*)
+POLICE 12 (*la police* 11, *lapolice* 1)
polisson v POLISSON
POLISSON 5 (*polisson*)
politesse v POLITESSE
POLITESSE 3 (*politesse* 2, *politesses* 1)
politesses v POLITESSE
+POMMADE 2 (*la pommade* 1, *lapommade* 1)
pomm' di terre v POMME+ DE+TERRE
POMME 1 (*pommes*)
pomme d'amour v POMME+ D'AMOUR
POMME+D'AMOUR 2 (*pomme d'amour* 1, *pommedamour* 1)
pomme di terre v POMME+ DE+TERRE
pommedamour v POMME+ D'AMOUR
POMME+DE+TERRE 2 (*pomm' di terre* 1, *pomme di terre* 1)
POMME+RAQUETTE 1 (*pom' raquette*)
pommes v POMME
+POMPE 6 (*lapompe*)
pompé, pompééé v POMPER
POMPER 4 (*pompé* 3, *pompééé* 1)
ponde v PONDRE
pondre v PONDRE
PONDRE 5 (*ponde* 4, *pondre* 1)
pont v PONT
PONT 4 (*pont*)
por, port₁ v PORT
port₂ v PORTER₁
PORT 30 (*por* 1, *port₁* 28, *pôrt* 1)
pôrt v PORT
port', porte v PORTER

+PORTE 84 (*la port* 10, *la port'* 2, *la porte* 15, *laporte* 51, *la-porte* 1, *lapôrte* 2, *laportes* 3)
porté, porter₁ v PORTER
porter₂ v **PORTER**
PORTER₁ 26 (*port₂* 11, *port'* 2, *porte* 2, *porté* 11)
PORTER₂ 1 (*porter₂*) [mot angl.]
PORTEUR 1 (*porter₁*)
portrait v PORTRAIT
PORTRAIT 3 (*portrait* 2, *portré* 1)
portré v PORTRAIT
pose₁ v POSER
pose₂ v PAUSER/ (RE)POSER
posé v PAUSER/ (RE)POSER
POSER 18 (*pose₁* 13, *poz₁* 5)
posère v POSEUR
POSEUR 1 (*posère*)
position v POSITION
POSITION 1 (*position*)
poss' v POCHE
possib', possibe, possible v POSSIBLE
POSSIBLE 3 (*possib'* 1, *possibe* 1, *possible* 1)
posson, pôsson, possons v POISSON
poste v POSTE
postè v POSTER
POSTE 5 (*poste*)
POSTER 1 (*postè*)
pot v POT
POT 3 (*pot*)
+POT 1 (*les pots*)
POT+DE+CHAMBRE 1 (*pôdeçambe*)
poteau v POTEAU
POTEAU 4 (*poteau* 1, *poto* 3)
poti v PETIT₁
potié v POTIER
POTIER 2 (*potié*)
poto v POTEAU
pou, pou' v POUR
pouce v POUCE
POUCE 5 (*pouce* 4, *pouces* 1)
pouces v POUCE

283

+POUDRE 8 (*la poude* 3, *la poudre* 1, *lapoude* 4)
Poudre d'or v POUDRE+ D'OR
POUDRE+D'OR 1 (*Poudre d'or*) [toponyme]
+POUDRE+D'OR 1 (*la poudre d'or*)
poul, poul' v POULE
poulailler v POULAILLER
POULAILLER 2 (*poulailler* 1, *poulaillers* 1)
poulaillers v POULAILLER
poule v POULE
POULE 32 (*poul* 1, *poul'* 1, *poule* 22, *poules* 8)
poules v POULE
poupon v POUPON
POUPON 1 (*poupon 1*)
pour v POUR
POUR 1452 (*pou* 7, *pou'* 1, *pour* 1442, *pour'* 2)[29]
pour' v POUR
pouritir v POURITURE
POURITURE 1 (*pouritir*)
pourki fair , pourkifair
  v POUR+QUE+ FAIRE
pourkoa v POURQUOI
POUR+QUE+FAIRE 54 (*pourki fair* 4, *pourkifair* 10, *pourqui faire* 1, *qui fair* 1, *qui fair'* 1, *qui-fair'* 3, *quifaire* 5, *qui faire* 20, *qui fer* 1, *qui fère* 7, *qui fère* 1)
pourqui faire
  v POUR+QUE+ FAIRE
pourquoi, pourquoy
  v POURQUOI
pouquoi v POURQUOI
POURQUOI 43 (*pourkoa* 1, *pouquoi* 1, *pourkoa* 8, *pourquoi* 32, *pourquoy* 1)
pouri, pourri v POURRI

[29] Malheureusement, ces données chiffrées ne distinguent pas entre le nombre relativement petit d'exemples de *pour* en tant que marqueur de futur et tous ces autres usages. Cette distinction est souvent difficile à établir en raison de contextes insufisants.

POURRI 8 (*pouri* 1, *pourri* 6, *pourrie* 1)
pourrie v POURRI
pourtan, pourtant
  v POURTANT
POURTANT 19 (*pourtan* 2, *pourtant* 17)
pourvi v POURVU
POURVU 1 (*pourvi*)
pous, pousée, pouss' , pousse
poussé v POUSSER
POUSSER 63 (*pous* 2, *pousée* 1, *pouss'* 3, *pousse* 42, *poussé* 15)
+POUSSIÈRE 3 (*la poussier* 2, *la poussière* 1)
pouvoar, pouvoir v POUVOIR
POUVOIR 3 (*pouvoar* 2, *pouvoir* 1)
poux v POUX
POUX 1 (*poux*)
+POUX 7 (*li pou* 2, *lipou* 4, *lipoux* 1)
pov, pov', pôve, povre v PAUVRE
poz$_1$ v POSER
poz$_2$ v PAUSER/ (RE)POSER
poz', poze, pozé
  v PAUSER/ (RE)POSER
praline v PRALINE
PRALINE 2 (*praline* 1, *pralines* 1)
pralines v PRALINE
pran, prand v PRENDRE
pran gar v PRENDRE+GARDE
pran gard
  v PRENDRE+GARDE
prangar' v PRENDRE+GARDE
prangard
  v PRENDRE+ GARDE
pratique v PRATIQUE
PRATIQUE 1 (*pratique*)
pratiqué v PRATIQUER
PRATIQUER 1 (*pratiqué*)
pré v PRÉ
PRÉ 1 (*pré*)
+PRÉ 4 (*lépré*)
précaution v PRÉCAUTION
PRÉCAUTION 1 (*précaution*)
preche, préche, préché
  v PRÊCHER

PRÊCHER 11 (*preche* 1, *préche* 4, *préché* 6)
précipice v PRÉCIPICE
PRÉCIPICE 3 (*précipice*)
préfère v PRÉFÉRER
PRÉFÉRER 1 (*préfère*)
preince v PRINCE
premié, prémié, premier
  v PREMIER
PREMIER 45 (*premié* 2, *prémié* 1, *premier* 4, *prémier* 10, *première* 6, *primier* 3, *promié* 20)
prémier, première v PREMIER
prend v PRENDRE
prend gard', prend garde, prend gare
  v PRENDRE+GARDE
prend' v PRENDRE
prend' gard', prend' garde
  v PRENDRE+GARDE
prende v PRENDRE
prendgare
  v PRENDRE+ GARDE
prendre v PRENDRE
PRENDRE 282 (*pran* 72, *prand* 2, *prend* 197, *prend'* 2, *prende* 4, *prendre* 2, *prends* 3)
PRENDRE+GARDE 53 (*pangar* 23, *pangard* 3, *pendgare* 5, *pends gar'* 1, *pran gar* 1, *pran gard* 4, *prangar* 7, *prangard* 1, *prend gard' , prend garde* 1, *prend gare* 2, *prend' gard'* 3, *prend' garde* 2, *prendgare* 1, *prend gard'* 1, *prends garde* 1)
prends v PRENDRE
prends gard', prends garde
  v PRENDRE+ GARDE
prepar, prépar v PRÉPARER
préparacion v PRÉPARATION
PRÉPARATION
  1 (*préparacion*)
préparé v PRÉPARER
PRÉPARER 10 (*prepar* 1, *prépar* 6, *préparé* 3)
près v PRÈS
PRÈS 3 (*près*)

présent v PRÉSENT
PRÉSENT 3 (*prézant*)
président v PRÉSIDENT
PRÉSIDENT 2 (*président*)
presque v PRESQUE
PRESQUE 1 (*presque*)
pressé v PRESSER
PRESSER 7 (*pressé*)
prêt v PRÊT(E)
PRÊT(E) 1 (*prêt*)
préte, prête, prête₁, prété, prétte, pretté v PRÊTER
prête₂ v PRÊTRE
prétend, prétend' v PRÉTENDRE
PRÉTENDRE 2 (*prétend* 1, *prétend'* 1)
PRÊTER 8 (*préte* 1, *prête₁* 3, *prété* 1, *prêté* 1, *prétte* 1, *pretté* 1)
pretes, pretr, prétr, prêtr', prêtre v PRÊTRE
PRÊTRE 48 (*prête₂* 6, *prète* 1, *pretes* 1, *pretr* 5, *prétr* 20, *prêtr* 1, *prêtr'* 1, *prêtre* 11, *prêtres* 2)
prêtres v PRÊTRE
+PREUVE 3 (*la preuve* 1, *la prév* 2)
PRÉVENIR 1 (*prévini*)
prévini v PRÉVENIR
prézan, prézant v PRÉSENT
pri₁ v PRIS
pri₂ v PRIX
pridan v PRUDENT
prie, prïe, prié, priée, prier v PRIER
PRIER 23 (*prie* 1, *prïe* 1, *prié* 6, *priée* 2, *prier* 1, *priye* 5, *priyé* 6, *prye* 1)
+PRIÈRE 25 (*la prière* 10, *la priyer* 4, *la priyér* 6, *la-priér* 1, *lapriére* 1, *lapriére* 2, *la-prière* 1)
primier v PREMIER
prince v PRINCE
PRINCE 26 (*prince* 23, *preince* 3)
+PRINCESSE 1 (*la princesse*)
prinelles v PRUNELLE
pris v PRIS(E)
PRIS 5 (*pri₁* 2, *pris* 3)

prise v PRISE
PRISE 1 (*prise*)
+PRISE 1 (*la prise*)
prison v PRISON
PRISON 16 (*prison* 6, *prizon* 10)
+PRISON 1 (*la prison*)
prisonniers v PRISONNIER
PRISONNIER 3 (*prisonniers* 1, *prizonié* 2)
priv v PRIVER
privé v PRIVÉ
PRIVÉ 2 (*privé*)
PRIVER 1 (*priv*)
prix v PRIX
PRIX 11 (*pri₂* 1, *prix* 10)
priye, priyé v PRIER
prizon v PRISON
prizonié v PRISONNIER
proç', proce, proces, proche v PROCHE
PROCHE 44 (*proç'* 1, *proce* 8, *proces* 2, *proche* 1, *pros* 28, *prosh* 2, *pross'* 2)
proclamation v PROCLAMATION
PROCLAMATION 1 (*proclamation*)
prodir v PRODUIRE
PRODUIRE 4 (*prodir*)
proféci v PROPHÉTIE
profet, profét, profete v PROPHÈTE
profétizé v PROPHÉTISER
profit, profiter v PROFITER
PROFITER 3 (*profit* 1, *profiter* 2)
profonder v PROFONDEUR
PROFONDEUR 1 (*profonder*)
progrès v PROGRÈS
PROGRÈS 2 (*progrès*)
prolongé v PROLONGER
PROLONGER 1 (*prolongé*)
prom'né v PROMENER
+PROMENADE 1 (*la prom'nade*)
promenant v PROMENANT
PROMENANT 1 (*promenant*)
promène, promené, proméné, prôméné, promener v PROMENER

PROMENER 29 (*prom'né* 2, *promène* 1, *promené* 10, *proméné* 5, *prôméné* 1, *promener* 2, *promné* 3, *proumener* 1, *proumouné* 4)
promet, promette v PROMETTRE
PROMETTRE 7 (*promet* 2, *promette* 2, *promie* 1, *promis* 2)
prométère v PROMETTEUR
PROMETTEUR 2 (*prométère*)
promie v PROMETTRE
promié v PREMIER
promis v PROMETTRE
promné v PROMENER
PRONONCER 1 (*pronons*)
pronons v PRONONCER
prop, prope v PROPRE
PROPHÈTE 40 (*profet* 37, *profét* 2, *profete* 1)
+PROPHÈTE 1 (*le profét*)
PROPHÉTIE 1 (*proféci*)
PROPHÉTISER 2 (*profétizé*)
proposé v PROPOSER
PROPOSER 3 (*proposé* 1, *propoz* 2)
PROPOSITION 1 (*propozicion*)
propoz v PROPOSER
propozicion v PROPOSITION
propre v PROPRE
PROPRE 19 (*prop* 8, *prope* 9, *propre* 2)
pros, prosh v PROCHE
Prosper v PROSPER
PROSPER 2 (*Prosper*) [prénom]
pross' v PROCHE
prostitié v PROSTITUÉE
PROSTITUÉE 2 (*prostitié*)
prot' v PROTÉGÉ (?)
protectèrs v PROTECTEUR
PROTECTEUR 2 (*protectèrs*)
PROTÉGÉ 1 (*prot'*)
proumener, proumouné v PROMENER
prouve v PROUVER
PROUVER 1 (*prouve*)
+PRUDE 1 (*la pride*)
PRUDENT 1 (*pridan*)
PRUNELLE 1 (*prinelles*)

prussien   v PRUSSIEN
PRUSSIEN 1 (*prussien*)
prye   v PRIER
pti, p'tit₁,p'tit'   v PETIT₁
p'tit₂   v PETIT₂
pti fi, pti fiye   v PETIT+FILLE
ptit   v PETIT₁
ptit fill', ptit fille, p'tit fille,
ptitfille   v PETIT+FILLE
ptit poucet v PETIT POUCET
p'tits, ptits v PETIT₁
PUANT   2 (*piant*)
PUBLIC₁ 2 (*piblik*) [adj]
PUBLIC₂ 1 (*piblique*) [n]
publicain v PUBLICAIN
PUBLICAIN 3 (*piblicain* 2,
    publicain 1)
PUCE   4 (*pices*)
PUER   7 (*pi₁*)
pui, puis   v PUIS
PUIS   14 (*pui* 1, *puis* 13)
PUISQUE 3 (*pisqué* 2,
    puisqui 1)
puisqui   v PUISQUE
+PUISSANCE 1 (*la pouissans*)
PUNAISE 3 (*pinaise* 1,
    pinaises 2)
PUNIR   14 (*pini* 13, *pinie* 1)
punission v PUNITION
PUNITION 4 (*pinicion* 3,
    punission 1)
PURGER 1 (*pirzé*)
PUTAIN 1 (*pit...*)
Pym   v PYM
PYM   1 (*Pym*) [nom de
    famille]

Q

qirpip'   v CUREPIPE
qu'   v QUE/QUI
qu'a même, qu'à même
    v QUAND-MEME
qu'y   v QUE/QUI
qua même v QUAND-MEME
qualité   v QUALITE
QUALITE 17 (*kalité* 4,
    qualité 11, *qualités* 2)
qualités   v QUALITE
quaméme, quamême
    v QUAND-MÊME
qua, quan, quand   v QUAND

QUAND   590 (*kan* 142, *qua* 6,
    quan 18, *quand* 422,
    quant 2)
quand mêm', quand' même,
quand même, quand' même',
quand' même, quand-même
    v QUAND-MÊME
QUAND-MÊME 84
    (*quaméme* 1, *quamême*12,
    qua même 2, *qu'a même* 1,
    qu'à même 3, *quand*
    mêm' 31, *quand même* 30,
    quand' même' 1, *quand'*
    même 1, *quand-même* 1)
quant   v QUAND
quantité   v QUANTITÉ
QUANTITÉ 1 (*quantité*)
quarante   v QUARANTE
QUARANTE 5 (*karant* 2,
    quarante 3)
QUART   1 (*kar*)
quartier   v QUARTIER
QUARTIER 10 (*cartier* 1,
    kartié 2, *quartier* 5,
    quartiers 2)
quartiers   v QUARTIER
quat', quate   v QUATRE
quate-laroues v QUATRE,
    +ROUE
quatorze   v QUATORZE
QUATORZE 4 (*katorz* 2,
    quatorze 2)
quatre   v QUATRE
QUATRE 51 (*kat* 3, *katr* 1,
    quat' 2, *quate* 29,
    quatre 16)
QUATRE-VINGT-DIX-NEUF
    2 (*katro-vein-diz-nef*)
quatrième v QUATRIÈME
QUATRIÈME   5 (*katriem* 1,
    quatrième 4)
que   v QUE
QUE/QUI 3022 (*ki* 977, *qu'* 15,
    que 21, *qui* 2008, *qu'y* 1)
quein'   v *qu', ein'*
quel   v QUEL
QUEL   1 (*quel*)
QUELQUE   94 (*kek* 4, *kik* 13,
    quelques 1, *quéque* 1,
    quéques 1, *quiq* 23, *quiq'*
    4, *quiqu'* 2, *quique* 43,
    quiques 2)

QUELQUE+CHOSE 81
    (*kikçoz* 39, *quet chose* 1,
    quichose 1, *qui'çose* 1,
    quiqçoce 1, *quiqçose* 5,
    quiqçoz' 2, *quiq'cose* 1,
    quiq'çose 6, *quiq'çoze* 3,
    quiqu'çoze 2, *quiqeçose*
    15, *quiqeçoses* 3,
    quiqeçôses 1,
    qui-qu'soz' 1)
quelques v QUELQUE
QUELQUEFOIS 35 (*kikfoa* 1,
    quequ'fois 1, *quéqu'fois*
    6, *quequefois* 2,
    quiquefois 25)
QUELQUEPART
    1 (*quiquepart*)
QUELQU'UN 14 (*kikéne* 5,
    kikène 1, *quequ'zein* 1,
    quéqu'zein 1, *quéquein'*
    1, *quéquén* 1, *quiqu'in* 1,
    quiquéne 2, *quiquène* 1)
quème quème   1 [origine
    inconnue]
quequ'fois, quéqu'fois
    v QUELQUEFOIS
quequ'zein, quéqu'zein
    v QUELQU'UN
quéque   v QUELQUE
quequefois v QUELQUEFOIS
quéquein', quéquén
    v QUELQU'UN
quéques   v QUELQUE
quérelle   v QUERELLE
QUERELLE 1 (*quérelle*)
QU'EST-CE+QUE 1 (*quesque*)
QU'EST-CE+QUE+C'EST+ÇA
    15 (*ki ci ça* 1, *ki-ci-ça* 1,
    qui ci ça 5, *qui ciça* 2, *qui*
    ci-ça 2, *qui ciça* 1, *qui ci-*
    çà 1, *qui sis-ça* 2)
quesque v QU'EST-CE+QUE
QUESTION 5 (*kestion* 4,
    questions 1)
QUESTIONNER 2 (*kestionne*)
questions v QUESTION
quet chose
    v QUELQUE+ CHOSE
+QUEUE 61 (*la qué* 5,
    la-qué 2, *laqué* 4, *laquée*
    48, *laquèe* 1, *laquées* 1)

quhaullxllhauxnhaillent
    v **COLONEL**
qui   v QUE/QUI
QUI   v QUE/QUI
*qui ci ça, qui ciça, qui ci-ça,
qui çiça, qui ci-çà*
    v QU'EST-CE+QUE+C'EST+ÇA
qui'ose, quichose
    v QUELQUE+ CHOSE
*qui fair, qui-fair', qui fair',
quifaire, qui faire, qui fer, qui
fére, qui fère*
    v POUR+QUE+ FAIRE
quilé   v (RE)CULER
quilote, quilotte   v CULOTTE
quime, quimé   v ÉCUMER
quinine   v QUININE
QUININE 2 (*quinine*)
quinze   v QUINZE
QUINZE 3 (*quinze*)
quiq, quiq' v QUELQUE
*quiq'cose, quiq'çose, quiq'çoze,
quiqçoce, quiqçose, quiqçoz'*
    v QUELQUE+CHOSE
quiqu'   v QUELQUE
quiqu'çoze
    v QUELQUE+CHOSE
quiqu'in   v QUELQU'UN
qui-qu'soz'
    v QUELQUE+ CHOSE
quique   v QUELQUE
*quiqueçose, quiqueçoses,
quiqueçôses*
    v QUELQUE+ CHOSE
quiquefois v QUELQUEFOIS
quiquéne, quiquène
    v QUELQU'UN
quiquepart v QUELQUEPART
quiques   v QUELQUE
quir-pipe   v CUREPIPE
qui sis-ça
    v QU'EST-CE+QUE+C'EST+ÇA
*quité, quitt', quitte, quitté,
quitter*   v QUITTER
QUITTER 80 (*kit* 21, *quité* 3,
    quitt' 3, *quitte* 43,
    quitté 9, *quitter* 1)
quivettes   v CUVETTE
quoi   v QUOI
QUOI   7 (*koa* 1, *quoi* 6)

R

rabot   v RABOT
RABOT   2 (*rabot*)
RACCOMMODER
    1 (*racomod*)
race₁   v RACE
race₂   v ARRACHER
RACE   13 (*race₁* 12, *ras* 1)
racé   v ARRACHER
Racel   2 *RUSSELL
raci   v RASSIR
racine   v RACINE
RACINE   8 (*racine* 5,
    racines 3)
racines   v RACINE
râclé   v RÂCLÉE
RÂCLÉE   1 (*râclé*)
racomod v RACCOMMODER
racont, racont', raconte
    v RACONTER
RACONTER 30 (*racont* 3,
    racont' 2, *raconte* 25)
+RADE   3 (*la rade* 2,
    la rades 1)
raffiné   v RAFFINER
RAFFINER 1 (*raffiné*)
RAFIA   1 (*rafias*)
rafias   v RAFIA
raflé   v RAFLER
RAFLER   1 (*raflé*)
+RAGE   3 (*la raz* 1,
    la raze 2)
ragoutant v RAGOÛTANT
RAGOÛTANT 1 (*ragoutant*)
raid, raide v RAIDE
RAIDE   10 (*raid* 1, *raide* 6,
    rêd' 1, *réde* 2)
RAIDIR   3 (*rèd'* 1, *rèd'* 1,
    rédi 1)
+RAIE 2 (*la raie*)
+RAIL 1 (*lérails*)
raisin   v RAISIN
RAISIN   4 (*raisin* 1, *rézein* 3)
raison   v RAISON
RAISON   28 (*raison* 24,
    raisons 3, *rézon* 1)
+RAISON 4 (*la raison*)
raisonable v RAISONABLE
RAISONABLE 2 (*raisonable*
    1, *rézonab* 1)

RAISONNER 2 (*résonné* 1,
    rézonné 1)
raisons   v RAISON
rakét   v RAQUETTE
*ramas, ramass', ramasse,
ramassé* v (R)AMASSER
(R)AMASSER 61 (*armasse* 1,
    ramas 11, *ramass'* 4,
    ramasse 27, *ramassé* 18,
    rammasé 1)
ramé   v RAMER
RAMER   1 (*ramé*)
rammasé v (R)AMASSER
REMPART 3 (*Grampant* 1,
    Grampart 2) [toponyme :
    Rivière-du-Rempart]
rampli   v REMPLIR
rançon   v RANÇON
RANÇON 1 (*rançon*)
ranconte, rancontr
    v RENCONTRE
rand, randé v RENDRE
rantr, rantré v RENTRER
ranversé v RENVERSER
ranvoy, ranvoyé
    v RENVOYER
ranze, ranzé v ARRANGER
rapé   v RÂPER
RÂPER   1 (*rapé*)
raport   v RAPPORTER
rapp'lé, rappelé v RAPPELER
RAPPELER 6 (*rapplé* 1,
    rapp'lé 1, *rappelé* 3,
    rappelez 1)
rappelez, rapplé v RAPPELER
rapport₁   v RAPPORT
rapport₂   v RAPPORTER
RAPPORT 1 (*rapport₁*)
RAPPORTER 10 (*raport* 7,
    rapport₂ 3)
raquette, raquettes
    v RAQUETTE
RAQUETTE   4 (*rakét* 1,
    raquette 3, *raquettes* 1)
rare   v RARE
RARE   1 (*rare*)
ras ·   v RACE
RASOIR 3 (*razoir* 2, *razoire* 1)
rassamblé v RASSEMBLER
RASSASIÉ   3 (*rassazié*)
rassazié   v RASSASIÉ
rassemblé v RASSEMBLER

RASSEMBLER 12 (*rassamblé* 10, *rassemblé* 2)
rassi v RASSIR
RASSIR 2 (*raci* 1, *rassi* 1)
+RAT 51 (*le ra* 1, *lé ra* 2, *lé rat* 12, *lérat* 16, *lé-rat* 9, *lérats* 4, *lé-rats* 5, *lira* 2)
raté v RATER
RATER 1 (*raté*)
ration v RATION
RATION 4 (*ration* 2, *rations* 2)
rations v RATION
Ratsitatane v RATSITATANE
RATSITATANE 1 (*Ratsitatane*) [nom d'un prince malg.]
RAVAGE 2 (*ravaze*)
ravanne v **IRAVÂNAM**
ravaze v RAVAGE
rave v RAVE
RAVE 1 (*rave*)
ravenalle, ravenals, ravenelle v **RÁVINÁLA**
Ravet v RAVET
RAVET 1 (*Ravet*)
RÁVINÁLA 5 (*ravenalle* 1, *ravenals* 2, *ravenelle* 1, *ravnal's* 1) [mot malg.]
+RAVINE 1 (*la-ravine*)
ravnal's v **RÁVINÁLA**
razoir, razoire v RASOIR
REBÂTIR 1 (*rébatir*)
rébatir v REBÂTIR
recevoar, récévoar v RECEVOIR
RECEVOIR 17 (*recevoar* 5, *récévoar* 12)
RECHANGE 1 (*ressanze*)
+RECHERCHE 1 (*la recerce*)
RÉCIF 1 (*récifs*)
récifs v RÉCIF
+RÉCOLTE 6 (*la récolt*)
récolté v RÉCOLTER
RÉCOLTER 5 (*récolté*)
récommand v RECOMMANDER
RECOMMANDER 1 (*récommand*)
recommence v RECOMMENCER

RECOMMENCER 1 (*recommence*)
*récompans*₁ v RÉCOMPENSE
*récompans*₂, *récompense* v RÉCOMPENSER
RÉCOMPENSE 9 (*récompans*₁)
RÉCOMPENSER 4 (*récompans*₂ 3, *récompense* 1)
réconnét v RECONNAÎTRE
RECONNAÎTRE 1 (*réconnét*)
RECULER 6 (*arqilé* 1, *arquilé* 3, *arquiler* 1, *arquillé* 1)
(RE)CULER 1 (*quilé*)
rèd' v RAIDIR
rêd' v RAIDE
réde v RAIDE
rédi v RAIDIR
Redl v REDL
REDL 1 (*Redl* 1) [nom de famille prussien]
Réduit v RÉDUIT
RÉDUIT 1 (*Réduit*) [nom d'un village]
réfisé v REFUSER
RÉFLÉCHIR 1 (*réfléci*)
réfléci v RÉFLÉCHIR
réfusé v REFUSER
REFUSER 3 (*réfisé* 2, *réfusé* 1)
RÉGATE 1 (*régates*)
régates v RÉGATE
RÉGIME 5 (*rézime*)
régiment v RÉGIMENT
RÉGIMENT 4 (*régiment* 1, *réziman* 2, *réziment* 1)
+RÉGIMENT 1 (*le réziman*)
+RÈGLE 1 (*la règle*)
réglé v RÉGLER
RÉGLER 6 (*réglé* 4, *règue* 2)
Régnaud 1 [nom de famille]
RÈGNE 1 (*reïn*)
+RÈGNE 1 (*le reïn*)
règue v RÉGLER
+REIN 23 (*lé rein* 3, *lé reins* 2, *lé rin* 1, *lérein* 1, *lé-rein* 4, *léreins* 11, *lérin* 1)
reïn v RÈGNE
+REINE 29 (*la reine* 17, *lareine* 12)
reinté v ÉREINTER

REJETER 1 (*rézété*)
+RELIGION 2 (*la r'lizion* 1, *la religion* 1)
rémark v REMARQUER
REMARQUER 1 (*rémark*)
remercie, rémercié v REMERCIER
REMERCIER 4 (*remercie* 2, *rémercié* 2)
remet, rémet, rémette v REMETTRE
REMETTRE 5 (*remet* 3, *rémet* 1, *rémette* 1)
rémonte, rémontée v REMONTER
REMONTER 3 (*rémonte* 2, *rémontée* 1)
rémor v REMORDS
REMORDS 1 (*rémor*)
rempar, rempart v REMPART
REMPART 8 (*rempar* 1, *rempart* 7)
remplace v REMPLACER
remplacé v REMPLACER
REMPLACER 3 (*remplace* 2, *remplacé* 1)
rempli v REMPLIR
REMPLIR 12 (*rampli* 3, *rempli* 9)
remué v REMUER
REMUER 1 (*remué*)
rénar, renard v RENARD
RENARD 3 (*rénar* 1, *renard* 2)
RENCONTRE 9 (*ranconte* 5, *rancontr* 4)
rend, rend', rende, rendé, rendée, rendie v RENDRE
RENDRE 58 (*rand* 10, *randé* 1, *rend* 2, *rend'* 11, *rende* 21, *rendé* 12, *rendée* 1, *rendie* 1)
renfrogn', renfrogné v RENFROGNER
RENFROGNER 2 (*renfrogn'* 1, *renfrogné* 1)
renié, rénié v RENIER
RENIER 4 (*renié* 2, *rénié* 2)
rénomé v RENOMMÉE
RENOMMÉE 1 (*rénomé*)
+RENTE 1 (*la rente*)

rente, rentent, rentre, rentré,
rentrer   v RENTRER
RENTRER 135 (*rantr* 36,
  rantré 9, *rente* 43, *rentent*
  1, *rentre* 1, *rentré* 36,
  rentrer 2)[30]
renverse, renversée
       v RENVERSER
RENVERSER 2 (*ranversé* 1,
  renverse 1, *renversée* 1)
RENVOYER 15 (*ranvoy* 14,
  ranvoyé 1)
répand   v RÉPANDRE
RÉPANDRE 1 (*répand*)
répanti   v REPENTIR
réparation v RÉPARATION
RÉPARATION 1 (*réparation*)
répare   v RÉPARER
RÉPARER 1 (*répare*)
repentie, repentir v REPENTIR
REPENTIR 11 (*répanti* 7,
  repentie 4, *repentir* 1)
répère   v REPÉRER
REPÉRER 1 (*répère*)
répét, répète, répété
       v RÉPÉTER
RÉPÉTER 4 (*répét* 1, *répète* 1,
  répété 1, *répétez* 1)
répétez   v RÉPÉTER
répitation v RÉPUTATION
repond, répond, repond',
répond', réponde, repondé,
répondé   v RÉPONDRE
répondeir v RÉPONDEUR
RÉPONDEUR 1 (*répondeir*)
RÉPONDRE 109 (*repond* 2,
  répond 56, *repond'* 1,
  répond' 5, *réponde* 30,
  repondé 1, *répondé* 14)
répons, réponse v RÉPONSE
RÉPONSE 4 (*répons* 1,
  réponse 3)
+RÉPONSE 3 (*la réponse* 1,
  laréponse 1, *laréponses* 1)
reposé   v REPOSER
REPOSER 1 (*reposé*)
réproce   v REPROCHE
REPROCHE 4 (*réproce* 2,
  reprosh 2)

reprosh   v REPROCHE
+RÉPUBLIQUE
       1 (*la république*)
RÉPUTATION 1 (*répitation*)
requête   v REQUÊTE
REQUÊTE 1 (*requête*)
réquin   v REQUIN
REQUIN 1 (*réquin*)
RÉSISTER 1 (*rézist*)
rés'ment
       v HEUREUSEMENT
résonné   v RAISONNER
respect   v RESPECTER
RESPECTER 6 (*respect* 5,
  respée 1)
respée   v RESPECTER
ressamblé v RESSEMBLER
ressanze v RECHANGE
resse   v RESTER
RESSEMBLANCE
       1 (*samblance*)
ressemblant v RESSEMBLANT
RESSEMBLANT
       1 (*ressemblant*)
ressemblé v RESSEMBLER
RESSEMBLER 6 (*ressamblé*
  5, *ressemblé* 1)
rest   v RESTER
rést, rest'   v RESTER
restan, restant$_1$ v RESTANT$_1$
restant$_2$ v RESTANT$_2$
RESTANT$_1$ 7 (*restan* 2,
  restant$_1$ 5) [adj]
RESTANT$_2$ 1 (*restant*$_2$) [n]
+RESTANT 3 (*larestant*)
+RESTE 1 (*lerest*)
reste, réste, resté, rester
       v RESTER
RESTER 110 (*resse* 3, *rest* 17,
  rést 1, *rest'* 1, *reste* 41,
  réste 3, *resté* 41, *rester* 1,
  restez 2)
restez   v RESTER
RÉSURRECTION
       3 (*rézirekcion*)
+RÉSURRECTION 2
       (*la rézirekcion* 1,
       la rézirékcion 1)
RETENIR 1 (*rétien*)
rétien   v RETENIR
retourn, rétourn, retourné
       v RETOURNER

RETOURNER 7 (*retourn* 2,
  rétourn 3, *retourné* 2)
rev, rév   v RÊVE
RÊVE   6 (*rev* 3, *rév* 3)
rève, rêvé v RÊVER
RÊVER   5 (*rève* 2, *rêvé* 3)
REVENIR 2 (*revini* 1, *révini* 1)
révérence   v RÉVÉRENCE
RÉVÉRENCE 1 (*révérence*)
revini, révini v REVENIR
révolt, révolté v RÉVOLTER
RÉVOLTER 2 (*révolt* 1,
  révolté 1)
rézein   v RAISIN
rézété   v REJETER
réziman, réziment
       v RÉGIMENT
rézime   v RÉGIME
rézirekcion
       v RÉSURRECTION
rézist   v RÉSISTER
rézon   v RAISON
rézonab   v RAISONABLE
rézonné   v RAISONNER
rheisement
       v HEUREUSEMENT
rhum   v RHUM/**RUM**
RHUM/**RUM** 8 (*rhum* 5,
  rum 3)
+RHUME 4 (*la rhim'* 1,
  larhime 3)
riban   v RUBAN
RIBOTER 1 (*ribotté*)
ribotté   v RIBOTER
riç', rice   v RICHE
Rice-en-eau
       v RICHE-EN-EAU
rices, riche v RICHE
RICHE   26 (*riç'* 2, *rice* 17,
  rices 1, *riche* 1,
  rish 4, *risse*$_1$ 1)
RICHE-EN-EAU 1 (*Rice-en-
  eau*) [nom de lieu]
RIDE   1 (*rides*)
rides   v RIDE
rïe, rié   v RIRE
rien que   v RIEN+QUE
RIEN+QUE 2 (*rien que* 1, *rien
  qui* 1)
rien qui   v RIEN+QUE
riés   v RIRE
rigaudon v RIGAUDON

---

[30] Sens moderne en CM et en fr. : « entrer »

RIGAUDON 1 (*rigaudon*)	RÔLE 4 (*rôle*)	ROUPIE 15 (*roupies* 10, *Rs* 5)
rinté v ÉREINTER	*romanç'*, *romance*	*roupies* v ROUPIE
riperipé v RIPER	v ROMANCE	*roussi* v ROUSSIR
RIPER 1 (*riperipé*)	ROMANCE 3 (*romanç'* 1, *romance* 2)	ROUSSIR 1 (*roussi*)
rire v RIRE		+ROUTE 5 (*la rout'* 1, *la route* 4)
RIRE 106 (*rïe* 1, *rié* 101, *riés* 1, *rire* 2, *riyé* 1)	*rond₁* v ROND₁	
	rond₂ v ROND₂	*rouvri* v ROUVRIR
rise v RUSE	ROND₁ 2 (*rond₁*) [adj]	ROUVRIR 1 (*rouvri*)
rish, *risse₁* v RICHE	ROND₂ 5 (*rond₂*) [n]	*rouz*, *rouz'*, *rouze*, *rouzerouze*,
risse₂ v HISSER	+ROND 1 (*lérond*)	*rouzes* v ROUGE
risseaux v RUISSEAU	*rondaze* v RONDAGE	ROYAUME 43 (*roayom*)
Ristikéli 1 [nom de famille]	RONDAGE 1 (*rondaze*)	+ROYAUME 10 (*le roayom* 5, *lé roayom* 5)
Rita 2 [prénom féminin]	+RONDE 4 (*la ronde* 1, *laronde* 2, *la-ronde* 1)	
+RIVIÈRE 65 (*la rivier* 3, *la riviér* 3, *la rivièr'* 2, *la riviere* 1, *la rivière* 26, *lariviére* 1, *larivière* 28, *la-rivière* 1)		*rozo* v ROSEAU
	ronferonflé, *ronfl'*, *ronfle*, *ronflé* v RONFLER	*Rs* v ROUPIE
		RUBAN 3 (*riban*)
	RONFLER 20 (*ronferonflé* 1, *ronfl'* 1, *ronfle* 2, *ronflé* 16)	+RUCHE 1 (*la ruche*)
		+RUE 17 (*la ri* 3, *la rie* 9, *larie* 3, *laries* 2)
riyé v RIRE		
+RIZ 52 (*di-riz* 1, *douri* 8, *douriz* 35, *dou riz* 5, *du riz* 3)	*rose₁* v ROSE₁	*ruiné* v RUINER
	Rose₂ v ROSE₂	RUINER 1 (*ruiné*)
	ROSE₁ 9 (*rose*) [fleur, couleur])	RUISSEAU 2 (*risseaux*)
roastbeef v **ROAST+BEEF**		*Rule Britannia* v RULE BRITANNIA
ROAST+BEEF 1 (*roastbeef*) [mot angl.]	ROSE₂ 4 (*Rose*) [prénom]	RULE BRITANNIA 1 (*Rule Britannia*) [chanson anglaise]
	+ROSE 1 (*la rose*)	
roayom v ROYAUME	ROSEAU 1 (*rozo*)	
rob, *rob'*, *robe*, *robe*, *robes* v ROBE	*Rose Belle* v ROSE+BELLE	*rum* v RHUM/**RUM**
	ROSE+BELLE 3 (*Rose Belle*)	**RUM** v RHUM/**RUM**
ROBE 25 (*rob* 3, *rob'* 3, *robe* 13, *rôbe* 1, *robes* 5)	*rosse* v ROCHE	RUSE 1 (*rise*)
	rotein v ROTIN	+RUSE 1 (*la riz*)
+ROBE 1 (*larobe*)	*rôti* v **ROṬĪ**	*Russell 2 (*Racel*)
roce, *roces*, *roche* v ROCHE	**ROṬĪ** 3 (*rôti*) [mot hind.]	
ROCHE 94 (*roce* 70, *roces* 16, *roche* 4, *rosse* 4)	*rotin* v ROTIN	# S
	ROTIN 4 (*rotein* 2, *rotin* 2)	
+ROCHE 1 (*laroce*)	+ROUE 5 (*laroue* 2, *laroues* 3)	*sa*, *sà* v ÇA
rod, *rod'*, *rode*, *rôde*, *rodé*, *rôdé*, v RÔDER		*sab*, *sabe* v SABRE
	rougaill' v ŪRU-KĄY	+SABLE 11 (*di sab* 1, *di sabe* 3, *di sable* 1, *lasabe* 6)
	rouge v ROUGE	
RÔDER 73 (*rod* 8, *rod'* 3, *rode* 22, *rôde* 21, *rodé* 11, *rôdé* 8)	ROUGE 38 (*rouge* 3, *rouz* 2, *rouz'* 2, *rouze* 29, *rouzerouze* 1, *rouzes* 1)	*saboulé* v SABOULÉ
		SABOULÉ 1 (*saboulé*)
		Sabour v SABOUR
rogné v ROGNÉ	+ROUGEOLE 1 (*la rouzeole*)	SABOUR 34 (*Sabour*) [nom de personnage]
ROGNÉ 1 (*rogné*)	+ROUILLE 3 (*larouille* 1, *la rouy* 2)	
roi v ROI		*sabre* v SABRE
ROI 18 (*roi*) [adresse au roi]	*roul* v ROULER	SABRE 9 (*sab* 6, *sabe* 1, *sabre* 2)
	ROULADE 1 (*roulades*)	
+ROI 371 (*lé roa* 25, *léroi* 275, *lèroi* 1, *lé-roi* 16, *le roi* 3, *lé roi* 47, *lè roi* 2, *lérois* 3, *lé-roy* 1)	*roulades* 1 ROULADE	*sac* v SAC
	roule, *roulé* v ROULER	SAC 70 (*sac* 66, *sacs* 3, *saque* 1)
	ROULER 29 (*roul* 2, *roule* 15, *roulé* 12)	
		sa caine v CHACUN
	roulis v ROULIS	*sacalié* v ESCALIER
rôle v RÔLE	ROULIS 1 (*roulis*)	

saclave v ESCLAVE
sacouy, sacouye, sacouyé
    v SECOUER
sacré v SACRÉ
SACRÉ 4 (*sacré*)
SACRÉ+COQUIN
    1 (*crécoquin*)
sacrifice v SACRIFICE
SACRIFICE 3 (*sacrifice*)
sacs v SAC
safran v SAFRAN
SAFRAN 2 (*safran*)
SAGAIE 9 (*sagaïe* 2, *sagaye* 4, *sagayes* 3)
sagaïe, sagaye, sagayes
    v SAGAIE
sage v SAGE
SAGE 26 (*sage* 2, *saz* 2, *saze* 21, *sazes* 1)
SAGESSE 1 (*sazesse*)
+SAGESSE 1 (*la sagesse*)
sagrin, sagrinne v CHAGRIN
SAILLER 1 (*saiyé*)
SAIN 5 (*sén*)
saint v SAINT$_1$
SAINT$_1$ 11 (*saint* 3, *sainte*$_1$ 7, *saintes* 1) [adj]
SAINT$_2$ 1 (*sainte*$_2$) [n]
saint espri v SAINT+ESPRIT
sainte$_1$ v SAINT$_1$
sainte$_2$ v SAINT$_2$
+SAINTE+CÈNE 3 (*la sainte cène* 2, *la sainte-cène* 1)
+SAINTE+ÉCRITURE 1 (*le saint-ecritire*)
sainte esprit, sainte-esprit
    v SAINT+ESPRIT
sainte-rita v SAINTE+RITA
SAINTE RITA 2 (*sainte-rita*)
saintes v SAINT$_1$
SAINT+ESPRIT 15 (*saint espri* 8, *sainte esprit* 1, *sainte-esprit* 1, *saint-esprit* 5)
saint-esprit v SAINT+ESPRIT
sainteté v SAINTETÉ
SAINTETÉ 2 (*sainteté* 1, *saintété* 1)
saintété v SAINTETÉ
Saint Pierre v SAINT+PIERRE
SAINT+PIERRE 1 (*Saint Pierre*)
saisi v SAISIR

SAISIR 8 (*saisi* 5, *sézi* 3)
saison v SAISON
SAISON 3 (*saison* 1, *sézon* 2)
+SAISON 4 (*la sézon* 2, *lasaison* 1, *la-saison* 1)
saison d'hiver
    v SAISON+D'HIVER
SAISON+D'HIVER
    1 (*saison d'hiver*)
sais pas v SAIS+PAS
SAIS+PAS 101 (*ci pas* 1, *sais pas* 2, *sipa* 5, *sipas* 50, *si pa* 2, *si pas* 31, *si-pas* 5, *sis pas* 2, *sis-pas* 3)
saiyé v SAILLER
sakabar v **TSA+KABAR**
sal$_1$ v SALER
sal$_2$ v SALLE
salade v SALADE
SALADE 5 (*salade*)
SALAIRE 1 (*saler*)
salaison v SALAISON
SALAISON 1 (*salaison*)
salam v **SALAM** [mot ar.]
SALAM 17 (*salam*)
sale v SALE
SALE 12 (*sale*)
salé v SALÉ
SALÉ 10 (*salé* 8, *salée* 2)
salée v SALÉ
saler v SALAIRE
SALER 1 (*sal*$_1$)
saleté v SALETÉ
SALETÉ 1 (*saleté*)
salié v SALUER
Salie-Marie
    v SALUER+MARIE
+SALINE 1 (*la saline*)
SALLE 1 (*sal*$_2$)
+SALLE 11 (*la sal* 2, *la sall'* 1, *la salle* 3, *lasalle* 5)
sallon, salon v SALON
SALON 7 (*sallon* 1, *salon* 6)
salue v SALUT
SALUER 5 (*salié*)
SALUER+MARIE 1 (*Salie-Marie*)[31]
SALUT 3 (*salue*)
+SALUT 1 (*le salue*)

---

[31] Prière catholique qui commence *Je vous salue, Marie.*

sam'di, sam'dis v SAMEDI
sambe v ENSEMBLE
samblan v SEMBLANT
samblance
    v RESSEMBLANCE
same v ENSEMBLE
samedi v SAMEDI
SAMEDI 4 (*sam'di* 2, *sam'dis* 1, *samedi* 1)
san v SANS
sanctifié v SANCTIFIER
SANCTIFIER 1 (*sanctifié*)
sandèles v CHANDELLE
+SANG 33 (*diçan* 1, *disan* 1, *di san* 15, *di sang* 3, *disang* 12, *di sen* 1)
SANGLE 1 (*sangue*)
sangsie v SANGSUE
SANGSUE 6 (*sangsie* 4, *sansie* 2)
sangue v SANGLE
sans v SANS
SANS 128 (*san* 18, *sans* 110)
sans-façon v SANS+FAÇON
SANS+FAÇON 1 (*sans-façon*)
sansouci, san-souci
    v SANS+SOUCI
sans peine v SANS+PEINE
SANS+PEINE 2 (*sans peine*)
sans-souci v SANS+SOUCI
SANS+SOUCI 28 (*Sansouci* 4, *San-souci* 1, *Sans-souci* 16, *Sans souci* 7)[32]
santé v SANTÉ
SANTÉ 3 (*santé*) [toast]
+SANTÉ 2 (*la santé*)
santié v SENTIER
sanzé v CHANGER
sap, sape, sapé v ÉCHAPPER
sapeau, sapo v CHAPEAU
saperlotte v SAPERLOTTE
SAPERLOTTE 1 (*saperlotte*)
saplé v CHAPELET
saque v SAC
sa quène, saquène v CHACUN
sardine v SARDINE
SARDINE 1 (*sardine*)
sarment v SERMENT
sarretier v CHARRETIER

---

[32] 27 de ces formes sont des noms d'un personnage ou d'un animal.

sarette	v CHARRETTE	
sarrié	v CHARRIER	
sarron	v CHARRON	
sartié	v CHARRETIER	
sasse, sassé	v CHASSER	
Satan	v SATAN	
SATAN	4 (*Satan*)	
satin	v SATIN	
SATIN	2 (*satin*)	
satte	v CHAT	
+SAUCE	1 (*la sauce*)	
saucisse	v SAUCISSE	
SAUCISSE	2 (*saucisse* 1, *saucisses* 1)	
saucisses	v SAUCISSE	
saucisson	v SAUCISSON	
SAUCISSON	1 (*saucisson*)	
saut'	v SAUTER	
sautant	v SAUTANT	
SAUTANT	1 (*sautant*)	
saute, sauté, sauter		v SAUTER
SAUTER	78 (*saut'* 2, *saute* 50, *sauté* 24, *sauter* 2)	
sauterelle	v SAUTERELLE	
SAUTERELLE	15 (*sauterelle* 14, *sotrél* 1)	
sautres	v AUTRE₃	
sauvage	v SAUVAGE	
SAUVAGE	2 (*sauvage* 1, *sovaz* 1)	
sauvais, sauvait, sauve, sauvé		v SAUVER
SAUVER	78 (*sauvais* 6, *sauvait* 1, *sauve* 14, *sauvé* 38, *sauvés* 1, *sov* 14, *sové* 4)	
sauvés	v SAUVER	
sava	v ÇA+VA	
+SAVANNE	8 (*la savanne*)	
savant	v SAVANT	
SAVANT	2 (*savant*)	
SAVATE	2 (*savates* 1, *savatte* 1)	
savates, savatte	v SAVATE	
savon	v SAVON	
SAVON	3 (*savon*)	
saye, sayé	v ESSAYER	
saz, saze, sazes	v SAGE	
sazesse	v SAGESSE	
sazinée	v ASSASSINER	
SCÉLÉRAT	1 (*scélérats*)	

scélérats	v SCÉLÉRAT	
scellé	v SCELLER	
SCELLER	1 (*scellé*)	
+SCIE	3 (*la scie* 1, *lascie* 2)	
SCIPION	1 (*coudesipion*) [prénom]	
scrib	v SCRIBE	
SCRIBE	23 (*scrib*)	
sé	v C'EST	
SÉAU	3 (*séaux* 2, *séo* 1)³³	
séaux	v SÉAU	
sec	v SEC	
SEC	73 (*sec* 57, *séc* 12, *secs* 1, *séque* 1, *sèque* 2)	
séc	v SEC	
séclâv', séclaves	v ESCLAVE	
second	v SECOND²	
SECOND¹	17 (*sécond* 10, *second'* 1, *ségon* 3, *ségond* 3) [adj]	
SECOND²	1 (*second*) [n]	
sécond, second'	v SECOND¹	
SECOUER	23 (*sacouy* 1, *sacouye* 13, *sacouyé* 9)	
SECOURS	4 (*sicour²* 1, *sicoure* 1, *sicours²* 2)	
sécré	v SECRET	
SECRET	3 (*sécré* 2, *secret* 1)	
sécret	v SECRET	
sécrétaire	v SECRETAIRE	
SECRÉTAIRE	2 (*sécrétaire*)	
secs	v SEC	
sega, séga	v CEGA	
ségon, ségond	v SECOND¹	
seigneir, seigner, seignere, seigneur		v SEIGNEUR
SEIGNEUR	55 (*seigneir* 1, *seigner* 1, *seignere* 1, *seigneur* 8, *sénier* 39, *seniér* 1, *séniér* 4)	
+SEIGNEUR	13 (*le seigneur* 2, *le sénier* 10, *lé séniér* 1)	
+SEINE	7 (*laseine* 1, *la seine* 1, *lasèné* 2, *la séne* 3)	
seir, seirs	v SOEUR	
sel, sél, séle	v SEUL	
+SEL	7 (*di sel* 5, *disel* 2)	
sél'ment, selman, sélment		v SEULEMENT

³³ Forme dial. bisyllabique. Le mot standard, *seau*, est monosyllabique.

SELON	4 (*sélon*)	
sélon	v SELON	
sels, séls	v tout séls	
sem, sém	v SEMER	
SEMAINE	3 (*sémaine* 1, *sémen* 1, *simaine* 1)	
+SEMAINE	4 (*la s'maine* 1, *la semaine* 3)	
sémaine	v SEMAINE	
semb, semb', sembe, sembl'		v ENSEMBLE
semblant	v SEMBLANT	
SEMBLANT	19 (*samblan* 1, *semblant* 18)	
semble	v ENSEMBLE	
semblé	v SEMBLER	
SEMBLER	1 (*semblé*)	
semé, sémé	v SEMER	
sémen	v SEMAINE	
+SEMENCE	1 (*la semence*)	
semer	v SEMEUR	
SEMER	8 (*sem* 4, *sém* 1, *semé* 1, *sémé* 2)	
sémer	v SEMEUR	
SEMEUR	3 (*semer* 1, *sémer* 2)	
sén	v SAIN	
senger	v CHANGER	
sénier, seniér, séniér		v SEIGNEUR
s'en mélé	v S'EN+MÊLER	
S'EN+MÊLER	3 (*s'en mélé*)	
s'en passé	v S'EN+PASSER	
S'EN+PASSER	1 (*s'en passé*)	
sens	v SENS	
SENS	2 (*sens*)	
sensé	v SENSÉ	
SENSÉ	3 (*çançé* 1, *sensé* 2)	
senti	v SENTIR	
sentié	v SENTIER	
SENTIER	1 (*santié*)	
sentiment	v SENTIMENT	
SENTIMENT	10 (*sentiment* 8, *sentiments* 2)	
sentiments	v SENTIMENT	
sentinelle	v SENTINELLE	
SENTINELLE	4 (*sentinelle*)	
SENTIR	47 (*senti*)	
s'en vanté	v S'EN+VANTER	
S'EN+VANTER	1 (*s'en vanté*)	
séo	v SÉAU	
sépar, séparé, séparée		v SÉPARER

SÉPARER 4 (sépar 2, séparé 1, séparée 1)	servant', servante v SERVANTE	siéze v SIÈGE
SE+PLAINDRE 1 (souplaigné)	SERVANTE 5 (servant' 1, servante 3, servantes 1)	si-fais v SI+FAIT
sept v SEPT		sifait, si fait v SI+FAIT
SEPT 28 (sept 4, set 12, sète 1, septe 10, sette 1)	servantes v SERVANTE	SI+FAIT 30 (si-fais 1, sifait 3, si fait 14, si fé 1, sifé 5, sifet 1, sifét 5)
septe v SEPT	servi v SERVIR	
septembre v SEPTEMBRE	service v SERVICE	
SEPTEMBRE 1 (septembre)	SERVICE 9 (service)	si fé, sifé, sifet, sifét v SI+FAIT
septième v SEPTIÈME	servie v SERVIR	siffoqué v SUFFOQUER
SEPTIÈME 1 (septième)	serviette v SERVIETTE	sign' v SIGNE
séque, sèque v SEC	SERVIETTE 4 (serviette 1, serviettes 3)	signale v SIGNALE
ser, sèr' v SOEUR		SIGNALE 1 (signale) [n]
sérail v SÉRAIL	serviettes v SERVIETTE	signataire v SIGNATURE
SÉRAIL 1 (sérail)	SERVIR 39 (servi 31, servie 8)	SIGNATURE 2 (signataire)
serce v CHERCHER		$signe_1$ v SIGNE
sère v CHER	serviter v SERVITEUR	$signe_2$ v SIGNER
séré v SERRÉ	SERVITEUR 12 (serviter)	SIGNE 11 (sign' 1, $signe_1$ 2, $siin_1$ 8)
SERGEANT/SERGENT 1 (serzent)[34]	serzent v **SERGEANT** / SERGENT	
		signé v SIGNER
SERGENT v **SERGEANT**/ SERGENT	ses v SES	SIGNER 5 ($signe_2$ 1, signé 3, $siin_2$ 1)
	SES 1 (ses)	
sérié v SÉRIEUX	set, sète, sette v SEPT	$siin_1$ v SIGNE
serine, sérine v TISSERINE	SEUL 3 (sel 1, sél 1, séle 1) v aussi TOUT+SEUL	$siin_2$ v SIGNER
sérire v SERRURE		simaine v SEMAINE
SÉRIEUX 1 (sérié)	SEULEMENT 4 (selman 2, sélment 1, sél'ment 1)	simbou v **SIMBU**
serman, serment v SERMENT		**SIMBU** 1 (simbou) [mot tam.][35]
SERMENT 27 (sarment 2, serman 17, serment 8)	séver v SÉVÈRE	
	SÉVÈRE 2 (séver)	simiroués v **TSIMIROUHI**
sermon v SERMON	sévré v SÉVRER	simise v CHEMISE
SERMON 1 (sermon)	SÉVRER 1 (sévré)	sinagog v SYNAGOGUE
serpan, serpent v SERPENT	sévrettes v CHEVRETTE	Singer v **SINGER**
SERPENT 8 (serpan 4, serpent 2, serpents 2)	Seycelles v SEYCHELLES	**SINGER** 12 (Singer) [nom d'un magasin]
	SEYCHELLES 1 (Seycelles)	
serpents v SERPENT	seyé v ESSAYER	sipa, si pa, si pas, sipas, si-pas v SAIS+PAS
serr', serre v SERRER	sez v CHEZ	
serré v SERRÉ	sézi v SAISIR	sipèse v SOUPESER
serré v SERRER	sézon v SAISON	sipite v DISPUTER
SERRÉ 10 (séré 2, serré 7, serrée 1)	**SHERRY** 1 (serry) [mot angl.]	sippliie, sippliy, sippliye, sippliyé v SUPPLIER
	si v SI	
serrée v SERRÉ	SI 318 (si)	sipport, sipporte v SUPPORTER
SERRER 3 (serr' 1, serre 1, serré 1)	siç' v SUCER	sipri, siprit, siprits v ESPRIT
	sicanair v CHICANEUR	sir, sîr, sir' v SÛR
serrire v SERRURE	sicané v CHICANER	sirampeck v **CAMPETEKE**
SERRURE 5 (sérire 3, serrire 2)	sice, sicé v SUCER	Sirandale v SIRANDALE
	sicoupe v SOUCOUPE	SIRANDALE 9 (Sirandale) [nom de personnage][36]
serry v **SHERRY**	$sicour_1$ v OBSCUR	
	$sicour_2$ v SECOURS	sirandane, sirandanne v **CIRANDANI**
	sicoure v SECOURS	
	$sicours_1$ v OBSCUR	**SIRDAR** 6 (sirdars 5, sirdas 1)
	$sicours_2$ v SECOURS	
	sicriers v SUCRIER	
	SIÈGE 1 (siéze)	

[34] La prononciation du mot en CM est basée sur le fr. mais son sens vient de l'anglais.

[35] Mot tamoul pour 'coussinet'.
[36] Nom probablement lié à sirandane.

sirdars, sirdas[37]	v **SIRDAR**	SOIGNER	27 (sogn' 7, sogne 1, sogné 2, soigne 3, soigné 9, soin 1, soingne 4)	SORCIER	16 (sorcier 5, sourcié 1, sourcier 10)
sire	v SÛR	soin, soingne	v SOIGNER	sort, sort', sorte	v SORTE
sirement	v SUREMENT	soir	v SOIR	SORTE	40 (sort 18, sort' 2, sorte 16, sortes 4)
Sirius	v SIRIUS	SOIR	5 (soir 3, soirs 2)	sortes	v SORTE
SIRIUS	1 (Sirius) [nom d'un navire]	+SOIR	3 (lé-soir 1, lésoirs 1, les soirs 1)	sorti, sortie	v SORTIR
sirop	v SIROP	soirs	v SOIR	SORTIR	150 (sorti 68, sortie 1, sortis 2, sourt' 2, sourte 1, sourti 71, sourtie 1, sourtit 4)
SIROP	6 (sirop)	soixante	v SOIXANTE		
siroutes	v CHIROUTE	SOIXANTE	3 (soassant 2, soixante 1)		
sirs	v SÛR	SOIXANTE-DIX	1 (soassant-dis)	sortis	v SORTIR
sirtout	v SURTOUT			*SOSONA	2 (sousouna) [mot malg.]
sis	v SIX				
sise, sisé	v ASSEOIR	soizir	v CHOISIR	sosir	v CHOISIR
sis pas, sis-pas	v SAIS+PAS	solda, soldars, soldat	v SOLDAT	sot	v SOT
sisse	v SIX	SOLDAT	27 (solda 4, soldars 5, soldat 6, soldats 12)	SOT	1 (sot)
sitan, sitant	v SI+TANT			sotrél	v SAUTERELLE
SI+TANT	5 (sitan 1, sitant 4)			sottise	v SOTTISE
+SITE	1 (la site)			SOTTISE	1 (sottise)
sitot, sitôt	v AUSSITÔT	soldats	v SOLDAT	sou[1]	v SOU
siv', sive, sivre, sivré, sivrè, sivrée	v SUIVRE	solé, soleil	v SOLEIL	sou[2]	v SOÛL
six	v SIX	SOLEIL	46 (solé 3, soleil 14, soley 4, soléy 6, soleye 4, soléye 15)	SOU	11 (sols 1, sou[3] 3, sous[1] 8)
SIX	19 (sis 1, sisse 3, six 15)			SOUCOUPE	2 (sicoupe) [fr. dial.]
sixième	v SIXIÈME	soley, soléy, soleye, soléye	v SOLEIL	soue	v SOÛL
SIXIÈME	3 (sixième 1, siziem 2)	solid', solide	v SOLIDE	soufer, souffer, souffert	v SOUFFRIR
siz, size, sizé[1]	v ASSEOIR	SOLIDE	2 (solid' 1, solide 1)	soufflé[1]	v SOUFFLER[1]
sizé[2], sizet, sizets	v SUJET	sols	v SOU	soufflé[2]	v SOUFFLER[2]
siziem	v SIXIÈME	somey, someye, soméye, sômeye	v SOMMEIL	souffler	v SOUFFLER[1]
sizon	v SUZON	SOMMEIL	7 (somey 1, someye 2, soméye 2, sômeye 1, sommeye 1)	SOUFFLER[1]	15 (soufflé 13, souffler[1] 1, souflé 1) [v]
so[1]	v SON			SOUFFLER[2]	1 (soufflé[2]) [n.]
so[2]	v CHAUD			souffrance	v SOUFFRANCE
soaf	v SOIF	sommes	v SOMMES	SOUFFRANCE	1 (souffrance)
soassant	v SOIXANTE	SOMMES	1 (sommes)	souffri, souffrie	v SOUFFRIR
soassant-dis	v SOIXANTE-DIX	sommeye	v SOMMEIL	SOUFFRIR	23 (soufer 2, souffer 2, souffert 2, souffri 12, souffrie 5)
soda	v SODA	son	v SON		
SODA	1 (soda)	SON	1873 (so[1] 1336, son 537)		
SOEUR	33 (seir 22, seirs 7, ser 3, sèr' 1)			souflé	v SOUFFLER
soffé	v CHAUFFER	+SON[1]	3 (lé son 2, léson 1)	Souillac	v SOUILLAC
sogn', sogne	v SOIGNER	+SON[2]	3 (di son 1, disson 2)	SOUILLAC	2 (Souillac) [toponyme]
sogné	v SOIGNER	**SÓNJO**	8 (sonze 6, sonzes 2) [mot malg.]		
+SOIE	2 (la soie 1, lasoie 1)				
soif	v SOIF	sonn', sonne, sonné	v SONNER	soul	v SOÛL
SOIF	7 (soaf 5, soif 2)	SONNER	39 (sonn' 1, sonne 18, sonné 20)	SOÛL	7 (sou[2] 3, soue 2, soul 1, soule[1] 1)
+SOIF	3 (lasoif 2, la soif 1)				
soigne, soigné	v SOIGNER	sonze, sonzes	v **SÓNJO**	soulage, soulagé, soulagè	v SOULAGER
		sor	v tir o sor		
		sorcier	v SORCIER	SOULAGEMENT	1 (soulazement)

---

[37] Peut-être une erreur typographique pour *sirdar*.

SOULAGER 22 (*soulage* 1, *soulagé* 1, *soulagè* 1, *soulaz* 1, *soulaze* 17, *soulazé* 1)
soulard v SOÛLARD
SOÛLARD 1 (*soulard*)
soulaz, soulaze, soulazé v SOULAGER
soulazement 1 SOULAGEMENT
*soule*₁ v SOÛL
*soule*₂, *soulé*, *souler* v SOÛLER
SOÛLER 10 (*soule*₂ 3, *soulé* 6, *souler* 1)
soulié v SOULIER
SOULIER 13 (*soulié* 7, *souliers* 4, *souliés* 1, *soulièt* 1)
souliers, souliés, soulièt v SOULIER
+SOUPE 11 (*la soupe* 4, *lasoupe* 7)
*soupé*¹ v SOUPER¹
*soupé*² v SOUPER²
SOUPER₁ 3 (*soupé*) [n]
SOUPER₂ 2 (*soupé*) [v]
SOUPESER 2 (*sipèse*) [dial.]
soupiré v SOUPIRER
SOUPIRER 4 (*soupiré*)
souplaigné v SE+PLAINDRE
souque, souqué v SOUQUER
SOUQUER 12 (*souque* 3, *souqué* 8, *sousque* 1) [mot dial.]
+SOURCE 1 (*la source*)
sourcié, sourcier v SORCIER
sourcillé v SOURCILLER
SOURCILLER 1 (*sourcillé*)
SOURD 4 (*sourd* 3, *sourdes* 1)
sourd, sourdes v SOURD
sourement v SUREMENT
souricière v SOURICIÈRE
SOURICIÈRE 2 (*souricière*)
souris v SOURIS
SOURIS 20 (*souris*)
soursouri, soursouris v CHAUVRE-SOURIS
sourt', sourte, sourti, sourtie, sourtit v SORTIR
sourzin v CHIRURGIEN
*sous*¹ v SOU
*sous*² v SOUS

SOUS 1 (*sous*²)
sousque v SOUQUER
sousouna v *SOSONA*
souval v CHEVAL
souvan, souvant v SOUVENT
souvenir v SOUVENIR
SOUVENIR 20 (*souvenir* 1, *souvini* 18, *souvni* 1)
souvent v SOUVENT
SOUVENT 27 (*souvan* 2, *souvant* 2, *souvent* 23)
souvente fois v SOUVENT+ DE+FOIS
SOUVENT+ DE+FOIS 1 *souvente fois*
souvini, souvni v SOUVENIR
souye, souyé v ESSUYER
sov v SAUVER
sovaz v SAUVAGE
sové v SAUVER
sozir v CHOISIR
spère v ESPÉRER
stipid v STUPIDE
STUPIDE 1 (*stipid*)
SUCER 4 (*siç'* 1, *sice* 1, *sicé* 2)
+SUCRE 13 (*di sicre* 3, *disic* 10)
+SUCRE+D'ORGE 1 (*di sic' d'orze*)
sucrerie v SUCRERIE
SUCRERIE 1 (*sucrerie*)
SUCRIER 1 (*sicriers*)
SUFFOQUER 1 (*siffoqué*)
+SUIF 1 (*disuif*)
SUIVRE 103 (*siv'* 1, *sive* 2, *sivre* 26, *sivré* 68, *sivrè* 1, *sivrée* 5)
SUJET[38] 6 (*sizé*₂ 1, *sizet* 4, *sizets* 1)
SUPPLIER 9 (*sippliie* 1, *sippliy* 2, *sippliye* 4, *sippliyé* 2)
SUPPORTER 3 (*sipport* 2, *sipporte* 1)
SÛR 47 (*cire* 1, *sir* 16, *sîr* 23, *sir'* 2, *sire* 3, *sirs* 2)
SUREMENT 2 (*sirement* 1, *sourement* 1)

[38] Personne soumise à une autorité souveraine.

surtout v SURTOUT
SURTOUT 4 (*sirtout* 3, *surtout* 1)
synagog v SYNAGOGUE
SUSON 5 (*Sizon*) [prénom]
SYNAGOGUE 9 (*sinagog* 6, *synagog* 3)

T

tâ v TÂ
TÂ 5 (*tâ*) [onomat.]
ta l'heire, tà l'heire, ta lhére v TOUT+À+ L'HEURE
taba, tabac v TABAC
TABAC 18 (*taba* 1, *tabac* 17)
tabaquière v TABATIÈRE
TABATIÈRE 1 (*tabaquière*)
tablatire v TABLATURE
TABLATURE 1 (*tablatire*)
TABLE v À+TABLE
+TABLE 14 (*la tab* 2, *la tabe* 1, *latabe* 10, *latable* 1)
tablète, tablette v TABLETTE
TABLETTE 3 (*tablète* 1, *tablette* 2)
TABLIER 1 (*tabliers*)
tabliers v TABLIER
tablissement, tablissemment v ETABLISSEMENT
tac v TAC
TAC 9 (*tac*) [onomat.]
tacamaca v TACAMAHACA
TACAMAHACA 1 (*tacamaca*) [forme espagnole d'un mot azteque]
tace, tacé, tâcé v ATTACHER
+TÂCHE 1 (*la tace*)
TÂCHER 1 (*tassée*)
tach'ment v DETACHEMENT
+TAILLE 1 (*la taill'*)
taille, taillé, taillée v TAILLER
TAILLER 19 (*taille* 4, *taillé* 13, *taillée* 1, *tayé* 1)
TAILLEUR 1 (*tayèr*)
tais toi v TAIS+TOI
TAIS-TOI 1 (*tais toi*)
talan v TALENT
tale v ETALER
talent v TALENT

TALENT 14 (*talan* 12, *talent* 2)
taler, talèr, talheire, talhére, tàlhére, talhère
  v TOUT+À+L'HEURE
tam tam   v **TAM-TAM**
tamanicoque
  v *****TAMANIKOK**
*****TAMANIKOK**
  7 (*tamanicoque* 5, *tambalacoque* 2)
  [origine non-identifiée]
TAMARIN 6 (*tambarin*)
tambalacoque
  v *****TAMANIKOK**
tambarin   v TAMARIN
tambave   v **TAMBAVY**
TAMBAVY 1 (*tambave*)
  [mot malg.]
tambour   v TAMBOUR
TAMBOUR 9 (*tambour*)
tampl   v TEMPLE
tamtam, tam tam v TAM-TAM
TAM-TAM 3 (*tamtam* 2, *tam tam* 1) [mot hind.]
tan₁   v TANT
tan₂   v TEMPS
tand, tandé   v ENTENDRE
tandi ki, tandis, tandis ki, tandis qu', tandis qui
  v TANDIS+QUE
TANDIS+QUE 6 (*tandi ki* 1, *tandis* 1, *tandis ki* 1, *tandis qu'* 1, *tandis qui* 2)
tandr   v TENDRE₂
tandrac   v **TANDRAKA**
TANDRAKA 5 (*tandrac* 1, *tandraque* 1, *tangue* 1, *tanke* 1, *tanque* 1) [mot malg.]
tandraque, tangue, tanque
  v **TANDRAKA**
tangaze   v TANGAGE
TANGAGE 2 (*tangaze*)
+TANGAGE 1 (*la tangaze*)
tanguélé   v ÉTRANGLER
TANIÈRE 1 (*tannière*)
tanke, tanque   v **TANDRAKA**
tannière   v TANIÈRE
tans   v TEMPS
tant   v TANT
TANT 54 (*tan₁* 2, *tant* 52)
tantacion   v TENTATION

tantater   v TENTATEUR
tantine   v TANTINE
TANTINE 2 (*tantine* 1, *tantines* 1)
tantines   v TANTINE
tantôt   v TANTOT
TANTÔT 3 (*tantôt*)
tant-que   v TANT, QUE/QUI
TANTY 1 (*tente*) [mot malg.]
tap, tap'   v TAPER
tapage   v TAPAGE
TAPAGE 26 (*tapage* 1, *tapaz* 1, *tapaze* 24)
tapaz, tapaze v TAPAGE
tape, tapé   v TAPER
TAPER 36 (*tap* 1, *tap'* 1, *tape* 22, *tapé* 10, *tappe* 2)
tapeur   v TAPER-*ER*
TAPER-*ER* 1 (*tapeur*)
tapis   v TAPIS
TAPIS 2 (*tapis*)
tapisse   v TAPISSER
TAPISSER 1 (*tapisse*)
tappe   v TAPER
taque, taqué v ATTAQUER
tar   v TARD
TARANGAMBADI
  1 (*Tringbar*) [toponyme]
tard   v TARD
TARD 19 (*tar* 3, *tard* 16)
tarde, tardé v TARDER
TARDER 5 (*tarde* 1, *tardé* 4)
tas   v TAS
TAS 8 (*tas*)
tasse   v TASSE
TASSE 1 (*tasse*)
tassée   v TACHEZ
tâtant   v TÂTANT
TÂTANT 1 (*tâtant*)
tate, tâte, tâté v TÂTER
TÂTER 17 (*tate* 2, *tâte* 13, *tâté* 1, *tâtetâte* 1)
tâtetâte   v TÂTER
taureau   v TAUREAU
TAUREAU 2 (*taureau*)
tax   v TAXE
TAXE 7 (*tax*)
tayé   v TAILLER
tayèr   v TAILLEUR
TCAMPETEKE 1 (*çampéc*)
  [mot mak.]
tchéga   v **CEGA**

tchiombo, tchiômbo, tchiombô, tchombo, tchombô v TENIR+BON
te, té, tè   v ÉTÉ₁
tectec   v **TSITSIKY**
  [mot malg.]
teïn, teingné, teinié
  v ÉTEINDRE
tel   v TEL
TEL 1 (*tel*)
tellement   v TELLEMENT
TELLEMENT 8 (*tellement* 5, *telman* 3)
telman   v TELLEMENT
témoaniaz v TÉMOIGNAGE
témoein, témoin v TÉMOIN
TÉMOIN 9 (*témoein* 6, *témoin* 3)
TÉMOIGNAGE 2 (*témoaniaz*)
temp   v TEMPS
TEMPLE 8 (*tampl*)
+TEMPLE 9 (*le tampl* 7, *lé tampl* 1, *le templ* 1)
temps   v TEMPS
TEMPS 41 (*tan₂* 8, *tans* 1, *temp* 1, *temps* 31, *tems* 7)
+TEMPS 102 (*le tan* 1, *lé tan* 25, *le temps* 1, *lé temps* 27, *lé tems* 2, *letemps* 1, *létemps* 41, *lé-temps* 1, *lé-tems* 2, *litemps* 1)
tems   v TEMPS
tend, tend', tende, tendé, tendent, tendez, tendre₁
  v ENTENDRE
tendre₂   v TENDRE₁
TENDRE₁ 1 (*tendre₂*) [v]
TENDRE₂ 1 (*tandr*) [adj]
+TENDRESSE 1 (*la tendresse*)
téneb   v TENEBRES
TÉNÈBRES 2 (*téneb*)
TENIR 40 (*tiens* 1, *tient* 1, *tine* 4, *tini* 28, *tinie* 6) v aussi TENIR+ BON
TENIR+BON 43 (*tchiombo* 3, *tchiômbo* 1, *tchiombô* 16, *tchombo* 3, *tchombô* 3, *tiomb'* 1, *tiombo* 15, *tionbo* 1)
TENTATEUR 1 (*tantater*)
TENTATION 3 (*tantacion*)
tente   v **TANTY**
+TENTE 1 (*la tant*)

296

tenté v TENTER	*timbalo* 3 [origine inconnue]	*tombant* v TOMBANT
TENTER 1 (*tenté*)	*tine, tini, tinie* v TENIR	TOMBANT 1 (*tombant*)
térain, terrain v TERRAIN	*tintamarre* v TINTAMARRE	*tombe₁* v TOMBE
TERRAIN 11 (*térain* 2, *terrain* 8, *terrin* 1)	TINTAMARRE 2 (*tintamarre*)	*tombe₂* v TOMBER
	tiomb', tiombo, tionbo v TENIR+BON	TOMBE 3 (*tomb₁* 1, *tombe₁* 2)
terrasse v TERRASSE	*tioula* 2 [origine inconnue]	*tombé* v TOMBER
TERRASSE 1 (*terrasse*)	*tir, tir'* v TIRER	*tombeau* v TOMBEAU
terre v TERRE	*tirbouillon* v TOURBILLON	TOMBEAU 11 (*tombeau* 2, *tombo* 9)
TERRE 1 (*terre*), v aussi PAR+TERRE	*tire, tiré, tirer* v TIRER	
+TERRE 94 (*la ter* 38, *la ter'* 1, *latére* 4, *latère* 1, *la tère* 1, *la terr'* 1, *la terre* 36, *laterre* 12)	TIRER 139 (*tir* 13, *tir'* 8, *tire* 90, *tiré* 24, *tirer* 3, *tirez* 1)[39]	*tombée* v TOMBER
		TOMBER 150 (*tomb₂* 30, *tomb'* 4, *tombe₂* 49, *tombé* 66, *tombée* 1)
	TIRER+AU+SORT 2 (*tir o sor*)	
	tirez v TIRER	*tombo* v TOMBEAU
	tiroir v TIROIR	*ton* v TON
terrible v TERRIBLE	TIROIR 1 (*tiroir*)	TON 274 (*to₂* 197, *ton* 77)
TERRIBLE 2 (*terrible*)	*tir o sor* v TIRER+AU+SORT	*tondre* v TONDRE
terrin v TERRAIN	*tirques* v TURC	TONDRE 1 (*tondre*)
testament v TESTAMENT	+TISANE 1 (*la tisane*)	*toné, tôné, tonné* v ÉTONNER
TESTAMENT 5 (*testament*)	*tison* v TISON	*tonnell'* v TONNELLE
tété₁ v TÊTÉ	TISON 1 (*tison*)	*tonnelle* v TONNELLE
tété₂, tette v TÉTER	TISSERINE 2 (*serine* 1, *sérine* 1)	TONNELLE 11 (*tonnell'* 4, *tonnelle* 7))
TÊTÉ 8 (*tété₁* 3, *tétés* 5)		
+TÊTE 133 (*la tet* 7, *la tét* 7, *latêt* 1, *la têt'* 2, *la-têt'* 3, *la téte* 1, *la tète* 3, *la tête* 36, *latéte* 22, *latète* 2, *latête* 52, *la-tête* 2, *latêtes* 1)	*Titine* v TITINE	*tonnerre* v TONNERRE
	TITINE 4 (*Titine*) [prénom]	TONNERRE 5 (*tonnerre*)
	tlavai v TRAVAILLER	*tonnés* v ETONNER
	to₁ v TOI	*tonton* v TONTON
	to₂ v TON	TONTON 6 (*tonton* 5, *ton-ton* 1)
	toa v TOI	
	toc v TOC	*ton-ton* v TONTON
TÉTER 4 (*tété₂* 3, *tette* 1)	TOC 4 (*toc* 2, *toc-toc* 2)	*topet* v TOPETTE
tétés v TÊTÉ	*tocsin* v TOCSIN	TOPETTE 1 (*topet*)
tétère v TÊTER-*ER*	TOCSIN 1 (*tocsin*)	*tor, tort* v TORT
TÊTER-*ER* 1 (*tétère*)	*toc-toc* v TOC	TORT 15 (*tor* 2, *tort* 13)
tétrark v TÉTRARQUE	*toë'ne* v to, ene	+TORT 1 (*di tort*)
TÉTRARQUE 1 (*tétrark*)	*toi* v TOI	*torte* v TORTE
+THÉ 2 (*di thé* 1, *dité* 1)	TOI 1015 (*to₁* 426, *toa* 117, *toi* 276)	TORTE 3 (*torte*)
théatre v THÉÂTRE		*torti, torti'* v TORTUE
THÉÂTRE 1 (*théatre*)	+TOILE 9 (*latoéle* 1, *la toil'* 4, *la toile* 3, *latouéle* 1)	*tortillé* v TORTILLER
Thérèse v THERESE		TORTILLER 3 (*tortillé*)
THÉRÈSE 6 (*Thérèse* 1, *Thérèz'* 2, *Thérèze* 3)		TORTUE 80 (*torti* 11, *torti'* 1, *tourtie* 68)
	toilette v TOILETTE	
Thérèz', Thérèze v THÉRÈSE	TOILETTE 1 (*toilette*)	*tou* v TOUT
Thomas v THOMAS	+TOILETTE 1 (*la toilette*)	*tou de souit, tou de suit* v TOUT+DE+SUITE
THOMAS 1 (*Thomas*)	*toit* v TOIT	
ti₁ v ÉTÉ₁	TOIT 2 (*toit*)	*tou sel* v TOUT+SEUL
ti₂ v TU	+TOIT 2 (*lé toa* 1, *létoit* 1)	*tou ta lor* v TOUT+À+L'HEURE
ti₃ v PETIT	*tomb₁* v TOMBE	
tic 2 [onomat.]	*tomb₂, tomb'* v TOMBER	*touce, touche* v TOUCHER
tiéga v **CEGA**		TOUCHER 13 (*touce* 4, *touche* 9)
tiens, tient v TENIR		
TIGRE 28 (*tigre* 2, *tigue* 26)	[39] Certaines de ces formes sont probablement issue de « retirer ».	
tigre, tigue v TIGRE		

touc-touc v TOUQUER
toud souite
    v TOUT+DE+SUITE
touf, touffe, touffé
    v ÉTOUFFER
touille v TUILE
toujour, toujours v TOUJOURS
TOUJOURS 168 (*toujour* 9, *toujours* 43, *touzou* 1, *touzour* 12, *touzours* 103)
touldé v TOUT+LES+DEUX
tou le, tou lé v TOUS+LES
tou le monde
    v TOUT+LE+MONDE
toulézour, tou lézours
    v TOUS+LES, JOUR
touni v TOUT+NU
toupie v TOUPIE
TOUPIE 3 (*toupie*)
touque v TOUQUER
TOUQUER 7 (*touc-touc* 2, *touque* 5) [fr. dial.]
tour$_1$ v TOUR
tour$_2$ v TROUVER
TOUR 9 (*tour$_1$* 7, *tours* 2)
+TOUR 2 (*la tour*)
TOURBILLON 3 (*tirbouillon*)
tourdi$_1$ v ETOURDI
tourdi$_2$ v ÉTOURDIR
tourdis v ÉTOURDI
tourdissement
    v ÉTOURDISSEMENT
+TOUR+MALAKOFF
    1 (*La Tour Malakoff*)
tourman$_1$ v TOURMENT
tourman$_2$, tourmant, tourmanté
    v TOURMENTER
TOURMENT 1 (*tourman$_1$*)
tourmenté, tourmentée
    v TOURMENTER
TOURMENTER 5
    (*tourman$_2$* 1. *tourmant* 1, *tourmanté* 1, *tourmenté* 1, *tourmentée* 1)
tourn v TOURNER
tournant v TOURNANT
TOURNANT 1 (*tournant*)
tourne, tourné, tourné'
    v TOURNER
tournée$_1$ v TOURNÉE
tournée$_2$ v TOURNER
TOURNÉE 2 (*tournée*)

tourner v TOURNER
TOURNER 157 (*tourn* 1, *tourne* 92, *tourné* 61, *tourné'* 1, *tournée$_2$* 1, *tourner* 1)[40]
tournèr v TOURNEUR
TOURNEUR 1 (*tournèr*)
tournir' v TOURNURE
TOURNURE 1 (*tournir'*)
tourou, tourous v TROU
tours v TOUR
tourterel, tourterelle
    v TOURTERELLE
TOURTERELLE 5 (*tourterel* 1, *tourterelle* 4)
tourtie v TORTUE
tourve, tourvé v TROUVER
tous v TOUT
tous d'bon v TOUT+DE+BON
tousite v TOUT+DE+SUITE
tous les v TOUS+LES
TOUS+LES 38 (*tou le* 1, *tou lé* 10, *tous les* 24, *tout lé* 2, *tout les* 1)
tous lé zours v TOUS+LES, JOUR
toussé v TOUSSER
TOUSSER 3 (*toussé*)
tout v TOUT
TOUT 1054 (*tou* 253, *tous* 165, *tout* 613, *toute* 7, *toutes* 9, *touts* 7) v aussi TOUT+À+ FAIT, TOUT +À+L'HEURE, TOUT+ DE+BON, TOUT+DE+ SUITE, TOUT+D'UN+ COUP, TOUT+LES+ DEUX, TOUT+NU, TOUT+UNIMENT.
tout a fait, tout à fait
    v TOUT+À+FAIT
TOUT+À+FAIT 2 (*tout a fait* 1, *tout à fait* 1)
tout à l'her, tout à lher
    v TOUT+À+ L'HEURE

TOUT+À+L'HEURE 34 (*taler* 3, *talèr* 2, *talheire* 6, *ta l'heire* 1, *tà l'heire* 1, *talhère* 6, *ta lhère* 1, *tàlhère* 1, *talhère* 7, *tou ta lor* 1, *tout à l'her* 1, *tout à lher* 3, *tout-à l'hère* 1)
tout cèle v TOUT+SEUL
tout d'bon, tout' d'bon, tout-d'bon, tout di bon
    v TOUT+DE+BON
TOUT+DE+BON 27 (*tous d'bon* 1, *tout d'bon* 16, *tout-d'bon* 1, *tout' d'bon* 1, *tout di bon* 8)
tout d'ein coup
    v TOUT D'UN COUP
TOUT+DE+SUITE 9 (*tou de souit* 1, *tou de suit* 1, *toud souite* 1, *tout d'suite* 1, *tout de suite* 1, *tout site* 1, *tout suit'* 1, *tousite* 1, *toutsouït'* 1)
TOUT D'UN COUP 1 (*tout d'ein coup*)
tout d'suite, tout de suite
    v TOUT+DE+SUITE
tout lé v TOUS+LES
tout lébomatin v *tout lé bomatin*
tout lé bomatin v TOUS+LES, BON+MATIN
tout les v TOUS+LES
tout lésoirs v *tout lé soirs*
tout lé soirs v TOUS+LES, SOIR
tou lé tan, tout létemps, tout lé temps v TOUT+LE+TEMPS
TOUT+LE+TEMPS 3 (*tou lé tan* 1, *tout létemps* 1, *tout lé temps* 1)
tout l'mond'
    1 v TOUT+LE+MONDE
TOUT+LE+MONDE 2 (*tou le monde* 1, *tout l'mond'* 1)
tout s'el, tout seil, tout sejls, tout sel, tout sél, tout sèl, tout séle, tout sèle, tout sels, tout séls, tout sel', tout seul
    v TOUT+SEUL

---

[40] La plupart de ces formes sont sans doute issue de « retourner ».

TOUT+SEUL 91 (*tou sel* 21, *tout cèle* 1, *tout seil* 29, *tout seils* 1, *tout sel* 10, *tout sél* 15, *tout sèl* 1, *tout s'el* 2, *tout sel'* 2, *tout séle* 1, *tout sèle* 1, *tout selle* 2, *tout sels* 2, *tout séls* 1, *tout seul* 2)
tout site, tout suit'
    v TOUT+DE+SUITE
tout-à l'hère
    v TOUT+À+L'HEURE
toute, toutes v TOUT
tout-iniment
    v TOUT+UNIMENT
TOUT+LES+DEUX 5 (*touldé*)
TOUT+NU 7 (*tou ni* 1, *touni* 3, *tout ni* 3)
touts v TOUT
toutsouit'
    v TOUT+DE+SUITE
TOUT+UNIMENT
    1 (*tout-iniment*)
touy, touy', touye, touyé
    v TUER
touzou, touzour, touzours
    v TOUJOURS
traca v TRACAS
TRACAS 2 (*traca*)
tracasse v TRACASSER
tracassé v TRACASSER
TRACASSER 9 (*tracasse* 4, *tracassé* 5)
trace v TRACE
TRACE 3 (*trace*)
+TRACE 3 (*la tarace* 2, *la traces* 1)
tradition v TRADITION
TRADITION 3 (*tradition*)
trafic v TRAFIC
TRAFIC 1 (*trafic*)
trahir v TRAHIR
TRAHIR 11 (*trahir*)
train', traine, trainé, traîné
    v TRAÎNER
TRAÎNER X (*train'* 1, *traine* 3, *trainé* 2, *traîné* 1)
trait', traite, traité v TRAITER
TRAITER 6 (*trait'* 1, *traite* 2, *traité* 2, *trét* 1)
TRAÎTRE 1 (*traitres*)
traitres v TRAÎTRE

tramblé v TREMBLER
trambleman de ter
    v TREMBLEMENT+DE+TERRE
tramblman v TREMBLEMENT
tranglé v ÉTRANGLER
*trankil, tranquiile, tranquil', tranquile, tranquiles, tranquille*₁ v TRANQUILLE₁
*Tranquille*₂ v TRANQUILLE₂
TRANQUILLE₁ 39 (*trankil* 3, *tranquiile* 1, *tranquil'* 3, *tranquile* 3, *tranquiles* 2, *tranquille*₁ 27)
TRANQUILLE₂
    52 (*Tranquille*) [nom de personnage]
transpir', transpiré
    v TRANSPIRER
TRANSPIRER 5 (*transpir'* 1, *transpiré* 4)
transplanter
    v TRANSPLANTER
TRANSPLANTER
    1 (*transplanter*)
transport v TRANSPORT
TRANSPORT 1 (*transport*)
trant v TRENTE
trape, trappé, trapper
    v ATTRAPPER
*travail*₁ v TRAVAIL
*travail*₂ v TRAVAILLER
TRAVAIL 7 (*travail*₁ 5, *travaille*₁ 1, *travay*₁ 1)
travaill' v TRAVAILLER
*travaille*₁ v TRAVAIL
*travaille*₂, *travaillé*
    v TRAVAILLER
travailleir v TRAVAILLEUR
travaillent v TRAVAILLER
TRAVAILLER 83 (*tlavai* 1, *travail*₂ 10, *travaill'* 1, *travaille*₂ 52, *travaillé* 7, *travaillent* 2, *travaillez* 5, *travay*₂ 2, *travaye* 3)
TRAVAILLEUR 1 (*travailleir*)
travaillez v TRAVAILLER
*travay*₁ v TRAVAIL
*travay*₂, *travaye*
    v TRAVAILLER
traver, travers v TRAVERS
TRAVERS 8 (*traver* 4, *travers* 4)

traverse v TRAVERSER
TRAVERSER 3 (*traverse*)
tré v TRÈS
trébicé v TRÉBUCHER
TRÉBUCHER 1 (*trébicé*)
+TREILLE 2 (*la treille*)
tremblé v TREMBLER
TREMBLEMENT
    1 (*tramblman*)
TREMBLEMENT+DE+TERRE
    1 (*trambleman de ter*)
trembler v TREMBLER
TREMBLER 12 (*tramblé* 3, *tremblé* 8, *trembler* 1)
trempe, trempées v TREMPER
TREMPER 2 (*trempe* 1, *trempées* 1)
trente v TRENTE
TRENTE 12 (*trant* 5, *trente* 7)
très v TRÈS
TRÈS 2 (*tré* 1, *très* 1)
trésor v TRÉSOR
TRÉSOR 27 (*trésor* 16, *trésors* 1, *trezor* 1, *trézor* 9)
trésors v TRÉSOR
tresse v TRESSER
TRESSER 1 (*tresse*)
trét v TRAITER
trezor, trézor v TRÉSOR
tribi v TRIBU
tribinal v TRIBUNAL
tribu v TRIBU
TRIBU 2 (*tribi* 1, *tribu* 1)
tribunal v TRIBUNAL
TRIBUNAL 7 (*tribinal* 6, *tribunal* 1)
tricolore v TRICOLORE
TRICOLORE 1 (*tricolore*)
trielle v TRUELLE
TRIER 1 (*triye*)
Tringbar v
    TARANGAMBADI
trinqué v TRINQUER
TRINQUER 2 (*trinqué*)
TRIPE 13 (*tripe* 2, *tripes* 11)
+TRIPE 1 (*latripe*)
tripes v TRIPE
trique v TRIQUE
TRIQUE 1 (*trique*)
trist, triste v TRISTE
TRISTE 7 (*trist* 4, *triste* 3)

tristesse v TRISTESSE
TRISTESSE 1 (*tristesse*)
triye v TRIER
tro v TROP
troa v TROIS
troa zher v TROIS+HEURE
troaziem, troaziém
　　　　v TROISIÈME
troi, trois v TROIS
TROIS 121 (*troa* 17, *troi* 3, *trois* 101) v aussi TROIS-ISLOTS et TROIS SEIRS
troisièm', troisième
　　　　v TROISIÈME
TROIS+HEURE 1 (*troa zher*)
TROISIÈME 22 (*troaziem* 5, *troaziém* 2, *troisièm'* 1, *troisième* 13, *troizième* 1)
TROIS+ILÔTS 1 (*Trois-Islots*) [un district de l'île Maurice au 18e siècle]
Trois-Islots v TROIS+ILÔTS
Trois-Seirs v TROIS+SOEURS
TROIS+SOEURS 2 (*Trois-Seirs*) [nom de lieu fictif]
troizième v TROISIÈME
tromp, tromp', trompe, trompé, tromper v TROMPER
TROMPER 9 (*tromp* 2, *tromp'* 1, *trompe* 1, *trompé* 4, *tromper* 1)
trompet, trompette
　　　　v TROMPETTE
TROMPETTE 6 (*trompet* 2, *trompette* 4)
+TROMPETTE 1 (*la trompette*)
+TRONC 1 (*létroncs*)
trone, trône v TRÔNE
TRÔNE 5 (*trone* 2, *trône* 3)
trop v TROP
TROP 81 (*tro* 3, *trop* 71, *trôp* 7)
trôp v TROP
trou v TROU
TROU 48 (*tourou* 8, *tourous* 3, *trou* 31, *trous* 6)
+TROUBLE 1 (*lé troubl*)
troublé v TROUBLER
TROUBLER 2 (*troublé*)
Trou-Fanfaron
　　　　v TROU+FANFARON
TROU+FANFARON

1 (*Trou-Fanfaron*)
trouloulou v TROU, LOUP/ **LOLO**
troupeau v TROUPEAU
TROUPEAU 7 (*troupeau* 3, *troupo* 4)
troupo v TROUPEAU
trous v TROU
trou souffler
　　　　v TROU+SOUFFLEUR
TROU+SOUFFLEUR 1 (*trou souffler*)
trouv, trouv', trouve, trouvé, trouver v TROUVER
TROUVER 315 (*tour₂* 3, *tourve* 14, *tourvé* 2, *trouv* 38, *trouv'* 6, *trouve* 157, *trouvé* 83, *trouver* 2, *trouvons* 2)
trouvons v TROUVER
TRUELLE 1 (*trielle* 1)
TSA+KABAR 1 (*sakabar*) [mot malg. + mot ar.][41]
tsiaka v TSIAKA
*TSIAKA 4 (*tsiaka*) [onomat.]
TSIMIROHI 1 (*simiroués*) [mot malg.]
TSITSIKY 1 (*tectec*) [mot malg.]
TU 1 (*ti₂*)
tué v TUER
TUER 111 (*touy* 12, *touy'* 1, *touye* 68, *touyé* 29, *tué* 1)
TUILE 3 (*touille*)
TURC 1 (*tirques*)
tyena, ty en a v *ti, en a*
typographe v TYPOGRAPHE
TYPOGRAPHE 2 (*typographe*)

---

[41] *Tsa* est une forme dial. correspondent à *tsy* 'négatif' en malg. ; *kabar* est un mot arabe qui veut dire 'nouvelles, annonce, discussion' etc. Il est établi dans beaucoup de langues avec plusieurs sens, y compris le wolof, le mandinka, le malgache, les langues bantou de l'Afrique de l'est, et plusieurs langues de l'Inde.

U

un v UN
UN 1946 (*an₁* 1, *ein* 83, *ein'* 157, *eine* 214, *einne* 17, *en₂* 1, *èn* 1, *ene* 117, *éne* 1232, *ène* 50, *éné* 6, *enne* 39, *in* 1, *un* 26, *une* 1)
+UN 3 (*l'éne* 2, *l'einne* 1)
une v UN
UN+PEU 42 (*ein pé* 31, *ein pè* 1, *ein-pé* 1, *ein' pé* 4, *en pé* 1, *impé* 2, *inpé* 1, *in-pé* 1)
unuk v EUNUQUE
ŪRU-KẠY 1 (*rougaill'*) [mot tam.]
USÉ 1 (*isés*)

V

va v VA₁,₂
VA 1325 (*a₁* 75, *à₁* 5, *va* 1281, *và* 1, *vat* 35)[42]
và v VA₂
vacabond v VAGABOND
vacarme v VACARME
VACARME 2 (*vacarme*)
vace v VACHE
Vacer v VACHER
vaces v VACHE
VACHE 14 (*vace* 19, *vaces* 5)
VACHER 1 (*Vacer*) [nom de famille]
vacoa¹ v **VAKOA**
vacoa² v *Mare Vacoa*
vacoas v **VAKOA**
vag v VAGUE
vagabond v VAGABOND
VAGABOND 4 (*vacabond* 2, *vagabond* 1, *vagabonds* 1)
VAGABONDAGE 3 (*vagabondaze*)
vagabondaze
　　　　v VAGABONDAGE
vagabonds v VAGABOND
VAGUE 2 (*vag*)

---

[42] Le total inclut un petit nombre de cas où VA n'est ni auxiliaire, ni un marqueur TMA.

vaillant v VAILLIANT	*vat₂* v VA₂	+VENT 30 (*di van* 8,
VAILLIANT 2 (*vaillant*)	*va-t-an* v VA-T-EN	*divent* 14, *di-vent* 1,
+VAIRETTE 4 (*la vérèt'* 1,	VA-T-EN 2 (*va-t-an*)	*di vent* 6, *di vents* 1)
la vérette 3)	*vaurien* v VAURIEN	+VENTE 2 (*lavente* 1, *la vente* 1)
VAISSEAU 1 (*vaisseaux*)	VAURIEN 2 (*vaurien* 1,	*vente, ventes, ventre* v VENTRE
vaisseaux v VAISSEAU	*vauriens* 1)	VENTRE 49 (*vante* 8, *vantr* 1,
VAKOA 3 (*bacoua* 1, *vacoa*	*vauriens* v VAURIEN	*vente* 34, *ventes* 1, *ventre* 5)
1, *vacoas* 1) v aussi *Mare*	*vaut* v VALOIR	*venzance, venzeance*
Vacoa [mot malg.]	*vaut mié, vaut mieux, vaut-mié*	v VENGEANCE
valé v VALET	v VAUT+MIEUX	*ver* v VER
valer, valère v VALEUR	VAUT+MIEUX 34	VER 2 (*ver*)
VALET 1 (*valé*)	(*vaut mié* 25, *vaut mieux*	+VER 2 (*léver*)
VALEUR 4 (*valer* 2, *valère* 2)	1, *vaut-mié* 2, *vaux mieux*	*verd* v VERT
+VALEUR 1 (*la valer*)	1, *vo mié* 4, *vômieux* 1)	*vergue* VERGUE
valide v VALIDE	*vaux mieux* v VAUT+MIEUX	VERGUE 2 (*vergue*)
VALIDE 1 (*valide*)	*vavangues* v **VOA+VANGA**	*véritable* v VÉRITABLE
valles v *va, alles*	*vaz* v VASE	VÉRITABLE 1 (*véritable*)
VALOIR 8 (*vaut* 3, *vo* 5)	*vé* v VEUT+PAS	*vérité* v *en vérité*
VAN 1 (*vane*)	*vec* v AVEC	+VÉRITÉ 7 (*la vérité* 6,
vand, vande, vandé, vane, vané,	*veil* v VEILLER	*la verté* 1)
vaner v VANNER	*veillant* v VEILLANT	*verni* v VERNIR
vanille v VANILLE	VEILLANT 1 (*veillant*)	VERNIR 1 (*verni*)
VANILLE 1 (*vanille*)	*veille, veillé, veillée* v VEILLER	*verr', verre* v VERRE
VANNE 1 (*vannes*)	VEILLER 27 (*veil* 1, *veille* 8,	VERRE 12 (*verr'* 1, *verre* 7,
vanné v VANNER	*veillé* 7, *veillée* 1, *véy* 2,	*vérre* 1, *verres* 2, *vérres* 1)
VANNER 14 (*vane* 1, *vané* 3,	*véye* 3, *véyé* 5)	+VERRE 2 (*lé ver*)
vaner 1, *vanné* 9)	*veillése* v VEILLEUSE	*vérre, verres, vérres* v VERRE
vannes v VANNE	VEILLEUSE 1 (*veillése*)	*versé* v VERSER
vant v VANTER	+VEINE 2 (*la veine*)	VERSER 1 (*versé*)
vantar, vantard v VANTARD	*vela* v VOILA	*vert, vért* v VERT
VANTARD 14 (*vantar* 4,	VELOURS 4 (*vélours* 3,	VERT 10 (*verd* 1, *vert* 7,
vantard 9, *vantards* 1)	*v'lours* 1)	*vért* 1, *verts* 1)
vantards v VANTARD	*vélours* v VELOURS	*verté* v *en verté*
vante v VENTRE	*vend, vend'* v VENDRE	*vert, verts* v VERT
vanté v *s'en vanté*	*vendardi* v VENDREDI	*vestibile* v VESTIBULE
VANTER 1 (*vant*)	*vende, vendé, vendez*	VESTIBULE 2 (*vestibile*)
vantr v VENTRE	v VENDRE	*vétéran* v VÉTÉRAN
vapère v VAPEUR	VENDRE 54 (*vand* 6, *vande* 3,	VÉTÉRAN 1 (*vétéran*)
VAPEUR 1 (*vapère*)	*vandé* 3, *vend* 1, *vend'* 5,	*vetivert* v VÉTIVER
VARANGUE 1 (*varangues*)	*vende* 13, *vendé* 22,	VÉTIVER 8 (*vetivert* 1,
varangues v VARANGUE[43]	*vendez* 1)	*vitiver* 7)
+VARANGUE 4 (*la varangue*	VENDREDI 2 (*vendardi* 1,	*vev* v VEUVE
1, *lavarangue* 3)	*vendrédi* 1)	VEUT+PAS 5 (*vé pas*)
+VARIOLE 1 (*la vériol*)	*vendrédi* v VENDREDI	VEUVE 2 (*vev*)
vas' te v *va, acheter*	*venez* v (DE)VENIR	*véy, véye, véyé* v VEILLER
VASE 2 (*vases* 1, *vaz* 1)	VENGEANCE 2 (*venzance* 1,	+VIANDE 21 (*la viand'* 3,
vases v VASE	*venzeance* 1)	*la viande* 7, *laviande* 6,
vat₁ v VA₁	*veni, venir* v (DE)VENIR	*la-viande* 1, *lavianne* 4)
	VENIR v (DE)VENIR	*vice* v VICE
	vent v VENT	VICE 1 (*vice*)
	VENT 1 (*vent*)	*victoar, victoire* v VICTOIRE

---

[43] Erreur d'impression apparemment pour *vavangues* (espèce de fruit) [< malg. VÓA+VÁNGA].

301

VICTOIRE 3 (*victoar* 1, *victoire* 2)
Victor v VICTOR
VICTOR 1 (*Victor*) [prénom]
vid₁ v VIDE
vid₂ v VIDER
vide₁ v VIDE
vide₂ v VIDER
VIDE 12 (*vid₁* 1, *vide₁* 11) [adj]
vidé, vider v VIDER
VIDER 11 (*vid₂* 1, *vide₂* 6, *vidé* 3, *vider* 1)
+VIE 51 (*la vi* 16, *la vie* 18, *là vie* 1, *lavie* 16)
vié, viée, vieille v VIEUX
viélon v VIOLON
VIERGE 4 (*vierz*)
+VIERGE 1 (*la vierge*)
vierz v VIERGE
viés, viés-viés, vieux v VIEUX
VIEUX 135 (*vié* 123, *viée* 4, *vieille* 1, *viés* 2, *viés-viés* 1, *vieux* 1, *viévié* 3)
viévié v VIEUX
vilain v VILAIN
VILAIN 10 (*vilain* 9, *vilains* 1)
vilains v VILAIN
village v VILLAGE
VILLAGE 7 (*village* 1, *villaz* 5, *villaze* 1)
villaz, villaze v VILLAGE
+VILLE 47 (*la vil* 43, *la ville* 3, *laville* 1)
Ville Bague v VILLE-BAGUE
VILLE-BAGUE 1 (*Ville Bague*)
+VILLE-BAGUE 1 (*la Vill'bague*)
villemain v VUILLEMIN
+VILLE+NOIR 2 (*la ville noire*)
+VIN 33 (*divain* 1, *divin₂* 18, *di vein* 4, *di vin* 10)
vin' v VENIR
VINAIGRE 3 (*vinaigue* 2, *vinég* 1)
vinaigue v VINAIGRE
vine v VENIR
vinég v VINAIGRE
vingt v VINGT
VINGT 4 (*vingt*)
vini, vini', vinie, vinne v VENIR
viol v VIOLER

violan v VIOLENT
VIOLER 4 (*viol*)
VIOLENT 1 (*violan*)
violon v VIOLON
VIOLON 14 (*viélon* 5, *violon* 9)
viper v VIPÈRE
VIPÈRE 2 (*viper*)
vir, vir', vire, viré v VIRER
VIRER 53 (*vir* 1, *vir'* 1, *vire* 25, *viré* 22, *virevire* 2, *vireviré* 1, *vir'viré* 1)
virevire v VIRER
vireviré v VIRER
Virginie v VIRGINIE
VIRGINIE 1 (*Virginie*) [prénom]
vir'viré v VIRER
VISAGE 7 (*visaze* 4, *visazes* 1, *vizage* 1, *vizaz* 1)
vis-à-vis v VIS-À-VIS
VIS-À-VIS 3 (*vis-à-vis* 1, *vizavi* 2)
visaze, visazes v VISAGE
vise v VISER
VISER 1 (*vise*)
visite v VISITE
VISITE 4 (*visite*)
vit' v VITE
vit'ment v VITEMENT
vite v VITE
VITE 19 (*vit'* 2, *vite* 17)
vitement v VITEMENT
VITEMENT 33 (*vit'ment* 3, *vitement* 28, *vitman* 2)
vites v VITRE
vitiver v VÉTIVER
vitman v VITEMENT
VITRE 1 (*vites*)
viv, viv' v VIVRE
vivan, vivant, vivants v VIVANT
VIVANT 20 (*vivan* 4, *vivant* 15, *vivants* 1)
vive, vivre v VIVRE
VIVRE 13 (*viv* 3, *viv'* 2, *vive* 1, *vivre* 7)
vivres v VIVRES
VIVRES 6 (*vivres*)
vizavi v VIS-À-VIS
vizage, vizaz v VISAGE
vlà, v'la, v'là v VOILÀ

VLAKT 3 (*Flacq*) [mot néerl.]
v'le, v'lé, v'lez v VOULOIR
v'lours v VELOURS
vlé, vlé' v VOULOIR
vo v VALOIR
voal v VOILE
voar v VOIR
VOA+VANGA 3 (*vavangues*) [mot malg.]
VOEMAR 1 (*vohémar*) [toponyme malg.]
vohémar v **VOEMAR**
voi v VOIR
+VOILE 5 (*la voile* 4, *lavoile* 1)
voilà v VOILA
VOILA 24 (*vela* 1, *vlà* 2, *v'la* 6, *v'là* 11, *voilà* 3)
voile v VOILE
VOILE 2 (*voal* 1, *voile* 1)
voir v VOIR
VOIR 242 (*voar* 70, *voi* 1, *voir* 164, *voir'* 4, *voire* 1, *voit* 2)
voir', voire v VOIR
voisin v VOISIN
VOISIN 2 (*voisin* 1, *voisins* 1)
voisins v VOISIN
voit v VOIR
+VOIX 27 (*la voa* 6, *la voi* 1, *la voix* 7, *lavoix* 8, *la-voix* 4, *lé voix* 1)
vol v VOL
VOL 1 (*vol*)
VOLAGE 1 (*volaze*)
volaille v VOLAILLE
VOLAILLE 7 (*volaille* 1, *volailles* 6)
volailles v VOLAILLE
volant v VOLANT
VOLANT 1 (*volant*)
volaze v VOLAGE
vole, volé v VOLER
voleir, voleirs, voler v VOLEUR
VOLER 7 (*vole* 5, *volé* 2)
volér v VOLEUR
VOLEUR 25 (*voleir* 4, *voleirs* 9, *voler* 9, *volér* 2, *volor₂* 1)
VOLEUR+*E* 28 (*volor₂* 23, *voloré* 1, *volore* 4)

volonté	v VOLONTÉ	
VOLONTÉ	2 (*volonté* 1, *volontés* 1)	
+VOLONTÉ 6 (*la volonté*)		
volontés	v VOLONTE	
volor[1]	v VOLEUR	
volor[2], *volore*, *voloré*		
	v VOLEUR+*E*	
vomi	v VOMIR	
vo mié, *vômieux*		
	v VAUT+MIEUX	
VOMIR	4 (*vomi*)	
vos	v VOS	
VOS	1 (*vos*)	
votre	v VOTRE	
VOTRE	1 (*votre*)	
vou$_1$	v VOUS	
vou$_2$	v VOULOIR	
vou'	v VOUS	
voudré, voudrée, voulait, voulé, vouler, voulez, vouloir		
	v VOULOIR	
VOULOIR	318 (*lé*$_1$ 2, *oulé* 15, *vlé* 152, *vlé'* 1, *v'le* 1, *v'lé* 7, *v'lez* 1, *voudré* 2, *voudrée* 2, *voulait* 4, *voulé* 125, *vouler* 2, *voulez* 3, *vouloir* 1)	
vous	v VOUS	
VOUS	1815 (*ou*$_3$ 34, *ous* 31, *vou*$_1$ 568, *vou'* 1, *vous* 1182, *wou* 3, *wous* 1)	
vouti	v *vou*$_2$, *ti*$_2$	
vouve	v **VOVO**	
VOVO	1 (*vouve*) [mot malg.]	
VOYAGE 8 (*voyaz* 1, *voyaze*$_1$ 5, *vôyaze* 2)		
voyagé	v VOYAGER	
VOYAGER	3 (*voyagé* 1, *voyaze*$_2$ 1, *voyazé* 1)	
voyaz, *voyaze*$_1$	v VOYAGE	
voyaze$_2$, *vôyaze*	v VOYAGE	
voyazé	v VOYAGER	
vrai	v VRAI	
VRAI	77 (*vrai* 35, *vrais* 1, *vré* 41)	
vrais, *vré*	v VRAI	
VUILLEMIN 1 (*Villemain*)		

W

wagon	v WAGON
WAGON	1 (*wagon*)
Waterloo	v WATERLOO
WATERLOO	1 (*Waterloo*)
whoun	1 [interj.]
Willoughby	v WILLOUGHBY
WILLOUGHBY 1 (Willoughby) [nom de famille]	
wou, *wous*	v VOUS
Wyndam	v WYNDHAM
WYNDHAM 1 (*Wyndam*) [nom de navire]	

X

xepté	v EXCEPTÉ

Y

y	v *y faut*, *y en a*
yana	v IL+Y+EN+A
yang	v *****NYANG**
***YANGO**	1 (*yangot*) [mot d'origine inconnue]
yangot	v ***YANGO**
YANKEE	1 (*yankee*)
yankee	v YANKEE
yanna, y-ein-a, y en a, y en à, y en-a, y-en à, yena, yen-a, y-en a, y-en-a, y en ena, yenna, y enna	v IL+Y+EN+A
Y+ETE+EN+A 1 (*y ty en a*)	
y ty en a	v Y+ETE+EN+A
yève, yévre	v LIÈVRE
+YEUX 134 (*léziés* 1, *lisiés* 1, *li zié* 5, *lizié* 54, *li-zié* 8, *liziées* 1, *li ziés* 8, *liziés* 50, *li-ziés* 5, *liziès* 1)	
y faut	v IL+FAUT

Z

z'abé	v +ABBÉ
z'affaire	v +AFFAIRE
z'ami	v +AMI
z'andouille	v +ANDOUILLE
z'anglais	v +ANGLAIS
z'animau	v +ANIMAUX
z'attaque	v +ATTAQUE
z'autre, z'autres	v +AUTRE$_3$
z'employés	v +EMPLOYÉ
z'enfans, z'enfant, z'enfants	
	v +ENFANT
z'esclav'	v +ESCLAVE
z'habitans, z'habitant, z'habitants	v +HABITANT
z'habits	v +HABIT
z'herbaze	v +HERBAGE
z'hirondelle	v +HIRONDELLE
z'histoir, z'histoir', z'histoire	
	v +HISTOIRE
z'homm'	v +HOMME
z'huître	v +HUÎTRE
z'impots	v +IMPÔT
z'invalide	v +INVALIDE
z'istoire	v +HISTOIRE
z'officiers	v +OFFICIER
zabit	v +HABIT
zabitant	v +HABITANT
zabitants	v +HABITANT
zabot	v JABOT
zaco	v ***JAKO**
zaconat, zaconats	v JACONAS
zacot, zacots	v ***JAKO**
zacques	v **CHAKKA**
za fère, zafère, zafère, zaffair, zaffair', zaffaire, zaffaires, zaffairs, zaffer	v +AFFAIRE
zaffront	v +AFFRONT
zaigouïes	v +AIGUILLE
zairignée	v +ARAIGNÉE
zallimettes	v +ALLUMETTE
zaloux	v JALOUX
zalphant	v +ÉLÉPHANT
zamais	v JAMAIS
zamandes	v +AMANDE
Zambèse	v ZAMBÈSE
ZAMBÈSE 1 (*Zambèse*)	
zambon	v JAMBON
zambourzois	v **JAMBO-ROSA**
zambrevatte	
	v **AMBERIVATRY**
zamé, zamés	v JAMAIS
zami, zamie, zamies	v +AMIE
zamiral	v +AMIRAL
zamis	v +AMI
z'amitié	v +AMITIÉ
Zamor	v ZAMOR
ZAMOR	1 (*Zamor*) [prénom]

zamoureix	v +AMOUREUX	zécelle	v +ÉCHELLE	zéro	v ZÉRO
zamployé	v +EMPLOYÉ	zéclair	v +ÉCLAIR	ZERO	2 (zéro)
Zan₁	v JEAN	zéco	v +ÉCHO	zerrata	v +**ERRATA**
zan₂	v dé zan	zécolier	v +ÉCOLIER	zesclav	v +ESCLAVE
zanana	v +ANANAS	zéconomie	v +ÉCONOMIE	zési	v JÉSUS
zanblongue, zanblongues		zécritir	v +ÉCRITURE	zespèce	v +ESPÈCE

zanblongue, zanblongues v **JAMBOLÕES**
zédi JEUDI
zet, zet', zète, zété v JETER

zanse v GENS
zédication v +ÉDUCATION
zétoal, zétoile, zétoiles, zétoille

zancétr v +ANCÊTRE
zefféts v +EFFET
v +ÉTOILE

zanciein, zanciens v +ANCIEN
zeffort v +EFFORT
zétranzé v ÉTRANGER

Zane v JEANNE
zégl v +AIGLE
zette, zétte, zetté v JETER

zanf... v JEAN+FOUTRE
zégouie, zégouïes, zégui₁
Zézé v ZÉZÉ

zanfan, zanfant, zanfants
v +AIGUILLE
ZÉZÉ 3 (Zézé) [prénom]

v +ENFANT
Zégui₂ v ZÉGUI
zhabitans v +HABITANT

zangarna, zanguerna,
ZÉGUI 1 (Zégui₂) [nom de personnage]
zher v troa zher

zangarnah v **JAGAN-NATH**
zhistoire v +HISTOIRE

zanges v +ANGE
zeimpo v +IMPÔT
zhom, zhomme v +HOMME

zanglais, zanglé v +ANGLAIS
zeine, zeines v JEUNE
zhopital v +HÔPITAL

zangui, zanguïe v +ANGUILLE
zeinfirmité, zéinfirmité
zhuître v +HUÎTRE

zanimau, zanimaux, zanimo
v +INFIRMITÉ
zibié, zibier v GIBIER

v +ANIMAUX
zeintéré v +INTÉRÊT
zige v JUGE

Zan marie v JEAN-MARIE
zên' v GÊNER
zilet v GILET

Zanot v JEANNOT
zence, zences v GENS
zilots v +ÎLÔT

zanre v GENRE
zendarm', zendarme, zendarmes
zimage, zimages v +IMAGE

zans v GENS
v GENDARME
ziment v JUMENT

zape, zapé, zappe, zappé
zéne, zène v JEUNE
zimpot, zimpots, zimpôts

v JAPPER
zêne, zéné₁, zèné v GÊNER
v +IMPÔT

zapprenti, zapprentis
zéné₂ v JEÛNER
zindépendants

v +APPRENTIS
zenemi, zénemie v +ENNEMI
v +INDÉPENDANT

zarb, zarbe, zarbes, zarbre,
zénéral v +GÉNÉRAL
zindiennes v +INDIENNE

zarbres v +ARBRE
zenes, zènes v JEUNE
zinga v *ZINGANA

zardein, zardin, zardins
zênesse v JEUNESSE
*ZINGANA 1 (zinga) [mot malg.]

v +JARDIN
zênes-zens, zênes-zens

zaricots v +HARICOT
v JEUNE+GENS
zintéré, zintérê, zintérêts

zarmes v +ARME
zenfan, zenfans, zenfant.
v +INTÉRÊT

zassasein v +ASSASSIN
zenfants v +ENFANT
zinvités v +INVITÉ

zassiettes v +ASSIETTE
zénie v GÉNIE
zinzelis v GINGELY

zassociés v +ASSOCIÉ
zennemi v +ENNEMI
zinzembe v GINGEMBRE

zatte, z'attes v +ATTE
zénoux v GENOU
zipe, zipes v JUPE

zatteliers v +ATTELIER
zenr', zenre v GENRE
zipocrit v +HYPOCRITE

zaune v JAUNE
zens, zense v GENS
zipon v JUPON

zaut, zaut', zaute, zautes,
zentille v GENTIL
ziraumon v **JIRUMUN**

zautre, zautres v +AUTRE₃
zentillesse v GENTILLESSE
zirlandais v +IRLANDAIS

zavaries v +AVARIÉS
Zeorz' v GEORGES
ziroffle v GIROFLE

zavocat v +AVOCAT₂
zépaules v +ÉPAULE
ziromon v **JIRUMUN**

z'bitant v +HABITANT
zéprons v +ÉPERONS
zirondelle, zirondelles

Zean v JEAN
zépi v +ÉPI
v +HIRONDELLE

Zean-la-Guérite
zépol, zépole v +ÉPAULE
zis v JUSTE

v JEAN+LA+GUERITE
zéreigné v +ARAIGNÉE
ziska v JUSQU'À

Zeanne v JEANNE
Zérémi v JÉRÉMIE
ziska prezan, zisqu'à présent

zécasse v +ÉCHASSE
zergnée v +ARAIGNÉE
v JUSQU'À, À+PRÉSENT

ziskas ki	v JUSQU'À, CE, QUI	*zouli*	v JOLI
zisqu', zisqu'à, zisqua, zisquà		*zour, zour'*	v JOUR
	v JUSQU'À	*zourd'hi, zourdhi, zourdi*	
zisquà soir, zisqu'à soir			v AUJOURD'HUI
	v JUSQU'À, À+SOIR	*zoure, zouré*	v JURER
zisqué	v JUSQU'À	*zour-en-zour*	v JOUR-EN-JOUR
zisse, zist, ziste	v JUSTE	*zourite, zouritte, z'ouritte*	
zistice	v JUSTICE		v **+HORITA**
zistoire	v +HISTOIRE	*zournée*	v JOURNÉE
zivroïn	v +IVROGNE	*zours*	v JOUR
ziz₁	v JUGE	*zousqu'à, zousqua*	v JUSQU'À
ziz₂	v JUGER	*zout, zoute*	v +AUTRE₃
zize	v JUGE	*zoutils*	v +OUTIL
zizé, zizer	v JUGER	*zouvraze*	v +OUVRAGE
zizes	v JUGE	*zouvrié, zouvrières, zouvriers*	
zizman	v JUGEMENT		v +OUVRIER
zoder	v +ODEUR	*zouyé*	v JOUER
zoffans	v +OFFENSE	*zouzou*	v JOUJOU
zofficié, zofficier, zofficiers		*Zova*	v ZOVA
	v +OFFICIER	ZOVA	17 (*Zova*) [prénom]
zoffrand	v +OFFRANDE	*zozeau, zozeaux*	v +OISEAU
zoficié	v +OFFICIER	*zozef*	v JOSEPH
zoinde, zouindre, zoine		*zozo*	v +OISEAU
	v JOINDRE	*Zozon*	v ZOZON
zoli, zolie, zolies, zolis	v JOLI	ZOZON	1 (*Zozon*) [prénom]
zolivié	v +OLIVIERS	*zozos*	v +OISEAU
zom, zomme	v +HOMME		
zon'	v JAUNE		
zone	v ZONE		
ZONE	1 (*zone*)		
zongues	v +ONGLE		
zonions	v +OIGNON		
zopital	v +HÔPITAL		
zor	v JOUR		
zoranges	v +ORANGE		
zordes, zordr, zordre, zordres			
	v +ORDRE		
zoreill', zoreille, zoreilles,			
zorey, zoréy, zoreye, zoréye,			
zoréyes, zorèyes			
	v +OREILLE		
zoriés	v +OREILLER		
zot, zot', zote	v +AUTRE₃		
zoté	v +ÔTER		
zotre, zotres, zott, zotte			
	v +AUTRE₃		
zordi, zoudi			
	v AUJOURD'HUI		
zoué	v JOUER		
zouères	v JOUEUR		
zouinde	v JOINDRE		

Elements for a sociolinguistic history of Mauritius and its Creole (to 1968)[1]

Philip Baker

A poor start (1721-25)

After more than a century in Mauritius, the Dutch abandoned the island in about 1710. Ten years later, the Compagnie des Indes, aware that Mauritius had two natural harbours in contrast to its existing territory, Bourbon island (later renamed île de la Réunion) which had none, decided to occupy the island. To that end they dispatched two ships from Lorient, the *Diane* and the *Atalante*, in May 1721 carrying a governor (De Nyon), several employees of the Compagnie, 210 Swiss troops (some of whose senior officers were accompanied by dependants), and four Lazarist priests. There were no settlers on these ships, the Compagnie's hope being that a few families would be persuaded to move there from Bourbon.

The voyage of the two ships did not go well. There was a great deal of illness and mortality on board which led to a lengthy stopover in Brazil to allow passengers to recover their health. Towards the end of 1721, the authorities in Bourbon, having had no news of the whereabouts of these ships, sent 16 Bourbon men under the command of Le Toullec to Mauritius in December of that year. Mauritius has been permanently inhabited since this event.

The *Diane* and the *Atalante* did not reach Mauritius until April 1722. Less than half the original passengers survived the journey, and most of the survivors were in very poor health. (For example, only 90 of the original 210 Swiss troops reached Mauritius, and a further 23 of these died within three months.) A detailed account of all known arrivals and departures from December 1721 to the end of 1725 is given in Baker (1982a: 142-57). Table 1 gives the results of a population census at 18 October 1725.

Table 1

Officiers et employés	20
Troupes	100
Ouvriers	28
Domestiques	5
Femmes	13
Enfants	13
Noirs de la Compagnie	24
Noirs de divers particuliers	10
	213

(source: Kaeppelin 1908: 105)

The above figures appear to exclude the Lazarists, the men from Bourbon, and the maroons (see below). The main population movements during this four-year period were:

- Troops: All but two of the surviving Swiss troops had returned to Europe before the end of 1725. They were replaced by soldiers from France.

---

[1] I am grateful to Vinesh Hookoomsing and Guillaume Fon Sing for their comments on a draft of this article.

- Bourbon men: 10 of the 16 who arrived at the end of 1721 returned to Bourbon in March 1722 (before the arrival of the *Diane* and the *Atalante*). Thereafter there were small numbers of arrivals and departures; their numbers varied between 6 and 17.
- Slaves: 30 slaves arrived from Bourbon in June 1722. 25 of these had been sent back to their owners in Bourbon by April 1723. 65 Malagasy slaves arrived in November 1722, many of whom soon became maroons.
- By the end of 1725 there were still no settlers, from Bourbon, France, or elsewhere.

The earliest known eye-witness account by a visitor of conditions in Mauritius comes from Père Ducros who, in 1725, spent a few days there while waiting for onward transport to Asia (Barnwell 1948: 142-44). He described the island as *le royaume des rats*, noting that the hordes of rats attacked humans as well as their foodstocks. He also mentioned two other major problems: attacks by maroons, and an ever-present threat of starvation. A further problem, which the priest failed to mention, was the shortage of women. All-in-all, the first four years of Mauritius under French ownership can only be described as a failure.

A new start (1726-35)

Lenoir, the newly appointed chief of the Compagnie des Indes operations in the Indian Ocean, visited Mauritius in 1726 on his way to take up his post in Pondicherry. In a detailed report which he sent to the Compagnie's headquarters in France, he set out plans for the settlement of the island. His main proposal was that the Compagnie should send unmarried women from France. Soldiers who married them would be given land, a few slaves, and a discharge from the army. *Il[s] s'y accoutumeroient pendant les deux ou trois premieres années, personne ne penseroit a retourner en France, la colonie se peupleroit, les terres se defricheroient* (ANC C4 v1). This proposal, which Kuczynski (1948-1949, vol. 2) terms "military colonization', was implemented. The first group of 12 young women arrived from France in 1728 and at least three more ships brought others during the following two years (Baker 1982a: 160).

Lenoir's plans also required slaves for the soldier-settlers, and both slaves and skilled workmen to erect buildings and make roads, etc. There were only 30 slaves in the island (Malagasies) at the time of his visit. Between 1727 and the end of 1734, 1420 more were introduced bringing the total number of slave arrivals to 1450.[2] Their geographic origins were as follows:

Table 2

Gorée (Senegal)	517
Juda (Ouidah, Whydah; now part of Benin)	178
India (mainly from South India area but some from Bengal)	269
Madagascar	363
total	1327 (Baker 1982a: 196)

Lenoir envisaged that the skilled workmen would be brought from France, and there were indeed some who arrived by the end of 1734. But a nearer and less expensive source of skilled workmen was Pondicherry and 190 Tamil artisans, employed on contracts, are known to have reached Mauritius by 1734.

Note that all the above figures for slaves and Tamil workmen relate to *arrivals* only. A proportion of the slaves would undoubtedly have died, or escaped captivity and

---

[2] Chaudenson (1979) has challenged some of my figures but his information is based exclusively on secondary sources whereas I have in many cases been able to consult the original documents in archives. In addition, I have worked through all the available parish registers to 1737 – only the first Grand Port register covering the first few years is missing – and can demonstrate that e.g. substantial numbers of slaves from Juda were present because they are mentioned in the registers as having got married or given birth.

become maroons, before the end of 1734. West Africans, who had spent about four months at sea before reaching the island, were more likely to die soon after arrival than others. However, the Malagasy slaves, who had generally only spent a few days at sea, were considered the most likely to become maroons:

> ...every day the brigands [maroons] become more numerous. Blacks newly arrived from Madagascar shake off the yoke of slavery very easily, and prefer the air of the woods... they even have wars among between [sic] themselves, the blacks of Madagascar detesting the Guinea Coast blacks. (Letter from Père Gandon written in 1732, as translated from French in Barnwell [1948: 148]).

There are three sets of figures relating to the population of Mauritius in 1735, none of which provides all the information one would wish. I will restrict attention mainly to the first of these which states that the population on January 1st 1735 "montoit à... 1600 personnes de tout âge, de tout sexe, de toutte condition, et de toutte couleur" (G^1 505).[3] However, the only details of how this figure was composed are:

Table 3
67 habitants ayant concessions
504 Esclaves mâles et femelles en Estat de cultiver la terre
165 Enfants mâles ou femelles esclaves ["sur les seules habitations"]
116 Esclaves mâles ou femelles ["appts. à la Compag."]

The above figures amount to 852, little more than half the claimed total of 1600. However, information on some of the people these figures exclude can be derived from other sources. The Annex at the end of this article, which sets out details of the slave-owning population at 1 January 1735, was compiled by working through the parish registers up to that date.[4] The registers record births, marriages, and deaths but often provide additional information such as place of origin and ethnicity. The figures are necessarily incomplete since anyone who did not get married, who was not named as a newborn's parent, act as its godparent, or serve as a witness to someone's death would not be mentioned in the registers. Nevertheless, the two sets of figures can be reconciled (Baker 1982b: 14-33).

Labourdonnais[5] arrived in Mauritius as governor of the Mascarenes in June 1735. He established his seat of government in Port Louis because of its harbour. According to Toussaint (1973: 21), he immediately set about "converting the primitive harbour into a civilised port" which included a hospital, warehouses, ship-building facilities, offices, and an aqueduct. This required a considerable increase in the numbers of skilled artisans. His 1740 *Mémoire* (Lougnon & Toussaint 1937: 133-34) indicates that he used some of the latter to train about 150 Indians and West Africans in these skills. This plan worked well and by 1739 Mauritius had surpassed Réunion in importance (Barnwell & Toussaint 1949: 51). This was, of course, what the people of Réunion had long feared and was a major factor in their lack of cooperation in the settlement of Mauritius in the 1720s. Labourdonnais also arranged for some slaves, termed "noirs hussards", to be trained to work with settlers in tracking down maroons. These were paid the same wages as the Topasses, men of mixed

---

[3] The other two are (1) a handwritten note in a parish register entry for 25 March 1735 which gives the total population as 1922 (of whom 1676 were in "port au SE" and 246 in "port du NO"); (2) La Bourdonnais' own figures for the plantation-based population only when he arrived in the island in June 1735: familles (hommes 61, femmes 39, garçons 54, filles 18 [sic], économes 18) and esclaves (noirs 272, negresses 222, negrillots 106, negrites 48). The figure for "filles" looks to be a copying error. The word *économes* refers to non-concessionaires in charge of the day-to-day running of a plantation. For a fuller discussion of population figures in 1735, see Baker (1982b: 14-33).

[4] The first Grand Port (Port Sud-Est) register was destroyed during a cyclone in August 1728. At that time, the only slaves in Mauritius were the survivors of the 65 Malagasies introduced in 1722, whose numbers had declined to 30 by the start of 1727, and a further group of 20 Malagasies who arrived later that year (Baker 1982a: 187-88).

[5] His name is also written La Bourdonnais in some sources.

European-Indian descent from Pondicherry who were drafted into the troops in Mauritius in 1736 (Lougnon & Toussaint 1937: 15, 122). Thus, during Labourdonnais' governorship at least, not all slaves were engaged in domestic or agricultural work.

There was strong dissatisfaction with Labourdonnais among the people of Réunion who complained of his neglect of their island, of the offloading of goods intended for Réunion in Mauritius, and of the Mauritian habit of keeping the best of the newly arrived slaves for themselves and sending on to Réunion those judged to be less healthy or otherwise inferior.[6,7] Such complaints were partly responsible for Labourdonnais' recall to France in 1740 but on that occasion he was able to successfully allay any doubts the Compagnie des Indes had about his policies.

Some time after his return to Mauritius, Labourdonnais took the seemingly unprecedented decision to "use the slaves to make up a native island-navy..." (Toussaint 1966: 155). In 1746 he used this naval force to seize Madras from the British. But this and other activities brought him into conflict with both the Compagnie des Indes and with French policy in the Indian Ocean, and these things eventually led to his imprisonment in the Bastille.

From 1 January 1736 to 2 January 1740, the sources and numbers of slaves taken to the Mascarenes, i.e. both Mauritius and Réunion, are given in Labourdonnais' *Mémoire* as follows:

Table 4

Madagascar	1,176
Mozambique	671
West Africa	300
India	180
unknown	102
	2,429

(derived from Lougnon & Toussaint 1937: 155-56)

The West Africans all remained in Mauritius (see Baker 1982b: 13 for references) but details of the division of the rest between Mauritius and Réunion are not known. More than a quarter of the above were from Mozambique and this proportion was to increase slowly thereafter, overtaking those arriving from Madagascar by the end of the 1760s. Figures for slave arrivals in the period 1773-1794 derived from Toussaint (1967: 450-54) indicate that those from East Africa outnumbered Malagasies by 9 : 1.

The declining fortunes of the French in India from the 1740s onwards brought to the island "a sort of scum of bankrupts, ruined adventurers, swindlers, rascals of all kinds" (Bernardin de St-Pierre 1773.1: 177). The beginnings of their arrival towards the end of Labourdonnais' governorship, is mentioned in a letter from Grant, published by one of his descendants more than 50 years later (Grant 1801: 73). Of the resulting population in 1768-69, Bernardin de St-Pierre (1773.1: 182) wrote:

> De tant d'hommes de différents états, résulte un peuple de différentes nations qui se haïssent très-cordialement. On n'y estime que la fausseté.

A further consequence of the growing difficulties faced by the Compagnie des Indes from the 1740s is that the quality of written records, so extraordinarily good during the 1720s and 1730s, declines rapidly. There are nevertheless some comments and documents which merit attention. A letter written in 1754 contains the following remarks on the different groups of slaves then in the island:

---

[6] Due to the wind patterns in the western Indian Ocean, it was always the case, from the start of French occupation of Mauritius, that all ships, whether from Europe, Madagascar, East Africa, or Asia, called at Mauritius before going on to Réunion.

[7] For one example of such a complaint, see the letter from Réunion to the Compagnie des Indes reproduced in Lougnon (1937: 37-38).

> Ainsi estime-t-on d'avantage icy les nègres Yeulloffes, Guinés, Mozambiques et Cafres que les Mallegaches... parceque les premiers vont rarement au maron (*RHL* 5: 245)

At around the same time, Noble visited the island. His comments include:

> Most of the *Slaves* come from Goree, an island on the coast of *Guinea*, belonging to the [French] *East India* Company, *Madagascar*, the East coast of *Africa*, and *Bengal*. The domestic *Slaves*, of both Sexes, are generally those of the last Place, of the *Gentoe* or *Portuguese* castes, they being more cleanly, docile, and serviceable in the House, than the others, who, on the other hand are stronger, and fitter for clearing the Woods, cultivating the Plantations, and other laborious Works (Noble 1755: 15)

In the parish registers in the 1730s there is a clear distinction between slaves from Senegal (described as 'Yolof' or 'Sénégal') and those from Whydah (described as 'Juda' or 'Guiné') and this distinction is maintained in the 1754 letter. However, in most documents consulted from the second half of the 18th century, 'Guinée' or 'Guinea' appears to refer to West Africa in general, as in the above quotation from Noble.

Another source of slaves is mentioned for the first time in a letter from Pierre Poivre who was responsible for introducing many valuable plants from Indonesia:

> Je vous ai ouvert une nouvelle veine de commerce à Timor, ou les Portuguais n'ont rien oublié pour m'engager à revenir tous les ans. Ils promettent annuellement trois cens esclaves à meilleur marché que ceux de Madagascar. (...)
> J'ai acheté 19 esclaves et 15 pics de cire brute. J'aurois trouvé une beaucoup plus grande quantité de l'un et l'autre, mais je n'[avois] ni place dans la cale pour la cire, ni assés de monde pour contenir plus d'esclaves. (Ly-Tio-Fane 1958: 69)[8]

The words Timorien and Malay (in diverse spellings) are found as ethnic labels for slaves in various documents up to the 1820s (see, for example, Table 8, *infra*).

Three interesting documents relating to 1758 are contained in ANC C4, carton 86 (liasse 1757/8). These are reproduced below as Tables 5, 6, and 7.

Table 5

Etat général des esclaves appartenants à la Compagnie du distric [sic] du Bureau des travaux existants au 1/7bre/1758[9]

	Recapitulation		
	Noirs	Negresses	Total
Guinées	220	310	530
Mozambiques	173	72	245
Malgaches	259	181	440
Indiens	103	39	142
Macaos	5	1	6
			1432
	Enfants de touts ages		242
			1674

Since most of the Yolof and "Bambara" slaves who arrived from 1730 onwards worked for the Compagnie, it seems clear that they and their descendents are include in the figures for 'Guinées' here (see also the quotation from Noble above).

In modern MC, /makaw/ is a mildly pejorative term for a person of Chinese descent but nothing has been found to suggest that this word has this meaning in the 18th or 19th centuries. Given that the Portuguese are known to have taken slaves from Indonesia to Macau in former times, it cannot be assumed that it refers to Chinese people here.

---

[8] Filliot (1974: 171) erroneously suggests that the first slaves from Indonesia did not arrive in the Mascarenes until the 1770s.
[9] 7bre refers to September.

Table 6

Etat des Malabards aux service de la Compagnie a l'isle de France au 1er 7bre 1758

Maçons [stone masons]	35
Coulis [coolies]	24
Briquetiers [brickmakers]	7
Charpentiers [carpenters]	19
Forgerons [(black)smiths]	10
Rotineurs []	6
Chaudroniers [braziers]	5
Plombiers [plumbers]	2
Ecrivain [scribe]	1
Pions [messengers]	52
Palfrenier [groom]	1
Menatte [?][10]	3
Gardien de magazin	1
	166

Table 7

Etat des gratiffications accordées aux esclaves de la Compagnie cy après dénomméz, pour talents à eux commise

mettiers

Forgerons [(black)smiths]	28
Charons [wheelwrights]	4
Charpentiers [carpenters]	45
Briquettiers [brickmakers]	6
Chauffourniers [lime-kiln workers]	7
Menuisiers [cabinet-makers]	11
Invalides – *revenus des guerres de l'Inde en 1756* [disabled slaves *returned from the wars in India in 1756*]	2
Armurier [armourer]	1
Vanniers [basket-makers]	2
Rotineurs [makers of rattan ware]	2
Jardinier [gardener]	1
Aux magazins [in the stores]	2
Charettiers [carters]	2
Gardien de troupeau [herdsman]	1
Boucher [butcher]	1
Mere de famille *pour lui aider à elever sa nombreuse famille* [mother *to help her raise her large family*]	1
Plombiers [plumbers]	3
Commandeurs [overseers of a gang of slaves]	13
Testuariers [assistant stone masons?][11]	17
Faiseurs de mortier [mortar makers]	9
Botaniste *Vadeboncoeur, avec M Aublet* [botanist *Vadeboncoeur, with M Aublet*]	1
	119

---

[10] I have not been able to identify the meaning of this word.

[11] I have been unable to find *testuariers* in any French dictionary. Annegret Bollée (p c) has suggested that it might be related to "mfr. nfr. testu 'marteau à tête carrée qui sert à abattre la pierre près des arêtes' [...] nant. ang. têtu 'gros marteau de maçon' (also in many other dialects; FEW 13/1: 278b). Given that Labourdonnais is on record as having arranged for some slaves be trained to work with Indian artisans (see Table 6 above), there seems every possibility that *testuariers* might have been the word applied to such people.

In the middle years of the 18th century the financial problems of the Compagnie des Indes went from bad to worse until in 1764 it went bankrupt. Mauritius and its dependencies became a French crown colony in 1767.

The period from 1767 to the French Revolution is described by Toussaint as "the Good Old Days" (1973: 44-45). Cultural advances during this time include the arrival of the first printing press (1767), the publication of its first newspaper (1773), the first college providing secondary education in the island (1778), the first literary society (1786), and the first theatre (1790).[12]

One of the earliest issues of this newspaper carried the following small advertisement:

> Un jeune Négrillon Mozambique, nommé Favori, âgé de 13 ans, appartenant au Sr Pierre Maheas, habitant à la Montagne Longue, a disparu depuis le 31 Janvier. Comme ce jeune noir s'est probablement égaré & qu'il n'entend pas la langue créole, il n'aura pu dire le nom de son maître ni retrouver sa maison, On prie ceux qui en auront connoissance d'en donner avis audit Sr Maheas. (*Annonces, affiches et avis divers pour les colonies des isles de France et de Bourbon*, 10 février 1773; original italics removed).[13]

This is the earliest known attestation of the word *créole* applied to a French-based Creole. But the advertisement is far more important than that because it indicates or at least implies:

- that this form of speech, distinct from French, existed by 1773;
- that this was what slave immigrants were expected to acquire (rather than French); and
- that knowledge of this was needed to find one's way around the island.

Apart from the nine earliest short texts (pp 3-4 in this volume), there is regrettably no other information on the nature of "la langue créole" in the 18th century. In the three years during which this newspaper existed there is no other use of *créole* to refer to a form of speech. The word is used only as an ethnic label, as in Table 8. Nor are any comments on the linguistic situation yet known from any other source in the last quarter of the 18th century.

One feature of *Annonces...* which is of some interest is a section in each issue listing slaves who had been arrested for travel without authorization. These were held in detention until their owners collected them. The newspaper printed not only the names of these slaves but also applied an ethnic descriptor to each of them. From these lists I have compiled Table 8 (overleaf; reproduced from Table 7 in Baker 1982b: 47). While "Bengali", "Indien", "Lascar", and "Malabar" all obviously relate to people from India, the precise distinctions between the meanings of these terms is unclear. I have not been able to determine the meanings of "Ambolambe" and "Malambou", nor is it clear how "Portugais" should be interpreted in this context.

---

[12] Toussaint claims that both the printing press and the theatre were the first in the southern hemisphere (1969: 16). I am somewhat dubious about both claims, suspecting that earlier dates for either or both could be found in Brazil or some other South American country.

[13] This text was reprinted earlier in Baker (1982a: 248).

Table 8

Summary of slaves held in detention for travelling without authorization in the years 1773 – 1775, by ethnic description applid

Ethnic label	1773	1774	1775	Total	%
Ambolambe			1	1	0.1
Bengali	33	29	13	75	7.6
Chinois		1		1	0.1
Créole	7	11	24	42	4.3
Créole de Bourbon			1	1	0.1
Guinée	6	4	4	14	1.4
Indien	12	3	12	27	2.7
Lascar	2	1	1	4	0.4
Malabar	7	25	12	44	4.5
Malambou	1		2	3	0.3
Malet		2		2	0.2
Malgache	115	156	125	396	40.3
Mosambique	65	123	162	350	35.6
Portugais	1		2	3	0.3
Timorien	15	1	4	20	2.0
Totals	264	356	363	983	99.9

Information derived from all issues of *Annonces, affiches et avis divers pour les colonies des isles de France et de Bourbon* published in the years 1773-1775.

The French Revolution appears to have caused only a limited amount of social disorder in Mauritius, mainly in 1790-91, and without disrupting life on the plantations. "It was slavery which held the colonists together and prevented class conflict" (Toussaint 1973: 53). Nevertheless some sans-culottiste groups were formed and a guillotine was even installed (but never used!). But when the commissioners Baco and Burnell arrived from France in 1796 with the task of ending slavery, they were quickly expelled from the island. From then until the arrival of Decaen as Napoleon's representative in 1803, Mauritius was effectively independent.

Three changes in the island's population followed in the wake of the French Revolution. First, substantial numbers of slaves were given their freedom and a consequence of this was that the free coloured population threatened to outnumber the whites. (In the 40 years to the 1807 census, the number of whites had doubled to 6,489 whereas the number of free coloureds had increased tenfold to 5,912.) Second, there was an increase in the number of white settlers arriving in Mauritius – 1,673 in the period 1787 – 1797 compared with 197 (1767–1777), 624 (1777–1787) and a mere 5 (1797–1807).[14] Third, British naval activities in the Indian Ocean from 1806, aimed at suppressing the slave trade, produced a late surge in the proportion of Malagasy slaves as compared to those from East Africa in the last few years of French rule.

The origins of MC

Having shown above that something sufficiently distinct from French to be termed by a plantation owner "la langue créole" in 1773, it is appropriate at this point to break off from social history and to consider the origins of Mauritian Creole (MC).

The general belief within Mauritius has always been that MC developed within the island from the range of languages formerly spoken there. This belief was challenged by Chaudenson (1974) who wrote:

---

[14] These figures come from D'Unienville (1838) as cited by Kuczynski (1948-49: 761).

> (...) réunionnais, mauricien, seychellois, et rodriguais sont en effet tous quatre issus d'une souche unique: le créole "bourbonnais" parlé à Bourbon au début du XVIIIe siècle.
>
> (...) l'Ile de France est peuplée *d'abord et surtout* à partir de l'Ile Bourbon.[15] Les esclaves introduits dans l'île, en plus grand nombre, après 1730, se trouvent donc en présence homogène sur le plan linguistique, puisque maître et esclaves déjà installés y parlent une seule langue: le créole "bourbonnais" (1974: 446; italics added).

This claim was unexpected, not least because MC and Reunion Creole are not mutually intelligible (as even Chaudenson [1974: 414] has acknowledged). Speakers of these two Creoles have to resort to French in order to communicate with each other. This contrasts sharply with the situation in the Caribbean area where all varieties of Creole French remain mutually intelligible.

Chaudenson's claim led me to carry out detailed research over several years, in France, Britain, and Mauritius, on the peopling of the island. This culminated in the publication of Baker (1982a) and the completion of a PhD thesis (1982b). These demonstrated clearly that the settler population of Mauritius had come from France, not Reunion. Thereafter Chaudenson attributed the transmission of "créole bourbonnais" among slaves in Mauritius mainly to the small numbers of Réunionnais who worked in that island at various times during the 1720s. In particular, it was claimed that the Reunionnais Creoles had the task of instructing slaves on the work they had to do. While this may initially have been the intention, it is not what actually happened, as is clearly indicated in the correspondence between De Nyon and his deputy De Hauville covering the period 1722-24 as well as in a letter from Lenoir to the Compagnie written in 1726 (see Baker 1982a: 157).

Underlying Chaudenson's claim was the assumption – never doubted until very recently – that such a thing as "créole bourbonnais" existed in 1722. The main evidence for this was a sentence said to come from a record of court proceedings in Bourbon in ca. 1722 (Chaudenson 1974: 444),[16] as reported in an article published in Reunion in the 19th century.[17]

> *Moin la parti marron parce qu'Alexis l'homme de jardin l'était qui fait à moin trop l'amour*
> 'I ran away because Alexis the gardener was making excessively amorous advances to me' (Chaudenson 1974: 444)

The 1722 sentence also includes three grammatical features which, in 1974, were known to be well attested in Réunionnais from the first half of the 19th century: preverbal *la* marking the perfective, preverbal *l'était qui* marking the imperfective, and a pronoun preceded by *à* in post-verbal position. This led Chaudenson to claim that:

> ...le créole [bourbonnais] est constitué dans sa forme définitive dès la première moitié du XVIIIe siècle (1974: 445).

Although none of these three features is attested in MC or Seychellois at any time, Chaudenson went on to claim that:

---

[15] Chaudenson's footnote here is a quotation from Toussaint 1936: 13: "Une embarcation de 25 tonneaux... expédiée de Bourbon débarquait quinze colons, un aumônier et un chirurgien barbier. M Duronguouët [sic] le Toullec était à la tête de ce premier contingent que de nouveaux envois de personnes allaient bientôt venir renforcer". See pp 307-08 above for further information.

[16] For the dating of this, see Baker & Corne (1982: 4).

[17] Chaudenson does not indicate the year in which this was published. On p 444, the author is given as H Azéma in volume 1 of *Bulletin de l'Académie de la Réunion* but his bibliography lists the author as V Azéma and gives the volume number as IX (p 1217). On the same page, Chaudenson indicates that his efforts to locate the original document in the Reunion archives proved unsuccessful.

> ...le "bourbonnais" parlé par les immigrants de Bourbon qui débarquent à l'île de France en 1721 est déjà celui que parleront en 1770 ceux qui s'embarqueront à leur tour pour les Seychelles (1974: 449).

New light on the nature of early Réunionnais Creole came with the recent discovery of two religious texts by RP Caulier which were probably written in the 1760s,[18] and which between them contain more than 4,000 words. A provisional transcription of these was made available on the internet by Baker & Bollée (2004). A printed version of these, with some minor corrections, is now available (Bollée 2007) and is accompanied by a detailed analysis of the texts together with a very thorough examination of the relevant historical background.

If MC was historically derived from *créole bourbonnais* one would expect Caulier's texts to resemble MC more closely than do 19th century Réunionnais texts, but this is very far from the case. The only respect in which this is true is the preverbal perfective marker *fini* which occurs far more frequently than the alternative perfective marker written as *l'a* by Caulier; the relative frequency of these two alternatives is reversed in modern Réunionnais. (MC has at all times had only *fini*, and abbreviated forms of this, as its perfective marker.) In all other respects the language of Caulier's texts is at least as remote from MC as all subsequent Réunionnais texts.

Of the three grammatical features in the 1722 text which are also current in the 19th century, two occur in Caulier's texts: object pronouns following *à* and, as already mentioned, *l'a* as the perfective marker. But there is no trace of *l'était qui* which, apart from the 1722 text, is not found until 1828 in the spelling *l'a té qui*.[19] Indeed the entire 1722 sentence is wholly consistent with 19th century Réunionnais whereas Caulier's texts are very definitely not. In a paper presented at Halle in 2006 (Baker, *forthcoming*), I discussed this and several other problems which the 1722 text raises, including the fact that that *était* has its modern spelling whereas, during the 18th century, this word was written *étoit*.[20] My conclusion was, and remains, that the supposed 1722 sentence was not written in 1722. I have no doubt that the trial to which this relates took place at that time and that the written records, in French, of what the accused said would have included something corresponding closely in meaning to the sentence quoted above. But it is my belief that the author of the article translated this into the Réunionnais spoken in his day. In other words, the supposed 1722 sentence is identical with mid-19th century Réunionnais precisely because it was written in the mid-19th century. Had a form of speech closely resembling 19th century Réunionnais existed in the mid-18th century then that is what Caulier would obviously have used to write his *Profession de Foy* and *Petit Catechisme*.

As indicated above and demonstrated in considerable detail in the past (Baker 1982a, 1982b), the number of visitors from Bourbon in the 1720s was always too small for them to have had any major impact on the development of MC, even if they had spoken "créole bourbonnais" as was formerly assumed. But Bollée's (2007) analysis of Caulier's texts and detailed examination of the relevant aspects of the history of Réunion Creole indicate very clearly that no such language could have existed in the 1720s. What the small numbers of slaves and free citizens of Bourbon island would have spoken was one minority variety of French among a range of others. Probably the only way in which they might have been more influential, linguistically, than their small numbers would otherwise suggest is in supplying names for flora and fauna for which those arriving from Europe had no name, as I suggested 25 years ago (Baker 1982a: 242).

In short, MC can only have originated in Mauritius. There was the potential for some lexical influence from Réunion is the earliest years but, after Labourdonnais established

---

[18] On the dating of these texts, see Bollée (2007: 5-9).

[19] *L'était qui* and *l'a té qui* occur as apparent variants in several Réunionnais texts in the 19th century as well as in Fourcade (1930); see Baker (1982a: 229-31).

[20] It is of course entirely possible that the modernization of the spelling was made, consciously or unconsciously, by the author of the article.

his headquarters in Mauritius in 1735, linguistic influences between the two islands are at least as likely to have travelled from Mauritius to Réunion as in the opposite direction.

The Mauritius

In 1809, the British occupied Rodrigues and, in the middle of 1810, they took control of Réunion. In August of the same year they attempted to take Mauritius but were heavily defeated in "the Battle of Grand Port". Four months later, they returned with 10,000 troops, many of them Indian. Decaen had just 4,000 troops and knew that there was no hope of getting help from outside. He capitulated, thereby avoiding any loss of life.

The terms of the capitulation were unusually generous. The free population were given the right to preserve their religion, customs, and laws, and to leave the island, with all their property, if they so wished, within two years. Few appear to have left.

The loss of Mauritius meant that "there was no rallying point left in Asia for French agents or French forces (Carrington 1968: 247). And while Britain returned most of the former French colonies, including Réunion, to France in 1815, it held on to Mauritius "not because of its own positive importance as a colonial possession but because of its harbour, and of the mischief it had caused when in the hands of France" (Egerton 1932: 223). The island thus had a new administration, a new name, *the* Mauritius,[21] and a new coat of arms bearing the words *stella clavisque maris indici* 'star and key of the Indian Ocean'. It also had another language, English. Nothing appears to have been done in the short term to promote knowledge or use of the latter. All official documents continued to be in French until the Colonial Office in London in 1832 – after two decades of British rule! – requested that henceforth all documents sent to London should be in English. Even then the policy adopted locally for several years was to print official documents in both English and French. And the island's leading educational establishment, the Royal College, did not even appoint its first teacher of English until 1833. Thus the change of administration had minimal impact on the local linguistic situation for many years.

Under British rule, slaves could not be brought to the island from East Africa, Madagascar, or elsewhere. But the Seychelles were then a dependency of the Mauritius where it was more difficult to control the illegal introduction of new slaves, and it was legal for slaves in the Seychelles to be transferred to the Mauritius. This created the possibility for the slave trade to continued through the "back door" of the Seychelles. Strenuous efforts were made to stamp this out by checking whether the transferred slaves could speak Creole fluently. If they could not, then they were deemed to be illegally introduced slaves. Declarations of the following kind can be found during the early years of the British administration:

> J'atteste qu'ils parlent le langage créole bien, et mieux peut-être que certains de mes noirs de la même caste, dont je puis prouver l'existence dans la colonie depuis plus de vingt ans. D'ailleurs quand ils se trouvent beaucoup de noirs de même caste sur une habitation, ils se réunissent entr'eux, parlent leur langue et se bornent à apprendre du François ce qui tient à leurs besoins, et à ce qu'ils ont à demander [sic] à leurs maîtres, qui souvent encore pour les entendre ont besoin d'interprêtes pour comprendre de 10, 15 et 20 ans de colonies. Il suffit encore d'aller sur les habitations pour convaincre de ce que j'avance.
> Signé Husson, 27/4/1818 (*Further papers and communications relative to the slave trade at the Mauritius and Bourbon, and the Seychelles*, p 45).

---

[21] How or why the definite article came to be regarded as part of the island's name is unclear. 'The Mauritius' was the usual name in English for several decades and the preceding definite article did not disappear until the second half of the 19th century.

In the 1820s, a Protector of Slaves was appointed, enabling slaves to complain about their ill-treatment.[22] In the same decade it became apparent that slavery itself would be abolished within a few years. This led to many owners of domestic slaves giving the latter freedom in advance of that event.

Relations between the Franco-Mauritians and the British appear to have been cool rather than hostile. The former did not participate in the administration in any way but, so long as their way of life and prosperity were not threatened, they had no serious cause for complaint. But the potential for major conflict arose with the approach of abolition. Plantation owners wanted to be compensated for their loss of slave labour, in Mauritius as in other British colonies. The Anti-Slavery Movement considered that compensation was unnecessary and in 1826 proposed that emancipation without compensation be tried out as an experiment in the Mauritius – the British colony with the smallest proportion of British slave-owners! The Franco-Mauritians quickly became organized and sent a representative to London. They eventually won their case, receiving £2 million as compensation, a very considerable sum at that time.

Comments about Creole languages are generally held to be largely negative and the first two descriptions, "corrupted French" (Grant, writing in 1749) and "mauvais patois" (Bernardin de St-Pierre 1773) may seem to conform to that but it is important to realise that both were writing for non-Mauritians so these descriptions can be seen as at least partly explanatory, preparing the reader for the fact that the quoted MC words do not conform to written French standards of the times. Whatever the case, comments on MC during most of the 19th century are distinctly more positive. The first such comment relates to a visit to Mauritius in 1818 (see **1818a, 1818b** for more information):

> Indépendamment du français, qui forme la base du langage à l'Ile de France, une sorte de patois a été inventé par les noirs, qui, ne pouvant se plier à notre syntaxe, prononcer nos mots difficiles, et saisir la valeur propre de quelques-unes de nos expressions, les ont travestis à leur manière. Peu à peu l'usage a fait loi ; et peut-être ne seroit-il pas sans intérêt aujourd'hui d'examiner les règles de cette langue créole, qui n'est pas dénudée de charmes (Freycinet 1827: 406).

The earliest comment from a British settler is:

> The "patois" or jargon of the Blacks is simple in its construction, and euphonical to the ear, though made up of the "membra disjecta" of several languages (Telfair 1830; 680)

A year later, the first Mauritian to use MC for literary purposes, described MC in the introduction to the second, enlarged edition of his work as "le patois naîf de nos heureux climats" (Chrestien 1831, dedication).

Slavery was abolished on February 1st 1835. The intention was that field slaves would continue to work for their former owners for six years while domestic slaves would do so for only four years. Most slaves moved away from their former owners as soon as they could.[23] This created a shortage of labour on the plantations but this problem was quickly resolved by recruiting indentured labourers from India on a truly massive scale. The total population on the Mauritius in 1835 was just over 100,000. In the following 35 years no fewer than 365,000 Indians were brought to the island and, of these, only 81,000 returned to India when their contracts expired. The net intake of Indians was three times as large as the slave labour force they replaced. The reason for this is that the area under sugar cane increased enormously at this time, and many of the new plantations initially had British rather than French owners.

---

[22] Written records of the evidence presented are held in the Public Record Office in Kew (London) – but the surviving evidence is all written or printed in French and/or English. The bulk of the evidence must have been given in MC but, if any of this survives, its location remains to be discovered.

[23] My understanding is that the planned apprentice scheme failed and that few if any plantation slaves continued to work for their former owners for six years, but I am unable to confirm this.

Charles Darwin visited Mauritius in 1836 on his return journey from Australia to Europe. His comments include the following:

> Although the island has been so many years under the English Government, the general character of the place is quite French: Englishmen speak to their servants in French, and the shops are all French; indeed, I should think that Calais or Boulogne was much more Anglified. There is a very pretty little theatre, in which operas are excellently performed. We were also surprised at seeing large booksellers' shops, with well-stored shelves; -- music and reading bespeak our approach to the old world of civilization; for in truth both Australia and America are new worlds.
>
> The various races of men walking in the streets afford the most interesting spectacle in Port Louis. Convicts from India are banished here for life; at present there are about 800, and they are employed in various public works. (...) These men are generally quiet and well-conducted; from their outward conduct, their cleanliness, and faithful observance of their strange religious rites, it was impossible to look at them with the same eyes as on our wretched convicts in New South Wales (Darwin 1845).

Sugar was very profitable in the middle part of the 19th century and the period from about 1840 to 1865 is sometimes known as *L'âge d'or* ("the golden age") for that reason. The benefits of this prosperity included the establishment of a railway network covering 250 km with more than 60 stations and the introduction of gas street lighting in Port Louis. But the prosperity rapidly declined soon after as sugar became less profitable, added to which there was a very serious epidemic of malaria which killed 10% of the entire population in 1867 alone. With the railway from Port Louis to Mahébourg completed in that year, the better off citizens of the capital moved out en masse, the whites to Curepipe and the coloured population to Rose Hill and Beau-Bassin, commuting to and from the capital in first and second class carriages while their servants, carrying their lunch, travelled in third class. The cause of malaria was unknown at the time but it was generally assumed to be a contagious disease introduced by Indians. Anti-Indian feelings grew and pass laws were introduced which meant that Indians found to be without a valid contract of employment could be arrested for vagrancy, an offence potentially punishable by a period of hard labour. In 1869 alone, more than 30,000 such arrests were made (Tinker 1974: 242). This led to protests and, eventually, to the arrival of a Royal Commission which abolished the pass laws and made other improvement for Indians.

Not much has been published about what happened to the former slaves after abolition. What little there is barely goes beyond Baissac's comment that *les nouveaux affranchis s'arrangeaient (...) pour vivre sans travail* (1880: xviii) and Bowe's claim that former field slaves lived by thieving and begging, etc. (1976: 10). A more detailed account, written in 1840 but never previously published, is included as an annex at the end of this book (see Lloyd, *this volume*).

The census of 1846 introduced a new term to the island: General Population or *Population générale*. This designated the entire non-Indian population of the island,[24] but it reflected the idea or hope that, on completion of their contracts, Indians would return to India and that, at some point in the future the racial structure of the island would revert to what it had been in 1835. The term has remained in use ever since and plays a key role in the current electoral system.

In the middle years of the 19th century, three anglophone visitors published comments on MC:

> The language used [in the Mauritius] is French creole with the Bengalese, nega[25] and some odd words belonging to no nation, all intermixed, requiring but a graft of Chinese to make it a most unique tongue (Pridham 1846: 410).

---

[24] The Chinese were recognised as a separate census category from 1861. Indo-Mauritians were subdivided into Hindus and Muslims from the census of 1962.
[25] This word meant 'African' and is cognate with Negro and its offensive derivative, nigger.

> The patois of the creoles of the lower classes is the most extraordinary imaginable medley of French, English, and Malgaseh [sic], with at times a dash of Hindustani and Malabar. As spoken by the Indian coolies it is the most laughable jargon, and the veriest lingual olla podrida in the world (Mouat 1852: 95).

> The language which may be called vernacular in Mauritius is Creole, a sort of corrupt French. Chinese artisans, Indian coolies, Arab traders, Mozambique rescued slaves,[26] natives of Madagascar, and English soldiers, who might land on the same day, each utterly unable to comprehend any one of the others, would be found, after a year's residence, conversing together in this strange dialect (Ryan 1863: 5).

The Indian immigrants brought several languages with them. Nearly two-thirds of them came from north-east India and it is from the range of related languages they spoke that Mauritian Bhojpuri emerged. In the 19th century, these languages would probably have been regarded as somewhat aberrant varieties of Hindustani. About 30% of the others sailed from Madras and were speakers of Tamil and Telugu. Tamil was already represented in the island throughout the previous century. The remaining Indians were from the western coast of India and probably speakers of Gujarati and Marathi.

The most notable publications in MC in the middle years of the 19th century are Lolliot's *Poésies Créoles* (1855) and Descroizilles' *Navire fine engazé* (1867). See the Corpus (*this volume*, 1-62) for more information about these. One thing which emerges clearly from both of them is that MC is considered the property of the entire General Population, not merely former slaves and their descendants. Descroizilles has a few lines devoted to MC which merit inclusion here:

> Yena qui dimandé, pourquoi criole nous causé?
> Est-ce qui par hazard, vlé empèche moi parlé?
> dans langage qui, zenfant, nourrice fine montré
> Est-ce qui dans Tribunal, ça vous vlé empéché?
> Mo dire vous, tout dimounde, yena son la gazette,
> Tout yena son couler, yena son pavillon;
> Jisqu'à Malbar, Chinois, son langage imprimé,
> Et nous, nous vrai criole [sic], ou bon ou n'a pas bon;
> dans nous langage oussi, laisse nous faire nous la tête;
> Après tout, qui vous embras, si au lié dire "Monsieur"
> Mo viré mon causé, moi mo vlé dire *Misié*?
> Est-ce qui vous maziné, vous capab empècer?

> Translation: There are those who ask why we speak Creole.
> Is it perhaps that [they] want to prevent me from speaking
> in the language which, as a child, my nursemaid taught me
> [or] is its use in the Tribunal what you want to prevent?
> I say to you, everyone has his newspaper,
> his colour, and his flag;
> Even the languages of the Indians and Chinese are printed.
> And we, we true Creoles, whether good or bad,
> in our language too, let us make headway;
> After all, does it embarrass you if, instead of saying "Monsieur"
> I turn my language around [and] I wish to say *Misié*?
> [and in any case] do you think you can prevent me?

One point to note is that both Lolliot and Descroizilles apply the word Creole (or Criole) to the entire General Population including Franco-Mauritians. This conflicts with modern usage. No one would apply the word 'Creole' to a Franco-Mauritian today, and no one of mixed but predominantly European descent would apply this word to themselves (although it might occasionally be so used, pejoratively, by others).

---

[26] Africans rescued from slave-trading ships in the western Indian Ocean by the British navy.

It is also worth noting that, while Descroizilles commented on many of the problems facing the island, he overlooked what was to be a particularly important one: the Suez Canal which opened in 1869. The Mauritius was suddenly no longer 'the star and key of the Indian Ocean'. It was just a small island, and not an obvious port of call on the way to anywhere. And perhaps purely by coincidence, the use of the definite article, which had slowly declined over the years, ceased entirely at about this time.

The economic decline continued in the latter part of the 19th century. Some Franco-Mauritians took their sugar production skills to Natal where they started plantations (Pope-Hennessy 1964: 237). As many as 5,000 Britons are estimated to have been living in Mauritius in about 1860 (Flemyng 1862: 199) but the majority of them appear to have left before the end of the century.

Notre pauvre patois (1880-1945)

Baissac's *Etude sur le patois créole mauricien* was published in 1880. It was one of the earliest grammars of a French Creole to appear. The value of this and *Le folk-lore de l'île Maurice* which followed in 1888 is amply illustrated by the fact that they have remained the most quoted sources of information on MC for more than a century (as also evidenced by the number of references to him in the index of this book). However, in the present context it is his attitude towards MC which is of particular interest.

In his Introduction, the first example he brought to the attention of readers was:

Papa Moussié Pôl grand zhabitant quartier Moka
'Le père de M. Paul est un grand propriétaire du quartier de Moka'

The MC sentence contains no prepositions nor is there an overt copula.[27] The French equivalent requires three prepositions and a copula. This arguably impressive economy was not seen as a positive feature for he commented:

Un tel système peut-il permettre l'érection d'un édifice quelconque? Hélas! à peine d'une humble, d'une bien humble bâtisse; et encore, à la condition expresse qu'elle n'ait pas l'ambition de s'élever à plus de quelques pieds au-dessus du sol (1880: v).

This seems overly pessimistic given what had already been achieved by his fellow Mauritians (none of whom he mentioned). However he did concede that MC had some favourable attributes. It was at least "le commun moyen d'échange" between the different races in the island "émigrés du coeur de la civilisation ou des confins mêmes de la barbarie" (1880: vi). He also remarked that *L'originalité de la langue est tout entière dans le pittoresque de l'expression. L'image avant tout (...)*. The following examples were given to illustrate this:

Divent après fére polisson av mo robe
'Le vent polissonne avec ma robe'

Navire là dans loin; prend vouys longuevie, longuevie l~a va hisse li
'Ce navire est dans le loiuntain; prenez votre longue-vue, la longue-vue le traînera à vous'

Camaron natté dans ça bassin là
'Les camarons font natte au fond de ce bassin'

Commenting on the last of these, he wrote: *il y a dans le mot tout un enchevêtrement de barbes, de pattes et de pinces qu'une longue périphrase française ne rendrait pas avec le même relief* (1880: xxxviii-xxxix).

---

[27] It does in fact contain zero copula, the presence of which is signalled intonationally although it cannot be represented phonemically.

The only person Baissac mentions who had written about MC was Freycinet (1827) who, with regard to Chrestien's (**1818b**) version of a La Fontaine fable, had commented:

> Après un tel essai, il est permis de concevoir la possibilité de reproduire en créole un grand nombre de morceaux de notre littérature (pp 412-13).

Baissac disagreed strongly:

> Il nous coûte de nous inscrire en faux contre ce jugement; mais loin qu'il nous soit permis d'admettre qu'on puisse mener à bien une telle reproduction, nous croyons que la pensée même de l'entreprendre ne saurait venir à un homme de sens. L'horizon est étroit autour de notre pauvre patois (1880: 232).

It is curious that a man who devoted a great deal of time and effort to writing a grammar of MC and collecting folktales in it should express such negative views. Perhaps these were intended not for local consumption so much as for a metropolitan French readership, which might not readily consider the "corrupt" French of former slaves as a matter for serious study? Only two comparable studies had been published earlier, Thomas (1869) on Trinidadian French Creole and St Quentin (1872) on Guyanais. He is unlikely to have been aware of the former, published in Trinidad, and would not necessarily have known about the latter.

A striking different attitude to MC was held by one of his former pupils at Royal College, Samuel Anderson whose publications contain some grammatical features not found in Baissac's work. For further information about both men, as well as details of other publications in MC during this period, see the Corpus (*this volume*, especially pp 54-56).

The most damning comment ever on MC, and perhaps on any Creole language, occurs in the title of an article by Ducrocq (1901): Idiome enfantin d'une race enfantine.

A measure of political democracy was introduced with the 1886 constitution but the property owning requirements ensured that almost all electors were either Franco-Mauritians or from the coloured population. These two groups had separate political parties which were bitterly opposed to each other. In 1911, their mutual dislike led to street riots which left several dead and wounded (Toussaint 1973: 101).

A new political movement which wanted the retrocession of Mauritius to France was launched a few years later. Its founders were all members of the coloured population but they fully expected to win the Franco-Mauritians over to their cause. This failed to happen, all pro-retrocession candidates being defeated at the following election. Smith (1969: 80) attributes this partly to the increased prices they received from Britain for their sugar after World War I, and partly to fears that France was more likely to widen the franchise than Britain and thus diminish their political influence. Following that, a book entitled *L'Evolution Nationale Mauricienne* was published by Duclos (1924). The author argued that, while ["educated"] Mauritians were culturally closer to France than to any other country, they had absorbed aspects of British and other cultures and should strive towards "Mauritianism" rather than "un retour aux origines". This appears to be the earliest published expression in favour of the development of an independent Mauritian sense of identity.

All comments about MC so far in this article have come from Mauritians or non-Mauritians who had spent some time in the island. The next comes from the very distinguished Danish linguist Jespersen. In what was a highly influential book at that time, he devoted a few pages to MC. His information came from Baissac but the comments were very much his own. With regard to the preverbal TMA markers, he wrote: "the language has really succeeded in building up a very fine and rich verbal system with the simplest possible means and with perfect regularity" (1922: 227). He went on to say: "Left to itself it might develop into a really fine idiom without abandoning any of its characteristic traits", but then he added that he thought the teaching of "real French" might well prevent that from happening (1922: 228).

In 1936, the Labour Party (Parti Travailliste) was formed with an initial membership drawn mainly from the coloured population. It differed from pre-existing political parties in a number of respects. First, its basic aim was to obtain voting rights and improved living conditions for all the underprivileged, whether Indian or from the "General Population". Secondly, its leaders made political speeches in MC whereas other political parties had used only French for this purpose (naturally enough, since that was the first language of their voters). Thirdly, it could not hope to win any seats so long as the 1886 constitution remained in force. It could, however, make speeches in "the only language everybody understands" outside the elected assembly when not banned from so doing.

In 1941, Ward's *Report on Education in Mauritius* was published. It was concerned with language policy in primary schools. Ward circulated two questions to primary schoolteachers:

(a) How long will it take a child who speaks Creole as his mother tongue to understand lessons given in French?

(b) how long would it take a child knowing no Creole but speaking an Indian language as his mother tongue to pick up enough Creole to understand lessons in Creole?

He received 990 replies to question (a)

Under two years	297	(30%)
Two to three years	426	(43%)
Over three years	267	(27%)

901 replies were received to question (b):

Six months or less	390	(43%)
Six months to one year	293	(33%)
Over one year	218	(24%)

Like some later reports on language in education in Mauritius, having found strong evidence in favour of the use of MC for teaching purposes but knowing that those who commissioned the report would find any such proposal unacceptable, an escape route had to be found. In Ward's case, this took the form of the requirement that "a major purpose of primary education must be to make children literate in a major European language".

During the Second World War, many Mauritians joined the British Army. Most were non-whites and they naturally resented the fact that their conditions of service were inferior to those enjoyed by whites. Resentment grew as it became apparent that all promotions were given to whites. They complained and, when it became apparent that this was not going to change matters, a group of them stationed in Madagascar mutineed. This produced the desired outcome: thereafter all Mauritian soldiers had the same conditions of service and some non-whites were promoted (cf Smith 1969: 237-38). Given that, under the existing constitution, the majority of non-white soldiers lacked the right to vote, this was an important victory.

In contrast to all previous censuses, that of 1944 included questions about language. The answers to the question asking people to name the language habitually spoken were recorded as: Hindi 52.3%, Creole 35.6%, French 8.5%, Chinese 2.4% and, after 130 years of British rule, English 0.3% (Census table xxxviii).[28] The figures are unsatisfactory because it is obvious that all responses naming an Indian language (including unrelated Dravidian languages such as Tamil and Telugu) were recorded as 'Hindi'. But if 'Hindi' is interpreted as 'Indian languages', the figures do at least provide a first, very approximate

---

[28] 0.8% provided no answer to this question. Five or fewer speakers were also listed for several European languages.

indication of the situation. This census also asked if respondents could speak English; 6.6% of the total population said they could.

Towards independence (1946-1968)

In 1946, preparations were already being made for the independence of India the following year, an event which would mark the beginning of the end of the British Empire. Extensions of the franchise in Mauritius and other colonies became inevitable. A new constitution for Mauritius in 1947 gave the right to vote to everyone in each administrative district who:

> ...is ordinarily resident in that district and can speak and can read and write simple sentences in, and can sign his name in, any of the languages mentioned in the second schedule to this order to the satisfaction of the officer charged with the duty of registering electors in that district (Order in Council establishing the Legislative Council, 19 December 1947).[29]

The languages mentioned in the second schedule were "English, French, Hindustani, Tamil, Telegu [sic],[30] Urdu, Chinese, [and] The Creole Patois commonly in use in the Colony" (*idem.*, commas added). If one assumes that Bhojpuri was counted as a variety of Hindustani, the only notable omission from this list is Marathi. The inclusion of MC is of particular interest since lack of a standard written form for this language has always been one of the major reasons given for *not* using it in schools. Had MC not been included here, the numbers able to claim the right to vote would have been severely reduced.

The new constitution provided for 19 single member constituencies but the governor had the right to nominate a further 12 members. Candidates who were successful in the election which followed included eleven Hindus, seven who belonged to the coloured population, and one Franco-Mauritian. The governor used his 12 nominations to prevent there being an Indian majority. Only one of his nominations was Muslim. Since Muslims formed more than 16% of the island's population, they protested at their under-representation. This was eventually to lead to the subdivision of the Indo-Mauritian population into separate Hindu and Muslim communities for census purposes and, later, for electoral purposes.

From this point onwards at least, political, educational, and social reforms were rarely out of the news and appear to have caused some to reflect on the place of MC in Mauritian society.

> Notre pauvre vieux patois est nôtre uniquement, complètement, créé par tous pour l'usage de tous, non pas seulement d'élites et de privilégiés, mais du maître et de son serviteur, du patron et de l'ouvrier... Langue de tous, qui n'humilie personne, que chacun parle sans défaut, l'écolier comme l'analphabète...
>
> Comme toutes les langues, il prend son bien ailleurs quand il le trouve. La langue malgache, l'indienne, l'anglaise, lui prêtent de quoi accroître son pittoresque. Mais, par-dessus tout, il est français (Charoux 1953: 18-19).

Reflecting on education in Mauritius, Benedict wrote:

> If Creole can be said to be unifying because nearly every one speaks it yet no one wants to, English can be said to by unifying because hardly anyone speaks it yet nearly every one wants to (Benedict 1958).

---

[29] I am grateful to Vinesh Hookoomsing for sending me this quotation, as well as those from Charoux and Benedict further down the page, and the one from Prosper on p 326.
[30] In India, this name is generally written 'Telugu' but in Mauritius the spellings *Telegu* (in English) and *télégou* (in French) are normally used.

In 1959, a group of Mauritians concerned about the state of inter-ethnic relations published a collective work entitled *Vers une entité mauricienne*. Four contributors drew attention to the important role of MC in enabling all sections of the population to communicate with each other. But while a contributor named Saminaden could only note, sadly, that *le patois créole nous a servi pour nous comprendre jusqu'ici. Dommage qu'il ne soit pas une langue* (p 72), the volume's editor, Sidonie, was more positive:

> Reste notre cher patois créole, longtempts méprisé, auquel nous nous raccrochons comme un moyen d'identification. Lien fragile entre tous, mais en ce moment où une nette tendance a l'aparthéisme semble se dessiner, il est très important de rechercher ce qui peut nous unir et non nous diviser (p 83).

In the same year, the first university dissertation on MC was completed (Kiamtia 1959) but, written in French at a Welsh university, it remained unknown locally. Others were soon to follow.

In 1961, the Meade Report was published. In the part concerned with language policy, Meade took the view that "the greatest handicap to successful education in Mauritius is that imposed by the multiplicity of languages in use (p 208). While acknowledging that "practically everybody" could speak MC, he wrote that this could "do no more than serve as a rough-and-ready means of oral communication" (pp 208-09). Having thus disposed of MC, he went on to list his conclusions:

1. It is universally agreed that English must remain the official language of Mauritius and the medium of instruction in her secondary schools. Therefore
2. English should be taught at the earliest possible stage in the primary schools and should become the medium of instruction when it has been adequately mastered. Therefore
3. No other language should be formally taught in the primary schools or examined at the end of the primary course.
4. French and oriental languages might be taught out of school to those pupils whose parents so desired and should in any event be taught as second languages in the secondary schools (p 211).

These proposals, being entirely unacceptable to most Mauritians, were never implement.

In about 1963, the *Parti Mauricien*, which enjoyed the financial support of whites and the electoral support of a growing proportion of the General Population, followed the language policy of the Labour and other political parties and opted to use MC in future to address the crowd at its meetings. The General Population accounted for only about 30% of the electorate. To win a parliamentary majority. the party had to gain some support from minorities unhappy at the prospect of a government dominated by people of northern Indian descent,[31] a difficult task. It is significant that use of MC was identified as essential for this purpose.

An entirely different, and non-political, endorsement of MC appeared, rather unexpectedly, from a well-known Franco-Mauritian, the poet, painter, and journalist Malcolm De Chazal in the Parti Travailliste's flagship newspaper *Advance*:

> Nulle langue sur la terre n'est plus riche que notre patois en tant que forme et véhicule poétique. Et cette langue dit absolument tout ce qu'elle veut dire, crée éternellement des verbes, ruisselle de métaphores inouïes et finalement est la gaieté même (*Advance*, 6 juin 1964).[32]

---

[31] These minorities include the Tamils, accounting for around 7% of the total population. Although never officially recognized as a separate community, the Tamils have long considered themselves to be such.

[32] Had I discovered this quotation myself, I would certainly have wanted to include it on the back cover of this book. But I found this on the back cover of Furlong &Ramharai (2007) to whom I am indebted for having rescued De Chazal's words from obscurity.

A government controlled television service started in 1965. Programmes were in English, French, and Hindustani in the approximate ratio of 6 : 5 : 1, respectively. This policy contrasted sharply with that of the radio station (also government controlled) where broadcasting was mainly in French (all morning and evenings from 6 p.m. with only a token amount of English) and "oriental languages" (Hindustani in the afternoons with token token slots for other Indian languages as well as both the Cantonese and Hakka varieties of Chinese). Neither service gave airtime to Bhojpuri or MC at this time. The high proportion of English was heavily and frequently criticized in the (overwhelmingly francophone) newspapers, especially since the television service failed to account for this policy or to promise change.[33] Dissatisfaction diminished somewhat as France stepped in and made arrangements for its FR3 television service in Réunion to be accessible to most Mauritians.

In the run up to independence, language policy was a matter of widespread debate, not least because France was actively seeking to maintain the role of French as an international language and saw the possibility of French acquiring official language status in Mauritius. In 1967 several publications dealing with language appeared. Mamet and De Rauville separately published articles with exactly the same title: *Ile Maurice: Ile de la francophonie*. Another Mauritian more realistically wrote:

> Si la langue officielle à l'île Maurice demeure nécessairement l'anglais, (...), la langue nationale ne peut être et n'est déjà que le français, ce vers quoi d'ailleurs tend le patois créole après des étapes de purgation (J-G Prosper, *Le Mauricien*, 27 novembre 1967).

Other languages also had their champions. Bhuckory, in a book promoting the use of, and entitled, *Hindi in Mauritius*, included a poem he had written in Hindi and provided English and French translations of this in which Mauritius was described as "a little India beyond the seas" and "une Inde en miniature" (1967: 177, 180), concepts unlikely to find much favour in a political atmosphere where the leading opposition *Parti Mauricien*, fiercely opposed to independence, used such overtly racist slogans such as *Malbar nous pas oulé* and *Enveloppé nous pas oulé*.[34] Yet in the same book, Bhuckory also made a remarkable, perhaps unintentionally positive-sounding, comment on MC:

> It is inconceivable to find a Mauritian child today unable to speak the creole. Everybody speaks it as naturally as birds fly or fishes swim (1967: 142).

A new electoral system was introduced for the pre-independence elections. Apart from 20 three-member constituencies,[35] there were to be eight additional seats for "best losers" distributed according to a formula linked to the census which would ensure that the main ethno-religious "communities" were adequately represented in parliament. If, for example, the Muslims were seriously underrepresented in the directly elected seats, the first "best loser" to be chosen would be the unsuccessful Muslim with the highest percentage of votes in his or her constituency. However, the system only recognised four

---

[33] As an employee of the television station at the time, I know that the language policy was at the insistence of the then prime minister, Ramgoolam, who did not want the press to know of this since it would hurt his popularity.

[34] These mean (word for word) 'Indians, we don't want' and 'wrapped (in Indian clothing), we don't want'. *Malbar* (< Malabar) d may originally have been applied to people from southern India in the 18th century. In the 19th century, with the huge influx of indentured labourers, it appears to have been applied to Indians in general. In more recent times it has become a pejorative term and has tended to designate primarily Hindus of northern Indian descent, to the exclusion of Tamils and Muslims. While I can find no historical evidence to support this, the slogan *enveloppé nous pas oulé* is said to date back to a 19th century myth among the former slaves to the effect that, once the entire population of India had moved to Mauritius, there would be one more, final boat bringing cloths (i.e. dhotis, sarees, etc.) which they, the former slaves, would be forced to wear in order to complete the Indianization process.

[35] Two more members were to be elected to represent Rodrigues which has not previously had any form of political representation.

communities: Indo-Mauritian Hindu,[36] Indo-Mauritian Muslim, Sino-Mauritian, and General Population. This division did not satisfy minorities who felt that they constituted a separate community, particularly the Tamils. This had already led to minorities using the language questions on census forms to record as "language usually spoken in the home"[37] a language associated exclusively with their community even if they were unable to speak it (cf Hookoomsing 1986). This, combined with a tendency to name a language more statusful than the one usually spoken, e.g. Hindi rather than Bhojpuri, French rather than MC, has bedevilled attempts by the census authorities to gain an accurate picture of the language situation, but this has slowly improved, as will be indicated below.

In the 1967 election, candidates favouring independence won 56% of the votes and a clear majority of seats. An independent Mauritius was now a certainty. Without waiting for the day itself (12 March 1968), Dev Virahsawmy, who has just returned from Scotland where he had written an MA dissertation on Mauritian Creole, began publishing a series of newspaper articles in which he proposed that MC be adopted as the national language of the soon-to-be-independent country. He also proposed an orthography for the language which he felt should henceforth be known simply as **morisiê**, but he adapted the McConnell-Laubach system for Haitian Creole, dating from the 1940s, which had long since been abandoned in Haiti itself. While he was to persevere with this orthography for more than a decade, using it in his own numerous publications, it failed to win significant popular support. Nevertheless Virahsawmy ushered in a new era for MC where its role in society and how it should be written were constantly in the news, questions which have continued to be debated for forty years with little sign of their being resolved in the near future.[38]

The title of this article indicates that it deals only with the situation up to 1968. I would nevertheless like to conclude with a few words on what can be gleaned from the language questions in the censuses. Once it had become apparent that the question about language use at home had been used by minorities to register their numerical strength, a second question asking the language of their forefathers was introduced (in 1962). This enabled minorities to record both their linguistic ancestry and numerical presence but it was only partially successful in persuading respondents to indicate their current home language accurately. Meanwhile the figures for MC climbed have climbed steadily. In 1944, 35.6% gave MC as their habitual language compared with 52.3% recorded as "Hindi" (but in fact the figure for all Indian languages combined). By the 1972 census, MC was acknowledged for the first time as the usual home language by the majority of the population (51.9%) while the figure for all Indic and Dravidian languages combined was 41.7%. Few would doubt that the true figure for MC at that time would have been about 20 percentage points higher, but this was nevertheless a sign that the census figures were becoming more accurate. One problem, even in 1972, was the government's refusal to recognise Bhojpuri as a valid response. This was changed in 1983,[39] but the recording of its more prestigious relative, Hindi, as the home language declined only slowly. Another change was introduced in 1990 when respondents were allowed to name up to two languages as being those spoken by their forefathers and as those currently in use at home. Since two languages co-exist in many Mauritian households, this has made it possible to gain a far more accurate picture of the linguistics situation. The latest (2000) figures give MC as the sole language usually spoken at home of 69.2% but a further 6.9% record use of MC

---

[36] Indo-Mauritian Christians (about 2% of the total population) were included in this category although this was not widely realised at the time. The word 'Indo-Mauritian' was later dropped and the first two groups were thereafter known as simply Hindu and Muslim.

[37] The wording of this question varies from census to census.

[38] A harmonized orthography proposed by Hookoomsing and collaborators in 2004 appears to have had a generally positive reception but the diversity of views on all matters in Mauritius is such that general acceptance of this or any variant of it is likely to take several years.

[39] For this and several other details in this paragraph, I am indebted to Hookoomsing (p c) but I am wholly responsible for the interpretation given here.

alongside an Indian language while yet others acknowledge its use with French, English, or a Chinese language, producing a total figure approaching 80% for those who use MC at least some of the time at home. This increase, compared with earlier figures, has been at the expense of Indian and Chinese languages. And while the numbers who can and do speak French fluently have undoubtedly increased enormously since independence, there is as yet only limited evidence of this replacing MC in the home.

Mauritian Creole, the language which Baissac and others in the latter part of the 19th century saw as threatened by the massive influx of people speaking Indian languages, has in fact ultimately triumphed over all of them.

References

Advance [a daily newspaper published since the 1930s]
ANC, *see* Archives Nationales. Archives des Colonies
Annonces, affiches et avis divers pour les colonies des isles de France et de Bourbon 1773-1775.
Archives Nationales. Archives des Colonies, Série C4 vol. 1, C4 carton 86, liasse 1757/8, G^1 505.
Baissac Charles 1880 Etude sur le patois créole mauricien. Nancy: Impr. Berger-Levrault.
—— 1888 *Le folklore de l'île Maurice*. Paris: Maisonneuve & Larose.
Baker, Philip 1972 *Kreol. A description of Mauritian Creole*. London: C Hurst.
—— Baker, Philip 1982a On the origins of the first Mauritians and of the Creole language of their descendants. Baker & Corne (eds.) *Isle de France Creole: origins and affinities*. Ann Arbor: Karoma, 131-259.
—— 1982b The contribution of non-francophone immigrants to the lexicon of Mauritian Creole, DPhil, School of Oriental and African Studies, University of London.
—— [*forthcoming*] Some of the things that social history and old texts can and cannot tell us about the evolution of Creole languages. R Ludwig & B Schnepel (eds) *Multiple identities in action: Mauritius and the Antillean parallelism*. [provisional title]. Frankfurt: Peter Lang Verlag ["Sprache-Identität-Kultur"].
Baker, Philip & Bollée, Annegret 2004 Edition de deux textes religieux du XVIIIe siècle : Philippe Caulier C M: Profession de Foy, en jargon des Esclaves Nêgres; Petit Catechisme de l'Isle de Bourbon tourné au Style des Esclaves Nêgres. *Creolica*, ISSN 1762-598X, <www.creolica.net>.
Barnwell, P J 1948 *Visits and despatches (Mauritius 1598 – 1948)*. Port Louis.
Barnwell, P J & Toussaint, Auguste 1949 *A short history of Mauritius*.
Benedict, Burton 1958 Education without opportunity. *Human Relations* 11.
Bernarding de St-Pierre, J-H 1773 *Voyage à l'Isle de France (...)*. Paris, 2 vols.
Bhuckory, Somdath 1967 *Hindi in Mauritius*. Port Louis.
Bowe, Gerald 1976 *Venerable Father Laval, 1803-1864*. Port Louis.
Bollée, Annegret 2007 *Deux textes religieux de Bourbon du 18e siècle et l'histoire du créole réunionnais*. London: Battlebridge.
Carrington, C E 1968 *The British overseas*. Cambridge, 2nd edition.
Charoux, Clément 1953 *Chronique du pays créole*. Port Louis : Mauritius Printing.
Chaudenson, Robert 1974 *Le lexique du parler créole de la Réunion*. Paris: Champion.
—— 1979 A propos de la genèse du créole mauricien: le peuplement de l'Ile de france de 1721 à 1735. *Etudes créoles* 2: 43-57.
Chrestien, François [1822] 1831 *les essais d'un bobre africain*. Mauritius: Déroullède.
Colony of Mauritius 1945 *Census of Mauritius and its dependencies*. Port Louis: Government Printing.
Darwin, Charles 1845 *Journal of researches into the natural history and geology of the countries visited during the voyage around the world of HMS "Beagle" (...)*. London.
Descroizilles, H C 1867 *Navire fine engazé. the "Mauritius" in danger*. Mauritius.
Duclos, J A 1924 *L'évolution nationale mauricienne*. Paris.

Ducrocq, Louis 1902 Idiome enfantin d'une race enfantine. *Revue de Lille* 20.
D'Unienville, M C A Marrier 1838 *Statistique de l'Ile Oaurice et ses dépendances (...)*. Paris: G Barba.
Egerton, H E 1932 *A short history of British colonial policy, 1606 – 1909*. [revised by A P Newton]. London.
Filliot, J M 1974 *La traite des esclaves vers les Mascareignes au 18ième siècle*. Paris.
Flemyng, Francis P 1862 *Mauritius or the Isle of France*. London.
Freycinet, Louis Claude Desaulces de 1827 *Voyage autour du monde exécuté sur les corvettes de S.M. l'Uranie et la Physicienne pendant les années 1817, 1818, 1819 et 1820 (....)*,Paris, vol. 2.2.
Furlong, Robert & Ramharai, Vicram 2007 *La production créolophone. Vol. 1. Des origines à l'indépendence*. Mauritius: TIMAM.
Hookoomsing, Vinesh Y 1986 Langue et identité ethnique : Les langues ancestrales à l'île Maurice. *Journal of Mauritian Studies* 2 (1) : 126-53.
—— 1987 L'emploi de la langue créole dans le contexte multilingue et multiculturel de l'Ile Maurice. Une étude de son importance en tant que langue commune et des implications sociolinguistiques de son élaboration en Mauricien, Thèse de PhD, Universite Laval, Quebec.
—— [*to appear*] Language loss, language maintenance: The case of Bhojpuri and Hindi in Mauritius.
Hookoomsing, V Y and collaborators 2004 [Proposal for a harmonized orthography for Mauritian Creole].
Jespersen, Otto 1922 *Language. Its nature, development and origin*. London:
Kaeppelin, Paul 1908 *les escales françaises sur la route de l'Inde 1638-1731*. Paris.
Kiamtia, L R 1959 Une étude du patois créole de l'Ile Maurice. MA dissertation, University College of Wales (Aberystwyth).
Kuczynski, R P 1949 *demographic survey of the British Colonial Empire*. Londo, vol. II.
Labourdonnais, Mahé de 1740 Mémoire..., *see* Lougnon & Toussaint 1937.
Lolliot, Pierre 1855 *Poésies créoles*. Port Louis: Imprimerie du *Mauricien*,
Lougnon, Albert (ed.) 1935-1937 *Correspondence du Conseil Supérieur de Bourbon et de la Compagnie des Indes 23 janvier 1736 – 9 mai 1741 ensemble trois lettres de la Compagnie au Conseil Supérieur de l'Ile de France 17 février 1738 – 29 décembre 1738*. Réunion, fasc. I et II.
Lougnon, Albert & Toussaint, Auguste 1937 *Mémoire des isles de France et de Bourbon, adressé au Controleur général Orry de Fulvy*. Paris.
Ly-Tio-Fane, Madeleine 1958 *Mauritius and the spice trade. The odyssey of Pierre Poivre*. Port Louis.
Meade, G E et al. 1961 *The economic and social structure of Mauritius*. London.
Mouat, F J 1852 *Rough notes of a trip to Réunion, the Mauritius and Ceylon (...)*. Calcutta.
Noble, Charles F [1755] 1793 *Some remarks made at Mauritius, called by the French, Isle de France; and at the Island Bourbon*. London: Dalrymple.
Pope-Hennessy, James 1964 *Verandah. Some episodes in the Crown Colonies, 1867-1889*. London.
Pridham, Charles 1846 *England's Colonial Empire (...). Vol. 1: The Mauritius and its dependencies*. London.
Revue historique et littéraire de l'Ile Maurice. Mauritius, 1887-1894.
RHL, see *Revue historique et littéraire de l'Ile Maurice*
Ryan, Vincent W 1863 *Mauritus and Madagascar (...)*. London
Saint-Quentin, Auguste de 1872 Etude sur la grammaire créole. St-Quentin, Alfred de *Introduction à l'histoire de Cayenne, suivie d'un recueil de contes, fables et chansons en créole*, Antibes: J Marchand, pp 99-169.
Sidonie, M T (ed.) 1959 *Vers une entité mauricienne*. Port Louis.
Smith, Adele 1969 Politics in Mauritius since 1934. A study of decolonization in a plural society. DPhil thesis, University of Oxford.

Telfair, Charles 1830 *Some account of the state of slavery at Mauritus (...)*. Port Louis & London.
Tinker, Hugh 1974 *A new system of slavery*. London
Thomas, J J 1869 *The theory and practice of Creole grammar*. Port-of-Spain: *The Chronicle Publishing Office*.
Toussaint, Auguste 1966 *History of the Indian Ocean*. London: Routledge.
—— 1967 *La route des îles*. Paris.
—— 1973 Port Louis: a tropical city. London.
Virahsawmy, Dev 1967 Towards a re-evaluation of Mauritian Creole. MA dissertation, University of Edinburgh.
Ward, W E F 1941 *Report on education in Mauritius*. Port Louis: Government Printing.

Philip Baker worked in Mauritius for MBC TV and L'Express newspaper 1965-67 but the interest in MC which this aroused led him to study linguistics formally and many publications have resulted. He is currently Professor of Linguistics at the University of Westminster, <phildbaker@yahoo.co.uk>.

Annex

The slave-owning population of Mauritius at 1.1.1735, their places of origin, and the numbers of slaves they owned (insofar as this can be derived from the parish registers and other documents consulted)

Owner and family (and place of origin)	Slaves owned: Men	Women	Children
Aché (n s); wife: Morel (n s); 1 son and 2 daughters	1	5	5
Bacquet (Ile-de-France [Seine]); wife: Girardin	2	2	2
Bastien (Ile-de-France [seine]); wife: Lecor (Brittany [Finistère]); 1 daughter	3	6	2
Bellecourt (n s)	1	1	
Bermond (Languedoc [Haute-Loire]); wife: Schmilorge (Germany); 3 daughters	2[1]	1	1
Bernage (Ile-de-France [Seine et Marne])		3	3
Bernard (Artois); wife: Penhouet (Brittany [Ille-et-Vilaine]); 1 son and 1 daughter	3	2	
Bouloc, J-D (Guienne [Tarn-et-Garonne]); wife: Aignan (n s); 2 sons and 2 daughters; co-owned with brother:			
Bouloc, J (Guienne [Tarn-et-Garonne]); wife: La Rivière (n s); 1 son and 2 daughters			
Bourceret (Ile-de-France [Seine])		1	1
Bulle (France Comté); wife: Bert (n s); 3 sons and 2 daughters	5	4	1
Capieux (Languedoc [Hérault]); wife: Leblanc (Brittany [Morbihan])	2	1	1
Cauvelet (Ile-de-France [Seine]); wife: Lelay (Brittany [Morbihan]); 1 stepson and 2 stepdaughters	2	1	
Céré (Pondicherry); wife: Brouillet (n s); 2 daughters	1		
Coignard (n s); wife: Laurent (n s); 1 daughter		3	3
Cornet (Brittany [Morbihan]); wife: Taignan (Brittany [Loire-Atlantique]); 1 son and 1 daughter	2	1	1
Courbon (Avignon); wife: Cadiot (n s); 2 sons and 1 daughter	1	1	3
Curé (Lorraine [Meurthe-et-Moselle]); wife: Helant (n s); 1 son	1	2	2
Dabadie (n s)			
Dacqueville (Normandy [Cher]); 2 sons and 1 daughter	1	1	1
Dalbert (Ile-de-France [Seine])		3	2
Delie (Ile-de-France [Oise]); wife: Repos (n s); 2 sons	4	7	5
Delieur (n s)	1	1	
Desvaux (Brittany [Côtes-du-Nord]); wife: Paquet (Anjou); 1 son and 1 daughter		1	1
Dieu (Ile-de-France [Seine])		1	1
Drouet (Ile-de-France [Seine]); wife Durens (Ile-de-France [Seine])		1	1
	32	50	37

---

[1] Includes one adult slave whose sex was not determined.

Owner and family (and place of origin)	Slaves owned: Men	Women	Children
from previous page	32	50	37
Dumenil (n s); wife: Desjardins (n s)	2	4	1
Duplessis (Brittany [Ille-et-Vilaine]); wife: name n s; 1 daughter	3	5	1
Floch (n s)	16[2]	18	8
Gast (n s); wife: Guillot (n s); 2 sons and 2 daughters	4	4	1
Genu (Normandy [Seine-Maritime]); wife: Conan (Brittany [Morbihan]); 1 son and 1 daughter	1	2	1
Giblot (Brittany [Ille-et-Vilaine]); mother: Conuerse (Brittany [Ille-et-Vilaine])	1	1	1
Giblot-Ducray (Brittany [Ille-et-Vilaine])	3	5	3
Gonnet (Belgium); wife: Thibert (Ile-de-France [Seine])		1	1
Guimard (Brittany [Ille-et-Vilaine]); wife Duval (Brittany [Ille-et-Vilaine]); 2 sons		1	1
Guy (Angoumais); wife: Sanson (Normandy [Eure]); 2 daughters	2	2	
Herbault (Ile-de-France [Seine]); 1 daughter	2	2	1
Jacob (Ile-de-France [Seine-et-Marne]); Laguerche (Brittany [Morbihan]); 2 sons	1	1	1
Jocet (Brittany [Ille-et-Vilaine]); wife: Thomas (n s); 2 daughters	1	1	1
Jonchée (n s); (absentee concessionnaire. one of the Compagnie's captains)	6	8	6
Lefevre (Ile-de-France [Seine]); wife: Thiordel (n s); 2 sons			1
Legrand (Normandy [Cher]); 1 daughter	3	6	5
Le Prince (Sardinia); wife: Dacqueville (Normandy [Cher])	1	1	
L'Heur (Anjou); wife: Lorcy (Brittany [Morbihan]); 1 son		1	1
Maldaque (Belgium); wife: Wolfenbutel[3] (Germany); 1 daughter		1	1
Mallet (n s); wife; Daumont (n s); 3 daughters		1	
Mandrou (Orléanais [Loiret]); wife: Crampon (Normandy [Seine-Maritime]); 2 sons and 1 daughter		1	
Mariat (n s)	1	2	
Marteau (n s); wife: Lecornu (n s); 1 daughter	2	2	3
Martin (Languedoc [Hérault]); wife: Colnair (Lorraine [Meuse]); 1 daughter	1	1	
Mathieu (Ile-de-France [Seine]; wife: Arthur (Réunion); 3 daughters[4]	2	2	2
Maupin (n s)	3	3	4
Menot (Brittany [Côtes-du-Nord]); wife: Couillon (Brittany [Finistère]); 1 son and one stepdaughter	1	2	1
	88	128	82

[2] Includes one adult slave whose sex was not determined.
[3] Real name Danielson. See Le Juge de Segrais, René 1963 *Les deux princesses*. Port Louis..
[4] Mathieu and Arthur married in Réunion in 1734; the daughters are from an earlier marriage.

Owner and family (and place of origin)	Slaves owned: Men	Women	Children
from previous page	88	128	82
Milon (Ile-de-France [Seine]); wife: Pogan (Brittany [Finistère]); 1 son and 1 daughter	1		
[Neizein][5] (n s); wife: Dumanche (Brittany [Finistère]); 1 son and 1 daughter	3	3	
Nicole (Normandy); wife: Dumenil (Brittany [Loire-Atlantique]); 2 sons		1	2
Oscorne (Normandy [Seine-Maritime]); wife; Dovat (Brittany [Loire-Atlantique]); 1 daughter		1	2
Pautre (Ile-de-France [Oise]); wife: La Bosserie (Ile-de-France [Aisne]); 1 son and 1 daughter		1	
Penisseau (Berry [Cher]); wife: Lefort (Brittany [Morbihan]); 1 son and 1 daughter		2	2
Perrot (Brittany [Côtes du Nord]); wife: (Brittany [Finistère]); 1 son and 1 daughter	2	2	2
Petit (Normandy [Seine-Maritime])		2	2
Pignolet (Brittany [Morbihan]); wife: Mandrou (Orléanais [Loiret]); sister-in-law Crugeon (n s); 2 sons, 2 nephews, and two nieces	2	4	2
Pondart (Brittany [Morbihan]); Dumeny ("St Nicolas de Luxembourg")	4	6	4
Raffin (Brittany [[Loire-Atlantique]); wife: Denancy (Brittany [Ille-et-Vilaine]); 1 son and 1 daughter		3	3
Robin (Brittany [[Loire-Atlantique]); 1 son	1	1	1
Rogier (n s); wife: Leclerc (n s)		1	1
Romans (Lyonnais [Rhône]) wife: Pignolet (Brittany [Morbihan])	1	2	2
Routier (Normandy [Eure]); wife: Busson (Brittany [Morbihan]); 1 son	2	1	
Saint-Martin (n s); wife: Duhamel (n s); 2 sons	17	17	14
Sanson (Normandy [Eure]); wife: Hainfray (n s); 2 sons and 1 daughter	5	3	3
Vivien (Normandy [Calvados]); wife: Girard (n s); 1 daughter	2	2	1
Other slaves: Owner not stated	15[6]	10	17
Congrégation de la Mission (Lazarists)	8	6	6
Compagnie des Indes	37	22	21
Total	188	218	167

[5] Neizein died before 1735 but the plantation was continued by his wife.
[6] Includes two adults whose sex was not determined.

Letter to the Colonial Office
on the conditions of emancipated negroes in the Mauritius[1]

J A Lloyd

Athenaeum April 4th[2]

My dear Sir,

A few days since you expressed to me a wish, to receive some information as to that fact of so very large a proportion of the emancipated negroes in the Mauritius, having altogether retired from labour, and to give you some clue as to their present mode of existence, and the places where, limited as the area of the island is, so great a number of persons could have secluded themselves.

To a stranger in Mauritius and to its resources, it would be a matter of some difficulty to account for such facts, but on describing some peculiarities of this island, you will easily account for the present dislike of the planter, and be at the same time convinced, that we may not even at a remote period hope [for?] steady industry (at least as far as the landed proprietor is interested) from this class of people.

I may I think divide the individuals who have abandoned work on the estates into as many as four different classes.

First those wandering from one point of the Island to the other, having no settled place of residence.

Second others residing in or near the two suburbs of the south of Port Louis and Mahebourg, as well as along the high roads in almost every quarter of the island.

Third[3] Those (by far the largest proportion) residing as trespassers on the "pas geometriques"[4] renting either for provisions or labour, or lodging in the huts of others.

It is necessary to presume that the emancipated negress may be considered as a distinct class and that excepting as washerwomen, house servants, or nurses, not a tenth part of the whole number, do devote themselves to any labour whatsoever.

Their feelings and opinions of the word "slavery" is so intimately blended with the culture of the soil and the use of the degrading "pioche", that liberty to them must be wholly independent of any field labour whatsoever. They live therefore in hundreds dependent on their husbands, brothers, cousins, etc. and the main repugnance of the black maybe attributed to the unceasing efforts on the part of the women in dissuading them from any other work than fishing or (what is the acme of their pride) keeping a shop.[5]

I may venture here to describe a scene I was party to, one morning early near "Cure Pipe", on encountering a party of 6 or 8 negroes accompanied by a greater number of

---

[1] The word 'Mauritius' occurs 12 times in this letter (including margin notes). On seven occasions it follows the definite article 'the' but there are five occurrences without this article which might suggest that the use of the definite article had begun to decline.
[2] Date-stamped "RECEIVED C.O. APR. 8 1840"
[3] The fourth class is not mentioned until p 336.
[4] Here and throughout most of the letter, Lloyd does not bother to write French accents.
[5] Comment in the margin (not in Lloyd's handwriting): Very right.

women and children with their usual valuables, a four post bedstead, an armoria⁶ & a trunk, etc. (?).⁷

I found them near the banks of a little stream, the men asleep, the women cooking and washing.

After (?) their usual salut "Bozour Mushee"⁸ I enquired of them where they were going and whence from. They told me that they had been for some time employed on their late masters [sic] estate. But as "Bonhomme" too had removed to Port Louis where he had [illegible word] to work, they were going to see him and (to?) keep a shop.

They had consequently left in the night without any previous notice or [illegible word] and were now on their journey. I asked them if they had had good wages, if they had received good food and were regularly paid and kindly treated. Yes! All that --- One of the most forward women answered me as "A'ce terre, nous té lib, qui faire nous tlavai?["]⁹ I replied that all people should work, that I even was obliged to work hard and they ought also & become rich. Their immediate reply – "Sauts n'a pas ti¹⁰ besogne l'arzan, pour gagner lib fin gagner".¹¹ But I said they should get money for their children. "So they would, but they could make much more money in a shop than by working the land."

I told them, that the wife should keep the shop & the men should work, the offended reply was "Ah ben li¹² n'a pas negre"!¹³

Such is the feeling so deeply & generally prevalent amongst these people.¹⁴

The first class therefore of non working people, is of this description, constantly on the move, and such is their restless disposition that when disappointed, like hundreds of others in keeping a shop, they will again take to the road but in preference to hiring themselves to a respectable planter,¹⁵ they will probably obtain a small piece of land, from a coloured or black petty proprietor, on the condition of working for him and building a hut in their own time. The neighbouring forests are devastated, timber young and old is cut, the hut is built, but as soon built, the wily proprietor exacts rent, quarrels with them, turns them out, and again dupes some newcomer of his own blood.¹⁶

The 2ⁿᵈ class forms an alarming proportion of idlers. The small and miserable houses of every description in the extreme western suburbs of Port Louis are inundated by these unfortunate people – they live in comparative idleness; the greater part of the day is passed in wandering about the exterior of the town and on the banks of rivers or sea shore, all come home in the evening, with sufficient to pay their rent, some with packets of grass, others with cane purloined on the road, others with eels and chevrettes¹⁷ and a very large proportion with small fish or mullet.

---

⁶ Lloyd here uses the Latin word corresponding to *almyra* in Anglo-Indian (Yule & Burnell *Hobson-Jobson* 1886). While the initial *al-* might suggest that this is an Arabic word, it is indeed from Latin via Portuguese. Pronounced [almajrə], it continues to be used in Indian and Sri Lanka to designate a large wardrobe in which family valuables as well as clothes are kept. The word is cognate with Fr. *armoire*. There is, however, no known attestation of this in MC.
⁷ Lloyd's margin note: These parties are so frequent that they are denominated in the Mauritius "flits".
⁸ Lloyd's note in the margin: bonjour monsieur.
⁹ Lloyd's note in the margin: "a cette heure nous libres; que faire nous travailler"? 'now we are free what for should we work'.
¹⁰ Perhaps *te* rather than *ti* – PB.
¹¹ Lloyd's note in the margin: "Les autres n'ont pas besoin d'argent pour gagner leur liberté, c'est deja fini".
¹² In Lloyd's handwriting this resembles *lé* more closely than *li* but given his near-total disregard for French diacritics and the fact that *lé* is nowhere else attested as the third person pronoun it must be assumed that *li* was the intended spelling.
¹³ Lloyd's note in the margin: "Eh bien il n'est pas negre(sse)"
¹⁴ Margin comment not in Lloyd's handwriting: No harm in this.
¹⁵ Margin comment level with the middle of this paragraph, not in Lloyd's handwriting: They are not wrong.
¹⁶ Margin comment not in Lloyd's handwriting: The coloured man treats them ill.
¹⁷ A French word for prawns or shrimps.

Strings of sometimes eight or ten (boys and men of herculean strength) may be seen of a morning late sallying (?[18]) out, with each a hamber (?)[19] rod over his shoulder a wicker basket & a wallet, on their road to their days sport.

The Eastern suburb receives its proportion of idlers and to a great extent – but these from a still more objectionable class, they are men who have absconded, or who from various shades of crime(s), are secreted during the day by the lower class of Malabars. Arabs & Chinese. They steal (?) out under the protection of night and pilfer whatever may come in the way – to be sold to their landlords, who again trade, at an enormous (?) profit.

The extent to which these people are permitted to settle may be proved (?) by the following circumstance – Some weeks before my departure for the Mauritius I desired that a general survey of the town and suburbs should be made by the official of my Department and a schedule made of all the buildings in wood or other combustible material, and which had not been reported (?) to me by the Police, and whether (?) erected since the enactment for bidding constructions otherwise than in masonry (?).

A large number was reported and amongst others nearly 200 huts thatched in hair (?) or light wood on the scarp (?) of the signal mountain at the back of Moka Street and partly concealed from view by the larger houses in front. The greater portion of these buildings had been run up within a few months – all this happening (?) on Govt. ground.[20]

On visiting this spot one Monday morning I found the greater part of these houses with the doors closed. By pushing (?) I succeeded in entering in many of them and to my astonishment found from 8 to 10 to 12 to 14 persons in many (?) of them, men women & children all huddled together, a great portion of them in a state of inebriety or suffering from their previous night debauch.[21]

The 3rd class forms by far the largest proportion of persons living in a state of comparative idleness and affording the worst examples to their more industrious brethren.

Around the Island an annular land was set apart by the French Government called the "Pas Geometriques".[22] This land extends a distance of 250 feet inland from spring high water mark, including the same distance on either side, all creeks & "barachoix"[23] & where the tide ebbs and flows.

The object of this reserve was, to afford facilities and the means of military defence in case of invasion. By the laws of the in office (?) country, this reserve was unalienable, neither could it be granted in puissance but by consent of the commanding Engineer.[24]

The same restrictions and principle have been confirmed by the British Government and altho [sic] much has been conceded in puissances the greater portion still remains as a crown property (?) and is of great value on these Crown Lands. Numbers of individuals have from time to time settled and trespassed without any permission whatsoever, others have asked and received permission to construct huts &c on paying a certain annual rent. Their title deeds have been made out, they have occupied the land, but they have neither paid the expenses to Govt of such deeds nor have they paid one shilling of annual rent.

But it is of late only that such numbers have flocked to the sea coast and taken possession of land & built huts thereon without any permission whatsoever.

To this sacred ground therefore have the negroes taken refuge from work, living in almost incredible numbers in each hut. Either with a simple rod & line, or with a seine

---

[18] The second letter of this word looks like *u* rather than *a* but 'sully' (to defile) would not fit the context here
[19] Cf SOED *hamber* 'naut. Small line for seizings, lashings' – PB.
[20] Lloyd's note in the margin: I issued a notice that if in three months from its date these huts were not removed they would be pulled down by the police.
[21] Lloyd's note in the margin: I brought this matter to the notice of the Govt. I submitted officially a list of their buildings with an account of what steps I had taken.
[22] Lloyd's note in the margin: See "144 Code Decaen".
[23] A shallow, enclosed stretch of water used for fish-farming.
[24] Lloyd's note in the margin: a "puissance" permits a person to occupy & build on such lands under certain conditions amongst others that he shall on being required to do so (?) give it up in (?) 48 hours.

formed solely by collecting numbers of the creeper(s) from the beach, these people procure in a far locus (??), enough fish to afford ample nourishment to their family for the work, and moreover leave a surplus for sale by which they procure rice, tobacco & ardent spirits.

No quota, no tax whatever is paid by them to Government and therefore people live in one constant round (?) of idleness, amusement and debauchery.

Without this land or "pas geometriques" commences, in many points, the highest cultivation, and valuable cane fields extend to the very edge (?) with neither fence nor safeguard against maurauders [sic = marauders]. The consequence is that cane to a very great value, completely disappears being daily and nightly pilfered by these squatters on the pas geometriques & what is worse, are stolen by labourers of the estates, and brought for sale, in exchange for tobacco, opium, spirits &c. These stolen goods are afterwards found exposed for sale in the suburbs of the town& in the shops of the Malabars or Chinese.

A few months before my departure from the Mauritius, this evil became so intolerable to the planters, that I received constant complaint and solicitations to adopt some means of arresting this abuse.

I consequently gave an order that the whole of the "pas geometriques", from Port Louis by Pamplemousses & Mapou to Flacq, should be visited & and eye sketches taken of the various encroachments and trespasses along the whole length (?). After nearly a month's work of the qualified officer, I received a report in detail of all the trespasses, with a schedule of the various persons who had built, the epoch nearly, when they had been erected, and the supposed number of individuals on each lot.

After reading the greater portion myself, I issued a circular to the various civil commissioners, calling upon them in conformation with my officers to put a stop to these encroachments, and I also forwarded for communication, circulars to be read to the various parties warning them to quit the grounds they had so unwarrantably taken possession of, and intimating to them, that after a certain period, they would be ejected by force.

The whole of the schedule and copies of the documents I forwarded to His Excellency the Governor through the Colonial Secretary but having sailed from Mauritius in December I am not aware if my projects were carried into execution.

I am not prepared from memory to give a note of the number of persons following this mode of life, but thousands not hundreds may be safely taken as the amount of individuals withdrawn from industry and the culture of the soil, and passing their lives without religious or moral instruction.

The fourth and last description are emigrants, proceeding of their own wills in the "chasse marees" constantly sailing from Mauritius to Rodriguez, Diego Garcia, Agalega &c inhabiting without interruption the "pas geometriques" of the various islands passing their lives in idleness, hunting guinea fowl, partridges, quail & even wild hogs and bulls (?) & obtaining ample means of existence from the various reefs surrounding the islands and just cultivating so much soil, as will yield sufficient rice and bret (?)[25] to maintain themselves families [sic].

The large quantity of fish these people catch (?) & sell for exportation to the Mauritius and the aid, some likewise, give to the proprietors of cocoa nut oil [sic] establishments, and moreover the little injury they cause from theft a bad example, renders this class the most respectable of the least objectionable.

From this sketch I have briefly given of the occupations & haunts of this race of people, it only remains to draw a comparison between their former, and their present mode of existence, and it must convince the planter that to any extent, he must give up any hope of inducing them to return to their former regular habits & agricultural life.

---

[25] If the word is indeed "bret" this probably corresponds to the word normally written "brède(s)" in Mauritian French, which is applied to a wide range of edible leaves which are stewed and served with rice dishes. The word is of ultimate Portuguese origin – see the entry for /bred/ in Baker & Hookoomsing (1987).

Many of the present generation are from the savage coasts of Mozambique or Madagascar, they appreciate too clearly the recollections of their former habits of life, not to be biassed (?) in their present (?) choice of pursuits, and for ever to abandon the hoe. The Madagascan & Mozambique Languages are still in use amongst some of the old negroes, and whether in such dialect or in Creole the [illegible word] of their nightly songs in accompaniment to their wild "boussin" (?) is the sense of their early days and liberty.

Every negro can now enjoy that same liberty & independence unobtainable on a larger island or a continent. Nature has been (?) so bountiful to their beautiful island, that, at any time or any hour, a bamboo and a line twisted from the vacquois[26] or cocoa nut [sic], will provide him with the means of satisfying his hunger, in the bush, on the beach or amongst his comrades can he be, alike, sure of shelter and rest, and the nightly song and merry dancing fills up the measure of his happiness and romantic feeling of liberty.

Such my dear Sir is the condition and state of a large proportion of the coloured population of Mauritius, and such the dependence you may place in inducing the free man to again return to industry or in other terms (what would be in his unchangeable opinion) "slavery".

Partial remedies might however still be adopted to recover these more from idleness or at any rate, <u>prevent their full enjoyment of the means of living in that state.</u>[27] I would therefore have suggested that a compendious vagrant law should be established, meeting their peculiarities to provide (?) a reality (?) differing from other colonies.

1st – that the vacation of the "pas geometriques" should be most rigidly and promptly insisted on. That no individual having already received a puissance on the sea coast, should be permitted to lodge in his house or take into his employ more than a certain number of persons according to the area of his grant of land. That all persons found loitering on the roads or in the woods, not having any honest profession of trade should be arrested and punished or be employed on the repair of the roads.

That no individual whatsoever should be permitted to carry a gun, without a regular licence and which only should be granted to those possessing certain qualifications; and finally, that no individual should be permitted to fish in the rivers but by special licence, and that fishing likewise on the sea coast or pas geometriques should be under certain restrictions and a tax be paid by the person so employed.

To carry these regulations into execution, a disciplined and effective body of police is indispensable.

The present police establishment of the Mauritius, although it may be well officered and on an expensive scale, is notoriously the contrary. This may be accounted for in two ways.

First – The town police (excluding its officers) consists of a large body of men made up from the dregs of society: a great proportion have been sailors, who have either deserted or been discharged from their ships[28]... another part is drafted from those who have been discharged from regiments.

All, unhappily give way, more or less, to their passion for drink, which increases from the effects of the climate until they become enervated and gradually sink, victims to the known deadly effects of the use of ardent spirits,

The rural police under the immediate superintendance [sic] of the Civil Commissioner of the country districts with the exception of the Brigadiers is made up from the negro races. Such are their habits and want of courage, and such their connexion[s] either by "beauperes" "tantines" or some other fancied relationship with many of their own race, that it is unreasonable to expect efficiency from them.

---

[26] This word is normally written "vacoas" today.
[27] This underlining might well have been added by the recipient of the letter rather than be part of Lloyd's original manuscript – PB.
[28] Lloyd's note in the margin: There is no alternative in Mauritius but these men or discharged soldiers.

The second cause of failure arises from the administration of the law of the land, for so voluminous are the "proces verbaux" now (?) indispensable in all police matters, that this duty alone takes up three parts of the time of the officers and attendant men & necessarily [illegible word] all prompt and energetic action.[29]

Under these circumstances a really efficient police force can only be ensured from the mother country.[30]

A very effective auxiliary force might moreover be embodied from amongst the Indian convicts if from their position in society, an insuperable objection might not on that account be raized [sic].[31]

Some years since it was recommended by the Commission of Enquiry and I believe commanded by the Right Honorable The Secretary of State, that all the Indian convicts of known good character should receive their pardon and that a grant of Government land should be made over to each near the military posts.

For some reasons not known to me these directions have never been obeyed.[32]

From my thorough and intimate knowledge of these men, their commanding strength, their military bearing, and above all their high courage and fidelity – I know of no class on the spot, who if properly officered and commanded, would make a more efficient and powerful body of police.

Two hundred to two hundred and fifty might be picked from the finest of these men, high caste, intelligent, capable of enduring any fatigue & knowing every fastness (?) and pass in the mountains & forests, they speak both the Creole and Hindustannee [sic] languages, they may generally be securely confided in (provided their religious prejudices are not interfered with) and above all, no beverage ever passes their lips, but pure water.

To conclude, these men, most of them, from their high birth, and moral courage, command a respect amongst their more humble brethren and the black population of the Island to such an extent, as cannot be imagined but, by a person who has been a witness to it on the spot.

I remain, my dear Sir
Your very obedient
& obliged servant (?)[33]

J A Lloyd

---

[29] Lloyd's note in the margin: For a simple case [illegible word] of a negro on the road or for taking a cane a "proces verbal" must be drawn up signed by all the parties and often containing 3 to 8 or 10 pages of foolscap.
[30] Lloyd's note in the margin: colonial and expenses of the regiment in which nearly provide the expenses of the police (??).
[31] Margin note not in Lloyd's handwriting: Certainly preferable.
[32] Margin note not in Lloyd's handwriting: I hope not.
[33] The handwriting of this word resembles 'service' more closely than 'servant' [PB].

Index

A

Abney, S 85, 89
Aboh, E 201
Adger, D 93, 111, 180, 193
Adolphe, H 27, 61
Adone, D 126-27, 130
Africa(n) 1, 15, 17, 27, 30-31, 33, 115, 123, 198, 202, 319-20
Afrikaans 109
Agalega 338
agglutination 197, 202, 204-05, 210-14
Ah-Vee, A 70, 75, 89, 182-84, 193
Akan 212
Ambolambe 313-14
Anderson, S 2-3, 54-55, 59, 68, 89, 106, 111, 119, 125-26, 128, 144, 152, 322
Angolar 199
Annamalai, E 202, 214
Anon. (1810) 5, 59
Anon. (1818) 59
Anon. (1826) 59
Anon. (1846) 27-33, 59
Anon. (ca. 1950) 212, 214
Anon. (1980) 76, 89, 119, 130, 171-72
Anon.(1989) 191, 193
Anon. (2002) 89
Anon. (2004) 73, 75, 89, 173, 178, 195
Anon. (2007) 179, 193
Antelme, H 56, 59, 128, 140
Anthony, L 158
Antilles 171, 200
Anttila, R 135, 152
Arab(ic) 136, 150, 190, 199, 320, 336-37
Arends, J 67, 89
Aristotle 180
Armand, A 212, 214
Asgarally, R 71, 75-76, 89
Asher, R 202
Asia(n) 198, 308, 310, 317
Assamese 199
Atlantic Creoles 120, 123, 197-99, 213
Auroux, S 139, 152
Azéma H/V 315

B

Baggioni, D 212, 214
Baissac, C 2-3, 12, 14, 28-33, 35, 40, 54, 56, 59, 64, 68, 89, 106-07, 109-11, 117-18, 123, 125-28, 130, 140, 144-45, 147, 152, 159, 166, 168-69, 172, 174, 176, 194, 319, 321-22, 328
Baker, E 28-29
Baker, P 1-61, 64, 66, 71, 73-75, 80, 89, 93, 95, 106, 111, 113-14, 119, 121-22, 130, 133, 137, 150-51, 153, 172-76, 178-79, 185, 190-91, 194, 197-216, 218-20, 307-22, 328, 338
Baltin, M 194
Bambara 197, 201-02
Bantu 14, 115, 123, 125, 127, 129-30, 150, 173, 190-91, 193, 197-198, 202-03, 205, 207-09, 211-14
Barnwell, P 308-09, 328
Barthelmi, G 210, 214
Barwise, J 179, 194
Bemba 150
Benedict, B 324, 328
Bengal(i) 150, 197, 201-02, 308, 311, 313-14, 319
Benin 197, 201
Benoît, N 1, 15, 35, 59
Benveniste, E 153
Berbice Dutch 109, 199
Bernardin de St-Pierre 1, 4-6, 59, 310, 317, 328
Bernstein, J 66, 89
Besant, W 54-55, 59
BFBS, *see* British and Foreign Bible Society
Bhojpuri 109-10, 121-23, 130, 201-02, 320, 324, 326-27
Bhuckory, S 326, 328
Bickerton, D 5, 84, 89, 111, 134-35, 153
Bihari 201
Bini 212
Blanche-Benveniste, C 149, 153
Bollée, A 8, 60, 111, 123, 129-30, 150, 153, 157, 170, 172, 175, 192, 194, 200, 214, 218, 220, 312, 328
Bord la mer, see Anon. (1980)
Bourbon(nais), see Réunion(nais)
Bowe, G 319, 328
Bowers, J 179, 194
Brazil 198, 307, 313
Britain 3, 315, 322
British 4, 16, 29, 150, **175, 314,** 318, 320, 324
British and Foreign Bible Society 54-55
British Parliamentary Papers **14,** 60
Brousseau, A-M 202, 215
Bruneau-Ludwig, F 131
Bruyn, A 127, 130
Burnell, A 336
Bybee, J 135, 153
Bynon, T 111

C

Cambodian 151
Camle, G 71, 89
Campbell, L 135-36, 154
Canada 151
Cantonese 326
Cape Verde(an) 199
Cardona, G 214
Caribbean 6, 165, 171, 197, 200, 202, 211-12
Carrington, C 317, 328
Carlson, G 72, 89
Carpooran, A 72, 73, 76-77, 89, 178, 182, 185, 187, 194
Caulier, P-A 316
Cernéen, see Le Cernéen
Chandernagore 201
Channel Islands 8
Charoux, C 324, 328
Chaudenson, R 1-4, 22, 35, 40, 60, 64, 89, 110-11, 113-14, 118, 120, 123-24, 130, 133, 146-47, 152-53, 157, 166, 172, 174, 194, 202, 214, 218, 220, 314-15, 328
Cheung, G 183, 194
Chevalier, J-C 148, 153
Chierchia, G 63, 71-72, 88-89, 174, 194
Chiffone, S 69, 89
Chinese 71, 93, 134, 151, 174, 189, 193, 198, 311, 314, 319-20, 324, 328, 337-38
Chomsky, N 64, 84, 89, 93, 103, 111, 175, 179-80, 184, 189-90, 194
Chrestien, F 1-3, 7, 9, 12-17, 19-25, **35, 40,** 44-45, 60, 67, 90, 111, 119-20, 128, 140, 140, 153, 167, 172-73, 175, 178, 182, 318, 321, 328
Christophersen, P 78-79, 82, 90
Ciluba 123
Cirandane Çampéc 27-34, 45, 56
Clark, E 134, 153
Claudi, U 106, 112, 154
Colley, E 202, 212, 214
Collins, C 194
Colonial Office 14, 27, 60, 317
Colville, General 20, 22
Comrie, B 90, 131
Compagnie des Indes 307-08, 310-13, 315, 333
conjunction 113-32

convergence 150
Cooper, R 179, 194
copula 173-96
Corne, C 8, 60, 107, 109, 112, 174, 176, 190-94, 214, 315, 328
Creissels, D 133-34, 153
Créole (= locally born) 6, 314, 320
Croft, W 153
Crosbie, P 210, 214

D

Darwin, C 319, 328
Dasgupta, P 202, 214
Davidson, D 180, 194
De Chazal, E 2, 41, 52, 60
De Chazal, M 325
Decotter, N 2, 57, 60
definiteness 63-91, 94-101, 174-75
DeGraff, M 187-88, 194
De Hauville 315
De la Butte, A 35
De la Butte, F 40
Dem, S 202, 215
De Nyon 307, 315
Déprez, V 187-88, 194
De Rochecouste, A 41
De Salle Essoo, M 70, 90
Descartes 176
Descroizilles, F 1, 7, 60, 109, 112, 119, 125, 128, 140, 143, 153, 320-21, 328
Detges, U 135-37, 152-53
Dholah, V 77, 90
Dick, G F 55
Dick, Miss 55
Diego Garcia 338
ditransitives 123-32, 203
Dominican Creole French 199
Doneux, J-L 215
Donnellan, K 79, 82, 90
Dryer, M 90
Ducoeurjoly, S 60
Ducrocq, L 322
Dravidian 122, 198, 327
Dryer, M 131
Duclos, J 322, 329
Ducrocq, L 322, 328
Ducros, Père 308,
Duff, P 133, 151, 153
Dumas, A 16-17, 60
D'Unienville, M 314, 329
D'Unienville, R 29, 60
Dutch 197, 199, 307

E

East Africa(n) 197-98, 202, 213, 310-11, 314, 317
Echeruo, M 212, 215
Edo 212
Egerton, H 317, 329
Elizier, C 69, 71, 90
Enç, M 83, 90
English 54, 64-65, 68, 70-78, 80-83, 88, 103, 107-08, 123, 151, 174-75, 177, 184, 188-89, 192, 198-99, 205, 317, 319-20, 324, 326, 328
Epstein, D 84, 90
Esnouf, A 58
etymology 218-19
Europe(an) 27, 30-34, 114-15, 200, 203, 310, 320
Ewe 188
existence 133-54

F

Fal, A 215
Fante 212
Federation of Preschool Playgroups 74, 90
Fields, E 28
Filliot, J 311, 329
Flemying, F 329
Fodor, J 83, 90
Foley, W 93
Fon(gbe) 150, 201-04, 206, 208-09, 212
Fon Sing, G 1-61, 68, 130, 133-55, 173, 194, 203, 208, 214-15, 217-306
Forbes, D 212, 215
Foulet, L 96, 112
France 29, 54, 307-08, 310, 315, 318, 322, 326
François, D 154
Franco-Mauritian 318, 320-22, 324
Frank, D 214
Frege, G 179, 194
French 3-4, 8, 15-16, 18, 44, 53-55, 63-65, 67-68, 70-72, 74-78, 80-83, 88, 94-97, 99-101, 105-07, 110-11, 116-20, 123, 125, 129-30, 133, 135, 139, 146, 150-51, 158, 169, 173-78, 184-86, 188-89, 191-93, 197-99, 201-04, 206, 208-14, 218-19, 308, 310, 312-14, 316-28, 337-38
French Revolution 3, 29
F&R, see Furlong, R & Ramharai, V
Freycinet, L de S 1, 9-14, 44-45, 60, 112, 175, 318, 321, 329
Furlong, R 2, 19, 22, 29, 45, 53, 55-58, 60, 130, 325, 328

G

Gambia(n) 201-02
Gandon, Père 309
Gbe 197, 201, 209
General Population 319-20, 323, 327
genitives 107-10
German 165
Giacalone Ramat, A 151, 153
Giacomi, A 148, 151, 153
Gil, D 90, 131
Giusti, G 85, 87-88, 90
Givòn, T 154, 189-90, 193-94
Goglia, F 151, 154
Gomm, Lady 27-29
Goodman, M 5, 60
Gorée 197, 308, 311
grammaticalization 111, 117, 120, 135, 188, 193
grammatisation 137, 139, 142
Grant, A 64, 90, 151, 174, 194, 197-216
Grant, Baron de 1, 3-4, 60, 310, 318
Grant, C 3, 60, 310
Guadeloupe 5
Guillemin, D 4, 63-91, 93, 133, 142, 173-97, 203-04, 215
Guinea (Guinée) 3, 201, 309, 311, 314
Guinea-Bissau 199
Guinée, see Guinea
Gujarati 320
Guyanais 200, 210, 212, 322

H

Hagège, C 135, 154
Haiti(an) (Creole) 4-5, 115, 123, 147, 187-88, 199-200, 210-13, 327
Hakka 326
Harris, A 135-36, 154
Harris, M 96, 100, 112
Haspelmath, M 90, 114-15, 119-20, 125, 131, 136, 154, 188, 193, 195
Hawai'ian Creole English 134, 200
Hawkins, J 79-81, 90
Hazaël-Massieux, G 138
He, S 134, 154
Hebrew 190
Heim, I 78, 90
Heine, B 106, 112, 117, 120, 122, 131, 154-55, 188, 195
Henri, F 119-20, 122, 126, 131
Higginbotham, J 180, 195
Himmelmann, N 71, 90
Hindi 109-10, 121, 202, 326-27
Hindu 319, 327
Hindustani 201-03, 205, 207-09, 212, 320, 324, 326, 340
Höftmann, H 212, 215
Hollingsworth, D 27, 60
Holm, J 109, 112, 197-200, 213, 215
Hookoomsing, V 1-61, 73-76, 89-90, 95, 173, 178, 183-84, 195, 198, 210, 214, 218, 220, 324, 327, 329, 338
Hopper, P 101, 106, 112, 154, 188, 195
Hornstein, N 84, 90
Hünnemeyer, F 106, 112, 154

I

Iberian 199
Igbo 151, 212
India(n) 27, 54, 109-10, 121-23, 197, 202, 209, 308-10, 312-14, 318-20, 323-24, 326, 328,340
Indian Ocean (Creoles) 120, 123, 157, 165, 171, 198, 202, 213, 218, 308, 314, 320
Indic 123, 198, 201, 203, 205, 207-09, 212, 327

Indo-Mauritian 130, 319, 324, 327
Indonesia 312
Indo-Pacific 199, 213
Indo-Portuguese 150
Isle de France = Mauritius
Isle de France Creole 176
Italian 151

J

Jackendoff, R 129, 131, 134, 154
Jacobière, M 197
Jain, D 214
Jamaica(n) 199-200
Japanese 93, 174
Jeanjean, C 148, 154
Jespersen, O 78-79, 82, 90, 101, 112, 322-23, 329
Johanson, L 119, 122, 131
Juda, see Whydah

K

Kaeppelin, P 307, 329
Karipuna 109
Karttunen, L 78, 90
Kaufman, T 155
Kearns, K 78, 90
Kenya 150
Kiamtia, L 325, 329
Kisseberth, C 202, 215
Klein, W 154
Konig, E 154
Korlai 199-200
Kriegel, S 35, 56, 60, 113-32, 154, 203, 215
Krio 199
Kuczynski, R 308, 314, 329
Kuteva, T 117, 120, 122, 131

L

Labourdonnais 309, 312, 316, 329
Ladhams, J 214-15
La Fontaine 9, 12, 15, 19, 41, 117, 120, 321
L'Albion 57, 60
Lambert, R 1, 60, 105, 112, 119, 125, 128, 140, 154, 178, 181, 185
Langacker, R 134, 136, 154, 185, 195
Lascar 313-14
Latin 29, 93, 336
Lazarist(s) 307, 333
Le Brun, J 8, 29, 60
Le Cernéen 22, 24-27, 40, 44-45, 60, 167
Ledikasyon pu Travayer, see Anon. 2004
Lefebvre, C 123, 126, 131, 202, 215
Legallant, G 68, 77, 90
Lehmann, C 137, 139, 154
Le Juge de Segrais, M-J 58
Le Juge de Segrais, Père 114
Le Juge de Segrais, R 332
Le Juge de Segrais, X 58, 60, 69, 90, 114, 116, 118, 131
Le Mauricien 29, 40, 47-52, 61, 118, 170, 326

Lenoir 308, 315
Leon, E 214
Lesser Antilles 138
L'Essor 58, 61
Le Toullec 307, 315
Levinson, S 83, 90
L'Homme, L 57, 61
Li, C 189-90, 193, 195
Lightfoot, D 135, 155
Lionnet, G 210, 215, 218, 220
Lloyd, J 27, 61, 319, 335-40
Lolliot, P 2-3, 40-45, 52, 61, 106, 112, 117, 124, 128, 147, 155, 159, 169, 172, 320, 329
London Missionary Society 29
Longobardi, G 63, 71-72, 87, 90, 180, 195
Lougnon, A 309-10, 329
Louisiana(is) 109-10, 200
Ludwig, R 119-20, 122, 131
Luganda 123
Lyons, C 79, 85, 90
Ly-Tio-Fane, M 311, 329

M

Macau 311-12
Maconde 150
Madagascar 14, 29, 197-98, 308-11, 317, 320, 339
Madhesi 121
Madras 310, 320
Maingard, J 72, 91, 183, 195
Makhuwa 17, 150, 197, 201-02, 205, 207-09, 211-13
Malabar 312-14, 320, 326, 337-38
Malagasy 3, 17, 29-31, 123-24, 150, 198, 201-03, 205, 207-09, 211-12, 308-11, 314, 320, 324
Malambou 313-14
Malartic, General 27, 29
Malay 311, 314
Malchukov, A 126, 128, 131
Mali 201
Mallefille, F 16-17
Mandarin 189, 193
Manding 198, 201-02
Mandinka 150, 197-98, 201-02, 204, 206, 208-09, 212
Maples, C 202, 215
Marathi 320, 324
maroon(s) 17
Martinique 198
Mascarenes 309-10
Matthews, P 173, 195
Maure, A 22, 61
Mauricien, see *Le Mauricien*
Mauritian Bhojpuri, see Bhojpuri
Mauritius Archives 3-4, 27, 61
MB = Mauritian Bhojpuri
MC = Mauritian Creole
Mchombo, S 191, 193, 195
McWhorter, J 84, 90, 188, 195
Meade, G 325, 329
Meillet, A 106, 112, 135, 155
Melzian, H 212, 215

Mérédac, S 58
Mesthrie, R 122, 131
Michaelis, S 35, 56, 60, 113-32, 203, 215
Milbert, J-G 1, 5-6, 61
Milsark, G 68, 91, 97, 112, 174, 179, 195
Minimalist Program 64, 84, 176, 190
Mondesir, J 210, 215
Mouat, F 320, 329
Moussié Caraba 2, 35-40, 45, 168
Mozambique 6, 9, 197, 201, 310-11, 313-14, 320, 339
Muslim 319, 324, 326-27
Muysken, P 130

N

Nadal, P 178, 195
Nagamese 199
Nairac, L 1
Natal 321
Ndyuka 199
negation 138-39, 184
Negerhollands 109, 160, 199
Nicolay, W 1, 22, 61, 99, 112
Niger-Congo 120
Nigerian 151
Nkore-Kiga 123
Noble, C 311, 329
noun phrase 93-112
Nubi 199
Nyanga 150

O

Oesterreicher, W 154
orthography 5-6, 12-13, 44-45, 55, 58, 139-46, 158, 160, 327
Ouidah, see Whydah
ownership 133-54

P

Pagliuca, W 135, 153
Palenquero 199
Papen, R 191-93, 195
Papiamentu 109, 134, 199-200
Papua New Guinea 199
Parkvall, M 120, 123, 131, 217
Parsons, T 180, 195
Partee, B 83, 91
Patrick, P 197-200, 213, 215
Perdue, 154
Perkins, R 135, 153
Pesetsky, D 82, 91
Petit Robert 212, 215
Peyraube, A 135, 155
Philippi, J 112
pidgin 199, 216
Pinker, S 155
Pitcairnese 200
Pitot, C 61
Pitot, H 53, 61
Pitot, T 6-8, 44-45, 61, 112, 166, 174
plurality 101-07
Poivre, P 311
Polish 151

Pollock, J 189, 195
Pondicherry 308
Pope-Hennessy, J 321, 329
Port Louis 309, 319, 336, 338
Portuguese 151, 199-200, 311, 314, 336, 338
possession 133-54
Price, G 100, 112
Pridham, C 319, 329
propriété, *see* ownership
Prosper, J-G 54, 61, 324, 326

Q

Queen Victoria 23
Quine, W 83, 91

R

Raible, W 154
Ramchand, G 180, 193
Ramgoolam, Sir S 326
Ramharai, V 2, 19, 22, 29, 45, 53, 55-58, 60, 130, 325, 328
Ramnah, A 121-22, 130
Rasoloson, J 202, 215
Ratsitatane 14, 17
reanalysis 135-37, 193
reduplication 203, 207-09
resumptive pronoun 173-96
Réunion(nais) 12, 124, 176, 200, 202, 212, 307-10, 314-17, 326
Richardson, J 207, 212, 215
Rickard, P 96, 112
Rizzi, L 87, 91, 175, 195
Roberts, I 87, 91
Rodrigues 171-72, 176, 315, 317, 326, 338
Romaine, A 73-74, 91
Romance 71, 87-88, 93, 125, 174
Rosalie, M 114-15, 118, 126, 129-31
Rothstein, S 179, 195
Royal College 54-55, 317, 322
Rungoo, G 75, 91
Russell, B 78-79, 82, 91
Russell, J 212, 215
Ryan, V 320, 329

S

Sag, I 83, 90
Saint Jorre, D de 210, 215, 218, 220
Saint Lucia(n) 210, 212-13
Saint-Quentin, A 322, 329
Salamut, R 70, 91
Samuel, D 214
Santos, R 215
Sãotomense 200
Sauvageot, S 202, 215
Sauzier, T 14
SC = Seselwa
Scarr, D 5, 18, 61
Schmidt, R 202, 215
second language acquisition 151-52
Senegal 197, 201, 308, 311
Seselwa 66, 114-15, 118, 120, 123-24, 126, 129, 170, 175-76, 190-93, 197, 199, 210, 212-13, 315
Seuren, P 84, 91
Seychelles 55, 123, 127, 316-17
Seychelles Creole, *see* Seselwa
Shakur, T 197, 202
Shona 123, 150
Shukla, S 122, 131
Sidonie, M 325, 329
Sino-Mauritian 327
Slavic 93
Slobin, D 134, 155
Smith, A 322, 329
Smith, I 197
Soogumbur, S
Soulsobontemps, P 2, 58, 61
Spanish 151
specificity 63-91, 94-101, 175-76, 180
Sranan 200
Stassen, L 114-15, 119, 123, 131-33, 155
Steever, S 202, 214
Stein, P 1-2, 15, 44, 57, 61, 124, 157-72, 181, 195, 206, 216
Stolz, T 114, 132
Stowell, T 72, 85, 91, 176, 180, 195
Strandquist, R 64, 91, 174, 195, 211, 216
Strawson, P 79, 82, 91
Stroh, C 132
Subsaharan Africa 123
substrate 150
Suez Canal 321
Sukuma 150
Swadesh 211-12
Swiss 307
Swahili 123, 150, 188, 191
Syea, A 93-112, 203-04, 216
Szabolcsi, A 85, 91

T

Talmy, L 134, 155
Tamil 71, 123, 150, 197-98, 201-03, 205, 207-09, 212, 308, 320, 324-25, 327
Tanzania 150
Targète, J 210, 216
Taylor, J 109, 112
Tayo 200
Telchid, S 131
Telugu 320, 324
Telfair, C 318, 3330
Tersis, N 202, 216
Therrien, I 123, 131
Thomas, J 322
Thomason, S 155
Thompson, S 189-90, 193, 195
Timor(ien) 311, 314
Tinker, H 319, 330
TMA markers 124, 157-72, 176, 180, 182-84, 192-93, 203, 206-07, 322
Tok Pisin 199-200
Topas 309
Toussaint, A 27, 61, 309-10, 313-15, 322, 328-30
transparency 136-37, 150
Traugott, E 101, 106, 112, 154-55, 188, 195
Travis, L 188, 195
Trinidad 322
Tupi 30-31
typology 197-216

U

Uganda 150
Urdu 202, 324
Urdze, A 132
Urciolo, R 210, 216

V

van Gelderen, E 188, 195
Véronique, D 68, 93, 114, 132-55, 173, 194, 203, 215
Verrips, M 130
Vicars, () 18-19, 61
Victor, C 202, 216
Vinet, M-T 187-88, 194
Virahsawmy, D 70-71, 73-74, 76, 91, 173, 182, 184-85, 195-96, 327, 330
Virgil 29
Von Heusinger, K 82-83, 91

W

Wagner, R-L 148, 155
WALS = *World Atlas of Language Structures*
Waltereit, R 135-36, 153
Ward, W 323, 330
Wappo 190
Wekker, H 84, 91
Welmers, W 120, 132
Wesley, J 29, 61
West Africa(n) 120, 123, 198, 201-02, 213, 309-10
Wiredu, K 66, 91
Whydah 197, 209, 308, 311
Wolof 123, 150, 198, 201-04, 206, 208-09, 212
World Atlas of Language Structures 114-15, 123

Y

Yao 150
Yolof 197, 201, 311
Yoruba 212
Yule, H 336

Z

Zamboangueño 199-200
zero copula 4, 173, 185-86, 188-89, 199, 206-07
zero TMA 157-72
Zulu 123
Zway 190